TIP OF THE SPEAR

German Armored Reconnaissance in Action in World War II

Robert J. Edwards
with contributions from
Michael H. Pruett and Michael Olive

STACKPOLE
BOOKS

Copyright © 2015 by Robert J. Edwards

Published by
STACKPOLE BOOKS
5067 Ritter Road
Mechanicsburg, PA 17055
www.stackpolebooks.com

All rights reserved, including the right to reproduce this book or portions thereof in any form or by any means, electronic or mechanical, including recording or by any information storage and retrieval system, without permission in writing from the publisher. All inquiries should be addressed to Stackpole Books, 5067 Ritter Road, Mechanicsburg, PA 17055.

Printed in the United States of America

10 9 8 7 6 5 4 3 2 1

FIRST EDITION

Library of Congress Cataloging-in-Publication Data

Edwards, Robert J., 1954– author.
  Tip of the spear : German armored reconnaissance in action in World War II / Robert Edwards ; with contributions from Michael H. Pruett and Michael Olive.
       pages cm
  Includes bibliographical references.
  ISBN 978-0-8117-1571-3
1. Germany. Heer—Armored troops—History—20th century. 2. World War, 1939–1945—Reconnaissance operations, German. 3. Germany—Armed Forces—History—World War, 1939–1945. 4. World War, 1939–1945—Tank warfare. 5. World War, 1939–1945—Campaigns. I. Pruett, Michael H. II. Olive, Michael. III. Title. IV. Title: German armored reconnaissance in action in World War II.
  D757.54.E36 2015
  940.54'1343—dc23
                                                    2015020346

Contents

Foreword v
A Note on Style vii

CHAPTER 1:   Prewar Training 1
CHAPTER 2:   Baptism of Fire 81
CHAPTER 3:   Blitzkrieg in the West 103
CHAPTER 4:   The Balkan Campaign 159
CHAPTER 5:   North Africa 185
CHAPTER 6:   The Campaign Against the Soviet Union: Barbarossa Unleashed 207
CHAPTER 7:   1942: Debacle in the East 273
CHAPTER 8:   Stalemate in Italy 327
CHAPTER 9:   The Tide Turns in the East 345
CHAPTER 10: The End in the West 381
CHAPTER 11: The End in the East 431

Appendix 1:   School Exercises for Combat Training in Reconnaissance (1939) 487
Appendix 2:   Reconnaissance Formation Cross-Reference Guide 489
Appendix 3:   The Transition to Increased Firepower: 1932–45 498
Appendix 4:   Errata and Addenda to *Scouts Out* 501

Notes 505
Bibliography 517

Foreword

This book continues the topics introduced in our first book, *Scouts Out*, by further analyzing tactics and doctrine of the German armored reconnaissance forces of the World War II era, as well as providing additional information concerning their evolving organization and equipment. The narrative provides an overview of the major theaters of war, the forces employed, and the reconnaissance formations involved. Woven within the narrative are a number of after-action reports and firsthand accounts. As with the first book, the text is accompanied by the presentation of more than 600 images, most of which have not been seen before or only by a limited audience. The color section not only presents a number of unique period images of reconnaissance elements, but also displays interesting artifacts from the era that are preserved in collections today. Several appendices round out the narrative for those readers desiring more in-depth information. There is also a listing of errata from the first book as well as addenda to text from that volume, where additional information on a particular topic has been obtained since *Scouts Out* was published.

Efforts have been made to avoid overlap in the treatment of material. Obviously, some must exist, but generally we have tried to refer readers to *Scouts Out* when the subject has been covered before.

It cannot be stressed enough that the tables of organization and equipment listed are theoretical constructs and rarely reflect the actual organization of the unit in question, except, perhaps, when it was first formed. In some cases, vehicles were authorized that were not even rolling off assembly lines in any appreciable quantities. In others, combat attrition and other losses ensured that the unit was never at full strength. Even if all vehicles listed were on hand, it was the rare occasion when all were also ready for combat, due to battle damage or mechanical problems. The chapter on Normandy and the final fighting in the West will attempt to illustrate these disparities somewhat, but the issues highlighted there can be considered representative of the German Army's order of battle as a whole. In addition, illustrations are not to scale and have been resized due to space constraints.

A common criticism leveled at books like this is that there are no late-war images or not enough images of a particular type of force, for instance, the *Waffen-SS*. While there is no denying the fact that any author on this subject would like to use as many late-war images as early and prewar ones, there is also no denying that the images are simply not there or have yet to be discovered. There are numerous reasons for this, but post-1943 images of almost any quality are generally hard to find.

As far as coverage of the reconnaissance forces is concerned, the authors have tried to be as evenhanded as possible. We have used a number of sources that are available only in German in an effort to provide information that has not been presented to the English-reading public before. We cover the *Waffen-SS*, but do not dwell on it. There is already a wealth of literature on it, and to contribute more to what has often become non-reflective hagiography seems counterproductive to what we are trying to present here. The bibliography contains a list of books available in English on the subject, which the reader may wish to consult if interested in firsthand accounts and small-unit tactics.

As with the first book, we hope you enjoy our efforts. We welcome any comments you might have; these can be submitted to the publisher or directly to us at our website, www.battlebornbooks.com. Any errata and addenda to the book will also be published at the site.

Robert J. Edwards
Michael H. Pruett
Michael Olive
Winter 2014–15

A Note on Style

It is assumed that the reader of this book probably already has an interest in the subject. Since the authors rely on a number of German-language sources, in which technical, professional, and military terminology and soldier slang are used, it might be prudent to outline some of the preferences we have in terms of translation and presentation of material.

In general, German unit and formation titles will be given their full designation upon first introduction, with no effort made to produce a German-English hybrid, as is often the case where extensive reference is made to German formations, equipment, and ranks in English-language titles. Thus, the German 4th Armored Reconnaissance Battalion will initially be rendered as *Panzer-Aufklärungs-Abteilung 4*. If extensive reference is made to it, then an abbreviated form may be introduced, such as *Pz.Aufkl.Abt. 4*. In all instances, the abbreviations will follow German practice. To assist in "deciphering" these, extensive use will be made of endnotes.

Ordinal numbers are rendered by the use of a "." in German; thus the 1st Armor Division is the *1. Panzer-Division*. Subordinate units within formations are indicated by Arabic numerals in the case of company-size formations and Roman numerals for battalions. Generally, division and higher commands are indicated by ordinal numbers. Brigades are usually indicated by ordinal numerals when an organic part of a higher command, while separate brigades are indicated by the numerical designator following the unit designator. Of course, there were exceptions to this rule of thumb; regiments, battalions, and separate companies generally had the numerical designator following the unit designator.

The term *Abteilung* will generally be translated as "battalion" when it refers to a combat formation, and as "detachment" when it refers to an element of the training base. For instance, *Panzer-Ersatz-und Ausbildungs-Abteilung 4* would be the 4th Replacement and Training Detachment, even though it is a battalion-size element.

Generally, when the word "formation" is used, it refers to a battalion or higher element. The term "unit" is reserved for company-size elements and smaller. Although the term *Schwadron* is literally translated as "squadron," this is actually a troop (company) in U.S. usage. When the original German is unclear or a mixture of formations and units is being described, then the term "elements" will be used.

German ranks will be used throughout the text; thus captain will be rendered as *Hauptmann* or *Rittmeister*, depending on the type of unit or actual rank title. Ranks for *SS* personnel will use the prefix *SS*, which was the official way of describing the rank, with a 2nd Lieutenant in the SS, for example, being an *SS-Untersturmführer*. The prefix may be deleted, however, when translating firsthand accounts, since it was not used in colloquial German. For those who are unfamiliar with German ranks, a comparison table is also provided at the back of the book.

In cases where official German documents are translated, portions may be changed slightly to facilitate meaning (e.g., abbreviations written out or text added to "shotgun passages" to make complete sentences).

CHAPTER 1

Prewar Training

SETTING THE STAGE

As discussed in the authors' previous book, *Scouts Out*,[1] the German armored force had arguably the most advanced prewar conception of what the face of the next war would look like. This was not true across the board, since the German military, like all militaries, had its fair share of those who preferred hindsight to foresight; but the presence of forceful adherents for the use of armor, led by Heinz Guderian, ensured that the *Panzerwaffe* had its fair share of representation in the structure, organization, doctrine, and tactics of the German Army in the years leading up to the start of the European conflict in 1939.

DOCTRINE

As discussed at length in *Scouts Out*, German prewar armored reconnaissance was defined primarily by *Heeresdienstvorschrift 299/10, Ausbildungsvorschrift für die Kavallerie, Die Aufklärungs-Abteilung (mot)*.[2] Compared to equivalent modern-day military manuals, it is remarkable in its succinctness. While the basic missions of the reconnaissance battalion are defined to some extent, the methodology by which intelligence information was to be gathered was left primarily up to the commander and his subordinates. While the idea of *Auftragstaktik*—mission-type orders—was stressed throughout the German Army, it was particularly emphasized within the *Panzerwaffe* and probably reached its apex with the armored reconnaissance forces.

This *Sd.Kfz. 221* of *Aufklärungs-Abteilung 7 (mot)* of the *4. Panzer-Division* moves down a snowed-over street while a crowd of curious civilians observes. AKIRA TAKIGUCHI

Heeresdienstvorschrift 299/10, Ausbildungsvorschrift für die Kavallerie, Die Aufklärungs-Abteilung (mot), the prewar "bible" for the reconnaissance battalion commander.

The reconnaissance battalion commander was essentially free to organize his force to meet the dictates of his mission. In accordance with *Auftragstaktik*, it was incumbent upon him to know the intent of his commander so that the mission could still be executed if and when circumstances changed. This was particularly important for reconnaissance elements performing their traditional mission of battlefield and tactical reconnaissance: that is, the effort to determine the location of the enemy, the size of his force, his deployment for battle, and his intent, to name but a few. Because of the unique organization of the reconnaissance battalions, which had integrated scout elements, tactical reconnaissance forces, and heavy weapons, they were also ideally suited for screening and guarding missions as well as economy-of-force efforts. As was quickly discovered in the course of initial combat operations, the battalions were also uniquely suited to provide command and control for the formation of *Kampfgruppen*, since their relatively extravagant allocations of radio and other communications devices enabled them to communicate easily and effectively with subordinated units as well as maintain communications over extended distances with higher levels of command.

In keeping with the doctrinal requirement of "seeing but not being seen," the battalions largely possessed the means to do so through speed, maneuverability, and communications capability. However, they lacked the requisite firepower as the war progressed and long-range reconnaissance gave way to the increasing need for the conduct of battlefield reconnaissance (at best) and a mobile defensive fighting force (at worst).

TRAINING

Prewar training throughout the German Army was rigorous and frequent. The watchword was *Schweiß spart Blut* ("Sweat spares blood"). As with most peacetime armies, the German Army was a professional one, its ranks filled by highly qualified individuals who had undergone a rigorous filtering process. Because advancement was slow, the junior ranks were also highly competent. Training regimes were organized for recruits, systematic affairs that released men back into civilian life after the end of their compulsory military duty with ingrained soldier skill sets. Examples of these training exercises can be seen in the accompanying sidebar.

ORGANIZATION

On the eve of World War II, the German Armed Forces had six armored divisions (1, 2, 3, 4, 5, 10), four light divisions (1–4), and four mechanized infantry divisions (2, 13, 20, 29). There was also the *ad hoc Panzerverband Kempf* and reconnaissance assets among the various elements of the *SS-Verfügungstruppe*.

In general, the armored divisions had an armored reconnaissance battalion with fairly standardized organization: two armored car companies, one motorcycle infantry company, and one heavy company. The *1., 2.,* and *3. Panzer-Divisionen* also had a motorcycle infantry battalion; the remaining armored divisions did not. The armored reconnaissance assets of *Panzerverband Kempf* came from the motorized reconnaissance battalion of the *SS-Verfügungstruppe* and consisted of two motorcycle infantry companies and the equivalent of a heavy company, which had an armored car platoon, among other assets. In addition,

School Exercises for Combat Training in Reconnaissance

One of the many training primers produced by the German Army in the pre- and early war years was one written by a staff officer of the *4. Panzer-Division*, *Hauptmann* Hans-Wolfgang von Fabeck. The subtitle of the booklet is *The Crew of the Individual Vehicle Within the Reconnaissance Patrol, 1939/1940, 14 Exercises with Corresponding Situation Sketch Maps*. Unlike doctrinal manuals, which tended to give commanders great latitude in the accomplishment of a mission, training primers such as this one often spelled out details to a painstaking degree in an effort to inculcate rapid, almost intuitive response on the part of soldiers when reacting to situations encountered on the battlefield. The importance attached to these booklets can be gleaned from the foreword, written by then-*General der Panzertruppen* Heinz Guderian:

Our motorized and armored reconnaissance battalions can now look back upon a number of practical experiences, some of which were collected under dire circumstances. These are examined in this booklet by *Hauptmann* Fabeck in the form of examples that will make the training entrusted to young officers and noncommissioned officers easier. May the reconnaissance battalions learn from them that the best defense is an offense and that success in reconnaissance springs from audaciousness and a never flagging offensive spirit, coupled with reason and attentiveness and with technical and tactical proficiency.

Guderian
General der Panzertruppen

The table of contents demonstrates the multitude and variety of the training exercises:

A. Introduction
B. The Exercises
1. Meeting engagement with enemy horse-mounted or bicycle forces (Exercise purpose: Halting and remaining concealed)
2. Meeting engagement with enemy lead elements (Exercise purpose: Timely withdrawal)
3. Meeting engagement with enemy light armored car (Exercise purpose: Attack on the enemy vehicle)*
4. Meeting engagement with enemy heavy armored car (Exercise purpose: Withdrawal in the face of a superior enemy)
5. Encountering an enemy antitank gun (Exercise purpose: Overrunning an enemy antitank gun going into position)
6. Meeting engagement with an enemy antitank gun (Exercise purpose: Rapid withdrawal in the face of an antitank gun in position)

Cover of the training primer *Schulübungen für die Gefechtsausbildung im Aufklärungsdienst*.

*Only Exercise 3 has been translated for illustrative purposes.

School Exercises for Combat Training in Reconnaissance *continued*

7. Encountering an obstacle (Exercise purpose: Bypassing an obstacle)
8. Encountering an obstacle (Exercise purpose: Breaching an obstacle)
9. Taking a position as a screening vehicle (Exercise purpose: Finding the best place and the proper siting of weapons)
10. Actions taken by a screening vehicle during an enemy armored attack (Exercise purpose: Defending from the screening position)
11. Actions taken as a messenger (Exercise purpose: Properly bringing back a report in differing situations. Included: Attack by fire on a valuable target)
12. Reconnoitering a blocked creek crossing on foot (Exercise purpose: Evaluating and exploiting terrain by a dismounted crew)
13. Observing an advancing enemy (Exercise purpose: Maintaining contact with the enemy and determining its location)
14. Reconnoitering at night (Exercise purpose: Observing a road by sending dismounted scouts forward)

Fabeck spells out the intended purpose of his booklet in his introduction:

The purpose of the examples is to train the young soldiers of a **vehicle crew** to act in a unified manner. It is intended to advance by drill the foundations of a tactically proper response and decision making early on by means of certain well-defined school exercises.

The skills already gained in **individual training** (*Heeres Dienstvorschrift 470/3a*, Part B and *Heeres-Dienstvorschrift 299/8c*, Part B)—vehicle training; training as a ground scout by means of movement exercises and hearing perception; use of the map; training in reporting, such as the preparing, transmission and rendering of reports; and basic training in engineer tasks—are the necessary ABC's of the **individual soldier** and **prerequisite** for the seamless function of the **vehicle crew**.

The soldiers have to be able to master the tools given them: vehicle, weapons, equipment, etc.

The necessity of executing the prescribed crew drills in the most exact and fastest manner possible must be continuously stressed as an instructional point while going through the tactical exercises.

It is important that the **terrain** that is to be used for the execution of the missions be reconnoitered in a timely manner by the chief instructor and the training personnel prior to the start of the exercises. The terrain features and the sketch maps used in the individual examples are to be considered to be purely illustrative. They are solely intended to be recommendations and a help in selecting suitable terrain.

The **enemy** has to be briefed on-site in an exact manner with regard to what he has to do and which signal will be used to have him appear. These instructions can never be issued too thoroughly. They are of decisive importance for the success of the exercise. The actions of the enemy are always to be subordinated to the purposes of achieving the exercise goals.

The mission is to be rehearsed with the soldiers on a **sandtable** prior to its execution in the terrain where it will take place. The soldier must know precisely why he has to act in such and such a manner after the start of the incident. He needs to be or become firmly convinced of the properness of his countermeasures. When executing the example on the actual terrain, there can still be numerous mistakes, despite all that. This must be discussed immediately at the time and place of occurrence.

In a few of the **scenarios**, the **mission of the reconnaissance patrol** is not spelled out in detail, since the scenario does not concern the mission of the reconnaissance patrol. Instead, the scenario is concerned with the missions of the **individual vehicle within the framework** of the **reconnaissance patrol**. Only the **mission of the individual vehicle** is described in detail in order to prevent the recruit from confusing the missions of the reconnaissance patrol and the individual vehicle. The missions of the reconnaissance patrol are therefore only discussed in each case as much as is needed to understand the overall situation and allow the crew of the **individual** vehicle to act properly within context of the mission.

The information provided in the **scenario** and the **mission** is to be used when conducting the exercise in **direct orders** and in giving the situation. The **issuance** of short and clear **orders** is to be encouraged in all situations with the soldiers. At the start of the mission stress is to be placed on **repeating the mission** by the armor commander. Furthermore, it is to be stressed that the **mission** must be executed unconditionally. The young soldier is to be trained from the very beginning that everything is to be subordinated to the absolute completion of the mission; if necessary, even one's own life. When it is no longer possible to execute the mission exactly, then efforts must be made at a minimum to continue within its context. To that end, the reconnaissance patrol order is of paramount importance.

Decisive for the selection of terrain, scenario and mission is the **purpose of the exercise**.

During the **conduct of the exercises**, the **instructor** is to remain in the vicinity of the students. During the focal point of the exercise, an **assistant instructor** may be necessary to overwatch details.

It is fundamental that an **umpire** be at the location, who knows exactly what is going on.

It is not always imperative that the soldiers execute their individual tasks in the order given. The main thing is that everything occurs at the right time in accordance with the situation. It must be stressed that in the course of the **battle drills** that no action is forgotten, even those of seemingly minor importance, even if their execution appears to be of secondary importance or obvious for a soldier, who has already been trained. On the other hand, do not fall into mindless **templating**!

At the conclusion of the mission, every soldier must be informed on how he solved the problem and how he fulfilled the mission.

At the end of the exercise day, the enemy is to be heard, with an eye to whether something striking was observed with regard to the actions of the soldiers. This is then to be addressed at the **final briefing**. In addition, the local **situation** at the beginning and at the end of the mission is to be **evaluated** and what conclusions can be drawn from that for friendly actions. Insight into the **decision-making capability** and ability to estimate the situation on the part of the soldiers can also be gained in missions where the scouts and the drivers appear together and are occasionally asked during the after-action review, what should have been done if one man of the crew had been lost during the engagement.

The **paragraphs of the manuals** that are keyed to the individual exercises should be pointed out during the after-action review. In the missions, not only are the paragraphs of the manuals concerning the vehicle used in the mission listed, but the manuals and paragraphs of other possible vehicles that may be used are also listed in order to assist the trainers.

Usually, it is good if the soldiers, who are to undergo the same mission later on, are **spectators** at the location of the events and view the course of the exercise. Their attention must be drawn to the mistakes of their comrades by the exercise controller or assistant personnel, and they should also alert each other of mistakes they see. If the same fundamental mistakes keep resurfacing despite all that, then it is practical to demonstrate the mission once by the instructor personnel.

The exercise controller has to decide occasionally, who may be permitted to watch. For

School Exercises for Combat Training in Reconnaissance *continued*

those soldiers, who have already completed the mission, there is no useful purpose served having them view the events.

It is recommended that the mission be repeated at the same location in the terrain in one of its **modified forms**. The differences in the course of the exercises are to be pointed out ahead of time during a period of instruction. During the repetition, personnel who are not directly involved should be allowed to view it.

Once all of the modified examples have been practiced by all of the personnel, then the basic exercise should be repeated, but on different terrain and without having any viewers present and without having instructed them earlier on what will transpire. This repetition serves to test the **level of training** of the individual soldiers.

When **time is constrained**, it is advisable to initially only conduct individual basic missions in an exacting fashion as opposed to a superficial treatment of all of the examples. It is better for the soldier to feel confident in just a few areas than to not feel confident in all of them.

The **type of vehicle** used in the examples is the light armored car. If the missions are to be executed with other types of vehicles, then the preparation and execution of the exercises is to be tailored to the changed circumstances—especially with regard to the changed weaponry and the issuance of orders. In the case of vehicles with more than a two-man crew, ensure that an already-trained armor leader (exercise controller or assistant personnel) rides along in the vehicle. This armored leader must know exactly how the exercise will run. Whenever it becomes necessary in the course of the mission, he must be able to issue orders and commands without hesitation, so that the scout and the driver act properly. These orders must be limited to the bare minimum necessary. To foster decision-making abilities and self-sufficiency of the individual crewmembers, the additional armor leader must leave anytime, when the mission can be accomplished without any problems in the context of the exercise purpose without his presence.

If the appearance of the **reconnaissance patrol leader** is necessary in the missions, the exercise controller must decide ahead of time, whether the reconnaissance patrol leader and his vehicle are actually to be portrayed. It will frequently suffice if the exercise controller portrays the patrol leader and rides along on the vehicles in which the exercise is being conducted.

It should also be attempted to select a few of the missions that have already been conducted during the day as exercises for **night training**, without making large changes to the structure of the example. By doing that, one can quickly demonstrate to the soldiers the considerable difference in actions taken during the day and the night.

The missions can also be used for **more senior soldiers**, who have already been trained, as **repetitive drills** or as **advanced exercises**. In such cases, the degree of preparatory discussion is based on the degree of training of all of the participants. In most cases, it will be necessary to allow these types of exercises to run in an open and non-predetermined manner, in contrast to the battle-drill school exercises of the recruits. Nonetheless, it must be ensured that the desired individual exercise purposes are achieved. This is achieved by the structure of the scenario and the mission.

Examples of exercises can be found in Appendix 2.

the *SS-Standarte* attached to Kempf's force—*SS-Standarte "Deutschland"*—had an armored car platoon and a motorcycle infantry company; this was true of all three *SS-Standarten* and the *Leibstandarte SS Adolf Hitler*. The *Infanterie-Divisionen (mot)* had an armored reconnaissance battalion, but with only one armored car company (exception: *2. Infanterie-Division (mot)*) and no heavy companies. The motorized infantry divisions did not have motorcycle infantry battalions at the time.

The light divisions were generally not standardized in their organization.

- *1. leichte Division*: one motorcycle infantry battalion (organized slightly differently than described above, but with substantially the same fire- and manpower). The armored reconnaissance battalion followed the model of the armored divisions.
- *2. leichte Division*: one motorcycle infantry battalion and one armored scout battalion within a reconnaissance regiment. The *Kradschützen-Abteilung* did not have a machine-gun company; the armored scout battalion had a total of four armored car troops.
- *3. leichte Division*: one motorcycle infantry battalion and one armored reconnaissance battalion within a reconnaissance regiment. The *Kradschützen-Abteilung* did not have a heavy company (only an antitank platoon), and the machine-gun company was motorized as opposed to mounted on motorcycles; the armored reconnaissance battalion was the same as that of an armored division.
- *4. leichte Division*: one motorcycle infantry battalion and one armored scout battalion within a reconnaissance regiment. The *Kradschützen-Abteilung* had three line companies, no machine-gun company, and a standard heavy company; the armored scout battalion had a total of three armored car troops.

The most important organizations can be seen in the accompanying sidebars.

PREWAR TACTICAL OPERATIONS

Prior to the initiation of hostilities against Poland on 1 September 1939, the German Army was involved with the reoccupation of the *Saarland* (March 1935) and the occupation of Austria (March 1938), the *Sudetenland* (October 1938), and the remainder of Czechoslovakia (March 1939). In the latter three instances, reconnaissance assets from several armored and mechanized infantry divisions were employed, as were forces of the *SS-Verfügungstruppe*, the *SS-Totenkopfverbände*, the *Leibstandarte SS Adolf Hitler*, and the *Luftwaffe*'s "General Göring" Regiment.

All three occupations were conducted peacefully, albeit with each escalating in nature, scope, and potential for actual combat operations. Once the respective borders were crossed, operations initially proceeded as a typical movement to contact, with reconnaissance assets to the front, followed by an advance guard, and then the main body. Once the initial danger passed, the reconnaissance assets were still employed in typical fashion: that is, conducting route reconnaissance.

In the case of Austria in March 1938, German forces were greeted enthusiastically everywhere they went, with the resulting operations resembling those of an extended road march, sometimes administrative in nature, sometimes tactical. The primary lessons learned were logistical in nature, focusing on the supply and maintenance of large motorized and mechanized forces over extended distances.

Emboldened by the lukewarm reaction from the Western Powers to the *Anschluß* with Austria, Hitler set his eyes on the *Sudetenland*, which was occupied in October 1938. The stakes were higher, since it was not certain how the Czechs would react, despite their agreeing to Hitler's demands at the eleventh hour. Had armed resistance been offered, the outcome would probably have been the same, but Czechoslovakia's relatively modern military and weaponry would have given the Germans pause. As with Austria, however, operations soon became more administrative than tactical in nature, since the overwhelmingly ethnic German population of the area being occupied greeted the arriving Germans as liberators. The lessons learned also were essentially the same as in Austria, although winter weather and icy roads affected tactical operations.

The final occupation of what remained of Czechoslovakia occurred in March 1939. Once again, German forces had to contend with possible armed resistance, since the fate of the Czech Republic clearly hung in the balance. Operations proceeded accordingly, but there was only one instance of armed conflict,[5] thus setting the marker for the start of World War II in Europe with the invasion of Poland.

Prewar Organizations of Reconnaissance Forces:
Kradschützen-Bataillon

The prewar organization of a *Kradschützen-Bataillon* generally had three motorcycle infantry companies, one motorcycle infantry machine-gun company, and one motorized heavy company. The headquarters was organized under *Kriegsstärkenachweisung (KStN) 1109* of 1 October 1937.[3] Each of the motorcycle infantry companies was organized under *KStN 1111* (1 October 1937), while the machine-gun company followed *KStN 1118* (1 October 1938). The heavy company had a headquarters (*KStN 1121* / 1 October 1937), an antitank platoon (*KStN 1122* / 1 October 1937), a light infantry gun platoon (*KStN 1123* / 1 October 1937), and a motorized engineer platoon (*KStN 1124* / 1 October 1937). In the case of the heavy company, a building-block approach was used to add or subtract elements as needed, determined by the German Army's Force Structure Branch (*Organizationsabteilung*).

The Headquarters Company

KStN	Type of Unit	German	Date
1109	Headquarters of a Motorcycle Infantry Battalion (Not in a Regimental Formation)	*Stab eines Kraftradschützen-Bataillons (nicht im Regimentsverband).*	1 October 1937

Notes: Also designated as: Headquarters of a *SS* Motorcycle Infantry Battalion (*Stab eines SS-Kradschützen-Sturmbanns*). Updated 1 February 1941. Shown below: 1 October 1937

a) Command Group

5x Medium Motorcycle, 2x Sidecar Motorcycle	Medium Cross-Country Vehicle (*Kfz. 11*)	Medium Cross-Country Vehicle with Equipment Storage Box (*Kfz. 15*) for Medical Personnel

Total Command Group: 6x Officers, 1x NCO, 11x Enlisted Personnel; 11x Rifles, 7x Pistols; 2x Vehicles, 5x Medium Motorcycles, 2x Sidecar Motorcycles

b) Signals Section

Radio Vehicle (*Kfz. 15/2*)

1st Small Telephone Section c (Motorized)

Signals Vehicle (Kfz. *15/1*)	Radio Vehicle (*Kfz. 2/2*) (3 seat)	2x Motorcycle

2nd Small Telephone Section c (Motorized)

Signals Vehicle (Kfz. *15/1*)	Radio Vehicle (*Kfz. 2/2*) (3 seat)	2x Motorcycle

Backpack Radio Sections

1st Backpack Radio Section d (Motorized)

Radio Vehicle (*Kfz. 2/2*) (3 seat)

2nd Backpack Radio Section d (Motorized)

Radio Vehicle (*Kfz. 2/2*) (3 seat)

Small Armored Radio Sections

1st Armored Radio Section d (Motorized)

Small Armored Radio Car (*Sd.Kfz. 261*), 1x Submachine Gun

2nd Armored Radio Section d (Motorized)

Small Armored Radio Car (*Sd.Kfz. 261*)

Totals Signals Section: 7x NCOs, 18x Enlisted Personnel; 16x Rifles, 9x Pistols; 7x Wheeled Vehicles, 2x Armored Radio Vehicles, 2x Motorcycles

c) Combat Trains

Light Truck, Canvas Top, for Small Field Mess Stove   Ambulance (*Kfz. 31*)   Medium Motorcycle

Total Combat Trains: 2x NCOs, 5x Enlisted Personnel; 4x Rifles, 3x Pistols; 2x Wheeled Vehicles, 1x Medium Motorcycle

d) Maintenance Section

Light Utility Vehicle (4 seat)   Light Truck, Canvas Top, for Armorer's and Medical Section Equipment   Light Truck, Canvas Top, for Combat Engineer Equipment and Digging Equipment

Light Truck, Cross-Country, for Petroleum, Oil & Lubricants   Light Truck, Cross-Country, for Maintenance Equipment   Sidecar Motorcycle

Total Maintenance Section: 2x Civilian Officials, 2x NCOs, 12x Enlisted Personnel; 10x Rifles, 6x Pistols; 5x Vehicles, 1x Sidecar Motorcycle

e) Rations Trains (for the Entire Battalion)

Light Truck for Rations   Light Truck for Rations   Light Wheeled Vehicle for Rations Officer   Medium Motorcycle

Total Rations Trains: 1x NCO, 5x Enlisted Personnel; 5x Rifles; 3x Vehicles, 1x Medium Motorcycle

f) Baggage Trains

Light Utility Vehicle (4 seat)   Medium Motorcycle   Light Truck, Canvas Top, for Baggage and Equipment

Total Baggage Trains: 1x Civilian Official, 2x NCOs, 3x Enlisted Personnel; 4x Rifles, 2x Pistols; 2x Wheeled Vehicles, 1x Medium Motorcycle

Summary

	Officers	Civilian Officials	NCOs	Enlisted Personnel	Rifles	Pistols / Submachine Guns	Vehicles (Armored Vehicles)	Motorcycles	Sidecar Motorcycles
Command Group	6		1	11	11	7	2	5	3
Signals Section			7	18	16	9 (2)	5 (2)		
Combat Trains			2	5	4	3	2	1	
Maintenance Section		2	2	12	10	6	5		1
Rations Trains			1	5	5		3	1	
Baggage Trains		1	2	3	4	2	2	1	
Totals	**6**	**3**	**15**	**54**	**50**	**27 (2)**	**19 (2)**	**8**	**4**

The Motorcycle Infantry Company

KStN	Type of Unit	German	Date
1111	Motorcycle Infantry Company	*Kraftradschützen-Kompanie*	1 October 1937

Notes: Also known as: *Kraftradschützen-Schwadron* (Cavalry) and *Kraftradschützen-Sturm (SS)*. Updated: 1 February 1941. Renumbered, as of 1 November 1941: *KStN 1112*

a) Command Group

3x Motorcycle, 1x Sidecar Motorcycle | Medium Cross-Country Vehicle (*Kfz. 11*) | Tactical Vehicle, 3 ton (*Kfz. 18*)

Total Command Group: 1x Officer, 2x NCOs, 9x Enlisted Personnel; 9x Rifles, 3x Pistols; 2x Wheeled Vehicles, 3x Heavy Motorcycles, 1x Sidecar Motorcycle

b) 1st Motorcycle Infantry Platoon
Platoon Headquarters Section

2x Motorcycle | Medium Cross-Country Vehicle (*Kfz. 11*) | Tactical Vehicle, 3 ton (*Kfz. 18*)

3 Squads

3x Sidecar Motorcycle, 1x Light MG | 3x Sidecar Motorcycle, 1x Light MG | 3x Sidecar Motorcycle, 1x Light MG

Light Mortar Section

2x Sidecar Motorcycle, 1x Light Mortar

Totals for Motorcycle Infantry Platoon: 1x Officer, 4x NCOs, 34x Enlisted Personnel; 31x Rifles, 8x Pistols, 3 Light MG's, 1x Light Mortar; 2x Wheeled Vehicles, 11x Sidecar Motorcycles, 2x Heavy Motorcycles

c) 2nd Motorcycle Infantry Platoon
Platoon Headquarters Section

2x Motorcycle | Medium Cross-Country Vehicle (*Kfz. 11*) | Tactical Vehicle, 3 ton (*Kfz. 18*)

3 Squads

3x Sidecar Motorcycle, 1x Light MG | 3x Sidecar Motorcycle, 1x Light MG | 3x Sidecar Motorcycle, 1x Light MG

Light Mortar Section

2x Sidecar Motorcycle, 1x Light Mortar

Totals for Motorcycle Infantry Platoon: 1x Officer, 4x NCOs, 34x Enlisted Personnel; 31x Rifles, 8x Pistols, 3x Light MG's, 1x Light Mortar; 2x Wheeled Vehicles, 11x Sidecar Motorcycles, 2x Heavy Motorcycles

d) 3rd Motorcycle Infantry Platoon
Platoon Headquarters Section

2x Motorcycle | Medium Cross-Country Vehicle (*Kfz. 11*) | Tactical Vehicle, 3 ton (*Kfz. 18*)

3 Squads

| 3x Sidecar Motorcycle, 1x Light MG | 3x Sidecar Motorcycle, 1x Light MG | 3x Sidecar Motorcycle, 1x Light MG |

Light Mortar Section

2x Sidecar Motorcycle, 1x Light Mortar

Totals for Motorcycle Infantry Platoon: 1x Officer, 4x NCOs, 34x Enlisted Personnel; 31x Rifles, 8x Pistols, 3x Light MG's, 1x Light Mortar; 2x Wheeled Vehicles, 11x Sidecar Motorcycles, 2x Heavy Motorcycles

e) Heavy MG Section   Section Headquarters

2x Sidecar Motorcycle

1st Section   2nd Section

4x Sidecar Motorcycle, 1x Heavy Machine Gun   4x Sidecar Motorcycle, 1x Heavy Machine Gun

Total Heavy MG Section: 3x NCOs, 22x Enlisted Personnel; 17x Rifles, 8x Pistols, 2x Heavy MG's; 10x Sidecar Motorcycles

f) Combat Trains

| 2x Sidecar Motorcycle | Medium Cross-Country Vehicle with Equipment Storage Box (*Kfz. 15*) for Medical Personnel | Light Cross-Country Truck for Large Field Mess Stove |

| Light Cross-Country Truck for Petroleum, Oil & Lubricants and Equipment | Light Cross-Country Truck for Petroleum, Oil & Lubricants | Light Cross-Country Truck for Ammunition and Combat Engineer Equipment |

Total Combat Trains: 6x NCOs, 11x Enlisted Personnel; 12x Rifles, 5x Pistols; 6x Vehicles, 2x Sidecar Motorcycles

g) Baggage Trains

| Light Truck, Canvas Top, for Baggage | Motorcycle |

Total Baggage Trains: 4x Enlisted Personnel; 4x Rifles; 1x Vehicle, 1x Heavy Motorcycle

Summary

	Officers	NCOs	Enlisted Personnel	Rifles	Pistols	Light MG's	Heavy MG's	Light Mortars	Vehicles	Heavy Motorcycles	Heavy Motorcycle/ Sidecar Motorcycles
Command Group	1	2	9	9	3				2	3	1
1st Platoon	1	4	34	31	8	3		1	2	2	11
2nd Platoon	1	4	34	31	8	3		1	2	2	11
3rd Platoon	1	4	34	31	8	3		1	2	2	11
Heavy MG Section		3	22	17	8		2				10
Combat Trains		6	11	12	5				6		2
Baggage Trains			4	4					1	1	
Totals	4	23	148	135	40	9	2	3	15	10	46

Prewar Organizations of Reconnaissance Forces: *Kradschützen-Bataillon continued*

THE MOTORCYCLE MACHINE-GUN COMPANY

As there is only a theoretical construct for this company, it is not illustrated in detail. It is believed to have contained:
- Headquarters section: three motorcycles, one sidecar motorcycle, one heavy cross-country wheeled personnel carrier (*Kfz. 18*), and one cross-country wheeled personnel carrier (*Kfz. 70*).
  - Two light telephone sections, each with one medium cross-country wheeled personnel carrier (*Kfz. 15*).
- Two machine-gun platoons:
  - Headquarters section: three motorcycles, one medium cross-country utility vehicle (*Kfz. 11*), and one heavy cross-country wheeled personnel carrier (*Kfz. 18*).
  - Light telephone section: one medium cross-country wheeled personnel carrier (*Kfz. 15*).
  - Ammunition section: two sidecar motorcycles.
  - Two machine-gun sections: six sidecar motorcycles and two heavy machine guns.
- Mortar platoon:
  - Headquarters section: one motorcycle, one medium cross-country utility vehicle (*Kfz. 11*), and one cross-country wheeled personnel carrier (*Kfz. 70*).
  - Three mortar sections: one medium cross-country utility vehicle (*Kfz. 11*), two cross-country wheeled personnel carriers (*Kfz. 70*), and two mortars (81mm).

THE MOTORIZED HEAVY COMPANY

The company headquarters section was essentially an administrative entity for the subordinate combat elements.
- Headquarters: two motorcycles, two sidecar motorcycles, and one medium cross-country utility vehicle (*Kfz. 11*).

The antitank platoon of October 1937 was organized as follows:

Platoon Headquarters Section

Sidecar Motorcycle, 1x Medium Motorcycle	Wheeled Vehicle (*Kfz.69*)

Gun 1	Gun 2	Gun 3
Prime Mover (*Kfz. 69*) and 3.7cm AT Gun (*PaK 37*)	Prime Mover (*Kfz. 69*) and 3.7cm AT Gun (*PaK 37*)	Prime Mover (*Kfz. 69*) and 3.7cm AT Gun (*PaK 37*)

1x Prime Mover (*Kfz. 69*) (Ammunition), 1x Light Machine Gun

Totals: 1x Officer, 5x NCOs, 24x Enlisted Personnel; 15x Rifles, 15x Pistols, 1x Light MG, 3x 3.7cm AT Guns; 5x Prime Movers, 1x Medium Motorcycle, 1x Sidecar Motorcycle

Prewar Organizations of Reconnaissance Forces: *Kradschützen-Bataillon continued*

The light infantry gun platoon of October 1937 was organized as follows:

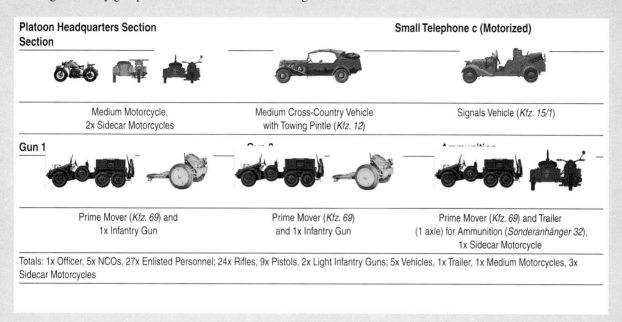

Totals: 1x Officer, 5x NCOs, 27x Enlisted Personnel; 24x Rifles, 9x Pistols, 2x Light Infantry Guns; 5x Vehicles, 1x Trailer, 1x Medium Motorcycles, 3x Sidecar Motorcycles

The motorized combat engineer platoon of October 1937 was organized as follows:

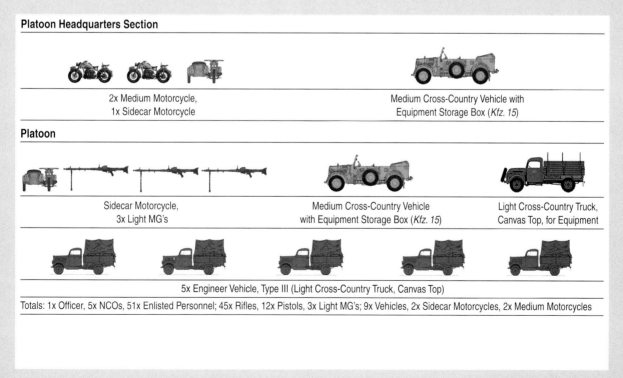

Totals: 1x Officer, 5x NCOs, 51x Enlisted Personnel; 45x Rifles, 12x Pistols, 3x Light MG's; 9x Vehicles, 2x Sidecar Motorcycles, 2x Medium Motorcycles

Prewar Organizations of Reconnaissance Forces:
Aufklärungs-Abteilung (mot)

The prewar organization of an *Aufklärungs-Abteilung (mot)* had a headquarters company (*KStN 1105* / 1 October 1937) with a subordinate signal platoon (*KStN 1191* / 1 October 1937) and a subordinate motorcycle infantry platoon (*KStN 1134* / 1 March 1939), two armored car companies (*KStN 1162* / 1 October 1938), a motorcycle reconnaissance company (*KStN 1111* / 1 October 1937), and a motorized heavy company. In the case of the motorcycle reconnaissance and the motorized heavy companies, the organization was identical to those of the analogous companies in the motorcycle infantry battalion. As such, they will not be illustrated again here.

The Headquarters Company

a) Command Group

| 2x Heavy Sidecar Motorcycle, 3x Medium Motorcycles | Medium Cross-Country Vehicle (*Kfz. 11*) | Medium Cross-Country Vehicle with Equipment Storage Box (*Kfz. 15*) for Medical Personnel | Heavy Cross-Country Armored Vehicle (*Sd.Kfz. 247*), 1x Submachine Gun |

Total Command Group: 6x Officers, 1x NCO, 9x Enlisted Personnel; 9x Rifles, 7x Pistols, 1x Submachine Gun; 2x Wheeled Vehicles, 1x Armored Vehicle, 2x Sidecar Motorcycles, 3x Medium Motorcycles

b) Combat Trains

| Sidecar Motorcycle | Ambulance (*Kfz. 31*) | Light Truck, Canvas Top, for Armorer and Medical Equipment |

| Medium Cross-Country Vehicle with Equipment Storage Box (*Kfz. 15*) | Medium Cross-Country Vehicle with Equipment Storage Box (*Kfz. 15*) | Light Truck, Canvas Top, for Small Field Mess Stove |

| Light Truck, Canvas Top, for Vehicle Maintenance Equipment | Light Truck, Canvas Top, for Vehicle Maintenance Equipment | Light Truck, Canvas Top, for Petroleum, Oil & Lubricants |

Total Combat Trains: 3x Civilian Officials, 6x NCOs, 20x Enlisted Personnel; 17x Rifles, 12x Pistols; 8x Wheeled Vehicles, 1x Sidecar Motorcycle

Prewar Organizations of Reconnaissance Forces: *Aufklärungs-Abteilung (mot)* continued

c) Rations Trains (for the Entire Battalion)

| Light Cross-Country Vehicle (*Kfz. 1*) | Light Truck, Canvas Top, for Rations | Light Truck, Canvas Top, for Rations | Light Truck, Canvas Top, for Rations |

Total Rations Trains: 1x NCO, 4x Enlisted Personnel; 8x Rifles; 4x Trucks

Summary

	Officers	Civilian Officials	NCOs	Enlisted Personnel	Rifles	Pistols/Sub-machine Guns	Vehicles	Armored Vehicles	Motorcycles	Sidecar Motorcycles
Command Group	6		1	9	9	7 / 1	2	1	3	2
Combat Trains		3	6	20	17	12	8			1
Rations Trains			1	7	8		4			
Baggage Trains		1		4	4	1	1			
Totals	**6**	**4**	**8**	**40**	**38**	**20**	**15**	**1**	**3**	**3**

The signals platoon had extended communications capabilities, adding significantly to those found within the armored car companies.
- Headquarters: one motorcycle, two motorcycles with sidecars, one light telephone communications vehicle (*Kfz 17*), and one medium telephone communications utility vehicle (*Kfz 15/2*).
- Light telephone section: one medium signals utility vehicle (*Kfz 15/1*).
- Two manpack radio sections, each with one light radio utility vehicle (*Kfz 2/2*).
- Two medium radio sections (armored), each with one medium cross-country radio utility vehicle (*Kfz. 15/2*) and one medium radio armored car (*Sd.Kfz 263*).
- Four light radio sections (armored), each with one light armored radio car (*Sd.Kfz 261*).[4]
- One light radio section (armored): one light armored radio car (*Sd.Kfz 260*).

The motorcycle infantry platoon attached to the battalion headquarters was identical to a line motorcycle infantry platoon of a motorcycle infantry company within a *Kradschützen-Bataillon*.

The Armored Car Company

a) Command Group   Company Headquarters Section

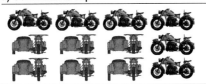

6x Sidecar Motorcycle,
3x Light Motorcycle,
3x Medium Motorcycle

Medium Cross-Country Vehicle (*Kfz. 11*), 1x Submachine Gun

Heavy Cross-Country Armored (*Sd.Kfz. 247*), 1x Submachine Gun

Total Command Group: 1x Officer, 2x NCOs, 15x Enlisted Personnel; 15x Rifles, 2x Submachine Guns, 3x Pistols; 1x Wheeled Vehicle, 1x Armored Wheeled Vehicle, 3x Medium Motorcycles, 3x Light Motorcycles, 6x Sidecar Motorcycles

b) Signals Section   Medium Armored Radio Section b (mot)

4x Light Armored Car (Radio) (*Sd.Kfz. 223 (Fu)*), 1x Light MG, 1x Submachine Gun

Radio Vehicle (*Kfz. 15*)

Armored Radio Car (*Sd.Kfz. 263*), 1x Light MG, 1x Submachine Gun

Total Signals Section: 5x NCOs, 15x Enlisted Personnel; 20x Pistols, 5x Submachine Gun, 5x Light MG's; 1x Vehicle, 5x Armored Vehicles

c) 1st (Heavy) Platoon

1st Section   **2nd Section**   **3rd Section**

Heavy Armored Car (*Sd.Kfz. 231*), 1x 2cm Main Gun, 1x Light MG, 1x Submachine Gun and Heavy Armored Car (Radio) (*Sd.Kfz. 232 (Fu)*), 1x 2cm Main Gun, 1x Light MG, 1x Submachine Gun

Heavy Armored Car (*Sd.Kfz. 231*), 1x 2cm Main Gun, 1x Light MG, 1x Submachine Gun and Heavy Armored Car (Radio) (*Sd.Kfz. 232 (Fu)*), 1x 2cm Main Gun, 1x Light MG, 1x Submachine Gun

Heavy Armored Car (*Sd.Kfz. 231*), 1x 2cm Main Gun, 1x Light MG, 1x Submachine Gun and Heavy Armored Car (Radio) (*Sd.Kfz. 232 (Fu)*), 1x 2cm Main Gun, 1x Light MG, 1x Submachine Gun

Total 1st (Heavy) Platoon: 2x Officers, 3x NCOs, 19x Enlisted Personnel; 24x Pistols, 6x Submachine Guns, 6x Light MG's; 6x Armored Vehicles

d) 2nd (Light) Platoon

1st Section   **2nd Section**   **3rd Section**

2x Light Armored Car (MG) (*Sd.Kfz. 221*), 2x Light MG, 2x Submachine Guns

2x Light Armored Car (MG) (*Sd.Kfz. 221*), 2x Light MG, 2x Submachine Guns

2x Light Armored Car (MG) (*Sd.Kfz. 221*), 2x Light MG, 2x Submachine Guns

Total 2nd (Light) Platoon: 1x Officer, 2x NCOs, 9x Enlisted Personnel; 12x Pistols, 6x Light MG's, 6x Submachine Guns; 6x Armored Vehicles

e) 3rd (Light) Platoon

1st Section	2nd Section	3rd Section	4th Section

Light Armored Car (MG) (*Sd.Kfz. 221*), 1x Light MG, 1x Submachine Gun and 1X Light Armored Car (2cm Main Gun, *Sd.Kfz. 222*)	Light Armored Car (MG) (*Sd.Kfz. 221*), 1x Light MG, 1x Submachine Gun and 1X Light Armored Car (2cm Main Gun, *Sd.Kfz. 222*)	Light Armored Car (MG) (*Sd.Kfz. 221*), 1x Light MG, 1x Submachine Gun and 1X Light Armored Car (2cm Main Gun, *Sd.Kfz. 222*)	Light Armored Car (MG) (*Sd.Kfz. 221*), 1x Light MG, 1x Submachine Gun and 1X Light Armored Car (2cm Main Gun, *Sd.Kfz. 222*)

Total 3rd (Light) Platoon: 1x Officer, 3x NCOs, 16x Enlisted Personnel; 20x Pistols, 8x Light MG's, 8x Submachine Guns; 8x Armored Vehicles

f) Combat Trains

2x Sidecar Motorcycle

Medium Cross-Country Utility Vehicle with Equipment Storage Box (*Kfz. 15*)

2x Light Cross-Country Trucks, Canvas Top, for Ammunition

Light Cross-Country Truck, Canvas Top, for Large Field Mess Stove

Light Cross-Country Truck, Canvas Top, for Vehicular and Engineer Equipment

Light Cross-Country Truck, Canvas Top, for Petroleum, Oil & Lubricants and Equipment

Light Cross-Country Truck, Canvas Top, for Petroleum, Oil & Lubricants

Light Cross-Country Truck, Canvas Top, for the Transport of Personnel

Total Combat Trains: 6x NCOs, 24x Enlisted Personnel; 25x Rifles, 5x Pistols; 8x Wheeled Vehicles, 2x Sidecar Motorcycles

Summary

	Officers	NCOs	Enlisted Personnel	Rifles	Pistols	Submachine Guns	Light MG's	Wheeled Vehicles	Armored Vehicles	Motorcycles	Sidecar Motorcycles
Command Group	1	2	15	15	3	2		1	1	6	6
Signals Section		5	15		20	5	5	1	5		
1st Platoon	2	3	19		24	6	6	6			
2nd Platoon	1	2	9		12	6	6	6			
3rd Platoon	1	3	16		20	8	8		8		
Combat Trains		6	24	25	5			8			2
Baggage Trains			4	4				1			
Totals	5	21	102	44	84	27	25	11	26	6	8

Photo Album: *5./Aufklärungs-Regiment 9 (mot)*

The images in this section came from a scout assigned to the *5./Aufklärungs-Regiment 9* of the *4. leichte Division (mot)* (later *9. Panzer-Division*). The 5th Troop was the first of the battalion's three armored car troops. At the time most of these images were taken, the troop commander was *Oberleutnant* Pössel, a transfer from the former Austrian Army and later recipient of the Knight's Cross as the commander of the *I./Panzer-Regiment "Großdeutschland"* (20 April 1943). Troop officers during this period were *Leutnant* Hardek and *Leutnant* Prinz zu Salm-Horstmar. (The latter is identified in several of the photographs in the album; he was killed in action in Poland on 9 September 1939.[6]) Much of the unit was Austrian, since the battalion was based in peacetime in Krems, Lower Austria.

The unidentified owner of the photo album, sometime in 1940 or later (based on his black overseas cap). The branch of service piping—*Waffenfarbe*—was golden yellow, a holdover from the time when the regiment was a part of the cavalry branch. MIKE DAVIS

Children clamber aboard an *Sd.Kfz. 232 (8 Rad)* during some sort of open house at the troop's garrison in Krems. In the second image, a scout checks his uniform during a pause in the activities. The license plate numbers were redacted in the original images in an effort to provide operational security and deny information about the unit. Since the vehicle has no national markings, these images were taken before the war. MIKE DAVIS

A crew dismounts a heavily smoking *Sd.Kfz. 232 (6 Rad)*. It is not certain whether the vehicle has been hit, caught on fire on its own, or is part of a training exercise. Since some of the crewmembers do not seem overly concerned and the photographer was in a position to capture both the front and rear of the vehicle, it was most likely a training exercise. Crew dismounting procedures and battle drills were of utmost importance in instilling almost instinctive responses in soldiers when seconds meant the difference between life and death, especially in the crowded confines of an armored vehicle. MIKE DAVIS

Several *Sd.Kfz. 222* medium armored cars stopped along a bridge, probably in prewar Germany. Tarpaulin covers have been placed over the turrets. The cylindrical device on the open door of the forward *Sd. Kfz. 222* is a portable fire extinguisher for the crew. MIKE DAVIS

Scouts amuse themselves during a break in operations or training. Note the effort to conceal the formation identity on the *Panzer* uniforms—a small piece of cloth was placed over the unit identifiers sewn into the shoulder straps on the tunics. Eventually, soldiers of all branches would be directed to remove any unit identification from their uniforms in the interest of operational security. It is believed that the center figure in both images is *Leutnant Prinz* zu Salm-Horstmar. MIKE DAVIS

Troop vehicles make their way down a street somewhere in Germany, most likely after the campaign in Poland. MIKE DAVIS

The officer next to the armored car appears to be wearing a version of the black overseas cap, which predates the official introduction of that same style of cap in 1940. Perhaps it is a dyed field-gray cap or a converted and dyed Luftwaffe officer's overseas cap, a modification occasionally seen. MIKE DAVIS

The troop lined up in a motor-pool setting, most likely sometime before or after the Polish campaign. This image provides a graphic example of the large number of different types of armored cars filling a unit's inventory at the time. MIKE DAVIS

Scouts on their early-model *Sd.Kfz. 221* await orders somewhere in Poland. The fascines on the rear of the vehicle were useful for recovering it whenever it had the misfortune of getting stuck. MIKE DAVIS

An *Sd.Kfz. 221* waits along a dirt trail somewhere in Poland. Although disliked by crewmembers, the steel helmet is worn by this vehicle commander, who presumably is fully cognizant of the limited ability of the vehicle's armor to protect him. MIKE DAVIS

This dramatic image shows armored cars and motorcycle infantry moving down a road toward a burning village. On the left, civilians appear to be fleeing the scene of the fighting. In the second image, an *Sd. Kfz. 232 (8 Rad)* appears to be maneuvering around a burning village, followed by a second vehicle. Finally, a column of *Sd.Kfz. 221's* passes by another burning village. MIKE DAVIS

"Der Chef und Kampfgruppenführer hilft „Sperren beseitigen."

Typical captioning for most of this album's photos is seen in the first image: "The Troop Commander and Battle Group Leader help remove obstacles." The officer is most likely *Oberleutnant* Pössel who, like the previously identified officer, appears to be wearing a non-regulation black overseas cap. The men appear to be wrapping a tow cable around a felled tree trunk in order to attach it to the heavy armored car and drag it away. In the second image, a more traditional method is used for dismantling the abatis. In the final image, tired troopers remove a section of fence from the road. While obstacles can be used to slow down a force, they are generally ineffective—or only temporarily effective—if not covered by the enemy. MIKE DAVIS

The troop headquarters pauses on an unimproved secondary road. The unusually large amount of traffic has transformed the packed dirt surface into a sea of sandy ruts. In the second image, elements of the troop's signals platoon speed down the road. Given the composition of the vehicles, it is most likely the platoon headquarters and an *Sd.Kfz. 263 (8 Rad)* from one of the two medium armored car signals sections. MIKE DAVIS

An *Sd.Kfz. 221* crosses an engineer bridge in a rear area. The crossing point seems to have its share of both military and civilian sightseers. MIKE DAVIS

A scout poses next to a knocked-out or abandoned Polish antitank gun, the 37mm *wz.36*, which was based on a Bofors design. MIKE DAVIS

The troop headquarters and an *Sd.Kfz. 263 (8 Rad)* from the signals platoon pause in a heavily damaged Polish town square. In the second image, an *Sd.Kfz. 263* crew poses for a picture in a wooded encampment. MIKE DAVIS

The turret crew of an *Sd.Kfz.222* strikes a martial pose. This close-up provides many details of the gun optics, 20mm cannon, and MG 34. Because the scouts are wearing black overseas caps, this image could not have been taken before 1940. MIKE DAVIS

Although not part of the battalion, the *15cm sIG 33 (Sf) auf Panzerkampfwagen I Ausf. B* was a heavy infantry gun that could have been attached to the scouts for immediate artillery support. Since this image was taken during the French campaign, when the battalion was part of the *9. Panzer-Division*, this rare vehicle probably belonged to *schwere Infanteriegeschütz-Kompanie 701*. The "C" denotes the third gun in the company. MIKE DAVIS

These scouts appear to appreciate their good fortune in walking away from this accident involving an *Sd.Kfz. 231/232 (6 Rad)*. Judging from the lack of battalion identifiers on the shoulder straps of the front scout, this image was probably taken in 1940. MIKE DAVIS

A scout poses in his *Sd.Kfz. 232 (8 Rad)* at the troop's home base in Germany. The spare tire is mounted in an unusual fashion, especially since it does not appear to be tied down or chained to the vehicle. MIKE DAVIS

This armored car—an *Sd.Kfz. 232 (8 Rad)*—was most likely knocked out during the fighting in the Balkans, as evidenced by the large "K" (*Kleist*) on the front slope and the tactical markings on the *Zerschellerplatte*, which were introduced in 1941. Note that the tactical insignia uses cavalry symbols to denote assignment to an armored car troop. In the second image, innumerable machine-gun penetrations can be seen in the *Zerschellerplatte*, the extra stand-off armor plate designed to provide additional protection against small-arms fire. MIKE DAVIS

Photo Album: Unidentified *Aufklärungs-Abteilung (mot)*

Troop canteens often provided a number of knick-knacks and souvenir items to remind service-members of their time with a unit or post. Likewise, photography studios often took company, platoon, and individual images of units and their soldiers. For those who did not possess cameras, which were still considered somewhat of a luxury at the time, small, generic photo albums were also available for purchase. The images here are from one such album, most likely from recruit training within a reconnaissance replacement detachment.

An unidentified reconnaissance company-grade officer, most likely the company commander. MICHAEL H. PRUETT

An officer, most likely the battalion commander, receives a report from a company first sergeant. In the second image, it can clearly be seen that he is a field-grade officer. MICHAEL H. PRUETT

Prewar driver training: learning how to negotiate water obstacles. This early *Sd.Kfz. 231 (6 Rad)* has a prewar stylized symbol for an armored car company below the radiator intake grill. In the second image, the vehicle is put through its paces in driving down a road covered in muck. The final two images show the less pleasurable side effect of that type of joyriding: cleaning an *Sd.Kfz. 221* and an *Sd.Kfz. 232 (6 Rad)*. MICHAEL H. PRUETT

This motorcycle messenger learns what his vehicle is capable of, while some of his comrades are reduced to pushing their machines through the muck. MICHAEL H. PRUETT

A noncommissioned officer briefs a section, most likely before conducting machine-gun training (two light machine guns are off to the side of the formation). MICHAEL H. PRUETT

Noncommissioned officers pore over a map while young soldiers look on. MICHAEL H. PRUETT

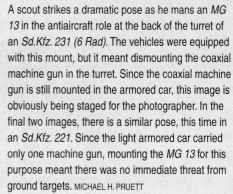

A scout strikes a dramatic pose as he mans an *MG 13* in the antiaircraft role at the back of the turret of an *Sd.Kfz. 231 (6 Rad)*. The vehicles were equipped with this mount, but it meant dismounting the coaxial machine gun in the turret. Since the coaxial machine gun is still mounted in the armored car, this image is obviously being staged for the photographer. In the final two images, there is a similar pose, this time in an *Sd.Kfz. 221*. Since the light armored car carried only one machine gun, mounting the *MG 13* for this purpose meant there was no immediate threat from ground targets. MICHAEL H. PRUETT

Armored cars—an *Sd.Kfz. 232 (6 Rad)* followed by a number of *Sd.Kfz. 221's*—lined up, perhaps before a movement. The stacked arms indicate this is probably a bivouac or training site. MICHAEL H. PRUETT

An *Sd.Kfz. 232 (6 Rad)* crosses a small berm. This image was frequently seen on period postcards. MICHAEL H. PRUETT

An *Sd.Kfz. 221* negotiates cross-country terrain at speed. MICHAEL H. PRUETT

Two static views of the predominant prewar medium armored cars: the *Sd.Kfz. 231 (6 Rad)* and the *Sd.Kfz. 232 (6 Rad)*. The latter image was also frequently seen on period postcards. MICHAEL H. PRUETT

Photo Album: *Aufklärungs-Abteilung 6 (mot)*

Aufklärungs-Abteilung 6 (mot) was assigned to the short-lived *1. leichte Division*, which was reorganized as the *6. Panzer-Division* after the Poland campaign. Upon reassignment, the reconnaissance battalion was redesignated as *Aufklärungs-Abteilung 57*. This battalion was among the army's oldest reconnaissance battalions, initially activated as *Kraftfahr-Abteilung Münster* on 1 October 1934. As such, the *Waffenfarben* seen here on the uniforms may have been either rose pink or golden yellow. The owner of this album was a scout in the battalion.

Portrait shot of the album's owner. He wears the first-pattern *Panzer* uniform with the narrow collar. His shoulder straps have the chain-stitched unit identifiers of his battalion (*A/6*). As is typical of prewar images, his only award is a sports badge. MICHAEL H. PRUETT

Scouts atop an *Sd.Kfz. 223* read a map on a training exercise. Two of the crew wear field-gray soft caps; the more iconic black cap was not introduced officially until 1940. MICHAEL H. PRUETT

Scouts pose for a group photo in front of an *Sd.Kfz. 222*. Given the presence of the Czech Model 35 Light Tank (*Lehký tank vzor 35*), which was adopted for service in the German Army as the *Panzerkampfwagen 35(t)*, this image was most likely taken sometime in 1939, after the German occupation. MICHAEL H. PRUETT

A swearing-in ceremony for new recruits, probably at the battalion's home garrison in Krefeld. Given the presence of the artillery pieces, this might have been a garrison-wide ceremony. Flanking the artillery and the speaker podium are two *Sd.Kfz. 232 (8 Rad)* armored cars. MICHAEL H. PRUETT

Battalion vehicles lined up in a town square in Czechoslovakia. Although the battalion was part of the *1. leichte Division*, one vehicle in the first image has the *Panzer*-style armored car tactical insignia as opposed to the more typical rectangle found in cavalry formations (*Sd.Kfz. 232 (8 Rad)* in the first image).
MICHAEL H. PRUETT

Prewar maneuvers. A 37mm *PaK 36* and limber from the division's antitank battalion can be seen clearly. The battalion's antitank platoon in the heavy company also had three of these types of guns and limbers. The front of a motorcycle from the battalion can be seen to the left. MICHAEL H. PRUETT

An *Sd.Kfz. 223* from the troop's headquarters signals section and an *Sd.Kfz. 222* from the mixed platoon have established themselves along an improved roadway somewhere in Czechoslovakia. In the second image, motorcycle infantry of the battalion cross the border into Czechoslovakia in March 1939. Finally, an antitank gun has set up along a street in another snowy setting. In this instance, it is uncertain whether it is in Czechoslovakia, since such shows of force were unusual during the occupation. It is more likely some sort of training exercise in Germany. MICHAEL H. PRUETT

Scouts take time to savor a hot meal in the open while lined up in a town square. Providing scouts with hot meals while out on extended patrols was nearly impossible, so any opportunity for warm food was greeted enthusiastically. MICHAEL H. PRUETT

Scouts and other members of the battalion gather around some confiscated Czech ordnance, in this case the *3.7cm KPÚV vz. 37* antitank gun, which was later adopted for German use as the *3.7cm PaK 37 (t)*. One of the guns has been placed in the back of a truck, while the one in the foreground has been limbered for towing, and a third gun, half-hidden by the soldiers, is also prepared for towing. The second image is of rarely seen Czech armored cars, which were also confiscated by the Germans. In the foreground is an *OA vz. 27 (Obrněný automobil vzor 27)* (rear view). Initially produced in 1929, it was armed with three 7.92mm machine guns; fifteen were built and nine fell into German hands.[7] The authors have been unable to identify the second armored car, perhaps a prototype of some sort. MICHAEL H. PRUETT

Scouts pose in front of their vehicles along a road. Of particular interest is the rampant lion insignia on the front of the *Sd.Kfz. 223*. Its significance is unknown, since it is not seen on other vehicles of the battalion. MICHAEL H. PRUETT

Battalion vehicles speed along an improved road, probably in Germany. Since there are a large number of images of this exact vehicle, it can be assumed that the album's owner was probably a crewmember on it or on the *Sd.Kfz. 223*, which is usually preceding it. MICHAEL H. PRUETT

Vehicles of the battalion display the distinctive white *Balkenkreuze* associated with the campaign in Poland. In typical gallows humor, German armor crews referred to them as aiming points for enemy gunners. MICHAEL H. PRUETT

Dusty scouts stand in front of the *Sd.Kfz. 223*, probably sometime after the start of the Polish campaign. Of interest in this image is the one scout to the right: he appears to be carrying his pistol unholstered in his pistol belt. MICHAEL H. PRUETT

An *Sd.Kfz. 232 (6 Rad)* makes its way across an engineer bridge set up next to a demolished one. MICHAEL H. PRUETT

Battalion vehicles have been adorned with flowers, indicating these images were taken around the October 1938 occupation of the *Sudetenland*, where this was a common practice. MICHAEL H. PRUETT

Photo Album: Unidentified *Aufklärungs-Abteilung (mot)*

The owner of this album was most likely assigned as a crewmember of an *Sd.Kfz. 223* (given the number of images of that particular vehicle) and the 2nd Company, thus making it one of the reconnaissance battalions of an armored division during the prewar era.

Typical prewar image of a scout manning an *MG 13* behind the turret of an *Sd.Kfz. 231 (6 Rad)*. Details of the antiaircraft mount and the vision ports can be seen. The vehicle appears to have been painted in the prewar two-tone camouflage scheme of dark brown and armor gray, which is very difficult to discern in black-and-white images. MICHAEL H. PRUETT

The scout's *Sd.Kfz. 223* has suffered a mechanical breakdown on the *Autobahn*. Note the oversize and stylized insignia of an armored car on the vehicle's rear stowage box. In the second image, the 9-meter mast antenna has been mounted, considerably extending the radio's range. MICHAEL H. PRUETT

The battalion has entrained for a rail movement to Putlos, Germany, for gunnery training. In the second image, heavy armored cars have lined up to fire, while personnel attend to range administrative details in the background. Finally, this moving target has been peppered with a number of hits. The cable for towing it can be seen along the ground. MICHAEL H. PRUETT

The stylized armored car insignia on a battalion truck and motorcycle. MICHAEL H. PRUETT

In this orders conference, some of the soldiers can be seen wearing the M1918 helmet, which featured unique ear cutouts and is popularly associated with cavalry units. The soldiers may have transferred into the battalion from the cavalry, a common occurrence. MICHAEL H. PRUETT

Prewar exercises involving the battalion.
MICHAEL H. PRUETT

Photo Album: *Aufklärungs-Abteilung (mot) 2*

This battalion was assigned to the *2. Infanterie-Division (mot)*, which later became the *12. Panzer-Division*. The owner of this album was most likely assigned to the *Sd.Kfz. 231 (8 Rad)* with license plate WH-27266, seen in many of the images.

An *Sd.Kfz. 232 (6 Rad)* prepared for rail movement. End ramps such as those seen here were much preferred for loading on trains, since the driver simply had to stay centered on the rail cars. Sometimes it was only possible to load from the side, which was considerably more difficult as there was a danger of tipping the rail car when first boarding it at an oblique angle. Once on board and secured—a portion of the tie-down chains can be seen in the second image with the *Sd. Kfz. 231 (6 Rad)*—the side stakes were raised or inserted, and the rail cars could be safely moved.
MICHAEL H. PRUETT

The battalion was part of a festival and sheltered in large tents, which have benefitted from efforts to improve their "curb appeal," particularly with the large armored car drawn in colored sand. MICHAEL H. PRUETT

Exhausted and dirt-encrusted scouts take a break next to an *Sd.Kfz. 222* during a prewar training exercise, while a unit commander enjoys a more lighthearted moment with some of his men in the second image.

MICHAEL H. PRUETT

Portions of the scout company's heavy platoon lead this column of armored cars. As was frequently the case, the *Sd.Kfz. 231's* and *Sd.Kfz. 232's* were a mix of six- and eight-wheeled versions. An *Sd.Kfz. 222* brings up the rear. MICHAEL H. PRUETT

An *Sd.Kfz. 231 (8 Rad)* about the time of the campaign in the West. It appears to have been painted in the brown-and-gray two-tone camouflage pattern. The battalion number is painted next to the stylized armored car insignia (partially obscured by the taillight) above and to the right of the left rear license plate. MICHAEL H. PRUETT

Decorated with flowers, this *Sd. Kfz. 231 (8 Rad)* participates in victory celebrations following the fall of France in 1940. Evidence of the brown-and-gray two-tone camouflage scheme can be seen in the second image. MICHAEL H. PRUETT

Photo Album: *Aufklärungs-Abteilung 3 (mot)*

Aufklärungs-Abteilung 3 (mot) was another of the old-line reconnaissance battalions stemming from *Kraftfahr-Abteilung Wünsdorf*. Activated on 1 October 1934, it was redesignated on 15 October 1935, stationed in Stahnsdorf, and assigned to the *3. Panzer-Division*. In January 1941 it was reassigned to the *5. leichte Division* and served in North Africa.

Studio portrait of the album's owner. The scout wears the early-pattern *Panzer* uniform, allowing ready identification of his unit of assignment. MICHAEL H. PRUETT

Draftees becoming young recruits underwent an elaborate swearing-in ceremony. Local dignitaries and higher-ranking officers attended in large numbers, and the speaker's podium was often flanked with vehicles and equipment representative of the formation. In this instance, the two-tone prewar camouflage pattern can be seen on the gun shields of the *PaK 36* and the *Sd.Kfz. 231 (8 Rad)*. MICHAEL H. PRUETT

The generally cramped space inside the turret of a fighting vehicle can be seen in this image of two scouts in the fighting compartment of an *Sd.Kfz. 231 (6 Rad)*.
MICHAEL H. PRUETT

A column of *Sd. Kfz. 221's* and *223's* prepares to move out along a cobblestone street in a German town.
MICHAEL H. PRUETT

Time for a little horseplay while attempting to retrieve this stuck Krupp *L2H143 Kfz. 69* prime mover, generally used to tow the antitank and infantry guns of the battalion.
MICHAEL H. PRUETT

An *Sd. Kfz. 231 (6 Rad)* appears to be firing its main gun while moving along a range road. Given the location of the photographer, all of the targets must have been off to the vehicle's right. Based on other photographs in the series, this image may have been taken at the ranges in Putlos. MICHAEL H. PRUETT

The company commander with some of his senior noncommissioned officers and the company first sergeant. The company officer (second from the left) is a young *Leutnant* Gerd von Born-Fallois, who would later serve as a liaison officer within the battalion headquarters. He later served in North Africa and became commander of the *Panzeraufklärungs-Lehr-Abteilung 130*. He was awarded the Knight's Cross on 29 January 1945. In the second image, much of the company takes a break during maneuvers. MICHAEL H. PRUETT

At first glance, nothing seems out of the ordinary in this image; however, closer inspection reveals a carefully concealed 7.5cm *leichtes Infanteriegeschütz 18* issued to the infantry gun platoon of the battalion's heavy company. MICHAEL H. PRUETT

A bottomed-out *Sd.Kfz. 223* receives some assistance in being retrieved. The soldiers on the vehicle's right are attempting to add more ground pressure on the "free" side of the vehicle in an effort to facilitate the recovery. MICHAEL H. PRUETT

This *Sd.Kfz. 221* guards the entry point to the woods along an intersecting set of trails. Hasty camouflage has been applied to the vehicle, which, for some reason, is positioned nose-first toward the woods. The driver has joined the vehicle commander in the one-man turret, perhaps in an effort to keep warm in the unheated, open-top armored car. MICHAEL H. PRUETT

Company elements prepare to cross a water obstacle with the aid of an engineer ferry. Engineer assistance was required in the absence of bridges whenever suitable fording sites could not be found. Here, the ferry gets underway with its cargo. In training exercises such as these, when safety was paramount and there was no threat of attack when the vessel was at its most vulnerable, the engineers and the scouts could afford their relaxed stance. MICHAEL H. PRUETT

A column of company vehicles moves down an unimproved road. Even with relatively light vehicular traffic, massive clouds of dust soon developed, which not only impaired vision but also made life miserable for crews in the open vehicles.
MICHAEL H. PRUETT

The company poses for a group photograph in its dress uniform, the *Waffenrock*. In the second image, senior personnel pose for the camera. The company mascot, probably the commander's pet, seems unimpressed in both instances. MICHAEL H. PRUETT

Photo Album: *Aufklärungs-Abteilung 7 (mot) / Kradschützen-Bataillon 34*

This album belonged to a scout serving initially with *Aufklärungs-Abteilung 7 (mot)* of the *4. Panzer-Division*, one of the army's original reconnaissance battalions. Activated as *Kraftfahr-Abteilung München* on 1 October 1934, it was originally assigned to the short-lived *Aufklärungs-Brigade*. In 1937, the battalion was reassigned to the *2. Panzer-Division*, only to receive its final reassignment to the *4. Panzer-Division* in 1938. It was later redesignated as *Panzer-Aufklärungs-Abteilung 7*, before being consolidated with *Kradschützen-Bataillon 34* in May 1942. The scout served in the battalion's signals section, primarily on the *Sd.Kfz. 263*.

Prewar water-crossing exercises, demonstrating the crossing of an engineer bridge by a Krupp prime mover. MICHAEL H. PRUETT

A motorcycle messenger is positioned near an *Sd.Kfz. 263* in a field training exercise. The large mast antenna remained covered to protect it from the elements; radio communications are being conducted via the frame antenna. MICHAEL H. PRUETT

Scouts clown around for the camera by wearing their gas masks. The soldier in the field-gray uniform also wears the *Schützenschnur*, the marksmanship lanyard, which is unusual in a field environment unless he just came from a range, where it was common to allow the soldier to wear his award on the field uniform the first day. Note that the scout on the left is carrying an obsolescent *MP 18* of World War I vintage. MICHAEL H. PRUETT

Scouts await movement in their Krupp prime movers. In an effort to maintain operational security, the unit identifiers on their shoulder straps have been covered with slides or patches of cloth. MICHAEL H. PRUETT

This *Sd.Kfz. 263 (6 Rad)* has slid off a road and overturned. Although the damage appears extensive, it was probably salvageable. Since only twelve of these were built, the maintenance personnel would have put extra effort into recovering the vehicle without further damage and repairing it. MICHAEL H. PRUETT

Another view of an *Sd.Kfz. 263 (6 Rad)*, probably the album owner's vehicle, this time in the Bavarian Alps during training. Even if the mast for the extended-range antenna cannot be seen, the vehicle can still be identified by the two support staffs for the frame antenna that are located to the front of the non-traversing turret and by the elliptical tube framing that allowed the mast to extend through the frame antenna (seen here in shadow). MICHAEL H. PRUETT

The album's owner in his *Sd.Kfz. 263 (8 Rad)* somewhere on the Russian Front. Note the generous application of whitewash, including one of the crew helmets. In the second image, the scout proudly displays his Iron Cross, Second Class, and his War Service Cross, both just awarded. By then, the reconnaissance battalion had probably been consolidated with the motorcycle infantry battalion. MICHAEL H. PRUETT

Photo Album: *Aufklärungs-Abteilung 3 (mot)*

Another prewar album from an unidentified scout assigned to the *1./Aufklärungs-Abteilung 3 (mot)* of the *3. Panzer-Division*, which was later reassigned to the *60. Infanterie-Division (mot)* (future *Panzergrenadier-Division "Feldherrnhalle"*) as part of *Aufklärungs-Abteilung 160 (mot)*.

The album owner as a young recruit and, in the second image, an unidentified company *Unteroffizier*. In both instances, it is easy to tell the unit of assignment because of the shoulder strap insignia.

A view inside the rear driver's compartment of the *Sd.Kfz. 231* or *232 (6 Rad)*.

The battalion participates in a parade in occupied Czechoslovakia, probably the *Sudetenland*. The relatively rarely seen *Sd.Kfz. 247 (6 Rad)* serves as a standard-bearing vehicle. One of these vehicles was supposed to be assigned to each battalion headquarters, functioning as a command and control vehicle for the battalion commander. Production shortfalls account for its rarity, and the lack of integral radio equipment for its relative unpopularity. Note the battalion headquarters insignia on the left front mudguard.

This series of images was probably taken on the Russian Front in the city of Stalino. The scouts have received the Iron Cross, Second Class, in some of the photographs (normally worn in ribbon form, the Iron Cross was worn as a medal on the first day a soldier received it). By then, the 1st Company had been transferred to *Aufklärungs-Abteilung 160 (mot)*, as evidenced by the divisional emblem in the form of the double yellow crosses on the vehicle's left fender. Hasty "urban" camouflage has been applied to these light armored cars parked outside an apartment building, which has been transformed into the battalion headquarters. In the third image, an *Obergefreiter* poses in front of a dirty and slightly battle-damaged *Sd.Kfz. 232 (8 Rad)*. In the last image, he is joined by several comrades in front of the same vehicle.

Company portrait of the *1. (Panzerspäh-)/Aufklärungs-Abteilung 1 (mot)*. Everyone in the company, with the exception of the commander and his company officer, pose in their issued black *Panzer* uniform. The company First Sergeant can be seen to the commander's right, identifiable by the two rings of silver braid on his lower sleeves. These were referred to in soldier jargon as *Kolbenringe* ("piston rings"). The company is flanked by the two heavy armored cars it had at the time, the *Sd.Kfz. 231 (6 Rad)* and the *Sd.Kfz. 232 (6 Rad)*, both of which have been christened in typical reconnaissance-unit fashion with names (white lettering on the sides of the hull). The date of the image is unknown.

German reconnaissance elements in infantry divisions still had horse-mounted scouts before the war started and well into the early part of the war. Horse cavalry continued to play an important role on the Eastern Front until the end of the war.

An unidentified *Reichswehr* unit participates in winter training in a mountain setting with vehicles meant to represent armored fighting vehicles. These mock-ups were built on an *Adler Standard* truck chassis and were present within the *Kraftfahr-Abteilungen*. Vehicle 2 has the early three-tone camouflage scheme of yellow, brown, and green.

Civilians check out the unusual sight offered them via the maneuvers. Due to prewar Versailles Treaty restrictions, Germany was only allowed to have armored cars for police duties. In the second image, the same line of armored cars is seen from the rear.

These motorcycle infantry or messengers have the unenviable task of attempting to negotiate the snow and icy conditions on their motorcycles. It appears that some sort of ski-type board has been affixed to the motorcycles, perhaps in an effort to improve their stability in the wintry conditions.

Unit vehicles lined up in the snow.

Although technically belonging to the infantry branch, motorcycle infantry battalions quickly became the *de facto* partners of the fledgling reconnaissance forces, since they were the fastest formation in an armor division and could provide reconnaissance elements with additional ground manpower and relatively high concentrations of automatic small-arms fire. In addition, each prewar reconnaissance battalion had a company of motorcycle infantry. A popular postcard of the period shows a column of *Kradschützen* from a reconnaissance battalion rolling down the road. In the next two images, motorcycle infantry assets are neatly lined up in a motor pool and preparing to move out on training. Another postcard emphasizes the potential threat posed by chemical weapons, which all armies took seriously both before the start of hostilities and until relatively late in the war. Although the motorcyclist seen in the final image is probably a messenger, the photo shows details of the rubberized overgarment issued to riders to protect them from the elements and, to lesser extent, road splash and debris. LAST IMAGE: MICHAEL H. PRUETT

Kradschützen im Vormarsch

An unidentified reconnaissance battalion has lined up to participate in a party function of some sort. It is believed this may have been for one of the annual parades held in April to celebrate the birthday of the *Führer*.

Vehicles of an unidentified reconnaissance battalion bivouac in the shade. Based on the all-white *Balkenkreuze* on the vehicles, this image was taken around the time of the campaign in Poland. Four different types of armored cars are parked close together.

Scouts in the motor pool of *Aufklärungs-Abteilung 5 (mot)* take a break and pose for a comrade's camera. In the second image, scouts work on their vehicles in front of motor-pool bays. Note the vehicular nomenclature stenciled on each of the vehicles on the upper portion of the left front hull. JIM HALEY

Elements of a reconnaissance battalion are thronged by curious civilians during a rest break while on maneuvers. Most of the armored cars have their custom-fitted tarpaulins mounted, indicating the battalion might be bivouacking there for the night. JIM HALEY

Several varieties of armored cars, led by the *Panther*, an *Sd.Kfz. 231 (8 Rad)*, are parked along a narrow cobblestone street. Given the small swastika banner on the *Sd.Kfz. 222*, the vehicles may be staging for participation in an event somewhere. MIKE HARPE

Vehicles of a reconnaissance battalion move through a Czechoslovakian town during the occupation. MIKE HARPE

Vehicles of a heavy scout platoon line up in an open area during maneuvers. The crewmembers wear coveralls, a common practice in many reconnaissance units. MIKE HARPE

A *Reichswehr*–era reconnaissance battalion, fielding a variety of early armored cars, including the already obsolete *Kfz. 13 Adler*. The first two *Adler* cars have had tarpaulins placed over the crew compartment, clearly showing the camouflaged, form-fitting covers produced for these vehicles and, analogously, for other armored cars. The second image shows more covered *Adler* cars belonging to a different unit, with the two-tone camouflage pattern. JIM HALEY

A makeshift motor pool and maintenance facility has been established in this farmer's barnyard for a reconnaissance element during prewar maneuvers.

This *Sd.Kfz. 221* of the *2./Aufklärungs-Abteilung 5 (mot)* appears to have needed some assistance in getting unstuck. Curious civilians look on as a scout returns to his vehicle. Although these vehicles possessed a modicum of cross-country mobility, their light weight and relatively low power-to-weight ratio was not enough to keep them from bogging down in even relatively benign situations such as this. JIM HALEY

Scouts of the *Aufklärungs-Abteilung 5 (mot)* observe for the "enemy" from their *Sd.Kfz. 221* during prewar maneuvers. Note the presence of additional fuel cans and concertina wire on the rear deck of the vehicle. Reconnaissance assets not only had to contend with extended missions involving great distances, but also master the art of conserving or obtaining fuel, since battalion supply elements could not be pushed forward to them. JIM HALEY

The men perform maintenance and consume rations during a rest break for a road march involving these *Sd.Kfz. 221's* and other vehicles of *Aufklärungs-Abteilung 5 (mot)*. JIM HALEY

Images of the *Sd.Kfz. 222* in prewar service. This vehicle has had a *Zerschellerplatte* mounted on the front to provide additional protection against small-arms fire. The canvas top for the turret remains in place over the grenade screens. The scout behind the gunsight wears the prewar field-gray overseas cap. AKIRA TAKIGUCHI

In this atmospheric setting, scouts pose on the balcony of a mountain cabin next to an *Sd.Kfz. 222*, which has its weapons elevated in an air-defense mode. Apparently, some local youngsters may have had their fun by writing *Sau* ("pig") in the fresh coat of snow on the front slope of the vehicle. AKIRA TAKIGUCHI

While two scouts appear to be dozing in the warming rays of a winter's sun, others work industriously on their *Sd.Kfz. 222's*. Other vehicles of *Aufklärungs-Abteilung 7 (mot)* flank them and bring up the rear. AKIRA TAKIGUCHI

An *Sd.Kfz. 222* in profile on an open plain somewhere in Germany. In the second image, a scout poses with the business end of the vehicle's weapons. JIM HALEY

An *Sd.Kfz. 222* sets off its smoke candles as part of an exercise in clearing an obstacle. Note the officer or noncommissioned officer off to the side, who is probably grading the exercise. MIKE HARPE

Wherever they went, armored vehicles proved to be an irresistible attraction to children of the area. MIKE HARPE

Images of the *Sd.Kfz. 223* in prewar service. A scout poses in the vehicle commander's position. A large "E" has been painted on the front and sides of the vehicle, possibly indicating its position within the platoon. The tactical sign for a motorized cavalry platoon appears on the front slope of the hull, as do several other markings that have not been identified. AKIRA TAKIGUCHI

This *Sd.Kfz. 223* was apparently assigned to *Panzer-Nachrichten-Abteilung 37* of the *1. Panzer-Division*, but is shown here because it provides interesting details of the commander's turret and also was widely present in reconnaissance battalions. AKIRA TAKIGUCHI

A scout stands guard in the field motor pool of a reconnaissance battalion. Of interest here is the shelter half-mounted around the stowage box on the front slope of the *Sd.Kfz. 223*.

Scouts pose in a lighthearted manner in front of an *Sd.Kfz. 223*, whose machine gun appears to have suffered some sort of severe maneuver damage. It is doubtful these scouts would have retained the same expressions when their superiors came by. In the second image, scouts from the same unit pose next to their vehicle, with some imposing scenery in the background. HENNER LINDLAR

A company bugler practices his craft in front of a rail-loaded *Sd.Kfz. 223*. While drills were still sometimes conducted by bugle calls before the war, the practice was discontinued by its start. JIM HALEY

Images of the *Sd.Kfz. 231 (6 Rad)* in prewar service. The *Boelke* is an early *Sd.Kfz. 232 (6 Rad)* in an unidentified *Reichswehr Kraftfahr-Abteilung* or *Aufklärungs-Abteilung (mot)*. Behind it is an *Sd.Kfz. 232 (6 Rad)*. The scouts wear *Reichswehr* work/drill uniforms and caps. Some of the scouts wear the *Panzer* beret/crash helmet, but the only insignia on it is a national wreath, placing this image in the early 1930s.

A canteen postcard image of an *Sd.Kfz. 231 (6 Rad)*.

Images of the *Sd.Kfz. 231 (8 Rad)* in prewar service. A pristine *Sd.Kfz. 231 (8 Rad)* parked outside a company building shows the three-tone camouflage scheme popular in the mid-1930s. As was typical in a garrison environment, the weapons were not mounted in an effort to minimize wear and tear and keep them in a secure environment in the arms room. AKIRA TAKIGUCHI

A scout strikes a dramatic pose with the turret of his *Sd.Kfz. 231 (8 Rad)* traversed to 270 degrees. This image comes through the estate of later Knight's Cross recipient Ulrich Kreß, who was assigned to the *2./Aufklärungs-Abteilung 20 (Kradschützen-Bataillon 30)* of the *20. Infanterie-Division (mot)*. AKIRA TAKIGUCHI

The unidentified scouts of this *Sd.Kfz. 231 (8 Rad)* have decided to take an ice cream break in a German town while on maneuvers. HENNER LINDLAR

This second-story view of an *Sd.Kfz. 231 (8 Rad)* provides details of the rear deck and top of the hull and turret. JIM HALEY

Scouts pose with their weathered vehicles, an *Sd.Kfz. 231 (8 Rad)* and an *Sd.Kfz. 232 (8 Rad)*, in the motor pool of an unidentified training area.

Members of the Hitler Youth enthusiastically inspect an *Sd.Kfz. 231 (8 Rad)*. Based on the vehicular insignia, the photograph was probably taken sometime after the campaign in France. MIKE HARPE

Images of the *Sd.Kfz. 232 (6 Rad)* in prewar service. In the first photo, scouts appear to be performing some sort of maintenance at the rear of the vehicle. The two-tone camouflage scheme can be seen. Of interest is the open access panel to the crew compartment, which retains the interior buff color even though portions of hatches exposed to the outside when opened were supposed to be painted in a color matching the exterior scheme.

An officer and several scouts of *Aufklärungs-Abteilung 8 (mot)* of the *5. Panzer-Division* appear to be studying a map in front of their *Sd.Kfz. 232 (6 Rad)*, which has its turret traversed to 90 degrees. Most of the hatches appear to have been opened, perhaps in an effort to cool off during a hot spell. The soldiers continued to wear full regulation attire, including closed shirts and ties, in their wool uniforms, which could become uncomfortably hot in even warm weather. Also of interest in this image is the "8" appearing on top of the stylized armored car. Usually, battalion numbers were located to the right and slightly below the armored car symbol. AKIRA TAKIGUCHI

Scouts pose around a railcar loaded with an *Sd.Kfz. 232 (6 Rad)*. The vehicle has had a tarpaulin placed over the turret to protect it in case of inclement weather. The small cabin at the end of the railcar was for the brakeman, who would ride in it at the end of a train, the German equivalent of the American caboose. JIM HALEY

This *Sd.Kfz. 232 (6 Rad)* has traversed its turret to the nine o'clock position. It has a light coat of dust on its superstructure and is more heavily weathered along its chassis. Based on the orientation of the turret and the presence of what appears to be a target in the far-right corner of the image, this may be a gunnery range, possibly at Putlos. JIM HALEY

A scout poses in front of a row of *Sd.Kfz. 232 (6 Rad)* armored cars in a dirt motor pool, possibly at a training area. JIM HALEY

A popular period canteen postcard featured this *Sd.Kfz. 232 (6 Rad)* from an unidentified reconnaissance battalion. MICHAEL H. PRUETT

Images of the *Sd.Kfz. 232 (8 Rad)* in prewar service. Scouts pose in front of their vehicle. A large stowage box has been placed behind the turret, and the license plate has been obscured by a wartime censor in the interests of operational security.

These scouts take advantage of a feature of the *Sd.Kfz. 232 (8 Rad)* that would probably have the original designer cringing. Given the large "K" on the front slope of the armored car, this photograph was probably taken during the campaign in France, when field laundry service was obviously not available.

Details of the *Sd.Kfz. 232 (8 Rad)* can be seen to good advantage in this oblique view of an armored car assigned to *Aufklärungs-Abteilung 5 (mot)* of the *2. Panzer-Division*.
JIM HALEY

This *Sd.Kfz. 232 (8 Rad)* of *Aufklärungs-Abteilung 5 (mot)* has taken up a concealed position during maneuvers, although the local citizenry seems well aware of its location. JIM HALEY

An *Sd.Kfz. 232 (8 Rad)* parked on a cobblestone road in mountainous terrain.

The only armored elements within the *SS* prior to the outbreak of war were its reconnaissance assets. This *SS Sd.Kfz. 232 (8 Rad)* has had flowers and greenery attached to it, thus identifying the image as having been taken about the time of the Austrian *Anschluß* or the march into the *Sudetenland*.

The *Sd.Kfz. 247*, designed to be a command and control vehicle for a battalion commander, was produced in limited quantities in both a four-wheeled and six-wheeled version. This particular vehicle has been upgraded with the addition of radio communications equipment, which was not integral to the factory-delivered vehicles. AKIRA TAKIGUCHI

Images of the *Sd.Kfz. 263 (6 Rad)* in prewar service. A crew poses in front of this rare vehicle, which had been issued to *Aufklärungs-Abteilung 7 (mot)* of the *4. Panzer-Division*. AKIRA TAKIGUCHI

Another *Sd.Kfz. 263 (6 Rad)* from *Aufklärungs-Abteilung 7 (mot)*. The 9-meter antenna appears to have been fully extended. AKIRA TAKIGUCHI

This *Sd.Kfz. 263 (6 Rad)* from *Aufklärungs-Abteilung 7 (mot)* is prepared for inspection. Of interest are the access panels to the rear driver position and the fold-down mount for the spare tire. AKIRA TAKIGUCHI

Scouts strike a casual pose by their *Sd.Kfz. 263 (6 Rad)* armored radio cars. In the last image, two of the crew take a break in their tent, while another two peer from the vehicle. The men may be on radio watch during an exercise, requiring the radios be manned twenty-four hours a day. JIM HALEY

This *Sd.Kfz. 263 (6 Rad)* was assigned to the signals platoon of *Aufklärungs-Abteilung 2 (mot)* of the *2. Infanterie-Division (mot)*. MICHAEL H. PRUETT

CHAPTER 2

Baptism of Fire

SETTING THE STAGE

With the breakdown of political discussion concerning the "Danzig Corridor," and sensing continued weakness on the part of the Western European powers, Hitler decided to invade Poland. *Fall Weiß* (Case White) started on 1 September 1939 and marked the start of World War II in Europe, with France and the United Kingdom declaring war on Germany, even though the Western European nations would not see ground combat against Germany until the following year. The Soviet Union and a small Slovakian contingent also participated in the hostilities, with the Soviets launching their invasion of the country from the east on 17 September 1939, one day after concluding hostilities with Japan and one week after signing a non-aggression pact with Germany. Hostilities ended on 6 October, although there was no formal surrender on the part of the Polish government.

This fighting represented the baptism of fire for Germany's armed forces and the limited testing of *Blitzkrieg* tactics, represented principally on the ground by the new *Panzertruppe*.

Motorcycle infantry line up to move out on an operation. Motorcycle infantry had the distinction of being the fastest ground combat force in the German Army. It also possessed a lot of firepower for its relative size: two heavy machine guns, nine light machine guns, and three 50mm mortars. Its speed allowed it to move across the battlefield very quickly, assuming it had access to relatively good roads behind the front, but the soldiers normally still needed to dismount in order to fight, since they were extraordinarily vulnerable while riding on their motorcycles. NATIONAL ARCHIVES

DOCTRINE

Doctrinally, the reconnaissance forces were not immediately employed in the predawn crossing of the Polish frontier in most sectors, since that effort represented a deliberate attack and initial reconnaissance had been conducted by the assault forces. Once the enemy lines had been penetrated, however, it was the task of the reconnaissance forces to range deeply into the enemy rear area to determine the location, size, and intent of enemy forces, as well as the suitability of the terrain and road network for motorized and mechanized forces.

HDv 299/10 called for a battalion to be able to cover between 200 and 250 kilometers a day, and up to 40 kilometers an hour for scout patrols. (The entire text of *HDv 299/10* can be found in Appendix 1.) Of course, these figures were for planning purposes and did not take into account enemy contact or the absence of a suitable road network. While the latter was not as much of an issue in Poland, it was to become a crippling limitation in much of the Soviet Union.

According to the manual, the mission of the initial reconnaissance effort

> is to ferret out the enemy and determine his location in a specific area or to establish contact with enemy forces reported by aerial reconnaissance. To that end, a scouting of only the most important roads and traffic nodes will generally suffice. To determine the location of the enemy force, his organization for combat and the actions of the enemy force that has been identified, the reconnaissance effort is to be intensified.

These actions generally worked in Poland, although the speed of the armored forces was often held in check by its relative tethering to traditional foot infantry formations, since conservative elements of the military hierarchy did not fully trust the concept of maneuver warfare. Due to lack of combat experience on one hand and the tough defense offered by Polish forces on the other, casualties tended to be relatively high, both in men and materiel.

As with all maneuver elements, the reconnaissance battalion also organized its elements to generally have scouting elements out front, followed by a smaller advance guard, and then the main body, which generally also contained the reconnaissance reserve. In paragraph 54 of *HDv 299/10*, the reader finds that the

> reconnaissance battalion establishes a reconnaissance reserve, reporting points and backup for its reconnaissance patrols. It moves forward by bounds. The length of the bounds is influenced by the closeness of the enemy and the nature of the terrain and its vegetation. As the distance to the enemy becomes closer, the length of the bounds is to be shortened.

Once combat had been joined, it was quickly determined that scouting forces and even the organic motorcycle infantry of the reconnaissance battalion were inadequate to deal with a determined foe, especially if he had antitank weaponry. In the case of the armored divisions, the motorcycle infantry battalions soon became habitual partners of the reconnaissance forces. In addition, reconnaissance battalions were beefed up with additional heavy weaponry, often in the form of tanks, antitank assets, artillery batteries, and/or combat engineers, to help them conduct battlefield reconnaissance more effectively. With these additional assets, the reconnaissance battalions frequently then served as the command and control headquarters for the division advance guard.

Enemy elements, once found, were often bypassed, with maneuver combat forces, such as rifle or armor elements, brought forward to develop the situation. If the enemy force could not be bypassed, then the reconnaissance forces were usually held in place until relieved by heavier combat elements, or pulled back to provide flank guard or screening missions for the division. It was up to the relieving forces to perform the necessary battlefield reconnaissance to further develop the situation. Once the bottleneck had been cleared, scouting elements were again sent forward to begin the process anew.

Reconnaissance Assets of the Major Armored Combat Formations

Parent Organization	Reconnaissance Assets	Notes
Armored Divisions / Formations		
1. Panzer-Division	Kradschützen-Bataillon 1	Assigned to the *1. Schützen-Brigade*. Each of the two rifle battalions in *Schützen-Regiment 1* also had a motorcycle infantry company (organized as the analogous company in the motorcycle infantry battalion). The battalion had a headquarters (*KStN 1109* / 1 October 1937), three motorcycle infantry companies (*KStN 1111* / 1 October 1937), one motorcycle machine-gun company (*KStN 1118* / 1 October 1938), and one motorized heavy company (*KStN 1121* / 1 October 1937) with one antitank platoon (*KStN 1122* / 1 October 1937), one light infantry gun platoon (*KStN 1123* / 1 October 1937), and one combat engineer platoon (*KStN 1124* / 1 October 1937).
	Aufklärungs-Abteilung 4 (mot)	Division troop asset. The battalion consisted of a headquarters (*KStN 1105* / 1 October 1937) with an attached signals platoon (*KStN 1191* / 1 October 1938) and a motorcycle infantry platoon (*KStN 1134* / 1 March 1939), two armored car companies (*KStN 1162* / 1 October 1938), one motorcycle reconnaissance company (*KStN 1111* / 1 October 1937), and one motorized heavy company (as with *Kradschützen-Bataillon 1*).
	Armored Car Platoon	Attached to division headquarters through the end of the Polish campaign. Organized under *KStN 1165* of 1 March 1939, consisting of one sidecar motorcycle, four *Sd.Kfz. 221's*, and four *Sd.Kfz. 222's*.
2. Panzer-Division	Kradschützen-Bataillon 2	Assigned to the *2. Schützen-Brigade*. Each of the two rifle battalions in *Schützen-Regiment 2* also had a motorcycle infantry company (organized as the analogous company in the motorcycle infantry battalion). *Kradschützen-Bataillon 2* was organized the same as *Kradschützen-Bataillon 1* above.
	Aufklärungs-Abteilung 5 (mot)	Division troop asset. The battalion was organized like *Aufklärungs-Abteilung 4 (mot)* above.
	Armored Car Platoon	As with the *1. Panzer-Division* above.
3. Panzer-Division	Kradschützen-Bataillon 3	Assigned to the *3. Schützen-Brigade*. Each of the two rifle battalions in *Schützen-Regiment 3* also had a motorcycle infantry company (organized as the analogous company in the motorcycle infantry battalion). *Kradschützen-Bataillon 3* was organized the same as *Kradschützen-Bataillon 1* above.
	Aufklärungs-Abteilung 3 (mot)	Division troop asset. The battalion was organized like *Aufklärungs-Abteilung 4 (mot)* above.
	Armored Car Platoon	As with the *1. Panzer-Division* above.
4. Panzer-Division	*Aufklärungs-Abteilung 7 (mot)*	Division troop asset. The battalion was organized like *Aufklärungs-Abteilung 4 (mot)* above. The division did not have a motorcycle infantry battalion. The division did not have an armored car platoon in the division headquarters.
5. Panzer-Division	*Aufklärungs-Abteilung 8 (mot)*	Division troop asset. The battalion was organized like *Aufklärungs-Abteilung 4 (mot)* above, with the following exceptions: The motorized heavy company did not have an antitank platoon, but it did have two light infantry gun platoons. The division did not have a motorcycle infantry battalion, although each of the rifle regiments (*Schützen-Regiment 13* and *Schützen-Regiment 14*) had a motorcycle infantry company. The division did not have an armored car platoon in the division headquarters.
10. Panzer-Division	*I./Aufklärungs-Regiment 8*	This battalion had been detached from its parent regiment in the *3. leichte Division* and served with the division throughout the campaign. Organized analogously to *Aufklärungs-Abteilung 4 (mot)* above, although companies were referred to as troops.
Panzer-Verband Kempf	*SS-Aufklärungs-Sturmbann (mot)*	The only reconnaissance battalion of the *SS-Verfügungstruppe*, the *Sturmbann* (battalion equivalent) was attached to the armored formation for the duration of the campaign in Poland. It had a battalion headquarters with an attached signals platoon, two motorcycle infantry companies (*KStN 1111a* / 1 October 1938), and the rough equivalent of a motorized heavy company, albeit without a company headquarters: one motorized antitank platoon (*KStN 1122* / 1 October 1937), one combat engineer platoon (*KStN 1124* / 1 October 1937), and one armored car platoon (*KStN 1136* / 1 March 1939).
	SS-Standarte (mot) "Deutschland"	The *Standarte* (regiment equivalent) had several reconnaissance assets, including a motorcycle infantry company (*KStN 1111* / 1 October 1937) and an armored car platoon (*KStN 1136* / 1 March 1939).

Parent Organization	Reconnaissance Assets	Notes
Light Divisions		
1. leichte Division	Kradschützen-Abteilung 6	The battalion headquarters and the three motorcycle infantry companies were organized the same as *Kradschützen-Bataillon 1* above. The machine-gun troop of the battalion was motorized instead of motorcycle borne and organized under *KStN 1116* of 1 October 1937. The battalion did not have a heavy troop; instead, there was a single antitank platoon, organized as the analogous platoon in *Kradschützen-Bataillon 1* above.
	Aufklärungs-Abteilung 6 (mot)	Organized analogously to *Aufklärungs-Abteilung 4 (mot)* above, although companies were referred to as troops.
2. leichte Division	Aufklärungs-Regiment 7	The headquarters was organized under *KStN 1101* of 1 October 1937. It had an attached signals platoon (*KStN 1191* / 1 October 1938) and a motorcycle infantry platoon (*KStN 1134* / 1 March 1939).
	I./Aufklärungs-Regiment 7	This *Kradschützen-Abteilung* had a headquarters organized like *Kradschützen-Bataillon 1* above but with an attached combat engineer platoon (*KStN 1124* / 1 October 1937). The three motorcycle infantry troops were organized under the same *KStN* as the analogous companies in *Kradschützen-Bataillon 1*. The motorized heavy troop had a troop headquarters, an antitank platoon, two light infantry gun platoons, and a mortar platoon. The mortar platoon was organized under *KStN 1126* of 1 October 1938 and had three sections of two 81mm mortars each, for a total of six medium mortars.
	II./Aufklärungs-Regiment 7	This battalion had the armored car troops of the regiment and was referred to as a *Panzer-Späh-Abteilung*. The battalion headquarters consisted of a headquarters (*KStN 1105* / 1 October 1937) with an attached signals platoon (*KStN 1191* / 1 October 1938). The four armored car troops were organized analogously to the armored car companies of *Aufklärungs-Abteilung 4 (mot)* above. Note this was the only battalion with four scout troops. The battalion did not have a heavy company.
3. leichte Division	II./Schützen-Regiment 9	This was the *de facto* motorcycle infantry battalion of the division and organized like *Kradschützen-Abteilung 6* (*1. leichte Division*) above.
	Aufklärungs-Regiment 8	The regiment's 1st Battalion served with the *10. Panzer-Division* during the Polish campaign. The headquarters was organized analogously to that of *Aufklärungs-Regiment 7*, although the organizational documents were slightly different.
	II./Aufklärungs-Regiment 8	Organized analogously to *Aufklärungs-Abteilung 4 (mot)* above, although companies were referred to as troops.
4. leichte Division	Aufklärungs-Regiment 9	The headquarters was organized analogously to that of *Aufklärungs-Regiment 7*, although the organizational documents were slightly different.
	I./Aufklärungs-Regiment 9	The motorcycle infantry battalion of the regiment, it was organized analogously to that of the *I./Aufklärungs-Regiment 7*.
	II./Aufklärungs-Regiment 9	The armored car troop of the regiment, it was organized analogously to the *II./Aufklärungs-Regiment 7* above, with the exception that it only had two armored car troops.
Motorized Infantry Divisions		
2. Infanterie-Division (mot)	Aufklärungs-Abteilung 2 (mot)	The reconnaissance battalions of motorized infantry divisions had one armored car company and one motorcycle infantry company. The battalion consisted of a headquarters (*KStN 1105a* / 1 October 1937) with an attached signals platoon (*KStN 1191a* / 1 October 1938), one armored car company (*KStN 1162* / 1 October 1938), and one motorcycle reconnaissance company (*KStN 1111*). There was no heavy company.
13. Infanterie-Division (mot)	Aufklärungs-Abteilung 13 (mot)	As with *Aufklärungs-Abteilung 2 (mot)*
20. Infanterie-Division (mot)	Aufklärungs-Abteilung 20 (mot)	As with *Aufklärungs-Abteilung 2 (mot)*
29. Infanterie-Division (mot)	Aufklärungs-Abteilung 29 (mot)	As with *Aufklärungs-Abteilung 2 (mot)*
SS-Verfügungstruppe		
Field Army Reserves	SS-Standarten	The *Standarte* (regiment equivalent) had several reconnaissance assets, including a motorcycle infantry company (*KStN 1111* / 1 October 1937) and an armored car platoon (*KStN 1136* / 1 March 1939). "Deutschland" was attached to *Panzer-Verband Kempf* (see above). The remaining three *Standarten* were initially attached to field armies as operational reserves: *Leibstandarte SS Adolf Hitler*—*10. Armee*; *SS-Standarte "Germania"*—*14. Armee*; and *SS-Standarte "Der Führer"*—*7. Armee*.

Headquarters of a Motorized Reconnaissance Regiment

Aufklärungs-Regiment 7 of the *2. leichte Division* and *Aufklärungs-Regiment 9* of the *4. leichte Division* were organized under *KStN 1101* of 1 October 1937. In addition to the headquarters proper, the regiment had a signals platoon and a motorcycle infantry platoon at its disposal. Those elements are detailed in the discussion of the headquarters of an *Aufklärungs-Abteilung (mot)* in Chapter 1.

MOTORIZED MORTAR PLATOON

The *I./Aufklärungs-Regiment 7* of the *2. leichte Division*, which was a motorcycle infantry battalion, had a mortar platoon in its heavy company. The platoon was organized under *KStN 1126* of 1 October 1938.

a) Command Group

| Medium Cross-Country Vehicle (Kfz. 11) | Heavy Cross-Country Armored Vehicle (Sd.Kfz. 247) | 3x Medium and 2x Heavy Sidecar Motorcycle |

Total Command Group: 3x Officers, 2x NCOs, 8x Enlisted Personnel; 8x Rifles, 3x Pistols; 3x Vehicles, 2x Sidecar Motorcycles

b) Combat Trains

| Medium Cross-Country Vehicle with Equipment Storage Box (Kfz. 15) | Light Cross-Country Truck for Petroleum, Oil & Lubricants and Equipment | Light Cross-Country Truck for Small Field Mess Stove | 2x Heavy Sidecar Motorcycle |

Total Combat Trains: 4x NCOs, 7x Enlisted Personnel; 8x Rifles, 3x Pistols; 3x Vehicles, 2x Heavy Sidecar Motorcycles

c) Rations and Baggage Trains (also for Signals Platoon)

| Light Utility Vehicle (4 seat) | Light Truck for Baggage and Rations |

Total Rations and Baggage Trains: 1x NCO, 4x Enlisted Personnel; 4x Rifles, 1x Pistol; 2x Wheeled Vehicles

Summary

	Officers	NCOs	Enlisted Personnel	Rifles	Pistols	Submachine Guns	Vehicles	Armored Vehicles	Medium Motorcycles	Sidecar Motorcycles
Command Group	3	2	8	8	5	1	1	1	3	2
Combat Trains		4	7	8	3		3			2
Rations Trains		1	4	4	1		2			
Totals	3	7	19	20	9	1	6	1	3	4

Headquarters of a Motorized Reconnaissance Regiment continued

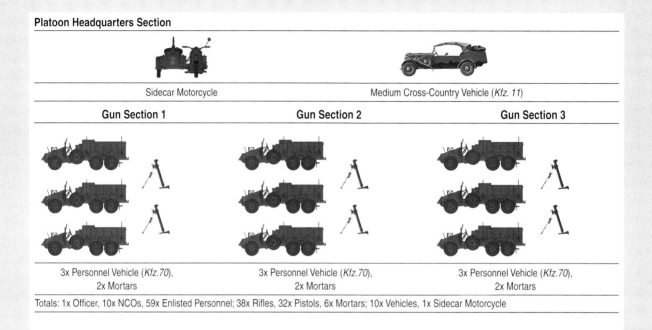

LESSONS LEARNED AND FIRSTHAND ACCOUNTS

Because of the relative quickness of the campaign and the respite that followed until the campaign in the West in 1940, numerous firsthand accounts concerning the fighting were written, and the German Army used the opportunity to take stock of its doctrine and operations. Of course, the postwar divisional and other unit histories have a wealth of material on the campaign, since there was substantially more in the way of documentation that survived the war, particularly in the form of the unit daily logs, often going down to company level.

The unofficial history of the Berlin-based *3. Panzer-Division* recounts the following concerning the first morning of operations:[1]

> Tank after tank followed, with the *Panzer-Lehr-Abteilung* in the lead. Following close behind, dispersed across a wide frontage, was the rest of the armor brigade. Interspersed were a few squads of riflemen, mounted in the few *SPW's* that were available. The rifle brigade followed closely behind the armor elements in two groups. *Oberst* Angern, the brigade commander, led one group, while *Oberst* Kleemann was in charge of the second one. The riflemen crossed the border on foot. The motorcycle battalion started moving through the barbed wire at 0500 hours and was committed behind the armor regiments.
>
> *Panzer-Regiment 5* rolled forward on the right-hand side of the attack zone, followed closely by the motorcycles of the *2./Kradschützen-Bataillon 3*. The battalion's 3rd Company followed it, leading a *Flak* battery, the 1st Company of the motorcycle battalion and the 4th and 5th Batteries of the divisional artillery into sector. *Panzer-Regiment 6* was employed on the left-hand side of the attack zone; its 1st Company was on the right, the 2nd Company on the left and the 4th Company following. The

remaining motorcycle elements, the 2nd and 3rd Companies of the divisional engineers and a light *Flak* battery followed the tanks. *General* Guderian rode at the front in an *SPW* among the regiment's tanks.

At this point, no mention is even made of *Aufklärungs-Abteilung 3 (mot)*, the division's reconnaissance battalion. In a deliberate attack, it was the responsibility of the maneuver elements to conduct their own battlefield reconnaissance; the reconnaissance battalion was held in reserve or used to conduct guard or screen missions. Since the front was continuous, the latter missions did not come into play until after forces had advanced into enemy territory. The division's motorcycle infantry battalion's companies were detached to serve as infantry backstop for the tanks after they had broken through the enemy's initial defenses and started to move forward to exploit the situation. Once the penetration had occurred, reconnaissance elements were usually passed forward through the lead combat elements to perform their traditional missions, as illustrated in the following passage:[2]

> The 1st Company of *Kradschützen-Bataillon 3* assumed the mission of protecting the division command post with one of its platoons. The remaining two platoons advanced into the woods north of Hammermühle. Two Polish infantry companies were wiped out in tough fighting. The two platoons lost two dead and four wounded in that engagement and only had 30 men altogether by the end of the evening . . .
>
> In the meantime, the motorcycle battalion had taken Klonowo with its remaining two companies and a few tanks from the *Panzer-Lehr-Abteilung*. Unconcerned about the sounds of fighting to their rear, the motorcycle infantry and reconnaissance troopers continued their advance east. The sun blazed mercilessly that day; with rain following in the afternoon. The tanks and riflemen moved, marched and advanced. The roads were poor and frequently only had a single lane. All of the traffic had to work its way around that. The roads became clogged and there were unpleasant stops. The reconnaissance battalion was far ahead of the division and moved right through the middle of enemy detachments, which were equally shocked and surprised and incapable of offering a defense. *Major* von Wechmar intended to reach the Vistula before the onset of darkness. But intertwined enemy columns or vehicles and trees that had fallen victim to *Stukas* blocked the way. The enemy was not falling back uniformly. Resistance around Rozana was especially hard.
>
> The reconnaissance battalion was unable to advance any further. The armored car crews, supported by the 1st Battery of the artillery regiment (*Leutnant* Hoffmann), had a hard fight on their hands at the Poledno Estate, which was being defended by Polish cavalry. The advance guard suffered its first officer casualties: The commander of the *2./Aufklärungs-Abteilung 3*, *Rittmeister* von Prittwitz und Gaffron, the former adjutant to *Generaloberst* von Fritsch,[3] was wounded in the stomach. The brave officer refused to be operated on at the main clearing station, insisting that the surgeons operate on the more severely wounded first. *Leutnant* Adam died on the battlefield at the head of his reconnaissance platoon. Once stopped, the battalion "circled the wagons" with its vehicles, the village of Rozana, set alight by air attacks and artillery, forming a backdrop.
>
> The motorcycle battalion pivoted from its movement east to head south in order to help the reconnaissance battalion. But the motorcycle infantry were not able to get beyond the line reached by the armored cars . . .

Here is another account of the initial fighting by the same elements:[4]

> . . . in the vicinity of the locality of Hammermühle, the reconnaissance battalion [*Aufklärungs-Abteilung 3*] succeeded in taking the bridge over the Brahe. That same night, the commander of the [battalion], *Major* von Wechmar, was entrusted with leading the advance guard: In addition to his [battalion], he had a battery from *Artillerie-Regiment 75* [the

divisional artillery] and a few tanks from the *Panzer-Lehr-Abteilung* [attached to the division for the campaign]. Objective: The Vistula. Shortly after the advance guard and *Kradschützen-Bataillon 3* had departed, strong elements of two Polish divisions and a cavalry brigade attacked the German bridgehead at Hammermühle . . . [description of fighting there] . . .

Unconcerned about the sound of fighting far to the rear, the men of the [reconnaissance battalion and the motorcycle infantry battalion] pressed on further to the east. The gigantic woods had an eerie effect. The yellow dust of the sandy roads rose into gigantic clouds and descended like powder on the vehicles, uniforms and faces of the men. That afternoon, it rained—the reconnaissance elements thundered on through shocked Polish troop elements, which did not offer any defense due to their surprise. Columns shattered by *Stuka* attacks blocked the route, and shredded trees lay across the road. Outside of Rozana, Polish rifle fire stopped the advance.

Polish cavalry stubbornly defended the estate at Poledno, which the [attached] battery shelled to pieces and the armored cars attacked. *Leutnant* Adam fell at the front of his reconnaissance platoon. *Rittmeister* von Prittwitz und Gaffron was badly wounded by a round to the stomach. Yellowish-red flames shot skyward from Rozana, which had been set alight and in front of which the [battalion] had circled its vehicles. The motorcycle infantry and the divisional engineers raced to help the reconnaissance force . . . as the 1st Company [of the motorcycle infantry battalion] attempted to take a rest behind the railway embankment at Belno, a train steamed towards them. The motorcycle infantry halted it, and had the passengers detrain: Four Polish officers and 128 enlisted.

In the meantime, the [reconnaissance battalion] moved parallel to the Vistula in the direction of Graudenz. The motorcycle infantry and the crews of the armored cars had gotten used to the danger by then and were in the process of seeing it as part of the daily routine. Scattered Polish soldiers fired occasionally from farmsteads and outbuildings. They no longer had a unified command. An occasional burst of fire from a machine gun caused them to surface from out of haystacks, gardens, vegetation and houses and raise their hands. The reconnaissance men moved through the dust, the rifle fire, the heat of the sun and the nights that were already appreciably cold. They had almost gotten used to doing without sleep; their eyes burned from tiredness. The roads were in miserable condition and the craters required attentiveness. Fuel lines and springs broke. On 5 September, the motorcycle infantry were the first to cross the Vistula towards Graudenz. The entire *3. Panzer-Division* was following them . . .

The perennial dilemma between the need for speed and providing security for the force surfaced in the first days of the war. Pressed by the division to move as rapidly as possible, a battalion commander usually had to push his patrols forward more rapidly than the situation might have otherwise dictated. The reconnaissance force had yet to develop that "sixth sense" that told the scout when he could speed up or needed to slow down.

Memoirs written after the campaign but published during the war suffered from the inevitable romanticizing that comes with wartime prose, but they also often provide an immediacy that gives the modern reader a sense for the *esprit de corps* that imbued the reconnaissance force. Here, for instance, are the exploits of a patrol leader from the *II./Aufklärungs-Regiment 9* of the *4. leichte Division*:[5]

From the high ground, I observed the bridge and the edge of Chocholow on the far bank for a long time. Nothing was stirring. Then, a man appeared next to the bridge. He waved to us. Was he trying to deceive us? The abatis in front of the bridge was opened and I correspondingly assumed that the bridge had been prepared for demolition. With my binoculars, I then discovered an object on the right side of the bridge that resembled a blasting device. But I was unable to make out anything more. To do that, I had to get closer. The driver allowed the armored car to roll forward carefully, while I kept a sharp eye on the surface of the ground. It would have been very easy for the enemy to set a trap, sending us sky high. Nevertheless, we reached the bridge without incident. The gunner screened; I jumped down from the vehicle and determined the condition of the bridge. I had been right; it had been prepared for demolition. Based on my mission, I was not to reconnoiter any further [at the bridge site]. A radio message was quickly sent off. In addition, a motorcycle messenger, who had ridden forward, was stopped at the bridge to keep anyone from crossing it for the time being.

While that was happening, my second vehicle had already reconnoitered a ford and reached the far bank. My driver was also able to master the somewhat difficult passage in superb fashion. We carefully felt our way into the village, but we did not find any trace of the enemy. So we proceeded to move in the direction of Carny-Dunajec. The road was straight and bordered on each side by fruit orchards. In front of us was a small group of farmsteads. My map showed another bridge there. I thought that perhaps the enemy had been surprised in Chocholow while preparing to blow the bridge and had not been able to destroy it based on our sudden appearance. That led me to believe that we might be able to prevent the bridge belonging to that group of farmsteads from being blown up if we were quick. Correspondingly, we sped through the hamlet at full throttle in the direction of the bridge. And what I had thought might happen, was happening: The Polish demolition party was in the process of preparing the charges. But they were too late! When the Poles saw us, they turned to flee. But our machine gun was already saying its piece. As a result, the bridge that had been prepared for demolition was intact.

After sending a message to that effect to the battalion, we moved on . . .

The small-unit example cited above provides good insight into the spirit of *Auftragstaktik* that was ingrained in junior leaders. Although the young officer could have easily waited for further orders, since he had accomplished his assigned mission, he chose to continue to scout to find another potential bridge site. With the concept of mission-type orders, a leader was free to take advantage of situations that presented themselves and fit with the overall concept of the commander. Of course, that concept only works well with leaders who are well trained and professionally competent.

The next passage details how easily the armored cars could be damaged by small-arms fire:[6]

> . . . All of a sudden, the enemy machine-gun fire was drumming against our armored car from another side. I soon came to the conclusion: We weren't going to advance any further there! We pulled back for a while.
>
> By then, the battalion command staff had advanced as far as the railway embankment. I dismounted and gave the Battalion Commander a situation report. Following that, I observed the battle damage on our armored cars. On two of the vehicles, some of the tires had been shot out; fenders and fuel cans had been penetrated. The driver of a 6-wheeled vehicle looked at his toolbox, which had been shot up. In his Swabian dialect, he badmouthed the Poles, who had completely shot up the hose for his air pump. "And how am I supposed to pump up my tires," he said to me. "The damned Poles have shot up everything!" I had to laugh at the outburst and I consoled him by saying he would get a new hose when the supply sergeant arrived from the rear.
>
> The tires were quickly changed. We then pushed our way forward towards the village.
>
> Our motorcycle infantry were attacking along both sides of the road, and the artillery was engaging the edge of the village. After a while, the enemy resistance collapsed completely.
>
> The road leading through the village was blocked in its entirety by felled trees. The *Unteroffizier* in the second vehicle turned off to the right. I remained on the road, however, and pushed all of the heavy trees out of the

way with my vehicle. Finally, the road was cleared and we continued in the direction of Novy-Targ.

While wheeled armored reconnaissance vehicles provided speed on improved road networks, their relative lack of heavy weaponry and armor protection made them prey to even heavy machine-gun fire. This was an issue that plagued armored reconnaissance forces of World War II and has carried on to ground reconnaissance forces in the modern era. Of course, the armored cars were doctrinally scouts and thus instructed to avoid combat, but when that failed, they were often at a disadvantage, especially against a defending force. It was in situations like those that speed, cunning, and initiative proved decisive, as illustrated in the next example:[7]

> At the crest of the hill, we found the first Polish field fortifications, which by then had been abandoned. The fact that they had been occupied was determined by the abandoned military equipment. Two armored car patrols, which had gone around Carny-Dunajec along the right-bank of the river, came back from Novy-Targ through the woods. The patrol leader reported to me that snipers and machine guns at the edge of the village made it impossible to enter the town.
>
> After thinking it over, I decided to get to the western outskirts on Novy-Targ by advancing along the riverbed. I would take along another scout section. From there, we would advance into the town. The third section was directed to fix the enemy in the woods during our approach and divert the undivided attention of Poles on it by making small advances. If we succeeded in entering the town, we would indicate it through signal flares. The two light armored cars remained behind; only the two 8-wheeled armored cars entered the river bottomland.
>
> I took point. The bottomland was filled with coarse sand and firm gravel. We were able to move rapidly forward without problems. However, just outside of Novy-Targ, we had to turn off to the left due to the railway bridge having been blown, blocking the entire riverbed. We then moved into marshy terrain. Despite that, we enjoyed good luck and were able to reach the railway embankment in front of us, which we soon crossed. During a short halt, I observed the edge of the town. A slope extended out in front of us, which led up to the road towards Krakow. It was under construction. I then observed where the road left Novy-Targ, and I could see extremely suspicious movements. They were bike riders in dark uniforms; they appeared to be assembling there to pull back. At that point, I was able to determine that they were the Polish State Police. It was a detachment of about 200 men. They had been putting up the previous resistance. We waited a bit until the detachment left the town. After two minutes, the lead elements could be seen on the road, which could be completely observed by us. A scout got the machine gun ready to fire; the *Unteroffizier* in the other vehicle let me know through a wave that he had identified the target. I gave the scout permission to fire; soon there were sprays of fire on the road. The Polish police then fled up the slope. The target no longer posed any threat; accordingly, I raced towards the edge of the town. The first few houses were soon reached. The field path we were on emptied into the main road at an acute angle. At that point, we needed to be careful. My vehicle pushed its way around the corner. Two vehicles were approaching us. A burst of machine-gun fire swept the street and brought the vehicles to a standstill. Button up and advance! Just before my head disappeared into the turret, I looked to see whether the *Unteroffizier* was still behind me. We then quickly moved into the town. About 100 meters in front of us, the road took a sharp turn to the right. We then found ourselves in front of the concrete and iron bridge that the Polish demolition parties had half destroyed. While the *Unteroffizier* and I dismounted and moved forward to check out the bridge, my radio operator also dismounted to search the [Polish] vehicles. He quickly determined that one of them was from the demolition party. By acting quickly, he

apprehended the driver. We found large quantities of explosives and igniters in the vehicle, along with a map with detailed information on the planned demolition targets . . .

In addition to combat experience, scouts also learned the limitations of their vehicles and equipment while on patrol:[8]

One day, we found ourselves in a position where we were no longer able to shoot, move and communicate—as the song goes—and found ourselves cut off and, with an overheated engine, a target for the Poles. You need to know: "Scouts out!" is easier said than successfully done. Fighting with the Poles was often only the last phase of a long battle with the vehicle, the routes and the weaponry. Right after the first few days of fighting, we were taught a lesson in how a small water obstacle can put an end to an entire scouting operation . . .

With its steel nose, the heavy vehicle felt its way forward across the vegetation and then moved into thin air with its first pair of wheels. It pushed forward deliberately, almost majestically, towards the water surface. Anything not nailed down slid slowly but surely towards the front driver, while his partner at the rear of the vehicle, released from the bonds of gravity, only saw blue skies above. A short while later, the feeling of being on a roller coaster was passed. The wheels firmly gripped into the sand, and all of the crew felt safe again. *U-Boot* time! The waves slapped against the starboard side and their whooshing mixed in with the sounds of the engine to a monotonous whole. Only a few meters separated us from the far bank. We were already starting to climb. The engine sounded louder and more powerful while the armored car pushed its way forward. The driver up front saw the sky and haze; the gunner saw colorful birds in his optics. The rear driver suddenly recognized what was to be our undoing. Before he could report, however, the result was already being felt. Water was being sucked into the intake ports; there was water in the carburetor! The engine stuttered, spat and shut down. That meant: That was all she wrote for any further movement! We could still fire and submit reports, however. We wound up not doing either. Instead, we helped the driver dry off the spark plugs. It was the best we could come up with. It must have looked pretty funny: Young guys in their underwear in the middle of enemy territory and under a blown-up bridge pulling maintenance!

One thing was certain, however: we had gained some experience. There was more to follow . . .

In the following account, a scout section has identified Polish forces in a town. While motorcycle infantry had engaged the Polish force, they were overwhelmed by an immediate counterattack and had to pull back. The vehicle commander and crew suddenly find themselves alone and with a stoppage on their machine gun:[9]

In the meantime, the situation changed. The Poles attempted to conduct a counterattack! Our motorized riflemen were unable to hold. They moved back down the road, firing, and disappeared into the village. We were all alone.

We pulled off into a covered position and waited. We could hear the slow-firing Polish machine guns firing bursts behind the burning houses of the village. The first few Polish infantry advanced. A burst from our weapons forced them back. They then attempted to attack from the flank. Turret traversed . . . sight picture . . .

Stoppage! Cock the bolt! Pull the trigger! A round went downrange and . . . stoppage! Of all the times! They were attacking. The scout section leader[10] worked feverishly on the machine gun. Nothing doing! The radio operator passed him a new bolt and took out a new barrel.

The Poles had recovered from the initial shock. They tried their attack for the second time. They saw that we could not fire and worked their way forward behind a garden fence. The first one jumped up and ran towards us. The others followed. Our machine gun still was not ready. Nonetheless, Ernst took up a sight picture and fired with the cannon. HE! It hit the first two at 15 meters in the chest. The effect was horrific. Not only for the Poles, but for us as well. They pulled back.

The motorized infantry then launched an immediate counterattack. They advanced far ahead of us. An antitank gun took up position next to us. We were relieved and were allowed to take off!

While most of the operations in these wartime narratives end relatively benignly for the participants, the following account shows the vulnerability of an armored car:[11]

It was 8 September, about 1700 hours and after several breakdowns, when we ran into our troop in Triziana with our 6-wheeled armored car. We had barely had time to freshen up a bit, when the word came: "Get ready to move out!" Another 6-wheeled vehicle and a machine-gun armored car, reinforced with some motorcycle infantry, formed the assault detachment, which was to be led by an *Oberleutnant*. The following was said during the short orders conference: "We are to advance in the direction of Rzeszow, occupy the road leading to the north from there, to include the north bridge. In doing so, we will cut off the retreat route north for the Poles."

We mounted up right away and took off. Our 6-wheeled vehicle was in the lead. We crossed a railway overpass. On the tracks were the burnt-out freight cars. We entered the first village. Nothing was stirring. Not a person was to be seen on the dusty streets. Everything looked dead.

Keep going towards the next village. Even from a distance, you could see smoke coming out of it and burning houses. As a result of the setting sun, everything looked like it had been bathed in blood. It was a terrible but beautiful picture! In the distance, figures appeared. Be careful! But it was only peasants. We moved through the village. People were standing around with defiant, grim expressions. They stared into the glowing and smoking rubble of their houses. Crying women, children . . .

When we reached the outskirts of the village, a destroyed bridge blocked our way. My vehicle commander reported this to the *Oberleutnant* and then jumped down from the vehicle to reconnoiter for a ford. He soon came back, however.

"You can't get through here," he reported.

That meant going back and finding another route. No one was moving in the same direction that we needed to take. Didn't matter! At the time, we were moving across a large section of pastureland to the front.

And we continued to move cross-country. Our vehicle was jumping around like a buck. The ground turned soft all of a sudden and only allowed us to move forward slowly, as if through thick porridge. We gave a sign to those behind us. Damn! They weren't going anywhere, either. Then, on top of everything else, the machine-gun vehicle bottomed out as well. Our wheels were turning round and round. The 6-wheeled armored car finally got moving and went to help the machine-gun vehicle. All around us, it was quiet. The sun had already disappeared. Its light was only to be seen in the illuminated puffs of clouds. Then there was a droning sound, which got closer and closer. A Polish artillery spotter! Just what we needed. It looped around and then flew off in the direction of Rzeszow.

Our motorcycle infantry were also unable to advance. The *Oberleutnant* sent them over to the road. It was just in the nick of time. A few minutes later, there was a whistling and hissing in the air coming towards us. A few rounds impacted far to our rear. Damn! Things were getting serious! Once again, it started humming and buzzing around us. This time, the rounds impacted a lot closer. Small-arms fire also started up against us.

Shortly thereafter, there was crash and explosion to the left and right of our vehicle. Then there was a dull thump. Air pressure pushed me away from my optics. I felt it: The vehicle was burning. I could scarcely breathe.

A scout from *Aufklärungs-Abteilung 4 (mot)* of the *1. Panzer-Division* poses next to his *Sd.Kfz. 231 (8 Rad)*, which has been christened the *Köln* ("Cologne"). The shiny round object under his tie is most likely his *Erkennungsmarke*, the German equivalent of the dog tag. Note that the white *Balkenkreuz* on the front of the vehicle has been covered in an effort to reduce its target signature. The *Sd.Kfz. 232 (6 Rad)* positioned to the rear still bears its large, white cross. AKIRA TAKIGUCHI

"Get out!" That was my initial instinctual reaction.

I wanted to open the rear turret hatch, since the vehicle commander was still trying to get out above me. Then it occurred to me that the rear driver could not get out through his hatch.

Damned heat!

The darting flames singed my hair and burned my hands held in front of my face.

Finally, the hatch opened. I did a somersault and was outside. The other ones were already running in front of me. Follow them! Then I saw the *Oberleutnant* disappear in a depression. We started receiving fire again all around us—a witch's cauldron! My head was throbbing and hurting, so much so that I hardly paid attention to anything any more. Then I looked over to the *Oberleutnant*. He pointed and then seemed to shout something.

Damn! I couldn't hear anything! The buzzing in my head was horrific!

The *Oberleutnant* signaled once again. He jumped up and ran towards the dark spot in the pasture behind a bush. I ran after him. It was my driver, who lay there curled up with a face full of blood. We applied first aid and then carried him away from the unprotected spot. In the distance was a potato field with a few bushes that offered some concealment. The wounded driver was soon brought there. The *Oberleutnant* indicated that I was to remain with the driver. He wanted to try to get help. Once more, there was some more artillery fire around us. After that, nothing stirred. It turned really dark. Finally, someone showed up with a sidecar motorcycle. We lifted the wounded man into it and sent him off to the doctor. We then worked our way in fits and spurts towards the burning village. Finally, we were at the church. There were some of our motorized riflemen there. But we didn't have time to tell them anything, because we started receiving fire from close by and tongues of flame could be seen. Get under cover and then try to get out of there, out of the village! The rear driver, a pistol in his hand, and I ran back along the way by ourselves through the roadside ditch and past the burning houses. We lost contact with the others. Then the *Oberleutnant* thundered down the road in a sidecar motorcycle. We were allowed to mount up with him and move back along the rough road to our unit. We thought we were safe, but another artillery round slammed into the field a few hundred meters ahead of us.

"That's the last straw," I thought to myself. The others probably thought the same thing.

But we reached our people without any further incident. It had been a hard but brave test of nerves for us.

As can be seen above, the early six-wheeled *Sd.Kfz. 231's/232's* and the *Sd.Kfz. 221's* often had difficulty traversing open ground once they left the road. In this instance, vehicles were lost to artillery fire because they bogged down in soft ground. Had they possessed the requisite cross-country mobility, it is likely that no losses would have been suffered. The lack of priority in the manufacture of reconnaissance vehicles resulted in the use of essentially *ad hoc* vehicles based on commercial designs. Although purpose-built vehicles such as the later series of armored cars and the introduction of light half-tracks in reconnaissance roles ameliorated this problem to a certain degree, they were never available in the numbers required, a problem that existed across the *Panzerwaffe*.

The *Aufklärungs-Lehr-Abteilung* was also committed to combat operations during the campaign in Poland, even though it was part of the Replacement Army. The German Army wanted combat-seasoned veterans as instructors at its schools, so the reconnaissance training battalion, along with all of the other school units for the respective branches, was regularly deployed at the front. The battalion adjutant at the time, *Oberleutnant Freiherr* [Count] von Esebeck, provided a firsthand account of the first day's fighting:[12]

> It was a pitch-black night. The battalion prepared for operations in some woods near Preußenfeld. Without any lights and practically without any noise, the elements took up their places along the narrow path. It was intended for the motorcycle infantry to initially cross the border, supported by the first wave of armored car sections and the heavy weapons. They would take the customs building and, by doing so, create a hole for the battalion to slip through. While it was still night, they moved directly up to the border.
>
> It was 0430 hours. The sky in the east started to turn color. There was a light ground fog covering the terrain. Probably no one had slept that night. All of our thoughts were directed towards what was to come. At exactly 0445 hours, the battalion moved out. Everything ran on schedule, as if we were at a training area. The Polish resistance was minimal and was soon broken by the motorcycle infantry. Without hesitating, the battalion advanced through the Polish position that had been taken. The motorcycle infantry mounted up and closed back up to the battalion. Our first wounded man was at the Polish customs building. A medic was looking out after him. The man looked at us with large, astonished eyes. He was badly wounded; he didn't say a word. It was with some difficulty that he raised his hand to wave to us, to take leave of us for our continued journey, in which he was no longer able to participate. Behind the customs building, we turned off the main road to find our way to our objective—Nakel—along secondary routes and the edges of fields. **It was not our mission to seek out a fight. That would interfere with our reconnaissance. But wherever we encountered resistance, it was broken by us with all means at our disposal.** [Emphasis added by authors.]
>
> That was the case in Dembowo. After we had gone around obstacles and penetrated 40

kilometers into Poland, the lead elements encountered resistance. We had to get through. We entered our first fight. The village was being held by the Poles; they were not intimidated by the armored cars that were supposed to clear the village. Once again, the motorcycle infantry moved out, supported by the heavy weapons. I stood with the commander on the road. The first few ricochets whistled past. The commander, a soldier from the first war, smiled. Then he said softly, wistfully: "There you are again, you little birds."

The motorcycle infantry reached the edge of the village in exact leaps and bounds and then entered it. Armored cars eliminated a Polish machine-gun nest in the church tower with their automatic cannon. After half an hour, the troop reported that it had the village in its possession.

A Polish bicycle troop was chased away; the route was clear. At that point a patrol reported: No significant resistance in Nakel; no obstacle at the western entrance. The commander had only one order for his battalion: "See you in Nakel." We reached the city without incident. No Poles were to be seen. A few civilians hid in the houses. We were at the marketplace. All of the exit points out of the city were blocked. The Poles were to the south of the Netze and didn't allow anyone to approach the bridges. But they weren't supposed to come over, either. We intended to blow them up.

Rounds whistled along the streets. All of a sudden, all hell broke loose. There were muzzle flashes coming out of windows, doors, roof-access panels and the depths of cellars. Machine-gun and rifle fire rattled and whipped past us. Hand grenades exploded next to the

Scouts from *Aufklärungs-Abteilung 5 (mot)* of the *2. Panzer-Division* pause to pose for a group picture near their armored cars. With the exception of the officer or noncommissioned officer smoking the pipe in the middle of the image, all of the junior-grade enlisted scouts appear to have removed the shoulder straps from their uniforms, perhaps in an effort to improve operational security. JIM HALEY

vehicles. We were sitting in a pocket. There was nothing to be seen of the Poles, and we were standing there on the streets like targets.

At the railway crossing at the northern part of the city was an open area. A few storage facility outbuildings were covering the houses in the city. We would at least have our backs covered there and could pull the vehicles out of the fire. There was a hellish racket in the city. The armored cars covered the non-armored vehicles. They fired with everything they had, traversing their turrets from side to side. The antitank and infantry guns had unlimbered and fired over open sights into the houses. It was burning at several spots. The men soon developed an excellent tactic: One round into the corner base of the house, one into the center above that and one in the roof. The Polish construction then came down with a crash . . .

That's how we avoided the worst of it. The battalion assembled at the northern part of the city, and the engineers started to clear the abatis. But the respite was not to last too long here, either. With the few men of the battalion, we were unable to clear a city like Nakel. It was not the Polish military that was fighting there. It was civilians and soldiers, who had taken off their uniforms. They were conducting a criminal, mean-spirited war. It had turned dark by the time we had left the inhospitable city. The sound of fighting fell silent. Behind us, the fiery torches of our first day of war colored the nighttime sky.

The battalion reconnoitered a few more days before it encountered fixed defenses, whereupon it was pulled out of the line. The battalion then moved to another area of operations (East Prussia), where it was attached to Guderian's *XIX. Armee-Korps (mot)*. It crossed the frontier again, albeit with more casualties the second time around. After following the *20. Infanterie-Division (mot)* for several days, the battalion was personally given an audacious mission by the commanding general, *Generalleutnant* Guderian: It was to seize the bridges over the Bug River at Tonkiele, more than 100 kilometers from the then-current German positions. *Oberleutnant Freiherr* von Esebeck again takes up the narrative:[13]

I went ahead with the commander of the battalion in order to establish contact with the lead regiment. Our mission: Reconnoiter from the south in the direction of Lomza, which was still stubbornly holding out. There, standing on the road, all by himself and armed with only his pistol and a radio crew was our *General* Guderian! The general mulled over the situation for a moment.

"Show me the map!"

I had always folded the map on my oversized map board, so that a decent day's march performance could be shown.

"No, no," the general said, "unfold the adjoining map below that."

And then he pointed to the map hanging down to the ground.

"See the bridge on the Bug there down below?" He asked. "I have to have it by early tomorrow morning."

I didn't believe what I was hearing. It was 100 kilometers as the crow flies!

. . . and then it started to turn dark. A short discussion of the situation followed.

"When can the battalion move out?"

"Immediately!"

"Good . . . then do a good job!"

With a patrol up front and to the right and left and moving by short bounds, the entire battalion followed close behind. Objective: The bridge over the Bug at Tonkiele. In the evening twilight, we moved through Zambrow. It had been taken by our infantry a half hour previously. There was a fire in the vicinity of the church. The local population, including a few Jews, hid shyly behind the corners of the buildings. At the southern outskirts, a bit outside of the city, were some large military facilities along the road.

Hmmm?

But nothing stirred. It had turned dark. We moved south, lights out, along a road that was quite good by Polish standards. The next town, Czyzewo, had burned to the ground. There was literally not a single house left. The remaining chimneys stared up to the nighttime sky in an eerie manner. Our pilots had done their work there in a major way.

At Ciechanowiec, we intended to turn off the main road. The patrol reported the city to be intact and still occupied [by civilians]. No soldiers; no obstacles. We went through the whistle-stop with our lights on. That way, we could see everything, the battalion column would not break up in the narrow, angular streets and any potential attackers were blinded. The civilian populace, mostly Jews with long beards, ran about helter-skelter, rousted out of bed. Things appeared to be going well. Up to that point, not a shot had been fired.

Damn it! We had celebrated too early. The main body of the battalion had already cleared the burg, but the trains were still in it. Signal flares went up into the air and flickered down. An ill-defined firefight started bellowing behind us in the night. We continued moving forward with the main body. The trains were soon back with us.

No one [up front] really knew what had just happened. A Polish motorcycle messenger had been captured, which had probably set off the entire nervous reaction. In the meantime, it had turned pitch black. The Polacks had to try to find us in that. But that *Kulturvolk* had also not made it easy for us to find our way. What appeared to be an improved road on the map turned out to be a sand trap. We could only drive in first and second gear. Occasionally, the path spread out to an indeterminate width, but then it appeared to become even more bottomless. A light wooden bridge collapsed under the weight of a heavy armored car. Thank God that the channel was dry and a detour quickly found. Regardless, the trains still had to get through that—but they got through. In one sand pit, every individual vehicle had to be guided through; all of the motorcycles had to be manhandled. Several trucks had to be towed by the heavy armored cars. But it all worked out. Everything practically went without a sound. At most, the parking lights were turned on. Not a single vehicle remained behind.

I had never before seen—and seldom later on—how much a person is capable of when he has to do something and there is no other way. The driver of our command vehicle asked me if I could relieve him for a while. His arms dropped down like blocks of wood. He was incapable of raising them. It was not easy to drive the armored vehicle at any time, let alone then. We already had 50 kilometers behind us after leaving Ciechanowiec. For the 15 kilometers of "desert," we needed almost as much time. That wasn't going to work; valuable time was being lost. That meant: Back to the main road. The patrols were redirected. But the commander did not want to wait until all that happened.

At that point, at the location of the lead elements, which had most likely just reached the main road, signal flares were going up. A few shots were fired. Then it was dark and quiet again. A short time later, a report came back from the lead elements: Moving from north to south along the main road were Polish forces of all combat arms in a lot of vehicles. At the same moment, we received a rather unusual confirmation [of that message]. A liaison officer from another reconnaissance battalion reported in to the commander, along with a light armored car, a *Kübelwagen* and a motorcycle. He was somewhat pale. He had moved along in the middle of that Polish column, hemmed in for a half hour. When he finally found a side road, he made himself scarce—and then ran into our lead elements! Everyone needs to have a little luck, especially a soldier!

We continued along on the secondary route, parallel to the Poles for 5 kilometers. And we also had our share of luck. The route improved, and we could move more rapidly. The Poles to the left would remain a lost opportunity; we had another mission. First light arrived. We were 10 kilometers from the bridge over the Bug. The lead patrol reported: Bridge intact; no one identified guarding it.

Let's go! An advance guard was formed: A few armored cars, motorcycle infantry and engineers. Mission: Occupy the bridge and, if necessary, disable demolitions. The battalion would follow directly. The city of Drohiczyn was bypassed; there was no need to become "popular." Barely half an hour had passed when the advance guard reported: "Bridge captured intact."

Damn!

A terrific feeling of happiness and pride overcame us: We had taken one of the most important east-west bridges between Warsaw and Brest-Litowsk more than 100 kilometers in front of our own forces and after an almost Herculean night march.

As luck would have it for the battalion, it was then ordered to pull back and blow up the bridges captured in a bold *coup de main*. Von Esebeck continues:[14]

Oberleutnant Knoblauch, our signals officer, handed an unencrypted radio message to me. That was something out of the ordinary. On it: Move immediately back to Czyzewo. Additional orders there. What? Damn it, we were there last night, weren't we? What's that all about? It was intended for us to give up "our" bridge? But orders were orders and the intuition of that old frontline soldier, my commander, led him to believe that something had not gone quite according to plan. But we didn't want to abandon the field where we had been that day without leaving some sort of memento. We got permission from the division and then the bridge went up in the air. For a long time after we started back—a march we initiated feeling heartsick—we could see the cloud of smoke coming from the burning bridge, "our" bridge, as it jutted vertically skyward. That was the least we could do. If we could no longer keep it, then they shouldn't be able to keep it, either.

Back at the division, we found out that the garrison at Lomza—about a division in size—had attempted to break out. Instead of following us, our division had had to turn around in order to interdict the breakout attempt. The main supply route had been cut off by the Poles. We didn't have a single drop of fuel! Polish cavalry had already broken through and was to our rear. Well then, cheers! We didn't have any more *Schnapps*, either. We'll just play infantry for a bit, since we still had plenty to shoot with. Just come our way, and we'll provide you with a warm welcome. And that's what happened in the small Polish village of Dmochi, after which we later christened a light armored car. The Polish division commander was killed. His second-in-command stood in front of our division commander, *General* Victorin, a former Austrian. Victorin laconically expressed his admiration for the brave actions of the Poles. The translator was supposed to translate into Polish. The Pole waved his hand, dismissively. "Not necessary," he said, "I was also an Austrian." An emotional moment.

Following is another account from the campaign in Poland, this time concerning *Panzer-Aufklärungs-Abteilung 4* of the *1. Panzer-Division*:[15]

The fight against Poland was also a campaign for the armored reconnaissance within the *1. Panzer-Division*, which attacked from the area around the upper Silesian town of Rosenberg against the Polish field army. The *1. Schützen-Brigade* moved out first: It was told to take [crossing points over] the small Liswarte River. Thirty minutes after the war started, three armored cars were already rolling across rapidly established crossing points and skillfully negotiating the marshland. Late in the morning, the reconnaissance patrols of the [division's] *Panzer-Aufklärungs-Abteilung 4* encountered enemy resistance at Truskiljassy. Providing more of a challenge than that, however, was the resistance offered by the terrain: Bad roads and worn-out river crossing sites hampered the flow of the columns. There were traffic jams and massed confusion. In the meantime, the [reconnaissance battalion] continued the chase in an effort to take the three bridges over the Warthe at Garnek, Gidle and Plawno. Each succeeded, but only at the last minute and under life-threatening circumstances: *Leutnant* Metzger [a platoon leader] was badly wounded.

The bridge at Garnek cost nerves and courage: Just as *Leutnant Graf* Dürckheim's patrol reached the bridge, Polish engineers lit the fuse. The engineers were driven off by fire, but the cord continued to burn on with each passing second. It proved possible to cut the cord prior to the ignition of the demolition.

After establishing bridgeheads, the armored reconnaissance sections fanned out again. One of them stopped a train headed for Tchenstochau on open track. It was filled with Polish reserves that had just been called up. The reconnaissance men thundered off into the countryside and witnessed an amazingly friendly reception in some of the villages by the locals: Women stood there waving and presenting flowers. The excitement soon faded when the citizenry realized that they were dealing with German soldiers and not the expected English . . .

Although the following account concerns the reconnaissance assets of an infantry division—*Aufklärungs-Abteilung 17* of the *17. Infanterie-Division*—and therefore is not related to the general focus of this book, the situation the infantry division faced on 18 September offers a vivid picture of what can happen when reconnaissance assets move too far too fast:[16]

On the morning of 18 September, the [reconnaissance battalion] received orders to advance rapidly into the Kutno Pocket, without regard to the flanks or rear. The usual security measures were throttled back in favor of a more expeditious advance, especially since recent experience had indicated that the enemy would no longer be putting up strong resistance: The Polish Army had already been beaten to the ground.

It would soon be seen, however, the difficult situation a reconnaissance battalion could face: A rapid, risk-intensive advance could take time away from the enemy that he needed to establish an effective defense, but it could also come at the cost of high casualties. A careful, cautious pursuit of the enemy—best accomplished by leapfrogging and overwatch by the heavy weapons—costs a great deal of time and allows the enemy to improve his defenses.

When the mounted troop of the [reconnaissance battalion] had reached the edge of the village in its entirety, it was hit by surprise on three sides by machine-gun and rifle fire. The riders dismounted and released their horses, but they were unable to establish a coordinated defense in the confusion and chaos. The bicycle troop raced to its help. But it received heavy rifle fire and even some artillery fire as it approached the stricken comrades. The cavalrymen had pushed their way into the village in the meantime, but they had given up hope of being relieved. In the end, however, they were rescued: After fighting for several hours, the Poles withdrew, since they were being threatened with being enveloped by another German division.

The mounted troop suffered 35 dead, including both of its officers, out of its assigned strength of 125 men. In addition, there were 8 missing and 41 wounded. The number of dead, wounded and runaway horses was likewise large—almost half of the mounts. The troop was only conditionally capable of conducting operations . . .

In general, the lessons learned from the campaign in Poland validated the theoretical doctrine relating to the employment of reconnaissance forces. Despite the increased "friction of war" that inevitably occurs when peacetime forces are committed to combat for the first time, the rigorous training of the prewar German Army allowed it to quickly assimilate the hard lessons of combat, even though some obvious needs—such as the requirement for increased cross-country mobility, armored protection, and firepower—would never be adequately addressed during the war, requiring creative combat leadership to counteract this issue. At this stage of the hostilities, that resource was still available in abundance.

An *Sd.Kfz. 231 (8 Rad)* and an *Sd.Kfz. 232 (8 Rad)* screen down a smoke-covered road, while motorcycle infantrymen cast a wary eye toward the building to the left. The immediate danger seems to have passed, however, given the rather nonchalant attitude of the civilian on the right. JIM HALEY

A column of vehicles moves down the road through a destroyed Polish village. An *Sd.Kfz. 263 (8 Rad)* is seen in the foreground. Although the radio car could have belonged to a signals detachment, the image comes from the album of a reconnaissance soldier. JIM HALEY

A scout in an *Sd.Kfz. 223* and a truckload of Polish prisoners appear to be observing something out of the viewer's sight. During offensive operations, scout sections had particular problems with prisoners, since they were usually ahead of the main body of the advance and sending them to the rear with an escort reduced the already small size of the force. Usually, an armored car would remain at the point of capture with the prisoners until the battalion could send someone forward to escort them to the rear. MIKE HARPE

These scouts in an *Sd.Kfz. 222* and an *Sd.Kfz. 231 (6 Rad)* are ready to move out on a mission. Although the unit cannot be positively identified, it is most likely from one of the light divisions since the tactical insignia is done in typical cavalry fashion. MIKE HARPE

Casualties of war. In the first image, a knocked-out *Sd.Kfz. 221* rests on its side in a roadside ditch. Judging by the damage, which appears to be confined mostly to the undercarriage, it may have run over an antipersonnel mine. The *Sd.Kfz. 231 (8 Rad)* in the second image appears to have been knocked out as a direct result of combat action, although it may have also been lost to a vehicular fire starting in the engine compartment, as evidenced by the open access panels, which seem to show fire damage. FIRST IMAGE: MIKE HARPE

Studio portrait of an *Oberfeldwebel* scout, probably taken about the time of the campaign in Poland, judging by what appear to be prewar decorations on his tunic. He wears the "A" cipher on his shoulder straps but no numerical designator for his battalion. SCOTT PRITCHETT

CHAPTER 3

Blitzkrieg in the West

SETTING THE STAGE

After the successful conclusion of the campaign in Poland and the *Sitzkrieg* that followed, plans began to be drawn up to invade and conquer France. Numerous plans were formulated, and initially they were all markedly conservative in their planned execution. The concept of a war of movement seemed a distant reality until von Manstein came up with his variation of the Schlieffen Plan from World War I and gradually convinced Hitler of its viability.

While riskier than the original planning concepts, which seemed to invite a war of attrition, it did offer the chance of a decisive victory—a victory that Hitler needed if he wanted to avoid a two-front war. Basically, the *Schwerpunkt* of the attack would occur in the Ardennes, a mountainous, wooded, and rural terrain with limited road capacity. It would avoid the virtually impregnable Maginot Line and, at the same time, drive to the English Channel in an effort to cut off the British and French forces that were predicted to race into the Low Countries to prevent a perceived German main effort there.

As it turned out, the plan worked beyond expectation, due partly to the overall German tactical superiority and the extremely plodding and reactive leadership of the Allies. The campaign started on 10 May 1940 and essentially lasted until its successful conclusion and the signing of the armistice on 22 June 1940. In less than six weeks (including an operational pause that lasted about a week), the main part of France had been conquered, the French government forced to capitulate and strike an accord with the German government, and the British Expeditionary Force driven off the continent.

A column of *Sd.Kfz. 221's* moves though a French or Belgian town. Of interest is the camouflage netting on the front slope of the lead vehicle, as well as the tow cable wrapped around the bumper.
JIM HALEY

The campaign allowed a maturation of tactics and doctrine by the reconnaissance forces, particularly in pursuit operations. It showed that armored reconnaissance forces, using the elements of speed and surprise, particularly against a demoralized enemy, could not only gain valuable tactical and operational information but also achieve remarkable tactical success in their own right.

DOCTRINE

As with the campaign in Poland, reconnaissance forces were generally not a part of the initial assault by the main German armored forces. They were only employed after the preliminary breach and river-crossing operations (Meuse) had occurred. Once committed, they were often used to provide flank guard for the armored divisions as they penetrated France on their way to the English Channel in Phase 1 (*Fall Gelb*) of the campaign.

In the second half of the campaign (*Fall Rot*), reconnaissance forces came into their own after initially being held back for the breakthrough through the Weygand Line. Once that was accomplished, they were used in an advance and flank guard role until French forces started to disintegrate and a pursuit was initiated. In those cases, the reconnaissance battalions were usually sent far ahead of the main bodies of the divisions in an effort to determine the location of the retreating forces and then cut off or entrap them. Little is mentioned in *HDv 299/10* concerning the pursuit, except for the following:

> 25. If the pursuit cannot be initiated from the wing or the way there is too far, then it is to be initiated from the point of breakthrough.
>
> The direction the pursuit is to be taken is to be selected in such a fashion that reconnaissance can be conducted at the same time against the withdrawing enemy force.

Although the manual is laconic in this regard, the *Reitergeist* ("cavalry spirit") of the force made little explanation necessary. *Auftragstaktik* and initiative were the order of the day, generally all that was needed against a dispirited force in the process of dissolution, particularly when aided and abetted by a relatively good road network and temperate weather conditions.

Reconnaissance Assets of the Major Armored Combat Formations, May 1940

Parent Organization	Reconnaissance Assets	Notes
Armored Divisions		
1. Panzer-Division	Kradschützen-Bataillon 1	Still assigned to the *1. Schützen-Brigade*. Each of the first two rifle battalions in *Schützen-Regiment 1* also had a motorcycle infantry company (organized as the analogous company in the motorcycle infantry battalion). The battalion was organized as before, with the exception that the number of motorcycle infantry companies (*KStN 1111* / 1 October 1937) was reduced from three to two.
	Panzer-Aufklärungs-Abteilung 4	No changes to the previous organization chart, other than redesignation.
2. Panzer-Division	Kradschützen-Bataillon 2	Still assigned to the *2. Schützen-Brigade*. Each of the first two rifle battalions in *Schützen-Regiment 2* also had a motorcycle infantry company (organized as the analogous company in the motorcycle infantry battalion). The battalion organization remained unchanged from the previous organization chart.
	Panzer-Aufklärungs-Abteilung 5	No changes to the previous organization chart, other than redesignation.
3. Panzer-Division	Kradschützen-Bataillon 3	Still assigned to the *3. Schützen-Brigade*. Each of the first two rifle battalions in *Schützen-Regiment 3* also had a motorcycle infantry company (organized as the analogous company in the motorcycle infantry battalion). Changes to organization the same as *Kradschützen-Bataillon 1* above.
	Panzer-Aufklärungs-Abteilung 3	No changes to previous organization chart. It is presumed that the battalion was redesignated analogously like the previous reconnaissance battalions, but there does not appear to be any documentation for it.
4. Panzer-Division	Panzer-Aufklärungs-Abteilung 7	No changes to the previous organization chart, other than redesignation. The division did not have a motorcycle infantry battalion. There were two motorcycle infantry companies in each of the 2nd Battalions of the two *Schützen-Regimenter* (*12* and *33*). The motorcycle infantry company of the *II./Schützen-Regiment 12* was organized under *KStN 1111a* of 1 October 1938 (see below).

Parent Organization	Reconnaissance Assets	Notes
Armored Divisions *continued*		
5. Panzer-Division	Panzer-Aufklärungs-Abteilung 8	Division troop asset. The battalion was reorganized like *Panzer-Aufklärungs-Abteilung 4* above and redesignated. (The battalion's heavy company lost one light infantry gun platoon and replaced it with an antitank platoon.) The division did not have a motorcycle infantry battalion, although each of the rifle regiments (*Schützen-Regiment 13* and *Schützen-Regiment 14*) had two motorcycle infantry companies, one in each of the battalions. In addition, those companies were all organized under *KStN 1111a*.
6. Panzer-Division	Kradschützen-Bataillon 6	Assigned to the *6. Schützen-Brigade*. The battalion had three line motorcycle companies, but they were organized under *KStN 1113* of 1 October 1937 (see below). There was no heavy company, but there was a motorized machine-gun company, which was organized under *KStN 1116* of 1 October 1938 (see below) and had an attached/assigned antitank platoon (*KStN 1122* of 1 October 1937 as described previously).
	Panzer-Aufklärungs-Abteilung 57	Division troop asset. The battalion was organized like *Panzer-Aufklärungs-Abteilung 4* above.
7. Panzer-Division	Kradschützen-Bataillon 7	Assigned to the *7. Schützen-Brigade*. The battalion had two line motorcycle companies organized under *KStN 1111a* of 1 October 1938 (see below). The motorized heavy troop had a troop headquarters, an antitank platoon, one light infantry gun platoon, and a mortar platoon. The mortar platoon was organized under *KStN 1126* of 1 October 1938 and had three sections of two 81mm mortars each, for a total of six medium mortars. There was no combat engineer platoon.
	Panzer-Aufklärungs-Abteilung 37	Division troop asset. The battalion was organized like *Panzer-Aufklärungs-Abteilung 4* above.
8. Panzer-Division	Kradschützen-Bataillon 8	The battalion was organized analogously to *Kradschützen-Bataillon 6* above.
	Panzer-Aufklärungs-Abteilung 59	Division troop asset. The battalion was organized like *Panzer-Aufklärungs-Abteilung 4* above.
9. Panzer-Division	Aufklärungs-Regiment 9	The headquarters provided command and control for the reconnaissance assets. It and the subordinate battalions were in the process of reorganizing, but it retained the same structure during the campaign in the West as it had had under the *4. leichte Division*.
	I./Aufklärungs-Regiment 9	No change to organization from previous chart.
	II./Aufklärungs-Regiment 9	No change to organization from previous chart.
10. Panzer-Division	Panzer-Aufklärungs-Abteilung 90	Division troop asset. The battalion was organized like *Panzer-Aufklärungs-Abteilung 4* above and formed from the *I./Aufklärungs-Regiment 8*. The division had no motorcycle infantry battalion.
Motorized Infantry Divisions		
2. Infanterie-Division (mot)	Aufklärungs-Abteilung 2 (mot)	No change to organization from previous chart. The division had no motorcycle infantry battalion.
13. Infanterie-Division (mot)	Aufklärungs-Abteilung 13 (mot)	As with *Aufklärungs-Abteilung 2 (mot)* above.
20. Infanterie-Division (mot)	Aufklärungs-Abteilung 20 (mot)	As with *Aufklärungs-Abteilung 2 (mot)* above.
29. Infanterie-Division (mot)	Aufklärungs-Abteilung 29 (mot)	As with *Aufklärungs-Abteilung 2 (mot)* above.
Field Army / Replacement Army Assets		
11. Schützen-Brigade		The brigade had no organic reconnaissance formations, but it did have an armored car platoon in its headquarters (*KStN 1137* / 5 January 1940) (see below) and an armored car section in each of the two regimental headquarters (*Schützen-Regiment 110 (mot)* and *Schützen-Regiment 111 (mot)*). The *KStN* for those sections is unknown, but it appears that they only had three light armored cars each (*Sd.Kfz. 221's?*). Each of the rifle regiments also had a motorcycle infantry company that was unique to the brigade: a headquarters section of unknown *KStN* and a motorcycle infantry platoon organized under *KStN 146* of 1 October 1937 (see below).[1]
Lehr-Regiment 900 (mot)	Reconnaissance Battalion	The battalion featured another unique organization with a headquarters and attached signals platoon (but using *KStN*'s intended for antitank battalions); two armored car platoons, each with two *Sd.Kfz. 222's* and one *Sd.Kfz. 223* (*KStN 371* / 1 October 1938); and a motorized antitank company with twelve antitank guns (*PaK 36*) and six light machine guns, organized under *KStN 1141* of 1 October 1937.
Separate Armored Reconnaissance Battalion	*Panzer-Aufklärungs-Lehr-Abteilung*	Organized like *Panzer-Aufklärungs-Abteilung 4* above.

Parent Organization	Reconnaissance Assets	Notes
Field Army / Replacement Army Assets *continued*		
Separate Armored Reconnaissance Battalion	Aufklärungs-Abteilung 1 (mot)	Organized like *Panzer-Aufklärungs-Abteilung 4* above and possibly redesignated as *Panzer-Aufklärungs-Abteilung 1* by the time of the campaign. This battalion was eventually assigned to the *3. Panzer-Division*.
SS-Verfügungstruppe		
SS-Verfügungs-Division	SS-Aufklärungs-Sturmbann (mot)	The battalion was reorganized for the campaign in the West. It continued to have a headquarters with attached signals platoon. The number of motorcycle infantry companies was increased from two to three (*KStN 1111a* / 1 October 1938), the armored car platoon was expanded to a company (*KStN 1162* / 1 October 1938), and the assorted heavy platoons were gathered together into a motorized heavy company with the following subordinate units: one antitank platoon (*KStN 1122* / 1 October 1937), one combat engineer platoon (*KStN 1124* / 1 October 1937), and one mortar platoon (*KStN 1126* / 1 October 1938).
	SS-Standarte (mot)	The division had three *SS-Standarten*: "Der Führer," "Germania," and "Deutschland." Each regiment equivalent had a motorcycle infantry company (*KStN 1111* / 1 October 1937) and an armored car platoon (*KStN 1136* / 1 March 1939).
SS-Totenkopf-Division	SS-T-Aufklärungs-Sturmbann	The battalion had a standard headquarters with a signals platoon detachment. It only had two motorcycle infantry companies (*KStN 1111a* / 1 October 1938) and a motorized heavy company. The heavy company was unique, with one antitank platoon and two platoons of light tanks (three *Panzer 35 (t)* each). There was no armored car platoon.
SS-Leibstandarte Adolf Hitler (mot)		Reconnaissance assets organized like those of an *SS-Standarte* (see above).

LESSONS LEARNED AND FIRSTHAND ACCOUNTS

As with the campaign in Poland, there is a wealth of information concerning operations in the Low Countries and France, written both during the war and later. The following excerpt from the divisional history of the *1. Panzer-Division* concerns the initial employment of *Panzer-Aufklärungs-Abteilung 4* after the Meuse had been forced:[2]

> [The reconnaissance battalion of *Major* von Scheele] was positioned on the high ground south and southeast of Chéhéry and screened to the south [along the division's left flank], after it had established contact with *Infanterie-Regiment "Großdeutschland" (mot)*.

> After [the reconnaissance battalion] was relieved by the leading elements of the *2. Infanterie-Division*, it raced after the *1. Panzer-Division*, initially assuming a flank-guard mission along the left flank, fighting south of *Gruppe Nedtwig*.

Since the tanks of *Panzer-Regiment 1*—reinforced by elements of *Kradschützen-Bataillon 1*—were making good progress on their own and in constant contact with the enemy, they were capable of conducting their own battlefield reconnaissance. At the same time, the reconnaissance battalion continued to guard the open left flank of the division:[3]

> It was only against the left flank of the division —in front of the outposts of the reconnaissance battalion, which had been reinforced with the *1./Panzer-Regiment 1* and the *3./Panzer-Pionier-Bataillon 37*, and Blocking Group "Müller"—that the French repeatedly attempted to attack the rear-area elements of the division and push them back. The attacks, with tanks and infantry, were primarily against Falvy and Essigny. The attacks were able to be turned back, however, after short albeit sharp engagements.

Motorcycle Infantry Company (1111A)

The motorcycle infantry company organized under *KStN 1111a* was similar to the original *KStN 1111*, with the exception that the machine-gun detachment was removed from the company headquarters, expanded in size, and given platoon status. It had two heavy machine-gun sections, each with two guns. While the three motorcycle infantry platoons were essentially organized the same way, each of the three squads within the platoon received an additional light machine gun, thus doubling the light machine guns in the company from nine to eighteen. (The number of mortars remained the same: Each platoon had one 50mm mortar.) The company was organized as follows:

- Headquarters
- Headquarters section: three motorcycles, one sidecar motorcycle, one medium cross-country utility vehicle (*Kfz. 11*), and one heavy cross-country wheeled personnel carrier (*Kfz. 18*).
- Three motorcycle platoons:
  - Headquarters section: two motorcycles, one medium cross-country utility vehicle (*Kfz. 11*), and one heavy cross-country wheeled personnel carrier (*Kfz. 18*).
  - Three infantry squads: four sidecar motorcycles, one infantry squad, and two light machine guns.
  - One mortar squad: two sidecar motorcycles and one 50mm mortar.
- One machine-gun platoon:
  - Headquarters section: one motorcycle, two sidecar motorcycles, one medium cross-country wheeled personnel carrier (*Kfz. 15*), and one heavy cross-country utility vehicle (*Kfz. 18*).
  - One light telephone section: one medium cross-country signals utility vehicle (*Kfz. 15/1*).
  - One ammunition section: two sidecar motorcycles.
  - Two machine-gun sections: six sidecar motorcycles and two heavy machine guns.

---

a) Command Group
Company Headquarters Section

| 3x Heavy Motorcycle, 1x Sidecar Motorcycle | Medium Cross-Country Vehicle (*Kfz. 11*) | Tactical Vehicle, 3 ton (*Kfz. 18*) |

Total Command Group: 1x Officer, 2x NCOs, 10x Enlisted Personnel; 10x Rifles, 3x Pistols; 2x Wheeled Vehicles, 3x Heavy Motorcycles, 1x Sidecar Motorcycle

b) 1st Motorcycle Infantry Platoon
Platoon Headquarters Section

| 2x Motorcycle | Medium Cross-Country Vehicle (*Kfz. 11*) | Tactical Vehicle, 3 ton (*Kfz. 18*) |

3 Squads

| 4x Sidecar Motorcycle (2x Light MG) | 4x Sidecar Motorcycle (2x Light MG) | 4x Sidecar Motorcycle (2x Light MG) |

Light Mortar Section

2x Sidecar Motorcycle, 1x Light Mortar

Totals for Motorcycle Infantry Platoon: 1x Officer, 4x NCOs, 34x Enlisted Personnel; 31x Rifles, 8x Pistols, 3x Light MG's, 1x Light Mortar; 2x Wheeled Vehicles, 11x Sidecar Motorcycles, 2x Heavy Motorcycles

c) 2nd Motorcycle Infantry Platoon
Platoon Headquarters Section

| 2x Motorcycle | Medium Cross-Country Vehicle (*Kfz. 11*) | Tactical Vehicle, 3 ton (*Kfz. 18*) |

3 Squads

4x Sidecar Motorcycle (2x Light MG)   4x Sidecar Motorcycle (2x Light MG)   4x Sidecar Motorcycle (2x Light MG)

Light Mortar Section

2x Sidecar Motorcycle, 1x Light Mortar

Totals for Motorcycle Infantry Platoon: 1x Officer, 4x NCOs, 34x Enlisted Personnel; 31x Rifles, 8x Pistols, 3x Light MG's, 1x Light Mortar; 2x Wheeled Vehicles, 11x Sidecar Motorcycles, 2x Heavy Motorcycles

d) 3rd Motorcycle Infantry Platoon
Platoon Headquarters Section

| 2x Motorcycle | Medium Cross-Country Vehicle (*Kfz. 11*) | Tactical Vehicle, 3 ton (*Kfz. 18*) |

3 Squads

4x Sidecar Motorcycle (2x Light MG)   4x Sidecar Motorcycle (2x Light MG)   4x Sidecar Motorcycle (2x Light MG)

Light Mortar Section

2x Sidecar Motorcycle, 1x Light Mortar

Totals for Motorcycle Infantry Platoon: 1x Officer, 4x NCOs, 34x Enlisted Personnel; 31x Rifles, 8x Pistols, 3x Light MG's, 1x Light Mortar; 2x Wheeled Vehicles, 11x Sidecar Motorcycles, 2x Heavy Motorcycles

e) Heavy MG Section
Section Headquarters   **Small Telephone Section c (Motorized)**

| 2x Sidecar Motorcycle, 1x Motorcycle | Medium Cross-Country Vehicle with Equipment Storage Box (*Kfz. 15*) | Tactical Vehicle, 3 ton (*Kfz. 18*) | Signals Vehicle (*Kfz. 15*) |

1st Section	2nd Section
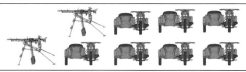	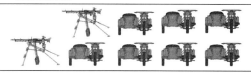
7x Sidecar Motorcycle, 2x Heavy Machine Gun	7x Sidecar Motorcycle, 2x Heavy Machine Gun

Total Heavy MG Platoon: 1x Officer, 7x NCOs, 43x Enlisted Personnel; 33x Rifles, 18x Pistols, 4x Heavy Machine Guns; 16x Sidecar Motorcycles, 1x Heavy Motorcycle

f) Combat Trains

2x Sidecar Motorcycle	Medium Cross-Country Vehicle with Equipment Storage Box (*Kfz. 15*) for Medical Personnel	Light Cross-Country Truck for Large Field Mess Stove
Light Cross-Country Truck for Petroleum, Oil & Lubricants and Equipment	Light Cross-Country Truck for Petroleum, Oil & Lubricants	Light Cross-Country Truck for Ammunition and Combat Engineer Equipment

Total Combat Trains: 6x NCOs, 11x Enlisted Personnel; 12x Rifles, 5x Pistols; 6x Vehicles, 2x Sidecar Motorcycles

g) Baggage Trains

Light Truck, Canvas Top, for Baggage	Motorcycle

Total Baggage Trains: 4x Enlisted Personnel; 4 Rifles; 1x Vehicle, 1x Heavy Motorcycle

Summary

	Officers	NCOs	Enlisted Personnel	Rifles	Pistols	Light MG's	Heavy MG's	Light Mortars	Vehicles	Heavy Motorcycles	Heavy Motorcycle/ Sidecar Motorcycles
Command Group	1	2	10	10	3				2	3	1
1st Platoon	1	4	43	34	14	6		1	2	2	14
2nd Platoon	1	4	43	34	14	6		1	2	2	14
3rd Platoon	1	4	43	34	14	6		1	2	2	14
Heavy MG Section	1	7	43	33	18		4		3	1	16
Combat Trains		6	12	12	6				6		2
Baggage Trains			4	4					1	1	
Totals	5	27	198	161	69	18	4	3	18	11	61

Motorcycle Infantry Company (1111A) *continued*

MOTORCYCLE INFANTRY COMPANY (1113)

This organization was only found in *Kradschützen-Bataillon 6* of the *6. Panzer-Division* and *Kradschützen-Bataillon 8* of the *8. Panzer-Division*. Unlike *KStN 1111a* above, the heavy machine guns remained in the company headquarters as a detachment with two weapons. As with *KStN 1111a* above, the number of light machine guns was doubled in the three line motorcycle infantry platoons. The mortar section allocations remained the same. The company was organized as follows:

- Headquarters
- Headquarters section: three motorcycles, one sidecar motorcycle, one medium cross-country utility vehicle (*Kfz. 11*), and one heavy cross-country utility vehicle (*Kfz. 18*).
- Machine-gun detachment: ten sidecar motorcycles and two heavy machine guns.
- Three motorcycle platoons:
  - Headquarters section: two motorcycles, one medium cross-country utility vehicle (*Kfz. 11*), and one heavy cross-country utility vehicle (*Kfz. 18*).
  - Three infantry squads: four sidecar motorcycles, one infantry squad, and two light machine guns.
  - One mortar squad: two sidecar motorcycles and one 50mm mortar.

MOTORCYCLE INFANTRY COMPANY (146)

The motorcycle company found in each of the regiments of the *11. Schützen-Brigade* was unique. In addition to the headquarters (unknown *KStN*), there were four motorcycle infantry platoons organized under *KStN 146 / 1 October 1937*. Each of these had a headquarters and three motorcycle infantry sections, which in turn each had an infantry squad with a light machine gun. In all, this company had twelve squads and twelve light machine guns.

MOTORIZED MACHINE-GUN COMPANY (1116)

Like the motorcycle infantry company organized under *KStN 1113* (above), this unit was unique to only two battalions: *Kradschützen-Bataillon 6* of the *6. Panzer-Division* and *Kradschützen-Bataillon 8* of the *8. Panzer-Division*. *KStN 1116* of 1 October 1938 was organized as follows:

- Headquarters
- Headquarters section: three motorcycles, one sidecar motorcycle, one heavy cross-country utility vehicle (*Kfz. 18*), and one personnel carrier (*Kfz. 70*).
- Two light telephone sections: one medium cross-country signals vehicle (*Kfz. 15/1*).
- Two machine-gun platoons:
  - Headquarters section: one sidecar motorcycle, one medium cross-country utility vehicle (*Kfz. 11*), and one heavy cross-country wheeled personnel carrier (*Kfz. 70*).
  - One light telephone section: one medium cross-country signals utility vehicle (*Kfz. 15/1*).
  - Two machine-gun sections: two heavy cross-country wheeled personnel carriers (*Kfz. 70*).
- One mortar platoon:
  - Headquarters section: one sidecar motorcycle, one medium cross-country utility vehicle (*Kfz. 11*), and one heavy cross-country wheeled personnel carrier (*Kfz. 70*).
  - Three mortar sections: one medium cross-country utility vehicle (*Kfz. 11*), two heavy cross-country wheeled personnel carriers (*Kfz. 70*), and two 81mm mortars.

Conducting operations to the front, *Kradschützen-Bataillon 1* soon found some of its movements reminiscent of prewar training:[4]

A patrol of *Kradschützen-Bataillon 1* had reported in the meantime that a completely intact bridge had been located at Quitteur. A constant stream of French columns, mostly trains, pulled back to the south over it. The commander of the motorcycle infantry battalion was immediately given the mission to take the bridge, located about 18 kilometers above Gray, in a *coup de main*. The battalion had had plenty of practice in that. During the preparatory phase before the campaign, it was quartered in Klotten an der Mosel, where it had constantly practiced all types of river-crossing operations. *Major* von Wietersheim was simply able to give the following order: "Cross like we did at Klotten: Exercise Number 2!" Enveloping the enemy on both sides, the motorcycle infantry succeeded in achieving this important mission, despite the stubborn resistance of the French. *Leutnant* Heinz Huppert ejected the forces guarding the bridge with his platoon, thus forcing a crossing over the undamaged bridge onto the south bank of the Saône . . .

Unlike the reconnaissance battalion, the motorcycle infantry were more or less expected to fight, even though the operations they conducted were similar to those of the reconnaissance battalion. Reconnaissance battalions were also capable of conducting raids against lightly guarded installations, key terrain, and certain types of infrastructure (usually bridges):[5]

. . . In addition its mission of guarding the flanks to the west of the advance route south, *Panzer-Aufklärungs-Abteilung 4* had also received the mission to blow up the rail lines leading into and out of Besançon. As it turned out, blocking detachments of the battalion under *Hauptmann* von Kuczkowski and *Oberleutnant* Riedinger succeeded in interdicting the rail lines at Franois and Misère, with the result that no less than 20 fully loaded trains stacked up in the space of two hours at Misère, where their journey came to an end.

This after-action report of *Panzer-Aufklärungs-Abteilung 4* was written at the conclusion of the fighting during the second phase of the campaign:[6]

Panzer-Aufklärungs-Abteilung 4 had the mission on 18 June 1940 to advance on [Fortress] Belfort via Hericourt. Based on reconnaissance conducted during the evening of 17 June, it was determined that Hericourt was full of the enemy and that motorized columns were moving from [there] to Belfort. Further: There was an antitank gun positioned at the south entrance to Hericourt. During the night of 17–18 June, Milititz' section was employed screening south of Hericourt, while most of the battalion rested at Aibre.

On the morning of 18 June, the battalion initiated its advance against Hericourt. *Oberfeldwebel* Dölling was employed as a reconnaissance section in front of the lead elements. The advance guard of the battalion under *Hauptmann* Stephan, consisted of the following units (also the order of march):

Armored group in the lead [although not mentioned here specifically, it is discovered later in the text that the author of the AAR is referring to an armored car platoon within the battalion]

Command of the advance guard
1st Motorcycle Infantry Platoon
Gun Platoon
Antitank Platoon
2nd Motorcycle Infantry Platoon
One engineer squad

Just before reaching the woods south of Hericourt, the reconnaissance patrol in the lead reported: "Machine-gun fire from the edge of the wood on the road." I showed the leader of the 1st Motorcycle Infantry Platoon the approximate location of the enemy machine gun and ordered him to attack it. By then, however, the machine gun had withdrawn. The advance guard then formed up to attack Hericourt. The gun platoon received orders to go into position and take the southern portion of the village under fire, while one platoon each of motorcycle infantry advanced to the right and left of the road. The reconnaissance patrol up front screened; the antitank platoon and the engineer squad initially remained at my disposal behind a small rise on the road. The command post of the advance guard was the small rise south of the locality, which was also the firing position of the gun platoon.

From a report by *Unteroffizier* Lampert from Milititz' patrol, I discovered that *Leutnant* Milititz' armored car had been hit by an antitank gun. The gun platoon received orders to place its fires on the position of the [enemy] antitank gun, which was correctly guessed to be located behind a curve at the entrance to the locality. Observation from the flanks by the motorcycle infantry revealed that crew manning the antitank gun jumped into the houses while under fire only to re-man the gun after the fire. While more fire from the guns was placed into the locality, the two motorcycle infantry platoons entered it. In a park on the west side of the road, the motorcycle infantry platoon employed on the left encountered three French light armored cars, whose crews abandoned the vehicles and ran away. Resistance in the park was eliminated by means of hand grenades. The motorcycle infantry platoon employed on the right had moved into the village east of the road in the meantime. The reports of enemy resistance in the eastern part of the locality and of flanking fires from gardens and houses caused me to employ the engineer squad with the right-hand motorcycle infantry platoon.

By then, some 100 prisoners came out of the village, including 2 officers. The enemy antitank gun had been abandoned during the attack by the motorcycle infantry, with the result that the armored elements in the lead (*Oberleutnant* Lienau) could move into the locality, while Dölling's reconnaissance section was employed to screen against a possible advance by the enemy into our flank south of the locality. The antitank platoon went into position along the southern edge of Hericourt. *Oberleutnant* Lienau established contact with the motorcycle infantry in the village and sent back constant reports on the progress of the attack. About 150 armed French were discovered in the courtyard of a factory. As a result of the courageous advance of some of my people, they were driven into the street and disarmed. In the meantime, the command post had been moved from the southern edge of the village to the large intersection there. The gun platoon also went into position there. When reports came in of enemy tanks, the antitank platoon was also employed at the crossroads. The enemy tanks did not materialize.

Further reconnaissance by *Oberleutnant* Lienau revealed that there were four enemy machine guns in houses on the far side of the bridge behind a bend in the road. There were two on each side of the road and two antitank guns next to one another as the road extended out into a small open area. *Oberleutnant* Lienau immediately took the antitank guns under fire with his light armored car. He obtained several hits through machine-gun fire, but then he had to abandon the vehicle, since it was hit by an antitank gun and rendered immobile. One gun was manhandled along the road far enough forward that it could engage the antitank guns over open sights. When the first rounds impacted, the French crews left their cannon. As a result of the gun firing into the houses where the machine guns had been identified, they were also silenced. Joining in engaging the antitank gun in the open area was the motorcycle infantry platoon employed on the right, which then thoroughly cleared the area. That meant that the locality was in our hands.

Just a short time before that, the 3rd Motorcycle Infantry Platoon had arrived, coming from another assignment. I kept it under my direct control. After the village of Hericourt had been taken, new orders arrived from the battalion: "New mission. Disengage from the enemy."

The enemy armored cars that were in the park were blown up by the engineer squad.

Summary: Approximately 400 prisoners and 80 French dead, as was determined later. Approximately just as many wounded. It was determined that 8 enemy machine guns and 10 antitank guns had been employed; not all of the latter were able to be employed.

Friendly losses: 1 officer and 1 noncommissioned officer dead; 1 noncommissioned officer and 4 men wounded.

By the end of the fighting in France, the reconnaissance assets of the *1. Panzer-Division*, the oldest armored division of the German Army, had won some impressive awards. *Hauptmann Graf* von Bellegarde of the *3./Panzer-Aufklärungs-Abteilung 4 (mot)* was one of six officers in the division to receive the Knight's Cross. The Commander-in-Chief of the Army, *Generaloberst* von Brauchitsch, sent a Certificate of Achievement to *Kradschützen-Bataillon 1* for the capture of Amiens and to *Leutnant* Huppert's platoon from *Kradschützen-Bataillon 1* for the *coup de main* against the bridge at St. Quitteur.[7] It was a distinction to be shared with most of the rest of the reconnaissance assets employed during the campaign as well.

Some of the armored divisions did not even see combat on the first day of the fighting, since the Ardennes turned out to be a bottleneck even without strong resistance. Approaching the border crossings in the north as part of the feint designed to lure the French and British forces into the Low Countries, the *3. Panzer-Division* employed its reconnaissance elements in the lead:[8]

The soldiers of the division were up early on the morning of 11 May. Many of them were entering combat for the first time and correspondingly nervous. Those who slept out in the open were awakened by the cold. The morale was good everywhere and the soldiers were confident of victory. They heard about the initial fighting along the border from the radios they had brought along, messengers passing through and the local populace.

The division started its movement towards the border with its lead elements, including the headquarters and the reconnaissance battalion, around 1000 hours. The movement was hindered by the congestion on the roads. The congestion was caused by the demolition of the bridges over the Meuse. Despite supreme efforts, it was not possible to guide the jammed-up formations over the provisional bridges quickly. The *XVI. Armee-Korps (mot.)* was delayed in its advance by exactly 24 hours.

The leading formations of the division, which started rolling forward at noon, reached the Dutch border around 1500 hours. The countryside was pretty and tidy; the soldiers had their first glimpse into Holland from the small, squat hills. The fruit trees were in bloom; it would have been a peacetime picture had it not been for the clouds of smoke that darkened the skies to the north and west.

The motorcycle infantry, reconnaissance elements and first tanks crossed the border at Locht. The move continued in fits and spurts via Simpelveld–Schin-op-Geul–Valkenburg. The motorcycle battalion was then outside the gates of Maastricht. It was shortly after 1500 hours. Long columns—tanks, engineers, *Flak*, medical vehicles—closed up on the attractive, broad streets of the city and waited for a crossing over the newly erected pontoon bridge. All of a sudden, *Flak* on both sides of the street went into position. Before the motorcycle infantry grasped what was going on, the first rounds were being fired. Twelve British Blenheims [the standard light twin-engine bomber of the Royal Air Force] raced in and dropped their loads on the bridges. The fireworks were soon over, however, and the motorcycle battalion was able to cross the bridge. *Leutnant* Schmidt and his platoon from the 3rd Company were the first to reach the far side.

The division participated in the fighting at Hannut and Gembloux, where it suffered heavy losses. Its reconnaissance assets—*Panzer-Aufklärungs-Abteilung 3* and *Kradschützen-Bataillon 3*—continued to be employed in a traditional manner:[9]

The forward-most elements—such as the motorcycle and reconnaissance battalion, as well as the two armor regiments, which were rapidly closing up, and the 1st Battalion of the divisional artillery—had already established contact with the enemy. The first prisoners, mostly from the Belgian 4th Infantry Division, had been brought in. The cannoneers of the 1st Battalion had even succeeded in capturing the 9th Battery of the Ardennes Light Infantry Regiment. The motorcycle battalion arrived at the battlefield around Hannut late in the afternoon, soon joined by the reconnaissance battalion. The antitank battalion, which had assembled in the Mopertingen area in the meantime, was also sent forward as soon as possible. Its 1st and 3rd Companies were attached to the armor brigade; its 2nd Company to the reconnaissance battalion. *Panzer-Regiment 6* followed the reconnaissance battalion through Heers and reached Hannut with its first battalion around 1800 hours.

The division received orders during the night: "Advance on Gembloux!" The Division Commander thereupon ordered an attack with the armor brigade in front with the main effort on the right. The attack was to cross the line Houtain–l'Eveque–Avernes–le Baudoin with the objective of taking the crossroads southwest of Jodoigne. *Major* von Wechmar's reconnaissance battalion was given the guard mission on the open right flank during the advance. It made its first enemy contact against reconnaissance elements at Hemitienne around 1000 hours. The rifle battalions formed up behind the armor regiments, with the 3rd Battalion held in reserve.

In the meantime, the tactical reconnaissance established contact with the enemy . . .

As with the *1. Panzer-Division*, the motorcycle infantry were often given direct ground-combat roles:[10]

The 3rd Company of the motorcycle battalion was finally given the green light to attempt a crossing at Renissart. While approaching, *Oberleutnant* Beck's company received heavy enemy machine-gun fire. The motorcycle infantry halted. *Unteroffizier* Lowa was sent forward to reconnoiter. His squad entered the village and called the neighboring squad of *Unteroffizier* Liebich forward. But both squads were unable to counter the fire from the Moroccans, who were able to take every movement in the village and in the open under fire from improved positions. Fortunately, light tanks arrived along with the rest of *Feldwebel* Hauff's platoon. The fighting vehicles were called back a few minutes later, after one tank flew into the air. That meant that the motorcycle infantry also had to pull back! Five dead men were left behind in the village (*Unteroffizier* Steinmetz, *Gefreiter* Müller, *Gefreiter* Maciejewskie, *Kradschütze* Feige and *Kradschütze* Wauer). The company set up to defend outside of Renissart. It did not advance again until that night. By then, *Hauptmann* Pape's 2nd Company had also arrived. Both companies succeeded in making it through the completely destroyed village and crossing the canal!

Even in France, which enjoyed a good road network, both the reconnaissance and motorcycle infantry forces experienced problems with cross-country mobility:[11]

The division moved out at 1000 hours [on 29 May] in stormy and rainy weather. Patrols from the 3rd Battalion of the rifle regiment could no longer find any enemy forces in Merville, with the exception of the area around the church, where a few prisoners were taken. Correspondingly, the battalion moved immediately into the town, supported by the 4th Company of *Panzer-Regiment 6* (*Hauptmann* Weiß). It moved through the town and then established contact with *MG-Bataillon 7* and *SS-Infanterie-Regiment "Deutschland"* just east and north of Merville. *Panzer-Regiment 6* then screened from the northern portion of the town with its 1st Battalion and the western portion with its 2nd Battalion. **The reconnaissance and motorcycle infantry battalions marched**

forward on foot due to the intractable mud and the continuously misting rains. [Emphasis added by authors.] The motorcycle infantry were able to establish a bridgehead at St. Tournant at 1200 hours, while the reconnaissance elements made it to the northern edge of the Hamont Woods!

In the second half of the campaign, the motorcycle elements and the reconnaissance battalion were habitually deployed forward, sometimes in front of the tanks and sometimes on separate routes. Since the forces were in a pursuit, speed was of the essence, although often at the cost of higher casualties:[12]

> *Oberst* Kühn's armor brigade was in the lead with both of its armor regiments, the motorcycle infantry battalion and the reconnaissance battalion. The first elements crossed the river at 1415 hours [on 12 June]. The rain misted from the heavens and placed a thin veil over the beautiful Marne Valley, which featured hills filled with deciduous trees on both sides. The reconnaissance and motorcycle infantry battalions passed through the positions of the *81. Infanterie-Division*—the Silesian division was commanded by *Generalmajor* von Loeper—and advanced into the enemy forces, which had been pulling back since noon as the result of heavy artillery fire.
>
> The 3rd Company of the motorcycle infantry sent a large patrol in the direction of Hill 222. The patrol, under the command of *Feldwebel* O.A. [*Offizier-Anwärter* = Officer Candidate] von Plessen, moved rapidly as far as the Railler Woods northeast of Soudan. **There it encountered surprisingly strong resistance and did not have time to turn around. The motorcycle infantry set up a desperate defense. But when the rest of the company arrived a few minutes later, it only found dead.** [Emphasis added by authors.] *Feldwebel* von Plessen, *Unteroffizier* Schörnborn, *Obergefreiter* Kurz, *Gefreiter* Müller and *Gefreiter* Zimmermann were the first dead of the division in its new sector.
>
> At the same time, the troops of the reconnaissance battalion were positioned in the woods south of Fontanelle. The village proper was full of enemy forces. The battalion had to hold up until the tanks had closed up. With their support, the village was taken in difficult house-to-house fighting by 2000 hours. Elements of the armor brigade had gone around the village by then and set up in the high ground to the south.

On 15 June the advance continued apace, sometimes with surprising results:[13]

> The division continued its movements without pausing and advanced via Cravant–Vermenton–Arcy to Avallon with both of its battle groups. The latter locality was reached during the night of 15–16 June around 0200 hours. The reconnaissance battalion was only able to enter and move through the village with the help of the 11th Company of the rifle regiment, which was quickly brought forward. In the process, several hundred prisoners were again taken.
>
> The French were surprised by the sudden appearance of the German tanks. Situations developed that bordered on the grotesque. For example, the lead armored cars of the reconnaissance battalion approached the La Côte de Chaux Mountain, south of Arcy. The tunnel through the mountain was completely illuminated. The French guards posted there greeted the waving armored reconnaissance soldiers in a friendly manner and seemed happy to encounter their British Allies. They were mightily disappointed when they looked down the barrel of a pistol after the tunnel was firmly in the hands of the few reconnaissance troopers.

Toward the end, combat abated but did not entirely disappear. Because the reconnaissance elements were far to the forefront, they were the ones who usually took the casualties:[14]

> To the soldiers of the division, it seemed they only moved in their vehicles and marched. The countryside grew prettier by the day. The

division found itself in the fruitful and rich Burgundy region. Small rivers snaked through the hilly countryside, which reminded the men of the wheat fields and blooming meadows of the Rhineland. The vineyards stretched for kilometers on the slopes of the wooded hills. The roads were good and straight as an arrow.

The reconnaissance battalion made it to the outskirts of Arnay. Nothing to be seen of the enemy far and wide. But, all of a sudden, there was a crack! The lead armored car was hit. There were two French tanks in front of it. An antitank gun from the battalion was immediately brought forward and was able to knock out one of the two fighting vehicles. The other vehicle cleared the route. *Major Freiherr* von Wechmar sent a motorcycle infantry platoon in pursuit. It was unable to enter the village, because it was halted outside by machine gun and antitank fire. The battalion halted its movements and waited for the rest of the advance guard to catch up. *Oberstleutnant* von Manteuffel ordered the 3rd Battalion of the rifle regiment to attack around 1600 hours. Valuable time was lost, since the battalion dismounted too early and tried to envelop too far to the west.

Kampfgruppe Oberst Kühn reached the Saône around noon [on 18 June] with most of his forces, crossing the river. The reconnaissance battalion continued to advance and turned in the direction of Mont Vaudery. *Oberst* Kleemann was with his forces at the same time outside of Aumont, while *Gruppe von Manteuffel* formed a bridgehead at Allery.

The enemy was generally falling back everywhere. In cases where a defense was being offered, there were strong officers in charge. There were frequent instances where machine-gun and carbine fire suddenly broke out far behind the lead elements. In one case, *Kradschützen* Pohl, Gerbsch and Kiebitz of the 3rd Company of the motorcycle infantry battalion noticed that the village of Chagny was still full of French soldiers! Under the direction of *Leutnant* Hiltmann, who was bringing up the rear because he was wounded, the three motorcycle infantrymen convinced the garrison there to surrender! Eight officers and 350 men surrendered! In addition, they also captured three intact freight trains and one hospital train!

Major Freiherr von Wechmar's reconnaissance battalion was turned in the direction of Champagnole. His troops did not encounter any serious resistance anywhere. The reconnaissance elements did run into columns of refugees again and again, however. Some soldiers tried to hide themselves among them, who were hoping to escape undetected . . .

The enemy no longer seemed capable of putting up organized resistance. It was only the reconnaissance and combat patrols that occasionally had it out in small skirmishes with enemy rear guards. For example, *Unteroffizier* Liebich of the 3rd Company of the motorcycle infantry was able to destroy six aircraft and a tank at an airstrip while conducting a patrol [on 21 June]. The noncommissioned officer, who received the Iron Cross, First Class for his efforts, had crossed the Rhône in a pneumatic craft with his squad.

After breaking through French lines during the second phase of the fighting in France in June 1940, *Panzer-Aufklärungs-Abteilung 90* was ordered south to exploit the situation and find weakness in the enemy front. On 8 June, the situation developed unexpectedly:[15]

A special adventure was to await *Panzer-Aufklärungs-Abteilung 90* in St. Just. The battalion, which had wanted to continue on to Verberie, another 40 kilometers distant—confident of victory and its abilities—wound up in an increasingly difficult situation at

1800 hours in the middle of two withdrawing but still thoroughly combat-capable forces that were also willing to fight. In the course of the evening, the battalion was ordered to hold St. Just and cover all entrances. But by 2100 hours, the ammunition was running out. A call for help from the battalion reached the division command post. It especially needed ammunition for its light infantry, antitank and machine guns. Soon afterwards, the battalion reported that a French column breaking out to the south had cut off the rearward lines of communication. The battalion had been cut off and was being pushed out of St. Just. It was being forced to occupy the dominant high ground at La Folie, where it was setting up an all-round defense. With its weak forces, the battalion was unable to interdict the French columns moving through St. Just. It had to be content with being able to save itself. Although the division sent a company from the *II./Schützen-Regiment 69* to help, it was unable to break through in the rapid onset of darkness.

At first light, the situation became even more critical for the battalion, which had been completely surrounded. Enemy tanks were attacking in small groups from all sides. Fortunately, they did not have unity of command. The lack of ammunition became ever more noticeable. The division was only capable of telling it to hold out and that help was on the way in the form of *Panzer-Regiment 7*. The intent was for the tanks to give the battalion 3.7cm ammunition.

But it was not until 1000 hours on 9 June that the armor brigade reached the cut-off reconnaissance battalion. The ammunition drop-off was a flop. The 3.7cm ammunition of the tank main guns did not fit the 3.7cm antitank guns of the battalion. Nevertheless, the battalion had been relieved.

The following account concerning *Aufklärungs-Abteilung 29 (mot)* of the *29. Infanterie-Division (mot)* provides some local color concerning scout operations during the pursuit south:[16]

. . . The bridge over the Doubs there was destroyed, but a suspension bridge was found at Torpes that was capable of bearing the necessary weight. Since it was a political matter of great importance to reach the Swiss border—even with only weak forces—a long-range scout patrol was formed from the advance guard. It consisted of three armored cars under the command of *Leutnant* Dietrich of *Aufklärungs-Abteilung 29 (mot)*. He received the mission to advance to the Swiss border at Pontarlier, without regard for consequences. *Leutnant* Dietrich, who was later killed in Russia, wrote about the bold operation:

"The scout section of *Leutnant* Dietrich received the mission at 0130 hours on 17 June at Saint Vitto: Advance to the Swiss border at Pontarlier by the quickest way possible. The mission was of political importance, it was said. Maps were unavailable for the last portion of the movement.

"After a short orders conference, the trip into uncertainty started off into the night. We had not been able to top off our vehicles completely, since fuel had not yet arrived. We moved without any type of lights; the gunners had orders to fire only if fired upon. I moved ahead in the cannon vehicle, followed by the light armored car. The rear was brought up by the radio car.

"At that point, our forward outposts were still able to give us some information; it was said that the enemy had pulled back a bit.

"We rolled into the uncertainty of the night along a small field path that paralleled the Doubs. It was pitch black. Nothing could be seen. Nonetheless, we moved on, feeling our way forward, since the small paths were not shown on the large-scale maps. Finally, we reached the road we were looking for. There was sinister movement everywhere. My gunner called out to me: "French! Leave them be and don't shoot!" [17] We rushed ahead, advancing past halting French columns. At the same time, we looked to the rear to see whether the second vehicle was still following. Keep going! Forward! The darkness and twilight hours had to be exploited since there were still 80 kilometers to the border.

"We fired into the darkness. A light was seen in front of us. A French soldier wanted to direct us into the column that was racing down the road. "Drive at him!" He jumped out of the way. We could not stop! I took a closer look: Heavy French artillery had halted on the road. It was starting to turn daylight and was getting lighter by the minute. French vehicles started to approach us. Just keeping on moving without hesitation! We couldn't do anything against those masses of forces. Our vehicles moved out at full throttle towards the border. Every town and village was occupied by the French. Large swastika flags were waving up front on our vehicles. Horrified, the French yielded. The French citizenry looked at us, flabbergasted. "The Germans are coming!" Salins was behind us, and it was already turning bright. We were approaching Pontarlier. The roads were partially blocked by obstacles. We were able to observe Pontarlier. Two enemy columns were getting entangled there. We wanted to turn off to the left or the right, but there was nowhere to do so from the road. I yelled to my driver: "Move through the middle of the columns!"

"We fired a few rounds into the columns! Horrified, everyone scattered. A few fearful French officers, who had been standing on the side of the road, hurried into a house. A few French got in front of our wheels, but it did not matter at that point: "Just don't stop!" Keep going, or everything was over! With some concern I looked to the rear, but our second vehicle was racing through the middle of the march columns. We then had to pass another column. "Step on it!" Finally, there was a path that led off to the left. I didn't know where it led, since we did not have any maps. We reached a small patch of woods and halted. The last few minutes had been a bit too exciting; we were only able to settle down with some *Schnapps*.

"It did not take very long before more French showed up. It was infantry this time; they were sneaking up on us, firing. That meant were needed to take off again. There was no sense in remaining there. We had to find the border. I looked through my binoculars: French were cowering around everywhere. We got a kick out of their horrified faces. We moved on into the pathless, difficult terrain. All of a sudden, a French border structure appeared in front of us. It was manned!

"Wire and road obstacles had been set up everywhere. We moved into a narrow, broken-up valley. All of a sudden, there was a sign in front of us: *"Frontiére à 500 m."* We were in front of a large abatis. The border had to be right around there. The wire fence along the border could be seen.

"It would have been impossible to turn around along the narrow wooded path. The slopes to either side rose sharply. We still weren't completely sure whether it was the border. Two of us climbed over the abatis and raced forward on foot. "There's a building up there!" I looked through my binoculars, and what I saw pleased us greatly. *"Douane Suisse."* The Swiss customs building was in front of us. We ran back, happy. A message was sent feverishly to the battalion: "Border reached!"

"At that point, we started receiving fiendish fire from the high ground to both the left and the right. We couldn't see anything, but the French had to be close, since we could hear them speak. We couldn't stay there, since the French could come at us from the impenetrable woods. The rounds smacked hard against the armor of the vehicles. There was nothing else to do but laboriously move backwards along the narrow wooded path. Finally, we were able to succeed in turning around on a somewhat wider stretch, thanks to repeated directions and knocking over trees. The French did not let go; we fired like wild men. We finally made it back to the exit point from that dreadful wooded valley. We waited for the enemy antitank guns; fingers on triggers, hand grenades and smoke bombs in our hands! Despite our concerns—we didn't know whether to believe it—we were able to get out of that bottleneck.

"We had barely reached another position, when the crazy firing started up again. There were French everywhere! That meant we had to keep moving! With our engines turned off, we rolled slowly forward. In front of us was a French guard post. A shocked guard attempted to take aim. Our machine gun fired. The guard contingent scattered, full of fear. Their will to resist had been broken. We rolled on. Soon, there was another guard post in front of us. It had been warned. But it also fled when we fired.

"There wasn't a single spot, where there weren't any French. We moved about among the French bunkers oriented towards the Swiss border. But we couldn't stay there. We only had a few liters of fuel left. Our effort to break into a gas station outside of Pontarlier had succeeded without a hitch, but the station was empty, with the result that our almost empty tanks could not be topped off. We started to approach Pontarlier again with the hope of being able to turn off to the right and attempt to hide ourselves in the woods there. It was swarming with French everywhere. Before we knew it, we were in the middle of a motorized French column. A wild ride ensued; the only thing that could help us was speed. The French stared at us, flabbergasted. They fired blindly in our direction. A large bus then attempted to ram us. We brushed up against it; we were lucky one more time. Finally, after about 5 kilometers in the midst of the column there was a road leading off to the left. We raced off into heavy vegetated terrain, where we were able to hide. All the while, the column continued to roll down the road.

"Our vehicles only had fuel for another 2 to 3 kilometers. Radio communications with the battalion had been lost. Correspondingly, there was nothing we could do at the time but sit there and wait. The terrain was good for conducting a defense; that was good, since the place was still crawling with French. We remained there overnight and took off the next morning in an effort to get fuel from French vehicles. We were successful, and we were soon back at the battalion location."

Oberleutnant von Mutius has provided an account of what was happening with the battalion at the time:

Aufklärungs-Abteilung 29 (mot) followed closely behind the scout section, but it was held up at various locations by the French. A crossing over the Saône was forced at Pontailler, a narrow bridge over the Doubs was taken in a *coup de main* at Dampierre and assorted pockets of resistance in the Jura Mountains west of Pontarlier were quickly eliminated. At first light on 17 June, the western outskirts of Pontarlier were reached. In an aggressively led attack along both sides of the road, the motorcycle infantry company forced its way into the city. As soon as the resistance abated, a reinforced platoon under *Leutnant* Metz was employed to advance further in order to pursue the enemy and reach the border east of the municipality. It was possible to prevent the demolition of the bridge in the middle of the village at the last minute. *Leutnant* Metz attempted to take the French border fort east of the city in a *coup de main*. He succeeded in entering the first gate of the fort with his motorcycle infantry platoon, but his demand for surrender was ignored. Dietrich's armored car section was rescued from a difficult situation. Around 1000 hours, the battalion was in possession of the municipality and had reached the border.

As in Poland, the cavalry school's *Panzer-Aufklärungs-Lehr-Abteilung* also participated in the campaign in the West. It was been alerted on 9 May, rolling to the border that night and entering Luxembourg early on 10 May, and moved ahead of the *2. Panzer-Division*, serving as a reconnaissance asset for Guderian's *XIX. Armee-Korps (mot)*. Its mission: "Reconnoiter along the right, open flank of the corps as far as the line Marche–Dinant–Givet." Armored car patrols covered up to 120 kilometers toward the Meuse on the first day. On 15 May, the battalion was attached to the *6. Panzer-Division*, where it received a typical order from the commander, *Generalmajor* Kempff:[18]

Moving ahead [of the division], the battalion crosses the pontoon bridge established at

Montherné and guards the right flank of the pursuit group of the *6. Panzer-Division*, which is advancing on Montcornet. Reconnoiter as far as the line Hirson–Vervins–Marle. Speed is of the essence!

Exhibiting the typical *Reitergeist* of the armored reconnaissance force, *Oberstleutnant* Cramer, the battalion commander at the time, wrote: "Neither the dark night nor the complete chaos on the clogged roads could hold up the pursuit."

Von Esebeck, the battalion adjutant, provides a firsthand account of the operations that followed:[19]

Happy to have a mission again and finally be able to move out, we reached Montherné, where numerous troop elements had already arrived, none of which wanted to be left behind in their unbridled desire to move forward. We cursed like sailors. What in the devil's name was the heavy artillery looking for there? God knows, it was blocking the way that the recon elements needed to use to get forward, where they belonged. But everyone was proud to be up front, and everyone wanted his piece of the French, who had had to yield to the unstoppable onslaught and give up the west bank [of the Meuse].

Finally we made it, boxing our way forward to the bridge with a lot of yelling and some choice words. A portion of the 1st Armored Car Troop had already crossed the pontoon bridge. They moved at a walking pace at large intervals in order not to overtax the bridge that had been taken with difficulty with too great a weight. Then, all of a sudden, a wild firefight broke out. The first impression was that the French had entered back into Montherné again from somewhere off to the side and that a fierce fight had flared up in the village.

All of the weapons were firing—but you could start to differentiate—it was the *Flak* on the surrounding high ground that was firing like crazy. In the blink of an eye and with admirable precision, the pontoon bridge was separated in the middle and disappeared along both banks of the river. And there they were! They roared in, brazenly low. Thirty to fifty meters above the slopes of the banks. French bombers, three . . . four . . . five of them. Anyone who didn't have something in his hand to fire just stared skyward, transfixed, at the silver birds, which flew around their target, most likely our pontoon bridge, in bold sweeps. But the bridge was gone and could no longer be hit. As a result, they opened up their bellies and indiscriminately dropped bombs on the town. At that low altitude, you could see the individual bombs tumble out.

Damn it! They were spinning down directly towards our heads! It was time to get out of there, pressing up against a wall or hiding behind an armored vehicle. The unfriendly greetings from the French exploded with a roar and a clatter, flinging dirt, stones and shrapnel everywhere. But nothing bad happened. They were probably prevented from a precision drop by the defensive fires of the *Flak* and our 2cm cannon and were happy to disappear behind the next bend in the river. One bomber did not succeed in doing that. It must have been hit. It headed straight for a hillside right in front of it and literally buried itself into the slope. Wild jubilation within our ranks!

But it appeared the Frenchies had not had enough. They turned around three more times and rained down their blessings anew. I started to doubt the old saying: Everything good comes from above. The *Flak* was unable to do anything; they were scurrying along too low—in some cases, along the river valley below the *Flak* positions. Our cannon on the road only had an extremely limited field of fire.

One of the men started to grumble: "Where's Hermann! He's never left us in the lurch before!"

"Be quiet, my boy! Just wait!"

All of a sudden, the *Flak* fell silent. Automatically, as if prearranged, our 2cm guns also stopped firing. There was a light singing and whistling sound that fell from the heavens and then the dull rattling of a long burst from aircraft machine guns. The first bomber acted as if it had been grasped by an invisible hand. It flipped over and shot vertically downward, as if struck by a large club. There was a dull explosion right behind the town, in the woods, followed by a gigantic shot of flame. Everything was then covered in a dark haze.

Visible for the first time, one of our fighters shot down from the blue, cloudless skies, quickly went over the area of the crash site and then disappeared behind the next hill, waggling its wings contentedly. Two other bombers did not have a better time of it, either. They didn't need to devote any more thought to the return flight home. Every "kill" was accompanied by a heady shout of jubilation from our people. Then the scare was over. The bridge was reassembled, and the march could be continued. The commander had already moved ahead with the elements moving forward from the armored car troop. A messenger came back to our location. It was directed for the battalion to follow the lead elements to Liart, some 40 kilometers further to the west. Valuable time had been lost to those damned bombers. Time to go!

Once again, the race was on with the forces that had already gained ground. The roads were bad and narrow. Both to the right and the left, the ditches were overflowing with abandoned military equipment of the French. Everything was scattered about, up to and including heavy howitzers and fighting vehicles. The small arms and the individual bits of equipment could not even be counted. The positions that had been assaulted were smoldering in the woods. The entire forest floor was black, with the underbrush carbonized, for kilometers on end. Those were the feeble remains of the Maginot Line, which had been considered to be a miracle of defensive artistry and impregnable by the French. It hadn't lasted three days. At that point, the only thing the position, in which so many dreams for resistance had been placed, showed was nothing but smoking and destroyed war materiel. It had been a dream that had had a bloody awakening. They must have fled in a panic there, once they realized that no obstacle could block the way against the German offensive spirit, the furor *teutonicus*. And so the battalion reached Liart, after it had fought its way forward to its own lead elements. It was already starting to turn dark.

It was there that we were to link up with the commander, who would finally be able to give us information concerning the situation and the objective. Messengers went through the village looking for him to report the arrival of the *ALA*. One after the other came back without any results. Finally, the last one brought the *Spieß* [First Sergeant (soldier slang)] of the 1st Armored Car Troop back with him. *Oberwachtmeister* Funk reported short and to the point: "All of the elements of the troop that arrived earlier have moved out as reconnaissance patrols."

"And the commander?"

"He's leading a patrol!"

Good grief! That could turn out interesting. We knew nothing, only that we were in Liart and that another pursuit group was supposedly advancing on Laon further to the south. We had received orders to guard the right flank and reconnoiter as far as the line Hirson–Vervins–Marle. What was to be done at that point, when everything seemed to be moving all at once? To start, I took the battalion off of the main road in the direction of Vervins and had it move to a small patch of woods behind the next village. Since it had turned dark by then, I had a "hedgehog" formed. I wanted to wait there for the return of the battalion commander and, presumably, spend the night there. We refueled and the meal was issued. As we did every time we halted, we got everything ready in case we had to move out again without notice for combat operations.

Half an hour later, the commander returned. Once again, he had been unable to contain his urge to participate in combat operations and do things. He had gone ahead with a patrol to reconnoiter the avenue of advance, since the battalion had been held up by the bombers. He brought back several prisoners; he had quickly rendered a French battery that he had encountered on the road combat ineffective and brought back valuable reconnaissance information. We breathed a sigh of relief that the "old man" was back with us in one piece.

He began asking questions: What? The battalion to remain here while the pursuit group on the southern avenue of advance was already 10 kilometers ahead of us? No, our objective is Vervins. We will reach it by tomorrow morning! We have the whole night to move.

That was our "old man" for you. Always forward, forward, forward! Just don't ask a lot of questions!

✠

Patrols formed up and disappeared into the night. They were to establish a thick reconnaissance screen, close in, and clarify the situation in front of the battalion, at least as much as was possible during the night. The first patrol reports concerning enemy contact soon arrived. In the distance, you could hear the dull bark of our 2cm cannon. Occasionally, there were individual reports from guns, which unmistakably sounded like enemy antitank guns. The right-hand patrol did not do so well; the left-hand group, on the other hand, established contact with the pursuit group and made good progress. And the patrol moving along the avenue of advance? It radioed like crazy for help; we needed to take its prisoners. Damn, what kind of nonsense was it doing? A reconnaissance patrol was intended not to fight; it needed to move forward and reconnoiter. Finally, the commander dispatched the patrol in front of our lead elements to clarify the mysterious situation.

But it did not take too long for the new patrol to also radio and report that even the two of them could not handle the hundreds of prisoners in Brunehamel. The battalion was requested to send reinforcements. The commander blew up at that point. Flying along, he led the battalion forwards, despite the darkness and uncertainty.

When we got near to Brunehamel, we were approached by a march column of French, led by a *Capitaine*. They had no weapons. So we sent them off. Direction of march: Berlin! So what had the patrol done this time. There were more than 200 men just at the one location!

At this point, the narrative continues with the first-hand account of *Leutnant* von Bäumen, a scout section leader:

At Montremé, an armored [car] pursuit group was formed. Our group consisted of thirteen men and four armored cars, which was sent forward as a patrol. When we were crossing the pontoon bridge that had just been built over the Meuse, three French bombers attacked. The bombs hit the water and along the banks. We tried to get out of the beaten zone by increasing our speed. We were soon able to observe the fact that all three enemy machines hurtled like torches towards the ground just moments after German fighters appeared. There was no time to reflect or have any feelings! Our orders were to pursue! Everyone was imbued with a single thought: "Forward!" "Forward" was the purpose and subject matter of all instruction, training and preparation for this fight. The patrol thundered "forward" on the ravaged roads, which had just been the targets of German bombs and artillery shells.

Shattered vehicles, tanks and guns covered the terrain; the smoking rubble of a strong position. In the woods to the right and left, tattered and scattered enemy soldiers were fleeing. A few of them senselessly fired a couple of times against our armored vehicles. We did not fire; the mission's objective was far in front of us and would require a lot of ammunition. The movements in the woods became more frequent and stronger. At some places along the road, we passed small groups of Negroes and French, all of them in terrible condition. We moved past vehicles that were full of fleeing soldiers. The retreating enemy forces became more and more numerous. They pulled back to the west in fairly large groups, up to platoon, demoralized and shocked. We weren't offered any resistance anywhere. For the most part, they probably did not even recognize we were German. But even there we could not allow ourselves to be held up under any circumstances. Our objective was still 80 kilometers in front of us.

For that reason, we left the main road. We continued along secondary roads. We were able to constantly observe the retreat routes of the French. The radio operators worked feverishly to transmit all of that which we had seen. As a patrol, we were to avoid a fight for as long as possible. Sometimes it was very difficult to allow high-value targets to pass us by without firing a round. As a result, however, we advanced rapidly.

All of a sudden, we had to cross the main retreat route of the French. Clustered thickly together, the enemy's horse-drawn and motorized columns pressed west. We observed for a while. There were no breaks in the column through which we could move without interference. There was only one thing to do: Break through by surprise! A short order was issued to the armored car commanders. We then moved concealed through the woods towards the road. The patrol leader gave the signal: There were flashes from all of the barrels. Our shells and rounds swept along both sides of the road. Orders . . . screams . . . vehicles tipping over . . . spooked horse teams . . . a sad conglomerate of humans, animals and equipment—it was complete chaos. Other than a few isolated rounds fired, there was no trace of a defense, and our four armored cars continued to roll along their route, leaving behind the bloody picture along the road.

After moving a short while, a village appeared in front of us. When we were within about 700 meters of it, enemy forces appeared on the road! A company of infantry marched towards us, followed by horse-drawn conveyances. We moved towards them. The enemy did not recognize who we were yet. No one probably thought there was German armor around there. We were then about 20 meters from the enemy. It might be possible to spare the lives and blood of the French in this instance. The patrol leader jumped down from his vehicle. Pistol in hand, he approached the French.

"*A bas les armes, haut les main!*" He yelled at the throng.

"*Allemands!*" The multi-voiced shout of terror echoed back. Everyone scrammed in all directions, seeking cover in roadside ditches and gardens. The driver of the first armored car observed a Frenchman raising his rifle against the patrol leader from behind. In a matter of seconds, a bullet from the driver's pistol firing from the hatch hit him. That was the first round. It unleashed a crazy racket from the houses, gardens and shrubs. But then our weapons issued their bloody statement. At the moment, the road, which had continued to fill with vehicles and soldiers coming from the rear, was a picture of panic. The vehicles could no longer get away. They were torn apart by our rounds, with many of them catching fire. The cannon and machine guns hammered away for several minutes. That bloody work was hard, but it could not be avoided. We had to get through there.

Two antitank guns going into position further to the rear were eliminated before they could point their dangerous fire-breathing gapes in our direction. The enemy started to flee as well he could. The French jumped from house to house and through gardens and fields, followed by a hail of our rounds. They were leaving behind everything on the road and in the village.

"Move out!" the patrol leader ordered.

The gray, heavy vehicles pressed forward slowly and irresistibly, moving through the inseparable entanglement of the grim rest of all that which had offered resistance to the

German armor. We repeatedly had to dismount and pry apart whatever it was that towered in front of our vehicles and proved a hindrance. We cleared a path. We continued on towards the objective of the mission.

Over the next hour, we repeatedly ran into enemy forces marching towards us. Each time, a similar drama played itself out in front of us. The encounters and engagements grew more frequent. In the end, we had to fight for almost every kilometer. Night started to descend gradually. All of our senses worked twice as hard. It was a situation of incredible tension to be out there all alone, far in front of the other friendly forces, moving in enemy territory. But it was also a proud moment to belong to the forwardmost portion of the German assault wave. With the increasing darkness, the march tempo became somewhat slower. We couldn't risk driving into an ambush. From the previous fighting, we were already well acquainted with the French mines. A look at the map revealed that we weren't too far from the French town of Brunehamel. We approached carefully and then rolled through the streets of a place that had died. There was a large marketplace in front of us; numerous streets emptied into it. There were two French trucks in the middle; not a soul was to be seen.

As a reconnaissance soldier, you started to get a feeling for the closeness of the enemy over time. That's why the situation seemed suspicious to us—despite or perhaps because of the deathly silence. We sent a vehicle a ways back to cover our rear, since an ambush in a built-up area can turn critical. The patrol leader then moved across the marketplace in his armored car; the others remained in place, ready to fire. Just as the vehicle was about in the middle of the square, an armored vehicle showed up in the half-darkness from a side street about 20 meters to the left. The gun flashed, but the round whistled past overhead.

Then the cannon of the armored car covering to the rear barked three times. The gunner had been on his toes. Three rounds tore open the body of the enemy vehicle along its side. The duel had been decided. The sound of tracks from the side street revealed to us that there were other enemy armored vehicles there, but that they were pulling back.

We wanted to pursue, but the commander of the second vehicle, which had pulled up in the meantime, yelled out: "Enemy to the rear!" You could hear the sounds of engines, and the lead elements of a vehicle column started coming out of a side street. We were able to identify an armored vehicle in front, followed by personnel carriers. A hail of fire from our side greeted them. The armored vehicle, badly hit, turned around and disappeared. Our rounds raced through the long row of trucks. Flames shot out of the engines and provided an eerie illumination. The vehicles, many of them missing their drivers, rammed into one another. We moved along the column. There were 40 vehicles in all, including 4 armored ones. About 100 men surrendered. The weapons were destroyed and then the French listlessly started their march into captivity. We sent them off to the east in the direction of our forces. Perhaps they would encounter French columns and temporarily escape their fate. But we couldn't take them along with us. At least their weapons had been destroyed.

In the darkness, we looked for the right way out of the village. The armor car commanders reported that their ammunition was getting low. That was nothing we wanted to hear. We had fired off almost everything. But that was unavoidable. But we were also still 20 kilometers from our objective of Vervins. We wanted to see how much further we could get. We sent a radio message to the battalion concerning the ammunition. When we were 500 meters outside of the village, we encountered two enemy motorized columns that had halted next to one another. Our route was blocked, but we had not been identified in the pitch-black night. According to the map and the terrain, it would be impossible to go around. Despite our ammunition situation, there was only one decision that could be made: Fight and, exploiting the confusion and the darkness, break through! Our weapons lit up the nighttime skies garishly, and our rounds hit the enemy in short bursts. An unholy noise accompanied the panic that was breaking out.

"Move out!" the patrol leader ordered.

But the first armored car had already gotten stuck between the vehicles that had been abandoned by the enemy and which were positioned helter-skelter next to one another. We couldn't get through. The road was on an embankment at that location; it could not be bypassed. Our spotlights lit up and scampered along eerily in the midst of the tumult. The rearward portions of the column attempted to turn around. Our machine-gun bursts responded to the shots coming from there.

The patrol leader and his noncommissioned officer jumped down from their vehicles and ran along the road, firing their pistols. After going about 100 meters, both of them saw the rearward elements of the column hightailing it out of there. They positioned themselves along the road and didn't let any more get away.

The noncommissioned officer then ran back to the patrol. Everyone, with the exception of the drivers needed to dismount. The men then cleared the area, pulling the fearful figures from out of the hiding places in and around the some 60 vehicles still there. The wounded were recovered, and the weapons taken away. We found a small turnoff from the road that led into a pasture. We had the French drive the undamaged vehicles there. Whatever was destroyed was pushed off the road. After that was done, we counted 130 men and 75 vehicles. But the last remaining magazines were in our weapons. In that situation, where the entire area around us appeared to be full of enemy forces, we could not continue on. We had to remain where we were. The situation was critical;

our presence had to be sufficiently known to the French by then. How long would it last until the next engagement took place? Would we get ammunition in the meantime? Of course, the battalion was well aware of what had happened up to that point and the enemy situation. But would the ones who were supposed to bring ammunition to us get through?

A lot of vehicular noise was coming over to us from the direction of Brunehamel. Two armored cars moved the short distance back [to Brunehamel]. The village was full of enemy forces. There was a vast number of vehicles at the marketplace. New columns arrived from different directions. French were plundering the houses. The two armored cars distanced themselves carefully and without being identified. The battalion was once again informed of our observations of the situation via radio traffic. From the other side of our location—according to the map, there was a crossroads not too far from us—the sound of heavy vehicular traffic could be heard. Reconnaissance indicated that there were strong enemy forces on the road there. We couldn't go in any direction without a fight. So we set up obstacles in front of us and behind us out of destroyed vehicles. Everything had to be done quietly. There were two armored cars behind each obstacle; each had its guns directed on the road. Only the drivers remained in the vehicles. The other men were divided along the obstacles with pistols, hand grenades, signal flare pistols and lanterns designed to blind the enemy. In case anyone attacked, they were to try to deceive them concerning our strength by means of a proper set of fireworks.

It took but 10 minutes before the French started approaching from Brunehamel. The sound of the engines got closer. Orders were issued in whispers. The enemy was about 20 meters from the obstacle. The first vehicle appeared to have spotted the obstacle; it stopped. At that point, our searchlight flashed on and a burst of machine-gun fire headed into the vehicle. We then banged away with our small arms from behind and to the sides of the obstacle. Three men ran along the column and fired pistols and tossed hand grenades. General confusion. The French surrendered after a short exchange of fire. Portions of them had fled after abandoning their vehicles. Five officers and about a hundred men were disarmed and led to the other prisoners in the meadows. They sat there, held in check by a captured French machine gun.

For incomprehensible reasons, however, they made no effort to escape or fight back. They probably did not understand that a small but determined group of Germans was fighting; the night hid our weakness. Our situation had improved as a result of the large numbers of captured weapons. French machine guns and rifles were integrated into our "defensive system." Despite that, we were concerned about the ammunition situation. Enemy vehicles, either individually or in small groups, repeatedly appeared at our obstacles; they were shot up. The number of prisoners grew more and more numerous; the battalion radioed that patrols were on their way to us.

✠

Midnight had long since passed. "Engine noises!" A subdued voice called out from the other obstacle on the western side. It was still pretty far away, but it was clearly coming closer. Putting our ears to the ground on the road, we heard the dull, heavy rattling. Could those be our armored vehicles? The question hovered eerily in the breathless silence. The prisoners were getting restless. With difficulty, they were controlled by the threat of pistol barrels. Three men had to pull guard duty over them. Everyone else was ready for anything to both sides of our obstacle. It was only by means of surprise and deception that we could help ourselves against the enemy. At nighttime, it was hard to differentiate between the muzzle flash of a cannon and a hand-grenade detonation. We intended to deceive them into thinking we had cannon. The noise came closer; slowly, terribly slowly, it approached us through the impenetrable night.

The silhouette of the first vehicle appeared. Another 50 meters . . . then 40 . . . 30 . . . the muzzle flash from the patrol leader's submachine gun lit up the night as a signal to initiate combat. The hail of fire tore apart the quiet and darkness of the night. We jumped towards the enemy on both sides of the road. Rifle fire and the detonation of hand grenades accompanied our run. The crack of main-gun rounds was not heard from the enemy side; individual rounds were the weak defensive response. They weren't armored vehicles!

We saw long barrels behind tracked prime movers. Disarming them and taking them prisoner were the work of several minutes. A heavy battery had been captured! The number of prisoners grew ever larger, causing concern.

There was still nothing to be heard nor seen of the patrols that were supposed to help us. Messages were radioed to the battalion. Morning was not too far away. We continued to crouch and wait. Then finally, finally . . . there was the hammering of German machine guns and rapid-fire cannon from far away. What a magnificent sound! Their signal flares arced skyward on two sides about a kilometer away from us. We replied in kind. The sound of fighting flared up, but it did not come any closer. Two patrols were hurrying towards us. By then, the battalion commander had gained a clear picture of the situation from the reports. It was not possible for just the patrols to advance any further where than they were!

He sent a radio message: "The battalion is coming!"

That was all we wanted to hear! And not much later, the lead armored car elements were stopping at our obstacle. Our reconnaissance mission had been accomplished. We had been 13 men: 4 armored vehicles, 500 prisoners, 400 vehicles and a heavy battery were an "incidental" result of our reconnaissance mission.

That concludes the firsthand account of Bäumen's patrol. The narrative continues with *Oberleutnant* von Esebeck:

We were in Brunehamel by then. We thought we were having a bad dream. At the marketplace and in front of the church of the small village were 400 disarmed French, Belgians and Negroes. Many were drunk; officers could not be found. Their weapons were in a gigantic, partially carbonized funeral pyre that had been doused in gasoline and lit up. It was a wild picture in the streets. Horse-drawn conveyances and motorized vehicles; the horses had not had their tack removed. Innumerable trains vehicles and several batteries, even a few heavy field howitzers. In a courtyard were two large command buses that undoubtedly had belonged to a higher headquarters as command and control vehicles. Despite our happiness in having caused such massive confusion within the ranks of the enemy, we still could not rid ourselves of a bitter feeling of soldierly shame. We felt ashamed for the once brave opponent of 1914/1918. We had not even seen such a pathetic scene in Poland. A Belgian sergeant stated almost apathetically, dully: We've been retreating for three days. The officers had taken off and not returned; enraged, we got drunk.

The battalion moved out again. We wanted to reach Vervins before it turned light. What we would then experience seems so improbable that I will run into the danger that half of it won't be believed. We had a hard time believing it ourselves.

We had barely moved for a quarter of an hour, when things didn't seem to be moving forward quite right up front. The commander attempted to move past to get to the commander of the lead elements. It wasn't possible. The road was generally good and wide, but it was plugged up by two columns. On the left was our battalion; on the right was a vast column of all types of troops, with a whole lot of horse-drawn conveyances—French! Not a shot was fired. We just honked our horns and cursed. The French coachmen lashed out at their horses. A lot of them wanted to be taken along on our trucks. They moved faster, after all, than the horses could. In some places, our drivers could only work their way forward at a walking pace, since vehicles and guns had flipped over into the ditch. The moon was appalled and crept away behind the clouds, ashamed of the spectacle it was seeing. It was like that for 10 kilometers.

The commander then lost his patience. We turned off of the main road to the south in an effort to be in Vervins in the morning, preferably before the French column. But the complete chaos on the road must have already torn the battalion apart, since it was not possible to get through by turning off and, after a few kilometers, our "forward move" was in front of a village, along with the rest of the lead scout troop, the signals platoon and a few motorcycle infantry. The village was occupied and did not want to let us pass through. On top of that, a storm came in, it turned pitch black and the radio sets had to be turned off. As a result, it was no longer possible to maintain contact with the other troops by that means. Two motorcycle messengers that we sent out we never saw again. Under those circumstances, a continued movement in the direction of Vervins did not make any sense. The battalion had to be brought together again first. But how?

Well, the way everyone got together will forever remain a puzzle to those who were part of it. In any event, all of the elements of the battalion, including the trains, were in the small patch of woods where the commander had originally crawled with his small band. The last vehicle had barely disappeared into the woods, when a French reconnaissance aircraft strained his eyes looking for us at 30 meters above the ground. We played "rabbit" and let him pass by without accomplishing his mission. It just then started to dawn on us what had happened the previous night. It seemed like a bad dream to us. We weren't even sure ourselves and what we remembered. Was that which we had done actually possible? We sent patrols to the rear to look at things in the daylight. They were no longer able to get through; all of the built-up areas were sealed off.

We then intended to establish contact with the neighboring pursuit group. The initial efforts failed; it was not until a combat-capable patrol was sent out that it was able to force its way through. The French knew that something was up, but they were still gun shy. They turned away to the north and disappeared behind the Oise. That meant that our mission had been accomplished. The reconnaissance had brought in the necessary information, and the French division marching against the flank of the pursuit group of the *6. Panzer-Division* had been scattered. In addition, *Leutnant* Waldow's patrol was able to knock out a French fighting vehicle and, by doing so, holding up an enemy armor attack until the necessary defensive weaponry was in place. A proud day for the *ALA* came to a conclusion. But there still wasn't any rest. That evening, we were told to keep going, follow the enemy and stay on his heels.

Despite extraordinary successes, after-action reports written after the campaign took a sharp look at operations of the force, as shown in this excerpt from the divisional report of the *7. Panzer-Division*:[20]

> In most cases, the armored reconnaissance battalion was unable to fulfill the demands placed on it *with regard to reconnaissance* in either the Campaign in Poland or in the Campaign in France. The reason for that is solely attributable to the more or less unusable reconnaissance vehicle, as was already reported after the end of the Campaign in Poland. In its differing versions, the armored car is confined to the roads and is, therefore, almost always quickly encountering antitank defenses or obstacles. Its armor protection is so poor that it is not proof against infantry armor-piercing rifle rounds and is, correspondingly, inferior to all of the weapons of the enemy. The tremendously high losses in armored cars, already sustained by the end of the first week of the Campaign in the West confirms these observations. On the 8th day of the war, the armored reconnaissance battalion of the division had only nine armored cars still available to it.
>
> It would be wrong to conclude from that fact that the armored reconnaissance battalion has no justification for its existence. For the indispensable ground reconnaissance needs of the division, it needs to be outfitted with vehicles that enable it to break through the enemy's antitank defenses or his obstacles off the road network. During the campaign in the West, as a consequence of the high losses sustained with its vehicles, the armored reconnaissance battalion was not employed as a whole. Nevertheless, it was employed with extreme success as follows:
> a) Reaching and occupying important sectors in front of and to the sides of the division, for which it is especially capable, given its speed.
> b) Shielding and adding density to an armor attack.
> c) Screening flanks.
>
> The organization of two armored car companies, one motorcycle infantry company and one heavy company proved itself. The number of companies is considered sufficient. An increase would only weaken the agility and maneuverability of the battalion.
>
> Operations demonstrated, however, the necessity of outfitting [the battalion] as follows:
> 1. Radio equipment:
> a) Within the reconnaissance section (previously notified one another through vocal calls, dismounting etc. in the face of the enemy).
> b) From the battalion commander to the patrol leaders for communications on the march and in operations with the armor.
> 2. *1 Antitank platoon* with at least three 5cm antitank guns. The 2cm armored car is *not* suited for defending against enemy armored vehicles.
> 3. *Mine detector* for the engineer platoon in order to be able to clear mined roads etc. quickly and without stopping while *in front of* the division.

4. As a heavy weapon, a second heavy mortar section.

5. As a replacement for the armored cars presently in service with the troops: A combination wheeled/tracked vehicle (hybrid) with a minimal road speed of 50 to 60 kph (rubber track pads) and an armament of either a 2cm [cannon] or a 4.7cm antitank gun with a machine gun in the turret and 1 to 2 machine guns in mantlets oriented both front and *rear*. With that type of vehicle, all of the missions that could be given to an armored reconnaissance vehicle could be completely accomplished.

Accordingly, the organization of an armored reconnaissance battalion is recommended as follows:

Headquarters with Signals Platoon (to include additional radio capability)
2 *Armored Car Companies*, as previously organized but with hybrid vehicles
1 *Motorcycle Infantry Company*, as previously organized
1 Heavy Company, comprised of
   1 Infantry Gun Platoon
   1 Antitank Gun Platoon
   2 Heavy Mortar Sections
   1 Engineer Platoon (including mine detector)

The armored reconnaissance battalion stands and falls with the development of a fully usable armored reconnaissance vehicle.

In the first image, soldiers, possibly scouts, pose in front of an *Sd.Kfz. 232 (6 Rad)*, which has had its weapons removed. In the second image, an early *Sd.Kfz. 223* serves as the backdrop for a posed photograph. Note the addition of a plate on the front of the vehicle. Since the vehicle already has its official license plate painted on the front slope, it must be assumed that this is a secondary marker, perhaps with the word *Fahrschule* ("driving school"), which was also a requirement for vehicles with unlicensed drivers on open roads. These images were most likely taken before the start of the campaign.

Motorcycle infantrymen, including the company first sergeant, of the *4./Kradschützen-Bataillon 3* (*3. Panzer-Division*) pose for a keepsake image. Based on the lack of decorations, this image was probably taken during prewar training. MARK MCMURRAY

These *Sd.Kfz. 221's* move down a road, probably somewhere in Germany between the campaigns in Poland and in the West. Interestingly, the vehicles do not appear to have license plates, although they are identified as army vehicles (*WH* = *Wehrmacht Heer* = Armed Forces—Army). JIM HALEY

This *Sd.Kfz. 232 (8 Rad)* was christened the *Biala-Podlaska* in honor of its baptism by fire in Poland. The vehicle was assigned to the *1./Aufklärungs-Abteilung 20 (mot)*, and the image was probably taken just before the campaign in the West. The same vehicle is seen in the second image, this time in a bivouac setting somewhere in France. Its name clearly stands out, as do the divisional tactical insignia for the campaign in the West and an unidentified insignia above it. In the final image of the *Biala-Podlaska*, the vehicle is somewhere in the Soviet Union. It has become the home of the crew, with all sorts of extra items, both personal and military, stowed outside the vehicle. JIM HALEY

A nice image of a heavy scout section, with an *Sd.Kfz. 222* bringing up the rear. Note the placement of a tarpaulin on top of the frame antenna on the *Sd.Kfz. 232 (6 Rad)*, perhaps in an effort to shield the commander from the elements.

Two *Sd.Kfz. 232's*—a *6 Rad* and an *8 Rad*—turn onto an unimproved road somewhere in France. Since crewmembers are riding outside the vehicles, perhaps in an effort to beat the heat or to avoid staying in cramped quarters any longer than necessary, it must be assumed that this unit is well behind the front. Note the aerial recognition panel on the rear deck of the trail vehicle.

Reconnaissance vehicles of the *Leibstandarte SS Adolf Hitler*. During the campaign in the West, the *Leibstandarte* had only one platoon of armored cars. This action sequence shows an *Sd.Kfz. 231 (8 Rad)* firing over its rear deck. Because of the rear driver, the vehicle could move forward or backward with equal ease and speed. In this instance, the vehicle commander may have chosen to engage a target in this manner in an effort to reduce the possibility of crew casualties in the case of a hit (since the round would have to pass through the engine compartment). In the fourth, an *Sd.Kfz. 232 (8 Rad)* fires while moving down a road. In the final image, an *Sd.Kfz. 221* fires over its side at a distant target. Fascines and what appears to be a shelter half are stowed on the vehicle's left side, while a bucket hangs from the rear tow pintle. NATIONAL ARCHIVES

In this sequence, soldiers of the *Standarte* encounter and clear rudimentary abatis along a road, with the assistance of an *Sd.Kfz. 231 (8 Rad)* of the armored reconnaissance platoon. NATIONAL ARCHIVES

Motorcycle infantry and armored cars of the *Leibstandarte* move into a French town and provide a show of force in the marketplace. French citizenry looks on bemusedly, while French boys seems to enjoy the close-up view of the armor. Although difficult to make out, it appears some of the scouts have branch-of-service piping (*Waffenfarbe*) around their tunic and rank collar tabs, which was neither authorized nor normally seen among the ranks of the *Leibstandarte*. By adding the piping, the scouts emulated the piping found around the collar tabs of their army counterparts. The distinctive *LAH* cipher can also be seen on some of the shoulder straps. It was supposed to have been removed or covered up for the campaign for operational security purposes, a directive that was obviously ignored in some instances. NATIONAL ARCHIVES

Kradschützen of the *Leibstandarte* roar through a French town and down French roads in an effort to keep up the pressure on enemy forces falling back. Sleep was a rare commodity and enjoyed every time the opportunity presented itself. NATIONAL ARCHIVES

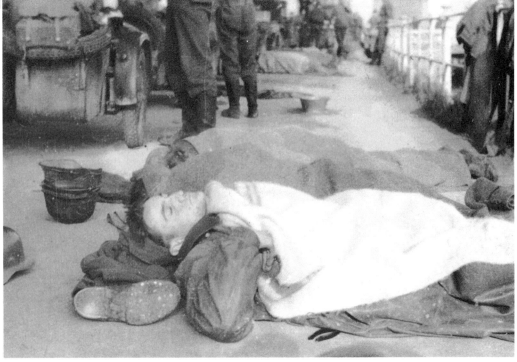

More images of *Kradschützen*, this time from the *SS-Aufklärungs-Sturmbann* of the *SS-Verfügungs-Division* and the reconnaissance elements of the *SS-Standarten* assigned to it. NATIONAL ARCHIVES

In a series of posed photographs, *SS-Kradschützen* and sections from the heavy weapons platoons "take up positions" for consumption on the home front. NATIONAL ARCHIVES

BLITZKRIEG IN THE WEST 139

Motorcycle infantry, possibly from the *SS-Standarte "Deutschland,"* continue the pursuit along dusty roads in the midst of army columns, through destroyed towns, and along improved roadways. NATIONAL ARCHIVES

BLITZKRIEG IN THE WEST 141

142 TIP OF THE SPEAR

In the first image, this *Sd.Kfz. 221*, christened the *Metz*, appears to be in a field workshop, having sustained some sort of mechanical failure or battlefield damage. All of its access panels are open, and trash and the vehicle's tarpaulin are strewn around the vehicle. Note its machine gun has been placed in an antiaircraft mount, as would be appropriate for a vehicle out in the open in a rear area, providing a tempting target from the air. Another view of a field repair facility is presented in the second image. In the background, an *Sd.Kfz. 222* has had its turret removed by a tripod gantry hoist (the turret can be seen in the upper-left corner of the image). Also of interest is the *Panzer 35(t)* in the right background. FIRST IMAGE: AKIRA TAKIGUCHI

BLITZKRIEG IN THE WEST 143

Soldiers and scouts from an armored reconnaissance unit strike a happy pose around this *Sd.Kfz. 221*, which has been christened the *Ströppchen*. It looks as though numerals have been removed from shoulder straps (where visible) but not the "A" of the reconnaissance force. This was done for operational security, but the covering of the "A" and/or numeral was enforced differently in different units.

In the first photograph, motorcycle infantry and scouts await orders to move out in this atmospheric image taken in a wooded staging area. The second image shows a long column of reconnaissance vehicles—mostly *Sd.Kfz. 221's* but also one *Sd.Kfz. 223* with an extended frame antenna—along with trains vehicles waiting to move out. LAST PHOTOGRAPH: MIKE HARPE

Typical scenes during the campaign in France, particularly after the start of *Fall Rot*. In the first image, a column of vehicles pauses outside a burning town while the situation is developed up front. The information provided by the lead elements allowed the commander to determine whether to deploy his force to eliminate the direct threat, bypass it, or wait for additional forces to be brought forward. The second image provides a similar viewpoint, although this image was shot during the campaign in Poland and features an *Sd.Kfz. 263*. The final image shows an *Sd.Kfz. 223* moving through the ruins of a French town after fighting has taken place. LAST IMAGE: JIM HALEY

The scouts of the *Sd.Kfz. 222* take time to eat a quick meal along the road. Feeding combat forces in the field was a difficult undertaking, but especially so for reconnaissance forces when they were on extended patrol and could not return to a base camp each day. They had to rely on living off the land or eating whatever food they happened to bring along at the onset of the operation. In dire circumstances, the crews were allowed to break into their so-called *eiserne Rationen* ("iron rations"), which were emergency rations normally kept under lock and key.

This battle-damaged *Sd.Kfz. 231 (8 Rad)* was assigned to either the *1.* or *2./Panzer-Aufklärungs-Abteilung 3* of the *3. Panzer-Division*. The divisional tactical insignia for the campaign in the West can be seen on the right front slope.
JIM HALEY

In the first image, we see a page from the album of future Knight's Cross recipient Ulrich Kreß, in which he pays tribute to those who paid the ultimate price in the campaign in the West. He originally joined the army as a scout in *Aufklärungs-Abteilung 5 (mot)* before he was later reassigned to *Aufklärungs-Abteilung 20 (mot)* of the *20. Infanterie Division*. The unidentified knocked-out *Sd.Kfz. 231 (8 Rad)* was moved to the side of the road to allow the remaining columns to pass by. Given the high density of vehicular traffic along an advance route, the number-one priority for a crew or other vehicles was to move damaged, disabled, or destroyed vehicles off of the road as quickly as possible. In the last image, a weary and tattered *Leutnant* Kreß stands next to his *Sd.Kfz. 231 (8 Rad)*, christened the *Leutnant Prohl*, in the Soviet Union.[21] JIM HALEY

A reconnaissance unit prepares to move out at a railhead. Tactical vehicles were always transported by train whenever possible in an effort to save wear and tear on them. The chock blocks in front of and behind the vehicle tires helped prevent them from sliding during movement. A cavalry-style reconnaissance symbol can be seen on the right rear mudguard on the trail *Sd.Kfz. 232 (8 Rad)*. Given the widespread wear of the black overseas cap, this image was probably taken after the campaign in the West. In the second image, crewmembers of this *Sd.Kfz. 221* of *Panzer-Aufklärungs-Abteilung 4* of the *1. Panzer-Division* seem to be enjoying their train ride. Their unit is probably being shipped home after the campaign in the West. The next image presents interesting details about rail-loading operations. While one train finishes loading its vehicles, the second is preparing to start the loading procedures. The short ramps between the cars allowed the vehicles to essentially drive down the railcars of the train. In the last two images, both heavy and light armored cars are loaded on trains and prepared for movement. SECOND IMAGE: MIKE HARPE. THIRD IMAGE: MICHAEL H. PRUETT

BLITZKRIEG IN THE WEST 149

Crewmembers of an *Sd.Kfz. 231 (8 Rad)* clown around for the camera with their officer. The three enlisted personnel wear "appropriated" French headgear, while the officer appears to be a sort of uniform dandy, wearing a polka-dot scarf and a *Luftwaffe* or SS–style cap that has apparently been dyed black and affixed with army insignia. Black caps for the crews of armored vehicles was not officially introduced until after the campaign in the West. JIM HALEY

In the first image, an *Sd.Kfz. 221* appears to have been knocked out in the vicinity of a road obstacle. It appears that a wartime censor eliminated the license plate numbers and made a rudimentary attempt to hide the vehicle's *Balkenkreuz*. Obstacles not covered by fire are generally ineffective; in this case, it appears the obstacle had been defended. In the second image, an *Sd.Kfz. 222* has fallen victim to enemy action, as evidenced by the shot-out headlights, the hole in the front slope of the vehicle, the missing weaponry, and what appears to be the burned-out interior. Generally somber motorcycle infantrymen are seen inspecting the grim reminder of war's consequences. The final image depicts another knocked-out *Sd.Kfz. 222*. LAST IMAGE: JIM HALEY

An impressive view of an *Sd.Kfz. 232 (8 Rad)* positioned atop a massive gun emplacement. This image was probably taken somewhere along the Maginot Line or the Belgian and Dutch equivalents farther north, albeit well after any immediate danger had passed, when there was some time for a bit of military "sightseeing." JIM HALEY

Soldiers and scouts of a reconnaissance unit in a staging area in an open field. The company first sergeant wears a bemused expression as he looks at one soldier adjusting the other's uniform. As the vehicles appear relatively pristine, this image may have been taken after the campaign. Of interest is the *Balkenkreuz* on the *Sd.Kfz. 263*, which runs parallel to the upper slope of the hull as opposed to the roof of the crew compartment, as is most commonly seen.

A *Kradschütze* intently paints the numerals of his vehicle's license on a blank plate. The fragile sheet-metal plates were easily damaged or ripped off during operations and frequently had to be replaced. Given the pristine condition of the motorcycle and sidecar, the vehicle may also be undergoing preparations for some sort of victory celebration or awards ceremony. At the time, the *Leibstandarte* only had a single motorcycle infantry company, the 15th. The distinctive *LAH* monogram appears on the front of the sidecar. NATIONAL ARCHIVES

SS-Gruppenführer Josef "Sepp" Dietrich decorates scouts of the armored reconnaissance platoon who are receiving the Iron Cross, Second Class, for their actions in the campaign. The piped collar tabs discussed earlier in this chapter can be seen quite clearly here. NATIONAL ARCHIVES

As with the *Leibstandarte*, the *SS-Verfügungs-Division* took time to decorate deserving soldiers after the fall of France. Heavy weapons are lined up as soldiers form up around them. In the last two images, scouts are also receiving awards. The *SS-Verfügungs-Division* generally removed rank insignia and telltale signs of unit affiliation during the campaign but, as can be seen in several of the photographs, the measures were not always adhered to. NATIONAL ARCHIVES

BLITZKRIEG IN THE WEST 155

A nice image of an *Sd.Kfz. 232 (8 Rad)* of *Panzer-Aufklärungs-Abteilung 37* of the *7. Panzer-Division* negotiating a small berm. Note the marker on the side of the hull for two crewmen killed in combat operations.
MICHAEL H. PRUETT

This *Sd.Kfz. 223* commander seems to be enjoying the ride as he races down the street of a large city. Since his cap appears to be black, the image was probably shot sometime after the campaign in the West.
MIKE HARPE

These soldiers and scouts of a signals section take a break during a movement in wintry mountainous terrain, most likely sometime in late 1940 or early 1941.
MIKE HARPE

156 TIP OF THE SPEAR

This series of images—most likely involving the heavy weapons of one of the *SS-Standarten* of the *SS-Verfügungs-Division* or the division's *SS-Aufklärungs-Sturmbann*—shows training being conducted under the watchful eyes of the division commander, *SS-Gruppenführer* Paul Hausser. In the first three images, engineers clear an abatis, allowing motorcycle infantry and unit vehicles to pass. In the next few images, gunners provide overwatch for infantry advancing through a breach in "enemy" defensive positions. Once the objective is taken, an aerial recognition panel is placed on the ground. The remaining images show heavy weapons associated with both the heavy company of the battalion—antitank guns and mortars—and the machine-gun platoon of one of the motorcycle infantry companies. The soldiers in training all wear the camouflage smocks uniquely associated with the *Waffen-SS*. Given the wintry nature of the scenes, these images were most likely shot in the late 1940.

A true rarity is this Trippel *SG6* amphibious car, in this instance issued to an unidentified element of the *Leibstandarte SS Adolf Hitler*. The use of amphibious cars for reconnaissance purposes found favor within the field formations of the *Waffen-SS* early on, although most of those were of the *VW-Schwimmwagen* type. Fewer than 1,000 of the Trippel *Schwimmwagen* found their way into military service.

CHAPTER 4

The Balkan Campaign

SETTING THE STAGE

Although the Balkan region of Europe was not initially on Hitler's radar, the military misadventures of his ally, Italy, under Mussolini, forced his hand. Italy invaded Greece in late October 1940, but its offensive soon stalled, the Greeks launched a counteroffensive, and Great Britain began sending forces and support. Partly to aid his struggling ally and partly to counter a perceived threat to Romanian oilfields, Hitler first sent forces to Romania and Bulgaria, and then had plans drawn up to invade Greece. The situation was further complicated by a *coup d'état* in Yugoslavia on 27 March 1941, prompting Hitler to include that country in his invasion plans.

The campaign was launched on 6 April 1941, with Yugoslavia falling by 17 April and mainland Greece by 30 April. On 20 May airborne forces stormed the island of Crete, which fell by 1 June when the remaining forces on the island surrendered. By the end of the fighting, Italy, Albania, Hungary, and Bulgaria had also joined the fray on the Axis side in an effort to expand their power bases in the region.

German forces essentially used the same maneuver warfare concepts against the Yugoslavians and the Greeks as they had used against France the previous year. They were aided and abetted by the almost complete dissolution of those forces once initial defensive lines were breached. The reputation of the Germans preceded them and contributed to the general lack of will to fight. The exception, of course, were the British forces deployed there, but there were too few to make a decisive difference (approximately 60,000 in theater).

An *SS* motorcycle infantryman intently observes a riverbank during a water-crossing operation.
NATIONAL ARCHIVES

Historians continue to debate the effect the operational "detour" had on the invasion of the Soviet Union that was to follow that summer, since it delayed the German offensive by several months.

DOCTRINE

With the doubling of the armored force, ordered by Hitler after the fall of France, the *Organizations-Abteilung* (Force Structure Branch) of the Army High Command instituted organizational changes that would allow the already limited numbers of vehicles and equipment to be further distributed across the force. At the same time, this represented an effort to standardize both armored reconnaissance and motorized infantry battalions. In general, the armored reconnaissance battalions of the armored divisions lost one armored car company out of their organization, essentially mirroring the organization already found in their sister battalions in motorized infantry divisions. All of the armored divisions were given a motorcycle infantry battalion, which was assigned to the respective *Schützen-Brigade*. The motorized infantry divisions all received a motorcycle infantry battalion organized the same as the one found in the armor divisions. In general, the additional motorcycle assets came from the rifle regiments, so there was no overall increase in the force; instead, existing assets were reorganized and reassigned. The new organizations and the *KStN's* that governed them—including the *Waffen-SS*, which continued to field a largely non-heterogeneous force—are discussed in detail below and in the next chapter.

Reconnaissance operations in the Balkans continued in essentially the same manner as they had in France and the Low Countries, with the exception that much of the fighting was conducted in hilly and mountainous terrain, which channelized movement much more than in the West. Forcing the way through the fortified passes leading into the countries along the respective borders proved challenging, and in such circumstances the motorcycle infantry took the lead in developing the situation. Once through the mountain defenses, operations took on the character of a pursuit. Thanks to the coupling of a lackluster defense offered by the Allies and the boldness and aggressiveness of small-unit leaders within reconnaissance elements, the Balkan campaign marked a sort of high-water mark in terms of classical offensive armored reconnaissance, with the fabled capture of Belgrade by a small motorcycle infantry detachment under the command of *SS-Hauptsturmführer* Fritz Klingenberg being one of the highlights.[1] Lesser known is the fact that army reconnaissance elements were among the first to enter Athens and lay claim to that city.

CHANGES IN ORGANIZATIONAL AUTHORIZATIONS (1 FEBRUARY 1941)

Headquarters, Motorcycle Infantry Battalion (1109)

The command group of the battalion remained essentially the same, with five motorcycles, three sidecar motorcycles, and two medium cross-country vehicles, albeit both of the latter were the *Kfz. 11*, as opposed to one *Kfz. 11* and one *Kfz. 15*. The signals section was reduced from a platoon to a detachment. The major change was the reduction of the two light telephone sections, which lost their motorcycles and one medium cross-country vehicle.

- Headquarters: five motorcycles, three sidecar motorcycles, and two medium cross-country utility vehicles (*Kfz. 11*).
- Signals detachment:
  - Headquarters: one light cross-country signals utility vehicle (*Kfz. 2*).
  - Two manpack radio sections: one medium cross-country radio utility vehicle (*Kfz. 15/2*).
  - Two light telephone sections: one medium cross-country signals utility vehicle (*Kfz. 15/2*).
  - Two light armored radio sections: one light armored radio car (*Sd.Kfz. 261*).

Motorcycle Infantry Company (1112)

This *KStN* was released in draft form in May 1940, intended to replace the former motorcycle infantry *KStN's* of the 1111 and 1113 series. It was formally released on 1 February 1941. It most closely resembled *KStN 1113*, from which the following comparisons are drawn. The company headquarters was essentially the same, although the integral machine-gun detachment was made into a separate heavy machine-gun detachment with a distinct headquarters (two sidecar motorcycles) and two heavy machine-gun

ORDER OF BATTLE FOR THE BALKANS CAMPAIGN, 6 APRIL 1941 (MAJOR RECONNAISSANCE ELEMENTS)

Parent Organization	Reconnaissance Assets
2. Armee / XXXXVI. Armee-Korps (mot)	
8. Panzer-Division	Kradschützen-Bataillon 8 and Panzer-Aufklärungs-Abteilung 59
14. Panzer-Division*	Kradschützen-Bataillon 64 and Panzer-Aufklärungs-Abteilung 40
16. Infanterie-Division (mot)*	Kradschützen-Bataillon 165 and Panzer-Aufklärungs-Abteilung 341
12. Armee / Army Reserve	
16. Panzer-Division*	Kradschützen-Bataillon 16 and Panzer-Aufklärungs-Abteilung 16
60. Infanterie-Division (mot)*	Kradschützen-Bataillon 160 and Panzer-Aufklärungs-Abteilung 160
12. Armee / 1. Panzer-Gruppe / XIV. Armee-Korps (mot)	
5. Panzer-Division	Kradschützen-Bataillon 55 and Panzer-Aufklärungs-Abteilung 8 (the motorcycle infantry battalion was assigned to the division after the campaign in the West)
11. Panzer-Division*	Kradschützen-Bataillon 61 and Panzer-Aufklärungs-Abteilung 231
12. Armee / 1. Panzer-Gruppe / XXXXI. Armee-Korps (mot)	
SS-Division "Reich" (Redesignated from SS-Verfügungs-Division)	SS-Kradschützen-Bataillon "Reich" and SS-Aufklärungs-Abteilung "Reich"[2]
Infanterie-Regiment (mot) "Großdeutschland"	17./Infanterie-Regiment (mot) "Großdeutschland," which consisted of a motorcycle infantry company (KStN 1111 / 1 February 1941) with an attached armored car platoon (KStN 1137 / 1 February 1941)
12. Armee / XVIII Gebirgs-Korps	
2. Panzer-Division	Kradschützen-Bataillon 2 and Panzer-Aufklärungs-Abteilung 5[3]
12. Armee / XXXX. Armee-Korps (mot)	
9. Panzer-Division	Kradschützen-Bataillon 59 and Panzer-Aufklärungs-Abteilung 9
Leibstandarte SS Adolf Hitler	SS-Aufklärungs-Abteilung Leibstandarte SS Adolf Hitler[4]
Army High Command Operational Reserves	
4. Panzer-Division	Kradschützen-Bataillon 34 and Panzer-Aufklärungs-Abteilung 7
12. Panzer-Division*	Kradschützen-Bataillon 22 and Panzer-Aufklärungs-Abteilung 2
19. Panzer-Division*	Kradschützen-Bataillon 19 and Panzer-Aufklärungs-Abteilung 19

Division formations marked with an "*" appear in the order of battle for the first time, as they were activated after the campaign in the West.

sections, each with four sidecar motorcycles and a heavy machine gun. The three motorcycle infantry platoons were essentially unchanged, although the new *KStN* provided each platoon headquarters with a trailer and the former infantry sections were now referred to as motorcycle sections.

- Company headquarters: three motorcycles, one sidecar motorcycle, one medium cross-country utility vehicle (*Kfz. 11*), and one heavy cross-country wheeled personnel carrier (*Kfz. 18*).
- One heavy machine-gun detachment:
  - Headquarters: two sidecar motorcycles.
  - Two heavy machine-gun sections: four sidecar motorcycles and one heavy machine gun.
- Three motorcycle infantry platoons:
  - Headquarters: two motorcycles, one medium cross-country utility vehicle (*Kfz. 11*), one heavy cross-country wheeled personnel carrier (*Kfz. 18*), and one equipment trailer.
  - Three motorcycle infantry sections: four sidecar motorcycles, one motorcycle infantry squad, and two light machine guns.
  - One mortar section: two sidecar motorcycles and one 50mm mortar.

Motorcycle Machine-Gun Company (1118)

As with the previous *KStN's*, this update brought about few substantive changes, with the major weapons systems remaining the same: eight heavy machine guns and six medium mortars (81mm). Support vehicles authorizations were reduced or substituted.

- Company headquarters
- Headquarters: three motorcycles, one sidecar motorcycle, one medium cross-country utility vehicle (*Kfz. 11*), and one heavy cross-country wheeled personnel carrier (*Kfz. 18*).
- Two light telephone sections: one medium cross-country signals utility vehicle (*Kfz. 15/1*).
- Two heavy machine-gun platoons:
  - Headquarters: one motorcycle, three sidecar motorcycles, one medium cross-country utility vehicle (*Kfz. 11*), and one heavy cross-country wheeled personnel carrier (*Kfz. 18*).
- Heavy machine-gun platoons:
  - One heavy machine-gun section: four sidecar motorcycles and one heavy machine gun.
  - One heavy machine-gun section: three sidecar motorcycles and one heavy machine gun.
- One mortar platoon:
  - Headquarters: one sidecar motorcycle and one medium cross-country utility vehicle (*Kfz. 11*).
  - Three mortar sections: three cross-country wheeled prime movers (light guns) (*Kfz. 69*), two 81mm mortars, and two ammunition trailers.

Headquarters, Motorized Heavy Company (1121)

The company headquarters had two motorcycles, two sidecar motorcycles, and two medium cross-country utility vehicles, an increase of one utility vehicle.

- Headquarters: two motorcycles, two sidecar motorcycles, and two medium cross-country wheeled personnel carriers (*Kfz. 15*).

Antitank Platoon (1122)

The assets of the platoon were reallocated but essentially remained the same.

- Headquarters: one motorcycle and one sidecar motorcycle.
- One ammunition section: two cross-country wheeled prime movers (light guns) (*Kfz. 69*) and one light machine gun.
- One gun section: three cross-country wheeled prime movers (light guns) (*Kfz. 69*) and three 37mm towed antitank guns.

Light Infantry Gun Platoon (1123)

The light infantry gun platoon was streamlined by the elimination or substitution of some wheeled support vehicles, but its combat power remained the same: two towed light infantry guns (75mm).

- Headquarters: one motorcycle and two sidecar motorcycles.
- One light telephone section: one medium cross-country signals utility vehicle (*Kfz. 15/1*).
- One ammunition section: two cross-country wheeled prime movers (light guns) (*Kfz. 69*) and one light machine gun.
- One gun section: two cross-country wheeled prime movers (light guns) (*Kfz. 69*) and two 75mm towed infantry guns.

Combat Engineer Platoon (1124)

As with the light infantry gun platoon, the assets were reallocated.

- Headquarters: two motorcycles, two sidecar motorcycles, and three medium cross-country utility vehicles (*Kfz. 11*).
- Three combat engineer sections: two 2-ton trucks, one combat engineer section, and one light machine gun.

Headquarters, Armored Reconnaissance Battalion (1105)

The headquarters remained essentially unchanged from its 1937 counterpart. In place of a signals van (*Kfz. 17*), the headquarters received two medium cross-country utility vehicles (*Kfz. 15*).

- Headquarters: three motorcycles, two sidecar motorcycles, one medium cross-country wheeled personnel carrier (*Kfz. 15*), and one heavy wheeled armored utility vehicle (*Sd.Kfz. 247*).

Signals Platoon, Armored Reconnaissance Battalion (1191)

The capabilities of the signals platoon remained essentially unchanged, although vehicular allocations were somewhat different.

- Headquarters: one motorcycle, two sidecar motorcycles, and one medium cross-country wheeled personnel carrier (*Kfz. 15*).
- Light telephone section: one medium cross-country wheeled personnel carrier (*Kfz. 15*).
- Two manpack radio sections: one light signals utility vehicle (*Kfz 2*).
- Two medium radio sections (armored): one medium cross-country wheeled personnel carrier (*Kfz. 15*) and one medium armored radio car (*Sd.Kfz 263*).
- Four light radio sections (armored): one light armored radio car (*Sd.Kfz 261**).
- One light radio section (armored): one light armored radio car (*Sd.Kfz 260*).

Armored Car Company (1162)

The new *KStN* represented no major changes from the previously issued one.
- Headquarters: six motorcycles, two sidecar motorcycles, one medium cross-country utility vehicle (*Kfz. 11*), and one heavy wheeled armored utility vehicle (*Sd.Kfz. 247*).
- One medium radio section (armored): one medium cross-country wheeled personnel carrier (*Kfz. 15*) and one medium armored radio car (*Sd.Kfz 263*).
- Four light radio sections (armored): one light armored radio car (*Sd.Kfz 261**).
- One heavy armored car platoon: three heavy armored cars (2cm) (8 wheeled) (*Sd.Kfz. 231*) and three heavy armored radio cars (8 wheeled) (*Sd.Kfz. 232*).
- One light armored car platoon: four light armored cars (MG) (*Sd.Kfz. 221*) and four light armored cars (2cm) (*Sd.Kfz. 222*).
- One light armored car platoon: four light armored cars (MG) (*Sd.Kfz. 221*).

LESSONS LEARNED AND FIRSTHAND ACCOUNTS

Greece

An impression of operations in the mountainous terrain of Greece can be gleaned from this account concerning *Kradschützen-Bataillon 55* of the *5. Panzer-Division* (23–24 April 1941):[5]

The 23rd of April was dedicated to organizing the formations and improving positions. The battalion command post was established 1 kilometer east of Delphinon.

That day, as in the past, logistics caused tremendous difficulties. Pack mule columns were set up from the donkeys that had been captured, in order to bring rations and ammunition forward. But they took more than 12 hours to reach the companies. The emergency rations were released for consumption.

Radio contact, which had been lost with *Aufklärungs-Abteilung 8 (mot)* (von Scheven) during the course of 22 April, was reestablished that afternoon. There was no longer any contact with the *I./Artillerie-Regiment 116*, and contact with the *I. (schwere) / Artillerie-Regiment 737*, was lost periodically, since the power source for the radio set of the forward observer was insufficient.

Friendly patrols from the 2nd and 3rd Companies made it as far as the area around Kuwela and to the lower serpentines of the pass road east of Delphinon. Heavy enemy forces and lively column movement was observed on the high ground 1 kilometer southwest of Skamnos, as were numerous improved machine-gun positions on both sides of the pass road that were reinforced with antitank obstacles. In addition, there were prepared road demolitions 3 kilometers southeast of Delphinon. All efforts to surprise the enemy by means of heavy patrols led by officers failed. Every approach by friendly patrols was observed in the terrain, which was especially suitable for the enemy, and made impossible by means of heavy and well-placed machine-gun and artillery fire.

The enemy also soon identified the penetration of *Kradschützen-Bataillon 55* in his left flank and set up his defenses accordingly, which was discerned by the reorganization of his artillery.

In order to execute their missions, the patrols needed 14 to 20 hours. All targets that

---
*The demand for the *Sd.Kfz 260* and *Sd.Kfz 261* could never be met, and wheeled signals vehicles, such as those in the *Kfz 15* series, usually had to take their place.

had been observed were transmitted to friendly artillery by radio. The fact that the distance was too great from the firing positions to targets south of Lamia made it impossible to engage the enemy. It was in this situation that the lack of infantry support guns and any type of artillery was painfully apparent, since friendly machine guns and mortars were unable to target the enemy effectively.

After all the patrol reports were in, the commander decided towards evening of 23 April to take the pass road on the high ground west of Skamnos by means of a *coup de main* in order to force a decision. The company commanders were briefed down to the last detail on the plan of attack and the attack was scheduled for 0600 hours on 24 April. Since friendly artillery support and the light infantry gun platoon of the battalion could not be counted on to provide support, it was directed that the companies approach as close as possible to the high ground at Skamnos without being seen and by exploiting the terrain. They were then to penetrate into the enemy machine-gun positions, supported by the heavy machine-gun platoons and a mortar section. For that reason, both the 2nd and 3rd Companies each received a heavy machine-gun platoon and a mortar section in attachment. The forward observer for the heavy artillery, a *Wachtmeister*, was relieved towards evening by an officer, who was then directed to support the 2nd Company. It was directed for the battalion to echelon in depth, with the 2nd Company up front, followed by the 3rd Company. It was to approach the enemy in column in order to then deploy on a broad front with both companies adjacent to one another in order to penetrate the enemy positions. The approach routes were established during the night. The men of the battalion enjoyed little rest that night.

Towards 2300 hours, heavy artillery fire was placed on the positions of the battalion. Although the companies were positioned more or less protected on the slopes facing away from the enemy, the battalion command staff was shot out of its command post. Since the battalion surgeon was not present, the wounded could only be treated in an emergency fashion. Many of the pack animals that had been brought along lost their lives that night. The enemy artillery fire lasted until morning.

24 April: Around 0500 hours, an artillery fire coordination party from the *I./Artillerie-Regiment 116* reported in to the battalion commander. The personnel appeared somewhat tired and out of it because of the approach route. An *Unteroffizier* from *Aufklärungs-Abteilung 8 (mot)*, who had found his way to the battalion command post during the night by crossing the steepest of cliffs, brought an attack order from the division. The attack was directed to start at 0700 hours on 24 April. The battalion was to conduct the attack on its own, with assistance from *Gebirgsjäger-Regiment 141*. That meant that *Kradschützen-Bataillon 55* was detached from *Kampfgruppe von Scheven*. Skamnos was designated as the objective for the attack; at the same time, the mountaineers were employed against Grawia by passing around the right flank of the battalion and moving through the mountains. It was intended for *Stuka* attacks starting at 0630 hours to destroy the enemy artillery positions and the main pockets of resistance southwest of Skamnos.

The *2.* and *3./Kradschützen-Bataillon 55*, which were already in their staging areas, were briefed on the new plan of attack. The *Stuka* attack started at 0630 hours. In accordance with plans and maneuvering well, the battalion entered the Asopos bottomland as follows: The 2nd Company was organized as the advance guard. The forward observer from the heavy artillery moved with the 2nd Company. Behind it was the battalion command staff. Following it was the 3rd Company, along with the forward observer from the light artillery, the remainder of the 4th Company and the battalion communications section.

Battlefield reconnaissance was initiated by the 2nd Company in the direction of Skamnos and the enemy-occupied high ground to the southwest. Patrols at Orias and on the Tapido established contact with the *I./Gebirgsjäger-Regiment 141*.

Identified enemy targets could only be engaged by friendly artillery with great difficulty. Once again, no radio contact could be established between the forward observer and friendly batteries due to the distance.

Whereas the light artillery had no presence whatsoever, the heavy artillery, which was probably in position around Kato-Brallos covered the eastern slopes of the hillcrests southwest of Skamnos with its fires.

At 1030 hours, when the first elements of the battalion reached the southern slopes and defiles of the vineyards at Porte by going around the tip of the hill there, the first enemy machine-gun fire was received from individual nests on the hill southwest of Skamnos. Shortly thereafter, enemy artillery fire also caught the elements of the battalion that were in the defile at the time. It appeared to be almost impossible to get out of the beaten zone by moving forward. Any movement by individuals was met with heavy machine-gun fire, stifling it. Initial casualties: one dead, one wounded.

Thanks to the tough determination of the men, it was possible over several hours to get to the northern slopes of the massif just west of Skamnos. The enemy also attempted to reach the defiles there with his artillery. His efforts were partially successful due to treetop detonations and rounds fired into the opposite slope. Elements of the *2./Kradschützen-Bataillon 55*, which had gotten past the protective high ground thanks to their aggressive attack, were literally nailed to the ground by the enemy fire. The pack animal column, which was following the battalion with ammunition and rations, was scattered at that point. Once again, the battalion had no choice but to use "iron rations" and the mountain creeks for its sustenance.

When the main body of the *I./Gebirgsjäger-Regiment 141* turned from Sklithron to the east around 1700 hours, in an effort to advance past Skamnos, the commander saw that the time had come to advance into the enemy on the hills southwest of Skamnos, employing all available heavy weapons and remaining ammunition (but without artillery support).

Both of the companies succeeded in getting into the defiles just west and south of Skamnos. Flanking fires from heavy machine guns in enemy nests were also received there. They had previously remained silent in well-camouflaged positions. Despite that, the forward momentum of the motorcycle infantry could no longer be stopped. While the heavy mortars were brought into position thanks to untold effort, the completely exhausted riflemen overcame the steep slopes. One enemy machine-gun nest after the other was engaged and silenced.

The village of Skamnos was taken at 1800 hours. The enemy positions on the hillcrest to the southwest were stormed at 1900 hours. When that happened, the enemy artillery at Brallos also stopped firing. It was possible to prevent road demolitions at Skamnos. As a result, the pass road across the Thermopile Mountains was firmly in the hands of *Kradschützen-Bataillon 55* on 24 April.

Lacking heavy weapons support and frequently losing radio contact with higher headquarters, the battalion commander was compelled to use his own initiative in storming positions that normally would have been very difficult to force. Thanks to the skillful use of his available forces and the tactical prowess of the force, coupled with an ultimately halfhearted defense of very defensible terrain, the motorcycle infantry were able to prevail and open a pathway for the division.

The next selection discusses the pitfalls of employing armored scouts in mountainous terrain and on a poor road network. Despite the difficulties, the situation was mastered, thanks to the initiative of small-unit leaders. This firsthand account, written by the division's Intelligence Officer, *Hauptmann* Kohlhardt, who was accompanying the battalion, concerns *Panzer-Aufklärungs-Abteilung 8* of the *5. Panzer-Division*:[6]

The road led through the middle of the mountains. It was richly blessed with potholes and so narrow in some places next to the precipices that we barely got through. But our drivers were great. We finally reached the highest point and then started descending into the valley. By then, it had turned so dark, that we had to drive with regular lights. The lead vehicle stopped. A bridge had been blown up. That, on top of everything else. Would our vehicles get across? The approach and exits to the ford were steep. We dismounted the vehicles and guided the drivers with flashlights. The engine noise between the cliffs sounded like thunder in the night. Another road. Get out the maps and take a look. No doubt . . . the road there headed to Kapandriti, to the right to Malakassa. After a short move, there was a railway track. The road started to climb sharply. Then another blown-up bridge. It was 0200 hours on 27 April. After three hours of sleep, the move continued at 0500 hours. Then the thought came to us. The road was untrafficable . . . but the railway tracks! There was the embankment; get up on the tracks. It worked. A few piles of rubble had to be moved here and there, but then there was no stopping us. The road ran parallel to the railway tracks. At five places, we saw how the road had been cratered extensively in an effort to hold up our advance. The vehicles performed gymnastics on narrow railway bridges; we moved through the tunnels. Finally, there was a larger village—Marussion. Cars on tracks—that was something new. Athens was only 17 kilometers, and the roads were negotiable. Time to get off the tracks and give it some gas. The road was good and broad. At that point, we were only thinking about our objective. Chalandri was the next village. We reached the outskirts of Athens. In front of us was a vehicle with a white flag. A Greek officer reported to us that he was an envoy from Athens. Radio message to the division: "Athens reached at 0835 hours on 27 April; envoy on site."

Although *Aufklärungs-Abteilung 8 (mot)* was the first formation to enter Athens, the capture of the city was later credited to the 6. *Gebirgs-Division*. *Kradschützen-Bataillon 55* was also employed during the airborne operations against Crete, where elements were inserted via both airlift and boats:[7]

Kradschützen-Bataillon 55, which had been earmarked for participation in *Unternehmen "Merkur,"* the operation against Crete, was loaded on fishing vessels on 20 May in Megara and Mylos. The convoy was scattered on 21 May by a British destroyer formation. The remaining elements reached the harbor at Piräus on 22 May. After it landed, the battalion received orders to move as quickly as possible to the field airstrips at Lamia and Topolia. It was then loaded on the good old *Tante Ju* ["Aunt Ju," soldier slang for the *Ju 52* tri-motor transporter]. The first unit to land, the 3rd Company, was unloaded from the aircraft at Maleme while under fire from Hill 107. The remaining companies followed on 27 May, but only with their motorcycles. The battalion was immediately employed in an advance to the south coast of the island, moving via Spilia to Paläochora.

The advance to Spilia on 26 May saw the battalion constantly entangled against organized snipers, who had occupied the high ground on both sides of the road. In contravention of all international law, they wore German uniforms and waved swastika flags to mislead patrols that had been sent out. The advance continued only in fits and spurts. The enemy was ejected from the high ground by means of enveloping attacks that were conducted only after tiresome climbing of the slopes. To the south of the mountain village, the enemy put up an especially stubborn resistance.

The village of Kandaros was also taken only after all available heavy weapons were employed. Even in cases where the enemy did not surface, terrain difficulties, poor and narrow roads and mountain paths impeded progress. Despite all that, the battalion reached Paläochora on the south coast of the island that same evening at 2300 hours. The city was devoid of people and demonstrated considerable damage inflicted upon it by German dive-bombers. An enemy warship had set course for Paläochora, but it later turned away at some distance.

On the next day, 27 May, the main body of the battalion was pulled back to Spilia. A reinforced company remained in Paläochora. A new mission awaited the battalion in Spilia: Pursuit of the withdrawing enemy to the east via Retimnon and Heraklion to relieve the encircled paratroopers and establish contact with the Italians, who had landed on the eastern part of the island.

On 28 May, the route led through Stylos, Neon-Chorion and Episkopi. Weak enemy forces east of Kalami were ejected, English rearguards at Tylos were scattered and an armored vehicle was captured. To the west of Kania, the lead elements received heavy fire from machine guns and armored vehicles. The English had dug in in the olive orchards and the mountain slopes and set up to defend. An enveloping attack created some breathing space for a while, but the enemy continued to bring up reinforcements and, in the end, initiated an attack himself. The company commander decided to conduct an immediate counterattack. The death-defying actions of two officers were crowned with success. The numerically superior enemy was ejected. A patrol, set out the next morning (29 May), discovered the British positions empty. The pursuit was immediately initiated.

Towards noon, the battalion reached Rethimnon, where approximately 400 Greeks were taken prisoner. A swastika flag was raised on the citadel. At Periodolia, to the east of Rethimnon, contact was established with the encircled paratroopers. The relief of those men, who had held out for a week in tough fighting against a superior enemy force, was the best payoff for the motorcycle infantry after the heavy fighting of the last few days.

On the next morning (30 May), an attack was conducted on Australian positions. The attack was supported by two tanks of the "Red Devils" (*Panzer-Regiment 31*).

Those tanks had been towed over to Crete on a pontoon boat and had landed at Kastelli during the night of 28–29 May. On the way to the battalion, they were greeted enthusiastically everywhere. After the heavy fighting recently, they were the symbol of an imminent victory.

Prisoner statements made later confirmed that the appearance of these tanks had a crippling effect on morale for the enemy forces. Their appearance seemed to be proof that strong German forces had already reached Crete using maritime routes.

In an aggressively conducted attack, the motorcycle infantry attacked enemy positions and overran them, despite being engaged by antitank guns. The airfield east of Rethimnon fell into German hands, and 1,500 Australians, including numerous officers, were taken prisoner. Artillery pieces and antitank guns were captured. In a tent camp, 300 captured paratroopers, including the badly wounded *Oberst* Sturm, were liberated. Likewise, it was possible to relieve another paratrooper battalion at Panormos.

Towards 1300 hours, the battalion reached Heraklion (Candia), followed a short while later by Jerapetra, a harbor town on the south coast of Crete. Contact was established with Italian forces at Chalochorian. That meant that Crete was finally in Axis hands.

In addition to the fighting with *frantireurs* and, in some cases, numerically superior enemy forces, it was the terrain and the road network that had demanded the utmost of everyone. Not used to mountain climbing, the motorcycle infantry had to overcome steep cliffs and rough terrain in scorching heat again and again. A constant stream of flat tires bore witness to the poor, stony roads and the mountain paths. Despite all that, in just three days and over the course of three larger engagements, 250 kilometers were covered; on the last day alone, 190 kilometers were registered.

Generalfeldmarschall List recognized the demonstrated performance during his visit on 1 July and presented *Obergefreiter* Brix with a gold watch for his terrific bravery. All of the personnel of *Kradschützen-Bataillon 55*, who participated in the difficult operation, were awarded either the 2nd Class or the 1st Class of the Iron Cross, as well as the *Kreta* cuff title.

Generalmajor Ringel, the commander of the *5. Gebirgs-Division*, praised the actions of

Kradschützen-Bataillon 55 in an order of the day. One of the sentences from that order:

> In true combat camaraderie, the battalion helped clinch victory on Crete along with my mountain troopers. The successful fighting at Stylos and Rethimnon are closely associated with the history of *Kradschützen-Bataillon 55*. No matter its location, the battalion constantly demonstrated aggressiveness and bravery.

Yugoslavia

An after-action report for the *Kradschützen-Bataillon 165* of the *16. Infanterie-Division (mot)*, written by the company commander of the 2nd Company, *Oberleutnant* Karl-Heinz Voigtmann, details the advance of the company through Nasice and Dakovo toward Vinkovci on 11 April 1941, about a week into the campaign in Yugoslavia:[8]

> 1. **Organization and Mission**: 2 Motorcycle squads, 1 heavy machine gun and one light mortar section. Leadership: *Oberleutnant* Voigtmann.
>
> **Mission**: Advance along the avenue of advance as far as Vinkovci. From there, reconnoiter routes and bridges in the direction of Brcko and Sabac.
>
> 2. **Execution**: Moving out at 1700 hours, the motorcycle infantry initially had to cross a demolished bridge with the help of combat engineers and prisoners. The following bridge demolition was bypassed and the motorcycle infantry moved onto the avenue of advance by means of a railway bridge.
>
> We moved out at high speed at 1745 hours. Nasice was reached before the onset of darkness, accompanied by the cheering of the Croatian populace. According to the locals, the last elements of Serbian forces moved through the area some 6-7 hours previously.
>
> Potnjani was reached towards 2030 hours, moving along good roads, when the lead motorcycles opened up fire with machine guns and machine pistols, when they received scattered carbine and pistol fire. The lead section immediately dismounted, entered a well-lit guesthouse and cleared it. A few Serbian officers and enlisted were killed; some of them slightly drunk. After stopping briefly, we moved out again.
>
> In Dakovo, we caught up to within about an hour of the withdrawing Serbs. A burned-out armored vehicle, shattered horse-drawn vehicles and tossed-away military equipment marked the retreat route. In several villages, Serb outposts were chased away with a short burst of fire; no time was used to clear the houses. Moving at high speed, the patrol reached Vinkovci around 0130 hours.
>
> Immediate interrogation of the city administrators revealed that Serbian forces were retreating hurriedly and under pressure in the direction of Zupanja, intending to cross the Sava there.
>
> The helpful civilians immediately prepared something warm for the soldiers, and the motorcycles were topped off.
>
> Around 0200 hours, the Division Commander arrived and issued new orders. Towards 0215 hours, the main body of the 2nd Company (Motorcycle) under the command of *Leutnant* Gärtner arrived in Vinkovci.
>
> 3. **Of note**: During the short engagements, *Unteroffizier* Kartscher distinguished himself as a decisive and plucky leader of the point element.

Alfred Hohnstein, an *Oberfeldwebel* at the time and a platoon leader in the *2./Kradschützen-Bataillon 165*, wrote the following in his diary:

> [in Vinkovci] . . . While we filled up our hungry bellies and the fuel tanks of the empty motorcycles, our *General* arrived. After receiving the report from *Oberleutnant* Voigtmann that the mission had been accomplished, he removed his Iron Cross, First Class from the 1st World War and pinned it on the chest of the commander of the *2./Kradschützen-Bataillon 165*.

The motorcycle infantry continued their fast-paced advance toward Sarajevo:[9]

In the meantime, the *2./Kradschützen-Bataillon 165* encountered stubborn resistance at Cerna and along the Sava; elements of *Aufklärungs-Abteilung 341 (mot)* were employed in support. The motorcycle infantry reported at 0900 hours that the area around Zupanja had been cleared of the enemy. It was then pulled back to Vinkovci. The main body of the reconnaissance battalion remained employed in the direction of Zupanja and Brcko, in an effort to take the bridge at Brcko. That was soon reported as having been blown up, however.

At 1000 hours, the following radio message was sent to the Division Commander, who was with *Gruppe Neumeister*, from the division command post: Corps was ordering the fastest advance possible on Lazarevac via Mitrovica and Sabac. Once there, it was to establish an all-round blocking position, especially along the Belgrade–Valjevo road. Contact was to be established with *Gruppe Kleist* coming from the direction of Kragujevac.

That mission was immediately given to *Kradschützen-Bataillon 165*, since the main body of the division had not closed up at the time. That type of mission was also perfect for that fast, agile and decisively led formation. Based on previous combat experience, letting the relatively weak forces advance so deeply into the enemy's sector was a risk that could be taken in an effort to further exploit the crippling effect of the unexpected appearance of enemy forces. As was often the case . . . the inferior numbers could be evened out by means of boldness, rapidity and maneuverability. [Emphasis added by authors]

Most actions had the character of pursuit and denial operations. Once again, an after-action report from the *2./Kradschützen-Bataillon 165*:[10]

1. **Organization and Mission**: The *2./Kradschützen-Bataillon 165* (only motorcycles) and a platoon from the *3./Kradschützen-Bataillon 165*. Advance via Zupanja to the Sava and prevent elements of the Serbian 27th and 60th Regiments from crossing [the river] to the south.

2. **Execution**: Moved out around 0300 hours in point formation. The first few villages south of Vinkovci were transited without enemy contact.

Outside of Cerna, the lead platoon received fire from a light machine gun and rifles from some high ground on both sides of the road outside of the village entrance. The lead platoon (*Oberfeldwebel* Hohnstein) pressed into the village aggressively, strongly supported by fires from the heavy machine-gun section and two light mortars. There were fully loaded horse-drawn ammunition wagons of a light infantry element along the village road.

Without stopping for long, the lead platoon moved on foot into the village. A few bursts of machine-gun fire convinced some of the Serbs to come out of their hiding places in the houses.

In the middle of the village, the sections advancing down both sides of the road were greeted by fire from the windows and dormers. The houses were forced open with hand grenades, bayonets and rifle stocks. By the onset of first light, the entire village was cleared in this manner.

Towards 0500 hours, ignoring small bouts of firing, the company moved out again with a new lead platoon (*Leutnant* Achenbach).

About 500 to 600 meters south of the village, the company received fire from light and heavy machine guns and rifles from the woodline that ran about 300 meters to either side of the road (approximately 4 light machine guns and 4 heavy machine guns).

The company, which immediately dismounted, initially found cover in the broad and deep ditches along the road, with the result that no casualties were taken. After a few minutes, all of the machine guns moved into position under the covering fires of the lead platoon. Employing all of its weapons, the company succeeded in silencing the majority of the machine guns. The light mortars distinguished themselves through the good effect of their fires on the individual farmsteads that were manned in strongpoint fashion.

The lead platoon moved out to attack, receiving covering fire from two platoons and the heavy machine-gun section. A few minutes later, the first men came out of the woods, surrendering with raised hands. To the right, a few enemy heavy machine guns continued to fire, but they were also silenced by the concentrated fires of the two platoons.

Approximately 500 to 600 prisoners, including a Battalion Commander, were sent to the rear; they had been elements of the 27th Infantry Regiment.

Leutnant Achenbach was slightly wounded in the head.

The company reassembled rapidly, while two platoons cleared the edges of the woods with hand grenades and bayonets. Around 0630 hours, Zupanja was reached. A few bursts of fire cleared the streets, which had been completely packed with bridging and supply columns. Oxen and horses ran around, minus their masters. The soldiers that belonged to them were hauled out of the houses.

A patrol reported heavy movement and concentrations about 4 kilometers south of Zupanja on the Sava.

While elements of the company cleared the village, the main body moved out without vehicles (the roads were completely muddy). It deployed for an advance against the crossing point. Around 0830 hours, the lead elements reached the embankments, which ran parallel to the river about 400 to 500 meters from the near bank.

The following was observed: Spreading out about 800 to 1,000 meters on this side of the river meadows were trains vehicles, weapons and equipment, about 1,200 to 1,500 horses and, mixed among them, soldiers. They were all tightly pressed together and were busily attempting to stow provisional ferries with equipment, so as to cross over the river. On the river proper, there were three ferries operating. On the far side of the river, slightly elevated, was the village of Orasje. There was movement around the houses and, in the meadowlands behind the village, there were soldiers pulling back, all tightly squeezed together.

The company's approach could not remain hidden. From the far bank, the company received light machine-gun fire. There was also poorly aimed heavy machine-gun fire. A heavy mortar started to register its fires.

Protected by the embankments, all elements approached to about 600 meters of the Sava. They then opened fire all at once with all available weapons. The enemy weapons were silenced; whoever had not yet saved himself on the far side of the river crawled behind horses and equipment. After about half an hour, the firing was stopped, since the enemy weapons were silent, the ferry operations had been interrupted and the jammed-up columns and trains vehicles shot to pieces.

Around 1200 hours, the company received orders from Neumeister's battalion to move to Vinkovci.

3. **Of Note**: a) Prisoners: Approximately 1,200 soldiers.

b) Spoils of war: Several light columns with munitions and equipment; a complete bridging column (new); all trains from two regiments at the crossing point.

c) Friendly losses: 1 officer wounded.

d) Ammunition consumption: Approximately 50% of the basic load expended; machine pistol ammunition completely expended.

Toward the end of the campaign in Yugoslavia, the advance of the German forces seemed unstoppable and resistance fruitless. The following is from the unofficial division history:[11]

The main body of *Aufklärungs-Abteilung 341 (mot)* did not arrive at the ferry point at Badovinci until around 1230 hours. Several armored cars were ferried across, one behind the other, followed by three combat elements of the 2nd Company. The company received orders to occupy. The village was reached by the company at 1530 hours. It pushed the enemy forces, consisting of a company and an infantry gun, back though the village. Based on a direct request from the corps, it relieved a weak airborne contingent that had landed at the airfield there at 1300 hours. At 1700 hours, the 2nd Company, reinforced with six armored cars and an antitank gun, advanced in the direction of Zvornik. In the process, several Serbian troop elements were forced to lay down their weapons, sometimes as entire units. Although the patrol continued to receive fire, it appeared that the will to fight on the part of the enemy had been broken. A 4-gun antitank-gun battery was captured in Branjevo. To the south of Kozluk, the patrol advanced through the open-field positions of an antiaircraft battalion, consisting of 12 guns. At 1757 hours, the company reached the eastern outskirts of Zvornik. It received orders from the Division Commander there, which were delivered by a liaison officer from *Infanterie-Regiment 60 (mot)*. They stated: "No combat activity until 2100 hours; Serbian 2nd Army negotiating surrender with division."

Oberleutnant Borchardt[12] of *Aufklärungs-Abteilung 341 (mot)* later wrote the following about his experiences during the advance on Zvornik on 14 April 1941 with his armored scout company:

I anxiously awaited my first operation. I was curious as to how I would perform, and that thought pushed all other thoughts into the background. From the very beginning, I conscientiously attempted to avoid any unnecessary losses of personnel, no matter how tired I was or whether there were other outside influences . . .

It was important to see to it that my orders were followed to the letter, since it was a matter of life or death. They had been thoroughly considered by me. Soon, everyone knew that I would not demand anything that I personally wasn't prepared to do.

On 14 April 1941, the battalion crossed the Drina at Badovinci and was then supposed to advance on Zvornik from the west bank. The mission was primarily to get the bridge over the Drina at Zvornik intact, so that the continued march of those elements of the division on the east bank of the river would not be delayed. After a short search at Badovinci, I found an old rope-line ferry across the Drina, which I immediately used to cross over the river with a few men, although we were under fire from snipers. In the course of the next three hours, I had three armored cars follow. I immediately moved ahead towards Bijeljina on the first one. We went through a village with ethnic Germans . . . I was deeply moved by the jubilation of the people there. Back then, I could not know what our arrival there would mean for them in the somewhat distant future.

Outside of Bijeljina, I encountered a Serbian artillery piece. I was able to fire twice and miss, before we could get under cover. Together with *Feldwebel* Weißmeyer, I went on a short detour though the farm fields and took it out, after the crew had fled when the first two hand grenades were thrown. Everything went quickly and without a lot of thought. It simply went the way we had learned it. As we got closer to Bijeljina, we saw 9 *Stukas* circling overhead. One after the other, they dove and dropped whistling bombs. It was an especially unpleasant sound, together with the detonation. We could see quite a few Serbian soldiers running back and forth in the village. After a short while, I thought they had been so shaken up by the *Stuka* attack that we could move *en masse* through the streets of the town at full throttle. Somewhat relieved, we reached open ground. We soon encountered numerous obstacles, however, that had been formed by the felling of the roadside trees in such a manner that they lay entangled across one another on the road. We had to tear them apart, sometimes with tow cables. In the process, we were fired upon several times. We determined that it was Serbian cavalry that was attempting to hold us up. We grabbed a couple of them. Most of them raised their hands after the first few rounds were fired. We had them put their rifles on the ground, and we broke off the stocks. We then sent them off in the direction we had come from, hoping that the rest of the battalion would soon follow.

Time was of the essence, and I pressed the men . . . In a village, it occurred to me that there was scarcely a person to be seen. As we approached the old stone bridge, there were the feared holes in the road that had been covered over. That was an indication of mines! I had them carefully dug out, as we had done so often in training. I could only hope that they weren't pressure sensitive. They were placed off to the side and marked with a warning sign. Gradually, the citizenry regained its trust. It was the first village we had seen with a mosque. The women wore pants and veils.

As we moved on, we heard heavy rifle fire not too far away. Before we entered curves in the road, I often dismounted and went forward on foot in order to observe. During one of those occasions, I received a sight that took my breath away somewhat. Twelve heavy antiaircraft guns were positioned in the vegetation of the bottomland of the river that our road went through. Their barrels were all positioned at right angles to the river, aimed at a road halfway up the slope of the rising ground on the far bank. Over there, in the middle of a motorized column of friendly forces, was great confusion. Apparently, the antiaircraft-gun fire was well placed. All of a sudden, the firing stopped, and I observed a mountain of casings next to each of the guns through my binoculars. Some 400 meters away, I fetched all of my people out of their vehicles. I showed them what was going on and told them that we were going to advance around the curve at the same time with all three vehicles. One vehicle each was going to move through the meadowlands on the right and left and that as they advanced, they had to fire into the enemy guns with all of their own machine guns and rifles. Surprise was of the essence, and we had to be in the midst of the enemy before he could swing his guns on us.

From the time we mounted up to the time we were in the midst of them couldn't have been more than three minutes. Only a few pistol and rifle rounds fell in our direction. The antiaircraft gun crews suffered a couple of dead and wounded before they gave up and were sent rearward. The guns were German-made 8.8cm *Flak*. I had the breeches taken out of all of the guns and thrown into the river. Feeling a bit proud, I radioed off a message. With some feeling of satisfaction, I saw my comrades across the river reorganize and continue their march.

The steel bridge at Zvornik had already been demolished and was lying in the water, when the first armored car carefully stuck its nose out from around the last curve. The scene there was completely different than the one with the antiaircraft guns. From the first moment forward, I knew that we had been expected and that there would be no *coup de main* there. I needed more assets than I had with me. The outskirts of the town were heavily manned with dug-in infantry with antitank guns. There were no friendly forces to be seen on the far bank. I had everyone turn around and get under cover. I radioed the battalion and asked for reinforcements. At the same time, I reported to the division that it would need engineers in Zvornik.

After about two hours, armored cars, motorcycle infantry and the Battalion Commander arrived. I briefed him on the situation and that things could get serious. He ordered me to move out to attack. The minimal resistance we had experienced up to that point allowed me to get past my doubts, and I issued a careful attack order. Before that, however, I sent a *Feldwebel* carrying a white flag over to the enemy, to have him inform them that it was hopeless to continue resistance and to surrender. To my surprise, the enemy forces accepted 10 minutes later. After a short period, about 250 men came out without weapons. We discovered that they were Croatians, whose Serbian officers gave up the fight when their [men] no longer wanted to fight. We moved into the town. I had the entrances and the post office occupied. Since the whole thing still did not sit well with me, I had my modest force assemble in the houses around the marketplace. When it turned dark, the initial elements of the division approached along the far bank of the Drina. I received instructions to prepare to move out in the direction of Sarajevo the following morning . . .

Fritz Klingenberg: The Motorcycle Infantry Officer Who Captured a Capital

Fritz Klingenberg, born on 17 December 1912 in Rövingshoven (vicinity of Rostock), received the Knight's Cross on 14 May 1941 as an *SS-Hauptsturmführer* and commander of the *2./SS-Kradschützen-Bataillon "Reich."* His spirited *Reitergeist* enabled him to achieve the award, which was presented for the almost single-handed "capture" of the Yugoslavian capital of Belgrade on 12 April 1941.

Born to the owner of a dairy, Klingenberg went on to university and entered the *NSDAP* early on as a member (1931). By 1934 he was an officer candidate in the *Leibstandarte SS Adolf Hitler*, and he attended the first officer candidate class held at the *SS-Junkerschule* in Bad Tölz in 1934–35. By the mid-1930s he had been transferred to the *SS-Verfügungstruppe*, serving in both the *"Deutschland"* and *"Germania" Standarten*. He attained the rank of *SS-Hauptsturmführer* before the start of the war (30 June 1939) and participated in the occupation of Austria, the *Sudetenland*, and, finally, the remainder of Czechoslovakia. In the campaigns in Poland and in the West, he served primarily as a staff officer to *SS-Gruppenführer* Hausser, although he did earn both classes of the Iron Cross during the latter campaign. By the fall of 1940, he commanded the *15. (Kradsch.-)/SS-Standarte "Der Führer"* and, when the motorcycle infantry battalion of *Reich* was being formed, his company became the *2./SS-Kradschützen-Bataillon "Reich."*

He next participated in the Balkans campaign, where on 12 April 1940 he received the mission to take a bridge over the Danube, north of Belgrade. He reached Pancevo at 0800 on 12 April and found the bridge over the Tamis River blown up. He proceeded to cross the river in fishing boats, taking a few motorcycles with him. He then reached the large bridge over the Danube north of Belgrade at 1130. That bridge had been destroyed early that same morning. Klingenberg, undeterred, found a motor launch by 1530 hours and attempted to cross the river in it, along with ten men, two machine guns, and five submachine guns. After several misadventures with the watercraft, he succeeded in reaching the far bank with his small force at 1630 hours, whereupon he

A period Hoffmann postcard of Fritz Klingenberg as an *SS-Hauptsturmführer*, shortly after the award of his Knight's Cross on 14 May 1941. Klingenberg has autographed this postcard, probably for a member of the *Hitlerjugend*, who often collected the signatures of Knight's Cross recipients.

sent the boat back to fetch more forces. He then continued on foot with his ten men, marching into the center of Belgrade. By taking approaching Serbian soldiers under fire, he was able to convince them to surrender. Using captured military vehicles, he then made his way to the War Ministry. Klingenberg found the building empty and destroyed. He sent a messenger to the mayor of the city, demanding that he appear and surrender the city. In the meantime, Klingenberg and a few men went to the German Embassy, found the military attaché, and raised the German flag. By then, the mayor had arrived. Under the impression that there were strong German forces present, he formally surrendered the city at 1845 hours. Awaiting reinforcements, Klingenberg's small group, which had

Fritz Klingenberg: The Motorcycle Infantry Officer Who Captured a Capital *continued*

been slightly augmented by additional forces from the motorcycle infantry battalion in the meantime, conducted deception operations in order to give the impression that there were large numbers of Germans present. In all, his men took in some 1,000 prisoners before the arrival of advance elements of *Gruppe Kleist* during the night. For these actions, Klingenberg was later awarded the Knight's Cross.

He continued to excel in the fighting in the east, promoted to *SS-Sturmbannführer* on 1 September 1941 and given acting command of the battalion. He not only distinguished himself in offensive fighting but also proved very adept in the defense. In January 1942 he suffered dysentery and had to be sent back to Germany to convalesce. Once there, he was selected to become part of the faculty at the *Junkerschule* at Bad Tölz. He returned to the front in early 1943, where he served as acting commander of the *II./SS-Panzer-Regiment 2*, only to be wounded again. Returning to the schoolhouse, he was given command of the institution on 12 December 1944. At the end of the war, Klingenberg, having been promoted to *SS-Standartenführer*, was given acting command of the *17. SS-Panzer-Grenadier-Division "Götz von Berlichingen."* He was killed in action on 23 March 1945 at Herzheim in the Pfalz region of Germany.

Command vehicles, personnel, and motorcycles of all three line battalions of *SS-Kradschützen-Bataillon "Reich"* can be seen in their approach march to Pancevo and the crossing of the Tamis River on 12 April 1940. In the first image, several expatriated British Bedford MWD trucks, most likely captured in France, are seen to the right. In the second image, Klingenberg's command vehicle for the 2nd Company can be seen. Air guards have been posted while crossing the river, even though the air threat was minimal. The distinctive SS camouflage smock is worn in most of the images. In the next-to-last image, the battalion commander, *SS-Sturmbannführer* Zehender, can be seen. Zehender would also be killed before the end of the war, dying in the fighting in Budapest on 11 February 1945. By then, he was an *SS-Brigadeführer und Generalmajor der Waffen-SS*, acting commander of the *22. SS-Freiwilligen-Kavallerie-Division "Maria Theresia,"* and recipient of the Oak Leaves to the Knight's Cross. NATIONAL ARCHIVES

In this series of images, more motorcycle infantry, possibly from the 2nd Company, cross an unidentified waterway during the Balkan campaign. NATIONAL ARCHIVES

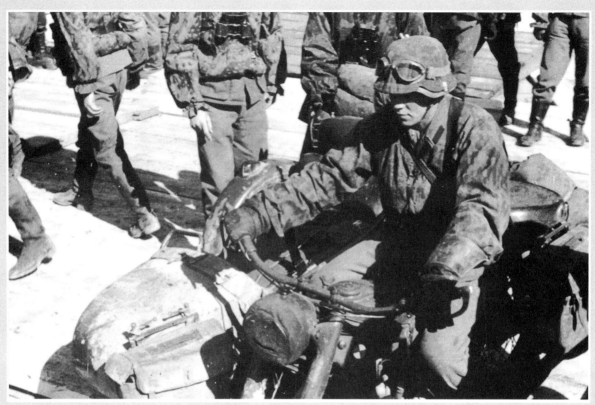

With regard to the attitude of his soldiers and the combat value of his unit, *Oberleutnant* Borchardt later wrote:

> On 7 January 1941, I assumed command of the armored car company of [*Aufklärungs-Abteilung 341 (mot)*]. The company had already had combat experience from Poland and France. I found opportunities to increase the company's military proficiency and combat value, in the process of which, my experiences in China helped a lot. I made it clear to my people that **proficiency and mastery of the weapons are better and more essential than enthusiasm.** To wish someone **good luck** should mean that he should **be successful in an operation and come home alive. For my people, all that mattered was that I understood my job. Discipline was very good and the relationship to the peoples of the occupied country was full of understanding and cordial as a result.**

The *Seydlitz*, an *Sd.Kfz. 232 (8 Rad)* from an unidentified reconnaissance unit, moves down a street in Greece, the commander observing through his binoculars. NATIONAL ARCHIVES

Motorcycle infantry of *SS-Kradschützen-Bataillon "Reich"* receive hand grenades in preparation for operations. In the next two images, motorcycle infantry listen intently as they are briefed by an officer. Given the attire, these images were probably taken during a training exercise sometime between the campaign in the West and the Balkans campaign, or during the approach march into its staging areas in Romania from 1–5 April 1940. NATIONAL ARCHIVES

A long column of vehicles from *SS-Kradschützen-Bataillon "Reich"* passes by long lines of supply trucks parked on either side of an unimproved muddy road. When columns met on a road march, the column with combat elements always had priority, unless medical vehicles were making their way to the rear. In the last image, one of the two light infantry guns of the battalion is being towed forward by a prime mover, the gun covered by a tarpaulin to protect it from the elements and ensure it was ready to fire as soon as it was pulled into a position and unlimbered. NATIONAL ARCHIVES

Motorcycle infantrymen of the 3rd Company have a difficult time as they attempt to make their way forward on a field trail that has been transformed into a quagmire by rainfall and heavy vehicular traffic, for which it was never intended. The sidecar motorcycles are essentially reduced to a walking pace, and many of the men had to get out and push whenever a vehicle got stuck.

Although some of the men in the lead manhandling the commander's vehicle manage a smile for the photographer, they probably had other expressions when the correspondent wasn't looking. The commander of the *3./SS-Kradschützen-Bataillon "Reich"* at the time was *SS-Hauptsturmführer* Christian Tychsen, who was awarded both the Knight's Cross and the Oak Leaves to the Knight's Cross in 1943 and later killed in action in Normandy on 28 July 1944. NATIONAL ARCHIVES

Additional images of the "march of misery." Tychsen can be seen lending a hand to bring an unruly sidecar motorcycle back to the roadway; and a medic and other motorcycle infantrymen have to use pickaxes, hoes, and manpower to free up the commander's vehicle. NATIONAL ARCHIVES

Desperate situations sometimes called for unorthodox solutions, as evidenced here in the efforts to keep the motorcycles and heavy weapons moving. NATIONAL ARCHIVES

Sometimes, the best method of moving when the road network was poor was along railway tracks. The foundation was solid, although the accompanying ride was hard on both vehicles and personnel. This method was used by *Panzer-Aufklärungs-Abteilung 8* of the *5. Panzer-Division* in Greece, as described in the text (see page 166).

THE BALKAN CAMPAIGN   183

The *Bussard* ("Buzzard") of *SS-Aufklärungs-Abteilung (mot) "Reich"* makes its way down a muddy main street. Note that its crew has added some sort of supplemental protection to the vehicle in the area of the mudguards, perhaps as additional protection against small-arms fire. In the second image, a utility vehicle from the 1st Company of *SS-Kradschützen-Bataillon "Reich"* also negotiates the muddy streets of a Balkan village while curious civilians look on. The truck with the white swastika aerial identifier painted on the hood is another ex-British Bedford MWD truck put to use by the Germans. NATIONAL ARCHIVES

An *Sd.Kfz. 222* and an *Sd.Kfz. 231 (8 Rad)* of the *1./SS-Aufklärungs-Abteilung Leibstandarte SS Adolf Hitler* during a break in operations somewhere in Greece. PRESS RELEASE PHOTOGRAPH COURTESY OF TODD GYLSEN

CHAPTER 5

North Africa

SETTING THE STAGE

As with the Balkans, the North Africa theater was not an area of interest to Hitler. It was only after the disastrous mishandling of the Italian forces there and the effective destruction of the Italian 10th Army by the British that Hitler agreed to help his friend Mussolini by dispatching German forces to the beleaguered theater of war. The Germans arrived in early 1941 under the command of the legendary Erwin Rommel. Operations against the British were initiated by the end of March that year, starting a series of offensives and counteroffensives that earned the Germans and Rommel the begrudging respect of the British and have captured the popular imagination ever since. What started out as a small "blocking force" (the essentially *ad hoc 5. leichte Afrika-Division*) turned into a corps—the famous *Deutsches Afrika Korps*—that summer.

Rommel turned out to be a much more effective tactical leader on the battlefield than an operational planner. He constantly took risks, despite an extremely precarious supply situation, that frequently caused him to pause or even call off operations due to a lack of fuel and other logistical support. The German lines of communications extended across the Mediterranean, thus making the *DAK* the only German force to fight overseas. Despite the relatively close distance to friendly Italian ports, the waters were controlled by the British and a large percentage of materiel—

A nice view of the *Sd.Kfz. 233*, the support variant of the heavy armored car, armed with a short 75mm main gun. These were issued to the heavy armored car platoons organized under *KStN 1138* (1 November 1942) and saw limited service in North Africa in all three of the major reconnaissance formations in 1943. Of interest in this image are the relatively pristine condition of the vehicle and the additional canteens hanging on the protective railing for the antenna. NATIONAL ARCHIVES

including precious combat vehicles—was sent to the bottom of the sea. By October 1942, the British had the upper hand in sheer numbers and were able to force the German forces back toward Tunisia after the Second Battle of El Alamein. A few weeks later, Allied forces landed in Algeria and Morocco, causing the collapse of the Vichy forces stationed there and directly threatening the Axis forces pulling back from Egypt and Libya.

Instead of realizing that the fate of his forces in Africa was sealed, Hitler ordered more troops into the theater, expanding what had essentially been a reinforced corps into a *Panzerarmee*. Stalemate ensued through the winter of 1942–43, followed by local victories on the part of the Axis—most famously at the Battle of the Kasserine Pass—but the end was inevitable, and the Axis capitulated on 13 May 1943.

DOCTRINE

Fighting in the desert is often compared to naval warfare, given its vast expanses of open terrain, dotted with the occasional "island" of civilization. A narrow strip along the North African coastline was sparsely inhabited and home to most of the infrastructure, including the only improved roads, while the hinterlands were desolate and largely uninhabited. This naturally occasioned fighting to control the coastal avenues, leaving the open desert for enveloping movements for forces to leapfrog their way forward.

The open flanks of the desert were the "homeland" of the reconnaissance forces of both sides. Since it was physically impossible to continuously man a static defensive line extending into untrafficable portions of the desert, strongpoints were established or standing patrols dispatched to serve as the "eyes and ears" of the higher-level commands. For that reason, the German reconnaissance battalions associated with the desert fighting—primarily *Aufklärungs-Abteilung 3 (mot)*, *Panzer-Aufklärungs-Abteilung 33 (mot)*, and *Aufklärungs-Abteilung 580 (mot)*—are prominently featured in histories of the campaign. It is interesting to note that these three reconnaissance battalions were often temporarily combined for operations, especially deception and economy-of-force missions. Because of the seesaw nature of the fighting, reconnaissance battalions were also used extensively as rear guards for the force whenever the German–Italian forces were pushed back. Due to their speed on the battlefield, they were also occasionally positioned behind Italian lines in an effort to provide moral support to their often wavering allies.

Since it was difficult to replace vehicles and other equipment, great value was placed on captured enemy stores and materiel. As such, the reconnaissance eventually came to have a battery of captured British guns added to its organizations. This was done unofficially—that is, through "command channels"—initially, but eventually the batteries became a *KStN* in their own right. That said, the forces in the desert often retained a sort of *ad hoc* organizational status since many of the changes that were applied to the organizations of the *Panzertruppe* on Continental Europe were never applied in North Africa.

LESSONS LEARNED AND FIRSTHAND ACCOUNTS

Among the first elements to be deployed in North Africa by an impatient *Generalleutnant* Erwin Rommel was *Aufklärungs-Abteilung 3 (mot)* of the *5. leichte Division*. Almost as soon as they arrived by ship at Syrte on 16 February, the armored cars of the battalion, were sent forward to determine the size, location, and disposition of the enemy:[10]

The Conquest of Cyrenaica

The first German combat forces, *Aufklärungs-Abteilung 3 (mot)* and *Panzerjäger-Abteilung 39*, arrived in Syrte on 16 February [1941]. On the same day, *Generalleutnant* Rommel assumed command of all German and Italian forces at the front. Deviating from his initial plan to establish a defensive line at Buerat, he proposed to the Italian High Command to employ a battle group east of Syrte, which would set up for defensive operations at En Nofilia. That formation, consisting of *Aufklärungs-Abteilung 3 (mot)* and an Italian battle group, had the mission of fending off small-scale attacks and, in the event of heavier attacks or the danger of being bypassed, to fall back to the positions at Syrte. In order to feign larger forces, dummy tanks were constructed.

ORDER OF BATTLE FOR THE NORTH AFRICAN CAMPAIGN, 1941–43 (MAJOR RECONNAISSANCE ELEMENTS)

Parent Organization	Reconnaissance Assets	Notes
5. leichte-Division	Aufklärungs-Abteilung 3 (mot)	Reassigned from the 3. Panzer-Division. Standard reconnaissance organization of the 1941 period: Headquarters (*KStN 1105* / 1 February 1941) with attached signals platoon (*KStN 1191* / 1 February 1941), one armored scout company (2nd Company) (*KStN 1162* / 1 February 1941), one motorcycle infantry company (3rd Company) (*KStN 1112* / 1 February 1941),[1] and one heavy company (4th Company) with headquarters (*KStN 1121*), antitank platoon (*KStN 1122*), light infantry gun platoon (*KStN 1123*), and combat engineer platoon (*KStN 1124*), all dated 1 February 1941. Shortly after arrival in theater, the battalion unofficially added a battery of captured British 25-pounders to its organization (four guns). The division did not have a motorcycle infantry battalion. The division was reorganized and redesignated as the *21. Panzer-Division* in August 1941 (see below)
15. Panzer-Division	Kradschützen-Bataillon 15	Organized like a standard armored division motorcycle infantry battalion of the period, with a headquarters (*KStN 1109* / 1 February 1941), three motorcycle infantry companies (*KStN 1112* / 1 February 1941), a motorcycle machine-gun company (*KStN 1118* / 1 February 1941), and a motorized heavy company with a headquarters (*KStN 1121* / 1 February 1941), an antitank platoon (*KStN 1122* / 1 February 1941), a light infantry gun platoon (*KStN 1123* / 1 February 1941), and an engineer platoon (*KStN 1124* / 1941). In April 1942, the battalion was reassigned to the *21. Panzer-Division*, where it was reorganized and redesignated as the *III./Panzer-Grenadier-Regiment 104*.
	Panzer-Aufklärungs-Abteilung 33	Organized analogously to *Aufklärungs-Abteilung 3 (mot)* when assigned to the *21. Panzer-Division* (see below).[2] Officially redesignated as *Panzer-Aufklärungs-Abteilung 15* in late April 1943, it retained the same organization.[3]
21. Panzer-Division	Aufklärungs-Abteilung 3 (mot)	The organization of the battalion started to morph from the time it arrived in theater until its reassignment to the *21. Panzer-Division* and beyond. The armored car company was slightly stronger than a normal company organized under *KStN 1162* (1 November 1941), reporting twenty heavy machine guns (2cm cannon) and forty light machine guns. The 3rd Company was redesignated as a (motorized) scout company, with an organization unique to Africa (*KStN 1113 (Afrika)* / 23 April 1942). The heavy company had only an antitank platoon (*KStN 1122a* / 1 December 1941) and an engineer platoon (*KStN 1124* / 1 November 1941) among its combat assets.[4] The division organization chart for April 1942 shows the impending arrival of a heavy armored car platoon (*KStN 1138* / 1 December 1942) and its presence in October 1942.[5] This platoon was at least administratively attached to the armored car company, although it is shown separately in organizational charts. In February 1943, the battalion was transferred to the *90. leichte Division*.
	Aufklärungs-Abteilung 580 (mot)	Reassigned to the division from the *90. leichte Division* in February 1943.
90. leichte Afrika-Division	gemischte Aufklärungs-Kompanie 580	The reconnaissance company was assigned to the division in July 1941, but it did not arrive in theater until January 1942. It had a special *KStN* created for it (*1163* / 25 June 1941) (see below). A battery of captured British 25-pounder field guns was attached to it in May 1942. It was expanded to a battalion in late September 1942, where it was organized analogously to *Aufklärungs-Abteilung 3 (mot)* when assigned to the *21. Panzer-Division* (shown above).[6]
10. Panzer-Division	Kradschützen-Bataillon 10	The battalion was a mixture of scout and motorcycle infantry elements, a structure devised when the motorcycle infantry and armored reconnaissance battalions of the mechanized force were consolidated in 1942 in Europe. As such, it had the following organization: headquarters (*KStN 1109* / 1 November 1941), one armored scout company (*KStN 1162* / 1 November 1941), one light armored reconnaissance company (*KStN 1113 (gp)* / 1 March 1942), two motorcycle reconnaissance companies (*KStN 1112* / 1 November 1941), and one motorized heavy company with a headquarters (*KStN 1121* / 1 November 1941), one antitank platoon with three 50mm antitank guns (*KStN 1122a* / 1 November 1941), two armored light infantry gun platoons (*KStN 1123 (gp)* / 1 November 1941), one combat engineer platoon (*KStN 1124* / 1 November 1941), and one antitank gun section with three 28mm antitank guns (*KStN 1127* / 1 November 1941). In March 1943, the battalion was redesignated as *Panzer-Aufklärungs-Abteilung 10*, retaining its old organization.

Changes in Organizational Authorizations (1 November 1941)

HEADQUARTERS, MOTORIZED RECONNAISSANCE BATTALION (1109)

In addition to the organization's name change, there were some equipment changes as well, with a substantial increase in signals resources, most likely due to the incorporation of scouting elements within the battalion in addition to the motorcycle infantry companies.

a) Command Group

8x Medium and 2x Sidecar Motorcycle	Medium Cross-Country Vehicle with Equipment Storage Box (*Kfz. 15*)	Medium Cross-Country Vehicle with Equipment Storage Box (*Kfz. 15*)	Heavy Cross-Country Vehicle (*Sd.Kfz. 247*), 1x Submachine Gun

Totals Command Section: 5x Officers, 4x NCOs, 15x Enlisted Personnel; 16x Rifles, 6x Pistols, 3x Submachine Guns; 2x Wheeled Vehicles, 1x Armored Vehicle, 8x Motorcycles, 2x Sidecar Motorcycles

b) Signals Platoon

Signals Vehicle (*Kfz. 15*)	Medium Motorcycle	Sidecar Motorcycle

Small Telephone Section c (Motorized)

1st Backpack Radio Section b (Motorized)	2nd Backpack Radio Section b (Motorized)
Radio Vehicle (*Kfz. 2*) (3 seat)	Radio Vehicle (*Kfz. 2*) (3 seat)

Small Armored Radio Section c (Motorized)

Small Armored Radio Car (*Sd.Kfz. 260*), 1x Submachine Gun

1st Small Armored Radio Section d (Motorized)	2nd Small Armored Radio Section d (Motorized)	3rd Small Armored Radio Section d (Motorized)	4th Small Armored Radio Section d (Motorized)
Small Armored Radio Car (*Sd.Kfz. 261*)	Small Armored Radio Car (*Sd.Kfz. 261*)	Small Armored Radio Car (*Sd.Kfz. 261*)	Small Armored Radio Car (*Sd.Kfz. 261*)

Note: *Kfz. 17* counts in lieu of *Sd.Kfz. 261*. Each vehicle has 1 Submachine Gun.

1st Medium Armored Radio Section b (Motorized)		2nd Medium Armored Radio Section b (Motorized)		3rd Medium Armored Radio Section b (Motorized)	
Armored Radio Car (*Sd.Kfz. 263*)	Radio Vehicle (*Kfz. 15*)	Armored Radio Car (*Sd.Kfz. 263*)	Radio Vehicle (*Kfz. 15*)	Armored Radio Car (*Sd.Kfz. 263*)	Radio Vehicle (*Kfz. 15*)

Note: *Kfz. 17* counts in lieu of *Sd.Kfz. 261*. Each vehicle has 1 Submachine Gun.

Total Signals Platoon: 1x Officer, 15x NCOs, 45x Enlisted Personnel; 16x Rifles, 44x Pistols, 9x Submachine Guns, 3x Light MG's; 7x Wheeled Vehicles, 8x Armored Vehicles, 1x Medium Motorcycle, 1x Sidecar Motorcycle

c) Combat Trains I

| Light Utility Vehicle (4 seat) | Light Cross-Country Truck, for Petroleum, Oil & Lubricants | Medium Cross-Country Truck, Canvas Top, for Large Field Mess Stove | Ambulance (*Kfz. 31*) | Sidecar Motorcycle |

Totals: 4x NCOs, 10x Enlisted Personnel; 9x Rifles, 5x Pistols; 4x Wheeled Vehicles, 1x Sidecar Motorcycle

d) Combat Trains II
Maintenance Section (Vehicles and Weapons)

| Small Maintenance Vehicle (*Kfz. 2/40*) | Medium Cross-Country Vehicle with Equipment Storage Box (*Kfz. 15*) | Medium Cross-Country Truck, Canvas Top, for Armorer's Equipment | Medium Cross-Country Truck, Canvas Top, for Maintenance Equipment |

| Medium Cross-Country Truck, Canvas Top, for Tires and Recovery | Medium Cross-Country Truck, Canvas Top, for Replacement Parts | Medium Cross-Country Truck, Canvas Top, for Armored Car Replacement Parts | Sidecar Motorcycle |

Supply Section

1x Light Utility Vehicle, 1x Motorcycle | Light Cross-Country Truck, Canvas Top, for Ammunition and Equipment for Armored Cars | Medium Cross-Country Truck, Canvas Top, for Ammunition and Equipment | Medium Cross-Country Truck, Canvas Top, for Ammunition and Equipment

4x Medium Cross-Country Truck, Canvas Top, for Petroleum, Oil & Lubricants transport

Totals: 1x Officer, 3x Civilian Officials, 5x NCOs, 41x Enlisted Personnel; 42x Rifles, 8x Pistols; 15x Vehicles, 1x Medium Motorcycle, 1x Sidecar Motorcycle

e) Rations Trains (for the Entire Battalion)

| Light Utility Vehicle | Medium Truck, 3 ton, Canvas Top, for Rations | Medium Truck, 3 ton, Canvas Top, for Rations |

Totals: 1x Officer, 1x Civilian Official, 2x NCOs, 5x Enlisted Personnel; 6x Rifles, 2x Pistols; 3x Vehicles

f) Baggage Trains

1x Motorcyclist, Messenger (Medium Motorcycle), 1x Rifle | Medium Truck, 3 ton, Canvas Top, for Baggage

Totals: 1x NCO, 4x Enlisted Personnel; 5x Rifles; 1x Vehicle, 1x Medium Motorcycle

Summary

	Officers	Civilian Officials	NCOs	Enlisted Personnel	Rifles	Pistols (Submachine Guns)	Light MG's	Wheeled Vehicles	Armored Vehicles	Motorcycles (Sidecar Motorcycles)
Command Section	5		4	15	16	6 (3)		2	1	10 (2)
Signals Platoon	1		15	45	16	44 (9)	3	7	8	2 (1)
Combat Trains I			4	10	9	5		4		1 (1)
Combat Trains II	1	3	5	41	42	8		15		2 (1)
Rations Trains	1	1	2	5	7	2		3		
Baggage Trains			1	4	5			1		1
Totals	8	4	31	120	95	65 (12)	3	32	9	16 (5)

Changes in Organizational Authorizations (1 November 1941) *continued*

MOTORIZED SCOUT COMPANY (AFRICA) (1113)

KStN 1113 (Afrika) of 23 April 1942 was a unique organization created by the *Organizations-Abteilung* for the reconnaissance battalions in North Africa. It was organized as follows:

- Headquarters: four motorcycles and three *Volkswagen* utility vehicles.
- Machine-gun section: seven *Volkswagen* utility vehicles and two heavy machine guns.
- Three scout platoons:
  - Headquarters section: one motorcycle and two *Volkswagen* utility vehicles.
  - Three scout squads: four *Volkswagen* utility vehicles and one light machine gun.
  - One antitank section: one 1-ton prime mover half-track (*Sd.Kfz. 10*) with towed 50mm antitank gun and one heavy wheeled personnel carrier (*Kfz. 70*) with one towed 28mm antitank gun.
  - Maintenance section: one sidecar motorcycle and one *Volkswagen* maintenance utility vehicle (*Kfz. 2/40*).
  - Company trains: one light cross-country wheeled utility vehicle (*Kfz. 1*) and eleven 3-ton trucks.

LIGHT RECONNAISSANCE COMPANY (ARMORED) (1113) (*gp*)

KStN 1113 (gp) was fielded on 1 March 1942 and had the following organization:

- Headquarters: four motorcycles, one sidecar motorcycle, and two light half-tracks (*Sd.Kfz. 250/3*).*
- Three reconnaissance platoons:
  - Headquarters section: one light half-track armored personnel carrier (*Sd.Kfz. 250/1*), and one light half-track armored personnel carrier with mounted 37mm antitank gun (*Sd.Kfz. 250/10*).
  - Three reconnaissance squads: two light half-track armored personnel carriers (*Sd.Kfz. 250/1*), one reconnaissance squad, and two light machine guns.

- One heavy platoon:
  - Headquarters section: one motorcycle and one light half-track armored personnel carrier (*Sd.Kfz. 250/1*).
  - Two heavy machine-gun sections: three light half-track armored personnel carriers (*Sd.Kfz. 250/1*) and two heavy machine guns.
  - One mortar section: two light half-track armored personnel carriers with 81mm mortars (*Sd.Kfz. 250/7*) and two light half-track armored ammunition carriers (*Sd.Kfz. 250/7*).
- Maintenance section: one sidecar motorcycle, one light half-track prime mover (*Sd.Kfz. 10*), and one light machine gun.
- Company trains: one medium cross-country utility vehicle (*Kfz. 15*), one 2-ton truck, one truck (medium), and two 3-ton trucks.

MOTORIZED HEAVY COMPANY COMPANY HEADQUARTERS (1121)

The *KStN* of 1 November 1942 offered little in the way of substantive changes to its predecessor.

ANTITANK PLATOON (1122A)

This *KStN* (1 December 1941) changed the weaponry from the 37mm antitank gun to the 50mm. In addition, the prime movers changed, with the trucks replaced by half-tracks. This is the organization of the platoon:

- Headquarters: one motorcycle, one sidecar motorcycle, and one medium cross-country utility vehicle (*Kfz. 15*).
- One ammunition section: two light half-track prime movers (*Sd.Kfz. 10*) with two trailers.
- One gun section: three light half-track prime movers (*Sd.Kfz. 10*) with three towed 50mm antitank guns and three light machine guns.

LIGHT INFANTRY GUN PLATOON (1123) (*gp*)

The armored variant of this *KStN* (1 November 1941) provided the towed light infantry guns with an armored prime mover (*Sd.Kfz. 251/4*). With the exception of the motorcycles, wheeled vehicles were removed from the platoon authorizations.

- Headquarters: one motorcycle, one sidecar motorcycle, and one medium half-track armored personnel carrier (*Sd.Kfz. 251/1*).

---

*This was the command and control variant of the vehicle. It featured a frame antenna with a variety of possible radio configurations.

Changes in Organizational Authorizations (1 November 1941) *continued*

- One gun section: three medium half-track armored personnel carriers (*Sd.Kfz. 251/4*)* with two light towed 75mm infantry guns.

COMBAT ENGINEER PLATOON (1124)
The update to *KStN 1124* of 1 November 1941 reduced vehicle allocations in the platoon headquarters while increasing them in the line squads, which were increased from three to four.
- Headquarters: one motorcycle, one sidecar motorcycle, one medium cross-country utility vehicle (*Kfz. 15*), and two 2-ton trucks.

---
*The full description of the vehicle: *Schützenpanzerwagen für Munition und Zubehör des leIG18* (Armored Personnel Carrier for Ammunition and Equipment of the Light Infantry Gun, Model 18).

- Four engineer squads: one 2-ton truck, one engineer squad, and one light machine gun.

ANTITANK GUN SECTION (1127)
KStN 1127 (1 November 1941) established an antitank gun section with three 28mm antitank rifles (guns).[7]
- Antitank gun section: one sidecar motorcycle, three cross-country wheeled personnel carriers (*Kfz. 70*), three 28mm antitank guns, and three light machine guns.

KStN 1127 (gp) (1 November 1941), illustrated below, had the guns mounted on the *Sd.Kfz. 250*.

Sidecar Motorcycle   3x Light Armored Personnel Carrier (Antitank Rifle, Model 41) (*Sd.Kfz. 250/11*) (*schwere Panzerbüchse 41*), 1x Light MG

Totals: 4x NCOs, 17x Enlisted Personnel; 10x Rifles, 8x Pistols, 3x Submachine Guns, 3x Light MG's; 3x Armored Vehicles, 1x Sidecar Motorcycle

HEAVY ARMORED CAR PLATOON (1138)
This *KStN* was introduced on 1 November 1942 and intended to provide armored scouts with heavy weapons support on a chassis that could keep up with the armored cars. It partially addressed a shortcoming that had been identified early on, but the short 7.5mm main guns of the vehicles were really only effective against infantry, soft-skinned targets, and other lightly armored vehicles by this point of the war.

a) Platoon

 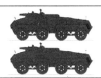 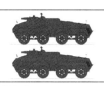

6x Heavy Armored Car (7.5 cm) (*Sd.Kfz. 233*), 6x Light MG's, 6x Submachine Guns, 6x 7.5cm Main Gun

Totals: 1x Officer, 11x NCOs, 6x Enlisted Personnel; 18x Pistols, 6x Submachine Guns, 6x Light MG's, 6x Main Guns; 6x Armored Vehicles

b) Trains (Moves with Combat Trains I of the Armored Scout Company)

Truck, 3 ton, Canvas Top, for Ammunition and Equipment   Truck, 3 ton, Canvas Top, for Petroleum, Oil & Lubricants

Totals: 4x Enlisted Personnel; 4x Rifles; 2x Wheeled Vehicles

Changes in Organizational Authorizations (1 November 1941) *continued*

MIXED RECONNAISSANCE COMPANY (1163)
This *KStN* was created on 25 June 1941 and only applied to *gemischte Aufklärungs-Kompanie 580*.[8] The company had a mixture of scout and reconnaissance assets and heavy weapons.[9]

- Headquarters:
  - Headquarters section: three motorcycles, two sidecar motorcycles, and two medium cross-country utility vehicles (*Kfz. 15*).
  - Light telephone section: one medium cross-country utility vehicle (*Kfz. 15*).
  - Two manpack radio sections (Type b): one light cross-country signals utility vehicle (*Kfz. 2*).
- One reconnaissance platoon:
  - Headquarters section: one motorcycle and three *Volkswagen* utility vehicles.
  - One machine-gun section: seven *Volkswagen* utility vehicles and two heavy machine guns.
  - Three reconnaissance squads: four *Volkswagen* utility vehicles, one reconnaissance squad, and two light machine guns.
  - One antitank section: three medium cross-country utility vehicles (*Kfz. 70*), three towed 28mm antitank guns, and three light machine guns.
- One armored car platoon: six medium armored cars (*Sd.Kfz. 222*) and two light radio armored cars (*Sd.Kfz. 223*).
- One antitank platoon:
  - Headquarters section: one motorcycle, one sidecar motorcycle, and one medium cross-country utility vehicle (*Kfz. 15*).
  - One gun section: five light half-track prime movers (*Sd.Kfz. 10*), three towed 50mm antitank guns, two ammunition trailers, and three light machine guns.
- One air defense platoon:
  - Headquarters section: three motorcycles and two medium cross-country utility vehicles (*Kfz. 15*).
  - One gun section: six medium cross-country utility vehicles (*Kfz. 70*), four towed 20mm antiaircraft guns, and two ammunition trailers.
  - Maintenance section: one sidecar motorcycle and one *Volkswagen* maintenance vehicle.
  - Company trains: two motorcycles, one sidecar motorcycle, one medium cross-country utility vehicle (*Kfz. 15*), one light truck, five 2-ton trucks, and one 3-ton truck.

Aerial reconnaissance reported concentrations of British formations on 18 February between El Agheila and Agedabia. En Nofilia was clear of enemy forces. At that point, the battle group was pushed further to the east and was able to take the important but salt-laden well there. Two days later, there was the first contact with the enemy. Armored scout sections from *Aufklärungs-Abteilung 3 (mot)* encountered British armored reconnaissance elements. At that point, Rommel wanted to know what forces were facing him. [The reconnaissance battalion] received orders to bring in prisoners. On 25 February—some sources state 24 February—armored reconnaissance sections ran into two combat vehicle sections of the King's Dragoon Guards and a section of Australian antitank forces. Wechmar's troops opened fire, destroying an armored vehicle, two small armored cars and a truck. Lieutenant Rowley of the Australian 6th Division and two soldiers from the Dragoons were captured with no friendly casualties.

The Armed Forces Daily Report of 26 February 1941 stated:

"During the morning hours of 24 February, a German and an English motorized scout section encountered one another along the

Libyan coast southeast of Agedabia. A number of English motorized vehicles, including several armored cars, were destroyed and a few prisoners taken. There were no losses on the German side."

This was the first mention of German forces being deployed on the African continent. Considering the important role reconnaissance forces played there, it is fitting that they were also the first combat elements mentioned. A reconnaissance officer, Hellmuth Schroetter, who was with the battalion from the beginning until the Second Battle of El Alamein, captured his impressions of that first meeting engagement:[11]

In the vicinity of the *Arco*,[12] the first contact took place between German and English forces on 20 February 1941. [This date is probably a typographical error in the German edition.] A battle group formed from motorcycle infantry and several armored scout sections had advanced east of the *Arco* without making enemy contact.

One of the armored scout sections received the mission to reconnoiter as far as the bottleneck at El Mugtaa, almost 70 kilometers east of the *Arco*. It was around 1500 hours and the section leader was contemplating turning around, when he suddenly thought he saw movement on the horizon. He then decided to take a closer look at the presumed enemy.

The same decision was reached by an armored scout section of the King's Dragoon Guards, which had been employed west of El Agheila, when it thought it saw several fighting vehicles. And so it came to pass—a strange and stubborn "movement towards one another" with an armored car from each side on the Via Balbia [the improved coastal road that was of vital importance to both sides during the campaign] and a wingman following to either the left or right of the road. The enemy armored cars, weapons blazing, rolled past one another.

There was a quick turning around and, once again, they rolled towards each other. Both parties were determined to reach "his side" by force of arms. Afterwards, they took off in a flash towards their respective lines.

From a respectful distance behind a sand dune—only the turret jutted out over the top of the dune towards the enemy—both of the section leaders reported the strange enemy contact to their battalions, once their nerves had calmed down.

The German section leader thought to himself: Why wasn't there any effect on the enemy from the 20mm ammunition? The hits were clearly seen because of the tracer elements. It was later determined that high-explosive ammunition had been loaded, and it simply shattered upon impact. The 20mm antitank rounds—solid shot, which would have penetrated the armor—had not been issued, since they were not considered "suitable for the desert."

For his part, according to English sources, the section leader from the King's Dragoon Guards thought he had seen 8-wheeled armored vehicles and *Balkenkreuze*.

My God! The Englishman thought. Those aren't Italians, those are Germans! His superiors did not believe his observations, however.

On the German side, there was a quick reaction. *General* Rommel appeared at the location of *Aufklärungs-Abteilung 3 (mot)* and issued orders:

- Increased reconnaissance in the direction of El Agheila.
- Advance of the main body of the [battalion] beyond the *Arco* and as far as the roadhouse (a building located on the Via Balbia).
- Reconnaissance from there to the east and to the south.

Over the next few days, reinforced armored scout sections advanced further to the east, destroyed enemy armored cars and took prisoners.

Schroetter was part of that first encounter only after he had first been sent out into the desert with his motorcycle infantry to acclimate themselves:[13]

As the platoon leader of a motorcycle infantry platoon, I received the mission . . . to reconnoiter 50 kilometers into the desert to the south/southeast. Our hearts were beating in our throats. We were directed to go out into the desert by ourselves for the first time. It was all so very strange to us still, and it appeared to offer little in the way of orienting us . . .

. . . An unending expanse and a flat surface tempted us to go fast. But caution was required, since the small runnels formed during the rainy period dried out later on in the sun and became rock hard. They gave short jabs to the chassis and posed a danger to the shocks and springs. We made our first few unpleasant discoveries and drove more slowly: It was at the slower tempo that we reached our objective, a certain "nothing" in the desert, 50 kilometers south/southeast of the battalion. We did not encounter the enemy. There weren't even any wheel tracks, which might have indicated the presence of English vehicles.

By March, Schroetter and his men also participated in the first few engagements with the British that are generally recorded in histories of the campaign, the fighting around El Agheila, Marsa el Brega, and Agedabia:[14]

After the desert fort of El Agheila had fallen into German hands on 24 March 1941, the motorcycle infantry company of *Aufklärungs-Abteilung 3 (mot)* assumed the screening mission there. The armored scout sections were sent in the direction of Agedabia and into the desert to the south to reconnoiter.

During that time, *Panzer-Regiment 5* moved past us: Armored scout sections had reported enemy forces at Marsa el Brega.

There was no longer any talk of a "Blocking Formation," as the *5. leichte Division* had been referred to when it was sent to North Africa. Our small formation, the *5. Leichte Division*, now received its honorable nickname: "*Die 5. Leichtsinnige Division*" (The 5th Foolhardy Division).

The increasing resistance of English armored formations at Marsa el Brega was broken on 1 April by the attacks of the *5. Leichte Division*. The Marsa el Brega area was a bottleneck, extending 13 kilometers between the dunes arrayed along the sea and the salt seas [to the south] that were difficult to negotiate by heavy vehicles. While *Panzer-Regiment 5*, supported by *MG-Bataillone 2* and *8*, advanced further along either side of the Via Balbia, our armored scout sections chased away English patrols along the sea and in the dunes. The motorcycle infantry company of [the battalion] was employed in the area between the sea and the Via Balbia. Widely dispersed, we went on the hunt across the largely dry salt seas and engaged English pockets of resistance. Generally, the resistance was slight. The English infantry mounted up on trucks that had been prepositioned and pulled back to Agedabia. A few English trucks got bogged down in the salt flats in the process; the mounted infantry was captured . . .

After his initial period of acclimation, Schroetter describes the routine of reconnaissance in the desert:[15]

After their defeat in June 1941, the English pulled way back into Egypt. There was only a screen of armored reconnaissance sections left behind to observe.

For their part, the Germans also positioned armored scout sections to screen along the Egyptian-Libyan border. The two reconnaissance battalions, *Aufklärungs-Abteilung 3* and *Aufklärungs-Abteilung 33*, swapped out their scout sections arrayed in front of the strongpoints every 14 days.

The following areas were designated as observation points: Point Bir Nuh; Point 205 (Sidi Suleiman); Point 204; and Point 200 (Fort Sidi Omar)

The armored reconnaissance sections were assigned one of those points, from which they had to conduct constant surveillance to their front. Small raids were allowed, but the mission dictated that the sections were not to allow themselves to be driven from their assigned points: Observe a lot; if necessary, fight; withdraw quickly and agilely, so as to show up in the flanks or rear at some other point. The "standing patrols" were required to be able to give information concerning the situation to their front at any time.

During that period—the beginning of September 1941—I was transferred to the 2nd Company, the armored car company [of the battalion]. I took over a light armored scout section. It consisted of three light armored cars, each weighing 4 tons. Two vehicles were outfitted with a 20mm automatic cannon and a machine gun; the third vehicle, a radio car, had the necessary radio equipment (40-watt transmitter) and a machine gun. All of the vehicles had all-wheel drive, with the front axle capable of being disengaged. All four wheels could also be engaged for turning.

So equipped, the scouting section was very agile and capable of cross-country movement. It was also extremely fast. In soldier jargon, they were like rabbits: The vehicles were too fast up front and too short in the rear to be knocked out. As a result of the low silhouette, the vehicles "disappeared" in the landscape; they were especially difficult to make out at long range.

The crew in the vehicle with the 20mm cannon consisted of the vehicle commander (also the patrol leader in the first vehicle), a gunner and a driver. In the radio vehicle, the crew was a vehicle commander, a radio operator and a driver. The vehicle commander also serviced the weapon.

When the missions were assigned, my section was given Point 205, the house ruins at Sidi Suleiman. As far as Capuzzo and around Sollum, I knew the terrain well from my previous operations. Nonetheless . . . what could I expect there?

I was being employed for the first time as the leader of an armored scout section. As the leader of a motorcycle infantry platoon, I was always connected to the company. Now I was on my own and responsible for an additional eight soldiers, whose well-being was dependent on my actions.

I reported to the commander and departed, moving along the Via Balbia in the direction of Capuzzo, the desert fort that had been so hotly contested. From there, we went in the direction of Sidi Suleiman, our objective.

Sidi Suleiman, a set of house ruins on top of a jutting piece of high ground, was a distinctive terrain feature. When there was good visibility, you could see from Hill 205 far out into the descending plain to the high ground almost 10 kilometers distant. The English scout sections were positioned there.

The lead of the scout section being relieved briefed me on the situation. There wasn't much to be identified in the midday air that glimmered in the heat.

The English were on the high ground to the east and reconnoitered in the morning and the evening into the plains below. My predecessor recommended I do the same. He then disappeared to the west with his armored scout section, wrapped in a cloud of dust.

I checked out the immediate environment. We followed the tracks made by my predecessor. They provided information about his activities. In the light of the setting sun—it was to my back—I saw the clouds of dust being churned up by the vehicles of my English "colleague."

I ventured towards him, somewhat cautiously, since I still did not know the terrain.

At a distance of about two or three kilometers—not a great distance for Africa—we faced each other. The English armored cars could be made out quite clearly in the evening sun. They were vehicles of a type we had not yet encountered.

We observed one another, the vehicles widely dispersed.

But what was the man in the vehicle in the middle doing? It was most likely the section leader. All of a sudden, the Englishman stood up on his vehicle and waved to us. Those English were sure polite. Standing on my vehicle, I also waved a friendly "good night" to him. A few artillery rounds impacting in the vicinity soon brought us back to reality. As night descended, we each pulled back to our respective high ground, one to the east and the other to the west.

We set out outposts around Sidi Suleiman and transitioned to nighttime rest. The stillness of the desert spread out before us. Not a sound was to be heard. The pale moon weakly illuminated the terrain in front of us.

At first light—it was around 0550 hours—we crawled out from under our blankets. The vehicles had to be warmed up. There was nothing to be seen of our Englishmen. We searched the horizon in vain for them. It wasn't until around 0700 hours that we caught a glimpse of them on the eastern heights.

You could tell which scout section it was by the way they deployed. The one section leader kept two vehicles close together and positioned the third one somewhat off to the side. The other leader had his vehicles dispersed at exact intervals from one another. A third one kept two vehicles up front and the third one somewhat to the rear. Each of those sections received a corresponding nickname from us.

In the glimmering morning sun, which put me to a great disadvantage when observing to the east, we met in the plain. Once again, the Englishman stood on his vehicle and waved a friendly "good morning" to me. I replied in kind. Once again, there were artillery rounds in the vicinity, followed by a withdrawal by both sides to their respective high ground.

In the heat of the day, observation was very limited by the glimmering air. It took a trained scout's eye to make out the three enemy armored cars in the mirage. The camel thorn bushes, which had taken on the appearance of "woods," had three thin fir trees spiking out of them.

All of a sudden, an artillery round landed in Sidi Suleiman. Thank God we had always avoided that distinct feature during the day.

But who was that single round intended for? It was a single round . . . nothing followed. By chance, I looked at my watch. It was exactly 1200 hours, noon . . .

We couldn't figure it out. From that time forward, we received that single round every day at the same time.

It goes without saying that the English took pains to prevent our forces from getting a glimpse into the area south and east of the general lines they occupied. As a result, our scout sections were frequently faced by three or more English patrols. As already described, the English often employed forward observers to direct the artillery employed behind the reconnaissance veil. Whenever reinforced patrols of the Germans advanced, the line of English scout sections would pull back like a wire screen. The enemy would then defend with artillery fire and self-propelled antitank guns, which were attached to the (English) scouts. They were also supported by low-level attacks by English fighters.

My first 14 days at the front as the leader of an armored scout section came to an end. It had been marked by mutual suspicion and lurking, by morning and evening "greetings" to one another that we both participated in and by the noontime impact of a single round on Sidi Suleiman.

Unlike the European theater, scouting sections frequently conducted operations at night:[16]

Late in the afternoon of 17 December [1941], we were positioned with three scout sections in an area marked by high plateaus, deep defiles and flat wadis. It was an extremely broken piece of terrain in the area around Signali, south of Derna.

Aufklärungs-Abteilung 3 (mot) had the mission to occupy a new position far to the west in the vicinity of Mechili. A battle group left behind by the Battalion Commander had withdrawn from its delay position and was on the march in that direction. Widely dispersed, only our armored scout sections were holding the position. All around us, we identified advancing English vehicles. Truck columns, increasing in number, advanced in our direction. It was a sign that the enemy was feeling confident. We were already in danger of being bypassed when the order to withdraw reached us around 1700 hours. It was both a surprise and a relief. We assembled and moved out to the west through a wadi. The three armored scout sections had a total of nine 4-wheeled armored cars. Moving along the Tregh Enver Bey, we reached a plain around evening that offered good visibility.

As the evening sun was setting, we suddenly saw a column of English vehicles, tanks and artillery, crossing our path ahead of us. They were moving from south to north.

At first, we hoped that they were captured vehicles, but a radio inquiry to battalion revealed that we had English in front of us!

We debated what we should do. Should we wait until the enemy formation had moved further north? But it did not appear to be continuing its march. We could also see that additional units were closing in. We thus decided to wait until it was night and then attempt to break through. We observed the enemy formation, which had halted in the meantime. Around 2200 hours—the moon had not yet risen—we started to move out, one scout vehicle behind the other, nose to tail, in an effort not to lose contact with one another. We tensely paid attention to the vehicle in front of us. On the first vehicle, I was positioned on the fender in order to give the direction and direct the driver. On the other fender was my radio operator, who was supposed to reply to any challenges by English guards.

In the course of that night march—the drivers could hardly see their hands in front of their faces—the vehicles had to tolerate a lot. They bounced over gravel and piles of rocks. The drivers had to hold the steering wheels firmly in their hands. The commanders of the individual vehicles observed the route and the terrain from their turrets.

"A little more to the left . . . a little bit more . . . now some to the right . . . now straight . . . slow . . . just a tad left . . ."

So went the night.

We slowly snuck up to the resting English column. We saw the first few tanks and trucks in front of us. A guard called out to us. The answer my radio operator gave appeared to satisfy him. They didn't appear to think there were any German soldiers in this area.

We got through the first "enemy contact" successfully. But we were still worried: Did everyone make it? Did a vehicle lose contact?

We were surprised that there was no enemy resistance. Didn't the English realize what was happening? A column of armored vehicles certainly had to stand out! They seemed to feel safe, and the darkness of the night helped us on the one hand not to be discovered, even if it made life difficult for us on the other. We carefully and slowly pushed our way through the English vehicles that were all around us. We passed by the small tents that had been set up for the sleeping crews and went by artillery pieces, tanks, trucks and antitank guns. It wouldn't be too long, it seemed. The massing of the vehicles was decreasing. We approached the outer edge of the English march column. None of the English guards had heretofore expressed any suspicions. It was not until the last vehicle of our column had left the English formation and was headed west, when one of the guards had second thoughts and fired a signal flare in our direction so as to better see who was "taking a Sunday drive." We had reached the open desert by then and disappeared into the night, when some rounds were fired in our direction.

All alone on the battlefield, the scout sections often charted their own destiny. Initiative, confidence, and tactical ability were all in great demand when separated by great distances from the main body of friendly forces or defensive lines:[17]

We soon encountered English patrols in that terrain, terrain that practically invited you to play a game of "Cat and Mouse." The fact that they were there was determined from the vehicle tracks.

As a scout section leader, who had participated in uninterrupted operations for several months, you not only got a sense for terrain but for tracks. The depth, to which the tires of the vehicles had pressed into the ground, the degree of blowover from the sand and the direction of the tread of the tires told us who, when and in which direction the tracks had been left. The tracks we saw came from English armored cars that had to have passed through there that morning. We needed to be careful! The English could still be nearby.

Soon we were receiving enemy machine-gun fire from a *dschebel* [hill, derived from the Arabic] in front of us. Seeking cover behind another plateau, we tried, for our part, to get behind the English. The hunt on the plateaus had started. Sometimes, we suddenly saw the enemy in front of us. He appeared to be lurking for us around a corner. Other times, he was suddenly to our rear. We chased each other around the plateaus, engines racing and constantly being on alert. But neither party could deliver a decisive blow, even though a few machine-gun rounds ricocheted off the armor of my armored car.

Our mission required that we shake off the English. They lost sight of us.

Aufklärungs-Abteilung 3 (mot) moved back west through that mess. For my part, however, I received the mission to reconnoiter to the east and into an area 20 kilometers southeast of Agedabia.

We were happy to get out of the chaos of columns and determine our own fate. Nothing was worse for the men of an armored scout section than to have to fight as part of a formation or to march in a column. We were used to executing missions based on our own decisions and responsibility. We were the "individualists" of the battlefield.

In the end, those types of operations took their toll on the men and equipment, a precious commodity the Germans could ill afford to lose:[18]

It was the 5th of February, 1942. *Aufklärungs-Abteilung 3 (mot)* was 20 kilometers south of Derna. The rain and an icy storm from the north forced us to crawl into our vehicles. We thought back wistfully: A year ago on that day, we had rail loaded in Berlin-Wannsee in order to head out to Africa.

What all had become of our once so proud *Aufklärungs-Abteilung 3 (mot)* in the meantime! How many comrades had we already lost?

We sat there: Exhausted, overexerted, chilled to the bone, burnt out, unwashed, no mail for a long time, rations that came from our enemy and in uniforms that were half German, half English and the occasional Italian item tossed in. The majority of us had long since lost any personal property; almost every one of us had either had his vehicle shot out from under him or had it burn out. Many no longer had any headgear or shoes. They ran around in sneakers . . . they wore berets or Arabic fezzes. But, in their core, they were still German soldiers. A saying was coined: "The German Army is fighting in Russia; the Fire Department in Africa."[19]

The experiences and lessons learned by soldiers and scouts in other reconnaissance battalions was similar, as evidenced in this passage from the unofficial history of *Panzer-Aufklärungs-Abteilung 33* discussing operations around Sollum in the summer of 1941:[20]

Patrols
Every patrol demanded a sense of responsibility, situational awareness, concentration, adroitness, inventiveness and, of course, courage. This was true not only of the armored patrol leader, but also from the crews of the vehicles. That also applied to the standing outposts that had been established by the motorcycle infantry and, in general, for every soldier of the battalion. Along the front at Sollum, the patrols regularly remained in contact with the enemy for several days, after which they were relieved by another patrol of the company. That was the rule while the battalion reported directly to the *DAK*.

Unteroffizier Trebi was employed as a patrol leader at Bir Nuh. He had only recently been given this type of mission for the first time. His patrol consisted of an 8-wheeled radio armored car (*Sd.Kfz. 232*) and two 2cm vehicles (*Sd.Kfz. 222*). Nothing was happening around Bir Nuh, but that didn't mean that combat preparedness could be allowed to falter. That was especially true during the evening hours, when the clear air that predominated then allowed better observation. Before it turned dark, every patrol got ready for the night. That was what we did, and it probably wasn't much different among the English. All of the personal belongings that had found a place off the vehicle in the course of the day had to be stowed again. In general, they were fastened to the outside of the vehicle, so as not to cramp the interior. When fighting, that was advantageous for the crew. Getting ready for the night didn't mean that all the work was done. Out of necessity, a small change of position was undertaken. If you didn't do that, it bordered on punishable foolhardiness. After all, the English knew where our patrols had been positioned during the day. Their positions hadn't remained hidden from us, either. During our evening changes of position, great stress was placed on keeping the new position hidden from the enemy. Of course, the outpost was not abandoned during the night. Otherwise, there was danger that you would then find the enemy there the next day. We got confirmation every morning that the enemy was still there. In general, he sent a salvo of artillery our way. The patrol had nothing to respond with. It was also not allowed to get involved in combat activities without express orders. This is, of course, unless there was an emergency situation that left no other choice but to fire.

Trebi's patrol was relieved by *Feldwebel* Lüdtke. On the way back to the battalion, one regularly passed by an area that was no-man's-land. There was no continuous front line at Sollum, after all. That was especially true for the forward outposts. They were kilometers apart from one another, and they had no visual contact to one another. At nighttime, it would have been possible for enemy movements to take place without ever catching wind of them. The only thing that would have been noticed was the sound of motors. On Trebi's return to the battalion, *Gefreiter* Kothy saw an aircraft in the distance that had landed. It had not been there the previous day. Trebi started steering towards the aircraft, along with the other two vehicles. At the same time, they saw two English scout vehicles distance themselves from the aircraft. They apparently had intended to take possession of it. The patrol pulled up to the aircraft, an Italian Fiat fighter. There was no sign of the pilot. Trebi, who had been an aircraft design engineer in civilian life, soon figured out what was wrong with the machine. After fixing the jammed-up oil line, Trebi thought the aircraft capable of flying again. It was soon hooked up for towing and taken to Upper Sollum. The Italian pilot was also soon found in the desert. The scout crews had possibly saved his life, since he might have died of thirst otherwise. Trebi turned out to be right. The machine could be repaired in Upper Sollum. It then took off along the coastal road, steering a course for its home airbase.

It most certainly was not a heroic deed to save the Italian comrade. It went without saying that one would come to the aid of an allied force that was in a difficult situation.

The other major armored reconnaissance battalion in the desert war was *Aufklärungs-Abteilung 580 (mot)*, which initially started operations in the desert as *gemischte Aufklärungs-Kompanie 580 (mot)*. A scout assigned to the unit, Otto Henning, recounted his experiences in his memoirs:[21]

<u>Our Armored Car Section</u>
We had already been in position in an outpost with our two 8-wheeled scout vehicles for three days. The terrain was hilly and broken. One of us was always on watch; because of the heat, we spotted each other every hour. The other scouts dozed apathetically; barely a word was spoken. Only the radio operator had a tough go of it; he had to sit at the box.

Our mission on patrol had less to do with fighting and more to executing the assigned screening mission and passing on reports to our battalion, the division and the field army in a timely manner in an effort to avoid unpleasant surprises on the part of the enemy and enable quick countermeasures to be undertaken. The mission changed, of course, depending on whether advancing forward or moving to the rear!

It was hammered into us as recruits during basic training that we were the eyes and ears of the division. We had to memorize the catchphrase of the scout: Who had seen whom, what, where and how.

The 8-wheeled radio armored car of our patrol leader had a large frame antenna and an 80-watt transmitter with a range of about 150 kilometers, if there was good terrain and weather conditions. Both the radio car and our vehicle had a radio set, the so-called "vehicle-to-vehicle voice set," which had a throat microphone and a range of about 8–10 kilometers. During my time in Africa and also, later on, with the *Panzer-Lehr-Aufklärungs-Abteilung*, we never used it while on patrol. It would have cramped us considerably, if we had needed to dismount in a hurry, what with all of its wires, rubber-cushioned headphones, throat microphone and talk switch on our chest.

Ever since first light we had been posted at another sector of the southern front as a "standing patrol." We approached the familiar location on a small rise with extreme caution. Likewise, about 3 or 4 kilometers away, an English patrol had set up shop. We immediately notice that a different patrol was there that day. They did things differently from our old friends. "Billy," the name we gave to the scout who brewed the tea, had always immediately started preparing it. The crew there seemed unsure of themselves and kept us under watch for a long time. But, after a while, they started to set up for the day.

Young officers in engineer units, who came to us from Russia, wanted to have mines emplaced there, whenever the patrols headed out for the night. Our company commander, *Oberleutnant* Kettler, and the other patrol leaders never would allow that. I never once heard of either German or English patrols engaging the enemy in such an underhanded manner. After all, there were plenty of other opportunities to beat our heads bloody with grenades and bombs. Nonetheless, we were always careful in the morning in moving to our location and always carefully scrutinized the terrain to see whether there had been any changes. You never could know what was going on in the heads of the fellows on the other side, and an extra ounce of caution is always appropriate in wartime!

The day started out slowly. The sun rose in the firmament, and the air flickered above the ground due to the heat. The hot wind sent dust devils across the desert, and their funnels reached up into the light blue skies. We were no longer able to see the enemy patrol in the distance due to the shimmering heat. It was not until evening, when the visibility was better, that we make out our counterparts on the other side again. Once again, there was an unbelievable heat, and we thought back wistfully to the time we were being reconstituted at El Daba. We had a slight breeze from the sea there, which brought with it some cooling effect from the Mediterranean. The torture started at 0900 hours and did not let up until 1800 hours. No one wanted to move, and we crawled under the small shelter half we had attached to the side of the vehicle. If you sat there without moving, you could see how the beads of sweat built up on the arms and legs and, after reaching a certain size, ran down, catching other beads of sweat and then forming small rivulets on your limbs. It stayed moist between your fingers and toes; once mixed with sand, it formed inflammations. Your shirt and trousers rubbed on your skin, with the result that you were always scratching. It was probably no different with the Tommy outpost across the way. In their case, however, they had more fruit and, most importantly, mineral water on hand. We slowly got ready to depart and started stowing our things. We also saw some movement on the other side as well, and the vehicle commanders scrutinized one another through their binoculars. Finally, we heard the command *Marsch!*, and we took off to our battalion. Once there, we topped off, grabbed some rations, received mail and, most importantly, took 40 winks, since we had to be at the outpost again with our patrol before the sun rose!

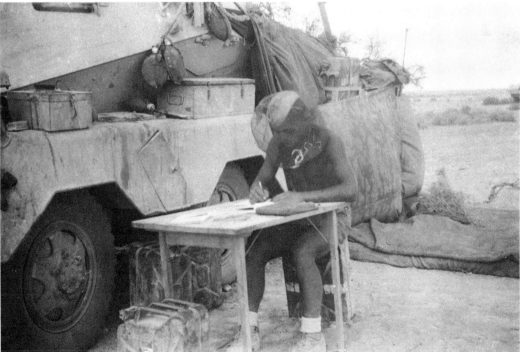

A scout has stripped down to shorts and shoes in an effort to beat the brutal heat of the Mediterranean Theater. The outsides of vehicles such as this *Sd.Kfz. 221* sometimes became hot enough to fry an egg. The crewmember wears netting to protect him from the constant plague of flies that seemed to follow the soldiers around in the desert. Based on the terrain, this image was probably not taken in North Africa. The next four candid shots show the crew of an unidentified scout unit resting, relaxing, and answering nature's call next to their *Sd.Kfz. 232 (8 Rad)*. Even in the middle of nowhere, soldiers were required to use a shovel to bury their waste, at least when the watchful eyes of a senior noncommissioned officer or officer were present. The fuel cans marked with large white crosses were used for carrying potable water, a precious commodity once away from the coastline. Regardless of location, most of the wells contained salty water, and a variety of elaborate methods were employed by soldiers in the field to eliminate the saline taste. LAST FOUR IMAGES: DAVE WILLIAMS

This *Sd.Kfz. 231 (8 Rad)* with a slightly mottled desert camouflage scheme—green on desert yellow—has been attributed to *Sonderverband 287*, which had an armored scout company, *Panzer-Späh-Kompanie 287*.
AKIRA TAKIGUCHI

This unidentified reconnaissance officer, a German Cross in Gold recipient, stands with a map well in front of his *Sd.Kfz. 232 (8 Rad)*, perhaps in an effort to get his bearings. In the barren landscape, small rises in the ground and the occasional manmade feature such as a well were decisively important in pinpointing locations on a map. Compasses were often used to set a general direction for a column, with frequent halts necessary to dismount and take a bearing; this had to be done some distance from a vehicle in order to avoid its magnetic interference.
JIM HALEY

A scout stands atop his *Sd.Kfz. 221* in order to gain a better vantage point for observing. This vehicle is unusual since it has had a radio installed, as evidenced by the antenna on the side of the turret.
NATIONAL ARCHIVES

Although a song intended for tankers, "Panzer rollen in Afrika vor" was also popular among scouts and reconnaissance soldiers and even printed on postcards intended for distribution through troop canteens.

Panzer rollen in Afrika vor

Worte von einem unbekannten Soldaten

Musik von Norbert Schultze

Über die Schelde, die Maas und den Rhein
stießen die Panzer nach Frankreich hinein.
Husaren des Führers, im schwarzen Gewand,
so haben sie Frankreich im Sturm überrannt.
    Es rasseln die Ketten . . . es dröhnt der Motor . . .
    Panzer rollen in Afrika vor!
    Panzer rollen in Afrika vor!

Heiß über Afrikas Boden die Sonne glüht.
Unsere Panzermotoren singen ihr Lied!
Deutsche Panzer im Sonnenbrand
stehen zur Schlacht gegen Engeland.
    Es rasseln die Ketten . . . es dröhnt der Motor . . .
    Panzer rollen in Afrika vor!
    Panzer rollen in Afrika vor!

Panzer des Führers, ihr Briten habt acht!
Die sind zu eurer Vernichtung erdacht!
Sie fürchten vor Tod und vor Teufel sich nicht!
An ihnen der britische Hochmut zerbricht!
    Es rasseln die Ketten . . . es dröhnt der Motor . . .
    Panzer rollen in Afrika vor!
    Panzer rollen in Afrika vor!

These grainy video captures were taken from the weekly German newsreel and show elements of a reconnaissance element, most likely from *Kradschützen-Bataillon 10* of the *10. Panzer-Division* since that is the only division in North Africa where the armored personnel routinely wore collar tabs on their tropical uniforms that were normally intended for wear on the black *Panzer* uniform.

CHAPTER 6

The Campaign Against the Soviet Union: Barbarossa Unleashed

SETTING THE STAGE

Feeling confident in the abilities of his armed forces after a string of unprecedented victories, in December 1940 Hitler formally announced his intent to invade the Soviet Union, with a planning date of May 1941 for the start of *Unternehmen* Barbarossa, the code name for the offensive. In doing so, he violated his own principles of not allowing Germany to be involved in a two-front war. Nevertheless, he sensed weakness on the part of the Western Allies and perceived no immediate threat emanating from them. He also felt the Soviet Union would topple like a house of cards, and that a calculated risk could be taken. Instead, the campaign that would cause "the world to hold its breath" turned out to be an immense strategic mistake, despite a series of decisive operational victories at the start of the war.

After a delay caused at least partially by the fighting in the Balkans, the attack order was given on 22 June 1941. Massed along the Soviet-occupied Polish zone and the frontiers of the Soviet Union was the largest concentration of forces the world had ever seen, including virtually all of the armored formations of the German Army and the *Waffen-SS*. The idea was to conduct a war of maneuver along the entire front, with the *Schwerpunkt* of the offensive in the center under the overall command of *Heeresgruppe Mitte*. The Germans were matched by a roughly equivalent number of troops but, as in France, outnumbered in totals of aircraft, armored vehicles, and artillery. In some cases, the Soviets' numerical superiority was immense—around fivefold the number of tanks and other armored fighting vehicles and sevenfold the number of aircraft.[1]

Sd.Kfz. 263's of a reconnaissance battalion churn up huge clouds of dust on an unimproved Soviet road during the rapid advance in the summer of 1941. JIM HALEY

Germany's armored forces were able to make significant gains from the onset of the offensive, partly due to the ill-advised forward positioning of the majority of the Red Army's combat forces, a move that has caused some historians to question whether Stalin was planning his own attack against Germany and her allies. Regardless, that disposition of forces; the virtually complete surprise achieved when the attack was launched; the destruction of much of the Red Army Force's tactical fleet on the ground; and the slow and inept response, starting with the commanders in the field and moving up the chain-of-command, led to unprecedented ground gains and a relatively quick breach of the Stalin Line. Victory seemed to be within grasp as the summer wore on, but a series of operational detours, especially the encirclement that led to the decisive victory at Kiev, deprived the Germans of the opportunity to take Moscow before the onset of winter weather, which proved to be the unhinging of the campaign in 1941. Funneling in fresh reserves from the East, Stalin was able to launch a counteroffensive that sent the Germans reeling for the first time and almost led to the destruction of a major portion of the German Army. The German Army would be able to recover and establish a winter defensive line, but its "nimbus of invincibility" had been shattered, with corresponding negative effects on German morale.

DOCTRINE

Although the military entered the conflict with some trepidation, based on the enemy's order of battle and the vastness of the terrain, it initially applied the same formula it had used in the past with unprecedented success. This worked well during the initial weeks of campaigning, when the Germans' martial reputation preceded them, but problems soon began to surface that would haunt the Germans for the rest of the war in the East. While not complete, this list addresses the major tactical issues that confronted the German armed forces on the ground:

- The topography of the Soviet Union varied widely, with vast tracts of forested terrain in the north proving to be essentially unsuitable for armored operations, while the harsh climate and vast distances of the steppes in the south accelerated wear and tear on combat and tactical vehicles of all types. While the center section of the Eastern Front had terrain features similar to Continental Europe, it had waterways approximately every 25 kilometers that could not be crossed without existing suitable infrastructure or engineer assistance, coupled with expansive forests and marshland.
- The transportation infrastructure was completely inadequate for fielding a modern army. The Soviet railway system used a different gauge than the European system, necessitating the conversion of track in order to transport supplies, logistical support, and reinforcements to the front by rail, and its capacity was further limited by long stretches of single rail. More important from a tactical perspective was the complete inadequacy of the road network, with only a few roads corresponding to the common "improved" roads of Western Europe. Most were of hard-packed dirt or gravel that quickly turned into dust bowls after just the first combat elements passed. Whenever it rained, they turned into rivers of mud. Likewise, bridges usually did not have the carrying capacity for most heavy military vehicles, having been constructed for light farm traffic.
- While the average Soviet soldier was initially poorly led and showed little to no initiative, he was stoic and stubborn in the defense, willing to lay down his life, even in hopeless situations. This was a new experience for the German soldier, who had been accustomed to foes who either surrendered with little or no fight or at least knew when there was no use in carrying on a struggle. The Soviet soldier also adapted well to life in the field, willing to forego creature comforts and endure hardships that were unfathomable to the average German soldier.
- The sheer numbers of men and materiel also came as a shock to German forces in the field. The Soviets had seemingly inexhaustible supplies of men, whom they were willing to commit no matter the cost. While the armored vehicles initially encountered were no match for the Germans—they were poorly led, committed piecemeal, and had hardly any radio capabilities—their sheer numbers proved daunting, and the

introduction of vastly superior tanks that summer—the vaunted T-34 and the KV series of vehicles—could scarcely be countered by German weaponry.

The above affected the entire force in the field, forcing changes in tactics for reconnaissance and motorcycle infantry forces. Initially employed to exploit penetrations along the frontier, the reconnaissance forces conducted deep reconnaissance, flank guard and screening missions, movements to contact (in cases where only slight resistance was expected), and long-range patrols. Increasingly, reconnaissance forces formed the advance guard for the armored formations, a mission for which they were also ideally suited, especially due to their excellent radio communications capabilities. In such cases, they were almost universally augmented with other combat arms in support—divisional engineers, artillery, antitank elements, and, of course, tanks or assault guns.

Since Soviet forces frequently allowed themselves to be bypassed, only to attack follow-on forces or strike advance-guard elements in the rear, reconnaissance elements found themselves fighting more than doctrinally conceived. In such cases, the limitations of the battalions' striking power often came painfully to bear, as the Soviets employed increasingly powerful weaponry against which the organic resources of the German reconnaissance or motorcycle infantry battalions were of limited utility.

Given the extended distances that supply elements and logistical forces had to cover as the advance penetrated ever deeper into Soviet territory, reconnaissance assets were also frequently employed as convoy escorts, since their speed allowed them to keep up with wheeled vehicles and their armament was usually enough to counter any rear-area threat.

By the time the fighting culminated outside the gates of Moscow, the reconnaissance and motorcycle infantry battalions had been severely depleted, resulting in the trend to consolidate both battalions into one, while still retaining the designation of *Kradschützen-Bataillon*. As the German Army was forced back during the first Soviet winter counteroffensive, it suffered tremendous losses in both men and materiel. Peacetime training for the German Army had not stressed large-scale retrograde operations and, coupled with the unusually severe winter, the lack of adequate winter clothing and a disastrous logistical situation made necessity the mother of invention. It was here that the reconnaissance assets often excelled. Due to their organic "combined arms" structure, they could perform economy-of-force missions, deception operations, and rearguard functions, often employing a combination of all three. In such a capacity, they could provide breathing room for other forces to pull back, regroup, and restructure their defense. Those types of operations took their toll, particularly on irreplaceable seasoned small-unit leaders, but they allowed the German forces to survive the first winter on the Russian Front.

ORGANIZATION

As mentioned above, the divisional armored reconnaissance and motorcycle infantry battalions started to consolidate in late 1941. The results of these consolidations and the implementation of new battalion structures and *KStN's* will be discussed in the next chapter.

At the start of the campaign in the East, it can generally be said that:

- The motorized armored reconnaissance battalions of the armored divisions were redesignated as armored reconnaissance battalions (*Panzer-Aufklärungs-Abteilungen*).
- The armored reconnaissance battalions of the armored divisions were not redesignated, remaining as *Panzer-Aufklärungs-Abteilungen*.
- The reconnaissance battalions of both the armored and motorized rifle divisions were reduced across the board by one armored scout company (largely to compensate for the rapid expansion of the armored force and inadequate production of armored reconnaissance vehicles).
- In the armored divisions, the motorcycle infantry battalions were assigned to the rifle brigade headquarters, with the latter bearing the numerical designation of the division (e.g., *5. Schützen-Brigade* was assigned to the *5. Panzer-Division*).
- In the motorized rifle divisions, the motorcycle infantry battalions were lumped together with the motorized rifle regiments, but there was no intermediate headquarters as in the armored divisions.

ORDER OF BATTLE FOR BARBAROSSA, 22 JUNE 1941
(MAJOR RECONNAISSANCE ELEMENTS)

Parent Organization	Reconnaissance Assets / Notes
Replacement Army (Army High Command Reserves) En route to the East on 22 June 1941. Scheduled to arrive in July 1941.	
5. Panzer-Division	Panzer-Aufklärungs-Abteilung 8 and Kradschützen-Bataillon 55. Armored reconnaissance battalion organized with *KStN's* going into effect on 1 February 1941: Headquarters (*KStN 1105*) with attached signals platoon (*KStN 1191*); one armored car company (*KStN 1162*); one motorcycle reconnaissance company (*KStN 1112*); one heavy company with headquarters (*KStN 1121*), antitank platoon (*KStN 1122*), light infantry gun platoon (*KStN 1123*), and combat engineer platoon (*KStN 1124*). Motorcycle infantry battalion organized with *KStN's* going into effect on 1 February 1941: Headquarters (*KStN1109*), three motorcycle infantry companies (*KStN1112*), one motorcycle machine-gun company (*KStN1118*), and one heavy company (organized the same as an armored reconnaissance battalion).
2. Panzer-Division	Panzer-Aufklärungs-Abteilung 5 and Kradschützen-Bataillon 2. Same organization as above.[2]
60. Infanterie-Division (mot)	Aufklärungs-Abteilung 160 (mot) and Kradschützen-Bataillon 160. Same organization as above.
Heeresgruppe Nord ***Panzergruppe 4 Reserves***	
SS-Totenkopf-Division	The division had an armored reconnaissance battalion but no motorcycle infantry battalion. Each of the three motorized infantry regiments, however, did have a motorcycle infantry company organized under *KStN 1112* of 1 February 1941. The reconnaissance battalion had a relatively unique organization: There was no armored car company; instead, there was a motorcycle infantry company. The two motorcycle infantry companies were organized under *KStN 1111a* of 1 October 1938. The battalion heavy company had not only the standard array of antitank, light infantry gun, and combat engineer assets, but also a mortar platoon (*KStN 1126*) and an armored car platoon (*KStN 1137*) (both dated 1 February 1941).
XXXXI Armee-Korps (mot)	
6. Panzer-Division	Panzer-Aufklärungs-Abteilung 57 and Kradschützen-Bataillon 6. Same organization as above.
1. Panzer-Division	Panzer-Aufklärungs-Abteilung 4 and Kradschützen-Bataillon 1. Same organization as above.
36. Infanterie-Division (mot)	Aufklärungs-Abteilung 36 (mot) and Kradschützen-Bataillon 36. Same organization as above.
LVI Armee-Korps (mot)	
3. Infanterie-Division 3 (mot)	Aufklärungs-Abteilung 53 (mot) and Kradschützen-Bataillon 53. Same organization as above.
8. Panzer-Division	Panzer-Aufklärungs-Abteilung 59 and Kradschützen-Bataillon 8. Same organization as above.
Heeresgruppe Mitte ***9. Armee—Panzergruppe 3*** ***XXXIX. Armee-Korps (mot)***	
7. Panzer-Division	Panzer-Aufklärungs-Abteilung 37 and Kradschützen-Bataillon 7. The armored reconnaissance battalion had two armored car companies, both equipped with French armored cars (*Panzerspähwagen Panhard 178(f)*), some additionally modified to serve as armored radio cars.
20. Panzer-Division	Panzer-Aufklärungs-Abteilung 92 and Kradschützen-Bataillon 20. The armored reconnaissance battalion had two armored car companies, both equipped with French armored cars (*Panzerspähwagen Panhard 178(f)*), some additionally modified to serve as armored radio cars.[3]
20. Infanterie-Division (mot)	Aufklärungs-Abteilung 20 (mot) and Kradschützen-Bataillon 30. Same organization as the 5. Panzer-Division above.
14. Infanterie-Division (mot)	Aufklärungs-Abteilung 14 (mot) and Kradschützen-Bataillon 54. Same organization as the 5. Panzer-Division above.
LVII Armee-Korps (mot)	
12. Panzer-Division	Panzer-Aufklärungs-Abteilung 2 and Kradschützen-Bataillon 22. Same organization as the 5. Panzer-Division above.
19. Panzer-Division	Panzer-Aufklärungs-Abteilung 19 and Kradschützen-Bataillon 19. Same organization as the 5. Panzer-Division above.
18. Infanterie-Division (mot)	Aufklärungs-Abteilung 18 (mot) and Kradschützen-Bataillon 38. Same organization as the 5. Panzer-Division above.

Parent Organization	Reconnaissance Assets / Notes
4. Armee—Panzergruppe 2	
XXXXVI. Armee-Korps (mot)	
SS-Reich-Division	The division had an armored reconnaissance battalion and a motorcycle infantry battalion, but they were organized slightly differently than their army counterparts. *SS-Aufklärungs-Abteilung "Reich"*: The same as a standard army armored reconnaissance battalion, but with its motorcycle infantry company organized under *KStN 1111a* (1 October 1938). In addition, the equivalent of two light platoons were taken from the armored car company in order to form standing reconnaissance companies within two of the division's motorized infantry regiments, *"Deutschland"* and *"Der Führer."* (The 15th Company of each of these regiments had an armored car platoon and two motorcycle infantry platoons.) *SS-Kradschützen-Bataillon "Reich"*: Its three motorcycle infantry companies were also organized under *KStN 1111a* (1 October 1938), and its machine-gun company was organized under *KStN 1116* (1 February 1941), using trucks as opposed to motorcycles to transport its weaponry (see below).
10. Panzer-Division	*Panzer-Aufklärungs-Abteilung 90* and *Kradschützen-Bataillon 10*. Same organization as the *5. Panzer-Division* above.
Infanterie-Regiment (mot) "Großdeutschland"	The reconnaissance assets of the regiment were contained in the 17th Company (4th Battalion). They consisted of a motorcycle infantry company organized under *KStN 1111* (1 February 1941) and an attached armored car platoon organized under *KStN 1137* (1 February 1941) (see below).
XXXXVII. Armee-Korps (mot)	
18. Panzer-Division	*Panzer-Aufklärungs-Abteilung 88* and *Kradschützen-Bataillon 18*. Same organization as the *5. Panzer-Division* above.
17. Panzer-Division	*Panzer-Aufklärungs-Abteilung 27* and *Kradschützen-Bataillon 17*. Same organization as the *5. Panzer-Division* above.
29. Infanterie-Division (mot)	*Aufklärungs-Abteilung 29 (mot)* and *Kradschützen-Bataillon 29*. Same organization as the *5. Panzer-Division* above.
XXIV. Armee-Korps (mot)	
1. Kavallerie-Division	The divisional reconnaissance asset was a bicycle reconnaissance battalion, but each of the horse cavalry regiments (*Reiter-Regimenter 1, 2, 21* and *22*) had a section of light armored cars, as did the headquarters of the *1. Kavallerie-Brigade* and the headquarters of the bicycle battalion.
4. Panzer-Division	*Panzer-Aufklärungs-Abteilung 7* and *Kradschützen-Bataillon 34*. Same organization as the *5. Panzer-Division* above.
3. Panzer-Division	*Panzer-Aufklärungs-Abteilung 1* and *Kradschützen-Bataillon 3*. Same organization as the *5. Panzer-Division* above.
10. Infanterie-Division (mot)	*Aufklärungs-Abteilung 10 (mot)* and *Kradschützen-Bataillon 40*. Same organization as the *5. Panzer-Division* above.
Heeresgruppe Süd	
6. Armee—Panzergruppe 1 Reserves	
16. Infanterie-Division (mot)	*Aufklärungs-Abteilung 341 (mot)* and *Kradschützen-Bataillon 165*. Same organization as the *5. Panzer-Division* above.
25. Infanterie-Division (mot)	*Aufklärungs-Abteilung 25 (mot)* and *Kradschützen-Bataillon 25*. Same organization as the *5. Panzer-Division* above.
13. Panzer-Division	*Panzer-Aufklärungs-Abteilung 13* and *Kradschützen-Bataillon 43*. Same organization as the *5. Panzer-Division* above.
Leibstandarte SS Adolf Hitler	As with the other *Waffen-SS* divisions, the *Leibstandarte* had anomalies in its organizational makeup. There was no motorcycle infantry battalion, and the armored reconnaissance battalion had an understrength armored car company equivalent[4] and two motorcycle infantry companies organized under *KStN 1111a* (1 October 1938). The heavy company was organized like its army equivalent.
III. Armee-Korps (mot)	
14. Panzer-Division	*Panzer-Aufklärungs-Abteilung 40* and *Kradschützen-Bataillon 64*. Same organization as the *5. Panzer-Division* above.
XXXXVIII. Armee-Korps (mot)	
11. Panzer-Division	*Panzer-Aufklärungs-Abteilung 231* and *Kradschützen-Bataillon 61*. Same organization as the *5. Panzer-Division* above.
XIV. Armee-Korps (mot)	
16. Panzer-Division	*Panzer-Aufklärungs-Abteilung 16* and *Kradschützen-Bataillon 16*. Same organization as the *5. Panzer-Division* above.
SS-Wiking-Division	The division had no motorcycle infantry battalion. Its armored reconnaissance battalion was organized like its army equivalent, except the motorcycle infantry company was organized under *KStN 1111a* (1 October 1938), as usually found in *SS* formations.
9. Panzer-Division	*Panzer-Aufklärungs-Abteilung 9* and *Kradschützen-Bataillon 59*. Same organization as the *5. Panzer-Division* above.

CHANGES IN ORGANIZATIONAL AUTHORIZATIONS (1 FEBRUARY 1941)

Motorcycle Infantry Company (1111)

The February 1941 version of the *KStN* represents no appreciable changes to the basic organization shown in Chapter 1.
- Headquarters: three motorcycles, one sidecar motorcycle, one medium cross-country wheeled personnel carrier (*Kfz. 15*), and one heavy cross-country wheeled personnel carrier (*Kfz. 18*).
- Machine-gun section: ten sidecar motorcycles and two heavy machine guns.
- Three motorcycle infantry platoons:
  - Headquarters: two motorcycles, one medium cross-country wheeled personnel carrier (*Kfz. 15*), and one heavy cross-country wheeled personnel carrier (*Kfz. 18*).
  - Three motorcycle infantry squads: three sidecar motorcycles, one motorcycle infantry squad, and one light machine gun.
  - One mortar section: two sidecar motorcycles and one 50mm mortar.

Motorized Machine Gun Company (1116)

This *KStN*, introduced on 1 February 1941, substituted trucks for motorcycles to transport its heavy weaponry.
- Company headquarters:
  - Headquarters: three motorcycles, one sidecar motorcycle, and one medium cross-country wheeled personnel carrier (*Kfz. 15*).
  - Two light telephone sections: one medium cross-country wheeled personnel carrier (*Kfz. 15*).
- Two heavy machine-gun platoons:
  - Headquarters: one sidecar motorcycle and two medium cross-country wheeled personnel carriers (*Kfz. 15*).
  - Two heavy machine-gun sections: two heavy wheeled personnel carriers (*Kfz. 70*) and two heavy machine guns.
- One mortar platoon:
  - Headquarters: one sidecar motorcycle and one medium cross-country wheeled personnel carrier (*Kfz. 15*).
  - Three mortar sections: one medium cross-country wheeled personnel carrier (*Kfz. 15*), two heavy wheeled personnel carriers (*Kfz. 70*), and two 81mm mortars.

Motorized Mortar Platoon (1126)

The mortar platoon of 1 February 1941 was substantially unchanged from its predecessor *KStN's* and had the following organization:
- Headquarters: one motorcycle and one medium cross-country utility vehicle (*Kfz. 11*).
- Three mortar sections: three heavy wheeled personnel carriers (*Kfz. 70*) and two 81mm mortars.

Armored Car Platoon (1137)

KStN 1137 of 1 February 1941 authorized the following for the platoon:
- Armored car platoon: one light cross-country utility vehicle, one 2-ton truck, four light armored cars (2cm) (*Sd.Kfz. 222*), and three light armored radio cars (*Sd.Kfz. 223*).

AFTER-ACTION REPORTS AND FIRSTHAND ACCOUNTS

As can be seen from the following quotations from the unofficial history of the *1. Panzer-Division*, the reconnaissance assets of the division were employed in fairly traditional roles at the onset of the campaign. On 6 July 1941:[5]

> The reinforced *Kradschützen-Bataillon 1* was able to expand its bridgehead in its sector that day without appreciable enemy resistance. *Kampfgruppe Westhoven* was pushed forward to Ostrow after midnight, with *Panzer-Aufklärungs-Abteilung 4* assuming the flank guard mission for the open left division flank in its place.
>
> 7 July 1941. Around 1300 hours, the *6. Panzer-Division* and the *1. Panzer-Division* moved out to attack north in the direction of Pleskau. *Kradschützen-Bataillon 1*, attached to *Kampfgruppe Westhoven* to cover its open left flank, took Pjudina and screened there. *Panzer-Aufklärungs-Abteilung 4* followed echeloned to

the left in order to guard the flanks to the northwest and the southwest.

During the same period, armored scouts were employed forward of the advance guard to determine enemy location and disposition:[6]

In a rapid advance, the advance guard reached Solovji. It should be noted that marshy terrain on both sides of the road hindered its advance in some places. At Solovji, armored scout sections of *Panzer-Aufklärungs-Abteilung 4* reported strong enemy forces advancing from the direction of Pleskau to the south. The *7./Panzer-Regiment 1* and the *2./Schützen-Regiment 1*, which were the point elements, were halted. They occupied positions at a crossroads north of Letovo, setting up an all-round defense.

The scouts were being used in a conventional way, serving as the "eyes and ears" of the lead elements in order to avoid surprises. Because the *1. Panzer-Division* was initially employed in the north, it encountered difficult terrain—forested tracts and marshland, coupled with a poor road network—before many of its counterparts to the south:[7]

During that period, the soldiers of both battle groups suffered greatly due to the poor roads and the terrain conditions. Even more oppressive was the heat. Without taking even that into account, 11 July 1941 had been a difficult day for the motorcycle infantrymen. In the engagements in the woods and along the advance route, it had to bring all of its equipment forward by foot, manhandling it. The enemy had heavily mined the woods and the roads.

But things were to turn worse for the brave battalion. Moving out again at 1445 hours, it reached Nowossjelje coming from the east, where it encountered enemy forces dug in up to their necks and supported by dug-in tanks and antitank guns. The village was already under fire from tanks and heavy weapons of the *SPW* battalion of *Schützen-Regiment 1*. While attempting to envelop Nowossjelje on both sides, the [battalion] slammed into an immediate counterattack being conducted by enemy tanks to the southeast. *Hauptmann* von der Chevallerie was killed at the head of his battalion. All of the company commanders were wounded, and many noncommissioned officers and enlisted men were lost. The battalion adjutant, *Oberleutnant* Huppert, assumed acting command of the battalion. After being reinforced by a section of the *1./Panzerjäger-Abteilung 37*, and the *11./Schützen-Regiment 1* (the infantry gun company), the motorcycle infantry battalion attacked again at 1900 hours. When that advance bogged down in the face of heavy fires from enemy antitank guns and numerous heavy machine guns, *Oberst* Westhoven ordered *Kradschützen-Bataillon 1* to occupy a screening line, adjacent to the *II./Schützen-Regiment 1*. The battalion dug in north of the advance route.

Against a determined foe who was dug in and possessed the will to fight, the motorcycle infantry had little chance unless they were supported by heavy weapons. Even then, as seen above, the results were not a foregone conclusion. Despite those setbacks, the morale of the force continued to remain high, since the average soldier was convinced he was superior to his enemy counterpart:[8]

As a result of the increased vehicular traffic flowing towards the Luga Bridgehead, the enemy increased his aerial attacks in the afternoon over the airspace of the division. The constant enemy air superiority weighed heavily on the nerves of the soldiers, but the leadership and the soldiers were able to put on a brave face. For instance, the commander of *Panzer-Aufklärungs-Abteilung 4*, *Oberstleutnant* von Scheele, radioed the command staff of the division at 1125 hours:
Der Russenflieger über uns viele,
sie suchen uns im Tiefangriff zum Ziele.
Wo bleibt Professor Messerschmitt?
Wir machen sonst hier nicht mehr mit!

After some back and forth:

Hurra, hurra, hurra—endlich sind mal Jäger da!

Leider keine Nazi-Flieger, alles Bolschewisten wieder![9]

The day-to-day routine of an armor scout and the inherent danger of reconnaissance operations are captured in this passage concerning operations of *Panzer-Aufklärungs-Abteilung 57* of the *6. Panzer-Division*, which was deployed in the north along with the *1. Panzer-Division*:[10]

It was a hard, tiresome and casualty-intensive fight, but it proceeded successfully—at least for the time being. The daily logs of the *6. Panzer-Division* give a glimpse of that in the radio messages from *Panzer-Aufklärungs-Abteilung 57* that were transcribed into plain text by the radio operators of the division headquarters. On 15 August 1941, the reports submitted by *Spähtruppe Krüger* reached the division:

"1745 [hours]. Location: 2 kilometers east of Prologi. Woods friendly artillery fire. Detouring to the west."

Spähtruppe Krüger was reporting in a succinct manner what was, in reality, a tense, life-threatening operation.

"1900. Kulznewo clear of the enemy."

Then . . .

"1955. Knjashewo occupied by the enemy. 2 enemy fighting vehicles. Locality under friendly artillery fire."

Then *Spähtruppe Krüger* fell silent. It was not until the following morning that the radio operators of the division command staff noted:

"0830. Woods 2 kilometers east of Treskowizy. Depression: Abatis with riflemen. Not possible to cross. Detouring north. 2 prisoners."

Krüger's soldiers were presumably tired, hungry and thirsty. They moved from one danger to the next. If a locality were occupied by the enemy, they encountered fire. If they approached a locality where there was not a single shot fired, then an antitank gun could be waiting for them in ambush, which would set the vehicles of the patrol alight from a distance, where it could not miss, and the crews would experience a horrible death. When entering a village it was possible that the men were moving into an ambush . . . the vehicles could run over mines . . . the crews taken prisoner. There were already rumors circulating at the time of what happened to reconnaissance personnel, who had been captured: Crucified on barn doors . . . beaten to death with hammers . . . bodies mutilated while still alive. The fear of being captured was often greater than that of dying . . .

"1130. Location: 100 meters south of Chimossowo. Locality occupied by the enemy."

An hour later: "1230. Location: Chimossowo. 25 prisoners. 1 heavy machine gun, 1 light machine gun captured. Tire damage on radio vehicle."

The *3. Panzer-Division*, deployed as part of *Heeresgruppe Mitte*, encountered similar problems to that of the *1. Panzer-Division* during its advance:[11]

The following elements of the tank regiment closed up. But there was no getting over the river in the dark night. *Generalleutnant* Model, who had ordered the attack on Brobruisk at 2100 hours, immediately ordered *Panzer-Aufklärungs-Abteilung 1* to reconnoiter south for a detour. The armored cars finally located a badly worn-out road. The columns then churned their way forward through the knee-deep sand. The route was marshy in spots; as a result, some of the wheeled vehicles became stuck. They could only be pulled out of the muck by means of prime movers and tanks. A small bridge broke under the weight of the trucks, but it could be repaired for the time being.

Despite the difficulties of the advance, there were still moments that recalled the glory days of the armored reconnaissance forces in France:[12]

Exactly 24 hours later, the enemy repeated the same attack. This time, he was able to break through the infantry lines. He encountered the *II./Panzer-Regiment 6* at Schesterowka. After hours of fighting, the enemy gave up, leaving behind 110 prisoners. *Oberleutnant* Klöber's tank company pursued the withdrawing enemy in the early morning hours, occupying Hill 203.8, where *Infanterie-Regiment 61* then dug in again for the second time in as many days. The *3. Panzer-Division*, the *4. Panzer-Division*, the *10. Infanterie-Division (mot.)* and the *7. Infanterie-Division* were all positioned south of the river and had driven a wedge into his front. The corps decided to capitalize on its advantage by launching a unified attack to the west. It was intended to tear open the Soviet front and cause it to collapse. On 7 August, the *3. Panzer-Division* committed a raiding party under *Major* Frank, which thrust through woods and marshland almost 100 kilometers into the enemy's rear area, where it blew up the rail line at Kletnja. The elements employed—*Panzer-Aufklärungs-Abteilung 1*, a company of *Panzerjäger-Abteilung 521*, a section of artillery and a platoon from the *3./Pionier-Bataillon 39*—all returned to the divisional area five days later. [6 August 1941]

The division's *Kradschützen-Bataillon 3* also enjoyed considerable success on occasion:[13]

Hauptmann von Cochenhausen's *1./Kradschützen-Bataillon 3* and *Oberleutnant* Lingk's *3./Panzerjäger-Abteilung 521* attacked Drjukowschtschina from the front. Despite considerable resistance, it was possible to enter the village, eject the Russians, capture two guns and six armored cars and take a number of prisoners. After the motorcycle infantry took a closer look at the Red Army men, they found out that they had captured the artillery commander of the 5th Army, Major General Ssetinski, along with his headquarters!
Most of the enemy forces were hiding in the two patches of woods and could not be driven out that evening. *Oberstleutnant* Wöhlermann's *II./Artillerie-Regiment 75* placed fires on the woods. At first light, *Hauptmann* Schneider-Kostalski's *III./Panzer-Regiment 6* and *Major* Pape's *Kradschützen-Bataillon 3* attacked the woods, while *Panzerjäger-Abteilung 521* and the *II./Panzer-Regiment 6* sealed off the area.
After five hours of struggling against stubborn resistance, the Russian defenses collapsed. The Soviets took considerable casualties. Fortunately, the German losses were negligible, although *Hauptmann* Schneider-Kostalski was wounded in the fighting. The motorcycle infantry of *Hauptmann* von Cochenhausen made a spectacular catch. When the soldiers searched the final portions of the woods for soldiers, who were hiding, a youngish, immaculately dressed officer came out of a hole in the ground. There were gold stars and two small gold-colored tin tanks on his collar tabs. It was the Commander-in-Chief of the Soviet 5th Army, Colonel General Potapow. [26 September 1941]

By November, the division's advance had slowed considerably, and it increasingly found itself fighting sharp engagements against an enemy determined to defend Moscow at all costs:[14]

On 13 November, the division ordered a *Kampfgruppe* under the command of *Oberstleutnant* Munzel to clear the bend in the Upa and block the western access roads to Tula. Munzel's battle group, consisting of the reconnaissance battalion, the three ad hoc tank companies, the *SPW* Company of *Schützen-Regiment 3* and the 5th Battery of the divisional artillery, combed the woods at Gorjuschino in extremely difficult circumstances. The temperature registered -25 degrees [-13 Fahrenheit]! It then crossed the high ground at Ugrjum and cleared the area of the enemy. The mission was already accomplished by noon, so that the battle group could be brought back to the combat outpost line, with the exception of the reconnaissance battalion, which continued to advance to the north and take the airstrip at Masslowo without encountering the enemy. The next day, a similar operation was conducted in the direction of Michalkowo. Four *Panzer IV*'s under *Leutnant* von Arnim and 12 motorcycles under *Feldwebel* Gradel (the

3./Kradschützen-Bataillon 3) started to enter the village. It was at that point that the small battle group encountered superior numbers of the enemy. Two fighting vehicles were lost to mines. *Oberfeldwebel* Ostwald, the forward observer from the 5th Battery, requested immediate fire support so that the battle group could pull back. At that point, the armor regiment was pulled out of the front and assigned to screen Jassnaja-Poljana again.

The *4. Panzer-Division* was also employed in the central section of the front. The following firsthand account is relayed by Ulrich Sachse, a platoon leader in *Kradschützen-Bataillon 34* at the time. He details the operations of the division in breaching the Stalin Line at Stary Bychow:[15]

Coup de Main on the Bridges Over the Dnjepr at Stary Bychow

For the fifth time since yesterday—when Detlev von Cossel's spearheading tanks were lost—the morning fog lifted up the steep riverbanks and spread across the ruins of Stary Bychow. The nighttime patrols returned from their activities from the unoccupied breadth of the riverbank area and occupied their positions back at the observation and firing ports, which had been bored into the walls of the east side of the huts overlooking the Dnjepr.

It was intended for the rifle regiments to force a crossing over the river with assault boats north of the city—and they did it. But it was out of the question to bring the heavy vehicles of the division through the bottomless marshland there. What was to be done? The road had been interdicted by the blowing up of the bridge and also rammed shut by the sheer impregnable defensive system beyond.

Impregnable?—*Oberleutnant* Rode, the Company Commander of the *2./Kradschützen-Bataillon 34*, took matters rapidly into his own hands. While he stormed down to the bridge at the head of a platoon, we took the firing ports of the field fortifications to the right and left of the bridge—which we had sighted on for days—under well-aimed carbine fire. There were no signs of defense as the commander and his men started their bold climbing over the ruins of the bridge. We followed, leaving the covering fire to our neighbors.

In the blink of an eye, it was swarming with *Landser* on the ruins of the bridge, who helped each other passing equipment along and got others across gaping holes. A small boat assisted in the process. Were the Russian obstacle guards gone or just asleep?

They woke up, but it was already too late. The first bunker-like positions had been eliminated with hand grenades. The bewilderment of the enemy in the face of the unexpected *coup de main* had apparently paralyzed them for the moment. Just sporadic defensive fires from the overrun Russians flared up. They barely disturbed the company advancing along the riverbanks.

The first group of prisoners, marching towards the ruins of the bridge, completed the confusion of the enemy. For a few moments, he may have thought they were an immediate counterattack by his comrades. But those few moments sufficed for *Feldwebel* Fritz Lützow to roll up in the dead space of the dangerous bunker north of the bridge. Lützow won the hand-grenade duel and, when the grenades blew up that he tossed back to the enemy, they succeeded in breaking into the position. The open terrain was crossed without casualties and even the second defensive line of the enemy was overrun.

The assault on the third line was broken off when the enemy was encouraged to launch an immediate counterattack. What happened along the road then demanded the full commitment of all the men at that location. *Oberleutnant* Rode headed straight as an arrow to the east with only one objective in his eyes: Taking the long wooden bridge over the marshland and capturing the arm of the Dnjepr, before the enemy could destroy it. Completely exhausted, he got there in just the nick of time to rip out the burning detonation cord before it could reach the demolitions.

At that point, it was imperative to reorganize the company in order to turn back the Russians' immediate counterattack. Just at that moment, our riflemen, the ones who had crossed the Dnjepr further to the north early that morning, also started to arrive from the east.

The bridges and the embankment were securely in our hands at that point. The tanks once again had an open road.

The *7. Panzer-Division* was employed along the northern wing of *Heeresgruppe Mitte*. In such cases, reconnaissance assets were often given the mission of not only guarding flanks but also maintaining contact with neighboring forces, assuming they were advancing at the same pace:[16]

Since the left (northern) wing of the division was still hanging completely in the air, *Panzer-Aufklärungs-Abteilung 37*, reinforced with a section of long-ranging 10cm cannon, was pushed to the north in an effort to deceive the enemy and place surprise fires from constantly changing positions on the depths of the enemy's area of operations, especially along the highway northeast of Jarzewo. The battalion, always terrifically led by *Major* Riederer, *Freiherr* von Paar, was able to significantly disrupt the introduction of enemy attack forces in the area around Jarzewo.

The division's reconnaissance assets were frequently used in direct combat roles, a situation that became increasingly common:[17]

In the southern sector of the division, the Russians had broken into [the German positions] at 0210 hours. The crossing points over the Wop were temporarily lost. The vegetated terrain favored . . . an unobserved approach of the Russian forces.

To clean up the situation, *Panzer-Aufklärungs-Abteilung 37* was employed under the personal leadership of the commander, *Major* Riederer, *Freiherr* von Paar, who distinguished himself through his circumspect leadership and personal bravery. At 0700 hours, *Kradschützen-Bataillon 7* reported that "the 1st Company of the battalion had taken the highway on the far side of the Wop in an immediate counterattack and the bridge was firmly in [German] hands." At the conclusion of the fighting on that day, *Panzer-Aufklärungs-Abteilung 37* was on the high ground south of the highway and "dominated the foreground." To that was added the fact that contact had been established with *Panzer-Regiment Rothenburg* and *Kradschützen-Bataillon 7*.

The following account concerns the first day of fighting by *Kradschützen-Bataillon 22* of the *12. Panzer-Division* in the area of operations of *Heeresgruppe Mitte*. It was written by Gerhard Möws, who eventually became the commander of the battalion, when he was still a motorcycle infantryman:[18]

22 June 1941. *Kradschützen-Bataillon 22* was in a staging area behind a clearing in the woods in the extreme outer tip of Suwalki–East Prussia. The Russians at the border were quiet. Morning was dawning. The clear crack of rifle fire whipped through the air ahead of us. Things came to life everywhere. The first hard bark of antitank and antiaircraft guns could be heard. The infantry in front of us took the bunker positions on the frontier. Siberians were in them . . . hard fellows. Bombers streamed above us towards the enemy. We were excited. Our attack objective was some 60 kilometers ahead of us: The bridge across the Njemen (Memel). We had been directed to hold it open and prevent it from being blown up. A messenger showed up: The bunker line had been penetrated.

The motorcycles were started. The lead sections raced out of the underbrush. Raffish figures squatted on the machines. The machine guns were ready to fire from their mounts on the sidecars. The riflemen had hand grenades in their belts and machine-gun belts slung over their shoulders. There were mountains of ammunition, smoke pots, mines and hand grenades in the sidecars. Who knew when we would see the trains and the ammo truck again.

I latched on behind the first squad. Vehicle-mounted *Flak* followed me. A cloud of dust enveloped us. The first prisoners approached us. Powerful figures with padded jackets. They had the typical Russian cap on their heads with the pointy top. We checked them out. No time, though. We had to move on . . . the bridge was our objective.

In front of us was a shot-up bunker. An 8.8cm *Flak* was in front of it. We passed by and took a short halt on some high ground. We oriented quickly and observed. Off we went! We were swallowed up by the sandy roads. Off to our right, a Russian machine gun bellowed. The rounds were already clattering from the machine gun in our sidecar. Get off the road; go around the next piece of high ground. It was between us and the Russians. Onward!

In the woods in front of us, the Russians were taking up positions. With a hand-and-arm signal, the motorcycles following us swung off onto some high ground. The machine guns from their section were soon whipping down on the enemy with their greetings. Our men were performing terrifically. It was like training; there was dash to it. We moved on. The *Flak* fired on the move. A cloud of dust marked our route. Russian infantry in trucks was moving off to our side. We took aim while moving. Complete confusion among the Ivans. There was no stopping; we moved on.

Also fighting in the center sector of the front under *Heeresgruppe Mitte* was the *18. Infanterie-Division (mot)*. The following three excerpts from after-action reports provide vivid accounts of combat operations conducted by the battalion. The first one concerns operations in mid-July 1941:[19]

On 13 July 1941, *Aufklärungs-Abteilung 18 (mot)* arrived in Saykowo, 3 kilometers south of Uskoje, in the afternoon. The village was cleared and the battalion assembled for further operations. *Leutnant* Meschkat's armored car section was sent in the direction of Uskoje with the mission to observe the road running Newel–Uskoje–Uswjaty. His report: Heavy vehicular traffic. *Kampfgruppe Proke* [two motorcycle infantry sections, an antitank gun, and a backpack radio section] received orders to disrupt the traffic and, in case of enemy attack of substantial proportions to pull back in a line towards the battalion. The battle group moved out at 1700 hours and reported enemy contact in Uskoje at 1925 hours. A short while later, there was another radio message: "Very unpleasant situation; disengagement from the enemy not possible."

The Battalion Commander, *Major* Sperling, received this message in Saykowo, just as he was briefing the Division Commander, who had arrived there, on the situation. The decision was made to attack Uskoje. To support the attack, an assault gun that had just arrived was directed to support the battalion. All immediately available forces and the assault gun were placed under the command of *Oberleutnant* Siegfried Schiller, the commander of the 2nd Motorcycle Infantry Company. Just before it turned dark, he succeeded in establishing himself as far as the bridge [in the village] with the platoon of *Leutnant* Reigber. *Leutnant* von Hagen's platoon, which had arrived by then, was employed in an enveloping maneuver to the left, in an effort to clear an isolated portion of the village and then move on from the flank against the church, its final objective.

On the way forward, the Battalion Commander ran into *Kampfgruppe Proske*, which was returning along a secondary route. It had been able to pull back by moving north and northeast. At 2100 hours, the Battalion Command Post was established on the high ground outside of Uskoje, in the former command post of *Oberleutnant* Schiller in a rye field. For the time being, *Leutnant* Konrad *Graf* von Hochberg's platoon was held in reserve.

Around 2230 hours, the adjutant arrived with directives from division to break off the engagement and to pull the battalion back to the high ground south of Uskoje. Based on the importance of the village for the continued advance of the division—dominance of the Newel–Uswjaty road—and based on the success already achieved against the hard-fighting enemy, the Battalion Commander decided to continue the attack under the cover of darkness. A few burning houses illuminated the battlefield on the enemy's side.

The reserve platoon was employed to reinforce Reigber's platoon. The concentrated fires of the assault gun and the infantry gun platoon were placed on the part of the village on the far side of the creek, especially the cemetery. At 2245 hours, Reigber's platoon was able to take the hotly contested bridge in the village. In that action, *Obergefreiter* Herbke, together with *Gefreiter* Roß, distinguished themselves by making a daring dash across the 20-meter-long bridge, enabling the platoon to continue operations in the next portion of the village and establishing contact with von Hagen's platoon. At first light and with the support of the assault gun, which had been brought forward, the enemy was finally ejected from the cemetery heights. The enemy pulled back into the vegetated terrain behind it and into the woods some 1,500 meters away. The fighting died down.

The slight casualties suffered during the bitter night fighting served to heighten the jubilation at the success. At 0320 hours on 14 July, the battalion was able to report to the division that the village of Uskoje was firmly in its hands.

Two platoons from *Kradschützen-Bataillon 38*, a battery from *Artillerie-Regiment 18 (mot)* and the remainder of the assault gun battery were then brought forward and attached to the battalion. They went into position in the village in such a way that they could take any tank attacks that might occur under fire. The battery was employed along the high ground to the southeast of the village in such a way that it could place fire on the vegetated terrain and the woods. There were large amounts of flour, butter and cheese that fell into the hands of the battalion, forming the basis for a hearty breakfast that was enjoyed after the fighting. Due to the lack of bread being supplied, some 600 loaves were baked by the next day in the bakery that was found in the village.

At 0645 hours that same day, the enemy fires came back to life. Heavy machine guns and some antitank guns that had been hidden and were well camouflaged in the vegetated terrain caused considerable disruption through their flanking fires. After taking a look at the situation, the Battalion Commander decided to organize a "hunt" to drive the enemy through and out of the vegetated area. An assault gun was directed to support each section. The guns fanned out of the village and stalked the area between the edge of the woods on the left and the open fields to the right. Surprisingly, two armored vehicles were caught and several machine guns and one antitank gun were captured. Peace and quiet finally settled in.

The second after-action report concerns operations conducted in late June 1941:[20]

Aufklärungs-Abteilung 18 (mot)
Russia, 13 August 1941

After-Action Report on the Engagement at Siedlisko on 27 June 1941

While at the Division Command Post during the night of 26–27 June 1941, the Battalion Commander received the mission to move out at 0600 hours from Hermaniski and advance through the wooded terrain around Siedlisko, move through Klewki and reach the Trokiele–Gieranony road. The battalion was to be reinforced with a battery from *Artillerie-Regiment (mot) 18* and a company from *Infanterie-Regiment 51 (mot)*. Reconnaissance was ordered for the time being as far as the line running Lipniszki–Bialozoryski–Subotniki. Three armored car sections

Leutnant Meschkat
Feldwebel Scheffler
Leutnant Dembowski

were sent out at 0500 hours, with the battalion following at 0530 hours. At Werenow, the Division Commander oriented the Battalion Commander on the exact situation. It was assumed that not only the battalion but also the reinforced *Infanterie-Regiment 51 (mot)*, advancing to the north, would encounter heavy enemy resistance. The reinforced *Infanterie-Regiment 30 (mot)* was still involved in heavy fighting to the area around Trokiele.

At 0730 hours, Scheffler's armored car section had its first enemy contact. As the result of two tire blowouts, it was right in front of the lead platoon. The weak enemy forces did not appear to be prepared for the advance of the battalion and withdrew immediately. The lead platoon remained mounted but on the heels of the enemy, who was fleeing in the direction of Siedlisko. It reached Siedlisko, disregarding the onset of individual fire from both sides. It intended to continue pursuing the enemy from there.

0745 hours. On the far side of Siedlisko, the platoon then started to receive such heavy machine-gun and mortar fire, that it had to dismount and deploy to attack along both sides of the avenue of advance. The platoon leader, *Leutnant* Reigber, who wanted to get a feel for the broken terrain and the enemy positions, jumped on board an armored car, whose weapon had jammed and was no longer functional, and moved to the high ground 400 meters southeast of Siedlisko. He was accompanied by the particularly plucky machine gunner, *Schütze* Langer. From there, he was able to observe the enemy positions in the wood line across from him. He was also able to take the enemy forces still withdrawing down the road under fire. By doing so, the lead platoon had successfully executed its mission, which was to prevent the withdrawing enemy from reestablishing himself. The platoon, which had taken its first casualties by then, moved out to attack the enemy forces, which were in improved field fortifications on both sides of the road. After tough fighting, it took the high ground 400 meters southeast of Siedlisko.

The fighting, conducted against the flanks and bridges of the enemy, went on for hours against enemy forces that seemed to come back to life. The platoon lost several riflemen and drivers, as well as the two attached armored cars (antitank guns). It was not possible to advance any further against the numerically superior and toughly defending enemy forces in the broken terrain. An antitank gun and a battery of light field guns were abandoned by their crews as the result of the rapid advance of the platoon. On the other hand, as a consequence of the large numbers of enemy antitank guns, it was not possible to use the armored cars, which had moved far ahead, to conduct an advance.

By then (0745 hours), the motorcycle infantry company, which was following the lead platoon, received heavy fires 2.5 kilometers northwest of Siedlisko. At that location, the company employed the platoon of *Leutnant Graf* von Hochberg, the machine-gun platoon and the machine-gun section to attack the enemy forces still firing out of Siedlisko and the patch of woods 1.3 kilometers north of the village.

Leutnant Günter von Hagen's platoon had not yet returned (0820 hours) from his mission of clearing the wooded terrain 4 kilometers northwest of Kondraciski (south of the avenue of advance), so that additional forces were not available to reinforce the 2nd Company and the platoon [at Siedlisko].

At 0825 hours, the Battalion Commander decided to employ the [attached] *9./Infanterie-Regiment 51 (mot)* and the battery of light howitzers against the apparently strong enemy force. The [infantry company] advanced on Siedlisko along both sides of the road. Right at the start of its operation, it lost its Company Commander, *Oberleutnant* Oddoy, by a round through the heart. *Oberleutnant* Galette's battery went into position 2.5 kilometers northwest of Siedlisko. It supported the attack from there, after first clearing the position of individual Russians.

At 0915 hours, the village of Siedlisko was finally in German hands after the personal involvement of the Company Commander and the section leader of the machine-gun section. By then, the platoon of *Leutnant* Konrad *Graf* von Hochberg, along with an individual infantry gun employed far to the front under the command of *Leutnant* Walter Felske, was involved in an attack against the patch of woods north of the village. There were heavy casualties. Once again, during this attack, there was repeated use of hand grenades. The platoon was prevented from advancing any further due to enemy fire from the east and the north.

1030 hours. After a lengthy attack, supported effectively by the infantry guns and the heavy machine guns, the enemy was finally driven from the patch of woods north of Siedlisko.

1100 hours. The platoon immediately faced to the right and engaged the enemy forces it then found on the wood lines east and northeast of Siedlisko. The infantry gun platoon and the machine-gun section were pulled out of their positions and sent to support *Leutnant* Reigber's platoon, which was still involved in heavy fighting. By then, *Leutnant* von Hagen's platoon had become available and was pushed forward to the right next to Reigber's platoon.

1050 hours. A liaison officer brought an order from the division to relieve the forces of *Infanterie-Regiment 30 (mot)*, which was attacking at Trokiele, by means of a deep flank against the enemy forces fighting there. In view of the current situation, the order had been overcome by events, especially since a disengagement from the enemy at that time could not occur without heavy casualties. A short while later, a radioed message was received from the division, which rescinded the order and stated that the original mission was still in effect. By then, von Hagen's platoon had reached its position to the right of Reigber's platoon, considerably relieving the latter force. The *9./Infanterie-Regiment 51 (mot)* plugged the gap between Reigber's platoon and *Graf* von Hochberg's platoon north of the village. The left flank of *Graf* von Hochberg's platoon continued to be engaged along its left flank, until the reserve platoon of the *9./Infanterie-Regiment 51 (mot)* arrived there on order of the Battalion Commander.

1040 hours. The Battalion Commander ordered the attack not be continued. Instead, the terrain taken and the village of Siedliske were to be held.

1102 hours. The Russians launched an immediate counterattack after a short preparation with machine guns and mortars. A few groups of infantry were supported by tanks. The engineer platoon, which had heretofore been held in reserve, as well as all available drivers, radio operators and messengers (under the command of *Leutnant* Ernst Korsawe) prepared a blocking position in front of the Battalion Command Post.

1140 hours. The counterattack, which was not conducted under unified command, was reported to the division as finally having been driven back. The firefight continued with undiminished intensity and brought with it some individual casualties. The battalion's success rested primarily on the verve and dedication of *Oberleutnant* Siegfried Schiller's well-led and plucky 2nd Company, which was supported during the entire engagement by the infantry gun and antitank gun platoons, which were located far forward, and the machine-gun section, which put down effective fires.

1210 hours. Receipt of a radio message from the division stating that *Infanterie-Regiment 51 (mot)* was advancing on Siedliske from the north to relieve the battalion.

1230 hours. The relief effort by *Infanterie-Regiment 51 (mot)* made itself felt; rearward movements by the enemy were observed.

1400 hours. Contact established with *Infanterie-Regiment 51 (mot)*. The battalion also moved out to attack, but it was held up by the division and pulled out of the line by the division and placed at its disposal.

The final after-action report from the battalion concerns operations that were conducted toward the latter part of August 1941:[21]

When the reinforced battalion—the *9./Infanterie-Regiment 30 (mot)*, the *6./Artillerie-Regiment 18* and the *3./Pionier-Bataillon 18*—moved out from Babino at 0630 hours on 26 August 1941 as the division advance guard, the Battalion Commander was of the opinion that the employment of the division along the only available (and marshy) route through the woods was something that did disservice to a motorized division.

The battalion's mission, to take the crossings over the Tigoda at Mjenjewscha, could only be successfully executed if the enemy, who was retreating along the main road, was denied the ability to reestablish himself from the outset by rapid actions that came as a surprise. For that reason, a reinforced, combat-capable armored car section was dispatched 10 minutes ahead of the lead elements of the battalion. It was under the command of *Oberleutnant* von Cotzhausen.

The battalion, which in Russia had a 15–20 kilometer-an-hour higher rate of march than the ponderous main body of the division, was only able to advance slowly that day, since the route had not yet completely dried out after the last rainfall.

At 0925 hours, von Cotzhausen's section had a short firefight with some 20–30 Russians at the wood line east of Gerjady. The Russians immediately disappeared into the woods. At 1027 hours, *Oberleutnant* von Cotzhausen took strong enemy elements under fire at the entrance to the woods just south of Mjenjewscha and identified a rifle company, about 50 men on horseback, one artillery piece and a few trains vehicles. After a few bursts of fire from the 16 machine guns of the motorcycle infantry company, the enemy left the village, abandoned his gun and disappeared into the woods.

The armored cars advanced to the wood line and were able to capture two trucks there, while the motorcycle infantry company advanced immediately as far as the Tigoda. It was expected that a [road bridge][22] was there, but there was none.

The Battalion Commander was faced with the decision of whether to wait for the engineer company, which was still far to the rear, and form a bridgehead after a time-consuming crossing or follow the fleeing enemy with the main body of the battalion to take the crossing over the river at Tur at the same time as the enemy did.

The Battalion Commander decided on the latter course of action.

The motorcycle infantry sprang onto their motorcycles and chased the enemy into the woods. Six armored cars joined them. The Battalion Commander issued orders to form a weak bridgehead at Mjenjewscha, with six armored cars screening that village. The remaining personnel of the 1st Company were carried across the river by the engineer platoon of the battalion. The engineer company repaired a broken bridge and the attached infantry company was sent by foot in the direction of Tur.

When the Battalion Commander arrived at the edge of the woods south of Tur at 1230 hours, the motorcycle infantry company was conducting an aggressive attack in the direction of Melechowa and the railway bridge. It was being effectively supported by the six armored cars and the infantry gun platoon. Clearly assessing the situation, *Oberleutnant* Proske had employed two platoons to the right against the railway bridge and one platoon and a machine gun section against the village. The platoon on the left (Reigber) entered the village despite strong defensive fires, employing one squad in the direction of the ford and the remaining squads against the railway bridge. Initially, both von Hochberg's and von Hagen's platoons made good progress on both sides of the railway embankment.

The Battalion Commander employed an armored car section in screening the railway station and issued orders to the *9./Infanterie-Regiment 30 (mot)* to screen the right flank of the battalion to the right of the railway tracks with a platoon. The main body of the company was to latch on to the attack of the motorcycle infantry, echeloned to the rear and left, thus making the attack on the bridge by the former easier. By then, *Leutnant* von Jordan had reached the ford across the river with an armored car, where he assisted *Feldwebel* Eisner's squad in attacking enemy elements still on this side of the river.

Together, the motorcycle infantry squad and the armored car were able to destroy or capture 32 trains vehicles and take 45 prisoners. The enemy on the far bank of the river was in a deeply echeloned and very well-improved defensive position with thick wooden and earthen bunkers. These were immediately taken under effective fire by the infantry gun platoon leader, *Leutnant* Felske, who brought a gun all the way forward. At 1245 hours, an armored train coming from the rear area moved through the attacking motorcycle infantry company, firing wildly in every direction. The fires from the infantry guns and the main guns of the armored cars ricocheted off the armor of the train without any effect. The Battalion Commander was afraid that as soon as the train crossed the bridge, it would fly into the air. The motorcycle infantry followed closely behind, however, and its forward elements made it to the bridge. They were able to pin down the enemy forces running into their positions so effectively that they were unable to trigger the demolitions that had been emplaced. The first effort to take the 200-meter bridge failed and bloody losses were suffered. That meant that a thorough fire preparation had to precede the effort. The enemy attempted several times to push his demolition party to the bridge, but it was always forced back into its holes by bursts of machine-gun fire from the motorcycle infantry company.

By then, the Division Operations Officer had arrived at the command post. He stated he did not agree with the battalion's employment at Tur. He was of the opinion that an attack with a platoon on Tur to the left of the Tigoda would have been better than a frontal attack by the battalion. The Battalion Commander did not share that opinion, because

1. An attack going through Mjenjewscha would not have been able to exploit the success achieved there, thus allowing the enemy time to blow up the bridge and

2. Based on the available enemy situation, the villages to the left of the Tigoda (Kusino–Berjosowik–Shar) were also heavily occupied by the enemy and the taking of the bridge at Tur could only be achieved after those villages had been taken.

Since the battalion was too weak to do that and the taking of the bridge did not appear possible at present, it was decided:

1. To call off the attack for the time being.
2. To leave the main body of the battalion in its present positions.
3. To place the approaches to the bridge under strong defensive fires, thus preventing its demolition.
4. To reinforce the bridgehead at Mjenjewscha with additional elements of the engineer company.

In order to accomplish the last-mentioned requirements, the Operations Officer left the battalion and made his way to Mjenjewscha.

An enemy air attack at 1530 hours demonstrated once again the importance the enemy placed on this railway bridge. In the meantime, the division had also been promised an attack by close-support aircraft, which was also carried out to good effect at 1735 hours. The motorcycle infantry company was still involved in an intense firefight along the river and at the bridge; antitank guns and armored cars screened the railway station and the right flank of the battalion together with the engineer platoon, which had arrived in the meantime. The lead elements of *Infanterie-Regiment 30 (mot)* were in the process of crossing the river at Mjenjewscha bridgehead, in order to carry out an attack left of the Tigoda. In order to avoid unnecessary casualties, the Battalion Commander pulled back those elements of the motorcycle infantry company that were in the village, without jeopardizing control of the bridge and the enemy positions behind it.

When the enemy defensive effort appeared to diminish around 1905 hours, *Oberleutnant* Proske, who had been reinforced with a platoon from *Infanterie-Regiment 30 (mot)* in the meantime, asked once again for permission to feel forward against the bridge. When that was done, *Leutnant* Jähnel and a few of his personnel from the *9./Infanterie-Regiment 30 (mot)* succeeded in jumping across the bridge. The immediate counterattacks launched by the enemy were thwarted by fires from the motorcycle infantry company. *Leutnant* Jähnel, who had already lost five of his seven men, could not be reinforced due to the heavy fires of the enemy, and he was brought back around 2200 hours. Despite that, the demolition of the bridge could still be prevented from the near side of the river.

During the night, the strong attack by *Infanterie-Regiment 30 (mot)* to the left of the Tigoda slowly gained ground, with its effect being felt around 0300 hours in the sector of the battalion, since the fire being received from the village of Tur became weaker. When friendly forces were observed in the village at 0400 hours, *Leutnant* Reigber ran across the bridge with his forces, which received heavy enemy fire. At 0500 hours, he was able to establish contact with an assault detachment from *Infanterie-Regiment 30 (mot)* along the railway line.

That meant the mission of the battalion had been accomplished and the bridge was firmly in friendly hands.

Fritz Langanke, who later went on to receive the Knight's Cross as a platoon leader in the *2./SS-Panzer-Regiment 2 Das "Reich,"* was a crewman on a heavy armored car in the *1./SS-AA "Reich"* during the summer of 1941 and has shared his experiences in the following account:[23]

Armor Scouts—The First and the Last

The short break to rest in the area around Smolensk after the fighting in the Jelnja Bend was over, and the *"Reich"* Division started marching again effective 1 July 1941 to the south and the pocket battle of Kiev. Those more than 450 kilometers were among the most unpleasant that we had to take in the course of the war. Only a small portion of the route at the beginning was along improved roads; they were followed by standard Russian country roads and worse. Heavy rainfall, that intensified into intense storms, ensured that the columns were always strung out. The cross movements of other units considerably increased the difficulties. The intense storms were often accompanied by such strong winds that the rain almost hit the vehicles horizontally. One of those cloudbursts was so horrific that we had standing water on the floor of the hull of our 8-wheeled armored car, even though only the small driver's visions slots were open. You could no longer identify the road. You oriented yourself by the tracks of a number of vehicles that had run somewhat parallel to yours, thus widening the road considerably.

The vehicles in front of us and behind us could no longer be made out, either. Then there was a wave of lightning making it impossible for our front driver, Walter Schulte, to drive anymore and forcing the vehicle commander, *Unterscharführer* Brandt, to stop the vehicle for a while. Unfortunately, it was right in the middle of an intersection. After a while, someone started hammering wildly on the vehicle, and I opened the side hatch. An *Oberst* immediately stuck his head inside, yelled at the top of his voice and tore us a new ass. It was the commander of a motorized regiment of an armored division that had to cross our route of advance there. We then moved our armored car a short distance back to free up the road. In the process, I—radio operator and rear driver—was practically unable to make out anything and simply moved straight back into the deeply rutted muck. The Army unit was just as strung out as our column, and we had to wait a considerable amount of time, even though the *Oberst* was continuously stomping around in the mud and driving his men forward. He must have had vocal cords like piano wires, since the volume never abated.

Once the visibility improved somewhat, we took advantage of a slightly larger gap in the column of the rifle regiment and started out again. The vehicles of our company that were following had not yet closed up.

When the reconnaissance battalion reached the area around Awdejewka–Kloenki, we were employed from the march. (Our battalion, together with the motorcycle infantry battalion and the *"Der Führer"* Regiment had formed the first march serial of the division.) Larger-sized Russian forces were continuously attempting to break through across our line of march. Our section was sent to a small locality to support some motorcycle infantry. Right outside the village, we received heavy fire from automatic weapons, mortars and cannon. Large numbers of Russians could be identified along the edge of some woods about 300–400 meters from the locality. They attempted to break out over and over again. We immediately joined the firefight. We had barely fired off a magazine for the cannon, however, when we started receiving aimed fire from Russian tanks and antitank guns. That meant we had to change positions as quickly as possible. For a long time we then proceeded as follows: As carefully and as well concealed as possible, we moved forward next to one of the huts. We fired and then pulled back immediately, looking for a new firing position as soon as possible, before the [enemy] cannon could finish us off, since our armor offered us no protection. I don't believe that my radio traffic was interrupted at any other point in the war as much as it was that day by the command: "Move back!" But we were able to fix the Russians along the edge of the woods, even though they were increasing in number. Our situation reports must have impressed the battalion, since *Hauptsturmführer* Weiß, the commander of our 4th Company, soon appeared with the bulk of his unit. He had us brief him and then he brought his heavy weapons into position. The Russians were unable to get through; they must have taken heavy casualties.

It rained almost the entire night. Our vehicle had taken up an outpost position at one of the exits of the village. Wet, frozen and practically without sleep, we awaited the coming morning. When it turned light, we saw that the Russians had pulled back. They were going to try it someplace else. And we reconnoitered again, this time in the direction of Mjna.

On 7 September, elements of the *"Reich"* Division took the bridge over the Desna at Mokoschin in a *coup de main* and formed a bridgehead there. The next day, the division rolled across the bridge that had been provisionally repaired to the south, with the reconnaissance battalion in the lead. While crossing the bridge, our vehicle—"Hans Metscher" [Battalion Liaison officer in the recon battalion, KIA in France on 14 May, apparently while running over a mine in his vehicle]—had some bad luck. The cover over a shell or bomb hole broke just as we were moving over it and one of our wheels got jammed in the bridgeworks. We were blocking the advance. You can just imagine the friendly commentaries we were receiving from all sides. I jumped out and set up the jack to raise the wheel so that it could be propped up. Everything was going just fine when there was a loud crack. The beam, on which I had placed the jack and on which I was also standing, broke—undoubtedly already cracked from being hit earlier—and fell into the Desna along with our jack. I myself was just able to hold on and hung wobbling over the hole, until my comrades could pull me up. The wheel was even deeper in the hole than before. In the blink of an eye, several men from other vehicles were at the scene with vehicle jacks and lifters. Beams were brought forward and as many hands as the small area would allow pitched in.

Russian artillery fire, which occasionally sought out the bridge, helped add to our cheerful disposition.

That drive, which animated everyone, that matter-of-factness, with which everyone helped others, whenever it was necessary, even without commands or orders, that constant and effective solidarity, which played an important role in the tumultuous advance of the German Armed Forces, fills all of us with pride and deep satisfaction even today, looking back across those many years, unless, of course, he belongs to that odd and pitiful group of people who do not think much of military comradeship.

The next two days kept all of our patrols moving in wide-ranging reconnaissance in the direction of Pliski–Bachmatsch. They were only braked somewhat by another bout of heavy rainfall.

When returning from one of those operations, an almost tragic incident occurred. We were just moments away from directing aimed fire with all of our weapons into a unit of the *"Der Führer"* Regiment. The heavy rain allowed only limited visibility. All of a sudden, we found ourselves behind a few groups of infantry, which were marching in column ahead of us.

We thought they were Russians and intended to start firing. Fortunately, we still had our doubts and moved closer. When we did that, we discovered that it wasn't a Russian unit but *DF*. Moreover, some of the groups were more than half Russian at the time. That was in the summer of 1941, when thousands of Russians in the Ukraine were prepared to fight for a free Ukraine against the Bolsheviks and the Soviets together with the German Armed Forces. The memories of the millions of victims that the Ukrainians suffered, especially as a part of the forced collectivization of the agrarian economy and the eradication of the *kulaks*, was still fresh and painful in wide circles of the populace. It would be idle conjecture to speculate on what could have happened politically or militarily back then given that situation. But a participant in the Campaign in the East, who was employed in those sectors, cannot eliminate those facts from his memory.

At first light on 11 September, out armored car was positioned once again as an outpost at a crossroads. During the night, it had rained heavily once more. It was not only the countryside, but also the roads and trails that were as soft as pudding. As was usually the case during that time, we were wet, chilled to the bone and tired. We screened in the direction of Alepowka, when one of our patrols moved past us to reconnoiter.

Led by *Hauptscharführer* Ritt, an armored car patrol consisting of three 4-wheeled cars was sent in the direction of Alepowka (one cannon vehicle, one machine-gun vehicle and one radio vehicle). *Hauptscharführer* Ritt was a well-proven man. His most important action had probably been the combat patrol conducted against Puchowitsche at the crossing site over the Swislotsch. In the presence of all of us, in front of the bridge over the river, the Division Commander later stated that his armored car section had looked as though the entire advance guard had rolled through there fighting. We had participated in that operation with our 8-wheeled car.

In our outpost position, we crossed our fingers for our comrades, who were moving on to the next locality. Nothing was stirring at our position. After some time, an odd-looking group of marching men appeared from the direction that Ritt's patrol had taken. Initially, we could not figure out what it all meant.

They were practically unarmed and some of the uniforms were torn or even shredded to pieces. Two or three of them had to be supported as they walked. When they had gotten closer, we noticed that some of their faces had a bluish tinge. The first one we recognized was Wiggerl Holzapfel, whereupon we knew that the men of the patrol were coming back without their vehicles. The way Sepp Schwarz recalled it—one of the guys from Seeboden in the Carinthian region [of Austria]—the operation went this way:

Ritt's patrol had had the mission of moving to Alepowka and blocking the road there that led from Komarowkato Borsna, so as to prevent the retrograde movements of the Russians to the east. Initially, the approach route ran parallel to a wood line that was about 100 meters distant. Ritt, who was a 2cm armored car commander in addition to being the patrol leader (gunner was Schwarz and driver was Weinhofen), actually wanted to move along the wood line, but because of the mud it was impossible to leave the road. Occasionally, rounds could be heard fired and individual Russians could be seen, some of whom waved.

About 200–300 meters in front of the locality, the lead vehicle received antitank-gun fire. Because of the dreary weather, the muzzle flashes of the guns were easy to make out. The first gun could be eliminated immediately. But because the village was too heavily occupied by the enemy, the patrol leader ordered the vehicles to turn around. While turning, the cannon vehicle received additional hits in the turret and along the suspension. The vehicle was immobilized, and the crew had to dismount. The gunner and driver had only slight shrapnel wounds; *Hauptscharführer* Ritt lost a portion of one hand. All three of them jumped on Holzapfel's vehicle, which had already turned around and was moving back slowly. Ritt was to the left front, Schwarz behind to the left and Weinhofen behind and to the right. The antitank guns were no longer firing, but high-explosive rounds were bursting above the vehicles. During the turning maneuver, the radio vehicle, which was now in the lead, had had difficulties in decoupling the 4-wheel-drive and, as a result, was moving in a different wheel rut than before. The same was true of the machine-gun vehicle that was following it. Then there was a murderous blast. The vehicles tipped over to one side, and the crews, who had not been terribly affected by the blast, bailed out. They thought they had been knocked out by enemy fire. What had really happened was that they had run over a mine. When they had been moving forward, luck would have it that that had taken probably the only route that led past the mines. Because of the extremely deep mud, the second and third armored cars had followed so closely in the tracks of the command vehicle that they might as well have been on rails.

Out of the two other dismounted crews, only Holzapfel had been wounded to some degree. The crewmembers of the knocked-out cannon vehicle, who had all clung to the outside of the machine-gun vehicle, had taken a beating. Sepp Schwarz had seen how there was an explosion at the location of the radio vehicle, before all three on his vehicle flew through the air. In the process, he lost consciousness. When he recovered, he was lying in a water-filled ditch and felt that he had been wounded pretty bad. Next to him was *Hauptscharführer* Ritt. The explosion had torn off both of his legs and a portion of his lower torso; he was dead. After a while, Sepp Schwarz sat up and determined that he could still hobble away.

Comrade Jantsch came running back to help him. Later on, in the reserve hospital, a portion of the mine's igniter was taken out of a wound on his hip, which had not wanted to heal. The driver of the cannon vehicle, Weinhofer, who had been hanging on the rear right of the machine-gun vehicle, got a bad scare but did not get too badly hurt, since the mine went up on the left front wheel. He was able to return to the company from the main clearing station. Later on, however, Russia still became his undoing: He was killed there in 1943.

Even during that incident something came to fore that emerged so often within frontline units of the German Armed Forces, especially in the most difficult of situations: An unbroken attitude and the firm determination to return back to the unit and the fighting that was accepted as a matter of course. In our units there were only a few who did not live up to that. And so I remember that bunch from our company, who had been tossed about wildly from the mines. On that 11 September 1941 they emerged as silhouettes from the mist of the rain-saturated countryside, gradually took on shape and, free of all panic, marched back to their company, always alert and with their wits about them. Although battered about and, in some cases, wearing ripped-apart uniforms, their spirit, discipline and determination remained unbroken.

Alepowka was stormed that same day by grenadiers of our division.

It was not until the next day when a *Kfz. 15* ran across a mine as it moved between the two armored cars that the actual reason for the loss of the 4-wheeled armored cars became clear. When the reconnaissance battalion took up the advance to the south again, engineers were in the process of clearing that section of the road of mines. The division advanced on Priluki. Our thrust was clearly aimed at the heart of the pocket. The fighting was correspondingly hard. For our crew there was another important patrol which, curiously enough, I have never found in the pertinent writings. When the lead elements of the division reached Priluki, it was directed that a long-range patrol be dispatched to establish contact with an Army division advancing from the south. Our company commander, *Obersturmführer* Pötschke, personally boarded our radio-equipped 8-wheeled armored car to command the vehicle and the patrol. Together with two 4-wheeled cannon vehicles, we took off at first light (it must have been either the 16th or 17th of September.)

Obersturmführer Pötschke fired us up by emphasizing that we were embarking on an "historical" operation.

As small fish in a big pond, who were fully engaged each momentous day with their own activities and who were not familiar with the big picture, we had interpreted the company commander's remarks as meaning that our actions would bring about the first closure of the Kiev pocket. It was only until I read material after the war that I realize my assumption was false. Instead, it was a bold thrust to the south. We encountered Russian columns of all types, big and small, whose movement ran parallel to ours or ran into us or whose direction of march crossed ours.

No matter what direction we took, we always avoided contact with the enemy, except when it was necessary to force passage. We were able to score one major success. We discovered a Russian airstrip behind a broad field with grain sheaves on it. Firing with everything we had, we raced across the field and the strip and shot up a large number of machines that appeared ready to take off.

A little later on, coming down a slope, we ran into the Army reconnaissance patrol that was coming from the other direction, not identifying it until it was about 200–300 meters away. If I remember correctly, they were equipped with the older 6-wheeled armored car made by Büssing. I did not partake in the exuberant greetings that were exchanged. Based on what Pötschke was telling me as we got underway again—I needed to get my report out concerning the contact faster than my counterpart in the Army—a death by firing squad would be the least of my worries. But my own pride was enough to spur me on. I encrypted as though the devil were behind me and sent out my message. Correspondingly, I was done considerably earlier than my compatriot in the Army division. The experience impressed me so much that I took the radio operator's pencil, together with its retaining ring, which belonged to the basic items issued with the armored car, along with me as a memento when I went home on leave. I still have it in my possession today, even if its value is considerably less than I had thought for many a year, based on knowledge of the development of the Kiev Pocket. I am quite certain that if Pötschke had not fallen towards the end of the war as a *Sturmbannführer* and recipient of the Oak Leaves, that one would still be talking about that long-range patrol "officially." (That's how the knowledge of many an event from the war years gets and got lost when the main participant dies.)

When we returned to our own lines, we were witnesses to and participants in an event that most certainly was experienced by only a few German soldiers during the war. As I remember it, the day had remained rain-free and visibility was still good late in the afternoon. The terrain rolled gently, and a small slope blocked our view as we approached our own lines. We heard the loud sound of a Russian battle cry and the heavy firing of German weapons. We carefully moved into firing positions along the reverse slope behind the crest and felt as though we had been transported into times past. It was like the portrayal of a battle in a museum. In the depression in front of us was a road running across our front, which almost looked like a railway embankment.

On the far side of the embankment were our grenadiers, dug in. (I am no longer certain which regiment they belonged to but I think it might have been *"Deutschland."*) They were defending and oriented in our direction. On the near side, a fairly large Russian cavalry unit was attempting to break through. They had ridden to the road with drawn sabers. The heavy fires from the defenders had stopped them, and they then proceeded to ride parallel to the road at a gallop, probably looking for a weak spot. We immediately took off with our three armored cars in the same direction as the Russians, firing with everything we had. Trapped in the pincers, it was soon over for the cavalry unit. It remains unforgettable to me how the last 5 to 10 of them spun their horses around one more time and rode towards us with brandished sabers, the last men of their unit. With a "Hurrah!" on their lips, they rode to their deaths before the barrels of our cannon and machine guns.

All of us were deeply impressed by what had happened and were happy to leave the scene of the fighting, which could truly be called a field of slaughter.[24]

On the next day or the day after, we were on the go again to the east in the advance of the division on Romny, where the same fierce fighting awaited us.

Among the motorized assets fighting within the area of operations of *Heeresgruppe Süd* was the *16. Infanterie-Division (mot)*. The following recounts the first contact with enemy forces on 29 June 1941:[25]

On **29 June 1941**, elements of the division—with the exception of the combat engineers that had been detached to Sokal—had enemy contact for the first time. Dubno was being attacked hard. There was a battalion from the *11. Infanterie-Division (XV. Armee-Korps)* there, as well as trains elements of the *11. Panzer-Division*. *Arko 108* of the *XXXXVIII Armee-Korps (mot)* was the local area command. It appeared there was a threat of complete encirclement! Because of that, the corps ordered *Aufklärungs-Abteilung 341 (mot)* to be pushed forward. The reconnaissance battalion was reinforced with armor-defeating weapons: 2 5cm antitank-gun platoons, 1 platoon from the *1./Artillerie-Regiment 146* (10cm cannon) and 2 mixed *Flak* sections from the *IV./Flak-Regiment "General Göring"* (each with an 8.8cm *Flak*, a platoon of 2cm *Flak* and a platoon of 3.7cm *Flak*). In addition, there were combat engineers with mines. That same morning, another 10cm battery was attached to the [battalion], coming from the *II./Artillerie-Regiment 64* (field army asset). "There's nothing more to give!" That was the succinct entry in the order concerning the operation.

An armored car section from the division observed during the morning hours that enemy tanks were moving through the gardens in the western part of the city. That was the reason that the *111. Infanterie-Division* had "confiscated" the two 5cm antitank-gun platoons of the *16. Infanterie-Division (mot)* and provided them to the local area command for Dubno. But before the arrival of the *44. Infanterie-Division*, which was coming from the northwest, the local area command for Dubno was able to fend off the tank and infantry attacks. At 1000 hours, the *44. Infanterie-Division* reached Muravica. The antitank guns of the division eliminated two of the tanks that were knocked out by guns and mines. *Aufklärungs-Abteilung 341 (mot)* lost three armored cars to Russian tanks.

The enemy fought stubbornly and employed heavy tanks, KV II's, for the first time (against the reconnaissance battalion). As was often the case later on, the 8.8cm *Flak* proved to be the salvation against the Russian tanks, against which the 3.7cm antitank gun proved to be completely ineffective . . .

Hauptmann Borchardt, the company commander of the *1./Aufklärungs-Abteilung 341 (mot)*, wrote the following concerning his first combat operation in Russia, which is the one described above:[26]

During the very first few days [of the campaign] a couple of hundred Russian tanks were encircled in the woods around Dubno. My first mission—one that was to be carried out under my command—was to prevent their breakout to the north along a frontage of 14 kilometers with a weak battle group. I took 10 of my armored cars, 2 howitzers, a couple of motorcycle infantrymen, a couple of antitank guns and a battery from *Flak-Regiment Göring* with me.

A road ran parallel to the wood line [where the Russians were], about one kilometer away, on average. I divided the battle group into smaller sections in such a fashion that groups of two vehicles each could pull back into defensive positions, which first had to be reconnoitered. I had the battery set up in a position where I thought the attack would most likely occur. I sent the armored cars out ahead with the mission to remain at their reconnaissance objectives as standing patrols.

Everything remained quiet until noon. I then received a radio message from one of the patrols that it had encountered Russian tanks. The message stopped abruptly midway through. A couple of thin smoke columns rose a half-hour later from the area where that must have occurred. I feared the worst.

I took a couple of motorcycle infantrymen and a self-propelled antitank gun and moved to that location. After moving for half an hour in the direction of Dubno—where the sounds of a large tank engagement could be heard ever more clearly—I saw the three armored cars burned out when I crossed some high ground. Still smoking, they were about 800 meters away and in a path cut through the woods on the opposite high ground. It was but moments later when we started receiving fire from several Russian tanks that had been concealed in the bottomland. I personally had to lead the antitank gun out of the defile a few times to the hilltop in order to fire off a couple of rounds. It might as well have been a cardboard cutout on a stage; the rounds did not penetrate those tanks.

I decided that the minimum I could do was determine what had happened to the three crews. I took 8 men and a huge detour by foot around the Russian tanks through marshland and high corn. Arriving at the burned-out armored cars, I found two dead and three slightly wounded scouts, whom I was able to bring back. It was good that the people knew that their commander would not leave them high and dry, even in an apparently hopeless situation.

I got back to the defensive sector just in time to see a massed Russian tank attack come out of the woods on the left wing, where the *Flak* battery was positioned. In the next half hour, 44 tanks, some of them heavy ones, were knocked out. Some of them were engaged from point-blank range. The 8.8cm *Flak* and their crews distinguished themselves in a magnificent manner. As a result, the day turned out to be a total success. That evening, all of the elements that belonged to the reconnaissance battalion were withdrawn. The neighboring division assumed the sector, and we continued our march, going around the battlefield where the tank engagement had taken place.

The following is taken from the daily logs of the 1st Platoon of the *2./Aufklärungs-Abteilung 341 (mot)*, the motorcycle infantry company:[27]

29 June 1941. The battalion was alerted at 0130 hours. The advance was continuing on Dubno. We frequently encountered destroyed Russian tanks on the avenue of advance. They often showed up like specters.

The avenue of advance is literally riddled with antitank guns . . .

The reconnaissance battalion has been divided into three blocking groups, which have been reinforced with antitank elements, *Flak* etc.

The 2nd group guarded the command post at Bokujina. The 1st group established a standing patrol/tank early-warning element at a position 6 kilometers southeast of Bokujina. The 3rd group also functioned as a tank early-warning element east of Smortwa. At night, they were pulled back to perform local security at the location of the 10.5cm artillery.

The 2nd group reconnoitered as far as the palace at Smortwa around noon. Valuable engineer equipment, especially pneumatic craft, were secured; the Russians had left a lot behind. At night, the group pulled back to the avenue of advance. The platoon leader conducted a "solo" patrol to Prloza, which was reported as clear of enemy forces. He returned back via Walkowyjc and Rudka.

Three armored cars of the 1st Company (*Feldwebel* Beierl and *Unteroffizier* Arnold) were knocked out by Russian tanks southeast of the Klesyczcka collective farm.

Another passage from the daily logs of the 1st Platoon of the *2./Aufklärungs-Abteilung 341 (mot)* concerns the fighting in the same area:[28]

30 June 1941: Today, Blocking Group 2 was attached to the *44. Infanterie-Division*. The 1st and 3rd groups reoccupied their positions as tank early-warning sections. The 2nd group moved to the location where the three armored cars had been knocked out the day before.

The terrain in front of us rose to become a small hill, across which the road appeared to only be a defile. Broad fields spread out to the left and right on either side. Just before the peak on the right-hand side of the road—halfway in the roadside ditch—were a radio and a cannon car. A little bit further on, at the top on the left and in the roadside ditch, was an additional vehicle. In the middle of the road was a *Wehrmacht* truck with trailer. It probably had gotten lost. Between the truck and trailer was a dead comrade. We took a look at the armored cars. The radio vehicle appeared to have gotten off lucky; only one of the tires had been shot up. It was repaired relatively quickly. Because of its condition, the condition of the other ones made an even greater impression. The turret had been ripped off of the cannon vehicle. The machine-gun vehicle was slit open in the front.

We went about creating a final resting place for the comrade, who found his death there. The machine gunner on the machine-gun car told us what happened. (He had dismounted and worked his way back to the German front.) The patrol had been attacked after it had entered the defile by artillery to the front and a Russian fighting vehicle to the rear. Our vehicles turned and prepared to take up the unequal fight. After the cannon vehicle had been knocked out, there was nothing left to do but dismount. *Obergefreiter* Lanzersdorfer remained in the machine-gun vehicle in an effort to turn it around. He was unable to do that. The comrade knew nothing about what happened after that, since he had to get out of the danger zone with the Russians.

By then, we had dug the grave. Comrade Gärtner had made a simple wooden cross out of a birch branch. When we saw the ring on the dead man, however, we figured out that it could not be comrade Lanzersdorfer. He wasn't married! The ring had the initials "FB"—Franz Breit, the driver of the vehicle. He had run to the machine-gun vehicle to remove the machine gun. Where, then, was Lanzersdorfer? Despite the machine-gun fire, it was possible that he had managed to dismount.

After we had paid our last respects to our dead comrade, we moved back to the command post.

The route back led past the truck. *Leutnant* Hahn, our platoon leader, stopped. His attention had been drawn to the [black] *Panzer* uniform of the dead man lying between the truck and the trailer. The *Soldbuch* there had a name completely unknown to us. The dog tag indicated that it belonged to our unit. A notebook containing mail cleared everything up: Franz Krebs, one of ours! A brave comrade! He had attacked the Russian tanks with the machine gun he had removed from his vehicle.

With a few short but moving words, *Leutnant* Hahn honored the dead man.

The following accounts relate to the operations order in the sidebar. First, the editor of the book, Fritz Memminger, sets the stage:[30]

During the afternoon, the armored car company of *Aufklärungs-Abteilung 341 (mot)* determined

The following is a typical written order for the reconnaissance assets of a division for the period. In this case, it is from the *16. Infanterie-Division (mot)*:[29]

16. Infanterie-Division (mot)
Division Command Post, 1 July 1941

Operations Section
1540 Hours
TO: *Kradschützen-Bataillon 165, Aufklärungs-Abteilung 341 (mot)*

1. The march attachment to *Gruppe Eisermann* is no longer in effect.

2. In accordance with special orders, reinforced *Kradschützen-Bataillon 165* is attached to the *11. Panzer-Division*, along with one tank battalion from this division, to clarify the situation northwest of Ostrog at the railway bridge at Brodow.

3. Reinforced *Aufklärungs-Abteilung 341 (mot)* has the mission to reconnoiter the routes leading via Nowomalin to Kuniow and Kamionka and determine crossing possibilities at those villages.

4. Attached:
a.) *Kradschützen-Bataillon 195*: The *4./Artillerie-Regiment 146*; *3./Pionier-Bataillon 675*; 1 *Flak* section; 1/2 fuel section (attached only for march purposes)
b.) *Aufklärungs-Abteilung 341 (mot)*: The *3./Panzerjäger-Abteilung 228*.

5. The *3./Flak 9* returns to the command of the commander of the *IV./Regiment "General Göring"* for the time being. Based on special directives, it is to be employed at Hulca–Wierzchow with one gun in an antitank role and two guns in an air-defense role.

6. Division Command Post: Northeast entrance to Wierzchow.

FOR THE DIVISION COMMANDER:
Division Operations Officer
/signed/ Gundelach

that the embankment around the mill south of Kuniow was only weakly manned by the enemy. It forded the Wilja to the south with some of its elements. They were under the command of their circumspect, energetic and brave commander, *Hauptmann* Borchardt, who occasionally was up to his neck in water.

Hauptmann Borchardt takes up the narrative:

It appeared the next day that the entire corps had bogged down outside of Ostrog along the Wilja. It appeared that a crossing was only possible after hard fighting because of the large number of forces on the far bank that were prepared to defend. In accordance with my mission, I employed several patrols to the right and was personally ordered to the corps. The Commanding General showed me the situation and stated that I was to attempt to find a crossing point up to 30 kilometers upstream. I only took an engineer *Leutnant* and a couple of men with me and moved along a road that had previously been declared clear of enemy forces. At Kuniow, I linked up with one of my patrols, which had just received artillery fire from the far bank. It did not take too long before we also had to seek cover. Despite that, I did not think that the enemy forces on the far banks were very strong, and I decided to take a closer look into the situation and, if possible, to cross over to the other side immediately. As was the case with most of the operations that followed, the certain feeling that the elements of friendly forces that were following would not leave you high and dry played a role. You could still have that certainty back then. **You had the feeling that a bold move could rally the troops that followed to close up. It was the bold move that proved itself during the first phase of the campaign in Russia to be the most effective one; it also proved to be the one that resulted in the least casualties. That was the first thing that reconnaissance personnel learned.** [Emphasis added by the authors.]

I cobbled together every available man and then through the village and downhill. We exploited the long firing breaks of what we determined to be the only battery there by observing. Despite that, I received shrapnel from a nearby impacting round. One piece lodged in the back of my head and another in my upper arm. I was able to pull the former out after I had recovered consciousness. Since I could also move my arm, we immediately took off again. When we got to the last houses, we only received weak rifle and machine-gun fire from the far bank. But there was no time to lose. In a last spurt, we reached the vegetation along the banks next to a mill. As a result, it appeared we were in the dead zone of the battery. After thoroughly observing the far bank—the river was only about 30 meters wide—I got the impression that the forces there could not be all too strong. I decided to cross. We moved hand over hand along the weirs of the mill across the canal and then ran across a footbridge. Once over, we initiated fire on the withdrawing Russians. The Russians recovered in the course of the afternoon, and we had to fend off two weak attacks with the two machine guns we had, all the while lying in water up to our necks. I immediately sent a messenger back to the patrol we had left on the high ground and had a radio message sent that we had established a bridgehead (6 men), but that we needed reinforcements as soon as possible. It took all afternoon before an artillery fire support team arrived and asked where I wanted to have artillery fire placed. The lead elements of a rifle battalion also arrived behind the high ground. As it started to turn dark, two companies and some heavy weapons came forward. At that point, we could attack the village in front of us from our small bridgehead. It was occupied without taking too many casualties. I organized outposts all around and determined where the bridge needed to go in. I then gathered my scouts and withdrew, turning over the bridgehead [to the follow-on forces].

I had myself driven back, since the loss of blood and the concussion to the back of my head had weakened me somewhat. The Division Commander, *General* Henrici, received me at Nowomalin. Beside himself with joy, he presented me with his own Iron Cross, First Class. The crossing was of great importance for the corps, because similar crossing attempts that day and the previous day had resulted in the loss of almost an entire *Panzergrenadier* battalion at one place and a motorcycle infantry company at another. I slept at the division for the first time in many days and returned to my company the following day with fresh dressings. It was crossing the new bridges just as I arrived.

In this account, we hear from *Oberstleutnant* Eisermann, the commander of *Kradschützen-Bataillon 165*, as it experienced its first combat in the Soviet Union:[31]

During the early morning hours of 1 July 1941, *Kradschützen-Bataillon 165*, reinforced with a battery of artillery and a company from *Pionier-Bataillon 675*, was attached to the command of the tank regiment of the *11. Panzer-Division*. It was directed that the battalion, supported by a tank battalion from [the regiment], take the railway bridge in the Chorow area at Brodow and establish a bridgehead.

The battalion reached Chorow without encountering enemy resistance and staged there for its attack. It was a warm day in the middle of summer, and the cornfields, which were almost ripe, did not allow too much of the terrain, which was broken up by a lot of depressions, to be observed.

There was nothing to be seen of the promised tanks from the *11. Panzer-Division*. There still weren't any definitive reconnaissance results. It was under those conditions that the battalion moved out to attack, supported by the attached battery and its own heavy weapons. After just a few hundred meters, it received heavy fires from enemy artillery, antitank guns, machine guns and infantry weapons. The Russians, for their part, had also moved out to attack. They were supported by tanks. The enemy attack was brought to a standstill, but the friendly attack did not make much progress after about a kilometer.

Since the tall corn did not allow good observation from the Battalion Command Post, the Battalion Commander[32] went forward to the lead elements. Based on his impressions, the attack was halted, and the battalion transitioned to the defense.

The battalion's casualties during the aggressive advance were considerable. Approximately 50 soldiers of all ranks had been killed or wounded. *Oberleutnant* Krause fell at the side of his attacking men!

The brave motorcycle messengers earned special praise for their efforts. They not only transmitted messages and orders under enemy fire, they also brought up ammunition when they went forward and wounded when they came back.

As the result of immediate counterattacks that were supported by strong local concentrations of fires, the enemy was stopped again and again in the course of the afternoon and the friendly frontline trace was improved. Strong patrols along the marshy Horyn prevented a threat to our right wing. Other patrols, which had been dispatched along the left wing, identified enemy movements with tanks in the patches of woods to the west of Brodow. After the onset of darkness, combat activities on both sides abated.

Based on an inquiry to the *11. Panzer-Division*, the reinforcement of tanks that had not taken place that day was promised for the resumption of the attack the next morning.

In general, the night of 1–2 July passed quietly. When it turned light, patrols determined that the enemy had withdrawn during the cover of night and, in the final analysis, due to the energetically conducted attack of the battalion the previous day.

Combat patrols under the circumspect leadership of *Hauptmann* Brede and *Oberleutnant* Hellfritsch pursued. They surprised the guards at the railway bridge at Brodow on both the near and far sides of the river and eliminated them or took them prisoner. Elements of the attached engineer company checked the bridge for demolitions and participated in the securing of the bridge.

Other elements of the battalion followed and formed a small bridgehead in the course of the morning.

After the battalion had completed its mission without the support of the tanks of the *11. Panzer-Division*, [those same tanks] crossed the railway bridge taken during the afternoon hours and rolled to the southeast.

At that point, the battalion was released from attachment and, conducting a tactical march via Grozow, reached Novomalin with its lead elements around 2200 hours, where it was placed at the disposal of the division.

Memminger recounts fighting conducted by *Aufklärungs-Abteilung 341 (mot)* that same July:[33]

Based on the reports of *Aufklärungs-Abteilung 341 (mot)* and aerial observers, the division was convinced that the enemy forces in its sector—both motorized and horse-drawn—were withdrawing. A further advance, however, was dependent on whether the enemy forces in the Miakoty area could be ejected. To that end, *Infanterie-Regiment 156 (mot)*, somewhat delayed due to poor road conditions, moved out of the bridgehead on a broad front.

Aufklärungs-Abteilung 341 (mot) moved out very early from Dobryn towards Zaslaw. Shortly after it moved out, it was attacked in the rear by enemy forces supported by artillery coming from the north out of Miakoty. Initially, it was thought that they were friendly forces. The Russians had been able to approach unseen in the high fields. The reconnaissance battalion immediately turned around and initiated an immediate counterattack. The fighting lasted until the afternoon, before the battalion could report: "Enemy ejected. One battery destroyed!" More than 1,000 dead Russia soldiers were counted on the battlefield.

The prolific *Hauptmann* Borchardt has again provided a very vivid account of events:

> The following morning, Kleinschmidt, the Battalion Commander, committed five patrols to the southeast. It was intended that they reconnoiter the entire sector of the division. He then also departed with almost all of the remaining combat elements of the battalion in an effort to take a bridge. I was directed to pull forward with the remaining elements, when called. Towards 0800 hours, I heard the sound of fighting from the area we came from yesterday. At first, I didn't believe it, but after a short period, it was obvious that there was a real Russian infantry attack supported by artillery. I split up what I still had with me, had the vehicles in the village take cover and posted all of the trains personnel at the edge of the village. Soon I was in a really tight situation, however. The 8 remaining armored cars had to move back and forth among the houses and fire in between them. The Russians had closed to about 400 meters, and it wasn't just a couple of hundred of them. At that point, I took 4 of the armored cars and moved out of the village, hoping to attack the Russians in the flank from some side route. I had the vehicles filled to the top with ammunition. Concealed by a small rise, we closed unseen to about 500 meters of the first Russians. They were in the process of staging in a long valley to take the final pounce on our village. The place was swarming with them. We crossed over the small rise, and I had the vehicles fire into the massed Russians along the valley from the side with everything they had. They soon took heavy losses and pulled back. We followed them carefully. The other vehicles then came out of the village, moving cross-country. The Russians left behind a large number of wounded and dead on the battlefield. They were in full flight. I was relieved like never before that everything had turned out so well.

As the battalion advanced farther into the Ukraine, an unidentified account, probably from Borchardt, recorded more impressions:[34]

> The route continued to the southeast. Elements of *Aufklärungs-Abteilung 341 (mot)* were already in the middle of the Ukraine. The corn in the vast fields was almost ripe. The villages made a decent impression. There were hardly any men remaining in the villages; the women and children usually required a little time to trust the Germans. Tidy garden patches were planted around the houses. The little livestock gave the impression of not being tended well at all. It was not difficult to live off the land. Because of the great march distances and the constant reconnaissance, it was difficult to bring fuel and ammunition forward in sufficient quantities. It was also not easy, as *Hauptmann* Borchardt assured, to have 20 of 26 armored cars ready for duty the next day. In general, the issuance of orders often took almost the entire night, because each of the patrol leaders had to be summoned and given his mission, with the route and actions to be taken discussed in detail with help of the map. It required the greatest of care to ensure that casualties were avoided. *Hauptmann* Kleinschmidt, the admirable commander of *Aufklärungs-Abteilung 341 (mot)*, had to accompany the battalion every other day in an ambulance, since he suffered in pain from stomach ulcers. . . .
>
> The terrain seemed to be made for motorized forces. It was only when it rained that everything got hopelessly stuck in the mud, remaining wherever it was at the moment. A lot of critical situations had already occurred for the reconnaissance battalion, where the crews were unable to help one another whenever they were attacked individually. On the other hand, there had not been any fighting yet with lots of casualties. That was primarily because the men of the battalion stayed true to the essence of reconnaissance: They only attempted to identify determined enemy resistance and then they sought ways to bypass that enemy.
>
> To counter that, the Russians soon developed the tactic of allowing the advance guards to move past and then attempting to encircle and destroy them later. The only thing that helped in those situations was keeping your

cool and waiting for relief forces. Soon, however, the only leaders who dared to operate far to the front of their own forces were those who firmly believed that they would be relieved in an emergency.

In the final quotation for this chapter from Memminger, we again hear from Borchardt, who recounts his experiences while encircled during the fighting for Berditschew:[35]

On one of the first days of July, I received orders to fight my way through to the headquarters of the *11. Panzer-Division* at Berditschew with the combat elements of the reconnaissance battalion. It seemed the Russians were pressing the headquarters hard. Although we got through without any serious fighting, the Russians closed the ring of encirclement right behind us. The days that followed were among the most critical that I experienced in Russia. I was directed to go the western portion of the city and close the defensive ring in the direction of the airfield. The nights passed quietly for the most part, but the Russians regularly attacked in great strength during the early morning hours. In general, the Russian artillery fire was extremely well placed. As we later discovered, that was due to the fact that it was being directed from secret radio outposts in the city. They reacted immediately and without error whenever we shifted positions.

During the afternoon of the third day, a massive Russian attack, supported by a large number of tanks, took place in my sector and that of my neighbor. In the neighboring sector, the combat outposts surrendered to the attacking Russians in the open field. It was something I had never seen before and never saw again. When the Russians resumed their attack shortly thereafter, they drove the prisoners in front of them. A few of them were even bound to the tanks. My sector was so thinly held, that I had the machine guns removed from the armored cars and the crews dig in along the outskirts of the city. That afternoon, the two howitzers and pair of antitank guns that had been attached to me knocked out 17 tanks from so-called ambush positions. They allowed the enemy vehicles to approach to within point-blank range.

I had feared that we would have to allow ourselves to be overrun in our foxholes; a thought that did not set well with me. But that attack was also brought to a standstill. With an audible sigh of relief, the sound of fighting could be heard on the morning of the 5th day in front of my sector. It indicated that the ring was being broken open from the outside. We were right. An hour later, a friendly tank appeared on the rise in front of us. A German general was waving with his arm. He could be seen from far away. He appeared to be giving orders with hand-and-arm signals. Using my binoculars, I could tell by the red face that it was *General* Hube, the commander of the *16. Panzer-Division*.

I suffered real casualties for the first time in Berditschew, even though my own company got off quite well. We received a half a day of time for the rest of the battalion to catch up. We replaced our losses and prepared for operations. We moved out again the next day. *General* Crüwll, the commander of the *11. Panzer-Division*, had me nominated for mention in the Honor Roll of the Army for my part in the defense of the encircled city of Berditschew (22 July 1941). When I saw him later in Africa, he recognized me immediately and asked, whether I ever thought about doing Berditschew again. He laughed when I said: "Only if it's with you!" He was general who was always there where things were the hottest—like Hube.

Also fighting in the south was the *13. Panzer-Division*, whose *Panzer-Aufklärungs-Abteilung 13* submitted the following after-action report, dated 28 June 1941:[36]

The mission of *Panzer-Aufklärungs-Abteilung 13*, which had been reinforced with a motorcycle infantry battalion, an artillery battalion and another engineer platoon because of the importance of the planned operation, had it moving out of Luck at 0400 hours on 26 June, echeloned to the right of *Kampfgruppe Panzer-Regiment*, in order to take a crossing point over the creek south of Rowne and establish a bridgehead on the far side. As soon as the force moved out of Luck, it made enemy contact, which took considerable effort to eliminate, since the elements attached to [the reconnaissance battalion] had not yet shown up. Despite [the lack of those forces], the crew of a self-propelled antitank gun, which performed in an especially industrious and bold manner, together with a [towed] antitank gun, were able to eliminate the attacking Russian tanks. . . . Despite having participated in the campaigns in both Poland and France, the antitank platoon had never been in such a situation before. It solved the problem by means of the aforementioned "kills," which also strengthened the confidence of the other soldiers in those weapons. The successful opening to the operation provided impetus to even the most recent replacement, and everyone looked forward to the almost 100-kilometer route full of confidence. . . .

The advance was continued under the stinging rays of the sun and the desert-like dust.

It was around 1600 hours, when the lead elements received fire from a village, when they turned onto the road leading to Rowne. Following that, the lead company also started to receive fire to the flanks. The road had to be cleared before the advance could continue. The Battalion Commander sent a company from the motorcycle infantry battalion (*Hauptmann* Fau) to the front. The company received orders to attack the houses along the road, clear them and then start screening the flanks to the southwest, so that the reinforced armored reconnaissance battalion could pull forward.

Two antitank guns were also employed, after several enemy armored cars on the road supported the resistance of the Russians with their fires. Once again, it was the one self-propelled gun and the one towed gun. Moving stealthily along the side of the road, they destroyed two armored cars.

It was anticipated that [the enemy would] press further into that sensitive flank in very unfavorable terrain. The way to combat that danger: "Forward!"

By then, elements of the main body were engaged in combat with the enemy forces that suddenly appeared that had allowed the armored reconnaissance battalion to pass through. It proved difficult to disengage from the enemy; whenever he noticed our intention to do so, he grew more active.

The new terrain encountered along the main road turned more open and, as a result of the onset of evening twilight, new tactics became necessary. In addition to the two armored cars and the antitank guns employed in the spearhead, a cannon from the attached *II./Artillerie-Regiment 13* was also added. The order to move out was issued.

The [reconnaissance battalion] succeeded in reaching the road with all of its elements and then moving north at 30 kilometers an hour. All of a sudden, a signal was given: "Stop! Pivot sharply right! Tank danger to the right!"

There was no doubt. To the south, you could see dust, and you could make out seven giants rolling towards us. It was imperative to employ the antitank defenses skillfully, so that the enemy, no matter from which depression he surfaced, would be eliminated. The cannon, the self-propelled gun and the antitank gun, which were all concealed, let the Russian tanks approach. Ready to fire and trusting in their weapons, they were unflappable as they let them approach. The first tank went into position along the corner of a house. It was in the process of traversing its turret in the direction of the battalion, which could be identified by its dust on the road. Five seconds later, it was burning. The second tank was put out of commission by the cannon from the 5th Battery, which was personally directed by *Oberleutnant* Schröder. *Unteroffizier* Dittmann's antitank gun took out the third one. The next tank was again eliminated by the artillery cannon. An artillery prime mover that was moving between the tanks was taken out next. The remaining tanks attempted to save themselves through flight.

Hand-and-arm signal: "Mount up! Move out!"

It had turned so dark by then that the armored car moving up front could no longer identify anything through its optics. The self-propelled gun had to take over the lead, and the march continued.

Orders: "Clear the road!"

Another dark point—2 rounds. We continued on without stopping. Moving past, we observed two trucks loaded with ammunition and similar items. All of a sudden, there was fire up front: A Russian armored car! The self-propelled gun was a better shot. The enemy fire died quickly. Most of the battalion did not observe any of this, since we always kept on moving.

The day's objective could not be reached. The heat had put a lot of wear and tear on the machines; even the good road did not make it easier for the motorcycles.

There was an attempt made to establish contact with the armor regiment, which was supposed to be not too far from us further to the north. That would allow us to go over to the defense for the night and allow the motorcycle infantry battalion to catch up. Radio traffic to that end was sent to the division. An answer from the division proved unnecessary, since the lead element ran into two vehicles that could not be identified with certainty. They were burning from rounds from the self-propelled gun. The engineer squad was sent forward to extinguish the flames. The vehicles were positioned in such a manner on the road that it did not appear advisable to attempt a bypass during the darkness. The Battalion Commander ordered: "Battalion closes up front, moves off the road into the fruit orchard, camouflages and sets up an all-round defense!" The road up front could have been mined; that was impossible to the southwest and to the rear.

All of the men were dead tired. The officers and noncommissioned officers needed to summon all their strength to establish security and maintain a defensive posture. The "hedgehog" was not finished until 0130 hours.

The battalion wanted to continue the advance at 0300 hours. The order to get ready to move had already been issued, when enemy infantry were observed digging in along the high ground to the right and left of the advance route as it started to turn increasingly light. That meant the advance route was blocked and, for the time being, could not be opened by means of an attack. Apparently, we had seen the enemy before he had seen us. The gun went into position and scattered enemy concentrations.

We needed reinforcements from the motorcycle infantry battalion and the artillery, which was also still hanging back. Orders were issued to expand the "hedgehog," go into position and to disperse the heavy weapons. While those orders were being carried out, a large Russian column with armored cars, trucks and tanks closed upon our position. A sharp fight ensued. The high corn in the fields made it easier for the enemy to approach us. During the first phase of his operations, the enemy only attacked from the southwest. When he was unable to get through there, however, he attempted to bypass us from the northwest and the southeast. The few operational armored cars screened the flanks, and the antitank guns shot the attacking armored cars and tanks to pieces. The concentrated fires of the two infantry guns were placed on the road, with the result that the Russian trucks were unable to advance any further. But the attacks continued. One thought predominated: The "hedgehog" defensive position had to be held under all circumstances; otherwise, the battalion would lose its vehicles and [it] would be out of commission for the rest of the campaign. As chance would have it, the battalion's "hedgehog" was in a somewhat reverse-slope position in the direction of the attacking enemy, which had the disadvantage that the enemy forces digging in had great fields of observation and were able to inflict casualties through snipers.

The Russians changed the main efforts of their attacks. Each time, we had to regroup individual weapons, whereby the armored cars conducted the battlefield reconnaissance in an excellent manner and frequently joined the fray decisively through defensive firepower.

When it was observed that three tanks were approaching the battalion from three different sides, it took a great deal of composure to prevent a panic from breaking out, which would have led to our own destruction. These efforts met with complete success.

It was thanks to the preparedness and alertness and also the agility of the self-propelled gun under the command of *Oberfeldwebel* Uhlmann (Gunner: *Unteroffizier* Melzer) that all three tanks were knocked out, thus stopping the attack one more time.

Ammunitions started to run low. The truck drivers sat behind a stone house. Boxes of ammunition were in front of them, and they belted the ammunition drums for the machine guns of the armored cars, which were rearmed after they had expended a load of ammunition. No one could afford to stand idly by; everyone had to be where duty called and help with heart and soul.

Occasionally, the situation turned more than a little threatening. Calls for help to relieve and support us were radioed out to the division and the armor regiment. The fight had started just after 0300 hours on 27 June; around 0900 hours, our tanks appeared on the far horizon and were directed towards us by means of white signal flares. They came too late to join the battle, however.

Around 1000 hours, four *Panzer I's* and *II's* arrived at the battalion's location. Despite that, it was a great relief, since the ammunition had run very low. We were especially low on armor-defeating ammunition. Due to their actions and bravery, the following are to be singled out:

- *Oberleutnant* von Boehn, the commander of the *3./Panzer-Aufklärungs-Abteilung 13*, was killed by a round to the head while at the observation point for his infantry gun platoon, where he had directed the fires.
- *Oberfeldwebel* Uhlmann and *Unteroffizier* Melzer and their crew.
- The self-propelled gun.
- The Infantry-gun crew under the command of *Stabsfeldwebel* Lange (wounded) and, later, *Feldwebel* Bein.
- The Machine-Gun Section of the 2nd Company.
- *Unterarzt* Wille, who personally help recover the badly wounded in the front lines with the stretcher bearers.
- The Engineer Platoon of *Leutnant* Wildaur, coming from the *4./Pionier-Bataillon 4*. He was wounded during the defensive fighting and during a counterattack.

Those are a few, who needed to be mentioned. A large number of soldiers performed in a likewise magnificent manner and deserve to be mentioned by name, but their names could not be determined in the thick of the fighting. Possible recommendations for awards will be submitted. Not to be forgotten is the work of the signals platoon, since the radio operators had to spend the entire period of the six hours of fighting at their equipment in their vehicles, which were usually unprotected. They did so, even though numerous rounds hit the vehicles.

It was not possible to take a closer look at the area where the fighting had taken place until the early afternoon, after the rifle brigade had arrived. There were shot-up tanks, armored cars and trucks. In a roadside ditch, lined up one after the other, were 30 corpses and a lot of wounded. Every member of the battalion can look back with pride to 27 June 1941 and hold the memory of those that fell that day close to heart.

The final extended excerpt in this chapter comes from Willi Kubik, who served as an armor scout in *Panzer-Aufklärungs-Abteilung 13* on the Eastern Front, until he was eventually captured toward the end of 1944:[37]

26 June 1941:

We got up at 0700 hours and went to work. The old Ukrainian from the neighborhood came up and gave us milk and white bread.

Seven men from a prisoner collection point scoured the local area for scattered Russians. All of a sudden, three Russian bombers approached. They were the first we had seen. By the time we figured out they were Russian, there were already explosions. I had been able to grab my binoculars from the armored car in order to be better able to observe. I went a few steps into the cornfield, put the binoculars up to my eyes and then, all of a sudden, I was flat on the ground.

I don't know whether I instinctively assumed that position or had fallen. I had the feeling that I had been hit. I felt a big bump on my forehead.

It didn't occur to me until later that the Russians had dropped four bombs on the heavy artillery battery that had halted on the road 30 meters away.

When I looked into the mirror on the vehicle, I saw that the cockade from my overseas cap had been half torn off and that there was a great deal of swelling on my forehead.

I was lucky, I said to myself. It was just a hair away. I didn't give it any further thought.

We quickly moved our armored car away from the road and under some trees.

Two *Me 109's* came racing in, but we were unable to observe the battle in the air. In any event, only one Russian bomber came back.

We quickly loaded everything up, washed and took off around 1400 hours, as an individual vehicle.

Whenever we asked about the *13. Panzer-Division*, no one could give us any information. When we got to a narrow field path, there were dead Russians and horses to the right and left of us, as well as cannon. Kalle became afraid and crawled into the armored car, even though there was really only room for the driver and me as the gunner. In front of us was a large tract of woodland. We got to a wide road, where the *14. Panzer-Division* was advancing. Up front, next to the road and along a wood line was Jesser's maintenance shop.

We were presented with a horrific image along the road. One Russian tank after the other was shot up along the edge. They had not even been able to deploy in a field. Most of the tanks were burned out. They were all light and medium tanks, with a few armored cars thrown into the mix.

The armor, which was only 3–4 centimeters thick, had been completely penetrated by many German antitank and main gun rounds. Some of the tanks had received more than 20 hits.

The woods were about two kilometers in length and full of troops.

It was a terrible picture of destruction, which made us shiver. The tanks were, at the most, some 100 meters from the road. Not a single one had gotten any further. The majority of the tanks were right next to the road or in the roadside ditch. The carbonized remains of tank crews, who had not been able to get out of their burning vehicles in time, stared out from some of the tanks.

We heard that there were about 200 Russian tanks altogether; all of them of light construction. Friendly losses during the armor engagement were 5 total write-offs and 11 damaged tanks. Many of the Russian tanks were literally perforated by the numerous hits; the armor had simply been too weak.

The German attack must have completely surprised the Russians.

We moved on. After about 5 kilometers, the ignition gave out. We halted at a small secondary road, and my driver attempted to fix the problem. Kalle warned him, but it was already too late: My driver lost small parts of the ignition.

At that point, we stood around, in the middle of the field, looking dumb. We were 5 kilometers from the closest German forces.

All around us were still plenty of scattered Russian soldiers. They presented a great danger to us. We needed to take a closer look at the surrounding terrain.

A house all by itself was burning about 100 meters in front of us. My driver and I headed in that direction; there was nothing in it. We then looked at the shot-up Russian tanks. The dead driver was looking out of one of them; one hand was outside of the hatch. He had been mortally wounded while trying to get out of the tank. In another tank, the carbonized remains of several Russians stared at us. The picture of the gruesome destruction became etched in my memory. In its very first few days, the war had shown us its horrible face.

By then, it had turned dark.

I rode back to the maintenance facility with a motorcyclist, who had come by. They were unable to tow us back until the next morning. I rode the 5 kilometers back in a staff car. What should we do?

In the end, a truck moving back to the rear towed us to his unit in the nearby woods. It was near the maintenance facility. A *Leutnant* there welcomed us with open arms.

They had already captured 10 Russians; others had escaped in the woods.

We lit up the wood line with our headlights. Guards called out and fired; they were overly nervous.

After a short while, I went to sleep in the armored car. You never knew what would come next.

This *Sd.Kfz. 223* from an unknown reconnaissance unit has veered off the side of the road and gotten stuck. Unable to free itself under its own power, it required the aid of a truck to help pull it out.

A scout performs maintenance in the engine compartment of his *Sd.Kfz. 222*. The vehicle driver was responsible for performing daily checks and services, applying lubricants, and reporting any deficiencies to his vehicle commander. In the event repairs were needed, he remained with the vehicle and helped the mechanics.

These scouts take in the vastness of the steppe in the southern part of the Soviet Union. As was typical on any armored vehicle, the crew of the *Sd.Kfz. 221* on the right has stowed a large portion of personal equipment and belongings on the outside, including assigned helmets.

Scouts of *Panzer-Aufklärungs-Abteilung 16* clown around for the camera while posing with a unit *Sd.Kfz. 222* in a Soviet village. The noncommissioned officer sitting on the back of the turret is possibly the unit first sergeant, as evidenced by what appears to be twin rows of silver braid on his lower left sleeve. Like the U.S. Army, first sergeant was a title and not a rank, although the holder was generally an *Oberfeldwebel*. Of interest is the suitcase fastened to the left front fender. AKIRA TAKIGUCHI

This *Sd.Kfz. 232 (8 Rad)* is carrying a 200-liter drum on its back deck, the exact purpose of which is unknown, although it may be for carrying potable water, since the placard on the telephone pole indicates this is a water point.

A trained radio operator and crewmembers of an *Sd.Kfz. 261* armored radio car from a battalion signals section display a wide variety of facial expressions in this photograph, as does the captured Soviet soldier, leaving open a wide number of interpretations. The image is attributed *Panzer-Aufklärungs-Abteilung 5* of the *2. Panzer-Division*. AKIRA TAKIGU

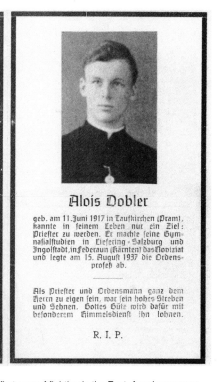

An assortment of obituary notices for soldiers of reconnaissance units killed in action during the first year of fighting in the East. Augsburger was a scout in a motorized reconnaissance battalion (30 June 1941); Degele was a motorcycle infantryman (1 October 1941); and Schröttle was also a motorcycle infantryman (11 August 1941). Dobler was not only a highly decorated enlisted man in a motorcycle infantry battalion (Infantry Assault Badge and Iron Cross, Second Class), but also a Heart of Jesus Missionary priest; badly wounded on 25 September 1941, he died a short time later.

This series of images all come from a motorcycle infantryman assigned to *SS-Kradschützen-Bataillon "Reich"* (part of *Heeresgruppe Mitte* during Barbarossa) and were probably taken shortly into the campaign in the East. In the first image, a bugler sounds a call while the battalion commander, possibly *SS-Sturmbannführer* Zehender, paces in the background. Based on the next image, the men are probably attending a field service for soldiers of the 3rd Company of the battalion who were killed in action in late September 1941, as indicated by the grave markers. In the next image, motorcycle infantrymen pose next to a sidecar motorcycle and a simple Russian hut while taking a break during operations. In the next two photographs, *SS-Hauptsturmführer* Fritz Klingenberg is seen presenting an award to one of his soldiers in the 2nd Company. Aside from his facial features, he can also be recognized by his height and his characteristic smirk. Finally, motorcycle infantry of the battalion negotiate an obstacle, apparently a tank ditch that has had its sides leveled out somewhat to facilitate crossing.

This group of photographs shows *Aufklärungs-Abteilung 18* of the *18. Infanterie-Division (mot)* in action in the center sector of the Eastern Front. The first image shows an *Sd.Kfz. 222* of the 1st Company with its guns raised in an air-defense role and trained on its prey, probably a Fieseler *Storch* light utility aircraft. In the second image, two *Sd.Kfz. 221's* move down an unimproved road. The stark contrast between the densely wooded tracts and wide-open spaces can be seen. When Soviet forces were bypassed, these types of woods became favorite hiding places. In the third image, scouts of the battalion have set up "shop" during a longer halt, as evidenced by the hull-down position of the *Sd.Kfz. 223*, the construction of what appears to be a wood-reinforced bunker—although it may also be a simple peasant root cellar—and the posting of an observer. In the fourth image, an *Sd.Kfz. 232 (8 Rad)* has been pulled into a tree line in an effort to conceal it from ground and aerial observation. Once again, there is evidence of a longer halt or pause in operations, since it appears scouts are taking advantage of the time allowed to wash clothes. The last photo is of the grave site of *Oberleutnant* von Bünau, the company commander of the *1./Aufklärungs-Abteilung 18 (mot)*, who was killed in action on 29 November 1941. JIM HALEY

THE CAMPAIGN AGAINST THE SOVIET UNION: BARBAROSSA UNLEASHED

This next series of images comes from the estate of *Oberleutnant* Kreß, a Knight's Cross recipient from the *1./Aufklärungs-Abteilung 20 (mot)*. The battalion was employed in the area of operations of *Heeresgruppe Mitte*. Kreß, an enthusiastic amateur photographer, had numerous pictures taken of him and his platoon, in addition to chronicling operations of the unit.* *Oberleutnant* Kreß was killed in action on 15 January 1943 while serving as the commander of the *1. (PzSpäh-) / Kradschützen-Bataillon 38*. In the first picture, Kreß poses with the crew of his *Sd.Kfz. 232 (8 Rad)*. During operations in the Soviet Union, he and his scouts all wore one-piece coveralls that were frequently devoid of all insignia, although Kreß himself wore the national eagle and officer shoulder boards. In the second image, a shot-up fender of Kreß's *Sd.Kfz. 232 (8 Rad)* gives mute testimony to the inherent danger of operating far forward of friendly forces. Next, Kreß poses for a formal studio portrait, taken shortly after the award of his Knight's Cross on 22 September 1941. He was probably on home leave at the time. In another studio portrait, Kreß poses in his black *Panzer* uniform for some formal occasion, as evidenced by his officer brocade parade belt. The aiguillette indicates that he was the battalion adjutant at the time. Based on the awards he wears, the image was probably taken after the campaign in the West. In the next image, we see an *Sd.Kfz. 232 (8 Rad)*—possibly Kreß's vehicle—positioned on a trail in the woods next to an unlimbered artillery piece, which appears to be ready to fire over open sights. The inherent danger of moving through woods is readily apparent here: forces are channelized along a narrow pathway that affords little visibility to the flanks, thus making any element a prime target for an ambush. In addition, the density of the woods would allow little leeway for bypassing knocked-out vehicles without first widening the trail or pushing the inoperable vehicle out of the way. Finally, a knocked-out *Sd.Kfz. 231 (8 Rad)* of the battalion awaits recovery and repair. Judging by the damage suffered to the front part of the chassis, the armored car probably ran over a mine. JIM HALEY

---

*Many more images of Kreß can be found in *Scouts Out*.

An atmospheric image of *Sd.Kfz. 263's* moving at speed down a dusty Soviet road in the summer of 1941. A large "G" for *Panzergruppe Guderian* is clearly visibly on the right front fender of the lead vehicle. JIM HALEY

While no longer considered fit for frontline service, older armored cars such as these *Sd.Kfz. 231 (6 Rad)* vehicles were useful for rear-area security, as evidenced by this photograph. JIM HALEY

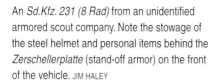

An *Sd.Kfz. 231 (8 Rad)* from an unidentified armored scout company. Note the stowage of the steel helmet and personal items behind the *Zerschellerplatte* (stand-off armor) on the front of the vehicle. JIM HALEY

Heavy armored cars of an unidentified scout company cross a waterway on engineer bridges. Based on the relatively relaxed poses, the unit is well behind the front lines and the *Luftwaffe* has local air superiority.
JIM HALEY

An armored scout company has lined up on a road in preparation to move out. In the lead is an *Sd.Kfz. 231 (8 Rad)*, followed by several *Sd.Kfz. 222's* and *221's*, and at least one *Sd.Kfz. 223*. Based on the terrain features, this photograph was probably taken in the southern sector of the Eastern Front. JIM HALEY

The crew of an *Sd.Kfz. 231 (8 Rad)* waits aboard its vehicle during a break in operations. These scouts all appear to be wearing standard field-gray, four-pocket tunics and corresponding trousers. The uniforms worn by scouts often varied. Because scouts were frequently called upon to dismount their vehicles to perform their duties, many preferred wearing uniforms with more neutral colors so as not to stand out against the terrain in their issue black *Panzer* uniforms. JIM HALEY

A scout—probably an officer, based on the headgear—stands atop an *Sd.Kfz. 221* in an effort to better observe the terrain ahead through his binoculars. In the better exposed second image, an *Oberfeldwebel* scout strikes a martial pose atop the same *Sd.Kfz. 221*, which is mostly concealed by the tall wheat. The *MG 34* has been mounted on the antiaircraft mount. JIM HALEY

Tired scouts pose atop their *Sd.Kfz. 232 (8 Rad)* wearing a hodgepodge of uniforms: black *Panzer* trousers, denim work overgarments, and what appears to be the reed-green HBT version of the *Panzer* uniform for armored vehicle crews. MARK MCMURRAY

Spirits appear to remain high for these scouts posing with an *Sd.Kfz. 222*, despite dirt, road dust, and probable exhaustion. JIM HALEY

Motorcycle infantry appear to be waiting to be briefed by the officer or senior noncommissioned officers standing next to the *Sd.Kfz. 232 (8 Rad)*. A bit of natural foliage has been added to the vehicle's front in an effort to break up its silhouette. Makeshift covers have been placed over the barrels in an effort to keep the weapons from becoming fouled. MARK MCMURRAY

Scouts pose in front of an *Sd.Kfz. 222*, which has had the name of a fallen comrade painted on the side. MIKE HARPE

Armored cars of an unidentified scout company intermingle with tanks as both move down the unimproved main road of a village. MIKE HARPE

A Panhard pressed into German service. Only two armored reconnaissance battalions were issued these vehicles: *Panzer-Aufklärungs-Abteilung 37* of the *7. Panzer-Division* and *Panzer-Aufklärungs-Abteilung 92* of the *20. Panzer-Division*. Both divisions reported to the *XXXIX. Armee-Korps (mot)*.
NATIONAL ARCHIVES

Scouts from an unidentified unit take a break on their *Sd.Kfz. 222*.
NATIONAL ARCHIVES

SS-Aufklärungs-Abteilung (mot) Leibstandarte SS Adolf Hitler

The *Leibstandarte SS Adolf Hitler*, still the equivalent of a reinforced brigade at the start of the campaign, was initially assigned to the field-army reserves of *Heeresgruppe Süd* at the start of Barbarossa. That status soon changed, and the *Leibstandarte* saw combat throughout the fateful year of 1941. Accompanying *SS-Aufklärungs-Abteilung (mot) Leibstandarte SS Adolf Hitler* for some of the campaign was *SS-Kriegsberichter* Augustin, who took the following images. In the first image, a KV-II heavy artillery tank (152mm) is knocked out next to a Soviet BA-64 armored car. The KV-II proved to be virtually impossible to knock out with German weaponry of the time unless it was taken under fire at relatively close range by the 88mm *Flak* or by artillery firing over open sights. This tank, along with the more frequently encountered KV-I and the T-34, were among the many unpleasant surprises that awaited the Germans in the summer of 1941. In the second photograph, motorcycle infantry move at speed down a Soviet road, followed by an Sd.Kfz. 222 of the scout company. The organization of the reconnaissance battalion was somewhat unique, with two motorcycle infantry companies, one understrength armored scout company, and a heavy company. In the third photograph, a scout or motorcycle infantryman conducts dismounted observation, using the camouflage of his early-pattern smock to help him blend in with the vegetation. Finally, an *Sd.Kfz. 231 (8 Rad)* moves past burning buildings in a Soviet town. NATIONAL ARCHIVES

As the campaign progressed and the Soviets proved to be a tough nut to crack, heavy weapons from other elements of the brigade were employed in support. The first two weapons seen here—a *Panzerjäger I* and an early-model *Sturmgeschütz III*—came from *Abteilung Schönefeld*, while the 50mm antitank gun came from one of the antitank assets of the brigade, possibly the heavy battalion. Note that the antitank gun has two "kill" rings on its barrel. NATIONAL ARCHIVES

Armored cars of the reconnaissance battalion move through the seemingly unending steppes of the southern Soviet Union. In the first image, an unidentified *SS-Untersturmführer*, probably a platoon leader within the armored scout company, receives a report while in his *Sd.Kfz. 223*. To his rear is a ground–air coordination noncommissioned officer from the *Luftwaffe*. Scouts observe from an *Sd.Kfz. 222* in the next two images, while another *Sd.Kfz. 223* is seen in the fourth and fifth photographs. The scouts and airman then dismount in the next two pictures in order to continue their observing. In the next two photographs, the reconnaissance elements appear to be coming under fire, with an *Sd.Kfz. 221* moving down the dirt road, followed by two other vehicles, perhaps in an effort to escape the incoming rounds. In the final image, an *SS-Obersturmführer* appears to be supplying a *Fliegerverbindungsoffizier* (air–ground liaison officer) with information on potential targets. The liaison officer was usually referred to by his position's abbreviation, *Flivo*. NATIONAL ARCHIVES

In this sequence, motorcycle infantrymen of the *Leibstandarte* bring in surrendering Soviets. A particular problem for all reconnaissance elements was the handling of prisoners. Given their missions, it was impossible to take prisoners along, but because of their generally small size, it was also difficult to leave forces behind to guard the men. In the early days of the campaign, when the Germans encountered formations surrendering *en masse*, a single man was often given the responsibility of escorting hundreds of prisoners to the rear. NATIONAL ARCHIVES

One of the light infantry guns of the battalion's heavy company in action. In the first image, a cannoneer cups his ears to protect them from the loud report of the gun. In the second picture, we see observers on a haystack giving corrections to the gunners. NATIONAL ARCHIVES

A sidecar motorcycle and crew move past burning Soviet vehicles during street fighting, while an *Sd.Kfz. 232 (8 Rad)* moves along railway tracks in a contested town. NATIONAL ARCHIVES

Period Color Imagery, Ephemera, Uniforms, Headgear, and Insignia

A fanciful rendition of armored reconnaissance forces in action. This postcard was available for sale in troop canteens throughout garrisons in Germany. The caption reads: "Armored cars screen far out in front." Of interest is the fact that the *Sd.Kfz. 231 (8 Rad)* sports the early *Reichswehr* three-tone camouflage scheme of yellow, green, and brown, which was officially discontinued in 1935.

Another watercolor postcard, this one featuring motorcycle infantry. The caption reads: "The advance guard encounters the enemy."

Awards belonging to Knight's Cross recipient Helmuth Spaeter, who received the decoration on 28 July 1943 as a *Rittmeister* and commander of the *2./Panzer-Aufklärungs-Abteilung "Großdeutschland."* From left to right: Knight's Cross of the Iron Cross (prepared for wear in the field by a shortened ribbon and attachment devices); Iron Cross, First Class; and Iron Cross, Second Class. Spaeter was also the recipient of the Close Combat Clasp in Bronze, the German Cross in Gold (*Oberleutnant / 2./Panzer-Aufklärungs-Abteilung "Großdeutschland"*), the Armored Assault Badge in Bronze, and the Wound Badge in Gold. The black-and-white images show Spaeter on the day of the presentation of his award by the division commander, *Generalleutnant* Walter Hoernlein. Additional information on the reconnaissance assets of *Panzer-Grenadier-Division "Großdeutschland"* can be found in Chapter 7 in the sidebar "*The Kradschützen-Bataillon* of *Infanterie-Division (mot) Grossdeutschland*," pages 303–309. SCOTT PRITCHETT

This particular field-gray officer's overseas cap with the *Braunschweiger Husaren* traditions badge has seen plenty of hard use in the field. The officer was either assigned to a prewar cavalry unit (*Kavallerie-Regiment 13*), one of the mounted reconnaissance battalions formed from it at the start of the war, or part of the *4. Kavallerie-Brigade*. Based on the wear and tear and the relative poor quality of the wool, it is assumed the cap belonged to an officer of the latter unit, which was both horse-mounted and motorized and fought with distinction on the Eastern Front at the end of the war. The small insert shows another traditions badge, this time for the *Schwedter Adler*, which was worn before the war by *Kavallerie-Regiment 6* and *Kradschützen-Bataillon 3*. Later it would be extended to *Aufklärungs-Abteilung 33 (mot)* and continued to be worn by *Panzer-Aufklärungs-Abteilung 115*. It was also worn by the *3. Kavallerie-Brigade* at war's end. The Schwedt Eagle was worn analogously to the Braunschweig Hussar badge. SCHWEDTER ADLER COURTESY OF SCOTT PRITCHETT

The unit cap badges shown above were created during the war. Although unofficial, the divisions usually issued award documents for the badges, thus restricting their wear to longstanding assigned soldiers or recent arrivals who particularly distinguished themselves. Unlike the traditions badges seen on the previous page, the cap badges were worn on the left-hand side of the cap. From left to right: *26. Panzer-Division*, *16. Panzer-Division*, and *116. Panzer-Division "Windhund."* A well-worn example of a black overseas cap for enlisted personnel is seen below; its owner marked it with handsewn initials in the lining. The golden-yellow soutache almost certainly identifies it as having been worn by a scout assigned to an armored car. In cases where a pink soutache is seen, the owner could have been either a tanker or a scout, since *rosa* was common to both. CAP BADGES COURTESY OF SCOTT PRITCHETT

A nice unissued example of a black overseas cap intended for wear by an armored scout. Unlike the cap on the opposite page, this one features regulation black-backed insignia. Manufacturer, year of manufacture, and size information can be seen inside, whereas the corresponding information on the previous cap has faded from wear.

Another well-worn cap, this time for an armored reconnaissance officer. A nametag has been sewn into the lining and a safety pin used in the crown to help pinch the sides together for a more "jaunty" look when worn. In addition, the upturns to the cap have been sewn into place at the front to prevent them from appearing loose. Although officer caps were made in accordance with regulation, a great deal of them were privately purchased, as was the case here and for the cap opposite. The tailor who made this cap for the officer was forced to use enlisted insignia. This is often encountered on officer caps, since the officer variants of the insignia were difficult to obtain.

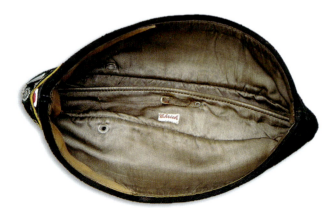

This field-worn cap was de-Nazified after the war by the removal of the national eagle. In addition, the owner removed a nametag that had been sewn into the lining. This particular cap does have the officer bullion cockade, however, implying that a bullion officer eagle was also in place at one time. Of note here is the addition of the death's head on the front of the cap, an unusual measure, especially for an officer. In addition to sewing the *Totenkopf* just above the soutache, the individual placed red cloth or felt behind the eyes; this enhancement is frequently seen on the collar tabs of black *Panzer* tunics, as illustrated in the two tunics that follow. RICO UNGER

This pristine example of an enlisted visor cap is noteworthy mostly for the unit stamping found on the leather sweatband. It is for the armored car troop of the reconnaissance school at Krampnitz, the *2. (Panzer-Späh-Lehr) Schwadron* of the *Kavallerie-Lehr-und Versuchs-Abteilung*. The *M38* officer field cap (old style), more commonly referred to as a "crusher," was popular with officers across all branches of the military. This cap can frequently be seen in photos of officers in armored cars. M38 COURTESY OF SCOTT PRITCHETT

Along the top row are examples of collar tabs worn on the black and field-gray special uniforms for armored vehicle crewmen. Prewar varieties have wool piping; tabs with rayon piping were introduced after the war started and eventually replaced the manufacture of wool-piped tabs. The shoulder straps on the bottom right are for a scout wearing the black *Panzer* uniform. They are attributed to the son of *General der Panzertruppen* von Manteuffel, seen standing to the right of his famous father. SCOTT PRITCHETT

The white summer uniform seen above belonged to a *Leutnant* assigned to *Kradschützen-Bataillon 3* of the *3. Panzer-Division*. Although it is not typically seen in wartime photographs, images do surface of this type of uniform being worn at the front during summer months. The insignia seen to the top right is a sleeve patch fashioned for members of the *23. Panzer-Division*. It was either designed and worn toward the end of the war, or produced on orders of their British captors in May 1945, depending on the source consulted. Either way, this is the version intended for wear on the black *Panzer* uniform; it is surrounded in white so it would stand out on the uniform. As such, it was worn by both tankers and scouts in *Panzer-Regiment 23* or *Panzer-Aufklärungs-Abteilung 23*. The last insignia seen on this page is for a *Leutnant* assigned to *Kradschützen-Bataillon "Großdeutschland."* Meadow green (*wiesengrün*) was worn in the battalion from approximately April 1942 to January 1943, except for the armored scout company, which wore golden yellow (*goldgelb*). After its redesignation as *Panzer-Aufklärungs-Abteilung "Großdeutschland,"* the battalion wore golden yellow. SHOULDER BOARD COURTESY OF SCOTT PRITCHETT

An example of the second-pattern *Panzer* tunic as worn by an *Unteroffizier* of an unidentified armored reconnaissance battalion. The jacket, which shows typical prewar quality and attention to detail, features a golden-yellow collar tab and collar piping in wool.

Details of the tunic seen on the previous page. The "A" cipher on the shoulder strap has been sewn on since the relatively fragile pins may have been broken off in the constant mounting and dismounting required of a scout in an armored car. As often seen, red fabric has been placed behind the eyes of the *Totenkopf* on the collar tabs. The bottom images show the various manufacturer stamps seen in prewar uniforms. On the left are the various garment measurements, with the "96" indicating the chest size in centimeters. The "B38" below it indicates the tunic was accepted by the Berlin Army depot sometime in 1938. The stamp on the right-hand side indicates the name of the garment manufacturer contracted to produce the tunic.

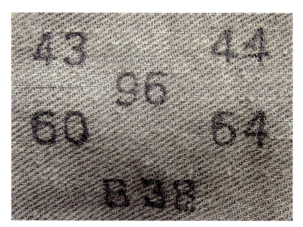

This last uniform is for a *Leutnant* assigned to an armored car company. The tunic is also a second-pattern variation of the *Panzer* uniform jacket. In place of an enlisted eagle (as was frequently encountered) or the relatively rare *Bevo*-weave metallic fabric eagle sometimes seen, the officer opted for the more common bullion officer-style eagle on a black base. SCOTT PRITCHETT

See Photo Section Notes at the end of this insert

See Photo Section Notes at the end of this insert

See Photo Section Notes at the end of this insert

See Photo Section Notes at the end of this insert

See Photo Section Notes at the end of this insert

See Photo Section Notes at the end of this insert

See Photo Section Notes at the end of this insert

See Photo Section Notes at the end of this insert

See Photo Section Notes at the end of this insert

See Photo Section Notes at the end of this insert

See Photo Section Notes at the end of this insert

See Photo Section Notes at the end of this insert

See Photo Section Notes at the end of this insert

See Photo Section Notes at the end of this insert

See Photo Section Notes at the end of this insert

Photo Section Notes

The first period color photograph shows an *Sd.Kfz. 222* from an unidentified armored scout company speeding down a dusty lane somewhere in the Soviet Union, probably around 1942. The guns have muzzle covers on them to help prevent the unrelenting dust from entering the barrels. The crewmembers were less fortunate and found themselves encrusted with dust even after short movements. It appears that the vehicle commander may be wearing a scarf to help keep out some of the contaminants. AKIRA TAKIGUCHI

This *Sd.Kfz. 263 (8 Rad)* is assigned to a signals detachment of some sort; as such, it could have served in a variety of units in addition to reconnaissance ones. The relatively pristine condition of the vehicle and the architecture of the building in the background suggest that the image was taken at a training establishment or replacement detachment in Germany. AKIRA TAKIGUCHI

The remaining color photographs, with the exception of the very last one, all come from the collection of Dave Williams, who graciously allowed these images, most of which have never been published before or only in relatively obscure publications, to be shown to a larger audience for the first time. The initial grouping shows elements of *SS-Aufklärungs-Abteilung "Totenkopf"* after it finally received some armored cars and was able to establish its armored scout company. These images were probably taken in mid- to late 1942. Two *Sd.Kfz. 222's* of the company can be seen on these two pages, showing two variants of the medium armored car's hull type: the first variant is on the bottom and the second variant hull is on the top. DAVE WILLIAMS

The crew of the *Sd.Kfz. 222* stands in front of its vehicle. In the middle is an *SS-Untersturmführer*, probably one of the platoon leaders. What is remarkable in these images, at least regarding the uniforms, is that two of the three scouts are wearing golden-yellow branch-of-service piping around their collar tabs and collars. Although pink-piped *SS* collar tabs for *Panzer* uniforms have been seen in collections before—also non-regulation and highly irregular—the application of this piping to these uniforms must have been for only a very short period. The collar tabs are the relatively rarely seen "vertical" death's head type (worn on both sides of the collar), as opposed to the standard issue ones. It is surmised that these scouts were trying to make their uniforms look like those of their army counterparts. Also of interest is the early-style black *Allgemeine SS* cap worn with the *Panzer* uniform. Although the more commonly encountered black M40 enlisted *SS Panzer* overseas cap was available at the time, most of these soldiers continue to wear the older version. The officer is the only one wearing a sleeve band, which appears to be the *Oberbayern* type (only a *Totenkopf*), as opposed to the regulation *Totenkopf* title. As will be seen in subsequent images, he appears to have been quite the "dandy" when it came to uniforms. DAVE WILLIAMS

The gunner on the *Sd.Kfz. 222* takes up a sight picture on his gun optics. He does not have the extra *Waffenfarbe* applied to his collar tabs and collar, although he wears the rare "vertical" *Totenkopf*. DAVE WILLIAMS

The *SS-Untersturmführer* seen previously takes his vehicle out for a test run. Details of his uniform can clearly be seen. Of interest is the officer's cap, which appears to be a "crusher"-style visor cap to which a chin cord has been added. In addition, it looks as though he is wearing an embroidered sleeve eagle on his cap, which appears to be piped in rose pink. DAVE WILLIAMS

The crew of an *Sd.Kfz. 223* poses in front of its vehicle. All three of these scouts have the additional piping applied to their tunics. The vehicle commander, the *SS-Rottenführer* in the center, is wearing the *M40* black overseas cap discussed earlier. In the second image, vehicles of the unit—two *Sd.Kfz. 222's* on the left and what appear to be *Sd.Kfz. 221's* taking up the rest of the row—are neatly parked in the motor pool. It seems to have been standard operating procedure for all the vehicles in the unit to mount a bundle of fascines on the front. DAVE WILLIAMS

After the Campaign in the West, a number of captured vehicles were pressed into service with the German Armed Forces, including these British Mark I scout cars, made by the Daimler firm and colloquially referred to as the "Dingo." (The dingo is a wild dog indigenous to Australia and known for its hunting abilities.) Given the chronic shortage of reconnaissance vehicles, it was only natural that they be reissued to new owners. The Daimler Scout Car was fast, agile, and very effective. It appears that all of them have been given a base coat of German *panzergrau*, the dark gray commonly associated with early-war German armor. Note the *SS-Rottenführer* on the left appears to be wearing standard *SS* collar tabs, with the rank tab on the left. The *SS-Unterscharführer*, on the other hand, has adopted the uniform peculiarities worn by many of the rest of the unit. DAVE WILLIAMS.

More views of the reflagged "Dingoes." Note one of the vehicles displays a prominent death's head on its right front fender. DAVE WILLIAMS

Company officers, wearing a variety of uniforms and headgear, pose in these images. In the top image, the officer initially seen with the *Sd.Kfz. 222* is seen again on the left. On the right is another *SS-Untersturmführer* who wears a black army officer overseas cap, which has been converted to *SS* use by the replacement of the cockade with the *Totenkopf*. It cannot be determined whether he also changed the national eagle from the army type to an *SS* one. In the bottom image, the *SS-Oberstumrführer* on the left may be the company commander. He wears a standard *SS* officer visor cap with metal insignia. The *SS-Untersturmführer* on the right wears a field-gray version of the *M40* overseas cap along with *SS* collar tabs without piping. DAVE WILLIAMS

In the last image from this series, the same *SS-Untersturmführer* appears again with some unit crewmembers who are proud to pose in front of their new vehicles, in this case, an *Sd.Kfz. 223* and an *Sd.Kfz. 222*. The bottom photograph shows a pass-in-review held in Oslo in late 1942 during the activation process for the *25. Panzer-Division*. The *Sd.Kfz. 263's* could be from the divisional signals battalion, the armor regiment, or *Kradschützen-Bataillon 87*, the reconnaissance asset of the division at the time. DAVE WILLIAMS

These two images were taken on a visit to front-line formations by *Generalfeldmarschall* von Kluge, the Commander-in-Chief of the *4. Armee*. An *Sd.Kfz. 221* from *SS-Aufklärungs-Abteilung "Reich"* has been assigned as part of the security detail for the visiting field marshal. Based on the uniforms and vehicular markings, these images were probably taken in mid-1941 before von Kluge assumed command of *Heeresgruppe Mitte*. In the first image, a Latin-style "A" can be seen as a slip-on over the scout's shoulder straps; the *SS* occasionally used the Latin "A" as opposed to a Gothic "A" to denote reconnaissance. DAVE WILLIAMS

These two images show radio communications vehicles of a signals detachment, probably for the signals battalion of an armored division. The top image shows an *Sd.Kfz. 251/3*, a *mittlerer Kommandopanzerwagen*, which was capable of fielding a variety of communications equipment and was recognizable by its large frame antenna. These were present in large numbers in the headquarters of reconnaissance battalions in *KStN's* issued in 1943 and later. The same officer featured in the first image is seen in the second holding the puppy and standing next to an *Sd.Kfz. 223*. DAVE WILLIAMS

This next series of images comes from a scout who was either assigned to the training base as an instructor; attending a course at the schoolhouse or one of the replacement and training detachments for reconnaissance units; convalescing at the home front and temporarily attached to a replacement detachment; or part of a detail assigned the mission of picking up new vehicles. The first is a combination of the old and the new, with an *Sd.Kfz. 234/2 "Puma"* positioned beside the venerable *Sd.Kfz. 223* next to typical German motor pool bays of the period. Both vehicles are painted in the standard dark yellow (*dunkelgelb*) applied to armored vehicles leaving the factories in 1943 and later. A driving school sign has been added to the front bumper of the *Sd.Kfz. 223*. Of interest is the fact that one of the vision port covers is missing from the front of the vehicle. In the second image, the scout poses on the 50mm main gun of the *Puma*. He has already seen some action at the front, as evidenced by his only award, a Wound Badge in Black, signifying a single combat wound. DAVE WILLIAMS

Several views of *Sd.Kfz. 233's* lined up. The vehicles look factory new and have had protective tarpaulins placed over the exposed gun compartments. They may be waiting for shipment to the front. DAVE WILLIAMS

Two more views of an *Sd.Kfz. 233*, with unit members or course attendees posing next to a vehicle and the owner of the images in front of one. Most of the scouts are wearing a one-piece protective coverall. Based on the condition of the vehicles, they may be going on a "shakedown" before taking the vehicles back to their unit. DAVE WILLIAMS

This video capture shows a unit surrender sometime in May 1945 and features a unique combination: the turret from a *Panzer II, Ausführung L Luchs,* and the chassis from an *Sd.Kfz. 234* series vehicle. Evidence suggests that this vehicle belongs to the *1./Panzer-Aufklärungs-Abteilung 17.** To date, the short video offers the only known image of this perhaps unique hybrid that seems to sum up the desperation of the Germans in fielding vehicles at the end of the war. CRITICALPAST

See the interesting discussion on the enthusiast website Missing Lynx (www.network54.com/Forum/47207/message/1193479661/Unit+ID) for more information.

SS-Totenkopf-Aufklärungs-Abteilung

Committed in the northern sector of the Eastern Front, the *SS-Totenkopf-Aufklärungs-Abteilung* also featured a unique organization at the start of the campaign, having only two motorcycle infantry companies and a heavy company. Organic to the heavy company at the time, however, was an armored car platoon, which is frequently featured in this sequence of images taken by *SS-Kriegsberichter* Baumann. In the first three images, an *Sd.Kfz. 222* and an *Sd.Kfz. 223* wait for motorcycle infantrymen to pass by before heading out on a dirt road. The distinctive *Totenkopf* of the division can be seen on the left rear mudguard of the *Sd.Kfz. 223*. In the fourth photograph, motorcycle infantry race down the road, churning up clouds of dust. The fifth and sixth pictures show another *Sd.Kfz. 223* with fascines tied to the front, as was typical for armored cars of the battalion (see the color section following page 264). The final series of images shows men of one of the motorcycle infantry companies. NATIONAL ARCHIVES

A motorcycle infantryman pauses to pay respects to fallen comrades. NATIONAL ARCHIVES

The effects of road dust are readily apparent in this image of a *"Totenkopf" Sd.Kfz. 223*. Besides being a nuisance to crewmembers, the dust also had the tendency to foul air filters prematurely and cause excessive wear and tear on mechanical components of the vehicle.
NATIONAL ARCHIVES

Motorcycle infantry advance through terrain typical of the northern theater of operations. Operations frequently led through thickly wooded terrain, which featured virtually nonexistent road networks. In cases of inclement weather, the primitive paths turned into muddy quagmires, necessitating the men to dismount and manhandle their vehicles forward. In the summer, the region was often unbearably hot as well, not to mention a haven for swarms of mosquitos.
NATIONAL ARCHIVES

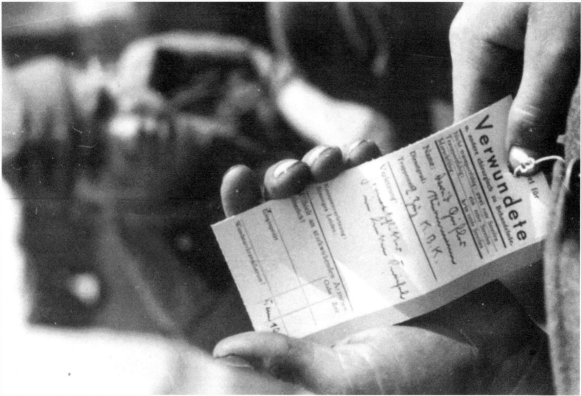

The evacuation of the wounded was trying even in the best of circumstances. For forces operating ahead of the main body it was doubly difficult, since recovery assets had to be brought forward and then returned through terrain that had usually not been cleared of enemy forces. The wound tag was affixed to the wounded soldiers by medics in the field so that medical personnel in the rear areas could rapidly perform triage on their incoming patients. NATIONAL ARCHIVES

THE CAMPAIGN AGAINST THE SOVIET UNION: BARBAROSSA UNLEASHED 271

Video captures from the weekly newsreel of 12 February 1941 show members of the *17. (Krad-)/Infanterie-Regiment (mot) "Großdeutschland"* conducting winter training on their motorcycles. This was the nucleus of what would become *Kradschützen-Bataillon "Großdeutschland"* and eventually *Panzer-Aufklärungs-Abteilung "Großdeutschland."* An *Sd.Kfz. 222* with snow chains mounted also participates in the exercise.

CHAPTER 7

1942: Debacle in the East

SETTING THE STAGE

After suffering its first operational setback in the winter of 1941–42, the German armed forces had to regroup and rebuild. The Eastern Front remained essentially static for the first half of 1942, except for local operations designed to streamline and improve defensive positions. Unable to conduct a major push along the entire front, the High Command eventually opted for its main offensive in the south, while *Heeresgruppe Nord* was to take Leningrad and link up with Finnish forces and *Heeresgruppe Mitte* was to conduct containment operations. To this end, large amounts of armored and motorized forces were transferred to *Heeresgruppe Süd*, and many formations that remained in the center and the north were forced to detach major elements to augment the new *Schwerpunkt*.

The overall plan in the south had a twofold objective, for which two army groups were eventually formed. *Heeresgruppe A* was tasked with crossing the Caucasus and reaching the strategically important oilfields around Baku. *Heeresgruppe B* was assigned the mission of covering the flanks of its southern neighbor while advancing toward the Volga and Stalingrad. This, in effect, created two competing *Schwerpunkte* that operated simultaneously instead of conducting a coordinated and multi-phased effort. Spectacular land gains were made in the direction of the oilfields, but continuing logistical problems meant that the offensive eventually sputtered to a slow crawl. To the north, *Heeresgruppe B* also found rough going, and its exhausted forces were unable to take the city of Stalingrad, despite controlling some 90 percent of the metropolis at one point. The *6. Armee* was overextended and

A column of heavy and light reconnaissance vehicles—led by an *Sd.Kfz. 231 (8 Rad)* and an *Sd.Kfz. 223*—moves down an unimproved road in a Soviet village. MIKE HARPE

relied on various Axis allies to protect the flanks. In the end, the Soviets launched counteroffensives that broke through the flank protection, encircled the forces in Stalingrad, and sealed their fate. This also forced the precipitous retreat of the forces of *Heeresgruppe A* in a difficult but ultimately successful effort to avoid encirclement and suffering the same fate as sister formations to the north.

It was largely thanks to the Soviets' overestimation of their capabilities that the Germans were eventually able to stop the enemy's offensive efforts, most notably at Kharkov, and reestablish some semblance of a defensive front, enabling them to plan another operational offensive for 1943.

DOCTRINE

The poor road networks in the Soviet Union, the protracted bouts of severe weather, and the sheer numbers and capabilities of Soviet weaponry compelled the planners of the High Command to analyze the requirements for the force as a whole. This included reconnaissance forces and resulted in the *Organizations-Abteilung* to issue a number of new or greatly modified *KStN's* for the force.

The force structure branch realized the need for greater cross-country mobility, crew protection, and firepower. That essentially spelled the end of the motorcycle infantry, even though the title was retained for some time. It was envisioned that the light half-track, the *Sd.Kfz. 250* series of vehicles, would eventually replace the venerable motorcycles. Because production of these vehicles never met demand, the conversion of the motorcycle infantry companies was a slow process, somewhat analogous to the attempts to field the *Sd.Kfz. 251* in larger numbers within motorized/mechanized infantry formations. As a result, parallel *KStN's* were developed which saw fieldings with light utility vehicles (the *Volkswagen*) or the motorcycle/half-track combination (*Kettenkrad*). Where even that was not possible, *KStN's* that still authorized motorcycles continued to be used.

In the case of the armored scout companies, older varieties of armored cars started to be phased out. However, it would still be some time before new types of vehicles would be introduced or armored scout *KStN's* developed to allocate the reconnaissance version of the light half-track, the *Sd.Kfz. 250/9*, or even fully tracked reconnaissance vehicles.

Because of the ongoing shortage of vehicles and the continued expansion of the force—Hitler often insisted on the activation of new formations instead of reconstituting decimated existing formations—the reconnaissance battalions were consolidated with the motorcycle infantry battalions in most of the divisions in the course of 1942. Because the armored scout companies were retained, they were still scouting and reconnaissance assets, despite keeping the designation of *Kradschützen-Bataillone*. The desire was to have at least one armored car company and one light reconnaissance company (light half-tracks) in each battalion.

The *Waffen-SS* became interested in the concept of so-called *schnelle Regimenter* (fast regiments), which were to be highly mobile forces able to respond to ever-changing situations on the battlefield. Since these regiments were composed primarily of motorcycle infantry and *Volkswagen*-equipped light reconnaissance companies, they are worthy of note here, even though there were not strictly reconnaissance assets. While the concept might have worked well on the advanced infrastructure of Western Europe, motorcycles and *Volkswagen* light utility vehicles did not hold up well to the rigors of the Soviet Union, and the regiments were soon disbanded, with their assets distributed among the division.

Given the static nature of most of the fighting in the first half of 1942, the reconnaissance battalions were generally held as ready reserves or actually occupied sections of the line. In cases where the frontages exceeded the doctrinal limitations, the reconnaissance battalions were often employed in economy-of-force missions, where strongpoints were occupied and standing mobile patrols were established to cover gaps in the lines. Once offensive operations were initiated in the south, the reconnaissance battalions were again employed in a classic role, either conducting longer-range reconnaissance or acting as advance guards for the divisions. If flanks were exposed, elements of the battalion were frequently employed in screening or flank guard missions.

After widespread withdrawals began in the south, the reconnaissance battalions were often the division favorite for rearguard actions, since their extensive firepower allowed them to "paint the picture" of a much larger force.

ORGANIZATION

As mentioned previously, 1942 saw the consolidation of the reconnaissance battalions of the armored and motorized divisions with the motorcycle infantry battalions, resulting generally in a battalion having a headquarters, one armored car company, three motorcycle infantry companies, and one heavy company. In some cases, a motorcycle infantry company was replaced by a light armored reconnaissance company. This generally occurred in armored divisions but was not universal. As before, the divisions in North Africa continued to field their own reconnaissance formations, which retained the designation of *Aufklärungs-Abteilungen*.

ORDER OF BATTLE FOR THE EASTERN FRONT, 28 JUNE 1942 (MAJOR RECONNAISSANCE ELEMENTS)

Parent Organization	Reconnaissance Assets / Notes
Heeresgruppe Nord	
16. Armee	
XXXIX. Armee-Korps (mot) (XXXIX. Panzer-Korps) (This motorized corps was not redesignated as a *Panzer-Korps* until 9 July 1942)	
8. Panzer-Division	*Kradschützen-Bataillon 8*: The battalion had a headquarters (*KStN 1109* / 1 November 1941); three motorcycle reconnaissance companies (*KStN 1112* / 1 November 1941); and one heavy company with a headquarters (*KStN 1121*), one motorized infantry gun platoon (*KStN 1123*), one antitank rifle section (*KStN 1127*), one antitank gun platoon (*KStN 1122a* / 1 December 1941), and one combat engineer platoon (*KStN 1124*). (All 1 November 1941, except as noted.) Some sources say the battalion did not have an armored scout company at the time.[1]
II. Armee-Korps	
SS-Totenkopf-Division (mot)	*SS-Totenkopf-Aufklärungs-Abteilung*: Organized with one armored car company, one motorcycle infantry company, and one heavy company (infantry gun platoon, antitank gun platoon (50mm), and company engineer platoon).
	SS-Totenkopf-Kradschützen-Bataillon: Organized with three motorcycle infantry companies, one motorized machine-gun company (*KStN 1116* / 1 November 1941), and one heavy company (infantry gun platoon, antitank gun platoon (50mm), and company engineer platoon).
X. Armee-Korps	
18. Infanterie-Division (mot)	*Kradschützen-Bataillon 38*: Organized as with *Kradschützen-Bataillon 8* (*8. Panzer-Division*) above, but also including one armored car company (1st Company) organized under *KStN 1162* of 1 November 1941.
18. Armee	
XXXVIII. Armee-Korps	
SS-Brigade 2 (mot)	*SS-Kradschützen-Kompanie 52*: Organized under *KStN 1112* of 1 November 1941, with an armored car platoon attached (*KStN 1137* / 1 February 1941)[2]
I. Armee-Korps	
20. Infanterie-Division (mot)	*Kradschützen-Bataillon 30*: Standard organization, with a headquarters; one armored car company; three motorcycle infantry companies; and one heavy company with one infantry gun platoon, one antitank rifle section, one antitank gun platoon, and one combat engineer platoon.
XXVIII. Armee-Korps	
12. Panzer-Division	*Kradschützen-Bataillon 22*: Standard organization, as with *Kradschützen-Bataillon 30* (*20. Infanterie-Division (mot)*) above.

Parent Organization	Reconnaissance Assets / Notes
Heeresgruppe Mitte	
2. Panzer-Armee	
XXXV. Armee-Korps	
4. Panzer-Division	*Kradschützen-Bataillon 34*: Standard organization, as with *Kradschützen-Bataillon 30 (20. Infanterie-Division (mot))* above.
LIII. Armee-Korps	
25. Infanterie-Division (mot)	*Kradschützen-Bataillon 25*: Standard organization, as with *Kradschützen-Bataillon 30 (20. Infanterie-Division (mot))* above, although armored car company was the 4th Company.
XXXXVII. Panzer-Korps	
18. Panzer-Division	*Kradschützen-Bataillon 18*: As with *Kradschützen-Bataillon 8 (8. Panzer-Division)* above, although sources agree there was no armored car company at the time.
17. Panzer-Division	*Kradschützen-Bataillon 17*: Standard organization, as with *Kradschützen-Bataillon 30 (20. Infanterie-Division (mot))* above.
4. Armee	
LVI. Panzer-Korps	
10. Infanterie-Division (mot)	*Kradschützen-Bataillon 40*: Standard organization, as with *Kradschützen-Bataillon 30 (20. Infanterie-Division (mot))* above.
19. Panzer-Division	*Kradschützen-Bataillon 19*: Standard organization, as with *Kradschützen-Bataillon 30 (20. Infanterie-Division (mot))* above.
3. Panzer-Armee	
20. Panzer-Division	*Kradschützen-Bataillon 20*: As with *Kradschützen-Bataillon 8 (8. Panzer-Division)* above, although sources agree there was no armored car company at the time. It is not certain why, since the battalion had two companies of Panhard armored cars at the start of Barbarossa.[3]
XXXXI Armee-Korps (mot) (XXXXI. Panzer-Korps)[4]	
36. Infanterie-Division (mot)	*Kradschützen-Bataillon 36*: Standard organization, as with *Kradschützen-Bataillon 30 (20. Infanterie-Division (mot))* above.
9. Armee	
XXVII. Armee-Korps	
14. Infanterie-Division (mot)	*Kradschützen-Bataillon 54*: Standard organization, as with *Kradschützen-Bataillon 30 (20. Infanterie-Division (mot))* above.
XXII. Armee-Korps	
1. Panzer-Division	*Kradschützen-Bataillon 1*: Standard organization, as with *Kradschützen-Bataillon 30 (20. Infanterie-Division (mot))* above.
XXXXVI. Panzer-Korps	
5. Panzer-Division	*Kradschützen-Bataillon 55*: Standard organization, as with *Kradschützen-Bataillon 30 (20. Infanterie-Division (mot))* above, except the heavy company did not have an antitank rifle section, and the antitank gun platoon had 37mm instead of 50mm antitank guns.
Gruppe Esebeck	
2. Panzer-Division	*Kradschützen-Bataillon 2*: Standard organization, as with *Kradschützen-Bataillon 30 (20. Infanterie-Division (mot))* above.
Heeresgruppe Süd	
Gruppe von Förster	
XIV. Panzer-Korps	
Leibstandarte SS Adolf Hitler	*SS-Aufklärungs-Abteilung (mot) Leibstandarte SS Adolf Hitler*: Standard organization, as with *Kradschützen-Bataillon 30 (20. Infanterie-Division (mot))* above, except a light armored reconnaissance company (*KStN 1113 (gp)* / 1 March 1942) replaced one of the motorcycle infantry companies (4th Company). The battalion kept its designation of *Aufklärungs-Abteilung*.
13. Panzer-Division	*Kradschützen-Bataillon 43*: Standard organization, as with *Kradschützen-Bataillon 30 (20. Infanterie-Division (mot))* above, except a light armored reconnaissance company replaced one of the motorcycle infantry companies (2nd Company).

Parent Organization	Reconnaissance Assets / Notes
XIV. Panzer-Korps continued	
SS-Wiking-Division (mot)	SS-Aufklärungs-Abteilung (mot) "Wiking": Organized like SS-Totenkopf-Aufklärungs-Abteilung above.

	Schnelles SS-Regiment "Westland": Composed of two battalions, it was formed from personnel levies against the motorized infantry regiments. The two battalions were organized identically.
	*** Regimental headquarters: headquarters, motorized infantry regiment (KStN 1104) and headquarters company, motorized infantry regiment (KStN 1153) (both dated 1 November 1941)
	** Two battalion headquarters: headquarters and motorcycle infantry battalion (KStN 1109 / 1 November 1941). Each battalion with:
	  * Three motorcycle infantry companies (KStN 1112 / 1 November 1941) or motorized infantry companies (Volkswagen) (KStN 1113 (VW) / 18 March 1942)
	  * One motorcycle machine-gun company (KStN 1118 / 1 February 1941)
	  * One heavy company: standard headquarters, antitank gun platoon (50mm), infantry gun platoon, and combat engineer platoon.

1. Panzer-Armee	
III. Panzer-Korps	
14. Panzer-Division	Kradschützen-Bataillon 64: Organized identically to Kradschützen-Bataillon 43 (13. Panzer-Division) above.
16. Panzer-Division	Kradschützen-Bataillon 16: Organized identically to Kradschützen-Bataillon 43 (13. Panzer-Division) above.
22. Panzer-Division	Kradschützen-Bataillon 24: Organized identically to Kradschützen-Bataillon 43 (13. Panzer-Division) above.[5]
60. Infanterie-Division (mot)	Kradschützen-Bataillon 160: Organized identically to Kradschützen-Bataillon 38 (18. Infanterie-Division (mot)) above.
6. Armee	
XXXX. Armee-Korps (mot) (XXXX. Panzer-Korps)[6]	
3. Panzer-Division	Kradschützen-Bataillon 3: Organized identically to Kradschützen-Bataillon 43 (13. Panzer-Division) above, although the armored light reconnaissance company was the 4th Company.
23. Panzer-Division	Kradschützen-Bataillon 23: Organized identically to Kradschützen-Bataillon 43 (13. Panzer-Division) above.
29. Infanterie-Division (mot)	Kradschützen-Bataillon 29: Organized identically to Kradschützen-Bataillon 38 (18. Infanterie-Division (mot)) above.
2nd Army (Hungary) **III Corps (Hungary)**	
16. Infanterie-Division (mot)	Kradschützen-Bataillon 165: Organized identically to Kradschützen-Bataillon 38 (18. Infanterie-Division (mot)) above.
4. Panzer-Armee	
XXIV. Panzer-Korps	
9. Panzer-Division	Kradschützen-Bataillon 59: Organized identically to Kradschützen-Bataillon 43 (13. Panzer-Division) above.
3. Infanterie-Division 3 (mot)	Kradschützen-Bataillon 53: Organized identically to Kradschützen-Bataillon 38 (18. Infanterie-Division (mot)) above.
XIII. Armee-Korps	
11. Panzer-Division	Kradschützen-Bataillon 61: Organized identically to Kradschützen-Bataillon 43 (13. Panzer-Division) above.
	Attached—Kradschützen-Lehr-Bataillon: Standard headquarters armored car company (1st), motorcycle infantry company (2nd), light armored reconnaissance company (4th), and heavy company (5th). The 3rd company was organized under KStN 1113 of 18 March 1942 as a light motorized reconnaissance company (Volkswagen).
XXXXVIII. Panzer-Korps	
Infanterie-Division (mot) "Großdeutschland"	Kradschützen-Bataillon "Großdeutschland": Organized with an armored car company (KStN 1162), a light armored reconnaissance company (KStN 1113 (gp)), a motorized light reconnaissance company (Volkswagen) (KStN 1113 (VW)), and a heavy company (standard organization with infantry gun platoon, antitank gun platoon, and combat engineer platoon, but no antitank rifle section).[7]
24. Panzer-Division	Kradschützen-Bataillon 24: Organized identically to Kradschützen-Bataillon 43 (13. Panzer-Division) above.
2. Armee	
SS-Brigade 1 (mot)	SS-Kradschützen-Kompanie 51: Organized under KStN 1112 of 1 November 1941, with an armored car platoon attached (KStN 1137 / 1 February 1941).

ORDER OF BATTLE: MAJOR RECONNAISSANCE ELEMENTS, 28 JUNE 1942 (NON-EASTERN FRONT)

Parent Organization	Reconnaissance Assets / Notes
Oberkommando der Wehrmacht—Armee Norwegen	
25. Panzer-Division	*Kradschützen-Bataillon 25*: Not yet formed. By February 1943, it was organized identically to *Kradschützen-Bataillon 38* (*18. Infanterie-Division (mot)*) above, with the armored scout company the last unit to join the formation.
Heeresgruppe D *15. Armee*	
10. Panzer-Division	*Kradschützen-Bataillon 10*: Organized identically to *Kradschützen-Bataillon 43* (*13. Panzer-Division*) above.
7. Armee	
Regiment "General Göring" (mot)	Still a reinforced regiment/brigade[8] in the summer of 1942, the formation was ordered to be expanded, reorganized, and redesignated into a division in October 1942. As the former formation, the reconnaissance assets were located in two companies, the 10th (Motorcycle Infantry) and the 13th (Armor) of *Schützen-Regiment "Hermann Göring,"* with an armored car platoon located within the latter company. The divisional reconnaissance battalion, which was later deployed to North Africa, had a unique structure, with a headquarters company and six line companies: 1st Company—motorcycle infantry company, 2nd Company—wheeled reconnaissance company, 3rd Company—armored scout company, 4th Company—antitank company, 5th Company—heavy company, 6th Company—antiaircraft company (2cm).[9]
6. Panzer-Division	*Kradschützen-Bataillon 6*: Organized identically to *Kradschützen-Bataillon 43* (*13. Panzer-Division*) above.
SS-Reich-Division	*SS-Aufklärungs-Abteilung "Reich"*: The battalion had one armored car company, one light armored reconnaissance company, and one heavy company, all organized like the standard army counterparts, although the heavy company did not have an antitank rifle section. The battalion kept its designation of *Aufklärungs-Abteilung*.

	Schnelles SS-Regiment "Langemarck": Composed of two battalions, it was formed from consolidation with *SS-Kradschützen-Bataillon "Reich"* and personnel levies against the motorized infantry regiments. The two battalions were organized identically.
	*** Regimental headquarters: headquarters, motorized infantry regiment (*KStN 1104*) and headquarters company, and motorized infantry regiment (*KStN 1153*) (Both dated 1 November 1941)
	** Two battalion headquarters: headquarters and motorized infantry battalion (*KStN 1108* / 1 November 1941). Each battalion with:
	   * Three motorized infantry companies (*Volkswagen*) (*KStN 1113* / 1 March 1942)
	   * One motorized machine-gun company (*KStN 1116* / 1 February 1941)
	   * One heavy company: standard headquarters, antitank gun platoon (50mm), infantry gun platoon, and combat engineer platoon.

1. Armee	
7. Panzer-Division	*Kradschützen-Bataillon 7*: Organized identically to *Kradschützen-Bataillon 43* (*13. Panzer-Division*) above.[10]
Panzer-Armee "Afrika"	
90. leichte Division	See Chapter 5.
Deutsches Afrika-Korps	
15. Panzer-Division	See Chapter 5.
21. Panzer-Division	See Chapter 5.

CHANGES IN ORGANIZATIONAL AUTHORIZATIONS (1 NOVEMBER AND 1 DECEMBER 1941)

Headquarters, Motorized Reconnaissance Battalion (1109)

In this update to the *KStN*, introduced on 1 November 1941, the command group of the battalion remained essentially the same, with motorcycle allocations and trucks changing slightly, and a command and control armored car added (*Sd.Kfz. 247*). The signals section was upgraded to a platoon, with all field telephone sections eliminated. The allocations of radio armored cars were increased substantially.

- Headquarters: eight motorcycles, two sidecar motorcycles, two medium cross-country wheeled personnel carriers (*Kfz. 15*), and one heavy wheeled cross-country armored personnel carrier (*Sd.Kfz. 247*).
- Signals platoon:
  - Headquarters section: one motorcycle, one sidecar motorcycle, and one medium cross-country wheeled personnel carrier (*Kfz. 15*).
  - Two manpack radio sections (Type *b*): one light cross-country radio utility vehicle (*Kfz. 2*).
  - One light armored radio section (Type *b*): one light armored radio car (*Sd.Kfz. 260*).
  - Four light armored radio sections (Type *c*): one light armored radio car (*Sd.Kfz. 261*).
  - Three medium armored radio sections (Type *c*): one medium cross-country wheeled personnel carrier (*Kfz. 15*) and one heavy armored radio car (*Sd.Kfz. 263*).

a) Command Group

8x Medium and 2x Sidecar Motorcycle	Medium Cross-Country Vehicle with Equipment Storage Box (*Kfz. 15*)	Medium Cross-Country Vehicle with Equipment Storage Box (*Kfz. 15*)	Heavy Cross-Country Vehicle (*Sd.Kfz. 247*), 1x Submachine Gun

Totals Command Section: 5x Officers, 4x NCOs, 15x Enlisted Personnel; 16x Rifles, 6x Pistols, 3x Submachine Guns; 2x Wheeled Vehicles, 1x Armored Vehicle, 8x Motorcycles, 2x Sidecar Motorcycles

b) Signals Platoon

Signals Vehicle (*Kfz. 15*)	Medium Motorcycle	Sidecar Motorcycle

Small Telephone Section c (Motorized)
1st Backpack Radio Section b (Motorized) — **2nd Backpack Radio Section b (Motorized)**

Radio Vehicle (*Kfz. 2*) (3 seat)	Radio Vehicle (*Kfz. 2*) (3 seat)

Small Armored Radio Section c (Motorized)

Small Armored Radio Car (*Sd.Kfz. 260*), 1x Submachine Gun

1st Small Armored Radio Section d (Motorized)	2nd Small Armored Radio Section d (Motorized)	3rd Small Armored Radio Section d (Motorized)	4th Small Armored Radio Section d (Motorized)
Small Armored Radio Car (*Sd.Kfz. 261*)	Small Armored Radio Car (*Sd.Kfz. 261*)	Small Armored Radio Car (*Sd.Kfz. 261*)	Small Armored Radio Car (*Sd.Kfz. 261*)

Note: *Kfz. 17* counts in lieu of *Sd.Kfz. 261*. Each vehicle has 1x Submachine Gun

280 TIP OF THE SPEAR

1st Medium Armored Radio Section b (Motorized)	2nd Medium Armored Radio Section b (Motorized)	3rd Medium Armored Radio Section b (Motorized)
Armored Radio Car (*Sd.Kfz. 263*) Radio Vehicle (*Kfz. 15*)	Armored Radio Car (*Sd.Kfz. 263*) Radio Vehicle (*Kfz. 15*)	Armored Radio Car (*Sd.Kfz. 263*) Radio Vehicle (*Kfz. 15*)

Note: *Kfz. 17* counts in lieu of *Sd.Kfz. 261*. Each vehicle has 1x Submachine Gun.

Total Signal Platoon: 1x Officer, 15x NCOs, 45x Enlisted Personnel; 16x Rifles, 44x Pistols, 9x Submachine Guns, 3x Light MG's; 7x Wheeled Vehicles, 8x Armored Vehicles, 1x Medium Motorcycle, 1x Sidecar Motorcycle

c) Combat Trains I

Light Utility Vehicle (4 seat)	Light Cross-Country Truck, Canvas Top, for Petroleum, Oil & Lubricants	Medium Cross-Country Truck, Canvas Top, for Large Field Mess Stove	Ambulance (*Kfz. 31*)	Sidecar Motorcycle

Totals: 4x NCOs, 10x Enlisted Personnel; 9x Rifles, 5x Pistols; 4x Vehicles, 1x Sidecar Motorcycle

d) Combat Trains II
Maintenance Section (Vehicles and Weapons)

Small Maintenance Vehicle (*Kfz. 2/40*)	Medium Cross-Country Vehicle with Equipment Storage Box (*Kfz. 15*)	Medium Cross-Country Truck, Canvas Top, for Armorer's Equipment	Medium Cross-Country Truck, Canvas Top, for Maintenance Equipment
Medium Cross-Country Truck, Canvas Top, for Tires and Recovery	Medium Cross-Country Truck, Canvas Top, for Replacement Parts	Medium Cross-Country Truck, Canvas Top, for Armored Car Replacement	Sidecar Motorcycle

Supply Section

Light Utility Vehicle, 1x Motorcycle	Light Cross-Country Truck, Canvas Top, for Ammunition and Equipment for Armored Cars	Medium Cross-Country Truck, Canvas Top, for Ammunition and Equipment	Medium Cross-Country Truck, Canvas Top, for Ammunition and Equipment

4x Medium Cross-Country Truck, Canvas Top, for Petroleum, Oil & Lubricants transport

Totals: 1x Officer, 3x Civilian Officials, 5x NCOs, 41x Enlisted Personnel; 42x Rifles, 8x Pistols; 15x Vehicles, 1x Medium Motorcycle, 1x Sidecar Motorcycle

e) Rations Trains for the Entire Battalion

Light Utility Vehicle	Medium Truck, 3 ton, Canvas Top, for Rations	Medium Truck, 3 ton, Canvas Top, for Rations

Totals: 1x Officer, 1x Civilian Official, 2x NCOs, 5x Enlisted Personnel; 6x Rifles, 2x Pistols; 3x Vehicles

f) Baggage Trains

 Motorcyclist, Messenger (Medium Motorcycles), 1x Rifle

 Medium Truck, 3 ton, Canvas Top, for Baggage

Totals: 1x NCO, 4x Enlisted Personnel; 5x Rifles; 1x Vehicle, 1x Medium Motorcycle

Summary

	Officers	Civilian Officials	NCOs	Enlisted Personnel	Rifles	Pistols (Submachine Guns)	Light MG's	Wheeled Vehicles	Armored Vehicles	Motorcycles (Sidecar Motorcycles)
Command Section	5		4	15	16	6 (3)		2	1	10 (2)
Signals Platoon	1		15	45	16	44 (9)	3	7	8	2 (1)
Combat Trains I			4	10	9	5		4		1 (1)
Combat Trains II	1	3	5	41	42	8		15		2 (1)
Rations Trains	1	1	2	5	7	2		3		
Baggage Trains			1	4	5			1		1
Totals	**8**	**4**	**31**	**120**	**95**	**65 (12)**	**3**	**32**	**9**	**16 (5)**

Motorcycle Infantry Company (1112)

This *KStN* was updated on 1 November 1941, replacing the provisional one issued in February of the same year. The heavy weapons were consolidated into a heavy platoon. The three 50mm mortars were replaced by two 81mm mortars and the number of heavy machine guns doubled from two to four. In addition, each of the line platoons received an antitank rifle.
- Company headquarters: four motorcycles, two sidecar motorcycles, and one medium cross-country wheeled personnel carrier (*Kfz. 15*).
- Three motorcycle reconnaissance platoons:
  - Headquarters: one motorcycle, two medium cross-country wheeled personnel carriers (*Kfz. 15*), and one antitank rifle.
  - Three motorcycle infantry squads: four sidecar motorcycles, one motorcycle reconnaissance squad, and two light machine guns.
- One heavy platoon:
  - Headquarters: one motorcycle, one sidecar motorcycle, and two medium cross-country wheeled personnel carriers (*Kfz. 15*).
  - Two heavy machine-gun sections: eight sidecar motorcycles and two heavy machine guns.
  - One mortar section: three heavy wheeled personnel carriers (*Kfz. 70*) and two medium mortars (81mm).

Light Armored Reconnaissance Company (1113 (*gp*))

This *KStN* was introduced on 1 March 1942 and represented one of the first efforts to upgrade the motorcycle infantry companies with armored vehicles in the form of variants of the light armored personnel carrier, the *Sd.Kfz. 250*. The antitank rifles were replaced by 37mm antitank guns mounted on the *Sd.Kfz. 250/10*. Structurally, it was similar to its predecessors, but it had substantially more cross-country, firepower, and radio communications capability and protection for the crewmembers and reconnaissance squads. There was an almost threefold increase in light machine guns due to the mounting of the *MG 34* on each of the authorized half-tracks.
- Company headquarters: four motorcycles, one sidecar motorcycle, and two light armored radio carriers (*Sd.Kfz. 250/3*).
- Three reconnaissance platoons:
  - Headquarters: one light armored personnel carrier (*Sd.Kfz. 250/1*) and one light armored personnel carrier with 37mm antitank gun (*Sd.Kfz. 250/10*).
  - Three reconnaissance squads: two light armored personnel carriers (*Sd.Kfz. 250/1*), one reconnaissance squad, and two light machine guns.
- One heavy platoon:
  - Headquarters: one motorcycle and one light armored personnel carrier (*Sd.Kfz. 250/1*).
  - Two heavy machine-gun sections: three light armored personnel carriers (*Sd.Kfz. 250/1*) and two heavy machine guns.
  - One mortar section: two light armored personnel carriers with 81mm mortar (*Sd.Kfz. 250/7*) and two light armored personnel carriers (ammunition carriers) (*Sd.Kfz. 250/7*).

a) Command Group

4x Medium Motorcycle, 1x Sidecar Motorcycle	2x Light Armored Radio Car (*Sd.Kfz. 250/3*), 1x Submachine Gun, 1x Light MG, 1x Radio Set (*Fu8 SE 30*) and Mount for 2 Sub-Units, 1x Radio Set a

Totals: 1x Officer, 3x NCOs, 10x Enlisted Personnel; 11x Rifles, 2x Pistols, 3x Submachine Guns, 2x Light MG's; 2x Armored Vehicles, 4x Motorcycles, 1x Sidecar Motorcycle

b) 1st Platoon
Platoon Headquarters Section

Light Armored Personnel Carrier (*Sd.Kfz. 250/1*), 1x Light MG, 1x Submachine Gun, 1x Voice Radio Set a	Light Armored Personnel Carrier (*Sd.Kfz. 250/10*), 1x Light MG, 1x 3.7cm *Pak*, 1x Submachine Gun, 1x Voice Radio Set a

1st Squad	2nd Squad	3rd Squad
Light Armored Personnel Carrier (*Sd.Kfz. 250/1*), 1x Light MG, 1x Submachine Gun, 1x Voice Radio Set a and 2x Light MG	Light Armored Personnel Carrier (*Sd.Kfz. 250/1*), 1x Light MG, 1x Submachine Gun, 1x Voice Radio Set a and 2x Light MG	Light Armored Personnel Carrier (*Sd.Kfz. 250/1*), 1x Light MG, 1x Submachine Gun, 1x Voice Radio Set a and 2x Light MG

Totals: 1x Officer, 8x NCOs, 36x Enlisted Personnel; 24x Rifles, 17x Pistols, 12x Submachine Guns, 14x Light MG's, 1x 3.7cm *Pak*; 8x Half-tracked Vehicles

c) 2nd Platoon
Platoon Headquarters Section

Light Armored Personnel Carrier (*Sd.Kfz. 250/1*), 1x Light MG, 1x Submachine Gun, 1x Voice Radio Set a	Light Armored Personnel Carrier (*Sd.Kfz. 250/10*), 1x Light MG, 1x 3.7cm *Pak*, 1x Submachine Gun, 1x Voice Radio Set a

1st Squad	2nd Squad	3rd Squad

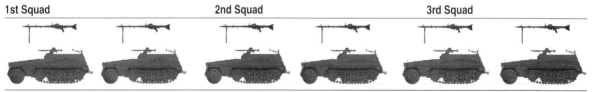

| Light Armored Personnel Carrier (*Sd.Kfz. 250/1*), 1x Light MG, 1x Submachine Gun, 1x Voice Radio Set a and 2x Light MG | Light Armored Personnel Carrier (*Sd.Kfz. 250/1*), 1x Light MG, 1x Submachine Gun, 1x Voice Radio Set a and 2x Light MG | Light Armored Personnel Carrier (*Sd.Kfz. 250/1*), 1x Light MG, 1x Submachine Gun, 1x Voice Radio Set a and 2x Light MG |

Totals: 1x Officer, 8x NCOs, 36x Enlisted Personnel; 24x Rifles, 17x Pistols, 12x Submachine Guns, 14x Light MG's, 1x 3.7cm *Pak*; 8x Half-tracked Vehicles

d) 3rd Platoon
Platoon Headquarters Section

Light Armored Personnel Carrier (*Sd.Kfz. 250/1*), 1x Light MG, 1x Submachine Gun, 1x Voice Radio Set a	Light Armored Personnel Carrier (*Sd.Kfz. 250/10*), 1x Light MG, 1x 3.7cm *Pak*, 1x Submachine Gun, 1x Voice Radio Set a

1942: DEBACLE IN THE EAST 283

1st Squad	2nd Squad	3rd Squad

| Light Armored Personnel Carrier (*Sd.Kfz. 250/1*), 1x Light MG, 1x Submachine Gun, 1x Voice Radio Set a and 2x Light MG | Light Armored Personnel Carrier (*Sd.Kfz. 250/1*), 1x Light MG, 1x Submachine Gun, 1x Voice Radio Set a and 2x Light MG | Light Armored Personnel Carrier (*Sd.Kfz. 250/1*), 1x Light MG, 1x Submachine Gun, 1x Voice Radio Set a and 2x Light MG |

Totals: 1x Officer, 8x NCOs, 36x Enlisted Personnel; 24x Rifles, 17x Pistols, 12x Submachine Guns, 14x Light MG's, 1x 3.7cm *Pak*; 8x Half-tracked Vehicles

e) 4th (Heavy) Platoon
Platoon Headquarters Section

Medium Motorcycle	Light Armored Personnel Carrier (*Sd.Kfz. 250/1*), 1x Light MG, 1x Submachine Gun, 1x Voice Radio Set a

1st (Heavy Machine Gun) Section   **2nd (Heavy Machine Gun) Section**

3x Light Armored Personnel Carrier (*Sd.Kfz. 250/1*), 1x Light MG, 1x Submachine Gun, 1x Voice Radio Set a and 2x Heavy MG	3x Light Armored Personnel Carrier (*Sd.Kfz. 250/1*), 1x Light MG, 1x Submachine Gun, 1x Voice Radio Set a and 2x Heavy MG

3rd Section (Heavy Mortar)

Light Armored Personnel Carrier (Heavy Mortar) (*Sd.Kfz. 250/7*) for the Gun Commander, 1x Submachine Gun, 1x Light MG, 1x Voice Radio Set a (Ammunition)	Light Armored Personnel Carrier (Heavy Mortar) (*Sd.Kfz. 250/7*) for Ammunition, 1x Submachine Gun, 1x Light MG, 1x Voice Radio Set a (Mortar)	Light Armored Personnel Carrier (Heavy Mortar) (*Sd.Kfz. 250/7*) for the Gun Commander, 1x Submachine Gun, 1x Light MG, 1x Voice Radio Set a (Ammunition)	Light Armored Personnel Carrier (Heavy Mortar) (*Sd.Kfz. 250/7*) for Ammunition, 1x Submachine Gun, 1x Light MG, 1x Voice Radio Set a (Mortar)

Totals: 1x Officer, 10x NCOs, 47x Enlisted Personnel; 29x Rifles, 23x Pistols, 17x Submachine Guns, 4x Heavy MG's, 11x Light MG's, 2x Heavy Mortars; 11 Armored Vehicles, 1x Medium Motorcycle

f) Vehicle Maintenance Section

Sidecar Motorcycle	2x Light Cross-Country Truck, Canvas Top, for Spare Parts	Light Prime Mover, 1 ton (*Sd.Kfz. 10*) Small Maintenance Vehicle, 1x Light MG (on Model 41 MG Mount) for Prime Mover

Totals: 1x NCO, 12x Enlisted Personnel; 10x Rifles, 3x Pistols, 1x Light MG; 3x Vehicles, 1x Sidecar Motorcycle

g) Combat Trains I (Combat Trains II with the Battalion Headquarters)

Medium Cross-Country Vehicle with Equipment Storage Box (*Kfz. 15*)	Light Cross-Country Truck, Canvas Top, for Petroleum, Oil & Lubricants	Medium Cross-Country Truck, Canvas Top, for Large Field Mess Stove	Medium Cross-Country Truck, Canvas Top, for Large Field Mess Stove (with Combat Trains II)

Totals: 4x NCOs, 9x Enlisted Personnel; 10x Rifles, 3x Pistols; 4x Wheeled Vehicles

Summary

	Officers	NCOs	Enlisted Personnel	Rifles	Pistols (Submachine Guns)	Heavy MG's (Light MG's)	Guns w/o Limbers (Mortars)	Wheeled Vehicles	Armored Vehicles	Motorcycles (Sidecar Motorcycles)
Command Section	1	3	10	11	2 (3)	(2)			2	5 (1)
1st Platoon	1	8	36	24	17 (12)	(14)	1		8	
2nd Platoon	1	8	36	24	17 (12)	(14)	1		8	
3rd Platoon	1	8	36	24	17 (12)	(14)	1		8	
4th Heavy Platoon	1	10	47	29	23 (17)	4 (11)	2		11	1
Vehicle Maintenance Section		1	12	10	3	(1)		3		1 (1)
Combat Trains I		4	9	10	3			4		
Baggage Trains		1	3	4				1		
Totals	5	43	189	136	82 (56)	4 (56)	5	8	37	7 (2)

Light Motorized Reconnaissance Company (Volkswagen) (1113)

This *KStN* was introduced on 18 March 1942. It likewise represented an effort to upgrade the capabilities of the standard motorcycle infantry company, while taking into account that Germany's production of light armored personnel carriers was insufficient to convert all of the latter into light armored reconnaissance companies. Its weaponry was the same as a motorcycle infantry company.

- Company headquarters: four motorcycles and three light cross-country utility vehicles (*Sd.Kfz. 1—Volkswagen*).
- Three motorized reconnaissance platoons:
  - Headquarters: one motorcycle, two light cross-country utility vehicles (*Sd.Kfz. 1*), and one antitank rifle.
  - Three motorcycle infantry squads: four light cross-country utility vehicles (*Sd.Kfz. 1*), one reconnaissance squad, and two light machine guns.
- One heavy platoon:
  - Headquarters: one motorcycle and three light cross-country utility vehicles (*Sd.Kfz. 1*).
  - Two heavy machine-gun sections: seven light cross-country utility vehicles (*Sd.Kfz. 1*) and two heavy machine guns.
  - One mortar section: three heavy wheeled personnel carriers (*Kfz. 70*) and two medium mortars (81mm).

1942: DEBACLE IN THE EAST

a) Command Group
Company Headquarters Section

| 4x Medium Motorcycle | 3x Light Cross-Country Vehicle (*Kfz. 1*) |

Totals: 1x Officer, 3x NCOs, 8x Enlisted Personnel; 9x Rifles, 2x Pistols, 1x Submachine Gun; 3x Vehicles, 4x Medium Motorcycles

b) 1st Platoon
Platoon Headquarters Section

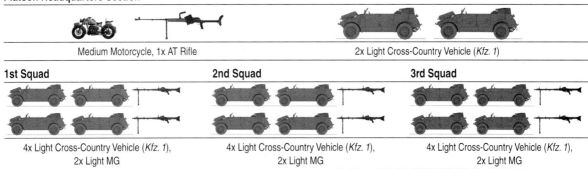

Medium Motorcycle, 1x AT Rifle | 2x Light Cross-Country Vehicle (*Kfz. 1*)

1st Squad — 4x Light Cross-Country Vehicle (*Kfz. 1*), 2x Light MG
2nd Squad — 4x Light Cross-Country Vehicle (*Kfz. 1*), 2x Light MG
3rd Squad — 4x Light Cross-Country Vehicle (*Kfz. 1*), 2x Light MG

Totals: 1x Officer, 4x NCOs, 38x Enlisted Personnel; 26x Rifles, 1x Submachine Gun, 1x AT Rifle, 6x Light MG's; 14x Vehicles, 1x Motorcycle

c) 2nd Platoon
Platoon Headquarters Section

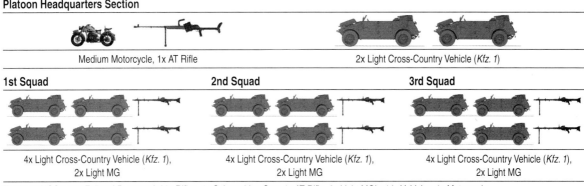

Medium Motorcycle, 1x AT Rifle | 2x Light Cross-Country Vehicle (*Kfz. 1*)

1st Squad — 4x Light Cross-Country Vehicle (*Kfz. 1*), 2x Light MG
2nd Squad — 4x Light Cross-Country Vehicle (*Kfz. 1*), 2x Light MG
3rd Squad — 4x Light Cross-Country Vehicle (*Kfz. 1*), 2x Light MG

Totals: 5x NCOs, 38x Enlisted Personnel; 26x Rifles, 1x Submachine Gun, 1x AT Rifle, 6x Light MG's; 14x Vehicles, 1x Motorcycle

d) 3rd Platoon
Platoon Headquarters Section

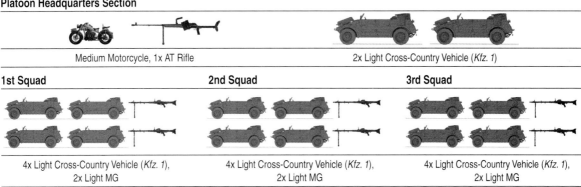

Medium Motorcycle, 1x AT Rifle | 2x Light Cross-Country Vehicle (*Kfz. 1*)

1st Squad — 4x Light Cross-Country Vehicle (*Kfz. 1*), 2x Light MG
2nd Squad — 4x Light Cross-Country Vehicle (*Kfz. 1*), 2x Light MG
3rd Squad — 4x Light Cross-Country Vehicle (*Kfz. 1*), 2x Light MG

Totals: 5x NCOs, 38x Enlisted Personnel; 26x Rifles, 1x Submachine Gun, 1x AT Rifle, 6x Light MG's; 14x Vehicles, 1x Motorcycle

e) 4th (Heavy) Platoon
Platoon Headquarters Section

Medium Motorcycle	3x Light Cross-Country Vehicle (*Kfz. 1*)

1st (Heavy Machine-Gun) Section | 2nd (Heavy) Machine-Gun Section

3x Light Cross-Country Vehicle (*Kfz. 1*), 2x Heavy MG	3x Light Cross-Country Vehicle (*Kfz. 1*), 2x Heavy MG	Light Cross-Country Vehicle (*Kfz. 1*)

3rd Mortar Section (Heavy)

2x 8cm Model 34 Mortar (*Granatwerfer 34*)	3x Personnel Vehicle (*Kfz. 70*)

Totals: 1x Officer, 10x NCOs, 57x Enlisted Personnel; 38x Rifles, 22x Pistols, 8x Submachine Guns, 4x Heavy MG's, 2x 8cm Mortar; 20x Vehicles, 1x Motorcycle

f) Vehicle Maintenance Section

Light Cross-Country Vehicle (*Kfz. 1*)	Small Maintenance Vehicle (*Kfz. 2/40*)

Totals: 1x NCO, 3x Enlisted Personnel; 3x Rifles, 1x Pistol; 2x Wheeled Vehicles

g) Combat Trains I (Combat Trains II with the Battalion Headquarters)

Light Cross-Country Vehicle (*Kfz. 1*)	Light Cross-Country Truck, Canvas Top, for Petroleum, Oil & Lubricants	Medium Cross-Country Truck, Canvas Top, for Large Field Mess Stove

Totals: 4x NCOs, 6x Enlisted Personnel; 7x Rifles, 3x Pistols; 3x Wheeled Vehicles

Summary

	Officers	NCOs	Enlisted Personnel	Rifles (AT Rifles)	Pistols (Submachine Guns)	Heavy MG's (Light MG's)	Heavy Mortars	Wheeled Vehicles	Motorcycles
Command Section	1	3	8	9	2			3	4
1st Platoon	1	4	38	26 (1)	13 (4)	(6)		14	1
2nd Platoon		5	38	26 (1)	13 (4)	(6)		14	1
3rd Platoon		5	38	26 (1)	13 (4)	(6)		14	1
4th (Heavy) Platoon	1	10	57	38	22 (8)	4	2	20	1
Vehicle Maintenance Section		1	3	3	1			2	
Combat Trains I		4	6	7	3			3	
Baggage Trains		1	3	4				1	
Totals	3	33	191	139 (3)	67 (20)	4 (18)	2	71	8

Motorized Heavy Company
Company headquarters (1121)

In the updated *KStN* of 1 November 1941, the company headquarters was reorganized slightly, with the addition of one motorcycle and a light field telephone section.
- Headquarters: three motorcycles, two sidecar motorcycles, and one medium cross-country wheeled personnel carrier (*Kfz. 15*).
- One light field telephone section (Type *c*): one medium cross-country wheeled personnel carrier (*Kfz. 15*).

Motorized Light Infantry Gun Platoon (1123)

The light infantry gun platoon of 1 November 1941 added a medium cross-country utility vehicle to the headquarters and eliminated one sidecar motorcycle. The light field telephone section was eliminated completely. The ammunition section lost one truck and its light machine gun, but the truck was replaced by a trailer. The gun section remained unchanged.
- Headquarters: one motorcycle, one sidecar motorcycle, and one cross-country wheeled prime mover (light guns) (*Kfz. 69*).
- One ammunition section: one cross-country wheeled prime mover (light guns) (*Kfz. 69*) and one trailer.
- One gun section: two cross-country wheeled prime movers (light guns) (*Kfz. 69*) and two 75mm towed infantry guns.

Combat Engineer Platoon (1124)

The capabilities of the combat engineer platoon were enhanced slightly with the *KStN* dated 1 November 1941. Motorcycle authorizations were reduced and truck types changed slightly in the headquarters. The number of combat engineer sections was increased from three to four, although the vehicular allocations were reduced for each section.

- Headquarters: two motorcycles, two sidecar motorcycles, one medium cross-country wheeled personnel carrier (*Kfz. 15*), and two 2-ton trucks.
- Three combat engineer sections: one 2-ton truck, one combat engineer section, and one light machine gun.

Motorized Light Antitank Rifle (Gun) Section (1127)

This section was introduced by *KStN 1127* (1 November 1941) and intended to augment the anti-armor capabilities of the heavy company and the battalion. It consisted of three 28mm towed heavy antitank rifles (guns).*
- Light Antitank Rifle Section: one sidecar motorcycle, three heavy wheeled personnel carriers (*Kfz. 70*), three towed 28mm heavy antitank rifles (guns), and three light machine guns.

Armored Car Company (1162)

The updated *KStN* of 1 November 1941 brought with it a number of organizational changes that streamlined the unit and eliminated several types of armored cars. Officially gone were the *Sd.Kfz. 221* light armored car, the *Sd.Kfz. 263* medium armored radio car, the *Sd.Kfz. 261* light armored radio car, and the *Sd.Kfz. 247* heavy wheeled armored utility vehicle. Organizationally, the light and medium radio sections were eliminated from the company headquarters. The total number of armored cars remained at twenty-four.
- Headquarters: two motorcycles, five sidecar motorcycles, and one medium cross-country wheeled personnel carrier (*Kfz. 15*).
- One heavy armored car platoon: three heavy armored cars, 2cm (8 wheeled) (*Sd.Kfz. 231*) and three heavy armored radio cars (8 wheeled) (*Sd.Kfz. 232*).
- Three light armored car platoons: four light armored cars (2cm) (*Sd.Kfz. 222*) and two light armored radio cars (MG) (*Sd.Kfz. 223*).

---

*The weapon was technically classified as a heavy antitank rifle (*schwere Panzerbüchse 41*), even though it had more in common with an artillery gun.

2x Medium Motorcycle, 5x Sidecar Motorcycle and 1x Medium Cross-Country Utility Vehicle with Equipment Storage Box (*Kfz. 15*)

Totals: 1x Officer, 3x NCOs, 9x Enlisted Personnel; 10x Rifles, 1x Submachine Gun, 2x Pistols; 1x Wheeled Vehicle, 2x Medium Motorcycles, 5x Sidecar Motorcycles

b) 1st (Heavy) Platoon

1st Scout Section	2nd Scout Section	3rd Scout Section
Heavy Armored Car (*Sd.Kfz. 231*), 1x 2cm Main Gun, 1x Light MG, 1x Submachine Gun and Heavy Armored Car (Radio) (*Sd.Kfz. 232*), 1x 2cm Main Gun, 1x Light MG, 1x Submachine Gun	Heavy Armored Car (*Sd.Kfz. 231*), 1x 2cm Main Gun, 1x Light MG, 1x Submachine Gun and Heavy Armored Car (Radio) (*Sd.Kfz. 232*), 1x 2cm Main Gun, 1x Light MG, 1x Submachine Gun	Heavy Armored Car (*Sd.Kfz. 231*), 1x 2cm Main Gun, 1x Light MG, 1x Submachine Gun and Heavy Armored Car (Radio) (*Sd.Kfz. 232*), 1x 2cm Main Gun, 1x Light MG, 1x Submachine Gun

Totals: 2x Officers, 4x NCOs, 18x Enlisted Personnel; 24x Pistols, 6x Submachine Guns, 6x Light MG's, 6x Main Guns; 6x Armored Vehicles

c) 2nd (Light) Platoon

1st Scout Section	2nd Scout Section

2x Light Armored Car (MG) (*Sd.Kfz. 221*), 2x Light MG, 2x Submachine Gun and 1x Light Armored Car (Radio) (*Sd.Kfz. 223*), 1x Light MG, 1x Submachine Gun	2x Light Armored Car (MG) (*Sd.Kfz. 221*), 2x Light MG, 2x Submachine Gun and 1x Light Armored Car (Radio) (*Sd.Kfz. 223*), 1x Light MG, 1x Submachine Gun

Totals: 1x Officer, 5x NCOs, 12x Enlisted Personnel; 18x Pistols, 6x Light MG's, 6x Submachine Guns; 6x Armored Vehicles

d) 3rd (Light) Platoon

1st Scout Section	2nd Scout Section
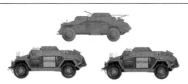	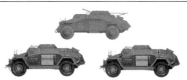
2x Light Armored Car (MG) (*Sd.Kfz. 221*), 2x Light MG, 2x Submachine Gun and 1x Light Armored Car (Radio) (*Sd.Kfz. 223*), 1x Light MG, 1x Submachine Gun	2x Light Armored Car (MG) (*Sd.Kfz. 221*), 2x Light MG, 2x Submachine Gun and 1x Light Armored Car (Radio) (*Sd.Kfz. 223*), 1x Light MG, 1x Submachine Gun

Totals: 1x Officer, 5x NCOs, 12x Enlisted Personnel; 18x Pistols, 6x Light MG's, 6x Submachine Guns; 6x Armored Vehicles

e) 4th (Light) Platoon

1st Scout Section	2nd Scout Section

2x Light Armored Car (MG) (*Sd.Kfz. 221*), 2x Light MG, 2x Submachine Gun and 1x Light Armored Car (Radio) (*Sd.Kfz. 223*), 1x Light MG, 1x Submachine Gun	2x Light Armored Car (MG) (*Sd.Kfz. 221*), 2x Light MG, 2x Submachine Gun and 1x Light Armored Car (Radio) (*Sd.Kfz. 223*), 1x Light MG, 1x Submachine Gun

Totals: 1x Officer, 5x NCOs, 12x Enlisted Personnel; 18x Pistols, 6x Light MG's, 6x Submachine Guns; 6x Armored Vehicles

f) Vehicle Maintenance Section

| Sidecar Motorcycle | Light Prime Mover (1 ton) (*Sd.Kfz. 10*) (as Small Maintenance Vehicle), 1x Submachine Gun | Light Cross-Country Truck, Canvas Top, for Vehicle Maintenance Section | Light Cross-Country Truck, Canvas Top, for Crews |

Totals: 2x NCOs, 10x Enlisted Personnel; 1x Pistol, 1x Submachine Gun, 11x Rifles; 3x Wheeled Vehicles, 1x Sidecar Motorcycle

g) Combat Trains I

| Medium Cross-Country Utility Vehicle with Equipment Storage Box (*Kfz. 15*) | Light Cross-Country Truck, Canvas Top, for Ammunition and Equipment | Light Cross-Country Truck, Canvas Top, for Petroleum, Oil & Lubricants | Medium Cross-Country Truck, Canvas Top, for Large Field Mess Stove |

Totals: 4x NCOs, 9x Enlisted Personnel; 9x Rifles, 4x Pistols; 4x Wheeled Vehicles

AFTER-ACTION REPORTS AND FIRSTHAND ACCOUNTS

In the fighting that ushered in the New Year, the remaining armored and reconnaissance assets of the division were employed as fire brigades in stopping Soviet offensive operations. In this passage, *Kradschützen-Bataillon 3* (*3. Panzer-Division*) assists in relieving infantry elements of various infantry divisions:[11]

The 13th of January saw *Infanterie-Regiment 528* [part of the *299. Infanterie-Division*] involved in hard fighting that resulted in a lot of casualties. It was only possible for the motorcycle infantry battalion to temporarily relieve the encircled *I./Infanterie-Regiment 245* [part of the *88. Infanterie-Division*] at Wypolsowa. The motorcycle infantry companies attacked in the direction of Machnino to the right of *Bataillon Müller*. Despite considerable terrain difficulties, the motorcycle infantry were able to take the enemy positions, which were being held by elements of an entire cavalry division. *Major* Pape and the commander of the 3rd Company, *Hauptmann* von Cochenhausen, served as examples in driving their men forward to attack. The enemy suffered a considerable setback. The rifle platoon of *Oberfeldwebel* Kruse, which was employed as a flank guard, was able to gain ground in the direction of Bynino and Schumakowo. After the successful attack of the motorcycle infantry battalion was concluded, Kruse's platoon went back to Milidowka that evening. The *I./Infanterie-Regiment 245* was still on its own, however. Only *Hauptmann* Markowski, who had taken over the 3rd Tank Company, was able to escort supplies to the infantry battalion.

Later that same month, the divisional reconnaissance assets were again employed in direct combat roles in support of operations designed to stop the Soviet advances and return the initiative to the Germans:[12]

On 26 January, the division was able to score a nice success with its two battle groups. *Major* Ziervogel and his reconnaissance battalion advanced from Schtschigry, along with some tanks and artillery, while *Oberstleutnant* Schmidt-Ott headed in the direction of Alekssandrowka with his battle group, consisting of elements of the armor regiment and *Infanterie-Regiment 133* [part of the *45. Infanterie-Division*, which was composed primarily of Austrians], from Poschidajewka, which had been taken that morning. The Russians were hit on two sides and ejected from Alekssandrowka after a short firefight. The battle groups exploited the success and continued the advance in the direction of Kriwzowka, which was reached in the evening. The enemy lost the will to fight and fled back.

The next mission for the division was the clearing of the valley depressions around

Kriwzowka. On 27 January, the motorcycle infantry battalion, transported by trucks, arrived in Werch-Olchowatoje from Wodjanoje. Once there, *Major* Pape assumed command of a battle group consisting of his battalion, an *SS infantry battalion* [based on additional information provided below, this was undoubtedly the *III./SS-Infanterie-Brigade 1 (mot.)*, which *SS-Hauptsturmführer* Alfons Zeitler commanded during this period], tanks and antitank elements. Shortly after 1330 hours, the men of the *Kampfgruppe* assaulted from Werch-Olchowatoje, overran the initial enemy strongpoints and positions and entered Solowjewka by surprise. Pape's men sustained few casualties—only three wounded! The regiments of the Soviet 32nd Cavalry Division that were holding there were completely surprised by the power and aggressiveness of the German attack. Despite that, they stubbornly defended in the impoverished huts and houses of the locality. *Major* Pape led from the front and rallied his men forward. The Soviet cavalrymen started to scatter in all directions. Their division commander was among those taken prisoner. The attached tanks continued rolling forward with their last few liters of fuel and were able to chase the remnants of a Soviet division out of Nikolskoje.

The 30th of January was marked by the crowning achievement of all of the heavy fighting and previous sacrifices. The division concentrated its forces for a concentric attack aimed at defeating the enemy forces in the Butyrki–Judinka–Stakanowo area. The main effort was with *Kampfgruppe Pape*, which was directed to advance on Stakanowo. The battle group staged for the attack with half of the *II./Infanterie-Regiment 246* and its tanks in Solowjewka and with the motorcycle infantry battalion and *SS-Bataillon Zeitler* in Rudino. *Oberst* Neubauer intended to only move his battalions out in the direction of Butyrki after *Kampfgruppe Pape* was successful.

Hauptmann Kersten's batteries, which had closed up, opened the attack with a short preparation on the enemy trenches. It was still dark across the snow-covered terrain when the men of *Kampfgruppe Pape* rose out of their trenches and advanced against the Russian positions. By 0630 hours, they had succeeded in entering Nowo-Danilowka; half an hour later, the attached tanks had reached Moskwinka. Both of the localities were in German hands after a short fight. The enemy left his positions fairly quickly. The battle group gained more ground by the hour and reached Stakanowo by 1100 hours with the tanks in the lead.

Kampfgruppe Oberst Neubauer moved out at 0800 hours and had to "chew" its way into Butyrki meter-by-meter against extremely tough resistance. The *I./Infanterie-Regiment 133* took heavy casualties, before it was able to take the village in hard house-to-house fighting. The *III./Infanterie-Regiment 156* [one of the motorized infantry regiments of the *16. Infanterie-Division (mot.)*], which was employed on the right wing and supported by tanks from the 9. *Panzer-Division*, moved through Orljanka and quickly closed on Judinka, although the tanks were then held up by the bottomland of the Kosorscha and the infantry could no longer follow.

At that point, the fighting vehicles of *Hauptmann* Markowski joined the fray. They advanced from Stakanowo to the southeast in the direction of Judinka, rallying *Kampfgruppe Oberst Neubauer* in the process. The enemy took extremely heavy casualties in the fighting and evacuated the battlefield. The battalions of *Oberstleutnant Dr.* Müller and *Major* Frank no longer needed to be committed; they remained to the rear to secure the area that had been taken. By the afternoon, the division had reached its attack objectives.

The weather that day was anything but nice. An icy wind from the east brought with it more snow, which was already meters deep. Fuel, ammunition and rations just did not make it forward. The men of the divisional signals battalion had to master extraordinary difficulties, just to lay wire. The radio sections were bogged down somewhere.

As a result, it was only possible to use tanks to reconnoiter as far as Chochlowka that afternoon. The results demonstrated, however, that the enemy was beaten everywhere. The same results were obtained when the reconnaissance battalion and *Kampfgruppe Major Frank* sent out patrols. The Soviets were pulling back along the northern flank of the division.

Major Pape, the commander of *Kradschützen-Bataillon 3*,[13] was awarded the Oak Leaves to the Knight's Cross for his leadership during this period. An Armed Forces Daily Report dated 31 January 1942 stated in part:

> A counterattack by German infantry and tanks led by *Generalmajor* Breith in the area northeast of Kursk has led to a complete success after several days of fighting.
>
> A group of enemy forces consisting of several [infantry] division and armor formations that had broken into the German lines was defeated, suffering heavy losses, and thrown back!

The winter fighting, which extended into March and beyond, continued to be bitter and saw the motorcycle infantrymen of the battalion constantly employed in both relief operations and defensive fighting:[14]

> *Kradschützen-Bataillon 3*, which was employed in the sector of *Kampfgruppe Mikosch*, was then subjected to continuous enemy attacks in the area around Ternowaja. There was not a single house in which to warm up, and it was impossible to dig into the frozen ground. Manning a sector of some 2–3 kilometers, the battalion turned back all attacks, in some cases by means of immediate counterattacks conducted by small groups. *Hauptmann* von Cochenhausen performed magnificently. Cases of frostbite increased. The battalion was soon at the end of its strength, after having suffered 11 dead and 47 wounded, including 5 officers, in the course of three days.

The following passage illustrates the expectations placed on the newly formed light armored reconnaissance companies in performing a variety of missions (26 May 1942):[15]

> Reporting directly to *Korpsgruppe Breith*, *Oberleutnant* Meister's light *SPW* company, the *4./Kradschützen-Bataillon 3*, received the mission to reconnoiter south through the pocket and establish contact with a Hungarian division advancing there. The company encountered resistance several times in the pocket, but it was also able to break it each time. The men thought they had found the Hungarians at Belikon, when a column of regimental size appeared in front of them, but it turned out to be Soviets. The company immediately attacked the marching infantry in the flank in an inverted wedge with 32 light *SPW's* and took 600 prisoners. Fleeing elements were pursued by *Oberfeldwebel* Hess' platoon and also captured. The platoon then encountered T-34's, but it was able to evade them. That operation by the recently formed 4th Company, whose soldiers came from the former reconnaissance battalion, was a decisive day for armored reconnaissance, since it proved that information had to be gained though fighting, and the reequipping of the motorcycle companies with light *SPW's* had been the proper decision.

After the launching of the summer offensive, *Kradschützen-Bataillon 3* was in the thick of things (13 July 1942):[16]

> Ever since the early morning hours of 13 July, *Major* Pape's motorcycle infantry battalion served as the advance guard for the advance south, attempting to leapfrog past the enemy cavalry and armor formations that were conducting a fighting delay. The lead company continuously encountered completely surprised Soviet rear guards and supply elements, which barely put up any resistance and, in most cases, could be captured intact.
>
> Late in the afternoon, an enemy reconnaissance aircraft could be shot down near Piechakoff by the concentrated employment of all available machine guns and rifles. As it turned dark, the day's objective was reached. The battalion turned west to encircle the enemy pulling back from the north by taking the villages east of Millerowo.
>
> The 2nd Company of the motorcycle infantry received the mission to take Karpowo-Russkiy

and to screen from there for the night. There were no signs of life in the extended "street" village, which ran about two kilometers long from east to west along the edge of a marshy creek bottomland. It was already dark when the motorcycle infantry entered the village. They noticed Russian tracked vehicles fleeing to the south. The onset of night did not allow for any reconnaissance of the surroundings. In a hurried move, the platoon leaders were given positions based on the map in order to establish a gap-prone and thin security line along the ridgeline to the north. The battalion was in a similar situation with its remaining units further to the east.

Since the company was supposed to receive reinforcements in the form of tanks during the night, the onset of engine and track noises coming from the northeast shortly after midnight were held to be coming from the promised reinforcements. But two or three tanks then rolled quickly through the dusty village and halted right in front of the provisional company command post. The tankers in the turrets were hanging out of the hatches. In the dust and the pale moonlight, the silhouette of the lead fighting vehicle was not clearly identifiable. For a few seconds, the company commander and the men of his headquarters section were indecisive, as to whether they had friends or foes in front of them. There were moments of intense uncertainty. All of a sudden, a signal flare shot vertically into the sky and, almost at the same time, the words *idi szuda* rang out from the tank commander to the frozen German soldiers. Both sides knew what was up by then. The Russians disappeared into the turrets of their tanks in the blink of an eye, followed by tracer rounds whipping through the darkness. The only available antitank gun was screening at the outskirts of the village. But the unexpected situation in the middle of the village was also unsettling for the Russians. Before anyone was in a position to approach the tanks with a bundled charge, the enemy fighting vehicles pulled back and took off quickly.

By then, however, the sound of tracked vehicles had increased in the eastern portion of the village. Accompanied by riflemen, the tanks were attempting to cross the marshy creek bottomland to get to the south. Sharp fighting ensued with the Soviet infantry, which had run into the strongpoints established by the motorcycle infantry. The Soviets thought they were facing a cohesive front. The enemy, who appeared to have been without adequate stocks of fuel and ammunition for some days and who also believed he was already encircled, left behind his vehicles and entered the village in an effort to escape to the south. In the confusion, it took some time to sort out what was happening. Contact with the battalion headquarters had been lost. The platoons had set up their defenses tied into the houses of the village. By first light, however, some order had been restored. Although the strongpoints were widely dispersed, the defensive positions were strong and suited for engaging the fleeing Soviets. In the morning haze along the creek bed, 16 T-34's were able to cross the narrow waterway and escape to the south. They had little ammunition, but their armor protected them from the 5-centimeter antitank gun doing any harm. The Russians were forced to leave behind numerous trucks, a few light guns and a large amount of light weapons and pieces of equipment. A few of the tanks got stuck in the bottomland. One of them fired into the village from time to time, thus providing the withdrawing infantry with some cover. It was not until the afternoon, when contact was reestablished with the battalion headquarters, that the enemy tank was destroyed by a light howitzer that was brought forward and fired over open sights.

The battalion headquarters and the remaining companies had also been involved in sharp defensive engagements a few kilometers further to the east. It wasn't possible to more-or-less reestablish the thin security line until 14 July. Fortunately, friendly losses were relatively small.

But that did not mean that the situation was no longer fluid. Millerowo still had not been taken and, from Karpowo-Russkiy, one could observe the fighting involving the *23. Panzer-Division* through binoculars.

The following night was another extremely critical one for the 2nd Company. Although the defensive positions could be improved, the left wing was still hanging in the air and there were unmistakable gaps between the platoons. The friendly forces to the right were two kilometers away in their positions.

Under the cover of darkness, an enemy cavalry troop—apparently the lead element of the regiment following—succeeded in entering the western portion of Karpowo-Russkiy from the north along a narrow pathway. Initially, the movements of the troop were not noticed. The unexpected neighing of horses alerted the guards in the village. When the white signal flares illuminated the main road, the chaos of the previous night returned. Murderous machine-gun fire slammed into the surprised troop and yielded a rich harvest. A short while later, the regiment that was following joined the fray with all of the forces at its disposal. Another night fight development, with all of the attributes of that type of combat. This time, the battalion was able to assist with the light *SPW's* of *Oberfeldwebel* Hess. At first light, coming from the east, the *SPW* Company attacked the cavalry formations by surprise in the flank and decided the unequal struggle for the German side with the aid of artillery. The day resulted in a large number of spoils-of-war in the form of weapons and materiel, as well as the capture of quite a few prisoners.

That signaled the end of a small episode on the periphery of the larger events. While the success may not seem to have been so great at first glance, the low number of forces was able to inflict considerable casualties on the enemy, hold up the enemy's weakened elements and gain some time.

Kradschützen-Bataillon "Großdeutschland" also participated in the initial offensive operations in the south. Helmuth Spaeter, the author of the three-volume unofficial history of the division and a Knight's Cross recipient of the reconnaissance battalion, has written the following account of some of those operations in July 1942:[17]

Kradschützen-Bataillon Großdeutschland, reinforced by a light battery of field howitzers and a combat engineer company, became the division's advance guard and was the first element to begin the march to the south. Rain and fuel shortages constantly hampered the advance, but there was nothing to be seen of the enemy. Nevertheless, increased attentiveness was the order of the day; the forces had reached an area, unlike the one further to the north, where German soldiers had not set foot before. Armored patrols were stepped up, and the division maintained a higher degree of readiness. Bogunoff was the division's intermediate objective on 14 July. In the last few days, more than 420 kilometers had been covered without any enemy contact. The first enemy forces were identified by the advance guard on the slope on the far side of Bogunoff following the capture of the town at 1900 hours. A horse-drawn Russian column was moving through, and it was quickly dispatched. The prisoners and spoils-of-war were the first taken since 7 July. Orders were immediately radioed to von Usedom's advance guard.[18]

14 July, approximately 1900 hours: "Move to the east-west road in the Kopani–Dederawski area, about 10 kilometers west of Kaschari, and block it."

It was around 2000 hours when new orders were received just after the reinforced 2nd Company had moved out: "For 15 July: Advance through Kaschari to the hills near Mirgorodskij and screen there."

As if that were not enough, more orders were radioed in to the battalion during the night, instructing it to reconnoiter as far as the line running Millerowo–Gruzynoff–Skassyrskaja–Morosowskaja road–north of Sstachoff. It was to determine the location of the friendly forces to either flank and where the enemy was.

The armored car sections of the 1st Company were on the go day and night to accomplish these missions and obtain the desired information. The operations, in which the scouts were completely on their own in totally unfamiliar terrain, proved very eventful. *Gefreiter* Karl Baur of the company has provided a firsthand account:

"It was night again. The battalion received orders to take up a hedgehog position. The armored car patrols and their drivers breathed a sigh of relief. Finally . . . a little rest. The vehicles we quickly topped off. Then, sleep. I was just about to crawl under the armored car, when a messenger came up with an order: *Wachtmeister* Weichert's section prepare for operations! Section leader and radio operator to the commander! So much for sleep. We quickly packed up our things again. Then *Wachtmeister* Weichert returned and the familiar order came: "Assemble!" Looking at the map, we learned about our mission. There was a village in front of us about 4 kilometers. It was next to a large stream. We were to establish a bridgehead there and hold it until the advance guard arrived the following morning. As a precautionary measure, we were to identify ourselves by means of a green signal from a flashlight in the event we had to return early, together or individually.

"As driver of the third 4-wheeled car, it fell to me to post the *GD* marker in a prominent place at every crossroads for the battalion that was to follow.

"It was just past 2300 hours when we moved out. Our previous movement had left our vehicles heavily coated with mud and almost unrecognizable. The Balkan Crosses were no longer visible. That was to prove lucky for us in the events that followed.

"After two kilometers, we ran into a Russian supply column that was heading east. The Russians were using tractors and *Panje* carts to move their fuel and ammunition back. Our vehicles moved past the unsuspecting Russians. No one recognized us, but we scarcely dared to breathe.

"Finally, at the entrance to the village, we came to a crossroads that had to be marked. I stopped my vehicle, while the other two 8-wheelers continued moving slowly.

"I dismounted quickly to nail a marker on a tree. But then I saw the Russians . . . barely 20 meters from the crossroads was an antitank gun and about 15–20 men. They looked at me calmly. I raced to my car and mounted swiftly, certain that the Russians would open fire at any minute.

"I started up the engine and raced after the other two cars. As we moved through the village, we noticed vehicle after vehicle positioned in front of the houses. The place was full of Russians and trains vehicles. My only wish was to get out of the village.

"But I couldn't find the road leading out. In the darkness, I had failed to notice it and missed the first turn, which veered off to the left. The other cars had gone that way. As our car rounded a curve in the middle of the village, we found ourselves facing two Russian tanks moving towards us. I couldn't get past them, but one of the tank commanders instructed his driver to move out of the way. My hair was standing on end. I was amazed that the vehicle commander, *Gefreiter* Grau, had not lost his nerves completely.

"Meanwhile, I saw another road that veered off to the left. Without hesitation, I stepped on the gas and moved down the road. I then saw a sight I would not soon forget: To the north, about 50 meters from the road, was an entire mounted Cossack troop! A real sight . . . truly unique!

"But all of that was hard to take! At first, we remained quietly where we were. We then moved back and looked for the other two cars. Finally, we were able to locate them. They had also had similar experiences. In light of the situation, we were unable to accomplish our mission of establishing a bridgehead."

Kradschützen-Bataillon 3 was frequently used as the advance guard during the division's advance (6 August 1942):[19]

As it turned first light the next day, the *3. Panzer-Division* started the advance that would take it into the Caucasus! *Kradschützen-Bataillon 3*, under its new and recently promoted commander, *Major* von Cochenhausen, left the outpost positions around Njewinnomyskaja at 0300 hours and moved along the railway embankment to the southeast. The other elements of the division likewise moved out from their assembly areas. The entire division, including the command section, was on the move by 0330 hours. The motorcycles and fighting vehicles of the *I./Panzer-Regiment 6* got as far as Kursawskoje without stopping and without encountering the enemy. It was there that Soviet forces threw down the gauntlet for the first time that day, but they were thrown back by the companies of the advance guard. The movement continued along the Grosny–Rostow oil pipeline. Whenever the lead elements approached a pumping station, it would go up in flames.

Willi Kubik, assigned to the *1./Kradschützen-Bataillon 43* of the *13. Panzer-Division*, which was also employed in the south, has provided vivid insights into life as an enlisted armored scout:[20]

10 June 1942:
The day we had waited for had arrived: Our new armored cars were coming. We were told to find camouflage material. We were a detail of 10 men and 4 noncommissioned officers. We went to the creek and made rush mats.

Over there, someone yelled. Everyone looked in that direction. Hurrah! The armored cars were coming over a rise, a long column of them.

At that point, none of us could hold back. We ran to the road. I grabbed my camera on the run; they were already approaching.

It was a proud moment and an unforgettable sight as the heavy guys pulled in. The vehicles with their 2cm cannon looked like bulldogs.

With a happy demeanor, Wagner, Buß, Fliesenberg, Staban and Becket reported that they had come back from the train transport; it had only taken a week to get from Magdeburg to here.

After about an hour, we resumed our rush mat work. We had waded into the marshland with rubber boots, where we cut the 2-meter green rush stems. By noon, we had finished a couple of the mats. During the afternoon, we made more mats and camouflaged the armored cars, which were parked closely to one another, due to a lack of space.

We camouflaged them with all sorts of vegetation.

11 June 1942:
. . . I wound up in the heavy platoon in the 8-wheeled radio car of *Unteroffizier* Westfeld. Walter Hein was the driver and Karl-Heinz Bues was the radio operator and rear driver. I was made the gunner. The scout section leader, in another 8-wheeled armored car, was *Unteroffizier* Waak. That meant that the scout section consisted of two vehicles with a crew of eight men.

After formation, we were told to go to the vehicles. We had bad luck with our vehicle, inasmuch as the armored car had a problem with water in the engine from the cylinder head gaskets. The bolts had not been tightened enough in Germany; perhaps it was sabotage. Hein and Bues got their tools; I unloaded the magazines and everything that belonged with it.

There was a long table in the garden; we put everything on it . . .

. . . I then took a look around in the vehicle's interior. I adjusted the sights, since I fired left, and then placed the 18 magazines for the main gun in their mounts (each magazine had 10 2cm rounds). The same for the bags for the machine-gun belts. Following that, I cleaned the submachine gun. That took up the afternoon. At 1700 hours, we all went to the creek and made a few more rush mats . . .

12 June 1942:
. . . Starting at 0300 hours, the maintenance section for our company pulled the engine from our armored car.

Formation at 0620 hours; then off to the vehicles.

In the morning, I removed the machine gun. More accurately: It was only with the help of our armorer that I got the machine gun out after about an hour.

Everything was still covered in cosmoline. The entire machine gun was covered in it. I had my work cut out for me until it was more or less clean. The gun had been coated in Germany; with the exception of the barrel, they had forgotten to clean it. The gas ports were completely fouled.

Together with *Unteroffizier* Westfeld, I removed the cannon during the afternoon. It took nearly half an hour, since the weapon was mounted in a way we were not familiar with. Then we started to remove the grease; a number of cleaning rags were used in the process.

The cannon had a number of rust spots, since it had not been cleaned after it had been test fired in Germany.

Something like that should not have happened. An hour was spent learning about the cannon. It was then remounted, totally cleaned up, with the help of my driver.

13 June 1942:
We were told that our commander, *Oberstleutnant* Scholz, was going to inspect the armored cars today.

I was tasked with placing all of my weapons on the long table for inspection.

Just before 0800 hours, he arrived. I briefed him on it, cocked it, etc.

Following that, the Commander rode cross-country for about 15 minutes in Brockmann's 8-wheel, along with *Oberleutnant* Eick and me. Once back, we went to the aid station to be immunized against cholera.

After that, I stowed all of the odds and ends in the armored car, cleaned the machine gun and the tripod.

My machine gun went with Tausend to the arms room.

In the afternoon, I went on a cleaning party. I swept thoroughly and scrubbed the tables.

One armored car conducted calibration firing. The new cannon fired amazingly fast . . .

In August, Kubik and his fellow scouts were regularly performing reconnaissance missions:[21]

9 August 1942:
. . . Wake-up was 0400 hours. Everybody topped off.

Once again, we received a major scouting mission. In the morning, it was still cool. The movement led once again through the fields.

We had not moved much, when we started to encounter the first enemy riflemen, horsemen, *Panje* carts etc. A *Panje* cart moved directly towards us; we provided it with a new march direction.

Soon, a village appeared in front of us. Russians were running around everywhere. In one spot, there was a large group of them. We halted and observed the village.

All at once, two *Me 109's* were above us. We received a long burst of fire. Tausend's hatch received a hit.

The aerial recognition flag was hastily displayed; the pilot in the *Me 109* recognized it.

A friendly fighter had almost knocked us out; we had been lucky.

We decided to move through the village. Moving at a moderate speed, we rode bunched up. The Russians were completely surprised. It was not until we had passed by them that they ran away. A bunch of fully manned trucks and *Panje* carts were lined up in the village, one behind the other. They were completely surprised.

We were happy to get out of there, nonetheless, and also to immediately find the embankment at a marshy spot.

Once out of the village, we moved along the railway tracks for a while. We then proceeded to go through enemy-occupied woods.

But we were lucky there, as well. Together with Knast, we then went back along the railway line . . . and into a sunflower field. We took a break there, since the engines had to cool off a bit.

We saw Russians pulling back along several field paths and reported everything by radio. After about 30 minutes, we continued moving, always in the middle of the fields. By then, it was unbearably hot. We moved along a *balka* [defile, from the Russian] that was winding through the terrain; in its bottomland was a marshy creek. Unfortunately, we did not find a crossing point. We moved about 4 kilometers in the *balka* and then arrived at a collective farm.

We had great fields of observation there.

Off to the right and left of us were two villages. Large Russian columns were moving in both directions.

We reported again by radio and then moved back some 150 meters to cross the creek at a ford.

We had some bad luck: The command armored car of *Unteroffizier* Waak bottomed out. From above, the ground had looked firm. Underneath it, everything was soggy manure.

The armored car sank up to its axles. At that point, we were stuck, with Russians to the right and left and friendly forces far to the rear.

Everyone started digging; Ferdinand and I manned the weapons. Later on, I also dug; I sweated like never before in my life.

No one even considered abandoning the armored car and taking off with the others. On several occasions, we had to put out our recognition panels, whenever friendly fighters came in too low.

We tried to pull Waak out with our vehicle, but in vain. In fact, in the process, we broke the short driveshaft.

Then, off to the right, some firing started. Apparently, it was an advance by friendly forces.

We had radioed our location by then and requested assistance. The firefight grew more and more intense; the situation stank to high heaven.

My vehicle driver, *Unteroffizier* Westfeld, went on foot to the slope and observed. There were a few Russian cavalrymen at the collective farm. More and more joined them, then rode away, while others took their place. We did not fire, in an effort not to betray our position. The Russians also appeared to be cautious.

A Russian trains element moved very close past us. We were ready to fire; we weren't about to give up our armored cars without a fight.

About 5 kilometers away, friendly forces moved past us. We were sitting in a trap. Finally, around 1500 hours, our salvation arrived. Our Company Commander, *Oberleutnant* Eick, came with a tank and pulled us out of the creek.

Without the radio sets, which we used to report our location, we would have been lost.

Protected by the *balka*, we then rode together through the left part of the large village. The other part of the village was still in Russian hands. A Russian antitank rifle engaged us but without success.

We soon reached our company. It had taken a halt. There was cabbage soup, but no one ate any.

We then moved out slowly. Through the fields, as usual. When we stopped again, there was firing to the left of us. Later, six Russians surrendered. To the right of the field trail, there were a number of shot-up *Panje* carts.

We got closer and closer to Maikop. There was the sound of fighting up front. We stopped one more time; far to our front, we could see a Stalin organ being fired. A short while later, there were impacts to our left at the location of another battle group.

I slept while we moved further; about 6 kilometers outside of Maikop, we set up for the night in a field.

Kradschützen-Bataillon 4 of the *24. Panzer-Division* participated in the drive on Stalingrad as part of *Heeresgruppe B*. The following firsthand account concerns operations of the 2nd Company, which was a light armored reconnaissance company with half-tracks. In this passage, the battalion was tasked with determining the location of bypassed enemy forces:[22]

We conducted an enveloping attack against the fruit orchard from the most favorable side. The armored vehicles were on the wings. The attack made good progress; I was personally manning a machine gun. I sent a burst of tracer ammunition into a bunch of Russians who surfaced just in front of us. We carefully entered the expansive plantation, widely dispersed. All of a sudden, something exploded in the middle of the vehicle. I thought it was a hand grenade tossed in from above. Jakob, the assistant driver and radio operator, was badly wounded. A thick stream of blood was running from his throat. At that moment, we were moving across a Russian trench. I looked over the side and fired an entire magazine from the submachine gun along the straight trench line. The bottom of the trench was transformed into a twitching, brown mass. The vehicle got stuck. I pulled Jakob from out of his seat and into my lap and dressed his neck. At the same time, I issued a radio order to the sections, which were only advancing cautiously, to enter the trenches as fast as possible. All of a sudden, something else exploded in the vehicle. Hädrich, my driver, cried out. I saw a small hole in the side of the armor to the left of him. The explosive round of the antitank rifle had shredded his rear. Then it exploded two more times. The dashboard was shattered, the radio destroyed. I had to lead the platoon with flags. Becker, my messenger, pulled the dead driver out of his seat and drove the vehicle. I then saw one armored vehicle set off smoke and pull back. We likewise disengaged from the enemy and assembled to pull back. On the way back, we were engaged from all sides. The armored vehicles moving ahead of us made only poor progress in the mud. All of a sudden, Hädrich stirred and said something. So he wasn't dead, after all. We picked up the pace; perhaps he could be saved. Finally, we got back to Jefrossinowka. I jumped out and made my report. The vehicle kept on going to the aid station, but Hädrich died on the way there.

There were six holes in the vehicle. There was a pool of blood in the vehicle hull. Everything had been splattered and sprayed with blood. Hundreds of casings were under the seats.

After we had cleaned up a bit and got the vehicle in order again, we were ready to go. In the evening, the Commander came by. My platoon had to form up; he praised it.

As a result of our reconnaissance-in-force, the actual strength of the enemy forces in the division flank had been established.

As the result of rapid advances, the fog of war frequently descended:[23]

After a very rapid advance, the reinforced *Kradschützen-Bataillon 4* reached Zymljanskaja at 0700 hours, where it established contact with the advance-guard battalion of the *29. Infanterie-Division (mot)* in an effort to attack the enemy forces on the north bank of the Don. Changing and different missions from the two divisions, which were widely separated from one another, had the negative effect of not allowing the intended attack to happen. At that point, *Kradschützen-Bataillon 4* screened the right flank of the advance guard battalion at the ferry crossing point at Zymljanskaja and from the high ground to the northwest.

From the diaries of a Platoon Leader from the *2./Kradschützen-Bataillon 4*, we discover how the next few days for the battalion, which was far forward of the division, went:

"17 July: A crazy night march! Due to the dust, you couldn't see the taillight of the man ahead of you. It's only when you you're right on top of them that you know you are still on the right route. One vehicle remained behind with a bent half-axle. Another hit the man in front of him, with the result that the idler broke off. On one vehicle, the gas line plugged up. It was the first time that vehicles were lost on a road march. We reached the Don for the second time with five vehicles.

"The advance guard of the *29. Infanterie-Division (mot)* had established a bridgehead over the river, but it was now in a difficult position due to a lack of ammunition. The Russian resistance finally appeared to be stiffening up again here. We had crossed almost all of the Don Steppe without serious resistance. The large pocket we had hoped for did not materialize. The enemy had masterfully pulled his head out of the noose. The enemy air force also started to become active again; it engaged the trains elements, which were following behind at great distance. That night, it started to rain. We were held in reserve on the near side of the Don.

"18 July: There was a wine storehouse somewhere in the city. The *Landser* [slang term for a German soldier] could hardly be contained. A few of them drank so much that they had to be laid back into their vehicles, completely out of action. It was a heavy, bluish-red wine from the Crimea. We took a small container of it along.

"I took a look at the Russian positions that had been set up there to protect the bridge. They had been constructed masterfully. Everything in accordance with the regulations: Vertical walls and exact measurements. Materiel was scattered about in great quantities. There were manuals in every hole. The way they were laid out, they were much better than the German ones. Faultless images of German armored vehicles and aircraft were illustrated in them.

"A dead Russian lay behind my vehicle. The top of his head had been blown off; flies were eating his brains.

"Russian flyers were very active here. Every man set up captured Russian machine guns and a wild firefight ensued.

"19 July: Fighting on its own, the **battalion was some 150 kilometers in front of the division** [emphasis added by the authors], which was still somewhere around Meschkow. Resupply with fuel was not functioning; the little bit that the division still had was being pushed forward to the battalion.

"20 July: This evening, we moved along the Don to the southwest to Nikolaijewskaja, where we had been directed to establish a bridgehead over [the river]. It turned out to be a nasty night move along poor, dusty roads in pitch-black darkness.

"21 July: We approached Nikolaijewskaja at first light. We could see movements and clouds of dust there. Armored scout patrols that had been sent forward reported that the 23. *Panzer-Division* had already taken [the town] and established a bridgehead. Between there and Zymljanskaja, about 100 kilometers away, there was not a single German soldier on the Don. Since the mission had been overcome by events, the entire battalion turned around in an effort to find additional ferry points and bridges over the Don. Enemy movements were identified at Marinskoje by patrols. The village was attacked while on the move and our troop went through it at high speed. While crossing a defile, my vehicle unfortunately got stuck. I immediately jumped on another and chased after my platoon, which had been the lead platoon going through the village.

"Once beyond the village, there was a broad, flat section of terrain with some sections of marsh. It led down to the banks of the Don. There were about 100 Russians fleeing across the flat land. About a dozen trucks, prime movers, three guns and some other odds and ends were distributed across the meadowland, camouflaged as haystacks. The Russians were running for their lives towards the large ferry, which was still positioned on this side of the Don.

"But my lead squad raced through their midst and reached the docking point. The ferry was sprayed down with fire, thus preventing it from shoving off. The Russians were encircled and taken prisoner. There were a number of good-looking women among them. On the far bank of the Don, which was about 200 meters wide, you could see prime movers and trucks driving off to the east through the woods. My 3.7cm antitank gun sent a few high-explosive rounds over, until apparently all of them had taken off.

"The ferry was captured intact, along with 20 working trucks. In addition, we got some useful things, e.g., homemade tomato paste, *Erbswurst* [a type of sausage made from dried bacon and pea flour, rehydrated and used to make a thick pea soup in the field], butter and onions. On one of the trucks, twin machine guns were mounted. They were American made and terrific. I fiddled around with the mechanism the entire afternoon without being able to break it down.

"After establishing outposts along the river, we pulled back to some rolling terrain. It was a scorcher. In the shadows of our trusty vehicles, the customary field cooking started up, since our field mess had not been seen for a long time. We found the most amazing things in the captured trucks. For instance, every *SPW* received a suitcase gramophone, a sack of sugar, tentage and new uniform articles."

Regarding the above operations of *Kradschützen-Bataillon 4*, a division after-action report noted:

Even if the advance did not lead to the desired bridge, it did succeed in finally thwarting Russian crossing efforts [across the Don] between Nikolaijewskaja and Zymljanskaja.

It was a great disadvantage during that advance, as had been the case elsewhere during that time, that the corps did not have [an aerial] reconnaissance section. As a result, it usually received important aerial reconnaissance information too late and, as a result, advance guards advanced into thin air, as was the case here . . .

The platoon leader from the *2./Kradschützen-Bataillon 4* kept a journal of combat operations in August:[24]

14 August 1942: After a short nighttime rest, we continued on into the steppe to the northeast. An unpleasant storm churned up so much dust that you could no longer see the man in front of you. The salty, ashen dust penetrated everything. The weapons looked like they had been covered with flour. We stood in powdery dirt up to our ankles in the vehicles. Shirts and faces wet with sweat had turned black and were covered in it. I had placed two sets of glasses over one another. Despite that, my eyes still got inflamed. Despite all that, the advance continued relentlessly, and we reached Aksai on the railway line.

15 August 1942: We continued on through the Kalmuck Steppe to the northeast in 136-degree heat and a continuous sandstorm. For days on end, you did not see any human settlements; the ground was barren, burned black and parched and cracked from the heat. There were no roads. We moved by compass over the hills.

The Kalmuck Steppe had swallowed us whole.

We reached the right wing of the *XXXXVIII. Panzer-Korps*, which was hanging in the air at Plodowitoje, and extended it to the northeast.

Our battalion advanced as far as the slopes of the Ergeni Hills, which stretched clear through the Kalmuck Steppe in a north-south direction. The eastern slopes are steep like the banks of the Don. We set up defensive positions there. Completely flat and stretching all the way to Volga in front of us was the salt steppe. At the foot of our hill, about 4 kilometers away, were Lakes Sarpa and Barmanzak, with broad expanses of reedy banks. Through the scissors scope, we were able to see the broad, silver glittery ribbon of the Volga. That meant that we were the first German soldiers to see the old Volga from the south.

16 August 1942: It was Sunday again; there was certain to be some sort of dance in store. The battalion was employed along a 15-kilometer sector. Between us and the 3rd Troop on the right was a gap of a kilometer with several unpleasant defiles running down to the east. A patrol reported that fairly strong Russian forces were approaching our hill position along those defiles. It was best that we proceeded to act offensively and beat back the enemy before he got closer and saw how weak we were.

The 1st Platoon and I quickly mounted and moved off in the direction of the enemy-occupied defile. It was directed that the 1st Platoon move out far to the east and cut off the enemy from the rear, while I attacked him. We moved carefully, with our right wing up against the defile, so that we could turn against the enemy at any time. All of a sudden, we received antitank rifle and machine-gun fire from a depression about 100 meters in front of us. I received several hits, but they ricocheted off.

Both plates of armored glass were shattered, however. As we moved forward slowly, I suddenly saw Russian helmets about 50 meters in front of me through my optics. Of course, the machine gun wouldn't fire. Because of the continuous fire from antitank rifles, I received orders by radio to attack dismounted. The depression the enemy was positioned in extended to the right to the defile. A company-sized enemy element had already moved past us in the defile and was continuing to advance on the high ground.

I decided to block the enemy's route back. I went around him to the east. I also had a squad rush through the depression, so that we could hit the enemy from two sides. We carefully approached the edge of the depression. The first man, who raised his head, was killed. We were hand-grenade distance from the enemy, whom we had not yet seen. He was stronger than we had thought, however, since several machine guns, a small mortar and two antitank rifles were firing like mad from the depression.

We tossed a lot of hand grenades all at once, which helped to give us some breathing room. We then wanted to make a charge against the Russian position, but we suddenly discovered Russians behind us on the high ground. The 1st Platoon had advanced too far to the east, we were unable to see it. The company commander ordered the dismounted attack called off and had us mount up. The 4th Platoon was pushed forward as well as the empty vehicles of the 2nd Platoon, which had remained in the position.

Finally, the 1st Platoon arrived and we advanced in concentric fashion against the depression in our vehicles. After close-in fighting that lasted only a short while, the enemy was eliminated. The enemy force had pulled back to a deep hole formed from rainfall and had defended to the last man. Even the badly wounded set off hand grenades as we cleared the rain ditch. Approximately 30 men were killed there. In addition, a heavy machine gun, three antitank rifles, three light machine guns and one mortar were captured.

Unfortunately, two of our men were killed.

After we had cleared the area, we turned back to the rear in order to attack the enemy force there. It had already reached the high ground and fired into our vehicles from above. A round hit next to my seat and shrapnel penetrated my right hand, with the result that I was unable to use it any more. Moving quickly and dispersed widely, we attacked the groups of Russians lying in the grass.

All of a sudden, about 20 meters in front of me, someone stood up and tossed a Molotov cocktail. My driver, Anton, had the presence of mind to step on the gas and run over the Russian, while the bottle flew over my head. I took out a lot of Russians that were nearby with my submachine gun. All of them had Molotov cocktails and the dried-out steppe grass was soon burning all around us.

The division, which was essentially wiped out at Stalingrad, reached the outskirts of the city in late August. The platoon leader cited previously takes up the narrative for 20 August:[25]

The armored spearheads advanced towards the bottleneck between the lakes. Before they knew it, they were running over mines. The entire bottleneck had been mined. Strong enemy defensive fires prevented any further advance. We mounted up and followed the attack. All of a sudden, we were also in the middle of a minefield. The 5 men of my engineer squad cleared 52 mines.

The motorized rifle brigade then started attacking to the north.

By evening, combat operations were in full swing, and we set up a hedgehog defense.

21 August 1942: Even before it turned first light, the attack started up again. The *14. Panzer-Division* advanced to the north along Jergeni Hill. Abutting it to the right was our armored spearhead. Moving out of Zaza and heading north, our armored infantry regiments were attacking in the wide bottomland between the chain of hills and the lakes. After overrunning a few positions, we sailed right through

the enemy artillery positions, and the armored group advanced over the smoking ruins of overrun artillery and mortar positions as far as the edge of the high ground deep in the enemy rear. The attack objective was the large bend in the Volga at Krasnoarmeisk.

Towards evening, we reached Hill 118 west of Tschapurkniki. From that dominant piece of high ground, one had a great view several kilometers away of the series of lakes that were ringed by villages. Beyond that, the glimmering steppe extended, transitioning from a garish yellow to a soft pink in the evening sun. It was bordered on the horizon by the scarcely perceptible leaden band of the Volga.

A few armored cars were sent down to reconnoiter in the direction of the lakes, and you could see them, looking like tiny beetles, moving rapidly east and churning up large clouds of yellow dust.

We were the northernmost attack spearhead of the corps. We wanted to reach the Volga by the next morning. The night descended quickly. After some back and forth, the armored group had set up a hedgehog position on the large, round crest of the hill. I was directed to screen to the east. Sitting on my vehicle, I observed how the sinking sun allowed the shadows of Jergeni Hill to wander ever faster to the east. They soon covered the lakes and, finally, night held the steppe in its embrace.

The trains did not arrive until after midnight. They were brought forward through the terrain, which was still swarming with Russians, by a tank troop. The usual aerial recognition signals that were fired to guide them in to the hedgehog indicated that they had arrived. The soldiers made a racket with their mess kits, and the fuel cans were gathered up.

22 August 1942: With the first rays of sunshine, our faithful aerial observer was overhead. I was able to monitor it on a certain frequency on the vehicle's radio set, and I entered its reports on my map in red pencil.

All of a sudden, the observer reported: Just to the northwest of us, some 15 enemy tanks were approaching. At the same moment, the sound of the long-barreled main guns firing could be heard bellowing though the morning stillness. Strong enemy infantry elements were then also reported behind the tanks. We were immediately pulled back from our position in the east. We were directed to extend the hilltop blocking position by occupying lower-lying high ground about one kilometer southwest of Hill 118.

My platoon, the furthest out front, quickly dismounted and set up a defense oriented to the north and west on the flat crest. We had scarcely arrived at the hill, when the first wave of Russians was spotted across from us. More and more of them kept coming and soon the slopes across the way were filled with hundreds of advancing Russians. We worked feverishly to dig in. After five minutes, both hands were completely blistered, and I had to wrap a handkerchief around them. The enemy was getting closer and closer, but then he started to receive well-directed artillery fire from the artillery accompanying the armored group.

The enemy went to ground. Apparently, he had not anticipated encountering strong resistance here. Then the sounds of a flight of *Stukas* could be heard roaring in the air. It dove on the assembled tanks and infantry. One of the *Stukas* blew apart in the air.

We spent the night at that position, moving our vehicles between us.

The *14. Panzer-Division* was hanging far back to the left of us. Its main body had moved past the rail station at Tinguta. Our armored infantry were fighting their way forward along Lakes Zaza and Sarpa so as to reestablish contact with us. The *XIV. Panzer-Korps*, advancing rapidly to the east from out of the great bend in the Don, reached the Volga at Orlowka, a city outside of Stalingrad. It was paramount at that point to advance rapidly to the north to take the southern edge of Stalingrad so as to establish contact with the *XIV. Panzer-Korps* and, as a result, the *6. Armee*.

Little did the platoon leader know what was to await him there.

The Kradschützen-Bataillon Of Infanterie-Division (mot) "Großdeutschland"

Despite its reputation as an elite formation, it took some time before *"Großdeutschland"* received armored elements, including a reconnaissance battalion. It was not until April 1940 that a motorcycle infantry company was activated for the regiment. The 17th Company—part of the regiment's 4th Battalion—received most of its start-up cadre from volunteers from *Kradschützen-Bataillon 3*. With the exception of a single platoon that reported directly to regimental headquarters, the 17th Company did not see any action in the campaign in the West.[26] In addition to its motorcycle infantry, the company also had a platoon of armored cars. When the regiment added a 5th Battalion in October 1940, the company was reassigned to it.

The first combat operations of the entire company were in the Balkan campaign in April 1941, although it was mainly employed in anti-partisan missions. In the initial stages of the fighting in the Soviet Union, the company performed typical reconnaissance missions for the rapid advance: flank-guard missions and pursuit operations to maintain contact with rapidly withdrawing enemy forces. That said, the company suffered a major setback in early July when it became encircled, lost its company commander, and was almost wiped out. It took substantial reinforcements from the rest of the regiment to get the company out of its predicament.

During the punishing fighting to take Moscow in December, the company again performed poorly when it failed to post adequate security in a nighttime base camp established in the village of Kolodesnaja. A Soviet ski unit infiltrated the perimeter and scattered the men of the company, which took extensive casualties and lost about half of its vehicles. The command post for the 5th Battalion was collocated in the village, and it was also attacked and almost wiped out. The battalion commander was killed. The company was able to redeem itself later that month when it launched a successful counterattack against superior Soviet forces. The incident at Kolodesnaja was the last time the company faltered; from then on, it acquitted itself well in all operations and engagements.

When the regiment was expanded to a division in the spring of 1942, the 17th Company was disbanded in order to provide the cadre for the formation of *Kradschützen-Bataillon "Großdeutschland."* The new battalion was organized like a typical motorcycle infantry battalion of an armored division of the period, with an armored car troop, an armored light reconnaissance troop, two motorized light reconnaissance troops (*Volkswagen*), and a heavy troop.

The battalion was placed under the command of *Major* Horst von Usedom and performed well during the summer offensive of 1942. It frequently pushed ahead of the division, maintaining contact with retreating enemy forces, developing fluid situations, and securing key terrain as launching pads for continued offensive operations. The division was spared some of the harsher fighting of the winter of 1942–43 when it was assigned to a relatively quiet sector and primarily involved in defensive operations against Soviet secondary efforts.

Company portrait of the *17. (Kradschützen-)/Infanterie-Regiment (mot) "Großdeutschland"* at the time of its formation. SCOTT PRITCHETT

Motorcycle infantry of the 2nd Platoon, 17th Company, are seen in Yugoslavia in April 1941. Soldiers assigned to the regiment/division are immediately recognizable by their distinctive *"Großdeutschland"* sleeve bands and the *GD* monogram on their shoulder boards and straps. SCOTT PRITCHETT

Horst von Usedom, the first commander of *Kradschützen-Bataillon "Großdeutschland."* He was awarded the Knight's Cross on 31 December 1941 while a *Major* and commander of *Kradschützen-Bataillon 61* of the *11. Panzer-Division*. After distinguishing himself as the commander of *"Großdeutschland"* motorcycle infantry battalion, he went on to successively higher commands and levels of responsibility, ending the war as a *Generalmajor*. Of interest in the first image is the fact that von Usedom is wearing an enlisted black *Panzer* overseas cap that has been upgraded for officer wear by the addition of silver twist cord piping along the crown and upturn. In the second image, von Usedom strikes a pose with some of his battle staff in a command and control half-track, the *Sd.Kfz. 250/3*. SCOTT PRITCHETT

Obergefreiter Gottfried Zetschke was a long-serving member of *Kradschützen-Bataillon "Großdeutschland,"* one of the first reconnaissance formations to be redesignated from *Kradschützen-Bataillon* to *Panzer-Aufklärungs-Abteilung*, eventually becoming *Panzer-Aufklärungs-Abteilung "Großdeutschland"* on 14 January 1943. Zetschke received the Wound Badge in Black in September 1942 from wounds sustained in July of that year. At the time, he was assigned to the heavy troop of the battalion. In October 1942 he received the Winter Medal. These were frequently awarded well after the fact, and he would have been assigned to a different unit when he earned it. In February 1943 he was awarded the Armored Assault Badge in Bronze. On 20 April 1944, Zetschke was awarded the War Service Cross, 2nd Class, indicating he may have been taken out of frontline service to perform administrative or logistical tasks. Finally, he received the Wound Badge in Silver on 28 September 1944, after suffering his third wound in July 1944. Although the document indicates he was assigned to the 4th Troop, that was still the heavy company of the battalion as a result of organizational changes initiated that year. SCOTT PRITCHETT

Besitzzeugnis

Dem __Obergefreiten__
(Dienstgrad)

__Gottfried Zetsche__
(Vor- und Zuname)

__5.(schw.)/Aufklärungs-Abteilung"Großdeutschland"__
(Truppenteil)

wurde das

Panzerkampfabzeichen
— Bronze —

verliehen.

Abt.-Gef.Std., 2.2.1943
(Ort und Datum)

(Unterschrift)

Rittmeister
und Abteilungs-Kommandeur
(Dienstgrad und Dienststellung)

BESITZZEUGNIS

DEM

__Obgefr. Gottfried Zetsche__
(NAME, DIENSTGRAD)
__4. Schwadron__
__Panzer-Aufkl.-Abteilung Großdeutschland__
(TRUPPENTEIL, DIENSTSTELLE)

IST AUF GRUND

SEINER AM __24. 8. 1944__ ERLITTENEN

drei MALIGEN VERWUNDUNG – ~~BESCHÄDIGUNG~~

DAS

VERWUNDETENABZEICHEN

IN __Silber__

VERLIEHEN WORDEN.

Abt.Gef.St. DEN __28. 9. 1944__

Schroeter
(UNTERSCHRIFT)

Rittmeister und Abt.-Kdr.
(DIENSTGRAD UND DIENSTSTELLE)

IM NAMEN DES FÜHRERS
UND
OBERSTEN BEFEHLSHABERS DER WEHRMACHT

IST DEM

Obergefreiten Gottfried Zetsche

AM 5. Oktober 1942

DIE MEDAILLE
WINTERSCHLACHT IM OSTEN
1941/42
(OSTMEDAILLE)

VERLIEHEN WORDEN.

FÜR DIE RICHTIGKEIT:

Oberleutnant und Schwadronschef

Gerhard Scheu was another reconnaissance soldier assigned to *Panzer-Aufklärungs-Abteilung "Großdeutschland."* His Armored Assault Badge in Bronze indicates he was assigned in 1943 to the 4th Troop, a light motorized reconnaissance company equipped with the *Volkswagen*. By October 1944 Scheu was serving in the battalion's 1st Company, a fully tracked armored scout company equipped with the *Aufklärungs-Panzer 38(t)*, one of only two such reconnaissance battalions in the German Army. The awards shown are attributed to Scheu; the Iron Cross, First Class, was probably awarded for his actions in helping to prevent the enemy from taking an important bridge. Finally, there are photos of Scheu in his black *Panzer* uniform, and an atmospheric image of comrades from his platoon while he was still in the *Volkswagen* reconnaissance troop. SCOTT PRITCHETT

A press-release image showing an *Sd.Kfz. 222* and an *Sd.Kfz. 250/11* of *Kradschützen-Bataillon "Großdeutschland"* during a halt in a Soviet village. TODD GYLSEN

Kradschützen-Bataillon 17/Panzer-Aufklärungs-Abteilung 27

The images seen here are from a soldier or officer, possibly the battalion surgeon, assigned to *Panzer-Aufklärungs-Abteilung 27* of the *17. Panzer-Division*. As the original images were not captioned, it is difficult to assign a definitive chronology to them.

A death notice for a scout who joined the army in *Aufklärungs-Abteilung 7 (mot)*. His date of death is listed as 5 November 1941, a short time after the official consolidation of the reconnaissance battalion (*Panzer-Aufklärungs-Abteilung 27*) with the motorcycle infantry battalion, thus explaining his assignment to a *"Kradschützen-Abteilung."* The *2./Aufklärungs-Abteilung 7 (mot)* was used to form the 1st Company of the battalion. The death notice was acquired separately from the album, so there is no direct connection. MICHAEL H. PRUETT

A highly decorated *Oberarzt*, *Dr.* Heinrich Hüls, of the battalion. The doctor, possibly the battalion surgeon, poses for the camera wearing the black *Panzer* uniform. He also wears his medical officer shoulder boards with metal caduceus. This photograph is dated 5 October 1944. MICHAEL H. PRUETT

Since the motorcycle infantry battalion was temporarily disbanded during the winter of 1941–42 and then organized like a motorized infantry battalion, this series of images may have been taken during the period of activation of the armored scout company for the establishment of *Panzer-Aufklärungs-Abteilung 27* in May 1943. An *Sd.Kfz. 231 (8 Rad)* can be seen on a road leading through a forest in what appears to be a staging area. In the third image, scouts take a breather. The final two images show a heavy armored car section in a forested bivouac site. The scouts have made themselves at home, pitching tents and setting up clotheslines. MICHAEL H. PRUETT

In the first photograph, division tanks move down a dusty road as armored cars of the scout company stage for continued operations. In the remaining images, vehicles of the battalion move at speed down an unimproved road in open terrain, occasionally two vehicles abreast.

MICHAEL H. PRUETT

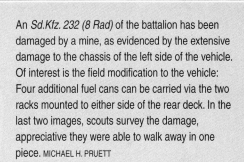

An *Sd.Kfz. 232 (8 Rad)* of the battalion has been damaged by a mine, as evidenced by the extensive damage to the chassis of the left side of the vehicle. Of interest is the field modification to the vehicle: Four additional fuel cans can be carried via the two racks mounted to either side of the rear deck. In the last two images, scouts survey the damage, appreciative they were able to walk away in one piece. MICHAEL H. PRUETT

These scouts have returned from an operation with a considerable haul in captured small arms, which are stacked on the front slope and rear deck. MICHAEL H. PRUETT

Vehicles from the battalion move down the road, while targets are taken under artillery fire in the distance. In the second image, it appears the convoy is also taking some fire. MICHAEL H. PRUETT

A quick downpour turned the unimproved roads found in the Soviet Union into quagmires of mud, as shown here. In the first image, an *Sd.Kfz. 223* makes its way through the deepest part, while the motorcyclist behind must surely be having second thoughts. To the right, soldiers are pushing a vehicle that has gotten stuck. In the second photograph, light armored cars line up in the mud. MICHAEL H. PRUETT

This group of images is believed to have come from a different scout assigned to the 1st Company of the battalion, although these images stem primarily from the campaign's early years.

Light and medium armored cars of the company line up on a road during a maintenance halt, while an *Sd.Kfz. 263* from the battalion signals detachment waits to move in the direction of a contested town. In the final image, an *Sd.Kfz. 263* advances along a smoke-filled road in a burning town believed to have been on the outskirts of Kharkov. JIM HALEY

This *Sd.Kfz. 232 (8 Rad)* appears to have run over a mine and possibly suffered extensive interior damage as well. JIM HALEY

Additional evidence of the incredible hardships endured by personnel during the muddy seasons in the Soviet Union, which occurred in the spring and fall. Under conditions like these, even motorcycles had to be towed out of the mud. JIM HALEY

Winter 1941–42 came early and with a vengeance in the Soviet Union. The scouts in the first photograph wear a variety of winter clothing, headgear, and footgear—some authorized, some impressed civilian clothing, and some "appropriated" Soviet items—in an effort to combat the cold. Despite all-terrain capability, most German armored cars were underpowered and had difficulty in mud and snow when moving cross-country. When roadways were not cleared off, as they are in the second image, the vehicles also had difficulties. The bent fenders and shattered headlight of the *Sd.Kfz. 221* in the final photograph show it has seen a lot of operations in the field. A talisman in the form of a horseshoe has been mounted to the right front bumper, perhaps in the effort to ward off further damage, or worse. JIM HALEY

This *Sd.Kfz. 231 (8 Rad)* has lost its left front mudguard. The thin sheet metals used for that purpose often proved no match for the objects encountered in the course of normal combat operations. JIM HALEY

Armored reconnaissance battalions tended to have a higher percentage of officers and, by extension, officer casualties, since the armored car sections and platoons often had officers in charge instead of the customary senior noncommissioned officers usually seen in artillery, infantry, and armor units. As with the *Panzertruppe* as a whole, many in the officer corps were noblemen, as evidenced here by the grave marker of *Leutnant* Karl Wendt, *Freiherr von Thüngen* (Count of Thüngen). JIM HALEY

Scouts check out prisoners, possibly cavalrymen, on the steppes of the Soviet Union. The crew in the *Sd.Kfz. 222* keeps a watchful eye while the enemy soldiers are patted down. JIM HALEY

A *Schwimmwagen* of the battalion has been placed in a partial defilade position. Although not nearly as numerous as the standard *Volkswagen Kübelwagen*, the amphibious version of the vehicle was issued to both army and *Waffen-SS* reconnaissance units, being seen more often in the latter. JIM HALEY

Battalion vehicles are entrained somewhere in Germany. These may be replacement vehicles for losses at the front. JIM HALEY

This scout from the armored car company or the headquarters of *Kradschützen-Bataillon 7* of the *7. Panzer-Division* applies a coat of whitewash to his *Sd.Kfz. 223* in anticipation of winter operations. The vehicle is about to be moved by rail. Of interest is the tire rim mounted on the side of the vehicle, which is missing its tire. In the second image, an *Sd.Kfz. 223* is recovered after bogging down. Despite all-wheel drive and tire chains, the underpowered vehicles could still get stuck in deep snow. The last photo shows grave markers from the headquarters of the battalion, belonging to men who fell in March 1943.

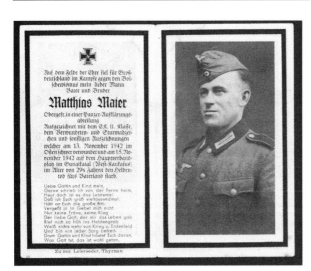

Death notices from the Eastern Front in 1942. Hans Eigner, a soldier assigned to a motorized reconnaissance battalion, was killed in action on 2 January 1942. Johann Kraus, an armored scout, succumbed to his wounds on 16 January 1942. Ludwig Schimpfhauser was a *Feldwebel* and an assistant platoon leader in a motorcycle infantry battalion when he was killed on 1 January. Franz Ferstl was assigned to a motorized reconnaissance battalion and killed in action on 1 April. Matthias Maier, an *Obergefreiter* in an armored reconnaissance battalion, fell on 13 November 1942. In the final image, scouts of a reconnaissance battalion pay their final respects next to an *Sd.Kfz. 222*. LAST IMAGE: HENNER LINDLAR

Scouts pose in front of their hastily camouflaged *Sd.Kfz. 231 (8 Rad)* in the dead of winter. Uniform regulations were generally ignored in winter, allowing the soldiers to garb themselves as needed to stay warm in the brutal cold. JIM HALEY

These images are attributed to *Kradschützen-Bataillon 24* of the *24. Panzer-Division* and were probably taken in early or late 1943, judging by the headgear. The brutal winters and primitive conditions along the Eastern Front are immediately obvious. JIM HALEY

The largely intact winter whitewash on this *Sd.Kfz. 231 (8 Rad)* from an unidentified reconnaissance battalion stands out in stark contrast to the springlike conditions. MIKE HARPE

These scouts, most likely in the battalion headquarters, take a lunch break in a bleak Russian winter setting. The *Sd.Kfz. 263 (8 Rad)* has been partially covered with hay, while a white tarpaulin has been spread over portions of the rear deck in an effort to break up the high, obvious silhouette of the vehicle. MIKE HARPE

Heinz Reverchon was a platoon leader in the *1./Kradschützen-Bataillon 43* of the *13. Panzer-Division* when he was awarded the Knight's Cross of the Iron Cross on 16 September 1942. The second image is a period press-release photograph of Reverchon and some of his men. At the time of his award, he was the youngest recipient in the German Army, thus sparking additional interest in him. The press-release note states: "21-year-old Knight's Cross recipient *Leutnant* Heinz Reverchon with his armored scout and radio crews, with whom he conducted numerous bold reconnaissance operations." The postwar-signed image seen last highlights his relative youth. Surviving the war, Reverchon died in Munich on 23 January 1999. It is interesting to note that the black *Panzer* uniform commonly worn by armored car crews is nowhere to be seen in these images. According to one of the officers assigned to the battalion, the black wool uniforms were not worn at the time because the weather was so hot (Walter Böhm in correspondence with Michael H. Pruett).

LAST THREE IMAGES: MICHAEL H. PRUETT

Armored cars, led by an *Sd.Kfz. 223*, park next to vegetation during a break in movement.

An *Sd.Kfz. 222* appears to be providing cover as a convoy moves down a snowy road in a Soviet town.

This press-release photo, dated 16 August 1942, shows scouts assigned to an *Sd.Kfz. 222* bartering with a local peasant. The accompanying note states that the scouts were engaged in a friendly conversation with the locals during a halt in the advance. The peasants were happy that the German forces had finally driven away the Soviets. TODD GYLSEN

Another press-release image, dated 11 September 1942, showing fighting during the advance on Stalingrad. The *Sd.Kfz. 250/3* is from an unidentified unit. TODD GYLSEN

CHAPTER 8

Stalemate in Italy

SETTING THE STAGE

Although the scene of bitter fighting, the Allied campaign in Italy was essentially a secondary theater from which forces and resources were regularly diverted to bolster the preparations for the invasion in Normandy and, a short while later, southern France. Likewise, Hitler regarded Italy as less important and only began to consider a stauncher defense after Commander-in-Chief South *Generalfeldmarschall* Kesselring convinced him that delaying the Allies as far south as possible would protect Germany's vulnerable sources of oil in the Balkans from air strikes. Due to frequently inept Allied leadership, constant transfers of forces, frequent bad weather that prevented Allied airpower from being used to its best advantage, tenacious German defense, and ideal defensive terrain, the fight for Italy continued until the end of the war.

Although mechanized forces were employed by the Germans, particularly in efforts to defeat Allied landings along coastal plains, the fighting was predominated by classical infantry defensive fighting for the most part, since the rugged mountain ranges and rivers that tended to run east–west favored the use of infantry. Many mechanized forces were also stationed in Italy for a short while in the course of being reconstituted, with several used to disarm Italian forces in September 1943 when Italy capitulated. As there was no direct combat role for those formations, they are not discussed here.

Scouts from an unidentified unit on their *Sd.Kfz. 250/9* on a railcar somewhere in the Mediterranean Theater. Of the army armored reconnaissance battalions serving in Italy, *Panzer-Aufklärungs-Abteilung 16* received its *Sd.Kfz. 250/9* in June 1943, with *Panzer-Aufklärungs-Abteilungen 103* and *129* starting to receive their allocations in July. *Panzer-Aufklärungs-Abteilung 26* did not receive any of the vehicles until April 1944.

DOCTRINE

The fighting in Italy increasingly saw the use of reconnaissance elements in economy-of-force missions, denial operations, rearguard actions, and direct combat. In the strictly defensive fighting, there was little need for scouting and reconnaissance in the classical sense, and battlefield reconnaissance was the responsibility of units on the line. As with armored assets, armored reconnaissance formations were frequently held back as a ready reserve in the event of Allied breakthroughs.

Because of the orders redesignating and reorganizing all reconnaissance assets in March 1943, the reconnaissance battalions of armored and mechanized infantry forces in Italy were officially redesignated *Panzer-Aufklärungs-Abteilungen*.

ORGANIZATION

Armored reconnaissance battalions were continuously upgraded in capabilities while essentially retaining a five-company structure. Within the theoretical construct, a heavy armored car platoon—consisting of six *Sd.Kfz. 233* heavy armored cars with the short 7.5cm main gun—was added to the organization, reporting to the headquarters but probably logistically attached to the wheeled armored scout company. In addition, there were now two types of armored scout companies, one wheeled and one half-tracked, with the latter outfitted with *Sd.Kfz. 250* light half-tracks including the newly introduced reconnaissance version, the *Sd.Kfz. 250/9*. The aim was also to reorganize all light reconnaissance companies into armored companies, although there were still companies organized in the generally same manner that used the *Volkswagen* utility vehicle or the *Kettenkrad* motorcycle half-track, or even retained motorcycles. The heavy companies were either armored or motorized, with most falling into the latter category. In the armored battalions, gun platoons using the *Sd.Kfz. 251/9* (with short 7.5cm main gun) were introduced. In light of increasing Allied air superiority and even dominance, antiaircraft platoons were also added as a possibility for a motorized heavy company.

ORDER OF BATTLE FOR ITALY, 1943

Parent Organization	Reconnaissance Assets / Notes
Oberbefehlshaber Süd (Commander-in-Chief South)	
XIV. Panzer-Korps	
16. Panzer-Division	*Panzer-Aufklärungs-Abteilung 16*: Headquarters and headquarters company (*KStN 1109* / 16 January 1943); heavy armored car platoon (*KStN 1138* / 1 December 1942); one armored scout company (half-track, *KStN 1162c* / 5 February 1943) (1st); one armored scout company (wheeled, *KStN 1162* / 1 November 1941) (2nd); two light armored reconnaissance companies (*KStN 1113 (gp)* / 1 March 1942) (3rd and 4th); one heavy company (armored, *KStN 1121a (gp)* / 1 March 1943) with one armored gun platoon (*KStN 1125 (gp)* / 1 May 1943), one armored light infantry gun platoon (*KStN 1123 (gp)* / 1 March 1943), one armored heavy antitank gun platoon (*KStN 1145 (gp)* / 1 March 1943), and one armored combat engineer platoon (*KStN 1124a (gp)* / 1 March 1943).[1]
3. Panzergrenadier-Division	*Panzer-Aufklärungs-Abteilung 103*: Organized identically to *Panzer-Aufklärungs-Abteilung 129* (*29. Panzergrenadier-Division*) below.[2]
15. Panzergrenadier-Division	No reconnaissance assets when initially formed. *Panzer-Aufklärungs-Abteilung 115* activated in October 1943. Headquarters and wheeled armored scout company formed from remnants of *Panzer-Aufklärungs-Abteilung 33* (capitulated in North Africa). Remaining assets formed from personnel and equipment levies against disbanded elements. Eventually: headquarters, one armored scout company (1st), three truck-borne light reconnaissance companies, and one heavy company. All elements seemed to have a non-standard organization.
29. Panzergrenadier-Division	*Panzer-Aufklärungs-Abteilung 129*: Organized identically to *Panzer-Aufklärungs-Abteilung 16* (*16. Panzer-Division*) above, except the wheeled armored scout company was the 1st Company, and the half-track scouts were in the 2nd Company.[3]
90. Panzergrenadier-Division	Theoretically organized along the lines of a *Panzer-Division 43*; the organization chart nonetheless shows no reconnaissance battalion.
Panzer-Division "Hermann Göring"	*Panzer-Aufklärungs-Abteilung "Hermann Göring"*: Organized similarly to *Panzer-Aufklärungs-Abteilung 129* of the *29. Panzergrenadier-Division* above, except the 4th Company was a *Volkswagen*-equipped light reconnaissance company (*KStN 1113 (VW)* / 18 March 1942) and there were two armored light infantry gun platoons in the heavy company (*KStN 1123 (gp)* / 1 March 1943).[4]

CHANGES IN ORGANIZATIONAL AUTHORIZATIONS, LATE 1942– EARLY 1943

Headquarters, Motorized Reconnaissance Battalion (1109)

This *KStN* was introduced on 16 January 1943, indicating it was an interim authorization document. The *KStN* officially eliminated a number of tactical vehicles that had until then been present in organizational documents: the *Sd.Kfz. 247* heavy wheeled command and control vehicle, the *Sd.Kfz. 260* light armored radio car, and the *Sd.Kfz. 263 (8 Rad)* heavy armored radio car. In their place—and also occurring more frequently throughout the headquarters—were variants of the light half-track *Sd.Kfz. 250* and, for the first time, variants of the medium half-track *Sd.Kfz. 251*. Gone was the manpack radio section of the signals platoon. Wheeled soft-skin vehicles had largely disappeared from the organization, except within the headquarters proper and, of course, within the battalion trains and maintenance sections.

- Headquarters: eight motorcycles, two sidecar motorcycles, two medium cross-country wheeled personnel carriers (*Kfz. 15*), and one light armored half-tracked radio vehicle (*Sd.Kfz. 250/3*).
- Signals platoon:
  - Headquarters section: one light cross-country utility vehicle (*Volkswagen*) and one light armored half-tracked radio vehicle (*Sd.Kfz. 250/3*).
  - One light armored telephone section: one medium armored wire signals vehicle (*Sd.Kfz. 251/11*).
  - One light armored radio section (Type *b*): one light armored half-tracked radio vehicle (*Sd.Kfz. 250/3*).
  - Four light armored radio sections (Type *c*): one light armored radio car (*Sd.Kfz. 261*).
  - Three medium armored radio sections (Type *c*): one medium armored radio half-tracked vehicle (*Sd.Kfz. 251/3*).

Heavy Company (Armored) Company Headquarters (1121a (*gp*))

The *KStN* introduced on 1 March 1943 continued the trend to complete mechanization of the company, at least within the headquarters and signals elements, by the addition of variants of the medium armored personnel carrier.

- Headquarters: two motorcycles, two sidecar motorcycles, one medium radio armored personnel carrier (*Sd.Kfz. 251/3*).
- One light armored field telephone section (Type *c*): one medium landline armored personnel carrier (*Sd.Kfz. 251/11*).
- One maintenance section: one light cross-country utility vehicle (*Kfz. 1 Volkswagen*), two 3-ton trucks, and one heavy 12-ton half-track prime mover (*Kfz. 8*).
- Company trains: one medium cross-country wheeled personnel carrier (*Kfz. 15*), one medium truck, and four 3-ton trucks.

Armored Light Infantry Gun Platoon (1123a (*gp*))

The primary change in the armored version of the *KStN* introduced on 1 March 1943 was the use of medium armored personnel carriers within the platoon for command and control and as prime movers for the guns.

- Headquarters: one motorcycle, one sidecar motorcycle, and one medium armored personnel carrier (*Sd.Kfz. 251/1*).
- Gun section: three medium armored personnel carriers (prime mover for light infantry gun) (*Sd.Kfz. 251/4*) and two light 75mm infantry guns (towed).

Armored Gun Platoon (1125a (*gp*))

This new *KStN*, introduced on 1 May 1943, represented an effort to provide the firepower present in the heavy armored car platoon equipped with the *Sd.Kfz. 233* (*KStN 1138*), while providing greater cross-country maneuverability, armored protection for the crew, and a lower silhouette.

- Headquarters: one motorcycle and one sidecar motorcycle.
- Gun section: six medium armored gun carriers (75mm) (*Sd.Kfz. 251/9*), one medium armored personnel (ammunition carrier) (*Sd.Kfz. 251/4*), and one 3-ton truck.

The above was the organization authorized for 1 May 1943, based on a working draft issued in November 1942. The illustrations below show the organization authorized on 1 November 1943.

Platoon Headquarters Section

Kettenkrad (*Sd.Kfz. 2*)

Medium Armored Radio Half-track (*Sd.Kfz. 251/3*),
1x Submachine Gun, 1x Light MG

Gun Section

6x Medium Armored Personnel Carrier (7.5cm Main Gun) (*Sd.Kfz. 251/9*), 1x Submachine Gun, 1x Light MG

Ammunition Section

Medium Armored Personnel Carrier
(Infantry Gun) (*Sd.Kfz. 251/1*) for Ammunition,
1x Submachine Gun, 1x Light MG

Truck, 3 ton, Canvas Top, Cross-Country,
for Ammunition and Equipment

Totals: 1x Officer, 8x NCOs, 26x Enlisted Personnel; 15x Rifles, 13x Pistols, 15x Submachine Guns, 8x Light MG's; 1x Vehicle, 8x Armored Vehicles, 1x *Kettenkrad*

Armored Combat Engineer Platoon (1124A (*gp*))

As with the previous authorization documents, *KStN 1124a*, issued on 1 March 1943, provided the combat elements of the platoon with armored protection in the form of variants of the medium armored personnel carrier, including an engineer-specific variant, the *Sd.Kfz. 251/7*.

- Headquarters: one motorcycle, one sidecar motorcycle, and one medium armored personnel carrier with 37mm antitank gun (*Sd.Kfz. 250/10*).
- Equipment section: three 3-ton trucks.
- Three combat engineer squads: two medium armored personnel carriers (engineer) (*Sd.Kfz. 251/7*), one engineer squad, and two light machine guns.

Armored Antitank Gun Section (1127a (*gp*))

Although authorized in organization charts from 1943, this organization does not appear to have been present in any reconnaissance battalions that year. This organization was intended to provide additional antiarmor punch in the form of light armored personnel carriers mounting a 28mm antitank rifle (gun) (*Sd.Kfz. 250/11*).

Armored Heavy Antitank Gun Platoon (1145A (*gp*))

This version of the antitank gun platoon, dated 1 March 1943, upgraded the antiarmor capabilities of the platoon and provided the crews with armored personnel carriers as prime movers.

- Headquarters: two motorcycles and one medium armored personnel carrier (*Sd.Kfz. 251/1*).
- Gun section: five medium armored personnel carriers (prime movers and ammunition carriers) (*Sd.Kfz. 251/4*) and three 75mm antitank guns (towed).

Armored Car Platoon (1138)

Introduced on 1 November 1942, the *KStN* authorized the following:

- Platoon: two 3-ton trucks and six heavy armored cars with 7.5cm main gun (*Sd.Kfz. 233*).

Armored Antitank Gun Section (1127a (*gp*))

Sidecar Motorcycle	3x Light Armored Personnel Carrier (Antitank Rifle, Model 41) (*Sd.Kfz. 250/11*) (*schwere Panzerbüchse 41*), 1x Light MG

Totals: 4x NCOs, 17x Enlisted Personnel; 10x Rifles, 8x Pistols, 3x Submachine Guns, 3x Light MG's; 3x Armored Vehicles, 1x Sidecar Motorcycle

Armored Car Platoon (1138)

a) Platoon

6x Heavy Armored Car (*Sd.Kfz. 233*), 6x Light MG's, 6x Submachine Guns, 6x 7.5cm Main Gun

Totals: 1x Officer, 11x NCOs, 6x Enlisted Personnel; 18x Pistols, 6x Submachine Guns, 6x Light MG's, 6x Main Guns; 6x Armored Vehicles

b) Trains (Moves with Combat Trains I of the Armored Scout Company)

Truck, 3 ton, Canvas Top, for Ammunition and Equipment	Truck, 3 ton, Canvas Top, for Petroleum, Oil & Lubricants

Totals: 4x Enlisted Personnel; 4x Rifles; 2x Wheeled Vehicles

Armored Scout Company (Half-track) (1162c)

This *KStN*, introduced provisionally on 5 February 1943 (see excerpt section) and formally codified on 1 November of the same year (see illustrations), introduced the light armored personnel carrier as the primary combat vehicle for the armored half-track scout company. Thanks to the development of the reconnaissance version of the light half-track, the *Sd.Kfz. 250/9*, the scouts had essentially the same firepower as before on their armored cars, while obtaining a greater degree of cross-country mobility and a lower silhouette. The absence of a rear driver, however, eliminated the ability to move away quickly in reverse as a tactical maneuver. The radio versions of the armored cars were also replaced by a similarly equipped version of the light half-track, the *Sd.Kfz. 250/5*.[5] The initial organization was planned as follows:

- Headquarters: three motorcycles, seven light half-tracks ($^1/_2$-ton) (*Sd.Kfz. 2 / Kettenkrad*), one medium cross-country wheeled personnel carrier (*Kfz. 15*), and one light observation armored personnel carrier (*Sd.Kfz. 250/5*).
- Four scout platoons (half-track), each with two sections consisting of: two light armored personnel carriers (2cm) (*Sd.Kfz. 250/9*) and one light observation armored personnel carrier (*Sd.Kfz. 250/5*).
- Maintenance section: one sidecar motorcycle, one light cross-country maintenance utility vehicle (*Kfz. 2/40*), two 3-ton trucks, and one light 3-ton half-track prime mover (*Sd.Kfz. 11*).
- Company trains: one medium cross-country wheeled personnel carrier (*Kfz. 15*) and five 3-ton trucks.

The November 1943 organization was organized as illustrated on the following pages.

a) Command Group
Company Headquarters Section

| 2x Light Motorcycle 350cc, 2x *Kettenkrad* | Light Utility Vehicle, Cross-Country (4 seat) | Light Armored Observation Half-track (*Sd.Kfz. 250/5*), 1x Submachine Gun, 1x Light MG |

Totals: 1x Officer, 4x NCOs, 5x Enlisted Personnel; 6x Rifles, 3x Pistols, 2x Submachine Guns, 1x Light MG; 1x Wheeled Vehicle, 1x Armored Vehicle, 2x Motorcycles, 2x *Kettenkräder*

b) 1st Platoon

| 1st Section | 2nd Section |

| Light Armored Observation Half-track (*Sd.Kfz. 250/5*), 1x Submachine Gun, 1x Light MG and 2x Light Armored Personnel Carrier (2cm) (*Sd.Kfz. 250/9*), 2x Submachine Gun, 2x Light MG, 2x 2cm Main Gun | Light Armored Observation Half-track (*Sd.Kfz. 250/5*), 1x Submachine Gun, 1x Light MG and 2x Light Armored Personnel Carrier (2cm) (*Sd.Kfz. 250/9*), 2x Submachine Gun, 2x Light MG, 2x 2cm Main Gun |

Totals: 1x Officer, 11x NCOs, 6x Enlisted Personnel; 18x Pistols, 6x Submachine Guns, 6x Light MG's, 4x 2cm Main Guns; 6x Armored Half-track Vehicles

c) 2nd Platoon

| 1st Section | 2nd Section |

| Light Armored Observation Half-track (*Sd.Kfz. 250/5*), 1x Submachine Gun, 1x Light MG and 2x Light Armored Personnel Carrier (2cm) (*Sd.Kfz. 250/9*), 2x Submachine Gun, 2x Light MG, 2x 2cm Main Gun | Light Armored Observation Half-track (*Sd.Kfz. 250/5*), 1x Submachine Gun, 1x Light MG and 2x Light Armored Personnel Carrier (2cm) (*Sd.Kfz. 250/9*), 2x Submachine Gun, 2x Light MG, 2x 2cm Main Gun |

Totals: 1x Officer, 11x NCOs, 6x Enlisted Personnel; 18x Pistols, 6x Submachine Guns, 6x Light MG's, 4x 2cm Main Guns; 6x Armored Half-track Vehicles

d) 3rd Platoon

| 1st Section | 2nd Section |

| Light Armored Observation Half-track (*Sd.Kfz. 250/5*), 1x Submachine Gun, 1x Light MG and 2x Light Armored Personnel Carrier (2cm) (*Sd.Kfz. 250/9*), 2x Submachine Gun, 2x Light MG, 2x 2cm Main Gun | Light Armored Observation Half-track (*Sd.Kfz. 250/5*), 1x Submachine Gun, 1x Light MG and 2x Light Armored Personnel Carrier (2cm) (*Sd.Kfz. 250/9*), 2x Submachine Gun, 2x Light MG, 2x 2cm Main Gun |

Totals: 1x Officer, 11x NCOs, 6x Enlisted Personnel; 18x Pistols, 6x Submachine Guns, 6x Light MG's, 4x 2cm Main Guns; 6x Armored Half-track Vehicles

e) 4th Platoon

1st Section	2nd Section

Light Armored Observation Half-track (*Sd.Kfz. 250/5*), 1x Submachine Gun, 1x Light MG and 2x Light Armored Personnel Carrier (2cm) (*Sd.Kfz. 250/9*), 2x Submachine Gun, 2x Light MG, 2x 2cm Main Gun	Light Armored Observation Half-track (*Sd.Kfz. 250/5*), 1x Submachine Gun, 1x Light MG and 2x Light Armored Personnel Carrier (2cm) (*Sd.Kfz. 250/9*), 2x Submachine Gun, 2x Light MG, 2x 2cm Main Gun

Totals: 1x Officer, 11x NCOs, 6x Enlisted Personnel; 18x Pistols, 6x Submachine Guns, 6x Light MG's, 4x 2cm Main Guns; 6x Armored Half-track Vehicles

f) Vehicle Maintenance Section

Truck, 2 ton, Cross-Country (Set up for Vehicle Maintenance Section)	Truck, 3 ton, Canvas Top, Cross-Country, for Replacement Parts	Truck, 3 ton, Cross-Country, for Workshop Equipment, with Basic Issue for Vehicle Maintenance Section	Light Prime Mover, 3 ton (*Sd.Kfz. 11*)

Totals: 4x NCOs, 9x Enlisted Personnel; 12x Rifles 1x Pistol; 4x Wheeled Vehicles

g) Combat Trains

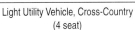

Light Utility Vehicle, Cross-Country (4 seat)	Truck, 3 ton, Canvas Top, Cross-Country, for Ammunition and Equipment	Truck, 3 ton, Cross-Country, for Petroleum, Oil & Lubricants	Truck, 3 ton, Canvas Top, Cross-Country, for Small Field Mess Stove

Totals: 4x NCOs, 8x Enlisted Personnel; 10x Rifles, 1x Pistol, 1x Submachine Gun; 4x Wheeled Vehicles

Summary

	Officers	NCOs	Enlisted Personnel	Rifles	Pistols (Submachine Guns)	Light MG's	Main Guns	Vehicles	Armored Vehicles	Motorcycles (Sidecars) [Kettenkräder]
Command Section	1	4	5	6	3 (2)	1		1	1	2 [2]
1st Platoon	1	11	6		18 (6)	6	4		6	
2nd Platoon	1	11	6		18 (6)	6	4		6	
3rd Platoon		12	6		18 (6)	6	4		6	
4th Platoon		12	6		18 (6)	6	4		6	
Vehicle Maintenance Section		4	9	12	1			4		
Combat Trains		4	8	10	1 (1)			4		
Baggage Trains		1	3	4				1		
Totals	3	59	49	32	77 (27)	25	16	10	25	2 [2]

AFTER-ACTION REPORTS AND FIRSTHAND ACCOUNTS

After-action reports and firsthand accounts concerning the operations of reconnaissance forces in Italy are relatively hard to come by. Here is a narrative concerning the history of *Panzer-Aufklärungs-Abteilung 115* of the *15. Panzergrenadier-Division* from the time of its activation—essentially as a successor organization to *Panzer-Aufklärungs-Abteilung 33* in Africa—to the end of its fighting in Italy:[6]

Panzer-Aufklärungs-Abteilung 33 had been forced to capitulate in Tunisia after 2 years of fighting in Africa. That spelled the end of the campaign in North Africa. The remnants of the battalion went into captivity and spent the rest of the war in Canada or America. Over time, everyone left who had once belonged to *Panzer-Aufklärungs-Abteilung 33* gathered at either the Armored Reconnaissance replacement Detachment in Berlin (Stahnsdorf) or at the convalescent company in Kleinmachow. The commander of the march company there was *Oberleutnant* Mertens, who had also served in Africa on the staff of the battalion. Among the officers: *Oberleutnant* Nehm, *Leutnant* Lüdtke and *Leutnant* Bensel. Time was spent with garrison duties and details involved with helping clear bomb damage in Berlin. At the same time, there were also rumors about the activation of a new armored reconnaissance battalion . . .

 . . . Eventually, Berlin decided to form a new battalion, this time as *Panzer-Aufklärungs-Abteilung 115*.

More and more former members of the old battalion arrived at Berlin (Stahnsdorf). Among them was *Rittmeister Freiherr* von Gienanth who, along with two other battalion officers, had been ferried out of Tunis on the day of the capitulation in an assault boat on orders of *General* von Vaerst.

Correspondence from *Freiherr* von Gienanth dated 10 November 1943, contains the following: "On 5 October 1943, we finally saw on paper that *Panzer-Aufklärungs-Abteilung 115* was to be formed using 'former Africans.' Preparations started. There was a tough fight with the replacement detachment in Stahnsdorf to get former battalion members released to us. They had become indispensable as instructors. I personally went to the Camp Senne Training Area to see what was available in terms of billeting and training opportunities."

On 9 October 1943, the battalion was moved by rail from Berlin-Grunewald station to the Camp Senne Training Area. On 11 October, the barracks camp at Staumühle was occupied by *Oberleutnant* Nehm (in charge), *Oberleutnant* von Salis-Soglio, *Leutnant* Bensel, *Leutnant* Krüger, 45 noncommissioned officers and 119 enlisted.

Training then commenced on the armored cars and other vehicles, which arrived on 22 October. Additional personnel arrived, including a battalion surgeon and a paymaster. Also arriving were *Leutnant* Lüdtke and *Leutnant* Peglow, both formerly of the *1./Panzer-Aufklärungs-Abteilung 33*. The new battalion commander was *Rittmeister* von der Borch, who assumed command of the battalion on 15 November 1943.

Rittmeister Freiherr von Gienanth travelled to the Italian Theater on 10 November 1943, in an effort to get a feel for the area of operations from *Oberleutnant* von Gaudecker, who was already there. On 16 November, the new cadre for the 115th was loaded on trains with vehicles for transportation to Italy.

On 22 November, the train was off-loaded at the eastern train station in Rome. The battalion personnel then moved by road march in the direction of Naples as far as the area around the front at Cassino. The armored car company, designated as the headquarters company, billeted at St. Giovanni. The other three companies, which had been formed in theater as armored reconnaissance companies, were already conducting operations. As far as the armored car company was concerned, there were no options for employing it in the mountainous terrain around Monte Cassino and along the Liri River.

The new battalion commander wrote the following on 12 December 1943: "Arriving at the division, we discovered that the three armored reconnaissance companies that had been activated in Italy for the battalion had already been in combat for some time and that our battalion, which still had not completed its activation process, would also be committed immediately. It should be noted that the combat operations that awaited us would be in high mountain terrain. It was rocky and filled with cliffs and the only way to provide logistical support—in a very laborious manner, to boot—was by means of mules and backpack. Truly a nice mission for an armored reconnaissance battalion! Despite that, we had to admit that we couldn't be standing around with our hands in our pockets when the grenadier regiments of the division were involved in extremely heavy fighting."

Another passage from the same correspondence: "At an altitude of 800 meters, I occupied a battalion command post with my staff in a cold and wet cave. We called it the "Camino Bar." During the first few days, the enemy only approached us with patrols. There were Americans to the left and Tommies to the right. The enemy's artillery and fighter-bombers were very active, but they didn't leave much of an effect initially. The combat engineer platoon was employed making positions. It has to be said that it was work that moved forward slowly due to the meager means and forces available.

"The free-for-all started on 2 December 1943. English and American forces moved out to attack the massif, which was occupied by us and two grenadier battalions. They were probably most interested in getting it because of the numerous observation posts it would offer their artillery. As a result, we and our poor companies experienced massive barrage fire. After the artillery preparation, the enemy attacked our two wings. After several attacks had been turned back in close-quarters fighting, in which our officers and men performed magnificently, the enemy did succeed in making penetrations on both wings. Our reserves were weak and immediate counterattacks were unsuccessful. It was in that position that the entire battalion experienced several intense days. It was truly extraordinary what the battalion demonstrated in terms of nerves, tenacity and bravery. That wasn't a smug judgment on my part, either. That was the call of the Division Commander of the *15. Panzergrenadier-Division*, *General* Rodt, who was very vocal in his praise and also had a general order of the day written that was very praiseworthy of the battalion.

"On 6 December 1943, the high command recognized that the high ground that had been lost could not be retaken with the forces at our disposal. Orders came to pull back. As a result of the capabilities of my company commanders, this occurred with practically no new casualties. On 9 December, we finally completed our disengagement from the enemy and pulled back to our rearward billeting area, which seemed like paradise to us. From the corps intelligence staff we discovered that we had fought against an English infantry division and an American regiment, both of which had been supported by 180 tubes of artillery of all calibers. It was our good fortune that Tommy was very circumspect in sparing blood and balked at taking up an infantry fight, instead hoping that artillery alone would be enough.

"During the days of its initial fighting in that sector, the battalion had suffered large casualties. It was terrain not suited for the battalion's training and equipment. There had been bad weather, storms and rain and the rocks and boulders of the mountains. There were 200 men killed, wounded and missing, including 5 officers. In addition, there were another 100 on sick call due to the extreme demands of fighting in the mountains and the terrible weather conditions.

"It was intended for us to have a week's worth of rest, before we would play infantry again in the next position. For a change of pace, we would be dealing more with rivers than with mountains.

"Despite all of the hardships, the morale of our terrific soldiers was good and among the officers, as one would expect, even better. I personally have enjoyed the fact that I am surrounded by an exceptionally capable officer corps, whose ranks are filled with nice people.

"18 December 1943: Monte Camino was abandoned. Heavy aerial attacks on Cassino. Heavy enemy bomber attacks on Pontecorvo, Ceprano and Arce as well. The ready-reaction platoon of the armored car company moved forward. All of the crews—noncommissioned officers, gunners, radio operators and rear drivers—were employed as infantry. Only the vehicle drivers remained with their vehicles in San Giovanni.

"24 December 1943. At present, the armored car company consisted of only about 20 men. Everyone else was up front in positions."

The 1st and 2nd Battles for Monte Cassino (Middle of January through 12 February 1944 and 15 through 18 February 1944)

On 17 January 1944, *Major* Ziegler, the commander of *Panzer-Aufklärungs-Abteilung 129* (formerly of *Panzer-Aufklärungs-Abteilung 33*) [*29. Panzergrenadier-Division*], wrote the following: "Every individual man has distinguished himself magnificently. To the right of me, Gienanth (the commander of the *5./Panzer-Aufklärungs-Abteilung 115*) and his warriors were likewise successful."

Especially distinguishing itself in the fighting in a forward position was the 2nd Company, under the acting command of *Leutnant* Wolff.

On 21 and 22 January, the 4th Company of *Oberleutnant* von Gaudecker was the bulwark in the fighting. By means of close-quarters combat, it suffocated any enemy attempts at breaking through. In the course of the day, 240 prisoners were brought in and 100 enemy killed counted, although the actual enemy losses in reality were considerably higher. All of the battalion, with the exception of the scout company, was in the Gustav Line.

22 January 1944: English and American forces conducting a landing north of Gaeta and established a beachhead at Nettuno. Alert! The armored scout company was employed to assist in eliminating the enemy forces. It was sent in the direction south of Rome (Anzio and Nettuno) . . .

. . . 30 January 1944: The armored scout company departed to Avezano in the Abruzzi Mountains, moving via Isoletta, Ceprano, Arce and Sorra. The narrow roadways, the snow walls that were meters high at altitudes of 2,000 meters all inserted themselves in front of the stunning image of the Gran Sasso. It demanded a lot of the drivers of the armored cars, who moved along the steep and curve-filled mountain passes.

Pescara on the Adriatic was reached early in the morning. The march objective for the company was Montesilvano and Silvi-Marina. The mission: "*Panzer-Aufklärungs-Abteilung 115* is attached to the *1. Fallschirmjäger-Division* and screens along the coast in the area from Pescara to Forli on the Adriatic."

At the beginning of March, the battalion was pulled out of the Gustav Line, where it had so successfully turned back the Americans.

Distinguishing themselves particularly were *Leutnant* Mann of the 3rd Company of *Oberleutnant* Möcker (5 March 1944) and *Oberfeldwebel* Kraus of the 4th Company of *Oberleutnant* von Gaudecker (12 March 1944), who earned the German Cross in Gold and the recognition of the Commanding General of the *XIV. Panzer-Korps*, *General der Panzertruppen* von Senger und Etterlin.

This round of fighting was followed by 8 days of operations against English forces in the mountains north of the former area of operations.

The 3rd Battle for Monte Cassino from 12 to 26 March 1944

The battalion was employed on the massif of Monte Cassino and attached to the *1. Fallschirmjäger-Division* of *Generalleutnant* Heidrich.

Officers of *Panzer-Aufklärungs-Abteilung 115* (As of 1 January 1944)

BATTALION HEADQUARTERS
Commander: *Rittmeister Freiherr* von der Borch
Adjutant: *Oberleutnant Freiherr* von Solis-Soglio
Liaison officer: *Leutnant* Bensel (formerly of *Panzer-Aufklärungs-Abteilung 33*)
Battalion surgeon: *Stabsarzt Dr.* Ruempler

1ST COMPANY
Commander: *Oberleutnant* Nehm (later: *Freiherr* von Türkheim zu Altdorf, formerly of *Panzer-Aufklärungs-Abteilung 33*)
Company officers: *Leutnants* Lüdtke, Unger, and Peglow (all formerly of *Panzer-Aufklärungs-Abteilung 33*)

2ND COMPANY
Acting Commander: *Leutnant* Wolff (formerly of *Panzer-Aufklärungs-Abteilung 33*)
Company officer: *Leutnant* Remy

3RD COMPANY
Commander: *Oberleutnant* Möcker
Company officers: *Leutnants* Schäfer and Mann (latter formerly of *Panzer-Aufklärungs-Abteilung 33*)

4TH COMPANY
Commander: *Oberleutnant* von Gaudecker (formerly of *Kavallerie-Regiment 6*)
Company officers: *Leutnants* Kessler and Hack (former formerly of *Panzer-Aufklärungs-Abteilung 33*)

5TH COMPANY
Commander: *Rittmeister Freiherr* von Gienanth (formerly of *Panzer-Aufklärungs-Abteilung 33*)
Company officers: *Leutnants* Henrici, Krüger, and Koerber (first two formerly of *Panzer-Aufklärungs-Abteilung 33*)

Under the leadership of the commander of the 5th Company, *Oberleutnant Freiherr* von Gienanth, who held acting command of the battalion in the absence of *Rittmeister Freiherr* von der Borch, who was on leave, the intrepid men of the 3rd Company, under the command of *Oberleutnant* Möcker, blew up seven enemy tanks in front of the German main line of resistance during the nights of 27–28 and 28–29 March 1944.

In the Daily Report of the Armed Forces High Command, *Rittmeister Freiherr* von Gienanth was mentioned by name for his exemplary bravery in the fighting in the area of operations around Cassino. On 20 April 1944, *Rittmeister Freiherr* von der Borch returned from leave and reassumed command of the battalion. On 21 April 1944, von Gienanth took leave of the battalion and, after attending a course, assumed command of *Panzer-Aufklärungs-Abteilung "Großdeutschland."* He was killed on 14 August 1944 in the vicinity of Jukniske (East Prussia).

On 2 May 1944, the battalion was pulled out of the line for a week to rest behind the front.

The 4th Battle for Monte Cassino from 11 May to 5 June 1944

Based on the thorough account of the Battalion Commander, it had to be assumed that the anticipated major offensive had already started. During the night of 11–12 May 1944, the enemy barrage fires commenced with approximately 1,600 guns. The sorties of the Royal Air Force reached an intensity never before experienced. After the preparation, the enemy moved out with such a numerical superiority in infantry and tanks that he was soon able to achieve six penetrations in the area from Cassino to the west coast. On orders of the Commanding general, *General der Panzertruppen* von Senger und

A letter of commendation from the division commander of the airborne forces speaks volumes concerning this fighting:

1. *Fallschirmjäger-Division* Division Command Post, 3 May 1944

TO: *Rittmeister* von der Borch!

Panzer-Aufklärungs-Abteilung 115 was attached to the *1. Fallschirmjäger-Division* in the period from 19 March to 2 May.

Under the circumspect and forceful leadership of its commanders, first *Rittmeister Freiherr* von Gienanth, and then *Rittmeister Freiherr* von der Borch, the battalion supported the paratroopers in a magnificent manner.

The decisive yet nimble *Reitergeist* of the armored reconnaissance battalion demonstrated itself again and again, even in difficult situations. By means of bold maneuver, the daredevil assault detachments of the battalion struck concentrations of enemy armor, surprising them and blowing a number of enemy tanks into the air without suffering any friendly casualties.

Deserving particular mention were the reconnaissance activities of the battalion, which were launched on its own initiative and executed successfully in a manner filled with a great deal of *élan*. They were able to provide the leadership of the division with valuable information about the enemy.

I extend my thanks and special recognition to the officers, noncommissioned officers and enlisted personnel of *Panzer-Aufklärungs-Abteilung 115* and wish all of them continued good luck and great success in future operations.

/signed/ Heidrich
Generalleutnant

Etterlin, the battalion, which had served as the corps reserve, was attached to the *44. Grenadier-Division "Hoch und Deutschmeister,"* commanded by *Oberst* Nagel, in an effort to contain a penetration. This resulted in desperate fighting against numerically superior enemy forces, which were heavily supported by aircraft, artillery and armor. Fresh reserves were continuously being pushed forward to rested and fanatically fighting Free French and Moroccan forces. Although our forces fought heroically under the most difficult of conditions, frequently all on their own, and were able to prevent some enemy penetrations, the positions had to be pulled back.

The Battalion Commander later wrote: "On 23 May 1944, I was pulled out of the line with a trench strength of 3 officers, 8 noncommissioned officers and 23 enlisted. We are now resting in a very pretty area. In order to reconstitute the battalion, a rest period of reasonable length is needed. I am fearful, however, that the battalion will be churned up based on the critical situation we are currently in before it has a chance to recuperate."

On 15 June 1944, the Battalion Commander wrote: "There was little to report of the battalion. It plodded around behind the front as a poor, weak little assemblage. Rome had already fallen. None of the wounded officers had returned as of yet. Instead of bringing in replacements, they were taking things like the communications centers away, thus making it even more difficult to rebuild the battalion. *Leutnant* Nehm's armored scout company operated for a few days with another armored division in another corps sector. The Battalion Commander had to assume acting command of a mechanized infantry regiment for about 14 days; its commander had been wounded. Based on orders, we transitioned from the defense to a delaying action; everything was moving towards the north . . ."

In June and July 1944, the battalion was pulled back in stages to the Po Valley.

On 8 July 1944, *Fahnenjunker-Feldwebel der Reserve* Ernst Schröer received the German Cross in Gold. He was a platoon leader in the 2nd Company of *Oberleutnant* Wolff.

On 15 August 1944, the battalion moved to Agno di Cetica and Quorle to engage in antipartisan operations. On 19 August 1944, *Major Freiherr* von der Borch received the Knight's Cross of the Iron Cross.

The armored scout company, which was employed along the Adriatic to guard the coastline, thus separating it from the battalion, was moved on 1 April 1944 from Silvi Marina to Guilianova. On 3 April 1944, it again moved, this time to Nereto. In the course of the withdrawal, the company conducted its operations from Nereto. On 27 June, the company returned to the battalion at St. Nicolo (near Ferrara). It was then employed in the areas of Olinella–Forli–St. Sofia.

The withdrawal [for the company] took place in stages as far as the Po Valley, sometimes accompanied by fighting against partisans.

The company moved from the area around Strada and headed north, moving through St. Sofia, St. Nicola and Bologna. It crossed the Po at night using a pontoon bridge. In Verona, the company was divided up into scout sections, which then moved separately through northern Italy, heading towards a contact point along the Brenner on 4 September 1944.

Augmented by personnel from two mechanized infantry divisions, the battalion was loaded on trains in Bozen and transported to the threatened Western front . . .[7]

Scouts from an unidentified company wear tropical uniforms and sit on their *Sd.Kfz. 250/1* somewhere in the southern theater of operations. In one instance, one scout has sun- or chemically bleached his *M40* tropical billed field service cap. The symbol for a half-tracked scout company can be faintly seen on the front of the vehicle, which features a two-tone camouflage scheme.

A death notice for a scout in Italy. Rupert Mittermaier was photographed as a highly decorated *SS-Hauptscharführer*, most likely assigned to *SS-Panzer-Aufklärungs-Abteilung 16* of *SS-Panzer-Grenadier-Division "Reichsführer SS."* That battalion had the dubious distinction of being the only reconnaissance battalion—army, *Luftwaffe*, or *Waffen-SS*—to have been charged with war crimes; its commander, *SS-Sturmbannführer* Walter Reder, became somewhat of a *cause célèbre* after the war, when he became one of the last war criminals to be released from prison. Mittermaier's death notice lists his rank as *Leutnant*, indicating he was promoted to *SS-Untersturmführer* before he died.

SS motorcycle infantry pause along a road during training somewhere in the Mediterranean Theater. These images are dated May 1943. NATIONAL ARCHIVES

An *Sd.Kfz. 250/1* of the *II./SS-Panzer-Grenadier-Regiment Leibstandarte SS Adolf Hitler* somewhere in Italy in September 1943, most likely involved in operations involving disarming the Italian military. The light half-track was usually found in armored reconnaissance battalions, but was also frequently seen in any motorized, mechanized, or armored headquarters. The vehicle has been painted in a two-tone camouflage scheme and has *Vorwärts* ("Forward") emblazoned next to the driver's station. NATIONAL ARCHIVES

Panzer-Aufklärungs-Abteilung 24 in Italy

These images come from a scout assigned to the armored car of future Knight's Cross recipient *Oberwachtmeister* Krüger. Except where noted, the images were taken during the time the battalion—along with the rest of the *24. Panzer-Division*—was being reconstituted in Italy.

This battle-damaged *Sd.Kfz. 222* has been loaded onto a short railcar. Apparently no passenger cars were provided for the crew, as evidenced by the pitched tent at the rear of the car. The vehicle is missing part of its hull, and its weapons are trained skyward as a precaution against aerial attack, to which rail-loaded units were particularly vulnerable. It is possible this image was taken shortly before or after the battalion's arrival in its reconstitution area, given the overall condition of the vehicle and the appearance of the scouts. JIM HALEY

A crewmember poses atop his *Sd.Kfz. 231 (8 Rad)* in his black *Panzer* uniform. Note the fuel cans strapped to the side of the superstructure. JIM HALEY

These scouts pose next to an *Sd.Kfz. 231 (8 Rad)* in Italy, possibly at a railhead. The *Zerschellerplatte* and part of its mounts, as well as other unidentified objects, are stacked on top of the turret. In addition, at least three spare tires have been placed on the rear deck of the vehicle, indicating once again that these initial images may have been taken after surviving elements of the battalion were returned to the West for reconstitution. The distinctive *springender Reiter* of the division can be seen on the upper hull. Of interest are the variety of uniforms being worn, including what appear to be the first version of the reed-green herringbone twill *Panzer*-type uniform, as well as tropical billed field caps. JIM HALEY

A scout rides outside his *Sd.Kfz. 222* during a rail movement, most likely in Italy. He also appears to be wearing the reed-green herringbone twill special-purpose uniform for reconnaissance scouts, to which he has added black shoulder straps. A tarpaulin has been placed over the mesh roof of the fighting compartment, and the barrels of the weapons have had muzzle covers placed on them. JIM HALEY

Three scouts pose on their *Sd.Kfz. 222* during a movement halt at a rail yard somewhere in Italy. JIM HALEY

The same scout atop an *Sd.Kfz. 231 (8 Rad)*, probably the same one featured in previous images. JIM HALEY

A scout of an *Sd.Kfz. 222*, christened the *Wien* (Vienna), enjoys the hot Italian sun during some downtime. JIM HALEY

A unit member has taken an image of several armored cars of the 1st Troop, including an *Sd.Kfz. 231 (8 Rad)* and an *Sd.Kfz. 223*, loaded on a train in a rail yard. Vehicles from another unit or possibly the troop's own trains have been marshaled next to the armored cars. JIM HALEY

CHAPTER 9

The Tide Turns in the East

SETTING THE STAGE

The year 1943 marked the turning point in the East for the Axis forces. The year started out with the disaster of Stalingrad and the operational victory of the German forces around Kharkov, effectively stopping the Soviet offensive in March. Both sides regrouped, with Hitler opting for a limited offensive to eliminate the large salient that had been created around Kursk during the fighting in the winter and spring. Hitler was uneasy about the offensive, and rightfully so. Unbeknownst to the Germans, the Soviets were generally aware of their enemy's intentions and prepared the Kursk salient accordingly. The resulting battle, launched at the beginning of July, bore witness to some the largest armored fighting along the Eastern Front. Although some gains were eventually made, especially in the southern end of the battlefield, the fate of the offensive was sealed when the Soviets launched their own counteroffensive on the northern part of the salient around Orel and the Western Allied forces invaded Sicily, forcing Hitler to draw off forces to combat this new threat in the Mediterranean. The fighting at Kursk resulted in a virtual tactical draw, tantamount to a Soviet operational victory, since the Germans could ill afford to lose large numbers of armored vehicles and trained personnel at that stage of the war, either directly through enemy action or through losses sustained while conducting withdrawals.

The efforts of *Generaloberst* Guderian to rebuild the *Panzertruppe* in his new role as the head of the armor branch in the early part of 1943 essentially came to naught, and the German Army was again forced to conduct defensive operations for

This *Sd.Kfz. 222* was assigned to the *SS-Aufklärungs-Abteilung Leibstandarte SS Adolf Hitler* reconnaissance battalion and was photographed in May 1943 during the buildup for Operation *Zitadelle*. NATIONAL ARCHIVES

much of the remainder of the year, with the Soviet forces reaching the prewar Soviet–Polish border at the turn of the year.

DOCTRINE

Faced with an ever-dwindling manpower pool, Hitler's incessant demands for more forces, and the inability of German industry to keep up with demand, the force-structure branch of the German Army resorted to several organizational tricks in an effort to maintain the force. For the armor branch, this resulted in fewer equipment and manpower authorizations for most formations, although the reconnaissance battalions were generally unaffected by the introduction of the Model 1943 *Panzer* Division.

In fact, these battalions gained additional firepower, armor, and maneuverability in the new armored reconnaissance structure, which continued with a five-company model, fielding two scout companies (one wheeled and one half-tracked), two light reconnaissance companies (also mounted on half-tracks), and an armored heavy company, which featured *SPW's* as the primary means of movement or maneuver for the battalion's heavy weaponry. In addition, each battalion was allocated a heavy armored car company, which had six *Sd.Kfz. 233* armored cars armed with the short 75mm main gun. The use of the light and medium *SPW* throughout the battalion saw considerable improvement in the ability to protect the force. In addition, the fact that each half-tracked vehicle generally had a light pedestal-mounted machine gun substantially increased firepower.

Of course, these were theoretical constructs that were never fully attained, with many battalions maintaining a hodgepodge of vehicles, but it was a step in improving deficiencies that had long been identified in the organization of the armored reconnaissance force. Since the battalions were increasingly being called upon to fight in an effort to reconnoiter, the steps taken to beef up the force were a natural progression.

In almost all of the major fighting conducted along the Eastern Front in 1943, the battalions conducted little in the way of traditional reconnaissance. In most cases, they were used as command and control elements in charge of armored *Kampfgruppe* or, when conditions were especially fluid, they assumed flank-guard and screening missions. Because of their increased maneuverability, firepower, and armor, the battalions were often seen as miniature mechanized infantry regiments. In fact, because of their large allocations of half-tracks, they often had more firepower and offensive striking power, if not an equal amount of manpower. Consequently, they increasingly began to be used as fire brigades as well, since they could be shunted across the battlefield with relative ease and the inherent *Reitergeist* of the formation allowed it to move, regroup, and change missions quickly and effectively.

ORGANIZATION

Most of the organizational changes for 1943 are discussed in the previous chapter. The chart that follows shows the theoretical organization for a Model 1943 *Panzer* or *Panzergrenadier* division armored reconnaissance battalion.

LESSONS LEARNED AND FIRSTHAND ACCOUNTS

The New Year on the Eastern Front started disastrously for the Germans, with their forces ever closer to capitulating in Stalingrad. Because of the nature of the Soviet encirclement operations, some divisions found themselves split and with elements outside of the pocket. Fritz Feßmann, commander of the *1./Kradschützen-Bataillon 64*, wrote down his experiences while convalescing in a hospital in Bamberg in February 1943:[6]

> Everything went without a hitch and, at 0800 hours, I rolled out with my armored cars at the head of the battle group to the northern outskirts of the village. The AT outpost stopped me there and pointed out a few vehicles moving around off to the west.
>
> "Watch out that you don't get your ass shot off in your tin cans," the AT *Leutnant* said to me.
>
> I observed the vehicles through the binoculars and identified them as tanks. They were circling around in the middle of the long column

PANZER-DIVISION AND PANZERGRENADIER-DIVISION, 1943 (MODEL)

Panzer-Aufklärungs-Abteilung	Reconnaissance Assets / Notes
Headquarters	Headquarters Company: *KStN 1109* (16 January 1943)
	Heavy Armored Car Platoon: *KStN 1138* (1 December 1942)
1st Company	Armored Scout Company (wheeled): *KStN 1162* (1 November 1941)
2nd Company	Armored Scout Company (half-track): *KStN 1162c* (5 May 1943)
3rd Company	Light Armored Reconnaissance Company (half-track): *KStN 1113 (gp)* (1 March 1942)
4th Company	Light Armored Reconnaissance Company (half-track): *KStN 1113 (gp)* (1 March 1942)
5th Company	Heavy Company (half-track)
	Company Headquarters: *KStN 1121a (gp)* (1 March 1943)
	Armored Infantry Gun Platoon: *KStN 1123a (gp)* (1 March 1943)
	Armored Combat Engineer Platoon: *KStN 1124a (gp)* (1 March 1943)
	Armored Gun Platoon: *KStN 1125 (gp)* (1 May 1943)
	Armored Antitank Gun Platoon: *KStN 1145 (gp)* (1 March 1943)

ORDER OF BATTLE FOR OPERATION *ZITADELLE*, JULY 1943

Parent Organization	Reconnaissance Assets / Notes
Heeresgruppe Nord	
18. Panzergrenadier-Division	*Panzer-Aufklärungs-Abteilung 118*: Standard headquarters and 1st Company (wheeled armored scout); 2nd through 4th Companies organized as motorcycle reconnaissance companies (*KStN 1112 /* 1 November 1941); 5th Company organized as motorized heavy company with headquarters (*KStN 1121 /* 1 November 1941); infantry gun platoon (*KStN 1123 /* 1 November 1941); antitank gun section (*KStN 1127 /* 1 November 1941); medium antitank gun platoon (*KStN 1122a /* 1 December 1941); combat engineer platoon (*KStN 1124 /* 1 November 1941).
Heeresgruppe Süd	
16. Panzergrenadier-Division	*Panzer-Aufklärungs-Abteilung 116*: Organized like *Panzer-Aufklärungs-Abteilung 118* above.
1. Panzer-Armee	
XXIV. Panzer-Korps	
17. Panzer-Division	*Panzer-Aufklärungs-Abteilung 17*: Organized like *Panzer-Aufklärungs-Abteilung 118* above.
23. Panzer-Division	*Panzer-Aufklärungs-Abteilung 23*: Organized like *Panzer-Aufklärungs-Abteilung 118* above, except the 2nd Company was an armored scout company (half-track) with *KStN 1162c* (5 May 1943), and the heavy company also had a light antiaircraft gun platoon (extrapolated from *KStN 192 /* 1 March 1943).
SS-Panzer-Grenadier-Division "Wiking"	*SS-Panzer-Aufklärungs-Abteilung "Wiking"*: Organized like older model for reconnaissance battalion of a motorized infantry division with headquarters (*KStN 1109 /* 1 November 1941); wheeled armored scout company; motorcycle reconnaissance company with attached antitank gun section (*KStN 1127 /* 1 November 1942); and motorized heavy company with infantry gun platoon, medium antitank gun platoon, and combat engineer platoon.
Armee-Abteilung Kempf	
III. Panzer-Korps	
6. Panzer-Division	*Panzer-Aufklärungs-Abteilung 6*: The battalion had a standard headquarters; a heavy armored car platoon; a wheeled armored scout company; a half-tracked armored scout company; two motorcycle reconnaissance companies (3rd and 4th); and a motorized heavy company with an infantry gun platoon, a medium antitank gun platoon, a heavy antitank gun platoon, an antitank gun section, and a combat engineer platoon.

Parent Organization	Reconnaissance Assets / Notes
III. Panzer-Korps continued	
7. Panzer-Division	*Panzer-Aufklärungs-Abteilung 7*: Organized the same as *Panzer-Aufklärungs-Abteilung 6* above, except the heavy company did not have a heavy antitank gun platoon; it had a second infantry gun platoon instead.
19. Panzer-Division	*Panzer-Aufklärungs-Abteilung 19*: Organized like *Panzer-Aufklärungs-Abteilung 118* above, except the heavy company also had a light antiaircraft gun platoon (extrapolated from *KStN 192* / 1 March 1943).
4. Panzer-Armee	
II. SS-Panzer-Korps	
SS-Panzer-Grenadier-Division "Totenkopf"	*SS-Panzer-Aufklärungs-Abteilung "Totenkopf"*: Standard headquarters, a wheeled armored scout company (1st), a half-tracked armored scout company (4th), two light wheeled reconnaissance companies (*Volkswagen*) (2nd and 3rd), and a motorized heavy company. The heavy company was organized like that of the *SS-Panzer-Aufklärungs-Abteilung "Wiking"* above, except it also had an armored gun platoon (*KStN 1125 (gp)* / 1 May 1943).
SS-Panzer-Grenadier-Division "Das Reich"	*SS-Panzer-Aufklärungs-Abteilung "Das Reich"*: Organized like *SS-Panzer-Aufklärungs-Abteilung "Totenkopf"* above, except it had a standard numbering system for the companies, and a motorcycle infantry platoon was attached to the wheeled armored scout company (extrapolated from *KStN 1112* / 1 November 1941).
SS-Panzer-Grenadier-Division Leibstandarte SS Adolf Hitler	*SS-Panzer-Aufklärungs-Abteilung Leibstandarte SS Adolf Hitler*: Standard headquarters with two light wheeled reconnaissance companies (*Volkswagen*) (1st and 2nd), a half-tracked armored scout company (3rd), and a wheeled armored scout company (4th). There was no heavy company. Instead, there was a motorized antitank gun company (*KStN 1140* / 1 April 1943) (5th), a motorized infantry gun company (based on *KStN 174* / 1 December 1942) with an attached self-propelled infantry gun platoon (established through command channels), and an armored combat engineer platoon (*KStN 1124a* / 1 March 1943).
XXXXVIII. Panzer-Korps	
3. Panzer-Division	*Panzer-Aufklärungs-Abteilung 3*: Organized with a standard headquarters; a wheeled armored scout company (1st); a half-tracked armored scout company (2nd); two motorcycle reconnaissance companies (3rd and 4th); and a motorized heavy company with two motorized infantry gun platoons, an antitank gun section, a medium antitank gun platoon, and a combat engineer platoon.
11. Panzer-Division	*Panzer-Aufklärungs-Abteilung 11*: Organized identically to *Panzer-Aufklärungs-Abteilung 3* above, except the heavy company had only one infantry gun platoon.
Panzergrenadier-Division "Großdeutschland"	*Panzer-Aufklärungs-Abteilung "Großdeutschland"*: Organized with a standard headquarters; a wheeled armored scout company (1st); a half-tracked armored scout company (2nd); two light wheeled reconnaissance companies (*Schwimmwagen*) (3rd and 4th); and a motorized heavy company with a motorized infantry gun platoon, an armored gun platoon (*KStN 1125 (gp)* / 1 May 1943), a medium antitank gun platoon, and a combat engineer platoon.
Heeresgruppe Mitte	
Gruppe Esebeck	
4. Panzer-Division	*Panzer-Aufklärungs-Abteilung 4*: Organized with a standard headquarters; a half-tracked armored scout company (1st); a light wheeled reconnaissance company (*Schwimmwagen*) (2nd); a motorized heavy company (3rd) with an infantry gun platoon, a medium antitank gun platoon, a heavy antitank gun platoon, and a combat engineer platoon; a wheeled armored scout company (4th); and a motorcycle reconnaissance company (5th).
10. Panzergrenadier-Division	*Panzer-Aufklärungs-Abteilung 110*: Organized like *Panzer-Aufklärungs-Abteilung 118* above.
12. Panzer-Division	*Panzer-Aufklärungs-Abteilung 12*: Organized like *Panzer-Aufklärungs-Abteilung 118* above, except the heavy company did not have an antitank gun section.
Other Reserves	
5. Panzer-Division	*Panzer-Aufklärungs-Abteilung 5*: Organized with a standard headquarters; a wheeled armored scout company (1st); two light wheeled reconnaissance companies (*Schwimmwagen*) (2nd and 3rd); a motorcycle reconnaissance company (4th); and a motorized heavy company (5th) with an infantry gun platoon, a medium antitank gun platoon, and a combat engineer platoon.
8. Panzer-Division	*Panzer-Aufklärungs-Abteilung 8*: Organized with a standard headquarters; a wheeled armored scout company (1st); three motorcycle reconnaissance companies (2nd to 4th); and a motorized heavy company (5th) with an infantry gun platoon, an antitank gun section, a medium antitank gun platoon, and a combat engineer platoon. In addition, the battalion had an attached light tank company consisting of three *Panzer 38(t)'s* and twelve *Panzer II's*.

Parent Organization	Reconnaissance Assets / Notes
9. Armee	
XXXXVII. Panzer-Korps	
2. Panzer-Division	*Panzer-Aufklärungs-Abteilung 2*: Organized like a Model 43 *Panzer* division, except there was no heavy armored car platoon.
9. Panzer-Division	*Panzer-Aufklärungs-Abteilung 9*: Organized like a Model 43 *Panzer* division.
20. Panzer-Division	*Panzer-Aufklärungs-Abteilung 20*: Organized like *Panzer-Aufklärungs-Abteilung 118* above, except there was a heavy antitank gun platoon instead of a medium one (*KStN 1145* / 1 April 1943).
XXXXI. Panzer-Korps	
18. Panzer-Division	*Panzer-Aufklärungs-Abteilung 18*: Organized like *Panzer-Aufklärungs-Abteilung 118* above.
2. Panzer-Armee	
LIII. Armee-Korps	
25. Panzergrenadier-Division	*Panzer-Aufklärungs-Abteilung 125*: Organized with a standard headquarters; three motorcycle reconnaissance companies (1st to 3rd); a wheeled armored scout company (4th); and a motorized heavy company with a standard headquarters, an infantry gun platoon, a medium mortar platoon (*KStN 1126* / 1 October 1938), a medium antitank gun platoon, and a combat engineer platoon.
3. Panzer-Armee	
XXXXIII. Armee-Korps	
20. Panzergrenadier-Division	*Panzer-Aufklärungs-Abteilung 120*: Organized like *Panzer-Aufklärungs-Abteilung 118*, except the antitank gun section in the heavy company was deleted and replaced by a medium mortar platoon (*KStN 1126* / 1 October 1938).

ORDER OF BATTLE—OTHER COMMANDS, JULY 1943

Parent Organization	Reconnaissance Assets / Notes[1]
Heeresgruppe D (France)	
21. Panzer-Division	*Panzer-Aufklärungs-Abteilung 21*: Standard headquarters but only two motorcycle reconnaissance companies.[2]
26. Panzer-Division	*Panzer-Aufklärungs-Abteilung 26*: Organized with a standard headquarters; a wheeled armored scout company (1st); three light armored reconnaissance companies (2nd to 4th); and an armored heavy company (5th) with a gun platoon, an infantry gun platoon, an antitank gun section, a heavy antitank gun platoon, and a combat engineer platoon (all armored).[3]
15. Armee	
24. Panzer-Division	*Panzer-Aufklärungs-Abteilung 24*: Model 43 armored reconnaissance organization, including a heavy armored car platoon, but the 1st Company was the half-track scout company and the 2nd Company was the wheeled company. In addition, the armored heavy company had a non-standard organization: a wheeled medium mortar platoon, an armored heavy antitank gun platoon, and an armored combat engineer platoon.[4]
9. SS-Panzer-Grenadier-Division "Hohenstaufen"	*SS-Panzer-Aufklärungs-Abteilung "Hohenstaufen"*: The proposed organization consisted of a standard headquarters; a wheeled armored scout company; a light wheeled reconnaissance company (*Volkswagen*); two light armored reconnaissance companies; and an armored heavy company with an infantry gun platoon, a heavy antitank gun platoon, and a combat engineer platoon (all armored).[5]
1. Armee	
14. Panzer-Division	*Panzer-Aufklärungs-Abteilung 64* (until May 1943) / *14*: Proposed organization in accordance with the Model 43 *Panzer-Division*.

Parent Organization	Reconnaissance Assets / Notes[1]
1. Armee continued	
10. SS-Panzer-Grenadier-Division "Frundsberg"	SS-Panzer-Aufklärungs-Abteilung "Frundsberg": Proposed organization in accordance with the Model 43 Panzer-Division.
LXXXIII. Armee-Korps	
Grenadier-Division "Feldherrnhalle"	Panzer-Aufklärungs-Abteilung "Feldherrnhalle": Proposed organization in accordance with the Model 43 Panzer-Division.
Heeresgruppe E (Adriatic)	
LXVIII. Armee-Korps	
1. Panzer-Division	Panzer-Aufklärungs-Abteilung 1: Standard Model 43 reconnaissance battalion organization, except there was no heavy armored car platoon.
Oberbefehlshaber Süd (See previous chapter)	
Oberbefehlshaber der Wehrmacht (OKW)	
Norwegen-Armee	
25. Panzer-Division	Panzer-Aufklärungs-Abteilung 25: Standard headquarters; a wheeled armored scout company; three motorcycle reconnaissance companies (2nd to 4th); and a motorized heavy company with an infantry gun platoon, an antitank gun section, a medium antitank gun platoon, and a combat engineer platoon (all wheeled).

of trucks and staff cars from the division trains that were headed west. They were shooting up vehicle after vehicle. There were flames above the column, flames and black spirals of smoke. In between, you could see the muzzle flash of the tanks again and again and the fuel explosions of the vehicles that had been hit.

"Everyone stop! I'm moving forward to reconnoiter!"

I then moved in my armored car on the road to Ljapitschew directly to the north in an effort to determine the enemy situation.

After two kilometers, I stopped and determined that the enemy had broken through with tanks between Ljapitschew and us. I saw a few of the Soviet tanks in the west, but there were also several of the ungainly giants to the north and northwest as well. I had my armored car turn around and raced back.

I ordered: "Motorcycle infantry follow the division trains withdrawing to the west! Silbermann, take these five armored cars and the third AT gun on the road to the north towards Ljapitschew. Judge for yourselves what you need to do, but don't get in the sights of the tanks!"

Oberleutnant Silbermann took the section that had previously been given to him and took off. At the same time, I headed north in the direction of Ljapitschew with my five armored cars and AT gun.

My vehicles maintained exemplary intervals. Together with the AT gun and the armored radio car, we looked like a proper force. And so it was! The impression we made must have been a good one. First one, then two and finally a third Russian tank that had been to the west of us took off to the north. They moved at high speed in a large arc to the northeast, joining up with their comrades there. They must have thought we were tanks and wanted to save themselves before getting cut off by us.

Later on, I discovered from *Oberleutnant* Silbermann that the Soviets had, in fact, previously been having great fun with moving around among our trains vehicles, because they could do so without repercussion. They had set a few of our vehicles alight.

It was thanks to Silbermann's aggressive intervention that the enemy tanks left the trains alone, even though he could have scarcely done anything against them. One of his two AT guns also had the great misfortune of having wanted to fire at a tank that was rolling past 10 meters away, when its firing pin broke.

For my part, my section and I had the enemy tanks positioned in front of us to the northeast while the trains moving west in columns were to my rear. We were out of a good firing range for our vehicles and were moving slowly.

The Soviets fired individual rounds with their main guns. They then slowly started to move out in our direction. We had to do something at that point. But what should I do? My armored cars only had two machine guns, and I could not stop the five T-34's in open terrain with a single AT gun. It was obvious that I would needlessly sacrifice my AT gun, if I attempted something like that. There was only one thing left to do: Move and delay!

I moved up with my armored car and directed the remaining vehicles to echelon to the side and rear by means of hand-and-arm signals. Moving past the Russians in an oblique fashion, I gave the impression I was possibly going to envelop them. They hesitated, stopped and fired.

Unfortunately, they were in a good shooting range by then, with the result that their rounds landed in front of us and smashed into the earth or behind us, where they whizzed past our ears. The crashing of the high-explosive rounds mixed in with the smacking sounds of solid shot hitting the earth. Steel shrieked as shrapnel into our vehicles or howled past our heads.

But the terrain was well suited for a tank engagement, since I was able to move ahead in a straight-line course at 25 to 30 kilometers an hour, until it was time to take another tack.

Moving in a zigzag fashion, the entire section moved alternately towards and away from the firing Soviet tanks. I looked back once. There were impacting rounds in front of and behind my five armored cars. Fountains of dirt, smoke from firing powder and the smell of cordite. Thank God, there were no hits. We were too quick for the gunners on the T-34's, who also served at the same time as vehicle commanders, who also had to observe. Because of that, they had a significant disadvantage compared to our tanks; they had a much slower rate of fire.

Of course, we could not fire. Otherwise, the light would have gone off in the Russians' heads: We only had machine guns. It was all quite exhilarating, and we got hot, despite the cold. Our zigzag driving was our salvation. Despite moving without being able to reply to the fire, I was left with the impression that I was calling the shots, and that is always a good feeling.

My vehicle driver moved quickly and confidently and reacted immediately. The changes in course I yelled out to him were executed uncommonly quickly. The men beside him were calm and controlled; the vehicles moving echeloned behind me maintained exemplary intervals. That told me that these men trusted me blindly. What choice did I have but to help them and the trains? And how could I do that without senselessly endangering all of them? It was a situation I had never experienced before.

Never before had we been deployed on the battlefield like we were then. I had the same feelings that perhaps an admiral would while conducting a passing maneuver. Unfortunately, I didn't have the artillery he would have had!

By then, the Soviet tanks were occasionally shifting to the left and then to the right. They were following our zigzag maneuver and getting increasingly closer. The situation became increasingly uncomfortable. If only one of the enemy tank commanders had had the courage to quickly thrust forward, he would have had forced us to flee or enjoyed a cheap victory. And that one advance would have had horrific consequences for our trains.

Closing to within 1,000 meters of the Russian tanks, I had the vehicles turn away to increase the distance to 2,000 meters, where I used a small swell in the ground to simulate a sort of blocking position.

The Soviets followed only hesitantly. They stopped again and again and fired. It was truly divine providence that none of my vehicles had yet been hit.

By means of hand-and-arm signals, I ordered my AT gun to go into position and had it open fire at the greatest possible distance. Of course, it was completely useless, when looked at a certain way, but the gaining of time was decisive and was the reason for the order. By analyzing the intent of my mission and adjusting it to meet the new situation, I had to hold up the Soviet tanks that had broken through until 1000 hours. That would prevent the Russian tanks from striking the rear of the trains moving out of Nowo-Petrowskij, as well as allowing our comrades in Ljapitschew to get away without being mowed down.

All at once, Silbermann's section appeared further to the rear on a slight rise. It joined up with us. I signaled over to Silbermann to come to me, and the *Oberleutnant*, whom I had learned to value in the weeks since I had joined the *14. Panzer-Division*, reported that the trains had already passed through and that the last vehicles of the division had passed the danger point, thus no longer needing his protection.

"Silbermann, we have to bluff the Russians. To that end, we are going to advance north with both sections without paying any attention to them. Perhaps we can get as far as Ljapitschew."

"Well, Feßmann, let's go!" was the answer from the exemplary officer.

We then moved out to the north with both sections together. But we had not quite yet arrived at Ljapitschew, when I saw that the Soviets had surrounded the village with a thick belt of tanks. Explosions rose skyward from the middle of the village. Then packs of riflemen turned up. They appeared from out of defiles and behind vegetation.

"We won't be getting into Ljapitschew, Silbermann!"

"It looks like our comrades in Ljapitschew are pulling out. The demolitions would lead you to believe that."

What Silbermann was saying was probably true. Our comrades were disengaging from the enemy. A quick look at my watch told me that it had turned 1100 hours in the meantime. We had held out an hour longer than was planned. That meant that we had fulfilled our mission to the best of our abilities. We then moved off to the west after we could no longer see any German soldiers. We linked up with our comrades at the Loshki bridgehead.

It turned out that *Gruppe Elbinger* had disengaged from the enemy in Ljapitschew in time and had already shown up in the new bridgehead before our armored car sections.

With the exception of the trains vehicles that had already been shot up by the enemy tanks before our arrival from Nowo-Petrowskij, we had made it through in one piece. All of the division supply trains and several rifle battalions had made it through to the west. And all that as a result of our crazy, outrageous bluff.

As discussed above, the operations conducted by the reconnaissance battalions of armored and mechanized infantry divisions increasingly took on the nature of combat operations in support of division plans. One such operation, a river crossing, is recounted by Helmuth Spaeter in his history of *Panzergrenadier-Division "Großdeutschland"*:[7]

Panzer-Aufklärungs-Abteilung "Großdeutschland," reinforced by *Sturmgeschütz-Abteilung "Großdeutschland,"* the *5./Flak-Bataillon "Großdeutschland"* and two howitzer batteries from the divisional artillery, moved out early that day for the intended crossing of the Merchik. The after-action report provides both a factual and exciting account of the operation:

"At 0515 hours on 9 March 1943, the 3rd Company moved out of Shuravli in the direction of Kirasirsky with a battery of assault guns, a 37mm *Flak* platoon and two 20mm *Flak* of the 1st Company. The village was taken after a brief firefight, and the battle group immediately continued in the direction of Sion. The strong resistance initially encountered was broken by the assault guns. The battle group's next objective was Hill 188.7, north of the village.

"At about the same time as the 3rd Company battle group had moved out, the 4th Company, together with the 1st Battery of the assault gun battalion (*Hauptmann* Magold), a 37mm *Flak* platoon and the 2nd Company (*SPW*), moved out to the east. It advanced on the Voytenkov collective farm, which was reached an hour later. The two companies immediately deployed behind the village, where the two artillery batteries went into position to further support the attack. They then advanced across the open plain toward the hills outside of Novy Merchik. The village itself, which was in the valley formed by the Upper Mok Merchik, could not be seen. The assault guns initially held back. The two companies advanced on the village, widely dispersed. Up to that point, there had been no defensive fires. The *SPW* company entered Dolina, which was further to the west. Soon afterwards, the assault guns and the 3rd Company entered the western portion of Novy Merchik, where the enemy stirred for the first time. The first mortar rounds landed some distance from the 37mm *Flak*, which had moved into position quite close to one another, in order to take enemy forces in the eastern part of the village under fire. The enemy soon adjusted his fires, however, and placed mortar fire in their midst. The *Flak* and the 4th Company suffered casualties.

"By then, the *SPW* company had moved through the village and continued its advance on Hill 199.3. Once there, it moved to the left and linked up with the 3rd Company on Hill 188.7. While that was happening, the assault guns and the 4th Company cleared the village of enemy forces. Crossing the Mok Merchik proved difficult, since the bridge had been completely destroyed and the ice, which had been thinned by the warmer weather, was no longer thick enough to support vehicular weight. A detour was eventually found, but not before one of the assault guns had broken through the ice.

"The 4th Company moved out again and attacked the village of Grigorovka across from Hill 199.3. Fleeing enemy sleigh columns on the hills north of Hill 188.7 were caught and quickly destroyed by the assault guns and the 37mm *Flak*. The advancing companies came under artillery fire from Alexandrovka, which was in the valley to the left of Hill 188.7. That scattered the vehicles that had concentrated in all directions. The 2nd Company then advanced on Tarasovka, where it turned toward Bayrak.

"At the same time, the 3rd Company aggressively assaulted down the hill and attacked the village of Alexandrovka, in spite of the heavy defensive fires. After the assault guns eliminated three 7.62mm antitank guns positioned along the edge of the village, the company entered the built-up area, where bitter house-to-house fighting ensued.

"The battalion battle staff had positioned itself on Hill 188.7 with the artillery forward observer. They observed Russian columns fleeing the large, gently sloped patch of woods northeast of Alexandrovka. The grouping of vehicles included guns, sleighs, trucks and even two tanks. The companies occupied defensive positions for the night, with the *SPW* Company in the western part of Kirasirsky, the 3rd Company (*VW*) in Alexandovka and the 4th Company (*MG*) in Grigorovka.

"It was the end to a very successful day, as the figures confirmed: 7 enemy tanks destroyed, including 3 T-34's; and 4 122mm guns, 21 76.2mm antitank guns and 16 47mm antitank guns captured. In addition, numerous sleighs, small arms, a backpack radio, antitank rifles and other weapons and equipment were also captured. About 300 enemy dead were counted.

"Around 0210 hours, the headquarters of *Panzer-Aufklärungs-Abteilung "Großdeutschland"* received radioed orders from the division that it was to be relieved by the reinforced *Füsilier-Regiment "Großdeutschland."* The battalion was to assemble at Kovjagi and await further orders."

The fighting around Kursk in July 1943 was some of the most intense seen on the Eastern Front. *Panzer-Aufklärungs-Abteilung 3* of the *3. Panzer-Division* was involved in operations in the southern half of the battlefield. This account is for the period of 7–8 July:[8]

The division headquarters sent the command staff to Werchopenje. *Hauptmann* Deichens' armored reconnaissance battalion, reinforced by a company from *Panzerjäger-Abteilung 543*

(Sfl), received orders during the night to relieve a mechanized infantry battalion from *"Groß-deutschland"* on the high ground north of Kruglick and, by doing so, screening the open left flank of the *3. Panzer-Division*, which was to attack north. That high-ground position became a bulwark of the front. During the relief, enemy riflemen, supported by fighting vehicles, attacked by surprise from the Kubasosskskij Defile against the outposts of the extended ridgeline. As a result of the critical situation that ensued, *Major* Franz' *Sturmgeschütz-Abteilung "Großdeutschland"* remained in its former positions and helped to turn back the enemy's attack. Soon after that occurred, *Major* Franz received new orders from his division and disengaged his assault guns.

The reconnaissance battalion had no contact with other forces in its two kilometers of sector. After the enemy attack had been turned back, the troops set about improving their positions only to soon report the approach of tanks and trucks about two to three kilometers away. They were headed south along a ridgeline further west. More tanks and other vehicles were constantly seen along the ridgeline road to the west of the Kubasosskskij Defile. They appeared to be concentrating for an operation northwest of Beresowka.

With the very first reports, the division started to fear that the enemy was preparing an attack against the open deep flank of the division and the *4. Panzer-Armee*. There was no contact with the *167. Infanterie-Division*, which was following to the left rear. The Operations Officer, *Oberstleutnant* Voß, was sent to the corps headquarters to gain permission for most of the division to hold up until the situation was clarified and to be able to be employed immediately, if a flank attack materialized. Even though the higher command did not share the same opinion and insisted on execution of the original orders, *Generalleutnant* Westhoven left the *II./Panzergrenadier-Regiment 394*, the antitank battalion and the divisional engineers behind.

When more reports came in from the reconnaissance battalion that enemy armor forces were continuing to advance, the *II./Panzer-grenadier-Regiment 394* and the antitank battalion received orders to immediately occupy Hill 258.5 west of Werchopenje. The Division Commander raced to the location to discuss the matter with the two battalion commanders. As they were conferring, Russian tanks appeared directly in front of the small group. The men jumped into a shell hole as fast they could and were overrun by the tanks. At that critical moment, the crack of antitank guns could be heard. Two Russian tanks were hit. The lead platoon of the antitank elements had unlimbered and fired at practically point-blank range. The confusion that erupted among the enemy forces was utilized by *Generalleutnant* Westhoven to run back, give instructions to the mechanized infantry battalion and issue orders from a communications center that had been sent forward as a precautionary measure to the artillery for concentrated fires on the new enemy grouping. The division's armored group received orders to turn around and launch an immediate counterattack.

Even those measures might not have come in the nick of time, had not *Hauptmann* Deichen saved the situation by means of a bold decision. Using his light *SPW* company and the brave self-propelled antitank-gun company, he attacked the surprised enemy in the flank. Several T-34's were knocked out and the enemy riflemen suffered heavy casualties from the machine guns firing from the *SPW's*. For his courageous decision, Deichen later received the Knight's Cross.[9]

While *Hauptmann* Deichen continuously struck at the enemy in the very essence of maneuver warfare, there was desperate fighting against the Soviet X Tank Corps between Hill 258.5 and Beresowka.

The armored reconnaissance battalion of *SS-Panzer-Grenadier-Division "Totenkopf"* was also involved in the thick of the fighting at Kursk.

Wolfgang Vopersal's massive history of the division contains numerous accounts from a senior corporal of the battalion's 3rd Company, *SS-Rottenführer* Hax, which put a human face on one of the largest battles of the war. The first account is from 5 July, the first day of the fighting:[10]

SS-Panzer-Aufklärungs-Abteilung 3 received orders to assemble at the location of its vehicles. The sun was burning down from the heavens. *SS-Rottenführer* Hax of the 3rd Company (*Volkswagen*): " . . . we marched off with our weapons and equipment. Damn it, why weren't our vehicles coming our way? Everyone was grumbling. We thrashed our way across the terrain for two hours and past our battery positions. We saw barrel bursts twice. In the case of the first gun, the accident must have just occurred. The dead cannoneers were lying about, just as the force of the explosion had scattered them. The fighting raged in the skies without any break . . .

" . . . We finally reached our objective. Has the world ever seen anything like this? The entire reconnaissance battalion and a tank battalion were drawn up on the open plain as if on parade. Lined up like there was no such thing as the Red Air Force. Our throats were parched, so the first question we had of the drivers was this: 'Do you have something to drink?' A few of us had already removed our sweat-drenched clothes, when a Russian 'butcher' formation [German soldier's nickname for the IL-2/M3 Sturmovik, a heavily armed and armored single-engine ground-attack aircraft] showed up. Naked and partially clothed men reached for their weapons, since there was no taking cover where we were. The dance started!

"The Russian pilots dove on us from out of the sun. In the blink of an eye, the heavens were filled with tracers. From off to the right, our scout vehicles were firing away, and there was a banging and crashing at the location of the tanks as well. The 2cm quad *Flak* of the antiaircraft platoon clattered away. The muzzle flashes from the aircraft weapons flashed red. Dark spots disengaged from the fuselages—bombs. They impacted amongst us. In the distance, one of the attackers was smoking; flames started shooting out of the fuselage. The Russian took off at a sharp angle. Then there was a crashing sound and a fiery blaze. His comrades turned away, but they attacked us again a short while later. Another 'butcher' was hit and crashed. That was enough for those that remained. They turned away . . . "

Another account, this time from 6 July:[11]

In the course of the morning, the division, divided into three groups, fought for and took the creek crossings west of Schopino, the high ground west of Ternowka and the high ground west of Nepohajewo.

At 1230 hours, it received the mission: " . . . to reconnoiter in the direction of Lutschki with an armored force and attempt to establish contact with [*SS-Panzer-Grenadier-Regiment "Der Führer"*], which is advancing on Lutschki."

To that end, the division employed elements of the reconnaissance battalion. All of the battalion company commanders were summoned to the command post at Gluschinskij.

SS-Rottenführer Hax wrote: " . . . our company commander, *Hauptsturmführer* Eichert, had hardly taken off, when the 'red butchers' came roaring in. They were firing like crazy from all barrels. Fortunately, the 'greetings' they were sending passed overhead. Unfortunately, however, their rockets hurtled into the village where the battalion headquarters was located. In the blink of an eye, the village disappeared in a cloud of smoke. That was followed by an eerie silence. Our commander came back—he was quite pale in the face—and told us that almost the entire headquarters was lost, including the vehicles. Several company commanders had been wounded." [The IL-2 was armed with 23mm cannon, bombs, and rockets—RS-82 and RS-132. The rockets were generally very inaccurate.]

By 13 July, the fighting for Kursk was in its final stages:[12]

The advance of the armored enemy forces from Wesselyj forced the armored group, which had advanced as far as Point 12 on the Beregowoje–Kartaschewka road, to turn and give up the terrain it had taken. On orders of the division, the tank regiment was pulled back to the expanded bridgehead behind Hill 226.6 so as "to have armored forces available as a mobile reserve."

SS-Rottenführer Hax wrote the following: " . . . During the last few hours in the platoon's sector at Kotschetowka, I 'procured' an abandoned T-34. The engine could not be started, but the main gun and the optics were intact. Skibinski, from the company headquarters, knew a little bit about the main gun. A test round landed right on target. We dug out an almost bombproof position under the tank. One of our machine-gun positions was located in front of us in the roadside ditch. A second one was further to the west, facing the marsh. Hugo Lechner and his squad screened along the forward slope. Further to the right, where the road started to drop off steeply in the direction of the enemy, another two of our heavy machine guns were in position. *SS-Untersturmführer* Radde had set up his platoon command post there. The 1st Platoon had dug in on the other side of the road to the right. The 3rd Platoon was positioned somewhat to the rear in the direction of the middle of the village on the other side of the embankment. The 4th Company was positioned to our right. It was said that elements of the *11. Panzer-Division* were off to our left.

" . . . Towards 1000 hours, the Russians suddenly covered our positions with a hail of fire. We were crawling around "our" T-34 at the time and were attempting to securely mount a machine gun. . . . We looked for cover under the Russian tank. *SS-Unterscharführer* Erwin Kopschiwa was hit by shrapnel. We yanked him into our covered position. He moaned softly as we dressed his wounds.

"Using the cover of their artillery, the Red Army men advanced as far as the 6th Squad, which was to the right of the road, and to our machine-gun nests. They were trying to get cover behind the houses and were firing from point-blank range at our comrades. But they were unable to advance any further, since our heavy machine guns were fixing them in position. Lechner's machine gun placed flanking fires from the left out of the vegetation. The 6th Squad fired from the right. The 7th Squad was unable to join in the fight. Its machine gun positions were too low. That meant we needed to take a 'sprayer' on top of 'our' tank. But even from that elevated position, we were unable to hit the Russians. What about the main gun of the T-34? We then fired like madmen into the ranks of the Russian infantry with Russian rounds from a Russian main gun. With every round we fired, the standing grain in the field blew over towards the ground. We cleared a path through the field. We soon learned how to reload rapidly. *Untersturmführer* Radde had a chain of men formed who called out target corrections to us. Although there was some difficulty in aiming against targets that could not be seen, the effect was devastating. The momentum of the Russian attack was soon a thing of the past . . .

" . . . The Russians moved an antitank gun forward. It was firing like crazy against 'our' T-34 from a fruit orchard. A new chain of men was formed; *Untersturmführer* Radde directed the fire. We were only able to identify the antitank gun by its muzzle flashes. The Russians had camouflaged themselves and their gun quickly and masterfully. The duel between the Russian antitank gun and our captured tank went on for some time. We adapted ourselves to the firing rhythm of the enemy.

"The Russian infantry stormed forward once more. A Russian machine gun fired without interruption against our 'iron skin.' The constant smacking of the machine gun bursts against the armor put us on edge. The forward hatch, through which the main gun rounds had been passed, had to be closed. Our comrades then passed the rounds through the escape hatch on the bottom of the hull. All of a sudden, *Unterscharführer* Hugo Lechner started waving and running about. Had he flipped out? No, a round had impacted right on the edge of his machine-gun position. He thought we had fired too short. But it had been Ivan.

"The round had hurt Meerkamp badly; the other members of the squad had only been slightly wounded. Meerkamp had to be evacuated as soon as possible. The medic and two stretcher-bearers jumped through the field like rabbits, trying to recover Meerkamp. We provided covering fire. They loaded Meerkamp on the stretcher behind a bush and then ran back with him at a devilish pace. Before they could reach cover, they got the medic. His hands, which had helped so many comrades, were shredded by a burst of machine gun fire. His blood was spraying everywhere. He needed to be dressed! Using the string from my tobacco pouch, I cut off the blood flow. The medic seemed to be unruffled. But what was happening with Meerkamp? Poor guy! Covered by the tank, we applied field dressings. There was hardly a place on his body that had not been torn open and was bleeding. The shrapnel had penetrated his body everywhere. Russian dirt had penetrated the skin and the wounds with the explosion. Some spots suffered burns. There was only a slight whimper emanating from his shattered body. His body reflected the entire horror of the war. May God grant that mothers never have to see their sons that way . . ."

When the Soviets launched their counteroffensive at Orel, *Panzergrenadier-Division "Großdeutschland"* was quickly moved from the south to the north to help stop the breakthrough. This account concerns fighting around Karachev in late July and early August 1943:[13]

The following firsthand account of a patrol near Karachev, provided by *Obergefreiter* Meissner of the *1./Panzer-Aufklärungs-Abteilung "Großdeutschland,"* provides insight into the difficulty of the missions facing the companies:

"First, we moved to Karachev. There was a halt just outside the city. Our general was there. He got our complete attention when he said that our mission was extremely dangerous and demanded the maximum amount of attention and caution. In Karachev proper, we were joined by *Unteroffizier* Karrasch and his section. It was the first time that four 8-wheelers drove a patrol together. That had to be a good sign. We then received the mission from *Leutnant* Gebhard, our patrol leader:

"'In spite of the heavy rainfall, the Soviets had succeeded in breaking through the front in the impassable forested terrain. They were currently threatening the main road from Karachev to Briansk and had also interdicted another, parallel road further to the north. Last night, a column had been ambushed near Kilometer Marker 23 and 28 out of 30 men there had been killed. We were being given the mission of advancing to the penetration point, supported by two *Tigers* and three flamethrower tanks, and plugging it until a recently detrained battalion could arrive.'

"We moved from the command post with the armored cars in front and the tanks behind. But our joy in having such strong support did not last too long. A *Major* took the tanks away from us at the last village before the point of penetration. After considering his options, *Leutnant* Gerhard decided to continue the mission with just the armored cars.

"As soon as we left the village, heavy mortar fire landed between and among our vehicles. Things were turning serious. Moving in the lead was *Unteroffizier* Karrasch. He was followed by *Leutnant* Gebhard's armored car. The third armored car was that of *Unteroffizier* Hartung, while *Unteroffizier* Schmidt covered the rear.

"Armored car personnel did not like this type of terrain: The road proper was primarily a raised, single-lane corduroy road. To the right and left were marshy ditches, followed by impenetrable woods that were untrafficable. We could not approach our objective unseen; neither could we move around it. The armored cars worked their way forward like a caterpillar. The enemy could be anywhere. We were extremely tense. I had to light one cigarette after another for the crew. We moved a short distance, stopped and observed. Then repeated the process. At each halt, the radio operator informed the command post of our location.

"We slowly approached the enemy's suspected point of penetration at Kilometer Marker 20. Nothing happened. The lead car moved forward, its engine making plenty of noise. We could definitely be heard deep into the woods. We continued. We passed Kilometer Marker 21 . . . again nothing. Kilometer Marker 22 . . . nothing. Just beyond Marker 23, there was an S turn. Halt! There were vehicles on the road. They were the vehicles from the shot-up column. It was a sorry sight. The vehicles were riddled with bullet holes, with the windows shot out and items of equipment scattered everywhere. A helmet here . . . a mess kit there . . . a wallet with money still in it.

"We continued forward; the enemy still had not been located. The lead armored car halted at the next bend in the road at Marker 24. A sharp crack ripped the stillness: an antitank gun! The enemy had been found. The next order was not long in coming: "Reverse, march!" We breathed a sigh of relief. We had completed our mission.

"Suddenly, there was a call from the rear: Tanks behind us! Were they ours or Russians? We then saw the crosses. They were German. They turned out to be assault guns with mounted infantry. A general was personally leading the battle group. *Leutnant* Gebhard reported and briefed the assault gun crews on the exact location of the antitank gun. The infantry fanned out to the left and right of the road. The assault guns were able to quickly destroy the antitank gun. We pulled back, and the order to move lifted the mental burden off of us . . ."

Another account from the same time period, this time concerning *Major* Deichen's *Panzer-Aufklärungs-Abteilung 3*:[14]

The enemy kept attacking with tanks and infantry and had enormous numerical superiority. The divisional armored reconnaissance battalion succeeded in entering Solotschew and establishing an all-round defense with the village as its pivot point. To the northwest of the village, it was possible to establish a defensive position with the light *SPW* company along Ridgeline 208.5. While the Soviets attempted to enter the village west of the rail line—mostly with infantry—from the north, they attacked from the east over and over again with tanks. They advanced past Solotschew to the south and separated the battalion for a while from its rearward lines of communication. Despite all that, it was possible to hold the village and also destroy two of the three enemy tanks that had entered it.

Major Deichen's men were able to hold the positions that had been hastily occupied and went after the tanks that had broken through with mines and shaped charges. *Oberleutnant* Kunze and *Pionier* Möhring of the *2./Panzer-Pionier-Bataillon 39* eliminated two T-34's in close combat.

Although German forces could gain tactical advantage on several occasions, they only succeeded in slowing down the Soviet advance to the southwest from Kursk in August and Kharkov reverted to Soviet control permanently late that month. Again, the *"Totenkopf"* reconnaissance battalion was deeply involved in the determined German attempts to slow down the Soviet juggernaut. The following account concerns the fighting around Murafa in the middle of August:[15]

The leading edges of the attack force turned to the southeast at Konstantinowka. They were to link up with the forces screening from the rail station at Wodjanaja to the station at Kolomak, which had turned back several enemy advances the previous night and during the morning hours. At 1235 hours, the main body of *SS-Panzer-Grenadier-Regiment "Totenkopf"* was advancing along the railway line west of Konstantinowka towards Ssurdowka. At the same time, elements of *SS-Panzer-Grenadier-Regiment 3* and *SS-Pionier-Bataillon 3* were moving along the tracks from the rail station at Wodjanaja to the southwest in the direction of the rail station at Kolomak. In the area around Panassenkoff–Zepotschkin, they linked up with *SS-Panzer-Aufklärungs-Abteilung 3* in order to continue the attack to the northwest, so as to advance in the direction of the forces attacking from Konstantinowka.

SS-Rottenführer Hax has provided the following account: "We deployed into an offensive wedge. Everything that was still part of the reconnaissance battalion was together. In addition, there were *Panzer III's* and *IV's*. We had no idea what the objective was. We had gotten used to the fact that we were no longer informed about the situation. You followed orders so that you could make your own decisions and act on your own at the right moment. The higher commands had a term for it: 'experienced combatants.'

"We rolled out. Four tanks to the front, which were followed by the *SPW's*. Everything else infiltrated into the formation.

"The sight of our formation was impressive. We hadn't seen anything like that for a long time. That made us feel good and confirmed our belief in the strength of the division . . . "

By then (1340 hours), elements of *SS-Panzer-Grenadier-Regiment "Theodor Eicke"* had taken Hill 186.7, northwest of Trudoljubowka, while advancing from Konstantinowka. They then occupied the village. At the same time, *SS-Panzer-Grenadier-Regiment "Totenkopf"* reached the area northwest of Ssurdowka in an attack. Hax continues: "A cloud of dust moved along with us. We passed a patch of woods, then Paschtschenkowka. The station buildings had burned to the ground. We swung to the right after crossing the railway line and approached a railway embankment. It ran perfectly parallel to the road we were advancing on.

"'Halt!'

"The lead tanks traversed their turrets to 9 o'clock and fired at a few individual peasant shacks. The *Schwimmwagen* moved off to the left and checked out the area.

"'Move out!'

"A short while later, the tanks up ahead halted again and fired. Our *SPW's* deployed to attack. The main body waited. We moved ahead by leaps and bounds. The ground rose gently. Along the road was a shot-up Russian infantry position. The lead tanks moved up to the railway embankment next to one another. Their main guns blazed and their machine guns rattled. The speed of the column picked up considerably. The vehicles raced over the railway crossing, which was higher than the surrounding area. Wild firing ensued and increased with every vehicle that crossed the railway line.

"At the embankment, an officer gave directions. It was only possible to take a short peek while making the leap across the embankment. It was swarming with Russians all over the broad, flat field. They were digging field fortifications or occupying them. We tensed up. At that point, the large group in front of us started to move. They were fleeing! That was a sight for sore eyes! Ascending slightly, the road that crossed the railway tracks led straight to a village (Ssurdowka). The tanks headed that way. Some of them fired while moving. Others moved by leaps and bounds: Alternately seeking cover . . . firing . . . moving again. They came to grips with the enemy.

"A few scout vehicles pressed forward, leaving the tanks behind them and advancing into the rear of the withdrawing Red Army men at the village. Between the *SPW's* and the armored cars, the *Schwimmwagen* bounced their way forward to the village in an attack line that was growing increasingly wider. Moving quickly and conducting a wide envelopment, the battle group rolled across the stubble fields. In front of us were the fleeing Russians. Their objective was the windmill at the north end of the village. Muzzle flashes could be seen there.

"We raced towards the village. The enemy could not be allowed to get a respite! He could not be allowed to establish himself again! By means of hand-and-arm signals, we communicated with the tanks. While they stopped and fired, we raced ahead. We caught up with the first fleeing men. We drove through the enemy forces in packs. They stared at us with eyes wide open, from which you could see fear and dismay. At that point, we were the ones doing the hunting and not the hunted, as had been the case recently. Finally, we had the opportunity to maneuver as we wished. I spontaneously thought of the cavalry attacks of days gone by, which crushed everything that stood in their path. The enemy defenses were getting stronger with every Ivan, who reached the edge of the village. The fire was also intensifying from the direction of the mill, even though the tanks were concentrating their fires there at the moment.

"We were the first to reach the road leading out of the village to the northwest. We had two *Schwimmwagen* and an armored car. Showing resignation, the Russians threw their rifles away or raised their hands. We only allowed ourselves to give them a single hand signal—'Head to the rear! Move out!'—we didn't have time for anything else. We needed to keep moving forward. The situation was one-of-a-kind; we didn't have time to worry about prisoners. We fired as we moved along the road. There was hardly any resistance coming anymore from the houses to the right. The group of trees to the left of the mill, on the other hand, was a dangerous wasp's nest! Halt! We were along the Russian flanks with our machine guns and the 2cm main gun of the scout vehicle. We fired with everything we had into the ranks of the defenders. Their defensive fires slowed down. Initially, they fled in small groups, groups that later turned large. A few tanks and *SPW's* had turned off the other road and swung towards the mill from the rear. The Russians from the mill ran right into the guns of our comrades.

"The vehicle commander of the scout car waved from his turret: 'Let's go! Get on them!'

"Without stopping its firing, the scout car rolled along the slightly curvy road. The turret then traversed to the right. The vehicle stopped. At that moment, we were next to it. What we saw took our breath away. While hundreds of Red Army men were running for their lives, a group of about 10–15 Bolsheviks were busy destroying the graves of German soldiers. The stop there lasted but a minute, and the affair then became part of the big picture. Perhaps they would find their graves next to those whose crosses they had destroyed."

At 1510 hours, Ssurdowka was taken by the reinforced [reconnaissance battalion] in its attack to the northeast. Hax continues: "The hunt continued, and we crossed through the edge of the village. Our right wing went around the village. Other vehicles were advancing in our direction from the left. (Vopersal's note: *SS-Panzer-Grenadier-Regiment "Totenkopf"*) While the armored vehicles formed up to the left of the road, the motorcycle infantry remained on it.[16]

"Beyond the last houses, the path took a dip and led into a defile. It appeared that the Russians were seeking refuge from the tanks there. By then, the tanks were rolling on another road about 1,000 meters away. We pursued the fleeing men with two *Schwimmwagen*. Two other amphibians moved along the upper edge of the road to the left. They had not been able to follow as quickly, since they had moved across rutted fields.

"'Don't fire. We'll be getting them regardless.' I was able to call that out to Fritz, before we entered the defile. Fritz had approached to within 10 meters of the Russians. With his submachine gun at the ready, he stood in his amphibian and called out: '*Stoi! Stoi!*'

"Despite their hopeless situation, the Russian soldiers continued running without stop. All of a sudden, a Russian as tall as a tree turned around and began firing with a submachine gun from the hip. Fritz's vehicle hurtled up the embankment, went off and rolled over onto the road. Fritz had been flung out of the vehicle. We stopped next to the amphibian. My rifleman had grasped the situation quickly and fired and fired with everything his weapon could give.

While jumping out of the vehicle, I saw how the tall Russian was swinging our way, when he collapsed from being hit. Both of the vehicles at the edge of the defile fired long bursts into the enemy masses . . . "

The [reconnaissance battalion] linked up with the elements of the division advancing from Konstantinowka. By doing so, the ring around the enemy forces in the area bounded by Medjanikij–Bidilo–Konstantinowka–Trudoljubowka–Alexejewka was closed. That same evening, Alexejewka was taken.

Vopersal and Hax describe offensive operations around Kharkov on 20 August, which took an unexpected turn:[17]

The *3.* and *4./SS-Panzer-Aufklärungs-Abteilung 3* were directed to reconnoiter to the north and attempt to establish contact with *Panzer-Grenadier-Division "Großdeutschland"* by moving through Lopuchowatyj. *SS-Rottenführer* Hax takes up the narrative: " . . . The lead element was formed by scout vehicles, followed by a group of motorcycle infantry. Behind them was a 5cm antitank gun which, in turn, was followed by the rest of the 3rd Company. We marched that way in a long column throughout the hot afternoon. The road crossed hills and valleys in treeless terrain in virtually straight fashion. Where was Ivan? As soon as we climbed a hill, everyone intently checked out the terrain. Nothing, nothing at all of the Russians was to be seen. Then a German aerial observer approached us. A tube hit the ground next to the road and a red smoke signal landed in the countryside. The report: 'A Russian tank is moving ahead of you!'"

In the meantime, the *1.* and *2./SS-Panzer-Aufklärungs-Abteilung 3* had been clearing the northern portion of Kolontajew. Following that, they moved out of the northern part of the village, together with the *I./SS-Panzer-Grenadier-Regiment "Totenkopf"* and some armored support. Towards 1500 hours, the [1st Company] reached the high ground around Point 167.5.

Together with the *II./SS-Panzer-Grenadier-Regiment "Totenkopf,"* the [2nd Company] attacked Ljubowka. The radio message dispatched to the division (command post at Kolontajew) reported the following: " . . . 2nd Company, together with the [aforementioned elements] is attacking Ljubowka. No reports concerning the reconnaissance initiated in the direction of Parchomowka." The *3./SS-Panzer-Aufklärungs-Abteilung 3* headed to the north. Hax again assumes the narrative: " . . . All of a sudden, the call with the bad news came from the lead elements: 'Tanks! Tanks!' Five tanks appeared in front of us. One of them was moving perpendicular to the slope in the direction of the road. What had appeared to be a haystack moments ago started to move. Sheaves of straw flew to the side. A second tank was rolling in our direction. It was time to get off the road. Along with other vehicles, we moved through the ditch behind a bunch of straw, seeking some concealment. Herd instincts lured other vehicles our way. The lead tank was already on the road. There was only about 600–700 meters between us. The main gun had to go off at any moment.

"*SS-Unterscharführer* Ehgartner called out to me: 'Let's get away from this pileup!'

"We drove off into the countryside. There still hadn't been a shot fired. The tanks got closer and closer, with more and more of them appearing in front of the high ground.

"'Man, those are German tanks!'

"We breathed a sigh of relief. They were *Panzer III's* and *IV's*, with *SPW's* among them. There was even an armored medical vehicle. It looked almost like an entire regiment. I was ordered to establish contact, so I headed cross-country down the hill, reaching Kotelewka. The first tanks rattled into the village from the other side. They were from *Großdeutschland*. The hatches opened. An *Oberleutnant* waved to me. I heard: 'Go to the *Graf*!' In the process, he pointed out a command tank. I thought a *Major Graf* was leading the formation. I reported by the book to him. He addressed me somewhat gruffly and told me:

'Report to your commander that the Russian tanks have been knocked out, and you can follow. We're turning back now!' I stood at attention and said, '*Jawohl, Herr Major!*' Then the following rained down to me: 'I am not a *Major*. I am *Oberst Graf* von Strachwitz! Don't forget it!'"

The continued use of reconnaissance elements as fighting units—in this case, infantry—is reflected in this account concerning *Panzer-Aufklärungs-Abteilung 5* of the *5. Panzer-Division* (6–7 September 1943):[18]

On 6 September, the division was attached to the *56. Infanterie-Division* of *General* Müller.

Panzer-Pionier-Bataillon 89 and [*Panzer-Aufklärungs-Abteilung 5*] received the mission to advance to the northwest from Point 227.2 and establish contact with friendly forces to the left. Two assault detachments were employed from out of Logatschewo. Assault Detachment 1 was formed by *Panzergrenadier-Regiment 14*. It advanced from Logatschewo to the north in order to turn east in the vicinity of Schatkowa. Following it was Assault Detachment 2 of *Panzergrenadier-Regiment 13*. It was directed to turn east at the Kossitschino collective farm and assault into the front lines of the pocket. Around 1600 hours, these forces were able to close the ring.

The commander of *Panzer-Aufklärungs-Abteilung 5*, *Hauptmann* Stephan, has provided a firsthand account of the fighting:

"After a day of rest in Borowka, the [battalion] received a special mission, which unfortunately had little to do with the missions of a reconnaissance battalion. The enemy had advanced via a corduroy road through the large tract of woods west of Klin with light motorized forces. He had set up an all-round defense east of Matwejewka. He waited for additional reinforcements there, which were supposed to be brought forward via the corduroy road. After a thorough briefing by the Operations Officer of the division, I received the mission to advance through the woods to the northwest with the dismounted companies (2nd, 3rd and 4th), reach the corduroy road and block it, both to the west and to the east. It was the division's intention to eliminate the enemy sitting in the woods.

"After rearming and refueling for three days—the mortars were dismounted so that the *SPW's* could be used for ground combat—the battalion departed late in the afternoon of 6 September. The march was conducted using a compass, with the companies arranged in a column without intervals between them. The woods had a primeval appearance. It was marshy in places. In some spots, the underbrush was so thick that engineers had to clear a path in front of me with axes. The advance was tiring; I directed a rest break of 15 minutes after every hour of marching. The distance to the corduroy road was about 5 kilometers, including the bypassing of the marshes. I believe we covered about two-thirds of the way by midnight. I directed a two-hour rest break. The night was still and already quite cold. The only thing you could hear was the snoring of the exhausted soldiers. Towards 0200 hours, I had the march continue. It was finally turning somewhat light in the east. I heard the sounds of engines from the north. After marching for an hour, the sound of the engines became increasingly loud. We had to be not too far from the corduroy road.

"I initiated a halt and ordered the company commanders to report to me. I then snuck up to the corduroy road with them. A Russian column with limbered guns on trucks moved slowly to the west. After the column had passed and no enemy force approached from the east, I had the companies close up to the embankment. The 2nd Company was positioned on both sides of the road, oriented to the west, while the 3rd Company oriented to the east. The engineer platoon was given the mission to block the embankment with mines. Towards 0500 hours on 7 September, I was able to report to the division: 'Corduroy road reached and blocked.'

"Not identified by the enemy and dug in into deep holes, we waited for the things that were surely to come soon. Towards 0800 hours, an outpost of the 3rd Company reported enemy approaching. I went to the 3rd Company and ordered it not to fire until the first vehicle had driven into the hasty mine obstacle. Everyone's heart was in his throat. With a thunderous blast, the first vehicle flew into the air. The 3rd Company then opened fire on the vehicles that had jammed up. The Russians left everything in a panic and ran into the fires of the company. Only a few were able to escape to the east. At that point, the enemy was aware of our presence, both to the east and to the west.

"The division informed me that the enemy forces that had broken through to the west were to be attacked by *Panzergrenadier-Regiment 14* from the north and *Panzergrenadier-Regiment 13* from the south on 8 September. The regiments had orders to establish contact with [*Panzer-Aufklärungs-Abteilung 5*].

"Towards noon on 7 September, the 3rd Company was attacked from the east. A grueling fight in the forested terrain developed. The enemy was turned back in close combat. At the same time, the enemy forces that had broken through to the west placed heavy mortar fire on the battalion. Men were wounded by tree bursts. By then, the 2nd Company was also being attacked from the west. The situation was turning critical. Our great ally was the night, which finally descended after heavy close-quarters combat.

"During the night, *Panzergrenadier-Regiment 13* established contact. With regard to *Panzergrenadier-Regiment 14*, which was employed north of the embankment, nothing was seen nor heard. Towards 0400 hours on 8 September, the loud sounds of the Russian battle cry and heavy weapons firing could be heard west and northwest of the embankment. The enemy had identified the gap to *Panzergrenadier-Regiment 14* and broke through it, leaving behind a portion of his equipment. The 2nd Company was able to push the enemy force, which was assaulting in its direction, back to the north through its fires. It was unable to halt it, however. [*Panzer-Aufklärungs-Abteilung 5*] was able to bring in approximately 100 prisoners, most of whom were wounded."

The *1. Panzer-Division* had been spared the inferno of Kursk in the summer, since it was still being reconstituted and performing occupation duties in Greece. It was summoned back to the Eastern Front in November 1943 and, due to the critical situation that existed, committed piecemeal as it arrived. Among the elements that were first to fight was *Panzer-Aufklärungs-Abteilung 1*:[19]

Panzer-Aufklärungs-Abteilung 1, which had been reinforced (including one antitank platoon and one platoon of combat engineers) and pushed forward, was already fighting by 12 November about 35 kilometers northwest of Biala Zerkwa. Thanks to the employment of almost all of the armored scout sections, the battalion succeeded in preventing a continuous expansion of the Red breakthrough to the southwest . . .

On 13 November 1943, *Panzer-Aufklärungs-Abteilung 1* backed up the success of the first day of operations with an aggressively conducted night attack on Pawolotsch. The reconnaissance battalion advanced into the Soviet assembly areas in front of the division as part of a reconnaissance-in-force, during which *Leutnant* Wallrodt, a scout section leader, was killed. The battalion took Pawolotsch. By doing so, it enabled the occupation of the approach positions by the battle groups that followed. That success was purchased with considerable loss in men and materiel, however, when the light *SPW's* of one of the armored reconnaissance companies ran into Russian T-34's that had been concealed and positioned in the middle of a village that had been reported as "clear of enemy" by the command. The company was only able to disengage from the enemy with great difficulty. The *SPW's* that had been left behind and were damaged were recovered a short while later, following an aggressively conducted counterattack, whereby the enemy was also cleared from the village.

Panzer-Aufklärungs-Abteilung 4 of the *4. Panzer-Division* conducted operations in the Chernobyl area in the middle of November 1943. *Leutnant* Ulrich Sachse, a platoon leader in the battalion, wrote his impressions of the fighting:[20]

16–22 November 1943—Chernobyl is a town on the lower course of the Pripjet, not far from where it joins the Dnjepr. It was a pretty pitiful one-horse town. For us, it came to be synonymous with the concept of a successful defense in the "wet triangle," as we called the area between the two rivers. We had just reduced a bridgehead north of the town, which the enemy had pushed across the river. We had repaired the front at just the spot where *Heeresgruppe Mitte* adjoined *Heeresgruppe Süd*.

We had taken care of that which we could take care of. Then, it happened south of the town. The boundary between the field army groups had been ripped open; the most recent Russian offensive had effectively wiped out the left wing of the southern field army. For the time being, we had been spared. Chernobyl remained a bulwark for *Heeresgruppe Mitte*. But we could not help our neighbors, even if we still had some reserves. At Chernobyl, the Usch River emptied into the Pripjet, coming from the west. It cut the rear area of the German front into a sharply defined north and south. It outlined in advance where the two field army groups would be torn apart.

The army corps to the south of us split and fell apart under the onslaught of the enemy thrust; its remnants continued to fall back to the west. Our front remained intact at Chernobyl but with a gaping open flank to the south, which continued extending to the rear by the day. Soon, we were also subjected to heavy attacks. Our last reserves stopped the enemy elements in an immediate counterattack, but by then they had moved along the Usch to the rear of Chernobyl along a stretch of 15 kilometers. As a result, the main line of resistance of the division had expanded to 40 kilometers.

Our standing armored car patrols guarded the deep flank of the division—the corps, the field army, the field army group—along the north bank of the Usch. They also felt their way into the abandoned area of the rear area of the neighboring corps. When would the enemy turn north, cross the Usch and advance into our rear? In the bandit-controlled woods within the Pripjet Marshes, it started to come alive. The partisans could smell a fresh breeze coming in. A hundred kilometers to our rear, the supply base at Owrutsch fell into their hands; barely 90 trucks full of rations could be saved by sending them forward to the division.

In the meantime, the division held fast in the face of the increasing pressure on both sides of Chernobyl.

On 15 November, information was received that the old front had been penetrated by the enemy in the vicinity of Lojew, along the middle Dnjepr. The measures taken by the field army resulted in a quite extraordinary mission for our armored reconnaissance battalion: Immediately form mobile *Kampfgruppen*, which were to initiate a high degree of activity along the main areas of the former main line of resistance of the division, so as to deceive the enemy concerning the evacuation of the positions west of the Pripjet.

The evacuation started at 2400 hours on 16 November. The rear-area services of the division had already flowed northward across the only useable Pripjet bridge at Dawljady, since the division had to be committed into the area of the breakthrough at Retschiza, moving there by means of expedited marches. The mission of the reconnaissance battalion was to keep the enemy from crossing the Pripjet for at least two days by means of delaying actions on the part of the *Kampfgruppen*, the holding of blocking positions by the rest of the companies and, in the end, through a defense of the bridgehead at Dawljady. The timeframe was necessary in order to allow the corps on the right wing to reorganize itself along a shorter line running Kalinkowitschi–Mosyr after giving up the open Chernobyl bend.

When the mission arrived at the battalion command post in Sapolje, there was only one hour of time until the gigantic division main line of resistance would start to expose itself at the stroke of midnight. On top of that, most of the battalion was located in the extreme right-hand sector of the division. It first had to be pulled out of its trenches and strongpoints, which meant that it was also participating in the same withdrawal movements that it was supposed to conceal. The armored car patrols were committed in guard missions far to the west along the Usch River. They were at Kabany, 20 kilometers deep in the open flank, and were engaging enemy forces that were pressing from the south across the Usch, as well as partisans that were coming out of the woods to the north.

The commander of the *Luchs* company, *Hauptmann* Kelsch, assumed responsibility for forming, leading and supplying the mobile *Kampfgruppen*. The commander, *Hauptmann* Westermann, employed the rest of the battalion in the blocking positions.

When it dawned on 16 November, revealing the abandoned positions of the division, the enemy attacked at the usual places of his main effort. To the south of Sapolje, he ran into the withering fires of the *Luchs* reconnaissance vehicles and the self-propelled *Flak*. They could not follow the enemy into the marshlands, however, where he pulled back. Therefore, it was also not possible to keep him from taking Sapolje. The *Kampfgruppe* blocked his continued advance to the north, however, along the high ground along the edges of the locality.

Ten kilometers to the east, *Kampfgruppe* Schöttl raced into Chernobyl just as the enemy was entering the town from the southeast. Schöttl dismounted with a couple of men and, supported by the vehicular weapons, drove the completely panic-stricken enemy out of town.

Eight kilometers upstream along the Pripjet, the *Kampfgruppe* positioned there drove the enemy out of the extended village of Lelew, after he had entered, and hunted him back across the river, inflicting heavy casualties. The two sections positioned further north did not become engaged with the enemy.

In an involuntary case of reconnoitering, the field mess of the Heavy Company discovered that its impression of the overall enemy situation was no longer valid after it started receiving heavy antitank-gun fire.

In a large arc extending 40 kilometers, the remaining three sections guarded to the west against the partisans in the woods. The most southern section overwatched the former reconnaissance line along the northern bank of the Usch. During the evening of 16 November, it had its first enemy elements on the near side of the river to its front.

With the exception of the entering of Sapolje, the entire main line of resistance was in our hands on the evening of 16 November.

It was then time to establish the rest of the battalion, principally the light *SPW* companies, in improved positions on the high ground outside of Tschistogalowka and Kopatschi, oriented to the south. Those intermediate positions blocked off the southern third of the area between Chernobyl and Dawljady. There were four *Kampfgruppen* operating in front of the blocking positions: North of Nowoselki–at Sapolje–in Chernobyl–at Lelew.

The first report of 17 November, however, came from the section far out to the west on the north bank of the Usch. It was pulling back slowly, fighting continuously, to the north. It was able to stop the enemy at the locality of Ilinzy.

Strong enemy forces moved out to the north from Sapolje. They had to attack six times in order to gain 2 kilometers by noon. Then they bypassed to the north, turning west. The section north of Nowoselki engaged those forces, after having waited in vain for enemy to approach from the south.

In the meantime, Schöttl had stopped all of the attacks on Chernobyl. Towards noon, he received orders to shift west to the area north of Sapolje. He raced off and encountered the enemy group—by surprise and with devastating effect—that was attempting to head north. Those enemy forces were only able to make small gains for the rest of the day.

The *Kampfgruppe* at Lelew was ordered south and encountered strong enemy forces halfway to Chernobyl. The enemy had been marching out of the town, heading upstream along the Pripjet. The *Kampfgruppe* engaged a compact march column while on the move, sending it back in an undisciplined fashion. A second effort from the enemy—an attempt to flank from the west out of Chernobyl—forced the *Kampfgruppe* to take up positions behind the intermediate position at Kopatschi. The enemy attack ended there that evening in the defensive fires coming from the blocking position.

Later that evening, the section located far to the west reported that the enemy moved out to attack the locality of Ilinzy after placing heavy fires on it. The enemy moved out against phantoms and conquered the village with an *Urrää*, even though it had not been defended by a single soul.

When it turned night on 17 November, that marked the two days that we were supposed to trick out of the enemy. The bridge over the Pripjet at Dawljady was still 24 kilometers behind the intermediate positions, however, along whose left portion the enemy had taken a bloody nose. To the north of Nowoselki and at Ilinzy, the sections were still even with Chernobyl.

On 18 November, the blocking positions on the hills outside of Kopatschi and Tschistogolowka held long enough against heavy enemy attacks for the last section, that of *Oberfeldwebel* Frank, to fight its way back from Maly Korogod. Frank's section then covered the jump of the 3rd Company from the first blocking position to the second one, 10 kilometers further to the rear and located around Nowy Schepelitschi, while the 4th Company jumped from Kopatschi to Dawljady, occupying the outer ring of the bridgehead. A hardworking construction battalion was busy constructing the fortifications there. On the far west flank, the section at Ilinzy had joined up with the southern anti-partisan outpost and prevented the advance of enemy elements, still striving directly northward, by continuous skirmishes.

On 19 November and halfway through 20 November, the 3rd Company held its blocking position at Nowy Schepelitschi. During the same time period, Frank's section, to the west at Stary Schepelitschi, prevented the enemy from exiting the woods until he suddenly found himself surrounded by the enemy in the middle of the village. The two sections in the west that had joined up were directed to Stary Schepelitschi, where they were able to break open the ring around Frank's forces. The brave leader of the section lost his life to fire from an antitank rifle.

During the evening of 20 November, the 3rd Company occupied bridgehead positions around Dawljady. The remaining anti-partisan outposts from the west were called in, since the enemy was threatening to cut off their withdrawal route from the south. The Russians tried in vain all of 21 November to break through the outer ring of fortifications. *Hauptmann* Winterling's battery, as well as an attached *Flak* platoon, which had already worked with the *Kampfgruppe* at Sapolje, decisively strengthened the defenses in the positions, along with the heavy weapons of the battalion. The six vehicles of the 8-wheeled cannon platoon flitted back and forth.

When the inner ring of defenses was occupied during the night of 21–22 November, it was only as part of the effort to initiate the evacuation. The battalion was desperately needed in the Korowatitschi area. The tracked and wheeled sections needed to assume missions along the open flank of the field army at Mosyr. According to the radio reports, the division was involved in heavy fighting. In the boundary area between the *2. Armee* and the *9. Armee*, things were reaching a crunch point.

Around midnight, on the night of 22–23 November, the battalion flowed north over the long wooden bridge over the Pripjet. It was covered by a rear guard. Despite the fires from the heavy weapons, the enemy followed hard on the heels of the rear guard and took the bridge with an *Urrää* just as it flew into the air with a mighty detonation caused by 1,500

Teller mines. They were what remained of the mines that could not be transported away from an ammunition dump.

Finally, an account concerning operations conducted by *Panzer-Aufklärungs-Abteilung 8* of the *8. Panzer-Division* at the end of the year:[21]

By the end of 1943, the division had been largely decimated and was in the laborious process of both defending a sector and attempting to reconstitute itself. The commander of *Panzer-Aufklärungs-Abteilung 8*, *Major* Mitzlaff, described one attack by his *Kampfgruppe* in an effort to regain lost ground:

" . . . In the meantime, we heard the sounds of fighting from the intermediate piece of high ground. That meant that *Hauptmann* Kloos had already encountered the enemy; the unmistakable sound of *MG 42*'s could be heard. Ivan only replied hesitantly . . . I then issued orders to advance north . . . The terrain was no longer so broken up. In front of us was a hill that looked like a dune. That meant that Janowka had to be behind it . . .

The armored vehicles crossed the dune. Ivan had woken up and was greeting us with heavy antitank-gun fire. . . . By then, we had disappeared into the far side of the depression between the dunes. One armored vehicle was firing towards the east and a few *SPW's* were up close to it . . . It turned out that everything up to that point had succeeded beyond all expectations. The Russians had been completely surprised and started fleeing after a short defense. The *SPW's* raced on to Janowka in an aggressive assault. They caught the Russians in the rear there. His artillery and antitank guns were overrun. As it turned out later, there was also an entire regimental headquarters . . . The *SPW's*, driven forward by the young *Leutnant* Corsepius, pursued the Russians fleeing from Janowka as far as the Pripet [River] . . .

"*Hauptmann* Kloos and I cobbled together everything we had in the way of vehicles in the area for an assault on the high ground . . . The hill was still occupied by the enemy. Nonetheless, they were surprised that we had approached from the rear . . . We churned our way through deep sandy soil up the hill and, at that point, the brave *Panzergrenadiere* appeared. Who had moved out from Chernobyl? It was *Oberleutnant* von Bredow's company!"

With the help of the mechanized infantry and a few *Panzer IV's*, the Soviets were driven off the hill, thus ending von Mitzlaff's mission successfully.

Tankers and scouts of *Panzergrenadier-Division "Großdeutschland"* show off a *Panzer IV, Ausführung G*, and an *Sd.Kfz. 232 (8 Rad)* to curious members of the Hitler Youth somewhere in Germany, possibly in Cottbus, the division's home base. Although the date cannot be certain, the preponderance of overseas caps worn by the military personnel—as opposed to the *M43* worn by one soldier—and the presence of the later-model *Panzer IV* indicate it might have been sometime in 1943.
AKIRA TAKIGUCHI

This press-release image dated 13 February 1943 shows the commander of an *Sd.Kfz. 231 (8 Rad)* intently observing toward the enemy along the Middle Don. TODD GYLSEN

Death notices from the Eastern Front in 1943. *Gefreiter* Simon Fehrer was killed in action in a motorcycle infantry battalion at Rostow on 21 January. *Oberfeldwebel* Xaver Meßner, an experienced reconnaissance soldier who participated in the campaigns in Poland and the West, was also assigned to a motorcycle infantry battalion when he was killed on 25 February. *Obergefreiter* Josef Gruber was assigned to a *Panzer-Aufklärungs-Abteilung* when he was killed at Ssewsk on 20 March 1943 during the fighting to retake Kharkov. *Gefreiter* Josef Reichkobler succumbed to his wounds from artillery shrapnel on 16 September 1943. Although the family listed him as being assigned to a motorcycle infantry battalion, he would have been in an armored reconnaissance battalion by the time of his death.

Scouts assigned to an *Sd.Kfz. 233* pose in front of their vehicle. Since most are wearing the *M43* field cap, which was not widely distributed until later in 1943, it must be assumed these images were taken in the East in the winter of 1943–44. Although the Model 1943 armored reconnaissance battalion was supposed to have a platoon of these vehicles within its structure, this was not frequently achieved due to shortfalls in production. JIM HALEY

Images taken from the album of a scout assigned to the vehicle of Erwin Krüger, who later went on to receive the Knight's Cross of the Iron Cross on 17 September 1944. These photographs were likely taken sometime after the division's return to the Soviet Union in late 1943 or the first half of 1944. Krüger's vehicle, an *Sd.Kfz. 231 (8 Rad)*, was christened the *König* (King) and can be seen in several of the shots. The scouts wear a variety of uniforms, and comfort seems to have been stressed over uniformity. This is somewhat surprising due to the fact that the armored car troop was detached from its parent battalion for much of late 1943 until late 1944, reporting directly to the division headquarters, where uniform regulations were normally more strictly enforced. The last image is of Division Commander *Generalleutnant* Maximilian *Reichsfreiherr* von Edelsheim, standing in his command and control half-track, most likely an *Sd.Kfz. 251/3*. Of interest in this last image is the *SS* camouflage field cap worn by the officer candidate in the vehicle. JIM HALEY

In late 1942 and early 1943, the *SS* fielded its own type of "fast" formation, the *schnelles Regiment*, which was intended to be the division's rapid-reaction force. To that end, much of the regiment was equipped with various versions of light wheeled utility vehicles. Most of these were the standard *Volkswagen Kübelwagen*, but a large number of the amphibious version, the *Schwimmwagen*, were also fielded. In addition to those produced by *Volkswagen*, a number designed by Hanns Trippel and designated the *SG6* entered military service. Although the idea of the *schnelle Regimenter* was later proven to be impractical, the elements of the regiments continued to see service in division line units, particularly in the reconnaissance battalions. NATIONAL ARCHIVES

THE TIDE TURNS IN THE EAST 373

Surrendering Soviet forces move along a tank ditch toward an *SS* soldier. The Germans often encountered this type of extensive obstacle network during the Battle of Kursk. Tanks could not cross the ditch, let alone the half-tracks and wheeled armored cars of a reconnaissance battalion. It either had to be bypassed or breached, a time-consuming and generally casualty-intensive operation since any obstacle like this was well covered by heavy weapons. NATIONAL ARCHIVES

Armored cars of an *SS* reconnaissance company make their way down a wooded trail, which appears to have been blocked by obstacles. These images were probably taken during a training exercise, given the number of bystanders seen in the second image.

Division Commander *SS-Obergruppenführer* Josef "Sepp" Dietrich and other high-ranking *SS* and army officers view vehicles of *SS-Aufklärungs-Abteilung Leibstandarte SS Adolf Hitler* during its reorganization in France in the late summer and fall of 1942. The object of attention is an *Sd.Kfz. 250/10*, the platoon leader's vehicle in a light armored reconnaissance company. Of interest in the first image is the *SS* version of the reed-green herringbone twill special-purpose armored crewman uniform, a variant rarely seen in photographs. NATIONAL ARCHIVES

Several images of the famous commander of *SS-Aufklärungs-Abteilung Leibstandarte SS Adolf Hitler*, *SS-Sturmbannführer* Kurt Meyer, during the operations associated with the retaking of Kharkov in early 1943. The battalion was used primarily in a combat role during the fighting; Meyer led one of the *Kampfgruppen* that took the city center in March.

An *Sd.Kfz. 250* from *SS-Panzer-Aufklärungs-Abteilung 1* during the fighting at Kursk. Of interest is the three-color camouflage scheme that was crudely applied by hand. The scouts all wear camouflage smocks and helmet covers. NATIONAL ARCHIVES

An *SS* medic talks to crewmembers of what appears to be an *Sd.Kfz. 250/10*, identifying this as part of *SS-Panzer-Aufklärungs-Abteilung 1*. NATIONAL ARCHIVES

Grainy images of *SS-Aufklärungs-Abteilung 5 "Wiking"* are identified as having been taken in May 1943, perhaps during the movement toward Slawiansk or the area around Kharkov, where the battalion served as the field army reserve of the *1. Panzer-Armee*. NATIONAL ARCHIVES

THE TIDE TURNS IN THE EAST 377

Elements of *SS-Panzer-Grenadier-Division "Totenkopf"* in September 1943, probably during efforts to eliminate the Soviet bridgehead at Krementschug. The motorcycles were probably from the motorcycle infantry companies that were still a part of the mechanized infantry regiments; the *Sd.Kfz. 222* images are most likely from the reconnaissance battalion. NATIONAL ARCHIVES

SS motorcycle infantry from an unidentified unit. The sidecar has a partially obscured martial slogan written on it: *Sieg oder...* ("Victory or..."), with the last part of the message not visible. NATIONAL ARCHIVES

Although dated 1943 and referring to the fighting around Kriwoi Rog, which took place late in that year, it is obvious from this photo that German reconnaissance formations still employed vehicles that long since had been considered obsolescent and even removed from organization documents. In this case, a scout section is employing an *Sd.Kfz. 223* and an *Sd.Kfz. 221*, vehicles of limited utility at that stage of the war. TODD GYLSEN

This press-release image dated 15 November 1943 indicates that these vehicles have just detrained to reinforce the southern front. The *Sd.Kfz. 250/9* features the tactical numbers "213," indicating it was most likely the third vehicle of the first section of the 2nd Company. TODD GYLSEN

In this press-release image dated 24 December 1943, the crewmember of an *Sd.Kfz. 223* looks downrange at fighting intended to "flush out remaining Bolsheviks from their hiding places." TODD GYLSEN

CHAPTER 10

The End in the West

SETTING THE STAGE

While the loss of North Africa and the ongoing slugging match in Italy was of some concern to Hitler and his senior leadership, it was the invasion of Normandy on 6 June 1944 that brought the realities of a two-front war home to the German command. Followed by an additional landing in southern France on 15 August, it was only a matter of time before the juggernaut of the Western Allies would close in on the *Reich* from the west. Although the Western Allies made numerous tactical and operational mistakes and seriously underestimated the ability of the Germans to reconstitute their forces, their sheer numerical superiority on the ground, coupled with air supremacy in the skies, meant a successful conclusion to the campaign was only a matter of time. Hitler contributed to his own demise by increasing his meddling in command and control of German forces, sacking competent commanders who dared not follow *Führer* directives unflinchingly, and insisting on an inflexible defensive strategy.

After struggling to break out of the *bocage* in June and July, the Western Allies conducted a rapid sweep through much of France in the months that followed and were poised to enter Germany in the fall. Logistical problems (lack of usable ports), divisiveness over grand strategy (narrow versus broad front strategy), unexpectedly tough German resistance and occasional tactical success (e.g., the failure of Operation Market Garden), high casualties among Allied ground forces (e.g., the forced deactivation of two British infantry divisions and the diversion of U.S. divisions intended for the Pacific), and the surprise launching of a German counteroffensive

A knocked-out *Sd.Kfz. 251/21* with the *Drilling* antiaircraft mount. Three army armored divisions—the 2nd, 9th, and 116th—had several of these in their reconnaissance battalions in November and December 1944. They were most likely acquired from the disbanded *Panzer-Brigaden*, which were consolidated with the divisions and had been relatively lavishly equipped with this lethal weapon. This knocked-out vehicle most likely came from one of the armored brigades. The *Drilling* came in two variants, each with three guns of the same caliber: 1.5cm or 2cm. In the second image, another knocked-out *Drilling* is seen, along with a dead crewmember. The guns appear to be the 2cm version.
NATIONAL ARCHIVES

in an unexpected location (the Ardennes), meant that the war in the West lasted until May 1945 instead of the winter of 1944–45.

DOCTRINE

For all practical purposes, German armored reconnaissance forces in the West were used as combat forces and generally employed in the line whenever fronts stabilized. As Hitler placed more and more demands on the establishment of new forces in the field while continuing to insist on the reconstitution of forces battered at the front, he continued to create an untenable position for force planners. As in the past, the staff officers in the *Organizations-Abteilung* had to "tighten the belt" of field forces by streamlining vehicle, equipment, and manpower allocations. For *Panzer* and *Panzergrenadier* divisions, this meant another attempt at standardizing the force and the introduction of a Model 44 organization.

Efforts were also made to lighten the logistical end of units and formations by introducing the *freie Gliederung* ("open organization") concept, by which combat units were essentially stripped of all organic logistical support. Because of the often bewildering array of equipment and combat vehicles in use, a number of variant *KStN's* were developed.

As with the standardization effort introduced by the Model 43 organization, the armored reconnaissance battalion generally benefitted from the changes due to the introduction of ever-more armored vehicles and firepower to the sub-elements. In many respects, they resembled a mechanized infantry battalion in terms of capabilities, fielding even more armored vehicles, albeit at the cost of fewer troops on the ground. Logically, the more combat power they had, the more likely they were to be employed in a direct combat role.

Under the Model 44 organization, the reconnaissance battalion's wheeled scout assets were consolidated with the headquarters company, resulting in four line companies instead of the traditional five. In addition, one of the light armored reconnaissance companies was supposed to be replaced by a medium armored reconnaissance company that was essentially identical to a half-track–equipped mechanized infantry company. Of course, these benefits were largely theoretical, as demonstrated by the detailed analysis of the actual organizations of reconnaissance assets within most of the divisions employed in the West from the start of the Normandy Invasion through the start of the Battle of the Bulge.

Indeed, most armored reconnaissance battalions in the West were still organized under the Model 43 template when the invasion started in June. In addition to fighting for sheer survival in the cauldron of Normandy, the reconnaissance battalions—along with the divisions, of course—started to make the transition to the Model 44 organization late in the summer. Correspondingly, the on-hand strengths of the battalions varied greatly month-by-month as commanders struggled to keep their formations intact, incorporate new changes, and deal with piecemeal employment. In many cases, divisions were pulled out of the line to conduct battlefield reconstitution, only to be recommitted—as a whole or piecemeal—when a new crisis arose.

The creation of the *Panzer-Brigaden* in August and September 1944 did nothing to help matters since they diverted considerable assets, especially combat vehicles, from divisions in the line. While most of the brigades were not authorized reconnaissance elements, they did possess vehicles for the most part that were sorely missed in both reconnaissance and mechanized infantry formations. Committed piecemeal and without much of a logistical backbone, the brigades were generally chewed up after being employed as fire brigades. By late September, most were absorbed into armored and mechanized infantry divisions, which helps to explain some of the spike in vehicle allocations seen in the November reports of the selected reconnaissance battalions under consideration below.

ORGANIZATION

The organizational changes for the Model 43 divisions were discussed in the previous chapters. Almost all of the divisions in the West were still following this model when they entered ground combat in Normandy in June 1944. The following chart shows the theoretical organization for a Model 1944 *Panzer* or *Panzergrenadier* division armored reconnaissance battalion.

PANZER-DIVISION AND PANZERGRENADIER-DIVISION, 1944 (MODEL)

Panzer-Aufklärungs-Abteilung	Reconnaissance Assets / Notes
Headquarters	Headquarters Company: *KStN 1109 (gp)* (1 April 1944)
1st Company	Armored Scout Company (half-track): *KStN 1162c* (1 April 1944)
2nd Company	Light Armored Reconnaissance Company (half-track): *KStN 1113 (gp)* (1 April 1944)
3rd Company	Medium Armored Reconnaissance Company (half-track): *KStN 1114c (gp)* (1 July 1944)
4th Company	Heavy Company (armored)
	Company Headquarters: *KStN 1121a (gp)* (1 April 1944)
	Armored Combat Engineer Platoon: *KStN 1124a (gp)* (1 April 1944)
	Armored Gun Platoon: *KStN 1125a (gp)* (1 April 1944)
	KStN 1126a (gp) (1 April 1944)

ORDER OF BATTLE IN THE WEST IN ORDER OF COMMITMENT, SUMMER 1944 TO WINTER 1944–45

The often-considerable differences between theory and practice are illustrated in the on-hand strength reports presented below. With the exception of the *Panzer-Lehr-Division*, no organization had its theoretical complement of vehicles at the time. Even those formations that had benefitted from reconstitution often deviated from the norm considerably, especially in overall numbers of combat vehicles.

Panzer-Aufklärungs-Abteilung 21 (21. Panzer-Division (neu))
(Started combat operations on the day of the invasion, 6 June 1944)

June 1944: At the time of the invasion, the reconnaissance battalion was organized using the Model 43 template. It was able to achieve that by its consolidation with the *Panzer-Aufklärungs-Lehr-Abteilung*, starting in September 1943.[1] Shortfalls were compensated for by incorporating equivalent captured French vehicles.

September 1944: As with many divisions involved in the fighting in Normandy, the *21. Panzer-Division* was heavily attrited when it submitted its status report for September. Only four line companies were reported, with evidence of a great deal of cross-leveling of assets. Of the sixty *Sd.Kfz. 250* variants authorized, only nineteen were on hand, of which two were in short-term and four in long-term maintenance. Nevertheless, there was still a wheeled scout company (2nd). In detail:
- Headquarters Company: four *Sd.Kfz. 250/3's* and one *leichter SPW U304(f)* (this was the French P107 medium half-track, converted for German use).
- 1st Company: four *leichte SPW U304(f)* (mounted with 2cm *Flak*).
- 2nd Company: nine *Sd.Kfz. 222's* and three *Sd.Kfz. 232's*.
- 3rd Company: four *Sd.Kfz. 250/1's*, two *Sd.Kfz. 250/3's*, and four *leichte SPW U304(f)* (one mounting a 3.7cm antitank gun).
- 4th Company: seven *Sd.Kfz. 250/1's*, two *Sd.Kfz. 250/3's*, and three *leichte SPW U304(f)* (one mounting a 7.5cm gun; two towing 7.5cm infantry guns).

October 1944: Late in September, *Panzer-Brigade 112* was consolidated with the division. Although the former had little left in the way of combat vehicles, it did provide needed manpower, tactical vehicles, and crew-served weaponry. Much of the division was withdrawn for reconstitution, but portions continued to fight through October (*Kampfgruppe von Luck*). The reconnaissance battalion reorganized and reported five line companies, retaining the Model 43 organization. The French personnel carriers also disappeared from the books. In detail:
- Headquarters Company: three *Sd.Kfz. 250/3's* and two *Sd.Kfz. 251/3's*.
- 1st Company (half-tracked scout): three *Sd.Kfz. 223's*, two *Sd.Kfz. 250/3's*, five *Sd.Kfz. 250/5's*, and nine *Sd.Kfz. 250/9's*.[2]
- 2nd Company (wheeled scout): two *Sd.Kfz. 231's*, two *Sd.Kfz. 232's*, and three *Sd.Kfz. 233's*.[3]
- 3rd Company (light armored reconnaissance): nineteen *Sd.Kfz. 250/1's*, two *Sd.Kfz. 250/10's*, and twenty-four light machine guns.
- 4th Company (light armored reconnaissance): eighteen *Sd.Kfz. 250/1's*, two *Sd.Kfz. 250/7's*, two *Sd.Kfz. 250/10's*, four *Sd.Kfz. 251/1's*, and thirty-three light machine guns.
- 5th Company (armored heavy): two *Sd.Kfz. 251/1s*, one *Sd.Kfz. 251/3*, six *Sd.Kfz. 251/7's*, one *Sd.Kfz. 251/9*, one *Sd.Kfz. 251/10*, and sixteen light machine guns.[4]

November 1944: The division continued to reconstitute as best it could while also fielding three *Kampfgruppen* involved in combat operations. The reconnaissance battalion was finally reorganized under the Model 44 template, although the new 3rd Company remained organized as a light armored reconnaissance company. In detail:
- Headquarters Company: two *Sd.Kfz. 222's*, three *Sd.Kfz. 223's*, three *Sd.Kfz. 231's*, two *Sd.Kfz. 232's*, three *Sd.Kfz. 233's*, three *Sd.Kfz. 250* variants, and two *Sd.Kfz. 251* variants (the armored personnel carriers are most likely the same ones listed in the previous month's report).

- 1st Company (half-tracked scout): thirteen *Sd.Kfz. 250* variants.
- 2nd Company (light armored reconnaissance): twenty-three *Sd.Kfz. 250* variants.
- 3rd Company (light armored reconnaissance): twenty-five *Sd.Kfz. 250* variants.
- 4th Company (armored heavy): one *Sd.Kfz. 250* variant and thirteen *Sd.Kfz. 251* variants.[5]

December 1944: For some reason, the status report for the division was submitted on 30 December. It reflected a relatively well-equipped battalion that had not changed much since the last report. In fact, it actually increased its overall number of combat vehicles. In detail:

- Headquarters Company: two *Sd.Kfz. 222*'s, five *Sd.Kfz. 223*'s, three *Sd.Kfz. 231*'s, three *Sd.Kfz. 232*'s, three *Sd.Kfz. 233*'s, two *Sd.Kfz. 250* variants, and three *Sd.Kfz. 251* variants.
- 1st Company (half-tracked scout): thirteen *Sd.Kfz. 250* variants.
- 2nd Company (light armored reconnaissance): twenty-four *Sd.Kfz. 250* variants.
- 3rd Company (light armored reconnaissance): twenty-two *Sd.Kfz. 250* variants.
- 4th Company (armored heavy): one *Sd.Kfz. 250* variant and seventeen *Sd.Kfz. 251* variants.

SS-Panzer-Aufklärungs-Abteilung 12 "Hitlerjugend"
(12. SS-Panzer-Division "Hitlerjugend")
(Started conducting combat operations in Normandy on 7 June)

June 1944: The division's reconnaissance battalion entered combat operations in Normandy under the Model 43 organization, with shortfalls in equipment primarily in armored cars. In detail:

- Headquarters Company: eleven *Sd.Kfz. 250/3*'s, three other *Sd.Kfz. 250* variants, and ten *Sd.Kfz. 251* variants.
- 1st Company (wheeled armored scout): six *Sd.Kfz. 223*'s, three *Sd.Kfz. 231*'s, and two *Sd.Kfz. 232*'s.
- 2nd Company (half-tracked armored scout): fifteen *Sd.Kfz. 250/9*'s and eight *Sd.Kfz. 250/4*'s.[6]
- 3rd Company (light armored reconnaissance): thirty-seven *Sd.Kfz. 250* variants, fifty-six light machine guns, four heavy machine guns, and two 8cm mortars.
- 4th Company (light armored reconnaissance): same as 3rd Company.
- 5th Company (armored heavy): one *Sd.Kfz. 250* variant, eleven *Sd.Kfz. 251* variants, six *Sd.Kfz. 251/9*'s, two towed infantry guns, three 7.5cm antitank guns, and six flamethrowers.

27 June 1944: The division submitted another status report toward the end of the month. This time, the reconnaissance battalion had started to reorganize under the Model 44 template, although it effectively had two light armored reconnaissance companies, as opposed to one light and one medium. Manpower was still reported as 100 percent.[7] In detail:

- Headquarters Company: The armored car assets of the battalion had been further reduced in June, with only three *Sd.Kfz. 223*'s and two *Sd.Kfz. 231*'s or *232*'s on hand.
- 1st Company (half-tracked scout): sixteen *Sd.Kfz. 250/9*'s and nine *Sd.Kfz. 250/4*'s.
- 2nd Company (light armored reconnaissance): unspecified total number of *Sd.Kfz. 250* variants (although two *Sd.Kfz. 250/7*'s and one *Sd.Kfz. 250/8* on hand) and forty-four light machine guns.
- 3rd Company (light armored reconnaissance): unspecified total number of *Sd.Kfz. 250* variants (although two *Sd.Kfz. 250/7*'s on hand), twenty-nine light machine guns, and four heavy machine guns.
- 4th Company (armored heavy): unspecified total number of *Sd.Kfz. 251* variants (although four *Sd.Kfz. 251/9*'s and six *Sd.Kfz. 251/2*'s on hand) and seventeen light machine guns.[8]

September 1944: Due to the heavy losses sustained from June through August, the division was ordered out of the line on 3 September to undergo battlefield reconstitution. As of 1 September 1944, the reported strengths were as follows:

- Headquarters Company: two *Sd.Kfz. 251/3*'s, one *Sd.Kfz. 231*, and three *Sd.Kfz. 222*'s.
- 1st Company (half-tracked scout): two *Sd.Kfz. 250/3*'s and seven *Sd.Kfz. 250/9*'s.
- 2nd Company (light armored reconnaissance): one *Sd.Kfz. 250/3*, five *Sd.Kfz. 250/1*'s, and one *Sd.Kfz. 250/8*.
- 3rd Company (light armored reconnaissance): twenty *Schwimmwagen*.[9]
- 4th Company (armored heavy): two *Sd.Kfz. 251/1*'s, one *Sd.Kfz. 251/3*, three *Sd.Kfz. 251/5*'s, and one *Sd.Kfz. 251/9*.

October 1944: By the middle of October, the entire division had been moved to Germany for reconstitution, which had to be welcome for the reconnaissance battalion since it had been further attrited, especially in armored cars and half-tracked armored scout vehicles. As can be seen by vehicles on hand, armored cars were present in both the headquarters and 1st Companies. In detail:

- Headquarters Company: two *Sd.Kfz. 251/3*'s, one *Sd.Kfz. 223*, and one *Sd.Kfz. 222*.
- 1st Company (half-tracked scout): five *Sd.Kfz. 221*'s.
- 2nd Company (light armored reconnaissance): sixteen *Sd.Kfz. 250* variants (of these vehicles, five were in long-term maintenance).
- 3rd Company (light armored reconnaissance): twenty-four *Schwimmwagen*.
- 4th Company (armored heavy): ten *Sd.Kfz. 251* variants.[10]

November 1944: Although much of the division continued to benefit from the reconstitution process, the reconnaissance battalion still had major shortages in combat vehicles. In terms of manpower, it had a slight overage in officers, a large underage in noncommissioned officers (only 62 percent on hand), and

a tremendous overage in enlisted (approximately 170 percent). Once again, a hybrid type of organization seems to have evolved, with the Headquarters and 1st Companies having armored cars while the 2nd Company has the *Sd.Kfz. 250/9*. In detail:
- Headquarters Company: one *Sd.Kfz. 251/3*, two *Sd.Kfz. 250/3's*, one *Sd.Kfz. 251/8*, four *Sd.Kfz. 234/1's*, and two *Sd.Kfz. 223's*.
- 1st Company (wheeled scout): five *Sd.Kfz. 222's* and one *Sd.Kfz. 223*.
- 2nd Company (half-tracked scout): four *Sd.Kfz. 250/1's*, two *Sd.Kfz. 250/3's*, four *Sd.Kfz. 250/9's*, and one *Sd.Kfz. 251/9*.
- 3rd Company (light armored reconnaissance): thirty-three *Schwimmwagen* and two *Sd.Kfz. 251/9's*.[11]
- 4th Company (armored heavy): three *Sd.Kfz. 251/1's* and six 8cm mortars.[12]

Panzer-Aufklärungs-Lehr-Abteilung (Panzer-Lehr-Division)
(Started combat operations in Normandy on 8 June 1944)

June 1944: Basically organized as a Model 43 armored reconnaissance battalion, with the 1st Company fielded under *KStN 1162a* as a *Puma* company. The battalion entered combat fully equipped and filled with well-trained personnel. The reconnaissance battalion was reorganized under the Model 44 template on 20 August.[13] The division suffered tremendous losses and was only a shell of itself by September.

September 1944: On the unit status report dated 3 September, the division reported its reconnaissance battalion at 35 percent manpower. The remaining assets of the 2nd and 3rd Companies were consolidated with the 1st Company. In addition, combat vehicles and equipment were likewise severely depleted. In detail:
- Headquarters Company: five *Sd.Kfz. 234/2's* and two *Sd.Kfz. 251/3's*.
- 1st Company (half-tracked scout): eight *Sd.Kfz. 250/1's*, three *Sd.Kfz. 250/9's*, and two *Sd.Kfz. 251/3*.
- 4th Company (armored heavy): four *Sd.Kfz. 251/1's*, one *Sd.Kfz. 251/3*, three *Sd.Kfz. 251/7's*, and one towed 7.5cm infantry gun.[14]

October 1944: The last of the formations employed in combat operations were pulled from the line in early October and transported to Germany to rejoin the rest of the division in the reconstitution process. When the division submitted its unit status report on 1 October, the reconnaissance battalion was essentially incapable of conducting any combat operations. The battalion reported three *Sd.Kfz. 234/2's* and four *Sd.Kfz. 250* variants. The 2nd through 4th Companies reported no vehicles at all.[15]

November 1944: The division continued the reconstitution process in November, recovering enough to be tasked with detaching two *Kampfgruppen* later in the month to deal with crises. One of the *Kampfgruppen* was spearheaded by the armored reconnaissance battalion. The situation had improved for the battalion since the last report, with all companies now reporting combat vehicles and equipment, and the overall manpower listed as 90 percent. The 1 November report in detail:
- Headquarters Company: seven *Sd.Kfz. 234/1's* and three *Sd.Kfz. 251* variants.
- 1st Company (half-tracked scout): fifteen *Sd.Kfz. 250* variants.
- 2nd Company (light armored reconnaissance): seventeen *Sd.Kfz. 250* variants.
- 3rd Company (medium armored reconnaissance): six *Sd.Kfz. 251* variants (supplemented by trucks).
- 4th Company (armored heavy): seven *Sd.Kfz. 251* variants.[16]

December 1944: The reconstitution of the reconnaissance battalion was essentially completed by the time the division submitted its status report on 1 December. In detail:
- Headquarters Company: thirteen *Sd.Kfz. 234/1's*, three *Sd.Kfz. 234/3's*, two *Sd.Kfz. 250* variants (probably *Sd.Kfz. 250/3's*), and two *Sd.Kfz. 251* variants (probably *Sd.Kfz. 251/1's*).
- 1st Company (half-tracked scout): twenty-two *Sd.Kfz. 250* variants (probably four *Sd.Kfz. 250/1's*, two *Sd.Kfz. 250/3's*, and sixteen *Sd.Kfz. 250/9's*).
- 2nd Company (light armored reconnaissance): seventeen *Sd.Kfz. 250* variants (probably thirteen *Sd.Kfz. 250/1's*, two *Sd.Kfz. 250/3's*, and two *Sd.Kfz. 250/7's*).
- 3rd Company (medium armored reconnaissance): twenty *Sd.Kfz. 251* variants (probably fourteen *Sd.Kfz. 251/1's*, two *Sd.Kfz. 251/2's*, two *Sd.Kfz. 251/3's*, one *Sd.Kfz. 251/9*, and one *Sd.Kfz. 251/17*).
- 4th Company (armored heavy): eleven *Sd.Kfz. 251* variants (probably two *Sd.Kfz. 251/1's*, two *Sd.Kfz. 251/3's*, two *Sd.Kfz. 251/7's*, and five *Sd.Kfz. 251/9's*).[17]

SS-Panzer-Aufklärungs-Abteilung 17 "Götz von Berlichingen" (17. SS-Panzergrenadier-Division "Götz von Berlichingen")
(The reconnaissance battalion entered the Normandy area of operations on 10 June)

June 1944: The division was in the process of completing its activation in France when the invasion started. It took heavy casualties and equipment losses during the fighting and was withdrawn to Germany by the end of July for reconstitution. The reconnaissance battalion was organized like a *Panzergrenadier-Division* prior to the introduction of the Model 43 template. As such, it had a wheeled scout company, three light reconnaissance companies, and a heavy company (motorized). The battalion's reconnaissance companies were issued the *Schwimmwagen* and appear to have been at full strength. In detail:
- Headquarters Company: No combat vehicles.
- 1st Company (wheeled scout): eighteen light armored cars (*Sd.Kfz. 222's* and *223's*)[18]
- 2nd Company (light armored reconnaissance—*Volkswagen*): fourteen *Schwimmwagen*, four heavy machine guns, twenty light machine guns, and two heavy mortars.[19]
- 3rd Company (light armored reconnaissance—*Volkswagen*): same as the 2nd Company.
- 4th Company (light armored reconnaissance—*Volkswagen*): same as the 2nd Company.
- 5th Company (motorized heavy): light infantry gun platoon, heavy antitank gun platoon, and combat engineer platoon (all motorized).[20]

Panzer-Aufklärungs-Abteilung 2 (2. Panzer-Division)
(Arrived in Normandy on 12 June)

June 1944: It appears the battalion was essentially organized along the lines of a Model 43 formation, with the addition of a heavy armored car platoon. The 1st Company (wheeled armored scout) was organized under *KStN 1162a* of 1 October 1943, thus equipping it with the *Sd.Kfz. 234/2 Puma* armored car.[21]

September 1944: Heavily attrited during the Normandy campaign, the battalion had been withdrawn from the front to be reconstituted, along with the rest of the division. It was reformed as a Model 44 reconnaissance formation, except the 3rd Company was also a half-tracked light reconnaissance company instead of an armored reconnaissance company (*KStN 1114c (gp) (fG)* / 1 July 1944).[22] In its status report dated 5 September 1944, it showed the following strengths:

- Headquarters: two *Sd.Kfz. 234/1's*, nine *Sd.Kfz. 234/2's*, three *Sd.Kfz. 243/3's*, and five *Sd.Kfz. 251* variants. Of the fourteen armored cars, three were in short-term repair.
- 1st Company (light half-tracked scout): three *Sd.Kfz. 250/3's* and seven *Sd.Kfz. 250/9's* were on hand; it is not known whether any were in maintenance.
- 2nd Company (light half-tracked reconnaissance): twenty *Sd.Kfz. 250/1's* and two *Sd.Kfz. 250/3's* were on the property books; it is not known whether any were in maintenance.
- 3rd Company (light half-tracked reconnaissance): twelve *Sd.Kfz. 250/1's* and one *Sd.Kfz. 250/3* were on the property books; it is not known whether any were in maintenance.
- 4th Company (heavy armored): thirteen *Sd.Kfz. 251* variants, distributed as follows: one *Sd.Kfz. 251/3* (company headquarters), one *Sd.Kfz. 251/1* and three *Sd.Kfz. 251/9's* (armored gun platoon), four *Sd.Kfz. 251/8's* (armored mortar platoon), and four *Sd.Kfz. 251/7's* (armored combat engineer platoon).[23]

October 1944: The battalion was committed to combat operations along the German western frontier in September, no doubt contributing to some of the reductions reflected in this 1 October 1944 report:

- Headquarters: two *Sd.Kfz. 234/1's*, one *Sd.Kfz. 234/2*, three *Sd.Kfz. 243/3's*, and three *Sd.Kfz. 251* variants. Of the six armored cars, two were in short-term repair.
- 1st Company (light half-tracked scout): no change from previous report.
- 2nd Company (light half-tracked reconnaissance): no change from previous report.
- 3rd Company (light half-tracked reconnaissance): no change from previous report.
- 4th Company (heavy armored): thirteen *Sd.Kfz. 251* variants, distributed as follows: no change from previous report.[24]

November 1944: The battalion did not pull out of the line until the middle of November. In addition, the 1st Company was temporarily detached from the division to serve with *Panzer-Brigade 150*:

- Headquarters: three *Sd.Kfz. 234/1's*, nine *Sd.Kfz. 234/2's*, three *Sd.Kfz. 233's*, and three *Sd.Kfz. 251* variants. Of the fifteen armored cars, four were in short-term repair.
- 1st Company (light half-tracked scout): detached for other duties and not reported. Officially listed as being reconstituted.
- 2nd Company (light half-tracked reconnaissance): nineteen *Sd.Kfz. 250* variants, of which two were in short-term maintenance and one in long-term maintenance.
- 3rd Company (light half-tracked reconnaissance): no vehicles listed; reported as being reconstituted.[25]
- 4th Company (heavy armored): no change from previous report.[26]

December 1944: At the start of December 1944, the battalion was still lacking a half-tracked scout company, its 3rd Company moved largely by bicycle, and its heavy company had a severe shortfall of vehicles, but it had received additional armored cars and *Sd.Kfz. 250* variants, thus making the wheeled scout and sole light armored reconnaissance companies fully equipped (albeit not completely with authorized vehicles). In detail:

- Headquarters: two *Sd.Kfz. 232's* (8 Rad), two *Sd.Kfz. 234/1's*, ten *Sd.Kfz. 234/2's*, three *Sd.Kfz. 233's*, one *Sd.Kfz. 250/3*, one *Sd.Kfz. 250/9*, one *Sd.Kfz. 251/1*, and three *Sd.Kfz. 251/3's*. Of the seventeen armored cars, three were in short-term maintenance.
- 1st Company (light half-tracked scout): no change from previous report.
- 2nd Company (light half-tracked reconnaissance): thirty *Sd.Kfz. 250* variants, as follows: twenty *Sd.Kfz. 250/1*, three *Sd.Kfz. 250/2's*, one *Sd.Kfz. 250/3*, one *Sd.Kfz. 250/5*, and five *Sd.Kfz. 250/7's*. Of the thirty-three *Sd.Kfz. 250* variants in the entire battalion, three were in short-term maintenance and five in long-term maintenance.
- 3rd Company (light half-tracked reconnaissance): one *Sd.Kfz. 250/3* listed.
- 4th Company (heavy armored): nine *Sd.Kfz. 251* variants, distributed as follows: two *Sd.Kfz 251/1's*, one *Sd.Kfz. 251/3*, two *Sd.Kfz. 251/7's*, two *Sd.Kfz. 251/9's*, and two *Sd.Kfz. 251/21's*.[27]

SS-Panzer-Aufklärungs-Abteilung 10 "Frundsberg" (10. SS-Panzer-Division "Frundsberg")
(Entered the Normandy area of operations on 24 June)

June 1944: The reconnaissance battalion was ordered to convert to the Model 44 organization in June 1944, just prior to its arrival in Normandy. While still organized under the Model 43 template, the reconnaissance battalion reported 100 percent manpower with the following assets:

- Headquarters Company: thirteen *Sd.Kfz. 250* variants, one *Sd.Kfz. 251* variant, and twenty light machine guns.
- 1st Company (wheeled scout): six light armored cars (*Sd. Kfz. 221's* and *223's*), twelve *Sd.Kfz. 222's*, six heavy armored cars (*Sd.Kfz. 231's* and *232's*).

- 2nd Company (half-tracked scout): sixteen *Sd.Kfz. 250/9's* and nine *Sd.Kfz. 250* variants.
- 3rd Company (light armored reconnaissance): thirty-three *Sd.Kfz. 250* variants (including three *Sd.Kfz. 250/7's* and two *Sd.Kfz. 250/10's*), forty light machine guns, and five heavy machine guns.
- 4th Company (light armored reconnaissance): thirty-three *Sd.Kfz. 250* variants (including three *Sd.Kfz. 250/7's* and two *Sd.Kfz. 250/10's*), forty-nine light machine guns, six heavy machine guns, and two 2cm main guns. [It apparently is not known whether these were the *Sd.Kfz. 250/9*.]
- 5th Company (armored heavy): twenty-three *Sd.Kfz. 251* variants (including four *Sd.Kfz. 251/9's* and one *Sd.Kfz. 251/10*), two towed infantry guns, three towed 7.5cm antitank guns, one half-track–mounted 5cm antitank gun, six flamethrowers, and thirty-five light machine guns.[28]

September 1944: By September, the battalion was still organized as a Model 43 battalion. Suffering heavy casualties in Normandy and subsequent fighting, the division status report dated 5 September 1944 showed the following:
- Headquarters Company: one *Sd.Kfz. 251/3*, four *Sd.Kfz. 250/1's*, and one *Sd.Kfz. 250/3*.
- 1st and 2nd Companies consolidated into the 1st Company: three *Sd.Kfz 231's*, six *Sd.Kfz. 222's*, and two *Sd.Kfz. 250/9's*.
- 3rd and 4th Companies consolidated into the 3rd Company: two *Sd.Kfz. 250/3's*, five *Sd.Kfz. 250/1's*, one *Sd.Kfz. 250/7*, and one *Sd.Kfz. 250/10*.
- 5th Company: three *Sd.Kfz. 251/1's*, one *Sd.Kfz. 251/3*, one *Sd.Kfz. 251/5*, and three *Sd.Kfz. 251/9's*.[29]

October 1944: The division continued to fight heavily. The organization remained the same (Model 43), while strength levels were reduced somewhat (based on a report submitted 12 October). The Headquarters Company lost two *Sd.Kfz. 250* variants, the 1st Company lost two *Sd.Kfz. 222's*, and the 5th Company lost three *Sd.Kfz. 251* variants. The 3rd Company, on the other hand, apparently gained one *Sd.Kfz. 250* variant.[30]

November 1944: Based on the status report of the division dated 1 November 1944, the reconnaissance battalion appears to have begun the switch to the Model 44 organization, although all of its armored cars remained in the 1st Company. The Headquarters Company increased its strength to a total of twelve *Sd.Kfz. 251* variants, with two *Sd.Kfz. 250* variants remaining on its books. The 1st Company had the same number of armored cars reported in October, but it appears to have increased its number of *Sd.Kfz. 250* variants from two to six. In addition, there was no 3rd Company, which would have been the medium armored reconnaissance unit. Finally, the 4th Company reported a total of twenty-three *Sd.Kfz. 251* variants, an increase of eighteen over the previously reported five.[31]

SS-Panzer-Aufklärungs-Abteilung 2 "Das Reich" (2. SS-Panzer-Division "Das Reich")
(started entering the Normandy area of operations on 29 June)

June/July 1944: By 1 June 1944 the division was supposed to be organized under the Model 43 guidelines. With regard to the reconnaissance battalion, it had a standard organization, except it did not have a heavy armored car platoon. The battalion reported aggregate manpower strength of 100 percent on 1 June 1944, as well as having thirty-five medium half-tracks and sixty-two light half-tracks. The 1st Company had no armored cars and the 2nd Company had no *Sd.Kfz. 250/9's*, although both companies may have been assigned some variant of the *Sd.Kfz. 250* series. In addition to an unknown number of half-tracks, the 3rd Company had three light machine guns and two 80mm mortars. The 4th Company had four light machine guns and two 80mm mortars. The heavy company had eleven machine guns, six *Sd.Kfz. 251/9's*, two towed infantry guns, and three towed heavy antitank guns (75mm).[32]

July 1944: By 1 July, the division was authorized to convert to a Model 44 structure and had initiated the process, although it still had the same number of light and medium half-tracks as reported in June, along with 100 percent manpower. The new 3rd Company was also organized under *KStN 1113 (gp)*, retaining its light reconnaissance status, as opposed to *KStN 1114 (gp)*, a medium reconnaissance company. At the time of the report, the division had not yet seen substantial commitment in the Normandy area.[33]

September 1944: After the fighting in Normandy, the battalion was reduced by more than half in terms of its armored personnel carriers, with only twenty-eight light and fourteen medium ones left. In terms of heavy weaponry, it had only one towed heavy antitank gun and one light infantry gun left.[34]

October 1944: With most combat units remaining in the line, the division continued to see combat, albeit not quite so heavy, in September. The October status report reflected the battalion as having its 1st Company (half-tracked armored scout) in Germany for reconstitution. With the exception of the 2nd Company, the remainder of the battalion was apparently drawn off the line, even if not officially reconstituting. The number of light and medium armored personnel carriers was essentially doubled (from twenty-eight to forty-nine and from fourteen to twenty-eight, respectively). Of the forty-nine light armored personnel carriers on hand, seven of them were in short-term maintenance. The only company remaining on the line, the 2nd Company (light armored reconnaissance), reported twenty *Sd.Kfz. 250* variants, twenty light machine guns, and two 8cm mortars on its books. In terms of personnel, the battalion had well over 100 percent manpower, except for officers (twenty-one of twenty-seven authorized).[35]

November 1944: Although additional equipment was issued to the battalion, it still had no armored cars in its headquarters company during the reporting period. In detail:
- Headquarters Company: two *Volkswagen Kübelwagen*, two *Schwimmwagen*, five *Sd.Kfz. 251/3's*, and one *Sd.Kfz. 251/11*.
- 1st Company: The half-tracked armored scout company did not have any *Sd.Kfz. 250/5's* or *Sd.Kfz. 250/9's* and was issued the *Sd.Kfz. 250/1* instead. It also had two 7.5cm light infantry guns on its books.[36]
- 2nd Company (light armored reconnaissance): at least fifteen *Sd.Kfz. 250/1's* assigned, along with two *Sd.Kfz. 250/3's* and two *Sd.Kfz. 250/7's*.[37]
- 3rd Company (light armored reconnaissance): twenty-one *Sd.Kfz. 250/1's*, two *Sd.Kfz. 250/3's*, and two *Sd.Kfz. 251/7's*.
- 4th Company (heavy armored): twelve *Sd.Kfz. 251/1's*, two *Sd.Kfz. 251/3's*, and three *Sd.Kfz. 251/16's*.[38]

December 1944: The division submitted its next status report on 8 December, and the overall vehicular situation of the reconnaissance battalion improved, including receiving armored cars for the headquarters company. Of the seventy-eight *Sd.Kfz. 250* variants assigned to the battalion, nine were in short-term repair. In detail:

- Headquarters Company: thirteen *Sd.Kfz. 234/1's*, three *Sd.Kfz. 234/3's*, six *Sd.Kfz. 251* variants, and four *Sd.Kfz. 250* variants. Interestingly, the headquarters company was able to keep a virtually 100 percent combat-ready rate for its armored cars through the end of December 1944.
- 1st Company: ten *Sd.Kfz. 250* variants.
- 2nd Company: thirty-two *Sd.Kfz. 250* variants.
- 3rd Company: thirty *Sd.Kfz. 250* variants.
- 4th Company: fourteen *Sd.Kfz. 251* variants.[39]

SS-Panzer-Aufklärungs-Abteilung 9 "Hohenstaufen" (9. SS-Panzer-Division "Hohenstaufen")
(Committed to the fighting in Normandy on 29 June)

June 1944: At the beginning of June 1944 when the division submitted its status report, the reconnaissance battalion still had a Model 43 organization. It was relatively full strength in both manpower (100 percent) and vehicles, although exact numbers of light and medium half-tracks are not available. In detail:

- Headquarters Company: vehicles unknown, and fifteen light machine guns.
- 1st Company (wheeled armored scout): twelve light and medium armored cars (including *Sd.Kfz. 221's*, *222's*, and *223's*) and six heavy armored cars (*Sd.Kfz. 231's* and *232's*)[40]
- 2nd Company (half-tracked armored scout): at least thirteen *Sd.Kfz. 250/9's*, although the total number is not available.
- 3rd Company (light armored reconnaissance): unknown number of light armored personnel carriers, but fifty-four light machine guns are indicated as being on hand, thus making the vehicular count probably close to that number as well.
- 4th Company (light armored reconnaissance): as with the 3rd company, but with even more light machine guns being reported (fifty-seven).
- 5th Company (heavy armored): Most platoons appeared to be close to full strength, although the armored gun platoon had only four *Sd.Kfz. 251/9's*, instead of six. In addition, the company had a 3.7cm antitank gun (half-track mounted) and six flamethrowers.[41]

September 1944: By the end of the fighting in Normandy and the withdrawal across France, the division was heavily attrited and officially referred to as *Kampfgruppe "Hohenstaufen."* The scout companies were consolidated into the 1st Company, and the 3rd and 4th Companies were consolidated into the 3rd Company. In detail:

- Headquarters Company: two *Volkswagen Schwimmwagen*, four sidecar motorcycles, one captured Humber Mark IV armored car, two *Sd.Kfz. 251/3's*, and one *Sd.Kfz. 251/1*.
- 1st Company: three *Volkswagen Schwimmwagen*, two motorcycles, three sidecar motorcycles, two *Sd.Kfz. 231's*, three *Sd.Kfz. 222's*, and five *Sd.Kfz. 250/9's*.
- 3rd Company: one *Volkswagen Schwimmwagen*, one *Volkswagen Kübelwagen*, one sidecar motorcycle, two *Sd.Kfz. 250/3's*, eight *Sd.Kfz. 250/1's*, one *Sd.Kfz. 250/7*, and one *Sd.Kfz. 250/10*.
- 5th Company (armored heavy): one *Volkswagen Kübelwagen*, one motorcycle, one *Sd.Kfz. 251/3*, two *Sd.Kfz. 251/1's*, and three *Sd.Kfz. 251/9's*.[42]

October 1944: During this reporting period, the division was being reconstituted and, at the same time, required to keep elements in the line for combat operations. Because of combat operations in the Arnhem area in September, the reconnaissance battalion had been further attrited. The battalion was effectively reduced to two understrength companies, with the armored cars assigned to the 1st Company and the armored personnel carriers to the 2nd Company.[43]

November 1944: The reconstitution of the entire division started in earnest in the second week of November. The status report dated 1 November showed the reconnaissance battalion at its most depleted state and in the process of converting to the Model 44 organization, although a light armored reconnaissance company was retained in lieu of a medium armored reconnaissance company. In detail:

- Headquarters: one *Sd.Kfz. 231*, four *Sd.Kfz. 222's*, and two *Sd.Kfz. 223's*. Of the armored cars, one was in short-term maintenance and two were in long-term maintenance.
- 1st (half-tracked scout), 3rd (medium armored reconnaissance), and 5th (heavy armored) companies all reported no vehicles.
- 2nd Company (light armored reconnaissance): three *Sd.Kfz. 250* variants and five *Sd.Kfz. 251* variants.[44]

December 1944: Although stocks of armored cars and armored personnel carriers steadily increased in anticipation of the Ardennes Offensive, the reconnaissance battalion still did not have a full complement of either as of the status report stated 8 December, although manpower was at 100 percent. In detail:

- Headquarters Company: four *Sd.Kfz. 222's* of four authorized (4/4), two *Sd.Kfz. 223's* (2/2), four *Sd.Kfz. 231's* (4/13), three *Sd.Kfz. 233's* (3/3), two *Sd.Kfz. 250/2's* (2/0), three *Sd.Kfz. 250/3's* (3/0), seven *Sd.Kfz. 251/3's* (7/7), one *Sd.Kfz. 251/8* (1/0), no *Sd.Kfz. 251/5's* (0/1), and two *Sd.Kfz. 251/11's* (2/2).
- 1st Company (half-tracked armored scout): two *Sd.Kfz. 250/3's* (2/0), three *Sd.Kfz. 250/5's* (3/9), and sixteen *Sd.Kfz. 250/9's* (16/16).
- 2nd Company (light armored reconnaissance): thirteen *Sd.Kfz. 250/1's* (13/22), four *Sd.Kfz. 250/3's* (4/2), no *Sd.Kfz. 250/7's* (0/4), and no *Sd.Kfz. 250/8's* (0/2).
- 3rd Company (light armored reconnaissance): six *Sd.Kfz. 250/1's* (6/22), two *Sd.Kfz. 250/3's* (2/2), one *Sd.Kfz. 250/7* (1/4), no *Sd.Kfz. 250/8's* (0/2), two *Sd.Kfz. 251/10's* (2/0), three *Sd.Kfz. 251/1's* (3/0), and one *Sd.Kfz. 251/3* (1/0).
- 4th Company (armored heavy): two *Sd.Kfz. 251/1's* (2/2), no *Sd.Kfz. 251/2's* (0/7), two *Sd.Kfz. 251/3's* (2/2), four *Sd.Kfz. 251/4's* (4/0), five *Sd.Kfz. 251/7's* (5/7), eight *Sd.Kfz. 251/9's* (8/6), one *Sd.Kfz. 251/10* (1/0), one *Sd.Kfz. 251/11* (1/1), and one *Sd.Kfz. 251/16* (1/0).[45]

SS-Panzer-Aufklärungs-Abteilung 1 Leibstandarte SS Adolf Hitler (1. SS-Panzer-Division Leibstandarte SS Adolf Hitler)
(Arrived in Normandy starting 4 July, staying in the West until shortly after the Ardennes Offensive)

June 1944: Still basically organized as a Model 43 *Panzer* Division armored reconnaissance battalion. The battalion was at 100 percent manpower, but suffered a serious deficiency in vehicles, weaponry, and equipment.
- 1st Company (wheeled armored scout): four *Sd.Kfz. 222*'s.
- 2nd Company (half-tracked armored scout): no vehicles.
- 3rd Company (light half-tracked armored reconnaissance): vehicle count incomplete; six light machine guns.
- 4th Company ((light half-tracked armored reconnaissance): vehicle count incomplete; six light machine guns.
- 5th Company (heavy armored): vehicle count incomplete (medium half-tracks); one 15cm howitzer (towed), two light infantry guns (7.62cm) (towed) (most likely the Soviet infantry gun *7.62 cm IKH 290(r)*), three heavy antitank guns (7.5cm) (towed), and one 2cm *Flak* (towed).[46]

July 1944: The reconnaissance battalion had begun the transition to a Model 44 formation. It had 100 percent manpower but still lacked a number of vehicles:
- Headquarters (with integral wheeled armored car sections): *KStN 1109 (gp)* of 1 April 1944. The company had sixteen *Sd.Kfz. 234/2 Puma* armored cars on hand, although only ten were combat ready. The four *Sd.Kfz. 222*'s reported above were also still on hand. Two *Sd.Kfz. 232*'s were also added to the vehicle inventory lists.
- 1st Company (half-tracked armored scout): *KStN 1162c* of 1 April 1944. No vehicles or equipment on hand.
- 2nd Company (light half-tracked reconnaissance company): *KStN 1113 (gp)* of 1 April 1944. Vehicle count uncertain (although one known *Sd.Kfz. 250/7*); forty light machine guns; two heavy machine guns; one 81mm mortar.
- 3rd Company (light half-tracked reconnaissance company): *KStN 1113 (gp)* of 1 April 1944. Vehicle count uncertain (although four known *Sd.Kfz. 250/7*'s); forty light machine guns; two heavy machine guns; four 81mm mortars.
- 4th Company (heavy armored): vehicle count incomplete (medium half-tracks); three heavy antitank guns (7.5cm) (towed), and nineteen light machine guns.[47]

August 1944: At the beginning of August, the battalion had been reduced to 95.2 percent manpower. Its vehicular and weapons situation was as follows:
- Headquarters: thirteen *Sd.Kfz. 234/2 Puma* armored cars on hand, although only seven were combat ready.
- 1st Company (half-tracked armored scout): no vehicles or equipment on hand.
- 2nd Company (light half-tracked reconnaissance company): vehicle count uncertain (although four known *Sd.Kfz. 250/7*'s); two heavy machine guns and four 81mm mortar. Light machine gun count uncertain.
- 3rd Company (light half-tracked reconnaissance company): no heavy weapons reported; light machine gun count uncertain.
- 4th Company (heavy armored): no heavy weapons reported; five light machine guns on hand.[48]

September 1944: After the fighting in France, most of the division was withdrawn from the lines for battlefield reconstitution. At the beginning of September, the battalion reported having eight *Sd.Kfz. 234/2*'s on hand, with two in short-term repair (less than two weeks). The half-tracked scout company still had not been formed. There were ten *Sd.Kfz. 250* variants in the 2nd Company and eight in the 3rd, of which only eleven were combat capable. The 4th Company reported six *Sd.Kfz. 251* variants on hand.[49]

October 1944: Orders were received in order to reconstitute the division to 100 percent of its manpower and heavy weaponry authorizations. The status report dated 6 October showed three *Sd.Kfz. 234/2*'s and three *Sd.Kfz. 234/1*'s on hand; one of the armored cars was in short-term repair (less than two weeks). The half-tracked scout company still had not been formed. There were eight *Sd.Kfz. 250* variants in the 2nd Company and two in the 4th, of which two were in long-term repair (more than two weeks). The 4th Company reported seven *Sd.Kfz. 251* variants on hand.[50]

November 1944: Reconstitution efforts continued in November, with the battalion receiving additional armored cars and both light and medium half-tracks but still unable to achieve 100 percent levels. Because of projected shortfalls in *Sd.Kfz. 250* vehicles, the 3rd Company was authorized to order *Schwimmwagen* as replacements, although it is unknown whether it would then reorganize that company under a *Volkswagen* reconnaissance *KStN*. In detail:
- Headquarters: twenty-one armored cars on hand, of which eight were in short-term and two in long-term repair. The armored cars consisted of five *Sd.Kfz. 234/1*'s, three *Sd.Kfz. 234/2*'s, eight *Sd.Kfz. 234/3*'s, two *Sd.Kfz. 223*'s, and one *Sd.Kfz. 222*. In addition, the company showed three *Sd.Kfz. 251* variants on its books.
- 2nd Company: thirteen *Sd.Kfz. 250* variants, of which two were in short-term repair.
- 3rd Company: four *Sd.Kfz. 251* variants and bicycles. This was apparently an interim measure until the *Schwimmwagen* could arrive.
- 4th Company: ten *Sd.Kfz. 251* variants.[51]

Panzer-Aufklärungs-Abteilung 116 (116. Panzer-Division)
(Committed to operations in Normandy on 24 July)

July 1944: The reconnaissance battalion of the division was organized under the Model 44 template. It is not certain how many and what types of vehicles it had on hand when it started combat operations.[52]

September 1944: The division was heavily attrited in the Normandy fighting, including the reconnaissance battalion. The number of armored cars was reported as three on 14 September, with a total of sixteen *Sd.Kfz. 250* variants and fourteen *Sd.Kfz. 251* variants spread among the four line companies.[53]

October 1944: The division fought in the area around Aachen during this period, frequently committed piecemeal. The report, dated 1 October, shows a marked improvement in the status of the reconnaissance battalion, at least in terms of armored personnel carriers. Across the battalion, there was a minimum of thirty-four *Sd.Kfz. 250* variants and thirty-nine *Sd.Kfz. 251* variants.[54] During the month, *Panzer-Brigade 108* consolidated with the division, which resulted in the reconnaissance battalion's receiving more vehicles and personnel. Based on allocations of *Sd.Kfz. 251's*, it appears that the 2nd Company served as the battalion's medium armored reconnaissance company.[55]

November 1944: The division status report dated 8 November showed a much stronger reconnaissance battalion. In detail:
- Headquarters Company: nine *Sd.Kfz. 234/1's* of thirteen authorized (9/13), two *Sd.Kfz. 234/3's* (2/3), six *Sd.Kfz. 251/3's* (6/7), one *Sd.Kfz. 251/8* (1/1), and one *Sd.Kfz. 251/11* (1/1).
- 1st Company (half-tracked scout): one *Sd.Kfz. 250/1* (1/0), four *Sd.Kfz. 250/5's* (4/9), eleven *Sd.Kfz. 250/9's* (11/16), four *Sd.Kfz. 251/21's*.[56]
- 2nd Company (medium armored reconnaissance): thirteen *Sd.Kfz. 251/1's* (13/9), two *Sd.Kfz. 251/2's* (2/2), one *Sd.Kfz. 251/3* (1/2), no *Sd.Kfz. 251/9's* (0/2), and no *Sd.Kfz. 251/17's* (0/6).
- 3rd Company (light armored reconnaissance): eleven *Sd.Kfz. 250/1's* (11/22), no *Sd.Kfz. 250/2's* (0/1), no *Sd.Kfz. 250/3's* (0/2), three *Sd.Kfz. 250/7's* (3/4), no *Sd.Kfz. 250/8's* (0/1), four *Sd.Kfz. 251/1's* (4/0), and one *Sd.Kfz. 251/3* (1/0).
- 4th Company (armored heavy): six *Sd.Kfz. 251/1's* (6/6), two *Sd.Kfz. 251/2's* (2/7), one *Sd.Kfz. 251/3* (1/2), five *Sd.Kfz. 251/7's* (5/7), and six *Sd.Kfz. 251/9's* (6/6).[57]

Panzer-Aufklärungs-Abteilung 9 (9. Panzer-Division)
(Committed in Normandy starting 4 August)

August 1944: Upon transfer from the Eastern Front to France for reconstitution in April 1944, the division was ordered to convert to the Model 44 organization. In addition, the division was authorized the fully tracked version of the scout organization document (*KStN 1162 b*) for its armored scout company and was issued the *Panzer II, Ausführung L*, commonly referred to as the *Luchs*. As with the other divisions involved in the Normandy fighting, it was heavily attrited, with an effective strength of one mixed armored scout company and one light armored reconnaissance company by the end of that round of fighting.[58]

September 1944: The September 1944 unit status report shows a relatively intact reconnaissance battalion that, at least structurally, bears all the hallmarks of a Model 44 organization. While there was a considerable shortfall in wheeled scouting assets, the *Luchs* company had almost 75 percent of its authorizations. In detail:
- Headquarters Company: five *Sd.Kfz. 234/1's*, three *Sd.Kfz. 251/3's*, and three *Sd.Kfz. 250/3's*.
- 1st Company (tracked scout): eighteen *Panzer II L Luchs*.
- 2nd Company (light armored reconnaissance): twenty *Sd.Kfz. 250* variants (fourteen *Sd.Kfz. 250/1's*, two *Sd.Kfz. 250/3's*, and four *Sd.Kfz. 250/10's*).
- 3rd Company (medium armored reconnaissance): eighteen *Sd.Kfz. 251* variants (fourteen *Sd.Kfz. 251/1's*, two *Sd.Kfz. 251/3's*, and two *Sd.Kfz. 251/9's*).
- 4th Company (heavy armored): eleven *Sd.Kfz. 251* variants (four *Sd.Kfz. 251/1's*, one *Sd.Kfz. 251/3*, three *Sd.Kfz. 251/7's*, and three *Sd.Kfz. 251/9's*).[59]

October 1944: On a 15 October 1944 status report,[60] the combat vehicles of the battalion had been attrited, with the exception of the *Sd.Kfz. 250* variants, which showed a net increase of three vehicles. The wheeled armored car strength was reduced from five to two, the tracked scout vehicles from eighteen to eleven, and the overall number of *Sd.Kfz. 251* variants from twenty-one to fifteen.[61]

November 1944: The division continued to see heavy fighting in November. The reconnaissance battalion seems to have been hit hard, with efforts made to cross-level combat vehicular assets throughout the battalion, including stripping the remaining armored cars from the headquarters company and consolidating them in the *Luchs* company. In detail:
- Headquarters Company: three *Sd.Kfz. 251* variants.
- 1st Company (tracked scout): three *Sd.Kfz. 234/1's*, one *Sd.Kfz. 234/3*, six *Panzer II L Luchs*, and four *Sd.Kfz. 250* variants.
- 2nd Company (light armored reconnaissance): six *Sd.Kfz. 250* variants and seven *Sd.Kfz. 251* variants.
- 3rd Company (medium armored reconnaissance): one *Sd.Kfz. 250* variant and eight *Sd.Kfz. 251* variants.
- 4th Company (heavy armored): two *Sd.Kfz. 250* variants and five *Sd.Kfz. 251* variants.

Of the thirteen *Sd.Kfz. 250* variants on hand in the battalion, four were in short-term and one in long-term maintenance on 1 November.[62]

December 1944: The month of December was used to continue the reconstitution process for the division and prepare it for the upcoming offensive operations. During the Ardennes Offensive, however, it only fought for about a week in December and actually ended the fighting in the salient with more personnel and equipment than when it started. The overall strength of the division was not reflected in the reconnaissance battalion, which continued to be understrength. During this period, it continued to field its forces in the organization described for the previous month. In detail (14 December 1944):
- Headquarters Company: no *Sd.Kfz. 234/1's* of thirteen authorized (0/13), no *Sd.Kfz. 234/3's* (0/3), one *Sd.Kfz. 250/1* (1/0), three *Sd.Kfz. 250/3's* (3/0), two *Sd.Kfz. 251/3's* (2/7), one *Sd.Kfz. 251/8* (1/1), and no *Sd.Kfz. 251/11's* (0/2).
- 1st Company (tracked scout): no *Sd.Kfz. 250/5's* (0/9), no *Sd.Kfz. 250/9's* (0/16), three *Sd.Kfz. 234/1's* (3/0), two *Sd.Kfz. 234/3s* (2/0), three *Sd.Kfz. 250/1's* (3/0), three *Sd.Kfz. 250/3's* (3/0), one *Sd.Kfz. 251/1* (1/0) variant, six *Panzer II's*, and four French armored vehicles armed with 3.7cm main guns. (It is not known whether these were the *Luchs* variant, or what type of French tanks these were.)
- 2nd Company (light armored reconnaissance): eleven *Sd.Kfz. 250/1's* (11/22), no *Sd.Kfz. 250/2's* (0/2), no *Sd.Kfz. 250/7's* (0/4), no *Sd.Kfz. 250/8's* (0/2), four *Sd.Kfz. 251/1's* (4/0), one *Sd.Kfz. 251/2* (1/0), one *Sd.Kfz. 251/3* (1/0), and three *Sd.Kfz. 251/21's* (3/0).
- 3rd Company (medium armored reconnaissance): one *Sd.Kfz. 250/7* (1/0), eight *Sd.Kfz. 251/1's* (8/11), no *Sd.Kfz. 251/2's* (0/2), one *Sd.Kfz. 251/3* (1/2), no *Sd.Kfz. 251/9's* (0/2), no *Sd.Kfz. 251/17's* (0/6), and four *Sd.Kfz. 251/21's* (4/0).
- 4th Company (heavy armored): two *Sd.Kfz. 250/1's* (2/0), one *Sd.Kfz. 250/3* (1/0), one *Sd.Kfz. 251/1* (1/2), no *Sd.Kfz. 251/2's* (0/7), no *Sd.Kfz. 251/3's* (0/3), two *Sd.Kfz. 251/7's* (2/7), eight *Sd.Kfz. 251/9's* (8/6), and no *Sd.Kfz. 251/11* (0/1).

Of the nineteen *Sd.Kfz. 250* variants on hand in the battalion, one was in short-term and one in long-term maintenance on 1 December.[63]

CHANGES IN ORGANIZATIONAL AUTHORIZATIONS, LATE 1943–44

Headquarters, Armored Reconnaissance Battalion (1109)

KStN 1109 (gp) (1 November 1943)

The *KStN* continued the trend established with the interim document released on 16 January 1943. Newly introduced in the headquarters proper was the *Sd.Kfz. 2 Kettenkrad* for the messenger section.

- Headquarters: three motorcycles, three *Sd.Kfz. 2 Kettenkräder*, two light cross-country utility vehicles (*Volkswagen*), one light armored half-tracked radio vehicle (*Sd.Kfz. 250/3*), one medium armored radio half-tracked vehicle (*Sd.Kfz. 251/3*), one medium armored ambulance (*Sd.Kfz. 251/8*), and three light machine guns.
- Signals platoon:
  - Headquarters: one light cross-country utility vehicle (*Volkswagen*), one medium armored radio half-tracked vehicle (*Sd.Kfz. 251/3*), and one light machine gun.
  - Two medium armored telephone sections (Type 10): one medium armored wire signals vehicle (*Sd.Kfz. 251/11*).
  - One light air-ground radio section (ultra short-wave) (Type 20): one light armored half-tracked radio vehicle (*Sd.Kfz. 250/3*) and one light machine gun.
  - Five medium armored radio sections (medium wave) (Type 80): one medium armored radio half-tracked vehicle (*Sd.Kfz. 251/3*) and one light machine gun. The 1st and 2nd Sections also had a manpack radio.

KStN 1109 (fG) (Type A) (1 November 1944)

This organizational document incorporated light armored cars into the headquarters and headquarters company as part of the *freie Gliederung* concept. The *Sd.Kfz. 247* was retained for the battalion commander and an *Sd.Kfz. 223* for the headquarters commandant (company commander). Eighteen light armored cars were authorized, distributed among three platoons of two three-car sections each. The signals platoon was motorized. This is the first of several variations that will be shown.

- Headquarters: three light motorcycles, one *Sd.Kfz. 2 Kettenkrad*, and one heavy armored utility vehicle (*Sd.Kfz. 247*).
- Headquarters Company:
  - Headquarters: two light motorcycles, two light cross-country utility vehicles (*Volkswagen*), one light armored car (radio) (*Sd.Kfz. 223*), and one light machine gun.
  - 1st Platoon (signals):
    - Headquarters: one light cross-country utility vehicle (*Volkswagen*).
    - Two medium telephone sections (Type 12) (motorized): one 2-ton cross-country truck.
    - 1st and 2nd manpack radio sections (medium wave) (Type G): one 2-ton cross-country truck.
    - Three light radio sections (medium wave) (Type 80) (motorized): one 2-ton cross-country truck. A light air-ground radio section (ultra-shortwave) (Type 20) (motorized) rode with the 1st light radio section.
  - 2nd Platoon (light armored scout): two light armored radio cars (*Sd.Kfz. 223*) and four light armored scout cars (*Sd.Kfz. 222*). It was further divided into two sections, each with two 2cm main guns and three light machine guns.
  - 3rd Platoon (light armored scout): same as the 2nd Platoon.
  - 4th Platoon (light armored scout): same as the 2nd Platoon.

a) Command Group

| 3x Light Motorcycle | *Kettenkrad* | Light Utility Vehicle, Cross-Country (4 Seat) | Heavy Cross-Country Armored Utility Vehicle (*Sd.Kfz. 247*) |

Total Command Group: 4x Officers, 3x NCOs, 9x Enlisted Personnel; 8x Rifles, 4x Pistols, 4x Submachine Guns; 3x Motorcycles, 1x *Kettenkrad*, 1x Light Utility Vehicle, 1x Heavy Armored Cross-Country Utility Vehicle

b) Headquarters Company (Type A with 3 Light Armored Scout Platoons)
a) Command Section

| 2x Light Motorcycles 125cc | 2x Light Utility Vehicle, Cross-Country (4 Seat) | Light Armored Car (Radio) (*Sd.Kfz. 223 (Fu)*) |

Total Command Group: 1x Officer, 5x NCOs, 5x Enlisted Personnel; 4x Rifles, 5x Pistols, 2x Submachine Guns, 1x Light MG; 2x Motorcycles, 2x Light Utility Vehicles, 1x Light Armored Car (Radio)

b) 1st Platoon (Signals)

Light Utility Vehicle, Cross-Country (4 Seat)

1st Medium Field Wire Section 12 (Motorized)	**2nd Medium Field Wire Section 12 (Motorized)**	**1st and 2nd Backpack Radio Section g Medium Wave (Motorized)**
Truck, 2 ton, Open Cargo Area, Cross-Country	Truck, 2 ton, Open Cargo Area, Cross-Country	Truck, 2 ton, Open Cargo Area, Cross-Country
1st Light Radio Section 80 Medium Wave (Motorized)	**2nd Light Radio Section 80 Medium Wave (Motorized)**	**3rd Light Radio Section 80 Medium Wave (Motorized)**
Truck, 2 ton, Open Cargo Area, Cross-Country	Truck, 2 ton, Open Cargo Area, Cross-Country	Truck, 2 ton, Open Cargo Area, Cross-Country

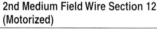

Light Air-Ground Radio Section 20   Shortwave (Motorized)**

Total Signals Platoon: 1x Officer, 8x NCOs, 26x Enlisted Personnel; 34x Rifles, 1x Submachine Gun; 1x Light Utility Vehicle, 6x Trucks

Notes: * *Sd.Kfz. 260* counts in lieu of truck. ** Loaded with 1st Light Radio Section 80 Medium Wave (Motorized)

c) 2nd Platoon (Light Armored Car)

4x Light Armored Car (2cm) (*Sd.Kfz. 222*) and 2x Light Armored Car (Radio) (*Sd.Kfz. 223 (Fu)*)

Total 2nd Platoon: 1x Officer, 5x NCOs, 12x Enlisted Personnel; 11x Pistols, 7x Submachine Guns, 6x Light MG's, 4x Main Guns; 6x Light Armored Cars

d) 3rd Platoon (Light Armored Car), same as 2nd Platoon (Except NCO Platoon Leader)

4x Light Armored Car (2cm) (*Sd.Kfz. 222*) and 2x Light Armored Car (Radio) (*Sd.Kfz. 223 (Fu)*)

Total 3rd Platoon: 6x NCOs, 12x Enlisted Personnel; 11x Pistols, 7x Submachine Guns, 6x Light MG's, 4x Main Guns; 6x Light Armored Cars

e) 4th Platoon (Light Armored Car), same as 2nd Platoon (Except NCO Platoon Leader)

4x Light Armored Car (2cm) (*Sd.Kfz. 222*) and 2x Light Armored Car (Radio) (*Sd.Kfz. 223 (Fu)*)

Total 4th Platoon: 6x NCOs, 12x Enlisted Personnel; 11x Pistols, 7x Submachine Guns, 6x Light MG's, 4x Main Guns; 6x Light Armored Cars

Total Type A Headquarters Company: 7x Officers, 33x NCOs, 76x Enlisted Personnel; 46x Rifles, 42x Pistols, 28x Submachine Guns, 19x Light MG's, 12x Main Guns; 5x Motorcycles, 1x *Kettenkrad*, 5x Utility Vehicles, 6x Trucks, 20x Armored Cars

KStN 1109 (fG) (Type B) (1 November 1944)

This organizational document also incorporated armored cars into the headquarters and headquarters company as part of the *freie Gliederung* concept. This variation substituted the eighteen light armored cars for fourteen heavy armored cars (plus an additional one in the company headquarters section). The armored cars were divided into two platoons of four and three sections, which were identically organized with two heavy armored cars each. The signals platoon remained motorized.

- Headquarters: three light motorcycles, one *Sd.Kfz. 2 Kettenkrad*, and one heavy armored utility vehicle (*Sd.Kfz. 247*).
- Headquarters Company:
  - Headquarters: two light motorcycles, two light cross-country utility vehicles (*Volkswagen*), one heavy armored car (*Sd.Kfz. 234/1*), one 2cm main gun, and one light machine gun.
  - 1st Platoon (signals):
    - Headquarters: one light cross-country utility vehicle (*Volkswagen*).
    - Two medium telephone sections (Type 12) (motorized): one 2-ton cross-country truck.
    - 1st and 2nd manpack radio sections (medium wave) (Type G): one 2-ton cross-country truck.
    - Three light radio sections (medium wave) (Type 80) (motorized): one 2-ton cross-country truck. A light air-ground radio section (ultra-shortwave) (Type 20) (motorized) rode with the 1st light radio section.
  - 2nd Platoon (heavy armored scout):
    - 1st Armored scout section: one heavy armored car (2cm) (*Sd.Kfz. 234/1*), one heavy armored car (7.5cm) (*Sd.Kfz. 234/3*), two light machine guns, one 2cm main gun, and one 7.5cm main gun.
    - 2nd Armored scout section: same as the 1st Section.
    - 3rd Armored scout section: same as the 1st Section.
    - 4th Armored scout section: same as the 1st Section.
  - 3rd Platoon (heavy armored scout):
    - 5th Armored scout section: one heavy armored car (2cm) (*Sd.Kfz. 234/1*), one heavy armored car (7.5cm) (*Sd.Kfz. 234/3*), two light machine guns, one 2cm main gun, and one 7.5cm main gun.
    - 6th Armored scout section: same as the 5th Section.
    - 7th Armored scout section: same as the 6th Section.

Under this organization, the *Sd.Kfz. 232* was authorized as a substitute, but was only supposed to be used to form sections with the same vehicles.

b) Headquarters Company (Type B with 2 Heavy Armored Scout Platoons)
a) Command Section

| 2x Light Motorcycle 125cc | 2x Light Utility Vehicle, Cross-Country (4 Seat) | Heavy Armored Car (*Sd.Kfz. 234/1*) |

Total Command Group: 1x Officer, 5x NCOs, 5x Enlisted Personnel; 4x Rifles, 5x Pistols, 2x Submachine Guns, 1x Light MG, 1x Main Gun; 2x Motorcycles, 2x Light Utility Vehicles, 1x Heavy Armored Car

b) 1st Platoon (Signals) (No change from Type A Headquarters Company)

Total Signals Platoon: 1x Officer, 8x NCOs, 26x Enlisted Personnel; 34x Rifles, 1x Submachine Gun; 1x Light Utility Vehicle, 6x Trucks

c) 2nd Platoon (Heavy Armored Car)
1st Armored Scout Section

| Heavy Armored Car (2cm) (*Sd.Kfz. 234/1*) | Heavy Armored Car (7.5cm) (*Sd.Kfz. 234/3*) |

2nd Armored Scout Section (Same as 1st Section except Platoon Leader is NCO)

| Heavy Armored Car (2cm) (*Sd.Kfz. 234/1*) | Heavy Armored Car (7.5cm) (*Sd.Kfz. 234/3*) |

3rd Armored Scout Section (Same as 1st Section except Platoon Leader is NCO)

Heavy Armored Car (2cm) (*Sd.Kfz. 234/1*)

Heavy Armored Car (7.5cm) (*Sd.Kfz. 234/3*)

4th Armored Scout Section (Same as 1st Section except Platoon Leader is NCO)

Heavy Armored Car (2cm) (*Sd.Kfz. 234/1*)

Heavy Armored Car (7.5cm) (*Sd.Kfz. 234/3*)

Total 2nd Platoon: 1x Officer, 11x NCOs, 20x Enlisted Personnel; 20x Pistols, 12x Submachine Guns, 8x Light MG's, 8x Main Guns; 8x Heavy Armored Cars

c) 3rd Platoon (Heavy Armored Car)
5th Armored Scout Section

Heavy Armored Car (2cm) (*Sd.Kfz. 234/1*)

Heavy Armored Car (7.5cm) (*Sd.Kfz. 234/3*)

6th Armored Scout Section (Same as 5th Section)

Heavy Armored Car (2cm) (*Sd.Kfz. 234/1*)

Heavy Armored Car (7.5cm) (*Sd.Kfz. 234/3*)

7th Armored Scout Section (Same as 5th Section)

Heavy Armored Car (2cm) (*Sd.Kfz. 234/1*)

Heavy Armored Car (7.5cm) (*Sd.Kfz. 234/3*)

Total 3rd Platoon: 9x NCOs, 15x Enlisted Personnel; 15x Pistols, 9x Submachine Guns, 6x Light MG's, 6x Main Guns; 6x Heavy Armored Cars

KStN 1109 (gp) (fG) (1 November 1944)

The primary difference between this organization and that of the one above is that the signals platoon had armored personnel carriers instead of trucks.

- Headquarters: four *Sd.Kfz. 2 Kettenkräder*, one light cross-country utility vehicle (*Volkswagen*), two medium armored radio personnel carriers (*Sd.Kfz. 251/3*), one medium armored ambulance (*Sd.Kfz. 251/8*), and two light machine guns.
- Headquarters Company:
  - Headquarters: two *Sd.Kfz. 2 Kettenkräder*, two light cross-country utility vehicles (*Volkswagen*), one heavy armored car (*Sd.Kfz. 234/1*), one 2cm main gun, and one light machine gun.
  - 1st Platoon (signals):
    - Headquarters: one light cross-country utility vehicle (*Volkswagen*), one medium armored radio personnel carrier (*Sd.Kfz. 251/3*), and one light machine gun.
    - Two medium telephone sections (Type 12) (armored): one medium armored cable vehicle (*Sd.Kfz. 251/11*) and one light machine gun.
    - Four medium radio sections (medium wave) (Type 80) (armored): one medium armored radio half-tracked vehicle (*Sd.Kfz. 251/3*) and one light machine gun.
  - 2nd Platoon (heavy armored scout):
    - 1st Armored scout section: one heavy armored car (2cm) (*Sd.Kfz. 234/1*), one heavy armored car (7.5cm) (*Sd.Kfz. 234/3*), two light machine guns, one 2cm main gun, and one 7.5cm main gun.
    - 2nd Armored scout section: same as the 1st Section.
    - 3rd Armored scout section: same as the 1st Section.
    - 4th Armored scout section: same as the 1st Section.
  - 3rd Platoon (heavy armored scout):
    - 5th Armored scout section: one heavy armored car (2cm) (*Sd.Kfz. 234/1*), one heavy armored car (7.5cm) (*Sd.Kfz. 234/3*), two light machine guns, one 2cm main gun, and one 7.5cm main gun.
    - 6th Armored scout section: same as the 5th Section.
    - 7th Armored scout section: same as the 5th Section.

Under this organization, the *Sd.Kfz. 231, 232,* and *233* were authorized as substitutes.

a) Headquarters

4x Motorcycle Messenger (*Kettenkrad*) (*Sd.Kfz. 2*), 4x Rifles

| Light Utility Vehicle, Cross-Country (4 seat) | Medium Armored Radio Half-track (*Sd.Kfz. 251/3*), 1x Submachine Gun, 1x Light MG | Medium Armored Radio Half-track (*Sd.Kfz. 251/3*), 1x Submachine Gun, 1x Light MG | Medium Tracked Armored Ambulance (*Sd.Kfz. 251/8*), 1x Submachine Gun |

b) Headquarters Company
a) Command Group

| 2x Light Utility Vehicle, Cross-Country (4 seat) | 2x *Kettenkrad* (*Sd.Kfz. 2*) | Heavy Armored Car (2cm) (*Sd.Kfz. 234/1*) |

Totals: 1x Officer, 5x NCOs, 5x Enlisted Personnel; 4x Rifles, 4x Pistols, 3x Submachine Guns, 1x Light MG, 1x Main Gun; 2x Wheeled Vehicles, 1x Armored Vehicle, 2x *Kettenkräder*

b) 1st Platoon (Signals)

| Light Utility Vehicle, Cross-Country (4 seat) | Medium Armored Radio Half-track (*Sd.Kfz. 251/3*), 1x Submachine Gun, 1x Light MG |

1st Medium Wire Section 10 (Armored)   **2nd Medium Wire Section 10 (Armored)**

| Medium Armored Signals Vehicle (Landline) (*Sd.Kfz. 251/11*), 1x Submachine Gun, 1x Light MG | Medium Armored Signals Vehicle (Landline) (*Sd.Kfz. 251/11*), 1x Submachine Gun, 1x Light MG |

| 1st Medium Radio Section 80 Medium Wave (Armored) | 2nd Medium Radio Section 80 Medium Wave (Armored) | 3rd Medium Radio Section 80 Medium Wave (Armored) | 4th Medium Radio Section 80 Medium Wave (Armored) |

Light Armored Reconnaissance Company

KStN 1113 (gp)

This organization, as updated on 12 July 1944, authorized a slight increase in armored personnel carriers, with one *Sd.Kfz. 250/1* in the headquarters earmarked for ammunition and the *Sd.Kfz. 250/8*'s replacing the *Sd.Kfz. 250/10*'s.

- Company headquarters: two motorcycles, two *Sd.Kfz. 2 Kettenkräder*, one light armored personnel carrier (*Sd.Kfz. 250/1*), two light armored radio carriers (*Sd.Kfz. 250/3*), and three light machine guns.
- Three reconnaissance platoons:
  - Headquarters: one light armored personnel carrier (*Sd.Kfz. 250/1*), one light armored personnel carrier (7.5cm) (*Sd.Kfz. 250/8*), one light machine gun, and one 7.5cm main gun.
  - Company 3 reconnaissance squads: two light armored personnel carriers (*Sd.Kfz. 250/1*), one reconnaissance squad, and four light machine guns.
- Company 1 mortar section: four light armored personnel carriers (Model 34 8cm mortar) (*Sd.Kfz. 250/7*) (two with mortars, one for the section leader, one for ammunition), one light machine gun, and two 8cm mortars.

396 TIP OF THE SPEAR

a) Command Group
Company Headquarters Section

2x Light Motorcycle, 2x *Kettenkrad*; Light Utility Vehicle, Cross-Country (4 seat); 1x Light Armored Radio Half-track (*Sd.Kfz. 250/1*) for Transporting Ammunition, 1x Light MG, 1x Submachine Gun; 2x Light Armored Radio Half-track (*Sd.Kfz. 250/3*), 2x Light MG, 2x Submachine Gun

Totals: 1x Officer, 5x NCOs, 11x Enlisted Personnel; 14x Rifles, 1x Pistol, 5x Submachine Guns, 3x Light MG's; 3x Motorcycles, 2x *Kettenkräder*, 1x Light Utility Vehicle, 3x Armored Half-tracks

b) 1st Platoon
Platoon Headquarters Section

Light Armored Personnel Carrier (*Sd.Kfz. 250/1*), 1x Light MG, 1x Submachine Gun   Light Armored Personnel Carrier (7.5cm Cannon) (*Sd.Kfz. 250/8*), 1x Submachine Gun, 1x Light MG

Totals: 1x Officer, 3x NCOs, 4x Enlisted Personnel; 3x Rifles, 4x Pistols, 3x Submachine Guns, 2x Light MG's

1st Squad   **2nd Squad**   **3rd Squad**

2x Light Armored Personnel Carrier (*Sd.Kfz. 250/1*), 4x Light MG   2x Light Armored Personnel Carrier (*Sd.Kfz. 250/1*), 4x Light MG   2x Light Armored Personnel Carrier (*Sd.Kfz. 250/1*), 4x Light MG

Totals for 1st Platoon: 1x Officer, 9x NCOs, 34x Enlisted Personnel; 24x Rifles, 16x Pistols, 12x Submachine Guns, 14x Light MG's, 1x 7.5cm Gun; 8x Armored Vehicles

c) 2nd Platoon
Platoon Headquarters Section

Light Armored Personnel Carrier (*Sd.Kfz. 250/1*), 1x Light MG, 1x Submachine Gun   Light Armored Personnel Carrier (7.5cm Cannon) (*Sd.Kfz. 250/8*), 1x Submachine Gun, 1x Light MG

Totals: 1x Officer, 3x NCOs, 4x Enlisted Personnel; 3x Rifles, 4x Pistols, 3x Submachine Guns, 2x Light MG's

1st Squad   **2nd Squad**   **3rd Squad**

2x Light Armored Personnel Carrier (*Sd.Kfz. 250/1*), 4x Light MG   2x Light Armored Personnel Carrier (*Sd.Kfz. 250/1*), 4x Light MG   2x Light Armored Personnel Carrier (*Sd.Kfz. 250/1*), 4x Light MG

Totals for 2nd Platoon: 1x Officer, 9x NCOs, 34x Enlisted Personnel; 24x Rifles, 16x Pistols, 12x Submachine Guns, 14x Light MG's, 1x 7.5cm Gun; 8x Armored Vehicles

d) 3rd Platoon
Platoon Headquarters Section

Light Armored Personnel Carrier (*Sd.Kfz. 250/1*), 1x Light MG, 1x Submachine Gun   Light Armored Personnel Carrier (7.5cm Cannon) (*Sd.Kfz. 250/8*), 1x Submachine Gun, 1x Light MG

Totals: 1x Officer, 3x NCOs, 4x Enlisted Personnel; 3x Rifles, 4x Pistols, 3x Submachine Guns, 2x Light MG's

THE END IN THE WEST

1st Squad	2nd Squad	3rd Squad

2x Light Armored Personnel Carrier (*Sd.Kfz. 250/1*), 4x Light MG	2x Light Armored Personnel Carrier (*Sd.Kfz. 250/1*), 4x Light MG	2x Light Armored Personnel Carrier (*Sd.Kfz. 250/1*), 4x Light MG

Totals for 3rd Platoon: 10x NCOs, 34x Enlisted Personnel; 24x Rifles, 16x Pistols, 12x Submachine Guns, 14x Light MG's, 1x 7.5cm Gun; 8x Armored Vehicles

e) Mortar Section

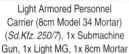

Light Armored Personnel Carrier (8cm Model 34 Mortar) (*Sd.Kfz. 250/7*), 1x Submachine Gun, 1x Light MG, 1x 8cm Mortar	Light Armored Personnel Carrier (Ammunition Carrier) (*Sd.Kfz. 250/7*), 1x Submachine Gun, 1x Light MG	Light Armored Personnel Carrier (8cm Model 34 Mortar) (*Sd.Kfz. 250/7*), 1x Submachine Gun, 1x Light MG, 1x 8cm Mortar	Light Armored Personnel Carrier (Ammunition Carrier) (*Sd.Kfz. 250/7*), 1x Submachine Gun, 1x Light MG

Totals for Mortar Section: 3x NCOs, 15x Enlisted Personnel; 8x Rifles, 9x Pistols, 5x Submachine Guns, 4x Light MG's, 2x 8cm Model 34 Mortars; 4x Armored Half-tracks

f) Vehicle Maintenance Section

Truck, 2 ton, Canvas Top, Cross-Country (Set up for Vehicle Maintenance Section)	Truck, 3 ton, Canvas Top, Cross-Country, for Vehicle Maintenance Section	Truck, 3 ton, Canvas Top, Cross-Country, for Maintenance Equipment (Set up for Vehicle Maintenance Section)	Light Prime Mover, 3 ton (*Sd.Kfz. 11*)

Totals for Vehicle Maintenance Section: 4x NCOs, 8x Enlisted Personnel; 12x Rifles, 1x Pistol; 3x Trucks, 1x Half-track Prime Mover

g) Combat Trains

Light Utility Vehicle, Cross-Country (4 seat)	Truck, 3 ton, Canvas Top, Cross-Country, for Petroleum, Oil & Lubricants	Truck, 3 ton, Canvas Top, Cross-Country, for Ammunition	Truck, 3 ton, Canvas Top, Cross-Country, for Large Field Mess Stove

Totals for Combat Trains: 4x NCOs, 9x Enlisted Personnel; 11x Rifles, 1x Pistol, 1x Submachine Gun; 4x Wheeled Vehicles

Summary

	Officers	NCOs	Enlisted Personnel	Rifles	Pistols	Submachine Guns	Light MG's	Main Guns	Vehicles	Armored Vehicles	Motorcycles (*Kettenkräder*)
Command Group	1	5	11	14	1	5	3		1	3	2 (2)
1st Platoon	1	9	34	24	16	12	14	1		8	
2nd Platoon	1	9	34	24	16	12	14	1		8	
3rd Platoon		10	34	24	16	12	14	1		8	
Mortar Section		3	15	8	9	5	4	2		4	
Vehicle Maintenance Section		4	9	12	1				4		
Combat Trains		4	9	11	1	1			4		
Baggage Trains		1	3	4					1		
Totals	3	45	149	121	60	47	49	5	10	31	2 (2)

KStN 1113 (gp) (fG)

In this organization, introduced on 1 November 1944, vehicular allocations for the company headquarters were reduced somewhat and one *Sd.Kfz. 250/1* was eliminated. The *Sd.Kfz. 250/8*'s previously authorized for each of the reconnaissance platoons were consolidated into a cannon section and reduced by one (from three to two).

- Company headquarters: three *Sd.Kfz. 2 Kettenkrad*, two light cross-country utility vehicles (*Volkswagen*), two light armored radio carriers (*Sd.Kfz. 250/3*), and two light machine guns.
- Three reconnaissance platoons:
  - Headquarters: one light armored personnel carrier (*Sd.Kfz. 250/1*) and one light machine gun.
  - Three reconnaissance squads: two light armored personnel carriers (*Sd.Kfz. 250/1*), one reconnaissance squad, and four light machine guns.
- One mortar section: four light armored personnel carriers (Model 34 8cm mortar) (*Sd.Kfz. 250/7*) (two with mortars, one for the section leader, one for ammunition), one light machine gun, and two 8cm mortars.
- One cannon section: one light armored personnel carrier (*Sd.Kfz. 250/1*), two light armored personnel carriers (7.5cm main gun) (*Sd.Kfz. 250/8*), one light machine gun, and two 7.5cm main guns.

a) Command Group

2x Light Utility Vehicle, Cross-Country (4 seat)   3x *Kettenkrad* (*Sd.Kfz. 2*)   2x Light Armored Radio Car (*Sd.Kfz. 250/3*), 1x Submachine Gun, 1x Light MG

Totals: 1x Officer, 7x NCOs, 9x Enlisted Personnel; 9x Rifles, 2x Pistols, 6x Submachine Guns, 2x Light MG's; 3x *Kettenkräder*, 2x Wheeled Vehicles, 2x Armored Vehicles

b) 1st Platoon   Platoon Headquarters Section

Light Armored Personnel Carrier (*Sd.Kfz. 250/1*), 1x Light MG, 1x Submachine Gun

1st Squad **2nd Squad** **3rd Squad**

2x Light Armored Personnel Carrier (*Sd.Kfz. 250/1*), 1x Light MG, 1x Submachine Gun, 2x Light MG   2x Light Armored Personnel Carrier (*Sd.Kfz. 250/1*), 1x Light MG, 1x Submachine Gun, 2x Light MG   2x Light Armored Personnel Carrier (*Sd.Kfz. 250/1*), 1x Light MG, 1x Submachine Gun, 2x Light MG

Totals: 1x Officer, 8x NCOs, 32x Enlisted Personnel; 22x Rifles, 7x Pistols, 12x Submachine Guns, 13x Light MG's; 7x Armored Vehicles

c) 2nd Platoon   Platoon Headquarters Section

Light Armored Personnel Carrier (*Sd.Kfz. 250/1*), 1x Light MG, 1x Submachine Gun

1st Squad **2nd Squad** **3rd Squad**

2x Light Armored Personnel Carrier (*Sd.Kfz. 250/1*), 1x Light MG, 1x Submachine Gun, 2x Light MG   2x Light Armored Personnel Carrier (*Sd.Kfz. 250/1*), 1x Light MG, 1x Submachine Gun, 2x Light MG   2x Light Armored Personnel Carrier (*Sd.Kfz. 250/1*), 1x Light MG, 1x Submachine Gun, 2x Light MG

Totals: 9x NCOs, 32x Enlisted Personnel; 22x Rifles, 7x Pistols, 12x Submachine Guns, 13x Light MG's; 7x Armored Vehicles

d) 3rd Platoon   Platoon Headquarters Section

Light Armored Personnel Carrier (*Sd.Kfz. 250/1*), 1x Light MG, 1x Submachine Gun

1st Squad	2nd Squad	3rd Squad

2x Light Armored Personnel Carrier (*Sd.Kfz. 250/1*), 1x Light MG, 1x Submachine Gun, 2x Light MG	2x Light Armored Personnel Carrier (*Sd.Kfz. 250/1*), 1x Light MG, 1x Submachine Gun, 2x Light MG	2x Light Armored Personnel Carrier (*Sd.Kfz. 250/1*), 1x Light MG, 1x Submachine Gun, 2x Light MG

Totals: 9x NCOs, 32x Enlisted Personnel; 22x Rifles, 7x Pistols, 12x Submachine Guns, 13x Light MG's; 7x Armored Vehicles

e) Mortar Section

Light Armored Personnel Carrier (*Sd.Kfz. 250/1*) for the Squad Leader and Ammunition, 1x Light MG, 1x Submachine Gun	Light Armored Personnel Carrier (Heavy Mortar) (*Sd.Kfz. 250/7*), 1x Submachine Gun	Light Armored Personnel Carrier (Heavy Mortar) (*Sd.Kfz. 250/7*), 1x Submachine Gun	Light Armored Personnel Carrier (Heavy Mortar) (*Sd.Kfz. 250/7*) for Ammunition, 1x Submachine Gun

Totals: 4x NCOs, 13x Enlisted Personnel; 4x Rifles, 8x Pistols, 5x Submachine Guns, 1x Light MG, 2x Model 34 Mortars; 4x Armored Vehicles

f) Cannon Section

Light Armored Personnel Carrier (7.5cm) (*Sd.Kfz. 250/8*), 1x Submachine Gun	Light Armored Personnel Carrier (7.5cm) (*Sd.Kfz. 250/8*), 1x Submachine Gun	Light Armored Personnel Carrier (*Sd.Kfz. 250/1*) for the Squad Leader and Ammunition, 1x Light MG, 1x Submachine Gun

Totals: 2x NCOs, 7x Enlisted Personnel; 2x Rifles, 2x Pistols, 5x Submachine Guns, 1x Light MG's; 3x Armored Vehicles

Summary

	Officers	NCOs	Enlisted Personnel	Rifles	Pistols (Submachine Guns)	Light MG's	Unlimbered Guns and Mortars	Kettenkräder	Utility Vehicles	Armored Vehicles
Command Section	1	7	9	9	2 (6)	2		3	2	2
1st Platoon	1	8	32	22	7 (12)	13				7
2nd Platoon	1	8	32	22	7 (12)	13				7
3rd Platoon		9	32	22	7 (12)	13				7
Mortar Section		4	13	4	8 (5)	1	2			4
Cannon Section		2	7	2	2 (5)	1	2			3
Totals	3	38	125	81	33 (52)	43	4	3	2	30

KStN 1113 (VW)

This organization was introduced on 1 November 1943 and modified in accordance with directives dated 7 June 1944.

- Company headquarters:
  - Headquarters section: three motorcycles and three light cross-country utility vehicles (*Volkswagen*).
  - Manpack radio section (Type G) (medium wave): one light cross-country utility vehicle (*Volkswagen*).
- Three reconnaissance platoons:
  - Headquarters: one motorcycle and two light cross-country utility vehicles (*Volkswagen*).
  - Three reconnaissance squads: four light cross-country utility vehicles (*Volkswagen*) and two light machine guns.
- 4th Platoon (heavy):
  - Headquarters: three light cross-country utility vehicles (*Volkswagen*).
  - 1st Section (heavy machine gun): seven light cross-country utility vehicles (*Volkswagen*) and two heavy machine guns.
  - 2nd Section (heavy machine gun): seven light cross-country utility vehicles (*Volkswagen*) and two heavy machine guns.
  - 3rd Section (heavy mortar): two 2-ton cross-country trucks and two 8cm mortars.

KStN 1113 (VW) (fG)

This organization, introduced on 1 November 1944, reduced the overall number of light utility vehicles in the line platoons and essentially halved the number of light machine guns and heavy machine guns, with authorizations for only nine light machine guns.

- Company headquarters:
  - Headquarters section: three motorcycles and three light cross-country utility vehicles (*Volkswagen*).
  - Manpack radio section (Type G) (medium wave): one light cross-country utility vehicle (*Volkswagen*).
- Three reconnaissance platoons:
  - Headquarters: one motorcycle and two light cross-country utility vehicles (*Volkswagen*).
  - Three reconnaissance squads: three light cross-country utility vehicles (*Volkswagen*) and one light machine gun.
- 4th Platoon (heavy):
  - Headquarters: two light cross-country utility vehicles (*Volkswagen*).
  - 1st Section (heavy machine gun): six light cross-country utility vehicles (*Volkswagen*) and two heavy machine guns.
  - 2nd Section (light radio section) (Type 30) (medium wave): five light cross-country utility vehicles (*Volkswagen*). (Based on an undated handwritten entry on the *KStN*, the 2nd heavy machine-gun section was deleted and replaced by this.)
  - 3rd Section (heavy mortar): two 2-ton cross-country trucks and two 8cm mortars.

THE END IN THE WEST 401

a) **Command Group**
Company Headquarters Section

Backpack Radio Section g
Medium Wave (Motorized)

3x Light Motorcycle and 3x Light Cross-Country Vehicle (*Kfz. 1*)   Light Cross-Country Vehicle (*Kfz. 1*)

Totals: 1x Officer, 6x NCOs, 10x Enlisted Personnel; 12x Rifles, 3x Pistols, 2x Submachine Guns; 3x Motorcycles, 4x Wheeled Vehicles

b) **1st Platoon**
Platoon Headquarters Section

2x Light Utility Vehicle, Cross-Country (4 seat)

1st Squad	2nd Squad	3rd Squad

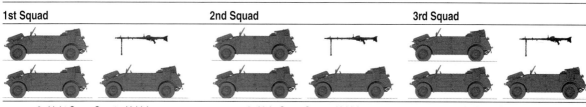

3x Light Cross-Country Vehicle (*Kfz. 1*), 1x Light MG	3x Light Cross-Country Vehicle (*Kfz. 1*), 1x Light MG	3x Light Cross-Country Vehicle (*Kfz. 1*), 1x Light MG

Totals: 1x Officer, 4x NCOs, 35x Enlisted Personnel; 32x Rifles, 4x Pistols, 4x Submachine Guns, 3x Light MG's; 11x Vehicles

c) **2nd Platoon**
Platoon Headquarters Section

2x Light Utility Vehicle, Cross-Country (4 seat)

1st Squad	2nd Squad	3rd Squad

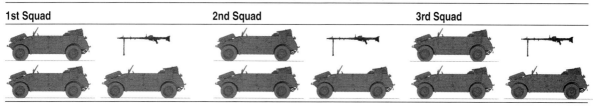

3x Light Cross-Country Vehicle (*Kfz. 1*), 1x Light MG	3x Light Cross-Country Vehicle (*Kfz. 1*), 1x Light MG	3x Light Cross-Country Vehicle (*Kfz. 1*), 1x Light MG

Totals: 5x NCOs, 35x Enlisted Personnel; 32x Rifles, 4x Pistols, 4x Submachine Guns, 3x Light MG's; 11x Vehicles

d) **3rd Platoon**
Platoon Headquarters Section

2x Light Utility Vehicle, Cross-Country (4 seat)

1st Squad	2nd Squad	3rd Squad

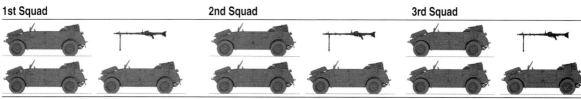

3x Light Cross-Country Vehicle (*Kfz. 1*), 1x Light MG	3x Light Cross-Country Vehicle (*Kfz. 1*), 1x Light MG	3x Light Cross-Country Vehicle (*Kfz. 1*), 1x Light MG

Totals: 5x NCOs, 35x Enlisted Personnel; 32x Rifles, 4x Pistols, 4x Submachine Guns, 3x Light MG's; 11x Vehicles

Summary

	Officers	NCOs	Enlisted Personnel	Rifles (AT Rifles)	Pistols (Submachine Guns)	Heavy MG's (Light MG's)	Heavy Mortars	Wheeled Vehicles (Trucks)	Motorcycles
Command Section	1	6	10	12	3 (2)			4	3
1st Platoon	1	4	35	29 (3)	4 (4)	(3)		11	
2nd Platoon		5	35	29 (3)	4 (4)	(3)		11	
3rd Platoon		5	35	29 (3)	4 (4)	(3)		11	
4th (Heavy) Platoon	1	10	49	34	20 (6)	4	2	14 (2)	
Totals	3	30	164	133 (9)	35 (20)	4 (9)	2	51 (2)	3

KStN 1114C (gp) (fG)

This version of the armored reconnaissance company, which essentially gave the battalion a mechanized infantry company, was only implemented in a few battalions. In comparison to the light armored reconnaissance company, it had substantially fewer light machine guns (thirty versus forty-three) and fewer armored personnel carriers (twenty-three versus thirty). In some respects, it had more assets—twenty-four more personnel, three heavy machine guns, and six 2cm *Flak* (*Sd.Kfz. 251/17*)—but both companies represented roughly equivalent capabilities.

- Company headquarters: three *Sd.Kfz. 2 Kettenkräder*, two light cross-country utility vehicles (*Volkswagen*), two medium armored radio carriers (*Sd.Kfz. 251/3*), and two light machine guns.
- Three reconnaissance platoons:
  - Headquarters: one medium armored personnel carrier (2cm) (*Sd.Kfz. 250/17*) and one 2cm *Flak*.
  - Three reconnaissance squads: one medium armored personnel carrier (*Sd.Kfz. 251/1*), one reconnaissance squad, and three light machine guns.
- One heavy platoon:
  - Platoon headquarters: one *Sd.Kfz. 2 Kettenkrad*, one medium armored personnel carrier (*Sd.Kfz. 251/1*), and one light machine gun.
  - 1st Section (antiaircraft and heavy machine gun): three medium armored personnel carriers (2cm) (*Sd.Kfz. 250/17*), three heavy machine guns, and three 2cm *Flak*.
  - 2nd Section (mortar): two medium armored personnel carriers (8cm mortar) (*Sd.Kfz. 251/2*) and two medium 8cm mortars.
  - 3rd Section (cannon): two medium armored personnel carriers (7.5cm) (*Sd.Kfz. 251/9*) and two 7.5cm main guns.

Sub-elements of a Heavy Company Armored Combat Engineer Platoon

KStN 1124A (gp)

In this organization, dated 1 November 1944, the combat engineers all have armored personnel carriers.

- Platoon headquarters: one *Sd.Kfz. 2 Kettenkrad*, one medium armored combat engineer vehicle (*Sd.Kfz. 251/7*), and one light machine gun.
- Three combat engineer squads: two medium armored combat engineer vehicles (*Sd.Kfz. 251/7*) and four light machine guns.
- Equipment section: one 3-ton cross-country, open bay cargo truck.

The *freie Gliederung* version of the document is essentially the same, except that there is no equipment section.

KStN 1124A (mot)

This organization, dated 1 November 1944, was for motorized combat engineers in an armored reconnaissance battalion. It has one more engineer squad, but no armored vehicles and considerably less firepower.

- Platoon headquarters: one sidecar motorcycle and one light cross-country utility vehicle (*Volkswagen*).

- Four combat engineer squads: one 2-ton cross-country, open bay cargo truck and one light machine gun.
- Equipment section: one 3-ton cross-country, open bay cargo truck.

Armored Gun Platoon

KStN 1125 (7.5cm) (gp)

Initially dated 1 November 1943 and then updated by hand to 7 June 1944, the cannon platoon had significant firepower, fielding six 7.5cm main guns, albeit they were only 24-caliber guns.
- Platoon headquarters: one medium armored radio carrier (*Sd.Kfz. 251/3*) and one light machine gun.
- Gun section: six medium armored personnel carriers (7.5cm) (*Sd.Kfz. 251/9*), six 7.5cm main guns, and six light machine guns.
- Ammunition section: one 3-ton cross-country, open bay cargo truck (ammunition), one medium armored personnel carrier (ammunition) (*Sd.Kfz. 251/1*), and one light machine gun.

KStN 1125 (7.5cm) (gp) (fG)

The *freie Gliederung* version of the document eliminated the 3-ton cargo truck used for hauling ammunition and also deleted the authorizations for light machine guns for the cannon vehicles.
- Platoon headquarters: one medium armored radio carrier (*Sd.Kfz. 251/3*) and one light machine gun.
- Gun section: six medium armored personnel carriers (7.5cm) (*Sd.Kfz. 251/9*) and six 7.5cm main guns.
- Ammunition section: one medium armored personnel carrier (ammunition) (*Sd.Kfz. 251/1*) and one light machine gun.

Armored Mortar Platoon

KStN 1126A (8cm) (mot)

Originally released on March 1944, the platoon called for six 8cm mortars transported by cargo trucks.
- Platoon headquarters: one sidecar motorcycle and one light cross-country utility vehicle (*Volkswagen*).
- Three gun sections: two 2-ton cross-country, open bay cargo trucks and two 8cm Model 34 mortars.
- Ammunition section: one 2-ton cross-country, open bay cargo truck (ammunition).

KStN 1126A (8cm) (mot) (fG)

This version of the platoon was authorized on 1 November 1944, increasing the firepower by the additional authorization of the *schwerer Wurfrahmen 40*.
- Platoon headquarters: two light cross-country utility vehicles (*Volkswagen*).
- Three gun sections: two 2-ton cross-country, open bay cargo trucks, two 8cm Model 34 mortars, and one *schwerer Wurfrahmen 40* (only in 1st and 2nd Sections).
- Ammunition section: one 2-ton cross-country, open bay cargo truck (ammunition).

KStN 1126A (8cm) (gp)

This version of the document, dated 1 November 1944, kept the six 8cm mortars but had them mounted on armored personnel carriers. In addition, the platoon leader and the ammunition section also each had a medium armored personnel carrier.
- Platoon headquarters: one *Sd.Kfz. 2 Kettenkrad*, one medium armored personnel carrier (*Sd.Kfz. 251/1*), and one light machine gun.
- Three gun sections: two medium armored personnel carriers (*Sd.Kfz. 251/2*) and two light machine guns.
- Ammunition section: one medium armored personnel carrier (8cm) (ammunition) (*Sd.Kfz. 251/2*), one 3-ton cross-country, open bay cargo truck (ammunition), and one light machine gun.

KStN 1126A (8cm) (gp) (fG)

The *freie Gliederung* version of the document, also dated 1 November 1944, had the same organization as above, but with the addition of the *schwerer Wurfrahmen 40* for the 1st and 2nd mortar sections and the elimination of the *Kettenkrad* in the platoon headquarters and the 3-ton truck in the ammunition section.
- Platoon headquarters: one medium armored personnel carrier (*Sd.Kfz. 251/1*) and one light machine gun.

- Three gun sections: two medium armored personnel carriers (*Sd.Kfz. 251/2*), two light machine guns, and one *schwerer Wurfrahmen 40* (only in 1st and 2nd Sections).
- Ammunition section: one medium armored personnel carrier (8cm) (ammunition) (*Sd.Kfz. 251/2*) and one light machine gun.

Armored Scout Company

KStN 1162 (1 November 1943)

This organization represented no substantial changes from the same *KStN* dated 1 November 1941.

- Headquarters: two light motorcycles, two *Sd.Kfz. 2 Kettenkräder*, and two light cross-country utility vehicles (*Volkswagen*).
- 1st Scout platoon (heavy): three heavy armored cars (2cm) (*Sd.Kfz. 231*), three heavy armored cars (2cm) (Radio) (*Sd.Kfz. 232*), six light machine guns, and six 2cm main guns. Organized into three sections.
- 2nd Scout platoon (light): two light armored cars (radio) (*Sd.Kfz. 223*), four light armored cars (2cm) (*Sd.Kfz. 222*), six light machine guns, and four 2cm main guns. Organized into two sections.
- 3rd Scout platoon (light): same as the 2nd Platoon.
- 4th Scout platoon (light): same as the 2nd Platoon.

a) Command Group
Company Headquarters Section

2x Light Motorcycles 350cc | 2x *Kettenkrad* (*Sd.Kfz. 2*) | 2x Light Utility Vehicle, Cross-Country (4 seat)

Totals: 1x Officer, 2x NCOs, 7x Enlisted Personnel; 7x Rifles, 2x Pistols, 1x Submachine Gun; 2x Utility Vehicles, 2x Motorcycles, 2x *Kettenkräder*

1st (Heavy) Platoon

1st Section	2nd Section	3rd Section
Heavy Armored Car (2cm Main Gun) (*Sd.Kfz. 231*), 1x Light MG, 1x Submachine Gun and 1x Heavy Armored Car (2cm Main Gun) (Radio) (*Sd.Kfz. 232 (Fu)*), 1x Light MG, 1x Submachine Gun	Heavy Armored Car (2cm Main Gun) (*Sd.Kfz. 231*), 1x Light MG, 1x Submachine Gun and 1x Heavy Armored Car (2cm Main Gun) (Radio) (*Sd.Kfz. 232 (Fu)*), 1x Light MG, 1x Submachine Gun	Heavy Armored Car (2cm Main Gun) (*Sd.Kfz. 231*), 1x Light MG, 1x Submachine Gun and 1x Heavy Armored Car (2cm Main Gun) (Radio) (*Sd.Kfz. 232 (Fu)*), 1x Light MG, 1x Submachine Gun

Totals: 1x Officer, 11x NCOs, 12x Enlisted Personnel; 24x Pistols, 6x Submachine Guns, 6x Light MG's, 6x Main Guns; 6x Armored Vehicles

2nd (Light) Platoon

1st Section	2nd Section

2x Light Armored Car (2cm Main Gun) (*Sd.Kfz. 222*)*, 2x Submachine Gun and 1x Light Armored Car (Radio) (*Sd.Kfz. 232 (Fu)*), 1x Submachine Gun	2x Light Armored Car (2cm Main Gun) (*Sd.Kfz. 222*)*, 2x Submachine Gun and 1x Light Armored Car (Radio) (*Sd.Kfz. 232 (Fu)*), 1x Submachine Gun

Totals: 1x Officer, 9x NCOs, 8x Enlisted Personnel; 18x Pistols, 6x Submachine Guns, 6x Light MG's; 6x Armored Vehicles

3rd (Light) Platoon

1st Section	2nd Section
	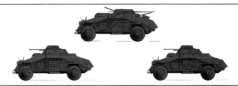
2x Light Armored Car (2cm Main Gun) (*Sd.Kfz. 222*)*, 2x Submachine Gun and 1x Light Armored Car (Radio) (*Sd.Kfz. 232 (Fu)*), 1x Submachine Gun	2x Light Armored Car (2cm Main Gun) (*Sd.Kfz. 222*)*, 2x Submachine Gun and 1x Light Armored Car (Radio) (*Sd.Kfz. 232 (Fu)*), 1x Submachine Gun

Totals: 10x NCOs, 8x Enlisted Personnel; 18x Pistols, 6x Submachine Guns, 6x Light MG's; 6x Armored Vehicles

4th (Light) Platoon

1st Section	2nd Section
	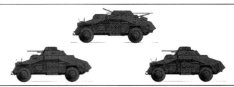
2x Light Armored Car (2cm Main Gun) (*Sd.Kfz. 222*)*, 2x Submachine Gun and 1x Light Armored Car (Radio) (*Sd.Kfz. 232 (Fu)*), 1x Submachine Gun	2x Light Armored Car (2cm Main Gun) (*Sd.Kfz. 222*)*, 2x Submachine Gun and 1x Light Armored Car (Radio) (*Sd.Kfz. 232 (Fu)*), 1x Submachine Gun

Totals: 10x NCOs, 8x Enlisted Personnel; 18x Pistols, 6x Submachine Guns, 6x Light MG's; 6x Armored Vehicles

f) Vehicle Maintenance Section

Light Truck, 2 ton, Canvas Top, Cross-Country (Set up for Vehicle Maintenance Section)	Medium Truck, 3 ton, Canvas Top, Cross-Country, for Replacement Parts	Truck, 3 ton, Canvas Top, Cross-Country, for Workshop Equipment (Set up for Vehicle Maintenance Section)	Light Prime Mover, 3 ton (*Sd.Kfz. 11*)

Totals: 4x NCOs, 9x Enlisted Personnel; 12x Rifles, 1x Pistol; 4x Wheeled Vehicles

g) Combat Trains

Light Utility Vehicle, Cross-Country (4 seat)	Truck, 3 ton, Canvas Top, Cross-Country, for Ammunition and Equipment	Truck, 3 ton, Canvas Top, Cross-Country, for Petroleum, Oil & Lubricants	Truck, 3 ton, Canvas Top, Cross-Country, for Small Field Mess Stove

Totals: 4x NCOs, 8x Enlisted Personnel; 10x Rifles, 1x Pistol, 1x Submachine Gun; 4x Wheeled Vehicles

Summary

	Officers	NCOs	Enlisted Personnel	Rifles	Pistols (Submachine Guns)	Light MG's	Wheeled Vehicles	Armored Vehicles	Motorcycles (Sidecars) [Kettenkräder]
Command Section	1	2	7	7	2 (1)		2		2 [2]
1st Platoon	1	11	12		24 (6)	6		6	
2nd Platoon	1	9	8		18 (6)	6		6	
3rd Platoon		10	8		18 (6)	6		6	
4th Platoon		10	8		18 (6)	6		6	
Vehicle Maintenance Section		4	9	12	1		4		
Combat Trains		4	8	10	1 (1)		4		
Baggage Trains		1	3	4			1		
Totals	3	51	63	33	82 (26)	24	11	24	2 [2]

KStN 1162A (1 November 1943) (Modified For 1944)

This particular organization document, along with *1162b*, was designed around a particular vehicle fielded in limited numbers: in this case, the *Sd.Kfz. 234/1 Puma*, one of the more famous armored cars of World War II.

- Headquarters: two light motorcycles, two *Sd.Kfz. 2 Kettenkräder*, one light cross-country utility vehicle (*Volkswagen*), one heavy armored car (5cm) (*Sd.Kfz. 234/2*), one light machine gun, and one 5cm main gun.
- 1st Platoon: six heavy armored cars (5cm) (*Sd.Kfz. 234/2*), six light machine guns, and six 5cm main guns.
- 2nd Platoon: same as the 1st Platoon.
- 3rd Platoon: same as the 1st Platoon.
- 4th Platoon: same as the 1st Platoon.

a) Command Group
Company Headquarters Section

| 2x Light Motorcycle 350cc, 2x *Kettenkrad* (*Sd.Kfz. 2*) | 2x Light Utility Vehicle, Cross-Country (4 seat) | Heavy Armored Car (5cm) (*Sd.Kfz. 234*), 1x Submachine Gun, 1x Light MG, 1x Main Gun |

Totals: 1x Officer, 3x NCOs, 7x Enlisted Personnel; 6x Rifles, 5x Pistols, 2x Submachine Guns, 1x Light MG, 1x Main Gun; 2x Wheeled Vehicles, 1x Armored Vehicle, 2x Motorcycles, 2x *Kettenkräder*

b) 1st (Heavy) Platoon

1st Section	2nd Section	3rd Section

2x Heavy Armored Car (5cm) (*Sd.Kfz. 234*), 2x Submachine Gun, 2x Light MG, 2x Main Gun	2x Heavy Armored Car (5cm) (*Sd.Kfz. 234*), 2x Submachine Gun, 2x Light MG, 2x Main Gun	2x Heavy Armored Car (5cm) (*Sd.Kfz. 234*), 2x Submachine Gun, 2x Light MG, 2x Main Gun

Totals: 1x Officer, 9x NCOs, 14x Enlisted Personnel; 24x Pistols, 6x Submachine Guns, 6x Light MG's, 6x Main Guns; 6x Armored Vehicles

c) 2nd (Heavy) Platoon

1st Section	2nd Section	3rd Section

2x Heavy Armored Car (5cm) (*Sd.Kfz. 234*), 2x Submachine Gun, 2x Light MG, 2x Main Gun	2x Heavy Armored Car (5cm) (*Sd.Kfz. 234*), 2x Submachine Gun, 2x Light MG, 2x Main Gun	2x Heavy Armored Car (5cm) (*Sd.Kfz. 234*), 2x Submachine Gun, 2x Light MG, 2x Main Gun

Totals: 1x Officer, 9x NCOs, 14x Enlisted Personnel; 24x Pistols, 6x Submachine Guns, 6x Light MG's, 6x Main Guns; 6x Armored Vehicles

d) 3rd (Heavy) Platoon

1st Section	2nd Section	3rd Section

2x Heavy Armored Car (5cm) (*Sd.Kfz. 234*), 2x Submachine Gun, 2x Light MG, 2x Main Gun	2x Heavy Armored Car (5cm) (*Sd.Kfz. 234*), 2x Submachine Gun, 2x Light MG, 2x Main Gun	2x Heavy Armored Car (5cm) (*Sd.Kfz. 234*), 2x Submachine Gun, 2x Light MG, 2x Main Gun

Totals: 10x NCOs, 14x Enlisted Personnel; 24x Pistols, 6x Submachine Guns, 6x Light MG's, 6x Main Guns; 6x Armored Vehicles

e) 4th (Heavy) Platoon

1st Section	2nd Section	3rd Section

2x Heavy Armored Car (5cm) (*Sd.Kfz. 234*), 2x Submachine Gun, 2x Light MG, 2x Main Gun	2x Heavy Armored Car (5cm) (*Sd.Kfz. 234*), 2x Submachine Gun, 2x Light MG, 2x Main Gun	2x Heavy Armored Car (5cm) (*Sd.Kfz. 234*), 2x Submachine Gun, 2x Light MG, 2x Main Gun

Totals: 10x NCOs, 14x Enlisted Personnel; 24x Pistols, 6x Submachine Guns, 6x Light MG's, 6x Main Guns; 6x Armored Vehicles

f) Vehicle Maintenance Section

Truck, 3 ton, Canvas Top, Cross-Country, for Spare Parts	Light Prime Mover, 3 ton (*Sd.Kfz. 11*)	Truck, 2 ton, Canvas Top, Cross-Country (Set up for Vehicle Maintenance Section)	Truck, 3 ton, Canvas Top, Cross-Country, for Workshop Equipment

Totals: 4x NCOs, 8x Enlisted Personnel; 11x Rifles, 1x Pistol; 4x Vehicles

g) Combat Trains

Light Utility Vehicle, Cross-Country (4 seat)	Truck, 3 ton, Canvas Top, Cross-Country, for Ammunition and Equipment	Truck, 3 ton, Canvas Top, Cross-Country, for Petroleum, Oil & Lubricants	Mess Truck, for Large Field Mess Stove	Truck, 3 ton, Canvas Top, Cross-Country, for Ammunition

Totals: 4x NCOs, 9x Enlisted Personnel; 9x Rifles, 3x Pistols, 1x Submachine Gun; 5x Wheeled Vehicles

Summary

	Officers	NCOs	Enlisted Personnel	Rifles	Pistols/ (Submachine Guns)	Light MG's	Main Guns	Wheeled Vehicles	Armored Vehicles	Motorcycles (Sidecars) [*Kettenkräder*]
Command Section	1	3	7	6	3 (2)	1	1	2	1	2 [2]
1st Platoon	1	9	14		24 (6)	6	6		6	
2nd Platoon	1	9	14		24 (6)	6	6		6	
3rd Platoon		10	14		24 (6)	6	6		6	
4th Platoon		10	14		24 (6)	6	6		6	
Vehicle Maintenance Section		4	8	11	1			4		
Combat Trains		4	9	9	3 (1)			5		
Baggage Trains		1	3	4				1		
Totals	3	50	83	30	103 (27)	25	25	12	25	2 [2]

KStN 1162B (1 March 1944)

This organizational document was used for fielding the fully tracked reconnaissance vehicles, the *Panzer II, Ausführung L, Luchs* or the *Aufklärungspanzer 38(t)*. In either case, the number of combat vehicles in the company was twenty-five:

- Headquarters: four *Sd.Kfz. 2 Kettenkräder*, two light cross-country utility vehicles (*Volkswagen*), one fully tracked reconnaissance vehicle (*Panzer II, Ausführung L, Luchs—Sd.Kfz. 123*), one light machine gun, and one 2cm main gun.
- 1st Platoon: six fully tracked reconnaissance vehicles (*Panzer II, Ausführung L, Luchs— Sd.Kfz. 123*), six light machine guns, and six 2cm main guns.
- 2nd Platoon: same as the 1st Platoon.
- 3rd Platoon: same as the 1st Platoon.
- 4th Platoon: same as the 1st Platoon.

THE END IN THE WEST 409

a) Command Group
Company Headquarters Section

3x Medium Motorcycle

7x *Kettenkrad* (*Sd.Kfz. 2*)

2x Light Utility Vehicle, Cross-Country (*Kfz. 1*), Volkswagen

Panzerkampfwagen II, Ausführung L (2cm) (Sd.Kfz. 123), 1x Submachine Gun, 1x Light MG

Totals: 1x Officer, 3x NCOs, 15x Enlisted Personnel; 13x Rifles, 6x Pistols, 1x Submachine Gun, 1x Light MG; 2x Utility Vehicles, 7x *Kettenkräder*, 1x Armored Vehicle, 3x Motorcycles

b) 1st Platoon

7x *Panzerkampfwagen II, Ausführung L (2cm) (Sd.Kfz. 123)*, 7x Submachine Gun, 7x Light MG, 7x 2cm Main Gun

Totals: 1x Officer, 7x NCOs, 20x Enlisted Personnel; 28x Pistols, 7x Submachine Guns, 7x Light MG's, 7x 2cm Main Guns; 7x Armored Vehicles

c) 2nd Platoon

7x *Panzerkampfwagen II, Ausführung L (2cm) (Sd.Kfz. 123)*, 7x Submachine Gun, 7x Light MG, 7x 2cm Main Gun

Totals: 8x NCOs, 20x Enlisted Personnel; 28x Pistols, 7x Submachine Guns, 7x Light MG's, 7x 2cm Main Guns; 7x Armored Vehicles

d) 3rd Platoon

7x *Panzerkampfwagen II, Ausführung L (2cm) (Sd.Kfz. 123)*, 7x Submachine Gun, 7x Light MG, 7x 2cm Main Gun

Totals: 8x NCOs, 20x Enlisted Personnel; 28x Pistols, 7x Submachine Guns, 7x Light MG's, 7x 2cm Main Guns; 7x Armored Vehicles

e) 4th Platoon

7x *Panzerkampfwagen II, Ausführung L (2cm) (Sd.Kfz. 123)*, 7x Submachine Gun, 7x Light MG, 7x 2cm Main Gun

Totals: 8x NCOs, 20x Enlisted Personnel; 28x Pistols, 7x Submachine Guns, 7x Light MG's, 7x 2cm Main Guns; 7x Armored Vehicles

f) Vehicle Maintenance Section

| Small Maintenance Vehicle (*Kfz. 2/40*), *Volkswagen* | 5x Light Utility Vehicle, Cross-Country (*Kfz. 1*), *Volkswagen* | | Truck, 3 ton, Canvas Top, Cross-Country, for Replacement Parts |

Truck, 3 ton, Canvas Top, Cross-Country, for Replacement Parts   Heavy Prime Mover, 18 ton (*Sd.Kfz.9*) and Lowboy Trailer for Armored Fighting Vehicles, 22 ton (*Sonderanhänger 116*) (Not Shown)   Truck, 3 ton, Canvas Top, Cross-Country, for Workshop Equipment

Totals: 4x NCOs, 17x Enlisted Personnel; 20x Rifles, 1x Pistol; 10x Wheeled Vehicles, 1x Trailer

Note: 18-ton Prime Mover later changed to a 12-ton Prime Mover

g) Combat Trains I

| Medium Cross-Country Vehicle with Equipment Storage Box (*Kfz. 15*) | 2x Medium Truck, 3 ton, Canvas Top, for Ammunition and Equipment | Medium Truck, 3 ton, Canvas Top, for Large Field Mess Stove | Medium Truck, 3 ton, Canvas Top, for Rations |

2x Medium Truck, 3 ton, Canvas Top, for Petroleum, Oil & Lubricants   4x Light Armored Vehicle (*Sd.Kfz. 250*) for Transport

Totals: 4x NCOs, 19x Enlisted Personnel; 18x Rifles, 5x Pistols; 10x Wheeled Vehicles, 4x Armored Vehicles

h) Combat Trains II

Light Cross-Country Truck, for Transport of Personnel

Total Combat Trains II: 1x NCO, 19x Enlisted Personnel; 12x Pistols, 1x Rifle; 1x Wheeled Vehicle

Note: The Combat Trains II was the holding area for spare (relief) crews for the armored cars.

Summary

	Officers	NCOs	Enlisted Personnel	Rifles	Pistols (Submachine Guns)	Light MG's	Wheeled Vehicles (Trailers)	Armored Vehicles	Motorcycles
Command Section	1	3	15	13	6 (1)	1	9	1	3
1st Platoon	1	7	20		28 (7)	7	7		
2nd Platoon	1	7	20		28 (7)	7	7		
3rd Platoon	1	7	20		28 (7)	7	7		
4th Platoon		8	20		28 (7)	7	7		
Maintenance Section		8	20	20	1		10 (1)		
Combat Trains I		4	17	18	5		10	4	
Combat Trains II		1	19	1	19		1		
Baggage Trains		1	3	4			1		
Totals:	4	46	154	56	143 (29)	29	31 (1)	33	3

THE END IN THE WEST 411

The illustrations below show the company as originally intended when the document was first released on 10 January 1943. The main difference is that the original fielding plane was for seven vehicles in each platoon, resulting in twenty-nine fully tracked reconnaissance vehicles authorized for the company, whether fielded with the *Panzer II, Ausführung L, Luchs* or the *Aufklärungspanzer 38(t)*.

The organization with the reconnaissance version of the *Panzer 38(t)*:

- Headquarters: four *Sd.Kfz. 2 Kettenkräder*, two light cross-country utility vehicles (*Volkswagen*), one fully tracked reconnaissance vehicle (*Aufklärungspanzer 38(t)—Sd.Kfz. 140/1*), one light machine gun, and one 2cm main gun.
- 1st Platoon: six fully tracked reconnaissance vehicles (*Aufklärungspanzer 38(t)—Sd.Kfz. 140/1*), six light machine guns, and six 2cm main guns.
- 2nd Platoon: same as the 1st Platoon.
- 3rd Platoon: same as the 1st Platoon.
- 4th Platoon: same as the 1st Platoon.

a) Command Group
Company Headquarters Section

2x Light Utility Vehicle, Cross-Country (4 seat)   4x *Kettenkrad (Sd.Kfz. 2)**   Panzerkampfwagen II, Ausführung L (2cm Kw.K.38) (Sd.Kfz. 123), 1x Submachine Gun, 1x Light MG, 1x 2cm Main Gun or 1x *Aufklärungspanzerwagen 38 (2cm) (Sd.Kfz. 140/1)*, 1x Submachine Gun, 1x Light MG, 1x 2cm Main Gun

Totals: 1x Officer, 4x NCOs, 8x Enlisted Personnel; 7x Rifles, 4x Pistols, 3x Submachine Guns, 1x Light MG, 1x 2cm Main Gun; 2x Utility Vehicles, 4x *Kettenkräder*, 1x Armored Vehicle

Note: *Sidecar Motorcycles count in lieu of *Kettenkräder*.

b) 1st Platoon

6x *Panzerkampfwagen II, Ausführung L (2cm Kw.K.38) (Sd.Kfz. 123)*, 6x Submachine Gun, 6x Light MG, 6x 2cm Main Gun or 6x *Aufklärungspanzerwagen 38 (2cm) (Sd.Kfz. 140/1)*, 6x Submachine Gun, 6x Light MG, 6x 2cm Main Gun

Totals: 1x Officer, 11x NCOs, 12x Enlisted Personnel; 24x Pistols, 6x Submachine Guns, 6x Light MG's, 6x 2cm Main Guns; 6x Armored Vehicles

c) 2nd Platoon

6x *Panzerkampfwagen II, Ausführung L (2cm Kw.K.38) (Sd.Kfz. 123)*, 6x Submachine Gun, 6x Light MG, 6x 2cm Main Gun or 6x *Aufklärungspanzerwagen 38 (2cm) (Sd.Kfz. 140/1)*, 6x Submachine Gun, 6x Light MG, 6x 2cm Main Gun

Totals: 1x Officer, 11x NCOs, 12x Enlisted Personnel; 24x Pistols, 6x Submachine Guns, 6x Light MG's, 6x 2cm Main Guns; 6x Armored Vehicles

d) 3rd Platoon

6x *Panzerkampfwagen II, Ausführung L (2cm Kw.K.38) (Sd.Kfz. 123)*, 6x Submachine Gun, 6x Light MG, 6x 2cm Main Gun or 6x *Aufklärungspanzerwagen 38 (2cm) (Sd.Kfz. 140/1)*, 6x Submachine Gun, 6x Light MG, 6x 2cm Main Gun

Totals: 12x NCOs, 12x Enlisted Personnel; 24x Pistols, 6x Submachine Guns, 6x Light MG's, 6x 2cm Main Guns; 6x Armored Vehicles

e) 4th Platoon

6x *Panzerkampfwagen II, Ausführung L (2cm Kw.K.38) (Sd.Kfz. 123)*, 6x Submachine Gun, 6x Light MG, 6x 2cm Main Gun or 6x *Aufklärungspanzerwagen 38 (2cm) (Sd.Kfz. 140/1)*, 6x Submachine Gun, 6x Light MG, 6x 2cm Main Gun

Totals: 12x NCOs, 12x Enlisted Personnel; 24x Pistols, 6x Submachine Guns, 6x Light MG's, 6x 2cm Main Guns; 6x Armored Vehicles

f) Vehicle Maintenance Section

Light Utility Vehicle, Cross-Country (4 seat)

Truck, 2 ton, Canvas Top, Cross-Country (Set up for Vehicle Maintenance Section)*

Truck, 3 ton, Canvas Top, Cross-Country, for Replacement Parts

Heavy Prime Mover, 12 ton (*Sd.Kfz.8*), 1x Lowboy Trailer for Armored Fighting Vehicles (*Sonderanhänger 115*), 10 ton (Not Shown)

Truck, 3 ton, Canvas Top, Cross-Country (Set up for Workshop Equipment)

Totals: 4x NCOs, 9x Enlisted Personnel; 12x Rifles, 1x Pistol; 5x Vehicles, 1x Trailer

Note: *Kfz. 2/40* counts in lieu of Light Truck

g) Combat Trains

Light Utility Vehicle, Cross-Country (4 seat)

Truck, 3 ton, Canvas Top, Cross-Country, for Ammunition and Equipment

Truck, 3 ton, Canvas Top, Cross-Country, for Petroleum, Oil & Lubricants

Truck, 3 ton, Canvas Top, Cross-Country, for Petroleum, Oil & Lubricants Transport

Truck, 3 ton, Canvas Top, Cross-Country, for Large Field Mess Stove

Totals: 4x NCOs, 9x Enlisted Personnel; 11x Rifles, 1x Pistol, 1x Submachine Gun; 5x Wheeled Vehicles

Summary

	Officers	NCOs	Enlisted Personnel	Rifles	Pistols (Submachine Guns)	Light MG's	Vehicle (Trailers)	Armored Vehicles	Kettenkräder
Command Section	1	4	8	7	4 (3)	1	2	1	4
1st Platoon	1	11	12		24 (6)	6		6	
2nd Platoon	1	11	12		24 (6)	6		6	
3rd Platoon		12	12		24 (6)	6		6	
4th Platoon		12	12		24 (6)	6		6	
Vehicle Maintenance Section		4	9	12	1		5 (1)		
Combat Trains		4	9	11	1 (1)		5		
Baggage Trains		1	3	4			1		
Totals:	3	59	77	34	102 (28)	25	13 (1)	25	4

KStN 1162c (fG) (1 November 1944)

Other than a slight change to vehicular allocations in the company headquarters and the disappearance of the company logistical tail, this company was organized identically to the organization introduced formally on 1 November 1943.

- Headquarters: two *Sd.Kfz. 2 Kettenkräder*, two light cross-country utility vehicles (*Volkswagen*), one light armored observation vehicle (*Sd.Kfz. 250/5*), and one light machine gun.
- 1st Platoon: two light armored observation vehicles (*Sd.Kfz. 250/5*), four light armored personnel carriers (2cm) (*Sd.Kfz. 250/9*), six light machine guns, and four 2cm main guns. Each platoon organized into two sections.
- 2nd Platoon: same as the 1st Platoon.
- 3rd Platoon: same as the 1st Platoon.
- 4th Platoon: same as the 1st Platoon.

THE END IN THE WEST   413

a) Command Group
Company Headquarters Section

2x Light Utility Vehicle, Cross-Country (4 seat)   2x *Kettenkrad (sd.Kfz. 2)*   Light Armored Observation Half-track (*Sd.Kfz. 250/5*), 1x Submachine Gun, 1x Light MG

Totals: 1x Officer, 6x NCOs, 5x Enlisted Personnel; 6x Rifles, 4x Pistols, 2x Submachine Guns, 1x Light MG; 1x Armored Vehicle, 2x Utility Vehicles, 2x *Kettenkräder*

b) 1st Platoon

1st Section	2nd Section

Light Armored Observation Half-track (*Sd.Kfz. 250/5*), 1x Submachine Gun, 1x Light MG, and 2x Light Armored Personnel Carrier (2cm) (*Sd.Kfz. 250/9*), 2x Submachine Guns, 2x Light MG, 2x 2cm Main Gun	Light Armored Observation Half-track (*Sd.Kfz. 250/5*), 1x Submachine Gun, 1x Light MG, and 2x Light Armored Personnel Carrier (2cm) (*Sd.Kfz. 250/9*), 2x Submachine Guns, 2x Light MG, 2x 2cm Main Gun

Totals: 1x Officer, 5x NCOs, 11x Enlisted Personnel; 11x Pistols, 7x Submachine Guns, 6x Light MG's, 4x 2cm Main Guns; 6x Armored Half-track Vehicles

c) 2nd Platoon

1st Section	2nd Section

Light Armored Observation Half-track (*Sd.Kfz. 250/5*), 1x Submachine Gun, 1x Light MG, and 2x Light Armored Personnel Carrier (2cm) (*Sd.Kfz. 250/9*), 2x Submachine Gun, 2x Light MG, 2x 2cm Main Gun	Light Armored Observation Half-track (*Sd.Kfz. 250/5*), 1x Submachine Gun, 1x Light MG, and 2x Light Armored Personnel Carrier (2cm) (*Sd.Kfz. 250/9*), 2x Submachine Gun, 2x Light MG, 2x 2cm Main Gun

Totals: 1x Officer, 5x NCOs, 11x Enlisted Personnel; 11x Pistols, 7x Submachine Guns, 6x Light MG's, 4x 2cm Main Guns; 6x Armored Half-track Vehicles

d) 3rd Platoon

1st Section	2nd Section

Light Armored Observation Half-track (*Sd.Kfz. 250/5*), 1x Submachine Gun, 1x Light MG, and 2x Light Armored Personnel Carrier (2cm) (*Sd.Kfz. 250/9*), 2x Submachine Gun, 2x Light MG, 2x 2cm Main Gun	Light Armored Observation Half-track (*Sd.Kfz. 250/5*), 1x Submachine Gun, 1x Light MG, and 2x Light Armored Personnel Carrier (2cm) (*Sd.Kfz. 250/9*), 2x Submachine Gun, 2x Light MG, 2x 2cm Main Gun

Totals: 12x NCOs, 6x Enlisted Personnel; 18x Pistols, 6x Submachine Guns, 6x Light MG's, 4x 2cm Main Guns; 6x Armored Half-track Vehicles

e) 4th Platoon

1st Section	2nd Section

Light Armored Observation Half-track (*Sd.Kfz. 250/5*), 1x Submachine Gun, 1x Light MG, and 2x Light Armored Personnel Carrier (2cm) (*Sd.Kfz. 250/9*), 2x Submachine Gun, 2x Light MG, 2x 2cm Main Gun	Light Armored Observation Half-track (*Sd.Kfz. 250/5*), 1x Submachine Gun, 1x Light MG, and 2x Light Armored Personnel Carrier (2cm) (*Sd.Kfz. 250/9*), 2x Submachine Gun, 2x Light MG, 2x 2cm Main Gun

Totals: 12x NCOs, 6x Enlisted Personnel; 18x Pistols, 6x Submachine Guns, 6x Light MG's, 4x 2cm Main Guns; 6x Armored Half-track Vehicles

Summary

	Officers	NCOs	Enlisted Personnel	Rifles	Pistols (Submachine Guns)	Light MG's	Main Guns	Vehicles	Armored Vehicles	Motorcycles (Sidecars) [Kettenkräder]
Command Section	1	6	5	6	2 (4)	1		2	1	[2]
1st Platoon	1	5	12		11 (7)	6	4		6	
2nd Platoon	1	5	12		11 (7)	6	4		6	
3rd Platoon		6	12		11 (7)	6	4		6	
4th Platoon		6	12		11 (7)	6	4		6	
Totals	3	28	53	6	46 (32)	25	16	2	25	[2]

Notes: Soldiers without assigned personal weapons are directed to use the vehicle small arms as personal weapons. Sidecar motorcycles count in lieu of *Kettenkräder*.

KStN 1162d (1 March 1944)

This organizational document was used for fielding the heavy armored car (2cm) (*Sd.Kfz. 234/1*):

- Headquarters: two *Sd.Kfz. 2 Kettenkräder*, two light cross-country utility vehicles (*Volkswagen*), one heavy armored car (2cm) (*Sd.Kfz. 234/1*), one light machine gun, and one 2cm main gun.
- 1st Light Platoon: six heavy armored cars (2cm) (*Sd.Kfz. 234/1*), six light machine guns, and six 2cm main guns.
- 2nd Light Platoon: same as the 1st Platoon.
- 3rd Light Platoon: same as the 1st Platoon.
- 4th (Heavy) Platoon: six armored cars (7.5cm) (*Sd.Kfz. 234/3*), six light machine guns, and six 7.5cm main guns.

a) Command Group
Company Headquarters Section

2x Light Motorcycle 350cc and 2x Kettenkrad (*Sd.Kfz. 2*) | Light Utility Vehicle, Cross-Country (4 seat) | Heavy Armored Car (*Sd.Kfz. 234/1*), 1x Submachine Gun, 1x Light MG, 1x 2cm Main Gun

Totals: 1x Officer, 4x NCOs, 6x Enlisted Personnel; 5x Rifles, 4x Pistols, 2x Submachine Guns, 1x Light MG, 1x 2cm Main Gun; 1x Wheeled Vehicle, 1x Armored Vehicle, 2x Motorcycles, 2x *Kettenkräder*

b) 1st (Light) Platoon

6x Heavy Armored Car (*Sd.Kfz. 234/1*), 6x Submachine Gun, 6x Light MG, 6x 2cm Main Gun

Totals: 1x Officer, 9x NCOs, 14x Enlisted Personnel; 18x Pistols, 6x Submachine Guns, 6x Light MG's, 6x 2cm Main Guns; 6x Armored Vehicles

c) 2nd (Light) Platoon

6x Heavy Armored Car (*Sd.Kfz. 234/1*), 6x Submachine Gun, 6x Light MG, 6x 2cm Main Gun

Totals: 1x Officer, 9x NCOs, 14x Enlisted Personnel; 18x Pistols, 6x Submachine Guns, 6x Light MG's, 6x 2cm Main Guns; 6x Armored Vehicles

d) 3rd (Light) Platoon

6x Heavy Armored Car (*Sd.Kfz. 234/1*), 6x Submachine Gun, 6x Light MG, 6x 2cm Main Gun

Totals: 1x Officer, 9x NCOs, 14x Enlisted Personnel; 18x Pistols, 6x Submachine Guns, 6x Light MG's, 6x 2cm Main Guns; 6x Armored Vehicles

e) 4th (Heavy) Platoon

6x Heavy Armored Car (*Sd.Kfz. 234/3*), 6x Submachine Gun, 6x Light MG, 6x 7.5cm Main Gun

Totals: 1x Officer, 11x NCOs, 12x Enlisted Personnel; 18x Pistols, 6x Submachine Guns, 6x Light MG's, 6x 7.5cm Main Guns; 6x Armored Vehicles

f) Vehicle Maintenance Section

| Truck, 2 ton, Canvas Top, Cross-Country (Set up for Vehicle Maintenance Section) | Truck, 3 ton, Canvas Top, Cross-Country, for Spare Parts | Truck, 3 ton, Canvas Top, Cross-Country, for Maintenance Section Workshop Equipment | Medium Prime Mover, 8 ton (*Sd.Kfz. 7*) |

Totals: 4x NCOs, 9x Enlisted Personnel; 12x Rifles, 1x Pistol; 4x Wheeled Vehicles

g) Combat Trains

| Light Utility Vehicle, Cross-Country (4 seat) | Truck, 3 ton, Canvas Top, Cross-Country, for Ammunition and Equipment | Truck, 3 ton, Canvas Top, Cross-Country, for Ammunition | Truck, 3 ton, Canvas Top, Cross-Country, for Petroleum, Oil & Lubricants | Truck, 3 ton, Canvas Top, Cross-Country, for Large Field Mess Stove |

Totals: 4x NCOs, 9x Enlisted Personnel; 11x Rifles, 1x Pistol, 1x Submachine Gun; 5x Wheeled Vehicles

Summary

	Officers	NCOs	Enlisted Personnel	Rifles	Pistols (Submachine Guns)	Light MG's	Main Guns	Vehicles	Armored Vehicles	Motorcycles (Sidecars) [*Kettenkräder*]
Command Section	1	4	6	5	4 (2)	1	1	1	1	2 [2]
1st (Light) Platoon	1	9	14		18 (6)	6	6		6	
2nd (Light) Platoon		10	14		18 (6)	6	6		6	
3rd (Light) Platoon		10	14		18 (6)	6	6		6	
4th (Heavy) Platoon	1	11	12		18 (6)	6	6		6	
Vehicle Maintenance Section		4	9	12	1			4		
Combat Trains		4	9	11	1 (1)			5		
Baggage Trains		1	3	4				1		
Totals	**3**	**53**	**81**	**32**	**78 (27)**	**25**	**25**	**11**	**25**	**2 [2]**

LESSONS LEARNED AND FIRSTHAND ACCOUNTS

Helmut Günther, who started the war as a motorcycle infantryman with *Das Reich*, was eventually transferred to *SS-Panzer-Aufklärungs-Abteilung 17 "Götz von Berlichingen,"* where he served as a platoon leader and acting company commander. He wrote several memoirs, which have appeared in English. He also contributed a great deal to the divisional history, where numerous accounts by him are related. This account concerns a patrol conducted in the latter half of June in Normandy against American forces. As is mentioned in the text, Günther wonders why his men are called upon to conduct battlefield reconnaissance—that is, frontline reconnaissance—when infantry forces were already on the line and opposite their opposing number. As with most operations conducted by reconnaissance forces at this stage of the war, the mission was not one found in doctrinal manuals:[64]

> With eight men, we sat behind an embankment and waited for darkness. We had arrived in the sector of a company of the *353. Infanterie-Division*, where we were supposed to determine whether a higher headquarters of the enemy was located in the village across from us. If possible, prisoners were to be taken!
>
> To be exact: It was two missions. Why the [infantry] division didn't execute the mission itself was beyond me. Maybe it had something to do with the fact that we were a "reconnaissance company" and those types of missions were associated with our "profession."
>
> The company commander, an *Oberleutnant*, briefed us. The terrain, similar to that in front of our own position, was just as marshy. As a result of reconnaissance conducted by the company that was already there, it had been determined that the only way to get into the village in question was across a man-made embankment on which there were railway tracks. In addition, that patrol leader had reported that there were outbuildings at the end of the embankment, where peat bales were probably prepared for shipment prior to the invasion.
>
> The mission didn't appear to offer any chance of success. Even the Americans couldn't be that stupid to forget what the embankment meant for them: They most certainly were keeping an eye on that strange crossing point.
>
> Until it turned dark, we killed time playing cards behind a mound of dirt in no-man's-land. The troopers in the Army company were no doubt amazed that we were playing cards in the face of the enemy and before just such an undertaking.
>
> We took off. We had three light machine guns. The rest of the men carried submachine guns. We crawled on our bellies for half an hour. It was a nasty feeling sliding over the wet, mushy ground. Unfortunately, there was no other way to move. Finally, I saw a rise in the ground, 1 meter high and even. It was the embankment, which was to offer us concealment for our continued advance. Unfortunately, that was only for a short distance, since it then headed straight for the village after making a right-angled turn. At the same time, the ground became even more marshy and impassable. We had no choice but to get up on top of the embankment. It was still probably a few hundred meters to the outbuildings, whose contours could barely be made out in the darkness.
>
> I left *Sturmmann* von Stein back at the bend. He was told to give us cover with his machine gun, in case we had to pull back quickly. He had a clear field of fire over the marsh to the village and, at the same time, to the aforementioned outbuildings. Then the damned slipping and sliding started. It was nerve-wracking. If only I knew whether there were any guards there! If so, then where were they posted? I had the constant feeling that someone had me in his sights and was only waiting for the right moment to squeeze the trigger.
>
> A bridge! That hadn't been part of the picture before. The marsh water in a big conduit babbled under our stomachs and headed in that direction. Still prone, I observed everything intently. On the far side of the conduit, a wire fence could be barely made out. At the end of the bridge, there was an open gate. Why was the gate so invitingly open? Was that laziness on the part of the Yanks or intentional?

I then held up with three men between the outbuildings. I had left the 2nd light machine gun in front of the bridge. It had taken us more than two hours to cover a lousy 1,000 meters. We were sweating and freezing at the same time. There were railway tracks, tipped-over railcars, a large quantity of iron and sheet metal between the outbuildings. All of it made it very difficult to advance.

I considered my options and decided to go ahead alone with Groß. Sander and Helbig remained behind. Helbig had some fields of fire and, in case of danger, could support us to a certain extent. I moved forward with Groß. Even Winnetou [an Indian character from the popular Westerns of German author Karl May] couldn't have done it better. A tin can laying around could have spelled the end of the operation. But nothing out of the ordinary happened. A half hour later, we were on the village street, right across from a house. The stillness around us was unnerving. Had we really not yet been discovered?

We caught our breath behind a low stone wall. I was just about to grab Groß by the arm to whisper to him that we needed to go a bit further to the left, when we heard steps. Talking loudly and in a carefree fashion, two GI's marched down the road about three meters from our noses. They disappeared into the house across the way. While the light shone briefly when the door was opened, I thought I had seen officers inside. Was this the place where the fabled headquarters was located?

I had to know. I didn't want to render only half a report. Damn it! If those guys hadn't appeared so suddenly, we could have snatched them! Now it was too late to do that!

We slowly pushed our way towards a gap in the stone wall. In two or three long strides, we ran across the street. We were pressed up against the wall of the house and waited to see whether there would be any firing. But nothing like that happened. Were all of the guards asleep?

It was our intention to wait at the door until one of the Yanks came out in order to find the little boys' room. If that took too long, we intended to rip open the door and, using the element of surprise, take one of the Americans prisoner . . .

. . . Groß nudged me slightly and pointed to a sign next to the door. A tactical symbol was painted on it. Nothing much could be identified in the darkness. We had to wait until the wisps of clouds in the heavens let some moonlight down for a bit. But the clouds didn't budge. I had to take a chance. I grabbed my flashlight, set it on its weakest beam and held it close to the small wooden sign, blocking the light with both hands and holding the flashlight by its cord between my teeth. A short blast of light was enough to have the sign stick to my memory.

Not too far from where we were was a small window. Unfortunately, it was nailed shut. Had the Yanks gone to bed? I pulled on Groß' arm and wanted to give him a sign that we had to go with the second option, knocking down the door. After all, we couldn't remain there until it turned first light.

Some distance away, where Stein was positioned, there was suddenly the sound of machine-gun fire. The house came to life immediately. Given those circumstances, we would never have gotten away with a prisoner. "Let's go," I hissed. Letting two hand grenades fall to the ground. Boooom . . . boooom! The explosions thundered behind us, as we reached Sander and Helbig, gasping for breath. Off to the sides, behind us and in front of us, all Hell had broken loose. There was the crash of firing everywhere. A Yank had to be close by, off to our right. Helbig fired from his machine gun, which he had jammed under his arm. It turned quiet.

We jumped over some debris and raced past tipped-over railcars. We had only one thought: To hopefully get over the bridge, since the machine gun we had posted there had also started to fire. We were gasping for breath. All the mutts in the village were barking, providing some mood music to the background. Groß tripped on a rail and landed on the full length of his body. He sprained his ankle. Sander and Helbig gave us covering fire.

Together with Groß, who weighed heavily on my arm, I reached the bridge and called out to the rifleman: "Another couple of bursts and then follow!" I staggered off with Groß. Because of the heavy volume of fire from the submachine guns and machine guns, the Yanks had become more careful. Parachute flares floated in the heavens and turned the night into day for a short while. We immediately hit the deck; every movement froze. "Can you make it?" I asked Groß abruptly. He had to be in some pain. "I'm going to have to!" He replied. I was burning with curiosity. "Tell me, what did you fasten on the door back there?" Despite his pain, Groß had to laugh: "The picture of old Götz . . . after all, we need to live up to our division's name." Some jokester somewhere had had the small pictures produced, which showed whoever was looking at them the picture of a knight with his pants pulled down, who was pointing to his rear end with his hand. Underneath was printed: "Götz von Berlichingen." Despite the screwed-up situation, I had to shake my head and laugh.[65]

After the festival-like lighting started to wane after a bit, the men coming from the bridge hit the deck next to us. Until we got to the aforementioned bend in the embankment, we lost no small amount of sweat. We linked up with von Stein there. He wanted to report to me why he had started the firefight. I waved him off: "Later!" At that point, we moved a lot faster, since we had better cover and concealment. We reached the first outpost of the Army company without taking any casualties.

I reported to the *Oberleutnant* at the command post. It was clear that we had only accomplished part of our mission. The tactical sign next to the door had, indeed, indicated a headquarters. Unfortunately we could not provide any prisoners. Well, not everything in a war goes the way you want it. The enemy has a vote as well! In any event, I was happy that we only had a sprained ankle and two surface wounds as a result of our efforts. We said our good-byes, mounted our *Schwimmwagen* and moved out.

So then . . . why had von Stein opened fire? For a long time, there had been nothing seen nor heard. Initially, the two had only heard noises that could not be identified. Then, when the moon looked down for a short while one time, they saw several Yanks, about 200 meters off the side of the bridge, push a plank or something similar across the water channel and then crawl to the other side. What were they to do at that point? They had received clear orders to keep the embankment open and ensure that our route back was not cut off.

Of course, it was still an open question: Had the Americans noticed us? Were they trying to sandwich us? Did they know anything at all about us? Were they starting their own operation? He had to do something: He opened fire. Those types of questions always plagued a patrol leader, whether conducting reconnaissance or leading a raid. It really didn't matter. The only thing that mattered was success, whether achieved by the book or without it and with as few casualties as possible.

Former *SS-Sturmbannführer* Ernst August Krag, commander of *SS-Panzer-Aufklärungs-Abteilung 2 "Das Reich"* during the fighting of the battalion in Normandy and the Ardennes, has provided a firsthand account of his experiences during the division's withdrawal through France toward Belgium. Once the Allies started pursuit operations through France, the paramount concern was saving as many men and as much equipment as possible:[66]

Fighting at Wassigny
Within the framework of the retrograde movements, the reconnaissance battalion had to assume a number of difficult blocking and screening missions. In the course of doing those, the strength of the battalion was always its fast and decisive actions. The battalion never changed position during the day when the weather was clear. That spared casualties caused by the air force. In addition, our Allied enemies only rarely attacked at night, and it was the exception to the rule, if they remained on our heels at nighttime.

While pulling back in the direction of the Belgian border, the reconnaissance battalion wound up in a very ticklish situation. Due to a lack of fuel, the battalion was stuck in Wassigny with all of its vehicles, *SPW's* and wheels. Tank units were outflanking us and left the reconnaissance battalion alone as a certain spoil-of-war. Based on the situation, it appeared that it would be impossible to secure fuel. The airfield at Peronne, the boats on the Somme and at St. Quentin and the abandoned or disabled vehicles along the retreat route were all searched for fuel. All of the searching yielded no success, but the battalion was not about to consider giving up and capitulation. In a detailed discussion, the battalion commander [Krag referring to himself in the third person] informed the company commanders of the seriousness of the situation.

We discussed how to fight our way back without *SPW's* and wheeled elements and prepared for that eventuality. With the few remaining liters of fuel, we intended to keep only a radio vehicle, one or two *Volkswagen* for route reconnaissance purposes and a wheeled ambulance running. The commander ordered the men to maintain their composure and avoid a fight wherever possible. At that point, the first miracle occurred in the hopeless situation: A patrol under *Oberscharführer* Pink reported that it had found a barge in the Ainse Canal with fuel on it. Near the barge was a disabled fuel vehicle. French civilians were in a hurry to secure the fuel for themselves. There were no enemy forces to be seen in the vicinity of the barge. A *Kfz. 15* with a few stout-hearted men was quickly sent with *Oberscharführer* Pink, an old hand who had seen a lot of difficult situations and who had found the fuel, towards the canal.

The *coup de main* was a success, and the French were chased away. More than 150 fuel cans were filled by means of buckets. The canisters had come from the aforementioned disabled fuel truck. After tiresome work, the barely believable had been accomplished. More than 3,000 liters of "life-giving elixir" made it to the command post towards 2300 hours. Everything had already been prepared in an exacting manner there, and the drivers of the companies all received the same amount of fuel distributed to them. The commander personally supervised the distribution, with the company commanders keeping a sharp eye out that everything was properly distributed within the companies. The fuel vehicle had been towed to the battalion command post by the *Kfz. 15* the patrol had. Around 2400 hours, the companies reported they were ready to move, and we could start our trip into the unknown.

There wasn't a single map of the area within the battalion. There was no more radio communication with the division due to the great distance. The reconnaissance battalion had already been stuck for more than 24 hours. The last radio message from the division: "The battalion had to get out." Towards 2400 hours, we deployed for combat in the direction of Oisy, moving out without any lights and with as little noise as possible. Around 120 *SPW's* and wheeled vehicles had enough fuel for about 100 kilometers. Everything went according to plan and without incident as far as Oisy on the Sambre Canal, to the northeast of Wassigny. Signs of light from the front far away showed us the direction, and the stars led the way.

There were still a lot of scattered elements in Oisy, including a platoon of paratroopers. The paratrooper platoon leader, an energetic young *Leutnant*, reported that the enemy was all around and that a breakthrough effort he had already attempted with his men had failed. At least the *Leutnant* had a map, albeit in a scale of 1:1,000,000. After assessing the situation, the Battalion Commander of the reconnaissance battalion decided to move out mounted with all elements in the direction of Etreux–La Capelle, attempting to establish contact with friendly forces there. The nighttime hours needed to be used, since the battalion would be served up on a platter to the enemy fighter-bombers during the day and under clear skies.

We had barely reached the outskirts of Oisy, when the battalion was forced to halt due to extremely heavy antitank-gun fire from a short distance along the road. Of the three *SPW's* with 7.5cm main guns that were in the lead, two were immediately knocked out by direct hits. The Battalion Commander was in the fourth position in the radio *SPW*, which served as the radio connection to the division. At least the two knocked-out *SPW's* were blocking the road and prevented a tank attack against the battalion, which had closed up tight in the meantime.

All of a sudden, there was heavy artillery fire from the flank. Fortunately, it was too short. It appeared that a breakthrough at that location was hopeless. The battalion turned around all at the same time to see what it could do in the opposite direction, that is, to the northeast. Together with *Oberscharführer* Pink, the Battalion Commander moved ahead of the battalion about 600 meters and guided the units forwarded with blink signals (flashlight). The lead was then taken over by three 7.5cm anti-tank guns and the armored engineer platoon. Just outside the entrance to La Croise, about five kilometers north of Oisy, the battalion received machine-gun and tank fire, which fell too short. The outposts the enemy had established there must have fallen asleep. Without firing a round in the locality, the battalion then moved east at a fast pace through some woods occupied by partisans. Contact had to be established with the friendly lines before the start of the day and the enemy's aerial activity. If not, our fate was sealed. In fact, the battalion reached the border via Le Chateau-Maubeuge with its last drops of fuel right around 0700 hours. It established contact with friendly elements there.

During that operation, the battalion suffered the loss of two men along with a few slightly wounded, as well as the two *SPW's* previously mentioned. After contact was established with the division by radio, the battalion joined in on the new fighting and retrograde movements. Once I reported back at the division command post, the division staff was happy to see that the once lost reconnaissance battalion had returned.

The following is a firsthand account by a soldier assigned to *SS-Panzer-Aufklärungs-Abteilung 10 "Frundsberg"* and concerns the withdrawal across the Ruhr during the fighting around Linnich in the first part of December 1944. The reconnaissance battalion was assigned a direct combat mission. Once the German forces had been enveloped, the primary objective was to withdraw across the Ruhr and live to fight another day:[67]

We had been conducting operations in the area around the Arnhem bridgehead up to 18 November 1944, when we were relieved by airborne units. We were only granted a few days to rest and recoup, when we were loaded on trains in Boetichen and sent to a new area of operations. The movement was short; we detrained in Reydt in the Rhineland. We road marched to the area of operations around Aachen. The reconnaissance battalion was assigned the sector around Wels–Rurdorf.

Early one afternoon, a young liaison officer came to the battalion with orders to reestablish contact with *SS-Panzer-Grenadier-Regiment 22*, which had been lost.

Extremely heavy artillery fire was being placed on the entire sector and enemy fighter-bombers hunted above the positions, making any and all movement impossible.

Since the situation was completely uncertain, we advanced to the northwest and, after a few hundred meters, saw soldiers digging in. We thought we had completed our mission, when we noticed to our shock, as we got closer, that they were Americans. The low December sun had blinded us, not allowing us to identify the Yanks earlier. Barely 50 meters separated us from the enemy. Maybe the Yanks thought we were going to desert? If that was the case, they were sadly mistaken. The moment of shock did not last long, and we turned tail and got out of there. Something had to be done to keep them from advancing further. We reported the situation to the battalion and requested reinforcements. It didn't take too long before an Army company was brought forward. It attacked immediately, but it was only able to advance a few meters before it was stopped, taking casualties. The acting company commander, a *Leutnant*, who had started to panic, wanted to pull back. We worked hard to prevent that. Fortunately, the penal platoon of the division arrived and was employed to our right. There was still no contact with the 22nd. Unfortunately, the Army company was pulled back during the night. In their place, we received elements of the [divisional combat engineer battalion] in the main line of resistance.

As it started to get lighter, the enemy's artillery fire intensified, making us conclude the enemy was going to attack again. But nothing happened before noon. Then, all Hell broke out. Fighter-bombers dove on our positions, not to mention unbelievable artillery fire. Then, smoke was fired. That was the sign that the enemy had started his attack. Everyone was ready to defend and strained his eyes to make out something through the fog. Infantry fires commenced and then the smoke finally started to clear. The Yanks had penetrated between us and the 22nd. The penal platoon was already pulling back! From the left flank we received the ominous message that there was no longer any contact with our battalion to the left. Signal flares that rose from the outskirts of Rurdorf announced out situation. It was clear that we had to hold our position until it turned dark in order to reestablish contact with our own forces. We requested artillery fire to make the enemy's advance more difficult. The fighter-bombers also helped us. They did not identify their own lines and dropped bombs among their own troops. As unfortunate as that undoubtedly was for the Yanks, it was just what we needed at the time. But then there was a new shock. The Yanks had tanks on the Linnich–Rurdorf road in front of the village. That was to our rear. We started receiving fire from there as well. When it turned dark, we were successful in disengaging without incident from the enemy. We immediately set up an all-round defense in Rurdorf. Late in the evening, a small assault detachment was formed to fetch a *Rottenführer*, who was supposed to be in a hospital. The hospital was halfway to Linnich and was occupied by the Yanks. We were able to get the *Rottenführer*, thus keeping him from being taken prisoner. *Sturmmann* Thomalla wasn't so lucky. He had had a high fever all day long, but he was unable to get back to the rear. When we were finally ready to take him back, he was killed by artillery fire. Thomalla had distinguished himself at Arnhem while destroying a bunker—all witnessed by the Battalion Commander—and had earned the Iron Cross.

There was heavy artillery fire all night long on our position. It got more intense as it neared morning. All of a sudden, there was a huge hue and cry; the Yanks had penetrated into Rurdorf. The elements of *SS-Pionier-Bataillon 10*, which were positioned to our left, had been enveloped. They were already pulling back. That meant we didn't have much time left there, either. The Yanks were in Rurdorf, and we were cut off once again. The most important thing was to get over the Ruhr in one piece.

Everything went relatively well. A footbridge over the Ruhr was being held by the penal platoon. We crossed over to the far bank at first light and towards a prepared passage point. The footbridge was then blown up. Then there was an unpleasant surprise. The passage point was supposed to have been occupied, but there was no evidence of that. We had to do it. Once again, there was no contact to the right or to the left. What was going on? The Yanks started firing again with artillery. They thought they could smoke us out with phosphorous. The men stood in the water with dampened clothes over their mouths and noses. The fighter-bombers provided a musical accompaniment. During the day, contact was finally established with the unit this sector belonged to. Towards evening, a platoon leader and messenger attempted to find the Army command post in order to get briefed on the situation. After some initial misunderstandings and give-and-take, the situation was soon clarified.

According to its orders, [the battalion] was to assemble in Hottorf. We were relieved as soon as it was possible and led back to Hottorf. Halfway there, two *SPW's* came our way in order to pick up the men, who had been through the wringer. All of the battalion, from the Battalion Commander on down, had had to swim the Ruhr, except for us, who had been able to use the footbridge.

Excerpts from Award Recommendations: SS Armored Reconnaissance Battalions, Western Front (1944)

While the quotation of award recommendations may run the risk of being tendentious, since the purpose of the document, after all, is to get the award approved, they nonetheless provide some insight into what actions were required in order to be eligible for an award. Unfortunately, there is no readily available source for army documents, unless one goes directly to the German Federal Archives, but the vast amount of secondary literature concerning the *Waffen-SS* allows a glimpse into the process.[68] Here is a sampling of award recommendations for some scouts and reconnaissance soldiers and officers who received high awards during the fighting in the West in the second half of 1944.

Berger, *Dr. med. Dent.* Arnold Oskar Richard. *SS-Hauptsturmführer* Berger was awarded the German Cross in Gold while assigned to *SS-Panzer-Aufklärungs-Abteilung 17 "Götz von Berlichingen"* as its battalion surgeon. His citation reads:[69]

12 June 1944 at Sainteny (Normandy): During the course of the difficult defensive fighting on the part of the battalion, friendly lines threatened to collapse as a result of the high losses. *Dr.* Berger remained in the front lines with his wounded until the last one received initial treatment and was evacuated. He then rallied the remaining 15 to 20 men, some of whom were slightly wounded, and launched himself against the enemy. He held them up until friendly forces had reorganized, and he was able to pull back under their protective fires. 17 July 1944 in the area around Remilly (Normandy): During a withdrawal, 12 men, including some badly wounded, remained behind. *Dr.* Berger, using 5 men, some of whom were slightly wounded, launched an immediate counterattack while advancing in a *Schwimmwagen*. He ejected the enemy, took care of the wounded and held the area until all of the wounded could be evacuated. No date; Hill 314 in the area around Mortain (Normandy): Acting on his own initiative, *Dr.* Berger supplied rations and ammunition for days on end to a friendly encircled battle group, evacuating wounded in the process. He accomplished this all by himself in a *Schwimmwagen* by breaking through the enemy encirclement while receiving extremely heavy enemy fire. 4 December 1944, Ebringen: During fighting in a village, after friendly forces had already pulled back, *Dr.* Berger personally evacuated wounded who had been left behind. He handed them over to slightly wounded men, who got them out of the enemy fire. Fighting all the while, *Dr.* Berger fought his way back to friendly lines as the last soldier. 4 January 1945, Großrederchingen: During an attack to relieve an encircled battle group in Großrederchingen, *Dr.* Berger rode forward in an assault gun with the lead attack elements. Heavy house-to-house fighting developed in the village. *Dr.* Berger raced past the houses occupied by the enemy, got through to the encircled battle group and took care of the wounded. Afterwards, he fought his way back to the lead attack elements, mounted an assault gun and broke through the encirclement for the second time and evacuated all of the wounded.

Bremer, Gerhard. Gerhard Bremer was the recipient of a number of high awards, including the Knight's Cross (28 October 1941), the Close Combat Clasp in Silver (25 November 1943), the German Cross in Gold (30 August 1944), and the Oak Leaves to the Knight's Cross (668th recipient) (26 November 1944). Here is the recommendation for the Oak Leaves, while serving as an *SS-Sturmbannführer* and commander of *SS-Panzer-Aufklärungs-Abteilung 12 "Hitlerjugend"*:[70]

August 1944, area around Rugles: When Bremer, who was with his battalion, which was in the process of battlefield reconstitution, heard about the advance of enemy armored elements in the direction of Chartres, he assembled all available forces and, using his own initiative, moved out against the enemy forces that had broken through. In the process, he provided

Excerpts from Award Recommendations: SS Armored Reconnaissance Battalions, Western Front (1944) *continued*

senior leadership valuable information concerning enemy movements. In addition, the scout troops he employed remained in constant contact with the enemy and considerably slowed down his advance. On 15 August 1944, the battalion was moved to the area around Evreux to continue its battlefield reconstitution. Thanks to reconnaissance initiated by the battalion on [Bremer's] own initiative, the advance of enemy armored forces on both sides of the Eure were identified in a timely fashion and a blocking position established. As a result of the reconnaissance initiated by Bremer, a clear picture was formed of the enemy situation and his advance was considerably delayed.

Gernt, Theo. Gernt received a number of high awards, including the Special Award for the Single-Handed Destruction of Armored Vehicles (1 September 1944) and the Close Combat Clasp in Silver (1 September 1944). Here is the award recommendation for the German Cross in Gold, which he received on 30 December 1944, while serving as an *SS-Oberscharführer* and platoon leader in the Headquarters Company of *SS-Panzer-Aufklärungs-Abteilung 1 Leibstandarte SS Adolf Hitler*:[71]

. . . Normandy operations, 1944, vicinity of [unreadable]: In the course of a counterattack against an enemy force that had entered a village with tanks, he stormed well ahead of his men and eliminated an enemy tank, which was influential in holding back the friendly attack, with a *Panzerfaust*. Fighting with cold steel and hand grenades, he and his platoon ejected the enemy from the point of penetration and restored the former main line of resistance. The enemy left five machine guns and two mortars behind. Normandy operations, 1944, in the Oise sector: During the withdrawal, Gernt and his platoon screened the movements of the battalion. He turned back reconnaissance efforts on the part of the enemy several times. Although he had already been bypassed by the enemy and he had received orders to pull back, he held the important position for the battalion and was able to report important information from there that assisted the continued defense of the Oise sector. Later, Gernt led his platoon through the enemy forces back to the new defensive positions without any friendly casualties. In the process, he inflicted heavy casualties on the enemy and destroyed two utility vehicles and a truck. Normandy operations, 1944, vicinity of La Capelle: After the battalion had been encircled and orders received to break out to the north, Gernt encountered an enemy outpost while reconnoitering. Together with the two men of his *Volkswagen*, he overpowered the enemy in close combat (three dead and six prisoners). Thanks to his decisive actions, Gernt enabled the entire battalion to move through the enemy's encirclement.

Gräbner, Viktor-Eberhard. Gräbner posthumously received the Knight's Cross to the Iron Cross on 23 August 1944 as an *SS-Hauptsturmführer der Reserve* and Battalion Commander of *SS-Panzer-Aufklärungs-Abteilung 9 "Hohenstaufen."* He had previously received the German Cross in Gold (15 May 1942) and the Close Combat Clasp in Bronze (25 July 1944). He was killed in action at Arnhem on 18 September 1944:[72]

16–20 July 1944, in Noyers-Bocage: On 16 July 1944, the battalion was attached to *Grenadier-Regiment 989* and received the mission to support the 1st Battalion [of the regiment] in its continued attack to restore the former main line of resistance and take the village of Noyers.

While still moving forward to the attack area, the enemy ejected the battalion that was to be supported and Noyers was taken by the English.

On his own initiative, Gräbner deviated from his mission, attacked the enemy and took back Noyers. During the days that followed, the village was in the middle of the fighting again and again. The enemy, supported and reinforced by artillery and armor, attempted to win back the village with all means at his disposal. He was turned back again and again,

Excerpts from Award Recommendations: SS Armored Reconnaissance Battalions, Western Front (1944) *continued*

during which Gräbner distinguished himself at the front through his superior leadership and personal actions. It was due to the efforts of Gräbner that Noyers, the hot spot of the entire front southwest of Caen, was held.

Harmstorf, Rudolf. Harmstorf had a long history serving in *SS* reconnaissance formations and was nominated for the German Cross in Gold as an *SS-Obersturmführer* and acting company commander of the *2./SS-Panzer-Aufklärungs-Abteilung 10 "Frundsberg."* He received the award on 27 October 1944:[73]

... 16 and 19 August 1944 [location not given; in the area around Falaise]: As the leader of the rearguard of the battalion, Harmstorf enabled the disciplined withdrawal of the division and, in the process, held up the enemy until the division was able to occupy new positions. 20 August 1944, in the Falaise Pocket: Harmstorf's company was the lead company in the breakout from the pocket. Harmstorf led an armored attack with his company, always ahead of his men, thus enabling the encircled friendly forces to break out... During all of those operations, Harmstorf especially distinguished himself through personal bravery and circumspect leadership.

Krag, Ernst-August. Krag, who received the German Cross in Gold on 9 April 1943, went on to receive both the Knight's Cross (23 October 1944) and the Oak Leaves (755th recipient) (28 February 1945). In both instances, he was an *SS-Sturmbannführer* and the battalion commander of *SS-Panzer-Aufklärungs-Abteilung 2 "Das Reich."* According to Jürgen Karl, the following actions got him nominated for the Knight's Cross:[74]

... Promoted to *SS-Sturmbannführer* on 20 April 1944, he was with his formation in defensive fighting in Normandy after the Allied landings. In the course of that, on 5 July 1944, he was slightly wounded one more time. On 10 July 1944, he replaced the commander of *SS-Panzer-Aufklärungs-Abteilung 2*, Heinrich Wulf, who had to depart because of wounds suffered. At the same time, *SS-Hauptsturmführer der Reserve* Roehder assumed command of the [divisional assault gun battalion].

On 15 July 1944, the enemy penetrated a blocking position northwest of Virges-des-Saints after hours of barrage fire. The position had been weakly held. *SS-Sturmbannführer* Krag was able to master the situation with his [battalion]. He inflicted heavy, bloody losses on the enemy while suffering only nominal casualties. Reeling from his defeat, the enemy requested a cease-fire for one hour, so that he could recover his many dead and wounded.

On 16 July 1944, the enemy attacked the positions of [the battalion] along its entire sector after an extremely intensive preparation. After hours of extremely heavy fighting, the enemy was able to slightly expand the penetration he had achieved the previous day. The immediate counterattack launched by [Krag], who showed reckless disregard for himself, was able to eject the enemy past the point of penetration of that day and the day before, all the while inflicting the heaviest of casualties on the enemy.

After the [division] had broken through to the southeast from the area around Avranches during the night of 28–29 July 1944, so as to establish a new main line of resistance along a line running from Percy to Sourdevall, [Krag] and his battalion, operating on his own initiative, blocked the enemy force that had penetrated into Gavray. By doing so, he prevented the enemy from launching a thrust into the deep flank of the division. [Krag] acted on his own accord, fully cognizant of the situation. With only the weakest of forces, he achieved a total defensive victory against numerically vastly superior enemy armored forces. The brave fight, which [Krag] and his battalion conducted, enabled the division and the other formations of the *LXXXIV. Armee-Korps* to establish a new front line. In the area around Gavray, [Krag] and his battalion destroyed nine enemy tanks, a large number of armored and soft-skinned vehicles and inflicted bloody losses on the enemy...

Studio portrait of a *Stabsgefreiter* assigned to the *Panzer-Aufklärungs-Lehr-Abteilung*. He wears the field-gray version of the protective clothing for armored vehicle crewmembers. Since all of the battalion was armored when initially deployed with the division, he might have been in any of the line companies. Of interest is that the stylized "L" on his shoulder strap appears to be considerably darker in color than the *Waffenfarbe* on his collar tabs, indicating he might have been assigned to one of the *Panzergrenadier* regiments initially, where the piping was meadow green. CARSTEN FRIES

Another studio portrait of a reconnaissance soldier, most likely in early 1944. He wears an earlier version of the *M43* billed field cap, as seen by the "T"-style national insignia machine-sewn to the front of his cap. CARSTEN FRIES

This *Sd.Kfz. 250/9* was knocked out somewhere in France in the summer of 1944. Most armored reconnaissance battalions fighting in the West at that time had some of these vehicles on hand, although rarely a complete complement of them (sixteen per half-tracked scout company). NATIONAL ARCHIVES

A knocked-out *Sd.Kfz. 222* in an unidentified French village. Some of the armored reconnaissance battalions that fought in Normandy still had this vehicle, especially in the *Waffen-SS* divisions. The veteran of many campaigns, it was being phased out toward the end of the war, along with the *Sd.Kfz. 223* armored radio car, which was also on hand in several formations. NATIONAL ARCHIVES

A knocked-out *Sd.Kfz. 231 (8 Rad)* in Normandy. The *21. Panzer-Division* and three *SS* divisions—the 9th, 10th, and 12th—all had several of these on hand when they entered the fighting in Normandy. NATIONAL ARCHIVES

This *Sd.Kfz. 234/2 Puma* was captured by Allied forces during the fighting in Normandy. Three divisions fielded this vehicle while fighting in the West: the *2. Panzer-Division*, the *Panzer-Lehr-Division*, and the *1. SS-Panzer-Division Leibstandarte SS Adolf Hitler*. NATIONAL ARCHIVES

A young reconnaissance *Leutnant* poses for a studio portrait in July 1944. Despite his youth, he has seen combat, as evidenced by his Iron Cross, Second Class, ribbon and his barely visible Armored Assault Badge in Bronze. SCOTT PRITCHETT

THE END IN THE WEST 427

These images are taken from the weekly German newsreel of 9 June 1943 and show factory production of *Sd.Kfz. 231's*. Despite the impressive display, production could never keep up with demand for these or any other German armored vehicle.

428 **TIP OF THE SPEAR**

These images are taken from the 13 July 1944 newsreel and show elements of *SS-Panzer-Aufklärungs-Abteilung 1 Leibstandarte SS Adolf Hitler* deploying for operations. The battalion commander, *SS-Sturmbannführer* Knittel, is seen in the first image.[75]

THE END IN THE WEST 429

CHAPTER 11

The End in the East

SETTING THE STAGE

As with the West, the Eastern Front in 1944 saw the beginning of the knockout blows that would be the death knell for the Third Reich. The first half of the year was marked by some continued give-and-take, but it was obvious the Soviets were clearly gaining the upper hand. By the time Operation Bagration was launched on 22 June 1944, the Western Allies had landed in Normandy, moved beyond the beachhead, and established a permanent presence, thus opening another front in the west—the one posing the greatest danger to Germany's western frontier.

By 1944 the Soviets also had become masters of maneuver warfare, and the aforementioned Operation Bagration effectively wiped out *Heeresgruppe Mitte*, thanks in part to the complete failure of German intelligence to divine the intentions of the Soviet forces for the summer campaigning season. Within ten days, the prewar Polish eastern border was reached by Soviet forces, and by August some 400,000 German personnel had fallen victim to the Soviet attack.

Although less effective in the north, Soviet forces eventually isolated and cut off *Heeresgruppe Nord*—the future *Heeresgruppe Kurland*—thus ultimately forming the Courland Pocket, which would be the scene of intense fighting through the end of the war. However, the Germans were able to regroup somewhat, and Soviet

This image of an *Sd.Kfz. 250/9* comes from a series of photos taken by *SS* war correspondent Ernst Baumann of the future 2nd Company of *SS-Panzer-Aufklärungs-Abteilung 11 "Nordland"* during new-equipment training on the vehicle in Croatia in late 1943. More images and amplifying text can be found in the sidebar "Employment of the *Sd.Kfz. 250/9* in *KStN 1162c* Armored Scout Companies," found on pages 467–77 in this chapter. HEINER DUSKE

offensive operations reached an initial culminating point in the fall of 1944. Once the Soviets had regrouped, reinforced, and reconstituted frontline forces, they initiated offensive operations again on 17 January 1945. Outnumbering the Germans in every category—five or six to one in personnel, and roughly six to one in armor and artillery—the only unknown was how long it would take to capture Berlin. Unlike the Western Front, the fighting in the East continued with a ferocity and ideological bent until the very end, with German forces fighting desperately for their homeland, especially after the initial wave of Soviet atrocities against German civilians were reported. Despite several offensive countermeasures, notably the failed attempts to relieve encircled Budapest and the fighting around Lake Balaton, the Red Army juggernaut could not be stopped. Vienna fell in late April and Berlin at the beginning of May. The German surrender was signed on 7 May (in the West) and 8 May (in the East).

DOCTRINE

By 1944 the armored reconnaissance battalions in the East were essentially reduced to the role played by their sister battalions in the West: direct-combat formations with very little being performed in the way of traditional reconnaissance. The battalions were usually employed in the line or held as divisional reserves, to be used as counterattack elements at hot spots. During withdrawals, they were typically employed as the divisional rear guard, augmented by other assets, as available. In cases where contact was lost between formations or the division was on a wing of higher commands—such as corps, field armies, or field army groups—then they usually performed flank guard or screening missions. As had frequently been the case in the desert, reconnaissance assets were occasionally detached from their parent divisions and combined into mobile battle groups, which usually covered long exposed flanks of higher headquarters and conducted deception operations. The most famous battle group of that type was probably formed for the third attempt to relieve Budapest, when the reconnaissance battalions of three armored divisions—the 1st, 3rd, and 23rd—were placed under unified command, reporting to the headquarters of the *3. Panzer-Division*.

The chaotic supply situation and inability of German industry to manufacture enough combat vehicles was also felt in the East, even though priority was given to that front. As a result of those factors and the ever-dwindling supply of suitable manpower, the *Organizations-Abteilung* introduced *Panzer-Division 45* and *Kampfgruppe Panzer-Division 45* in March 1945. All armored formations, including *Panzergrenadier-Divisionen*, were envisioned to convert to the new organization, even though many had never even fully converted to the Model 44 templates. The armored reconnaissance battalions were reduced in manpower, combat vehicles, and equipment, fielding only three line companies and no longer having a heavy company. The new organization is detailed below, although it must be considered a theoretical construct since it was only possibly fielded in a few cases for the units sent to the Milowitz Training Area for reconstitution in the late spring of 1945.

PANZER-DIVISION, 1945 (MODEL)

Panzer-Aufklärungs-Abteilung	Reconnaissance Assets / Notes
Headquarters	Headquarters Company: *KStN 1109 (gp) (fG)* (1 April 1945)
1st Company	Mixed Armored Scout Company: *KStN 1162f* (1 April 1945)
2nd Company	Light Wheeled Reconnaissance Company: *KStN 1113 (gp)* (1 April 1945)
3rd Company	Light Wheeled Reconnaissance Company: *KStN 1113 (gp)* (1 April 1945)

ORDER OF BATTLE IN THE EAST, 15 JUNE 1944[1]

Formation	Notes
Heeresgruppe Nord (Reserves)	
12. Panzer-Division	*Panzer-Aufklärungs-Abteilung 12*: The battalion was detached from the division and being reconstituted at the Wildflecken Training Area in Germany while undergoing reorganization under a Model 44 template. The battalion, minus the *KStN 1162c* company, rejoined the division in July, with the half-track scout company apparently not rejoining the battalion until after September.
Armee-Abteilung "Narwa"	
III SS-Panzer-Korps (germanisches)	
SS-Freiwilligen-Panzergrenadier-Division "Nordland"	*SS-Panzer-Aufklärungs-Abteilung 11 "Nordland"*: Although an organization chart for the division shows a pre–Model 43 organization for the reconnaissance battalion with an armored scout company (1st), three *Volkswagen*-equipped motorized light reconnaissance companies (2nd through 4th), and a motorized heavy company (5th), it is known that the battalion's 2nd Company was organized as a half-tracked scout company and assigned to the division by June 1944. The 1st Company (armored scout) also had the *Volkswagen* utility vehicle on hand until it received some armored cars in the June timeframe (apparently four light and six heavy armored cars).
Heeresgruppe Mitte	
4. Armee	
XII. Armee-Korps	
18. Panzergrenadier-Division	*Panzer-Aufklärungs-Abteilung 118*: Pre–Model 43 organization, with one wheeled scout company, three motorcycle infantry companies, and a wheeled heavy company. After Operation Bagration, only *Panzer-Späh-Zug 118* remained until the division was reconstituted (six armored cars of which four had 2cm main guns).
XXVII. Armee-Korps	
25. Panzergrenadier-Division	*Panzer-Aufklärungs-Abteilung 125*: Pre–Model 43 organization, with one wheeled scout company, three motorcycle infantry companies, and a wheeled heavy company. After Operation Bagration, only *Panzer-Späh-Zug 125* remained until the division was reconstituted (six armored cars of which four had 2cm main guns).
Heeresgruppe Nordukraine	
1. Panzer-Armee (Reserves)	
1. Panzer-Division	*Panzer-Aufklärungs-Abteilung 1*: Converted to a Model 44 organization in May, although the 1st, 2nd, and 4th Companies apparently all had soft-skinned vehicles until July 1944. The 1st and 2nd Companies received half-tracks in July 1944, but the 1st Company (half-tracked armored scout) apparently did not have any *Sd.Kfz. 250/9's* again until January 1945. The 4th Company (armored heavy) did not receive any half-track variants until September 1944.
7. Panzer-Division	*Panzer-Aufklärungs-Abteilung 7*: The battalion reorganized under the Model 44 template during this period.
8. Panzer-Division	*Panzer-Aufklärungs-Abteilung 8*: In June the battalion had a modified Model 43 organization, with its 4th Company still organized under a motorcycle infantry company *KStN*. The battalion started to convert to a Model 44 organization in July while attached to the *1. Panzer-Division* for an extended period. By August, the entire battalion was detached and sent to Germany to complete reconstitution and conversion to the Model 44 template. The battalion returned to the front in October, where it reported directly to the *8. Armee*. In November it rejoined the division.
17. Panzer-Division	*Panzer-Aufklärungs-Abteilung 17*: Organized under the Model 43 template in June, the battalion started its conversion to a Model 44 formation in July.
20. Panzergrenadier-Division	*Panzer-Aufklärungs-Abteilung 120*: Pre–Model 43 organization, with one wheeled scout company, three motorcycle infantry companies, and a wheeled heavy company. The battalion made a transition to a very modified Model 44 template in September 1944.

4. Panzer-Armee (Reserves)

4. Panzer-Division	*Panzer-Aufklärungs-Abteilung 4*: The battalion converted to the Model 43 organization in June 1944. In addition to the 1st Company (Wheeled Armored Scout), the battalion was also authorized a heavy scout platoon of six *Sd.Kfz. 233's*. Its 2nd Company was organized under *KStN 1162b* and equipped with the *Panzer II, Ausführung L Luchs*. The 3rd and 4th Companies were both light armored reconnaissance companies (motorized), while the 5th Company was organized under the motorized heavy company template.[2]
5. Panzer-Division	*Panzer-Aufklärungs-Abteilung 5*: By June 1944 the battalion had started the process to convert to the Model 44 organization, with most of its companies in Germany for reconstitution or reorganization. Only elements of the battalion were on hand with the division in the field.

Heeresgruppe Südukraine
6. Armee (Reserves)

3. Panzer-Division	*Panzer-Aufklärungs-Abteilung 3*: The battalion never converted to a Model 43 structure. It retained the following organization: Headquarters, 1st Company (Wheeled Armored Scout), 2nd Company (Motorcycle Infantry),[3] 3rd Company (Light Armored Reconnaissance), 4th Company (Light Armored Reconnaissance), 5th Company (Motorized Heavy). By July the battalion started to make the transition to a Model 44 organization, with its 2nd Company reorganized as a *KStN 1162b* armored scout company equipped with the *Aufklärungs-Panzer 38(t)*.
13. Panzer-Division	*Panzer-Aufklärungs-Abteilung 13*: Organized along the lines of a Model 43 reconnaissance battalion, it started converting to the Model 44 organization in August. It was badly battered in subsequent fighting and reported on 1 November 1944 that it had the following assets: a wheeled scout company (two light and five heavy armored cars), a light reconnaissance company (half-track; eighteen *Sd.Kfz. 250* variants and one mortar), and a wheeled heavy company (three light machine guns and one mortar).

XXXXIV. Armee-Korps

10. Panzergrenadier-Division	*Panzer-Aufklärungs-Abteilung 110*: Organized under the pre–Model 43 organizational framework, with a wheeled armored scout company (1st), three motorcycle infantry companies (2nd through 4th), and a motorized heavy company (5th). At an undetermined point in time, the motorcycle infantry companies became *Volkswagen*-equipped light reconnaissance companies. The battalion was essentially wiped out in August 1944.

8. Armee
Gruppe General Mieth

23. Panzer-Division	*Panzer-Aufklärungs-Abteilung 23*: Model 44 organization, most likely at full strength, although the reorganized and redesignated 4th Company (new 3rd Company) did not rejoin the battalion until the end of June.

Fourth Army (Romanian) (Reserves)

24. Panzer-Division	*Panzer-Aufklärungs-Abteilung 24*: Although it had formed under the Model 43 template by the beginning of 1944, the reconnaissance assets of the battalion were later subordinated to *Panzergrenadier-Regiment 26*, while the wheeled armored car troop reported directly to the division headquarters as *Panzer-Späh-Schwadron 24*.
3. SS-Panzer-Division "Totenkopf"	*SS-Panzer-Aufklärungs-Abteilung 3 "Totenkopf"*: The battalion was organized under the Model 44 template in June 1944 but severely understrength, reporting only five *Sd.Kfz. 250* variants and three *Sd.Kfz 251* variants in July.

Gruppe Knobelsdorff (Reserves)

14. Panzer-Division	*Panzer-Aufklärungs-Abteilung 14*: Modified Model 43 organization, with a light armored reconnaissance company taking the place of a medium armored reconnaissance company. The heavy armored car platoon with six *Sd.Kfz. 233's* was also fielded. The battalion began the transition to the Model 44 organization in August, although the headquarters company retained both light and heavy armored cars.

ORDER OF BATTLE IN THE EAST, 31 DECEMBER 1944[4]

Heeresgruppe Nord
18. Armee
III. SS-Panzer-Korps (germanisches)

4. SS-Panzer-Grenadier-Brigade "Nederland"	*Divisions-Füsilier-Bataillon 54 "Nederland"*: An organization chart for May 1944 shows this as a *Volkswagen*-equipped company-sized element with six armored cars (apparently *Sd.Kfz. 222's*), three heavy antitank guns, two medium mortars, four heavy machine guns, and twenty-one light machine guns. The actual figures are uncertain, as is the fact of whether this "battalion" was ever fielded with the brigade.

11. SS-Panzer-Grenadier-Division "Nordland"	SS-Panzer-Aufklärungs-Abteilung 11 "Nordland": See previous table.

II. Armee-Korps

14. Panzer-Division	*Panzer-Aufklärungs-Abteilung 14*: A status report dated 1 January 1945 shows the battalion having the following assets: Headquarters with one *Sd.Kfz. 250* variant, one *Sd.Kfz. 251* variant, sixteen light armored cars (presumably a mix of *Sd.Kfz. 222's* and *223's*), and four heavy armored cars (unknown variants); and 1st through 4th Companies with a small mix of light and medium half-tracks (numbers illegible on document reviewed).

16. Armee
VI. SS-Armee-Korps

4. Panzer-Division	*Panzer-Aufklärungs-Abteilung 4*: Same organization as previous table.
12. Panzer-Division	*Panzer-Aufklärungs-Abteilung 12*: Model 44 organization. In January the 3rd Company (medium armored reconnaissance) was detached to the Milowitz Training Area for reconstitution, never rejoining the division (see entry for *Panzer-Aufklärungs-Abteilung 7*).

Heeresgruppe Mitte (Reserves)

7. Panzer-Division	*Panzer-Aufklärungs-Abteilung 7*: Same organization as the previous table, although the battalion started to become heavily attrited. By the end of January 1945, it no longer had any *Sd.Kfz. 250/9's*.
18. Panzergrenadier-Division	*Panzer-Aufklärungs-Abteilung 118*: The battalion had recovered somewhat and planned for a Model 44 organization, although it never attained that status. The headquarters company was in relatively good shape, with sixteen armored cars (three with 7.5cm main guns, most likely *Sd.Kfz. 233's*, and thirteen additional cars, all with 2cm main guns). It only fielded two line companies, however; both were light motorized reconnaissance companies equipped with *Volkswagen* utility vehicles.
20. Panzer-Division	*Panzer-Aufklärungs-Abteilung 20*: The battalion had moved to the Wildflecken Training Area in April for reconstitution and reorganization as a Model 44 formation. In the course of that, the headquarters company received the *Sd.Kfz. 234/2 Puma*. Redeployed to the Eastern Front in July, it was attached to the *5. Panzer-Division* (see below), not returning to its parent division until September 1944.[5]

4. Armee (Reserves)

5. Panzer-Division	*Panzer-Aufklärungs-Abteilung 5*: While most of the battalion was in Germany for reconstitution and reorganization (see previous table), *Panzer-Aufklärungs-Abteilung 20* of the *20. Panzer-Division* was attached to the division in August and September to take its place.
Fallschirm-Panzer-Division "Hermann Göring 1"	*Fallschirm-Panzer-Aufklärungs-Abteilung 1 "Hermann Göring"*: The battalion converted to a Model 44 structure in September 1944, with the 1st Company organized under *KStN 1162c*.
Fallschirm-Panzergrenadier-Division "Hermann Göring 2"	*Fallschirm-Panzer-Aufklärungs-Abteilung 2 "Hermann Göring"*: Formed in September 1944, the battalion theoretically had a Model 44 organization. It is doubtful it ever had but a fraction of its authorized personnel and equipment. Since the battalion did not have a half-tracked armored scout company authorized, its place was most likely taken by a light armored or motorized reconnaissance company.

Heeresgruppe A (Reserves)

16. Panzer-Division	*Panzer-Aufklärungs-Abteilung 16*: The battalion converted to the Model 44 organization in June 1944, although the 3rd Company (presumably light armored reconnaissance) still lacked vehicles and returned to Germany in December 1944 for reconstitution. A status report for 1 January 1945 shows the battalion with five light and five heavy armored cars and fifty-one light and four medium half-tracks, although the battalion would be effectively destroyed by the end of the month.
17. Panzer-Division	*Panzer-Aufklärungs-Abteilung 17*: Although the battalion retained its Model 44 structure through the end of December, including fielding a complete *KStN 1162c* company, it was badly mauled in subsequent fighting, effectively losing most of its armored vehicles. By March it reported having only a light motorized reconnaissance company equipped with *Volkswagen* utility vehicles, although the situation improved dramatically upon the battalion's consolidation with *Panzer-Aufklärungs-Abteilung "Hirschberg"* later that month (the battalion came from *Panzer-Brigade 103*, which was disbanded that month). The battalion was then able to report a headquarters (with armored cars), two half-tracked armored scout companies (1st and 2nd), one motorized reconnaissance company (*VW*) (3rd), one motorized reconnaissance company (truck) (4th), and an armored heavy company (5th).
20. Panzergrenadier-Division	*Panzer-Aufklärungs-Abteilung 120*: Modified Model 44 organization with the first three line companies all organized as motorized light reconnaissance companies (*Volkswagen*). The heavy company was motorized as well.

19. Panzer-Division	*Panzer-Aufklärungs-Abteilung 19*: In June the division was in Holland for reconstitution as a Model 44 formation. Due to the situation on the Eastern Front, the division interrupted its reconstitution process and was dispatched to the East as *Kampfgruppe 19. Panzer-Division*, with the reconnaissance battalion's composition uncertain. By December the division was again heavily attrited, with the reconnaissance battalion reporting no combat vehicles. The situation improved slightly by February, although the battalion still only had one combat-capable company, a light armored reconnaissance company with uncertain composition.
25. Panzer-Division	*Panzer-Aufklärungs-Abteilung 25*: After having been effectively wiped out in February 1944, the battalion started its reconstitution process in July. It was organized initially under a modified Model 44 template, with no half-tracked armored scout company authorized. The future 1st Company was activated on 29 September; the rest of the battalion had reported back to the division earlier that month. The Headquarters was organized under the Type "A" version of the 1944 iteration of *KStN 1109* and correspondingly only authorized light armored cars. On 23 September the division reported the following combat vehicles for the reconnaissance battalion (minus its 1st Company): nineteen armored cars, sixty *Sd.Kfz. 250* variants, and thirty-four *Sd.Kfz. 251* variants. The *KStN 1162c* company rejoined the battalion in November with its full complement of authorized vehicles. On 30 December the division reported that the battalion had ninety-six *Sd.Kfz. 250* variants (eighty-three operational) and sixteen light armored cars (sixteen).
Kampfgruppe 10. Panzergrenadier-Division	*Panzer-Aufklärungs-Abteilung 110*: After having been reconstituted in October 1944 as a quasi–Model 44 battalion—the armored cars were moved into the headquarters company, the *Volkswagen* companies were retained (the new 1st through 3rd), and the heavy motorized heavy company became the new 4th—the battalion was again effectively wiped out in January 1945.

Heeresgruppe Süd (Reserves)

3. SS-Panzer-Division "Totenkopf"	*SS-Panzer-Aufklärungs-Abteilung 3 "Totenkopf"*: The battalion continued to be severely understrength, reporting the following combat vehicles on 15 January: six light armored cars (four operational), four heavy armored cars (three), and twenty-nine *Sd.Kfz. 250* variants (twenty).
5. SS-Panzer-Division "Wiking"	*SS-Panzer-Aufklärungs-Abteilung 5 "Wiking"*: The battalion converted to a Model 44 organization in June 1944, although it did not receive its half-tracked scout company until September. It appears that the headquarters company only had light armored cars and *Volkswagen* utility vehicles. The battalion did not rejoin the division at the front until August 1944. On 15 January the division reported the following combat vehicles directly attributable to the battalion: fifty-one *Sd.Kfz 250* variants (thirty-two operational), seven light armored cars (five), and one heavy armored car (one).

Armeegruppe Balck / 6. Armee
Gruppe Breith
Kavallerie-Korps

1. Panzer-Division	*Panzer-Aufklärungs-Abteilung 1*: Although an organizational chart for October 1944 shows a Model 43 template, it appears that the battalion went over to a Model 44 organization much earlier (see previous entry). At that time, the 3rd Company (Medium Armored Reconnaissance) was possibly equipped with a version of the *Maultier* half-tracked soft-skinned utility vehicle. A status report in November 1944 shows the division's reconnaissance battalion as having only eighteen *Sd.Kfz. 250* variants (fourteen operational), four light armored cars (three), and four heavy armored cars (one). The on-hand figures for December were the same, although the operational status changed somewhat.
23. Panzer-Division	*Panzer-Aufklärungs-Abteilung 23*: The reconnaissance battalion was involved in steady fighting throughout the fall and participated in the initial offensive to relieve Budapest at the beginning of January. On 15 January the division reported that the battalion had forty-seven *Sd.Kfz. 250* variants (thirty-six operational), ten light armored cars (eight), and two heavy armored cars (two). Other combat vehicles and equipment on hand cannot be determined since the figures are mixed with those of other formations of the division.

Gruppe Pape

3. Panzer-Division	*Panzer-Aufklärungs-Abteilung 3*: The battalion's 2nd Company was reorganized under *KStN 1162b* on 1 July 1944 and equipped with the *Aufklärungspanzer 38(t)*; the motorized heavy company was reorganized as an armored heavy company on 21 August 1944. The battalion officially converted to the Model 44 organization on 1 September 1944, although the new 3rd Company continued to be equipped with the *Sd.Kfz. 250* instead of the *Sd.Kfz. 251*. Due to reconstitution and reorganization efforts, the battalion rarely had more than two companies on hand during the summer and fall of 1944.
8. Panzer-Division (portions)	*Panzer-Aufklärungs-Abteilung 8*: Organized as a Model 44 reconnaissance battalion, it reported the following combat vehicle strength on 15 January: thirty-eight *Sd.Kfz. 250* variants (eighteen operational) and fifteen heavy armored cars (twelve).
6. Panzer-Division (portions)	*Panzer-Aufklärungs-Abteilung 6*: In June 1944 the only combat element of the battalion with the division was its half-tracked armored scout company, which sustained heavy losses in subsequent fighting. The remainder was in Germany being reconstituted. As was frequently the case, the 3rd Company (medium armored reconnaissance) was actually equipped with *Sd.Kfz. 250* variants. The armored cars apparently rejoined the battalion in August. The 4th Company (armored heavy) was still not with the battalion at this time.

Gruppe Kirchner

6. Panzer-Division (portions)	Panzer-Aufklärungs-Abteilung 6: See above.
3. Panzer-Division (portions)	Panzer-Aufklärungs-Abteilung 3: See above.
8. Panzer-Division (portions)	Panzer-Aufklärungs-Abteilung 8: See above.

IX. SS-Gebirgs-Korps

Panzer-Division "Feldherrnhalle"	Panzer-Aufklärungs-Abteilung "Feldherrnhalle": Organized under the Model 44 template, the battalion was reconstituted after its predecessor formation was wiped out in Operation Bagration. Although deployed to the field by the end of December, much of it was again wiped out in the fighting to relieve Budapest.
13. Panzer-Division	Panzer-Aufklärungs-Abteilung 13: The strength continued to dwindle (see previous table), and the battalion was essentially wiped out in the fighting around Budapest. A division report from December listed the following vehicles attributable to the reconnaissance battalion: one light armored car (none operational), seven (other) armored cars (seven), and twenty-two Sd.Kfz. 250 variants (twenty).

8. Armee
IV. Panzer-Korps

24. Panzer-Division	Panzer-Aufklärungs-Abteilung 24: On 15 November the division reported the following combat vehicles for the battalion: fifty-two Sd.Kfz. 250 variants (fifty operational), two light armored cars (one), and three heavy armored cars (one). The battalion officially adopted a Model 44 organization on 5 January 1945, although evidence suggests the KStN 1162c company became the 1st Troop as early as the summer of 1944.

ORDER OF BATTLE IN THE EAST, 12 APRIL 1945[6]

Heeresgruppe Kurland
18. Armee (Reserves)

14. Panzer-Division	Panzer-Aufklärungs-Abteilung 14: The battalion was detached from the division in March and became a part of Panzer-Brigade Kurland (see there).

16. Armee (Reserves)

Panzer-Brigade Kurland	An ad hoc organization formed to concentrate armored elements trapped in the Courland Pocket to serve as an operational reserve and ready-reaction force. Elements of the brigade included Panzer-Aufklärungs-Abteilung 12 and Panzer-Aufklärungs-Abteilung 14. In accordance with a status report for February 1945, the time the brigade was formed, Panzer-Aufklärungs-Abteilung 12 had the following combat vehicle assets: five light armored cars (presumably Sd.Kfz. 222's), four light armored radio cars (presumably Sd.Kfz. 223's), five heavy armored cars, forty-five Sd.Kfz. 250 variants (of which two were radio versions), and forty-two Sd.Kfz. 251 variants (of which ten were radio versions). Panzer-Aufklärungs-Abteilung 14 had the combat vehicle strength indicated in the previous table.

VI. SS-Armee-Korps

12. Panzer-Division	Panzer-Aufklärungs-Abteilung 12: In February, the battalion was detached from the division to become part of Panzer-Brigade Kurland (see above).

9. Armee (Reserves)

25. Panzergrenadier-Division	Panzer-Aufklärungs-Abteilung 125: Upon reconstitution in November 1944, the battalion was organized on the Model 44 template, albeit with just two motorized light reconnaissance companies using the Volkswagen utility vehicle. There was no half-tracked scout company or heavy company. By February a motorized heavy company had been added, as had an additional motorized light reconnaissance company (VW). An organization chart from 1 April 1945 shows the same organization but gives no strength figures.
Panzer-Division "Müncheberg"	Panzer-Aufklärungs-Kompanie "Müncheberg": The company was formed on 11 March 1945 from a company reassigned from Panzer-Aufklärungs-Abteilung "Sternberg" (see 10. Panzergrenadier-Division). In addition to the Volkswagen utility vehicle, it had both light and heavy armored cars, with Sd.Kfz. 234/1's and 234/4's constituting the latter.

XI. SS-Armee-Korps

20. Panzergrenadier-Division	Panzer-Aufklärungs-Abteilung 120: In March, the battalion was detached from the division for reconstitution at Milowitz Training Area. Only the armored car sections in the headquarters remained, with the company redesignated for a short while as Panzer-Späh-Kompanie 120. In April the remainder of the battalion rejoined the division, apparently with orders to convert to a Model 45 organization, although it is uncertain whether that occurred.

Armee Ostpreußen (ex 2. Armee)
Generalkommando Hela (Reserves)

7. Panzer-Division	*Panzer-Aufklärungs-Abteilung 7*: Appreciably attrited by this time, the battalion apparently only had four line companies of uncertain composition, one of them possibly a motorized reconnaissance company. In late April 1945 the personnel of the *3./Panzer-Aufklärungs-Abteilung 12*, which had been at the Milowitz Training Area awaiting reconstitution, were ordered transferred to the battalion.

XXIII. Armee-Korps

4. Panzer-Division	*Panzer-Aufklärungs-Abteilung 4*: Same organization as before, although a *KStN 1162c* company was authorized in the event the *Luchs* reconnaissance vehicles were consumed in combat operations. On 21 January 1945 sixteen *Sd.Kfz. 250/9's* were sent to the battalion and distributed among the 2nd through 4th Companies. In March the battalion was consolidated with *Panzer-Aufklärungs-Abteilung München*, while retaining its original designation.

XXVI. Armee-Korps

5. Panzer-Division	*Panzer-Aufklärungs-Abteilung 5*: Same organization as in previous table, except the 3rd Company was reorganized as a motorized reconnaissance company in February 1945 due to a lack of armored personnel carriers.
Panzergrenadier-Division "Großdeutschland"	*Panzer-Aufklärungs-Abteilung "Großdeutschland"*: The battalion converted to a standard Model 44 organization in June 1944, albeit with a *KStN 1162b* company substituted for the standard *1162c* company. The 1st Company was issued the *Sd.Kfz. 140/1*, the *Aufklärungspanzer 38(t)*. On 30 December the division reported the following combat vehicle strengths for the battalion: twenty-two *Aufklärungspanzer 38(t)'s* and thirty-six *Sd.Kfz. 250* variants.

Heeresgruppe Mitte (Reserves)

Führer-Begleit-Division	*Panzer-Späh-Kompanie 102* (*Führer-Panzer-Späh-Kompanie 1*): The exact composition of the company is unknown, but a 21 January division status report indicated the formation had thirteen armored cars on hand. Six days later, the number of armored cars was reported to be ten. By March no armored cars were reported as being on hand.

1. Panzer-Armee (Reserves)

8. Panzer-Division	*Panzer-Aufklärungs-Abteilung 8*: According to an organizational status chart dated February 1945, the battalion was in relatively good shape, with the headquarters reporting eighteen armored cars, three *Sd.Kfz. 250* variants, and nine *Sd.Kfz. 251* variants; the 1st Company, twenty *Sd.Kfz. 250* variants (apparently including nine *Sd.Kfz. 250/9's*); the 2nd Company, another twenty *Sd.Kfz. 250* variants; the 3rd Company, twelve *Sd.Kfz. 251* variants; and the 4th Company, another twelve *Sd.Kfz. 251* variants.
17. Panzer-Division	*Panzer-Aufklärungs-Abteilung 17*: As a result of the consolidation with *Panzer-Aufklärungs-Abteilung "Hirschberg,"* the battalion was still a formidable fighting force in March and April 1945. The battalion fielded a Model 44 headquarters company with integral armored cars, two half-tracked armored scout companies (1st and 2nd), a *Volkswagen*-equipped motorized light reconnaissance company (3rd), a motorized light reconnaissance company (4th), and an armored heavy company (5th).

XXIV. Panzer-Korps

10. Panzergrenadier-Division	*Panzer-Aufklärungs-Abteilung 110*: In February the battalion received replacements in the form of consolidation with *Panzer-Aufklärungs-Abteilung "Steinberg"* (formerly attached to *Panzer-Brigade 103*) and reorganized into a mixed scout company (armored cars and *Sd.Kfz. 250* variants) and an understrength *Volkswagen*-equipped motorized light reconnaissance company. The armored scout company was eventually reassigned to *Panzer-Division "Müncheberg"* for the formation of its reconnaissance assets. Later in March, it appears the battalion had the following organization: Headquarters, one armored car platoon, one light motorized reconnaissance company (*VW*), one 7.5cm cannon platoon (half-track), and one antitank company (towed).

LIX. Armee-Korps

19. Panzer-Division	*Panzer-Aufklärungs-Abteilung 19*: Status of the battalion at this date uncertain, although the division as a whole had been heavily attrited.
16. Panzer-Division	*Panzer-Aufklärungs-Abteilung 16*: In March, the battalion absorbed elements that had been earmarked for the formation of *Panzer-Division "Jüterbog."* On 4 March, the division reported the battalion had a headquarters, a half-tracked armored scout company, a wheeled armored scout company, and a light armored reconnaissance company. In April the battalion received its 3rd Company (light armored reconnaissance) back, but it had no combat vehicles. On 4 April the battalion reported a slightly different organization from the previous month: Headquarters, a light wheeled armored scout company, a heavy wheeled armored scout company, and a half-tracked armored scout company. Whether the differences are substantive or simply the result of differing designations is uncertain.

THE END IN THE EAST

17. Armee (Reserves)

18. SS-Panzergrenadier-Division "Horst Wessel"	*SS-Panzer-Aufklärungs-Abteilung 18 "Horst Wessel"*: Organized like a pre–Model 43 reconnaissance battalion, with a wheeled armored scout company, three motorized light reconnaissance companies (most likely *VW*), and a motorized heavy company. The actual strength of the battalion is unknown.
Fallschirm-Panzer-Division "Hermann Göring"1	*Fallschirm-Panzer-Aufklärungs-Abteilung 1 "Hermann Göring"*: In February 1945 the battalion unofficially reorganized as follows: Headquarters with three armored reconnaissance companies (1st through 3rd), an armored heavy company (4th), and a wheeled armored scout company (5th). The latter was equipped with *Sd.Kfz. 234* heavy armored cars. In March, it had the following combat vehicles on hand: twenty *Sd.Kfz. 250* variants, four light armored cars, and nine heavy armored cars. By March the 2nd Company had been effectively destroyed.

XXXX. Panzer-Korps

20. Panzer-Division	*Panzer-Aufklärungs-Abteilung 20*: A status report dated 1 April 1945 shows the battalion organized as follows: Headquarters (with ten *Sd.Kfz. 234/2's*, one *Sd.Kfz. 233* or *234/3*, and possibly one more armored car); one half-tracked armored scout company (with at least thirteen *Sd.Kfz. 250/9's* and an additional seven light machine guns); and one light armored reconnaissance company (combat vehicles uncertain but twenty-two light machine guns on hand). The status report indicates that the 3rd Company "does not exist at present" and the 4th armored heavy company had forty-six light machine guns but apparently no vehicles (none shown).

4. Panzer-Armee (Reserves)
Panzer-Korps "Großdeutschland"

Panzergrenadier-Division "Brandenburg"	*Panzer-Aufklärungs-Abteilung "Brandenburg"*: Formed on 13 September 1944, the battalion was organized using the Model 44 template.

Heeresgruppe Süd
2. Panzer-Armee

XXII. Gebirgs-Korps

9. SS-Panzer-Division "Hohenstaufen"	*SS-Panzer-Aufklärungs-Abteilung 9 "Hohenstaufen"*: Organized as a Model 44 organization, it had two light armored reconnaissance companies instead of one light and one medium. By February 1945 it had been so attrited that the two companies were consolidated. A 1 March report shows the battalion as having the following combat vehicles: forty-five *Sd.Kfz. 250* variants (forty-two operational) and eleven light and heavy armored cars (eight). At about the same time, the half-tracked armored scout company was disbanded. The battalion was detached from the division and reported to the *6. Panzer-Division* almost to the end of April.

I. Kavallerie-Korps

23. Panzer-Division	*Panzer-Aufklärungs-Abteilung 23*: On 1 March 1945 the battalion reported the following combat vehicles and equipment on hand: Headquarters Company with one *Sd.Kfz. 250* variant, six *Sd.Kfz. 251* variants, thirteen light armored cars, and eleven heavy armored cars; the 1st Company (half-tracked armored scout) with eighteen *Sd.Kfz. 250* variants; 2nd Company (light armored reconnaissance) with nineteen *Sd.Kfz. 250* variants and two *Sd.Kfz. 251* variants; 3rd Company (medium armored reconnaissance) with nine *Sd.Kfz. 250* variants and fifteen *Sd.Kfz. 251* variants; and 4th Company (armored heavy) with ten *Sd.Kfz. 251* variants.
3. Kavallerie-Division	*Panzer-Aufklärungs-Abteilung 69*: The battalion started to be formed in February and it was planned to have a Model 44 headquarters company, a light armored reconnaissance company, and a medium armored company. It is not known whether the battalion or elements thereof ever reached the division from the Milowitz Training Area, where it had been forming.
16. SS-Panzergrenadier-Division "Reichsführer SS"	*SS-Panzer-Aufklärungs-Abteilung 16 "Reichsführer SS"*: Originally organized like a pre–Model 43 reconnaissance battalion, with a wheeled armored scout company, three motorcycle infantry companies, and a motorized heavy company, it appears that the battalion may have never received any armored cars and used primarily *Volkswagen* utility vehicles for both scouting and reconnaissance.

6. Armee
IV. SS-Panzer-Korps

3. Panzer-Division	*Panzer-Aufklärungs-Abteilung 3*: At some point in 1945, the battalion adopted an *ad hoc* organization that fielded a mixed scout and reconnaissance company and a 3rd and 4th Company of undetermined composition (most likely soldiers without vehicles). In April the battalion was detached from the division, never to rejoin it.
5. SS-Panzer-Division "Wiking"	*SS-Panzer-Aufklärungs-Abteilung 5 "Wiking"*: The division did not report any combat vehicles directly associated with the battalion on 15 April.

1. Panzer-Division	*Panzer-Aufklärungs-Abteilung 1*: Probably organized as indicated in the previous table. Effective 3 March, the battalion was detached from the division and reported directly to the headquarters of the *6. Panzer-Armee* until the end of the war. In the middle of January, the battalion reported seventeen *Sd.Kfz. 250* variants (twelve operational), four light armored cars (two), and five heavy armored cars (two). In April the division reported forty-three *Sd.Kfz. 250* variants (twenty-seven operational), five light armored cars (two), and four heavy armored cars (two).

6. (SS)-Panzer-Armee[7]
I. SS-Panzer-Korps

1. SS-Panzer-Division Leibstandarte SS Adolf Hitler	*SS-Panzer-Aufklärungs-Abteilung 1 Leibstandarte SS Adolf Hitler*: The reconnaissance battalion was organized under the Model 44 template, with the headquarters company initially issued the *Sd.Kfz. 234/2 Puma*. In February the armored light reconnaissance company was issued the *Volkswagen* utility vehicle. On 5 March the division reported the following combat vehicle strengths for the battalion: thirteen heavy armored cars (five operational) and twenty-nine *Sd.Kfz. 250* variants (twenty-four).
12. SS-Panzer-Division "Hitlerjugend"	*SS-Panzer-Aufklärungs-Abteilung 12 "Hitlerjugend"*: Organized as a Model 44 reconnaissance battalion, the formation apparently had no armored cars left at this time. The 3rd Company (light armored reconnaissance) converted to a motorized company in February, using *Volkswagen* utility vehicles.

II. SS-Panzer-Korps

2. SS-Panzer-Division "Das Reich"	*SS-Panzer-Aufklärungs-Abteilung 2 "Das Reich"*: As with many of the other *SS* divisions, the headquarters switched from armored to motorized (in this case in January 1945). The 3rd Company also converted to a motorized reconnaissance company in February, using *Volkswagen* utility vehicles. By April its remaining elements (minus the 1st Company) were fighting against U.S. forces, surrendering on 9 May.
3. SS-Panzer-Division "Totenkopf"	*SS-Panzer-Aufklärungs-Abteilung 3 "Totenkopf"*: No definitive strength figures available, but it is assumed the battalion was even worse off than shown in the previous table. Starting on 5 May, the battalion was withdrawn from the front lines in the East and committed in the West against American forces.
Führer-Grenadier-Division	*Panzer-Späh-Kompanie 101* (*Führer-Panzer-Späh-Kompanie 2*): A mixed scout/reconnaissance company with both heavy armored cars and *Sd.Kfz. 250* variants. In January 1945 it reported the following combat vehicles on hand: thirteen *Sd.Kfz. 250* variants and six armored cars. In a March report, the following are listed: twelve *Sd.Kfz. 250* variants and eighteen armored cars, of which nine were probably *Sd.Kfz. 234* variants and nine *Sd.Kfz. 232*'s.
6. Panzer-Division	*Panzer-Aufklärungs-Abteilung 6*: The same theoretical organization as before, although the 4th Company did not rejoin the battalion until February 1945.

8. Armee
XXXXIII. Armee-Korps

25. Panzer-Division	*Panzer-Aufklärungs-Abteilung 25*: By the middle of March, the battalion had effectively lost one of its light reconnaissance companies and the remaining one had converted to a motorized organization (*Volkswagen*). On 3 April, the division reported only eleven armored cars (eleven operational) for the reconnaissance battalion.[8]

Panzer-Korps "Feldherrnhalle"

Panzer-Division "Feldherrnhalle 1"	*Panzer-Aufklärungs-Abteilung "Feldherrnhalle 1"*: After being effectively wiped out in the fighting for Budapest, the battalion was ordered reconstituted at the end of February. In the end, only a company was apparently formed. It was equipped with *Volkswagen* utility vehicles, but did not make its way back toward the front until 27 April.
Panzer-Division "Feldherrnhalle 2" (redesignated *13. Panzer-Division*)	*Panzer-Aufklärungs-Abteilung "Feldherrnhalle 2"* (redesignated *Panzer-Aufklärungs-Abteilung 13*): The battalion continued to refer to itself by its old designation, although there was not much left of it. There was an effort to reconstitute the formation in March as *Aufklärungsgruppe 13*, but it apparently was a glorified motorized light reconnaissance company equipped with *Volkswagen* utility vehicles. A status report from March 1945 also shows some armored cars on hand.

Oberkommando des Heeres (Reserves)
In area of operations of *Heeresgruppe Mitte*

21. Panzer-Division	*Panzer-Aufklärungs-Abteilung 21*: The battalion had a standard Model 44 organization, which was modified slightly in February when it was ordered to convert its medium armored reconnaissance company to a light one. Apparently the order was never completely carried out, since a status report dated 15 April 1945 shows the following combat vehicles:

	Headquarters Company with six light armored cars, thirteen heavy armored cars, four *Sd.Kfz. 250* variants, and ten *Sd.Kfz. 251* variants; 1st Company (half-tracked armored scout) with twelve *Sd.Kfz. 250* variants, of which seven were apparently the *Sd.Kfz. 250/9*; 2nd Company (light armored reconnaissance) with twenty-four *Sd.Kfz. 250* variants, two medium mortars, thirty-two light machine guns, two medium antitank guns, and one 2cm *Flak*; 3rd Company (light/medium armored reconnaissance company) with seventeen *Sd.Kfz. 250* variants, seven *Sd.Kfz. 251* variants, two medium mortars, thirty-five light machine guns, two medium antitank guns, and three 2cm *Flak*; and 4th Company (armored heavy) with one *Sd.Kfz. 250* variant, twenty-five *Sd.Kfz. 251* variants, five medium mortars, four 7.5cm (infantry) guns, two towed 7.5cm antitank guns, one (other) 7.5cm antitank gun, and fifteen light machine guns.
10. SS-Panzer-Division "Frundsberg"	*SS-Panzer-Aufklärungs-Abteilung 10 "Frundsberg"*: Organized under the Model 44 template, the battalion apparently consolidated the 1st Company (half-tracked armored scout) with the Headquarters Company in January 1945. A strength report in February noted the following: thirty-seven *Sd.Kfz. 250* variants (thirty operational), five light armored cars (one), and twelve heavy armored cars (eight). Later that month, the total number of armored cars on hand was reduced by one. The battalion, trapped in the Halbe Pocket, was able to break out and eventually surrender to U.S. forces along the Elbe.
In area of operations of *Heeresgruppe Vistula*	
18. Panzergrenadier-Division	*Panzer-Aufklärungs-Abteilung 118 / Panzer-Aufklärungs-Abteilung 18*: Presumably a variation of the structure listed in the previous table (through the end of March). The division was reconstituted in April and used equipment and personnel from the envisioned *Panzer-Divisionen "Schlesien"* and *"Holstein"* (*Panzer-Aufklärungs-Kompanie "Schlesien"* in the former case, and *Panzer-Aufklärungs-Abteilung 44* in the latter) to form the "new" reconnaissance battalion for the division, *Panzer-Aufklärungs-Abteilung 18*. It might have been organized as a Model 45 reconnaissance battalion.
In area of operations of *Armee Ostpreußen*	
Fallschirm-Panzergrenadier-Division "Hermann Göring 2"	*Fallschirm-Panzer-Aufklärungs-Abteilung 2 "Hermann Göring"*: See previous table.
24. Panzer-Division	*Panzer-Aufklärungs-Abteilung 24*: By February 1945 the headquarters company was essentially inactivated, although a headquarters element remained (reporting four *Sd.Kfz. 251* variants on 1 February 1945). Likewise, the 2nd Troop was also disbanded, with its assets distributed among the remaining elements of the battalion. The 1st Troop had apparently become an armored car troop again, reporting eight heavy and two light armored cars. The 3rd Troop had a mixed light and medium component, with twenty-four *Sd.Kfz. 250* variants and eight *Sd.Kfz. 251* variants. The 4th Troop (armored heavy) reported only nine *Sd.Kfz. 251* variants, six medium mortars, and six light machine guns.

CHANGES IN ORGANIZATIONAL AUTHORIZATIONS (1945)

Headquarters, Armored Reconnaissance Battalion (1109)

This organization, dated 1 April 1945 and only released in a hand-typed format, pared down the headquarters considerably and removed all armored cars and combat vehicles, except for the commander's.

- Headquarters: one light motorcycle, two sidecar motorcycles, two light cross-country utility vehicles (*Volkswagen*), and one heavy armored car (2cm) (*Sd.Kfz. 234/1*).
- Signals platoon:
  - Platoon headquarters: one motorcycle and one light cross-country utility vehicle (*Volkswagen*).
  - One medium field wire section (Type 12) (motorized): one 2-ton open bay, cross-country cargo truck.
  - Two medium radio sections (Type 80) (medium wave): one 2-ton closed, cross-country cargo truck. Each also allocated one man-pack radio.
  - Two light radio sections (Type 30) (medium wave): one 2-ton closed, cross-country cargo truck. First light section also allocated an air-ground radio section (Type 20) (shortwave).

a) Headquarters

| Motorcycle Messenger (1x 350cc Motorcycle), 2x Sidecar Motorcycle | Light Staff Car, Cross-Country (4 seat) | Heavy Armored Car (2cm) (*Sd.Kfz 234/1*); 1x Submachine Gun, 1x Light MG, 1x 2cm Cannon |

Totals (Headquarters): 3x Officers, 4x NCOs, 9x Enlisted Personnel; 8x Rifles, 5x Pistols, 3x Submachine Guns, 1x Light MG, 1x Main Gun; 1x Motorcycle, 2x Sidecar Motorcycles, 2x Staff Cars, 1x Armored Wheeled Vehicle

b) Signals Platoon   Platoon Headquarters Section

| Light 350cc Motorcycle | Light Staff Car, Cross-Country (4 seat) |

a) Headquarters   1st Medium Wire Section 12 (mot)

Truck, 2 ton, Canvas Top, Cross-Country

1st Medium Radio Section 80 Medium Wave (Motorized) | **2nd Medium Radio Section 80 Medium Wave (Motorized)**

| Truck, 2 ton, Hard Top, Cross-Country | Truck, 2 ton, Hard Top, Cross-Country |

1st Light Radio Section 30 Medium Wave (Motorized) | **2nd Light Radio Section 30 Medium Wave (Motorized)**

| Truck, 2 ton, Hard Top, Cross-Country | Truck, 2 ton, Hard Top, Cross-Country |

Totals (Signal Platoon): 1x Officer, 7x NCOs, 23x Enlisted Personnel; 30x Rifles, 1x Submachine Gun, 7x Light MG's; 1x Motorcycle, 1x Staff Car, 5x Trucks

Totals (Entire Battalion Headquarters): 4x Officers, 11x NCOs, 32x Enlisted Personnel; 38x Rifles, 6x Pistols, 3x Submachine Guns, 1x Light MG, 1x Main Gun; 2x Motorcycles, 2x Sidecar Motorcycles, 3x Staff Cars, 5x Trucks, 1x Armored Wheeled Vehicle

Notes: Light Staff Car Cross-Country (4 seat) counts in lieu of sidecar motorcycles. The driver for the armored vehicle uses the vehicular submachine gun as his personal weapon.

KStN 1113 (VW) (fG)

This organization, introduced on 1 April 1945, was substantially the same as the version authorized on 1 November 1944.

- Company headquarters:
  - Headquarters section: three motorcycles and three light cross-country utility vehicles (*Volkswagen*).
  - Manpack radio section (Type G) (medium wave): six light cross-country utility vehicles (*Volkswagen*) with five radios altogether.
- Three reconnaissance platoons:
  - Headquarters: two light cross-country utility vehicles (*Volkswagen*).
  - Three reconnaissance squads: three light cross-country utility vehicles (*Volkswagen*) and one light machine gun.
- 4th Platoon (heavy):
  - Headquarters: two light cross-country utility vehicles (*Volkswagen*).
  - 1st Section (heavy machine gun): six light cross-country utility vehicles (*Volkswagen*) and two heavy machine guns.
  - 2nd Section (heavy mortar): two 2-ton cross-country trucks and two 8cm mortars.

a) Command Group
Company Headquarters Section

| 3x Light Motorcycle (125cc) | 3x Light Utility Vehicle, Cross-Country (4 seat) |

Totals: 1x Officer, 5x NCOs, 8x Enlisted Personnel; 9x Rifles, 3x Pistols, 2x Submachine Guns; 3x Light Motorcycles, 3x Utility Vehicles

b) Radio Section
Backpack Radio Section g 5 Radio Sections (*Volkswagen*)
Medium Wave (Motorized)

| Light Utility Vehicle, Cross Country (4 seat) | 4x Light Utility Vehicle, Cross Country (4 seat)* |

Totals: 6x NCOs, 12x Enlisted Personnel; 18x Rifles; 5x Utility Vehicles

Note:* 3x Equipped with 1 Set of Signals Equipment for Light Radio Section 30 Medium Wave (Motorized) (*Volkswagen*)

c) 1st Platoon
Platoon Headquarters Section

2x Light Utility Vehicle, Cross-Country (4 seat) (as Tactical Vehicle)

1st Squad	**2nd Squad**	**3rd Squad**

3x Light Utility Vehicle, Cross-Country (4 seat), 1x Light MG	3x Light Utility Vehicle, Cross-Country (4 seat), 1x Light MG	3x Light Utility Vehicle, Cross-Country (4 seat), 1x Light MG

Totals: 1x Officer, 4x NCOs, 35x Enlisted Personnel; 29x Rifles, 3x Assault Rifles, 4x Pistols, 4x Submachine Guns, 3x Light MG's; 11x Utility Vehicles

d) 2nd Platoon
Platoon Headquarters Section

2x Light Utility Vehicle, Cross-Country (4 seat) (as Tactical Vehicle)

1st Squad	**2nd Squad**	**3rd Squad**
	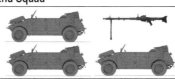	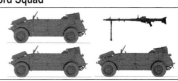
3x Light Utility Vehicle, Cross-Country (4 seat), 1x Light MG	3x Light Utility Vehicle, Cross-Country (4 seat), 1x Light MG	3x Light Utility Vehicle, Cross-Country (4 seat), 1x Light MG

Totals: 5x NCOs, 35x Enlisted Personnel; 29x Rifles, 3x Assault Rifles, 4x Pistols, 4x Submachine Guns, 3x Light MG's; 11x Utility Vehicles

e) 3rd Platoon
Platoon Headquarters Section

2x Light Utility Vehicle, Cross-Country (4 seat) (as Tactical Vehicle)

1st Squad	2nd Squad	3rd Squad
	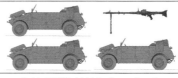	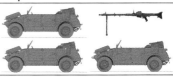
3x Light Utility Vehicle, Cross-Country (4 seat), 1x Light MG	3x Light Utility Vehicle, Cross-Country (4 seat), 1x Light MG	3x Light Utility Vehicle, Cross-Country (4 seat), 1x Light MG

Totals: 5x NCOs, 35x Enlisted Personnel; 29x Rifles, 3x Assault Rifles, 4x Pistols, 4x Submachine Guns, 3x Light MG's; 11x Utility Vehicles

f) 4th (Heavy) Platoon
Platoon Headquarters Section

2x Light Utility Vehicle, Cross-Country (4 seat) (as Tactical Vehicle)

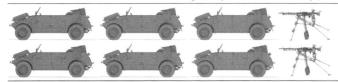 

6x Light Utility Vehicle, Cross-Country (4 seat)*, 2x Heavy MG's	2x Truck, 2 ton, Canvas Top, Cross-Country, for Transport of Personnel and Telephone Equipment, 2x 8cm Model 34 Mortars

Totals: 1x Officer, 7x NCOs, 33x Enlisted Personnel; 22x Rifles, 15x Pistols, 4x Submachine Guns, 2x Heavy MG's, 2x Heavy Mortars; 8x Utility Vehicles, 2x Trucks

Note: * Any utility vehicle counts in lieu of the Light Utility Vehicle.

Summary

	Officers	NCOs	Enlisted Personnel	Rifles (Assault Rifles)	Pistols (Submachine Guns)	Heavy MG's (Light MG's)	Mortars	Motorcycles (Sidecar Motorcycles)	Utility Vehicles (Trucks)
Command Section	1	5	8	9	3 (2)			3	3
Radio Section		6	12	18					5
1st Platoon	1	4	35	29 (3)	4 (4)	(3)			11
2nd Platoon		5	35	29 (3)	4 (4)	(3)			11
3rd Platoon		5	35	29 (3)	4 (4)	(3)			11
4th (Heavy) Platoon	1	7	33	22	15 (4)	2	2		8 (2)
Totals	3	32	158	136 (9)	30 (18)	2 (9)	2	3	49 (2)

MIXED ARMORED SCOUT COMPANY

1162E

This update to the armored scout company organization, dated 1 February 1945, might have been fielded by a few units, especially those formed in the beginning of 1945.

- Headquarters: two light motorcycles, one light cross-country utility vehicle (*Volkswagen*), one medium armored radio carrier (*Sd.Kfz. 251/3*), and one light machine gun.
- 1st Platoon:
  - 1st Section: one light armored personnel carrier (*Sd.Kfz. 250/1*), one light radio armored personnel carrier (*Sd.Kfz. 250/3*), one medium armored personnel carrier (MG 151 / *Drilling*) (*Sd.Kfz. 251/21*), two light machine guns, and one tri-barrel light antitank automatic cannon.
  - 2nd Section: same as 1st Section.
  - 3rd Section: same as 1st Section.
- 2nd Platoon: same as 1st Platoon, except only two sections, numbered 4 and 5.

a) Command Group

| 2x Light Motorcycle 350cc | Light Utility Vehicle, Cross-Country (4 seat) | Medium Armored Radio Half-track (*Sd.Kfz. 251/3*), 1x Submachine Gun, 1x Light MG |

Totals: 1x Officer, 4x NCOs, 3x Enlisted Personnel; 3x Rifles, 3x Pistols, 2x Submachine Guns, 1x Light MG; 2x Motorcycles, 1x Vehicle, 1x Armored Half-tracked Vehicle

b) 1st Platoon

1st Armored Scout Section	2nd Armored Scout Section	3rd Armored Scout Section
 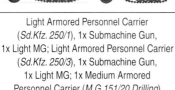		
Light Armored Personnel Carrier (*Sd.Kfz. 250/1*), 1x Submachine Gun, 1x Light MG; Light Armored Personnel Carrier (*Sd.Kfz. 250/3*), 1x Submachine Gun, 1x Light MG; 1x Medium Armored Personnel Carrier (*M.G.151/20 Drilling*) (*Sd.Kfz. 251/21*), 1x Submachine Gun, 1x Main Gun	Light Armored Personnel Carrier (*Sd.Kfz. 250/1*), 1x Submachine Gun, 1x Light MG; Light Armored Personnel Carrier (*Sd.Kfz. 250/3*), 1x Submachine Gun, 1x Light MG; 1x Medium Armored Personnel Carrier (*M.G.151/20 Drilling*) (*Sd.Kfz. 251/21*), 1x Submachine Gun, 1x Main Gun	Light Armored Personnel Carrier (*Sd.Kfz. 250/1*), 1x Submachine Gun, 1x Light MG; Light Armored Personnel Carrier (*Sd.Kfz. 250/3*), 1x Submachine Gun, 1x Light MG; 1x Medium Armored Personnel Carrier (*M.G.151/20 Drilling*) (*Sd.Kfz. 251/21*), 1x Submachine Gun, 1x Main Gun

Totals: 1x Officer, 11x NCOs, 24x Enlisted Personnel; 3x Rifles, 24x Pistols, 9x Submachine Guns, 6x Light MG's, 3x Main Guns; 9x Armored Half-tracked Vehicles

c) 2nd Platoon
4th Armored Scout Section   5th Armored Scout Section

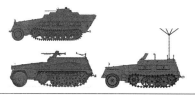

Light Armored Personnel Carrier (*Sd.Kfz. 250/1*), 1x Submachine Gun, 1x Light MG; Light Armored Personnel Carrier (*Sd.Kfz. 250/3*), 1x Submachine Gun, 1x Light MG; 1x Medium Armored Personnel Carrier (*M.G.151/20 Drilling*) (*Sd.Kfz. 251/21*), 1x Submachine Gun, 1x Main Gun

Light Armored Personnel Carrier (*Sd.Kfz. 250/1*), 1x Submachine Gun, 1x Light MG; Light Armored Personnel Carrier (*Sd.Kfz. 250/3*), 1x Submachine Gun, 1x Light MG; 1x Medium Armored Personnel Carrier (*M.G.151/20 Drilling*) (*Sd.Kfz. 251/21*), 1x Submachine Gun, 1x Main Gun

Totals: 1x Officer, 7x NCOs, 16x Enlisted Personnel; 2x Rifles, 16x Pistols, 6x Submachine Guns, 4x Light MG's, 2x Main Guns; 6x Armored Half-tracked Vehicles

d) Vehicle Maintenance Section b (Armored)

Light Utility Vehicle, Cross-Country (4 seat)   Truck, 2 ton, Canvas Top, Cross-Country (for Vehicle Maintenance Section)   Truck, 3 ton, Canvas Top, for Vehicle Maintenance Section

Totals: 1x NCO, 6x Enlisted Personnel; 7x Rifles; 3x Vehicles

e) Combat Trains

Light Utility Vehicle, Cross-Country (4 seat)   Truck, 3 ton, Canvas Top, Cross-Country, for Ammunition and Equipment   Truck, 3 ton, Canvas Top, Cross-Country, for Petroleum, Oil & Lubricants   Truck, 3 ton, Canvas Top, Cross-Country, for Small Field Mess Stove

Totals: 5x NCOs, 9x Enlisted Personnel; 11x Rifles, 2x Pistols, 1x Submachine Gun; 4x Wheeled Vehicles

Summary

	Officers	NCOs	Enlisted Personnel	Rifles	Pistols (Submachine Guns)	Light MG's	Motorcycles	Wheeled Vehicles (Trucks)	Armored Half-tracks
Command Section	1	4	3	3	3 (2)	1	2	1	1
1st Platoon	1	11	24	3	24 (9)	6			9
2nd Platoon	1	7	16	2	16 (6)	4			6
Vehicle Maintenance Section		1	6	7				1 (2)	
Combat Trains		5	9	11	2 (1)			1 (3)	
Baggage Trains		1	3	4				(1)	
Totals	**3**	**29**	**61**	**30**	**45 (18)**	**11**	**2**	**3 (6)**	**16**

1162f (fG)

Had it been fielded, this particular version of the armored scout company, dated 1 April 1945, would have packed a considerable punch.

- Headquarters section: two light motorcycles, one sidecar motorcycle, two light cross-country utility vehicles (*Volkswagen*), and two heavy armored cars (2cm) (*Sd.Kfz. 234/1*).
- 1st Armored scout platoon:
  - 1st Armored car section: one heavy armored car (2cm) (*Sd.Kfz. 234/1*), one heavy armored car (7.5cm Model 40 antitank gun) (*Sd.Kfz. 234/4*), two light machine guns, one 2cm main gun, and one 7.5cm main gun.
  - 2nd Armored scout section: same as 1st section.
  - 3rd Armored scout section: same as 1st section.
  - 4th Armored scout section: same as 1st section.
- 2nd Armored scout platoon: same as 1st Platoon, except only three sections, numbered 5 through 7.
- 3rd Armored scout platoon (half-track):
  - 8th Armored car section (half-track): one medium armored radio vehicle (*Sd.Kfz. 251/3*), one medium armored personnel carrier (Model 151/20 machine gun *Drilling*) (*Sd.Kfz. 251/21*), one medium armored personnel carrier (7.5cm Model 40 antitank gun) (*Sd.Kfz. 251/22*), one light machine gun, one tri-mount antiaircraft machine gun, and one 7.5cm antitank gun.
  - 9th Armored car section (half-track): same as 8th section.
  - 10th Armored car section (half-track): same as 8th section.

a) Command Group

2x Light Motorcycles 350cc, 1x Sidecar Motorcycle	Light Utility Vehicle, Cross-Country (4 seat)		Heavy Armored Car (*Sd.Kfz. 234/1*), 1x Submachine Gun, 1x Light MG, 1x 2cm Main Gun

Totals: 1x Officer, 6x NCOs, 5x Enlisted Personnel; 5x Rifles, 4x Pistols, 3x Submachine Guns, 1x Light MG; 1x 2cm Main Gun; 2x Motorcycles, 1x Sidecar Motorcycle; 2x Utility Vehicles, 1x Armored Car

b) 1st Armored Scout Platoon (Armored Car)

1st Armored Scout Section	2nd Armored Scout Section	3rd Armored Scout Section	4th Armored Scout Section

Heavy Armored Car (*Sd.Kfz. 234/1*), 1x Submachine Gun, 1x Light MG, 1x 2cm Main Gun and 1x Heavy Armored Car (*Sd.Kfz. 234/3*), 1x Submachine Gun, 1x Light MG, 1x 7.5cm Main Gun	Heavy Armored Car (*Sd.Kfz. 234/1*), 1x Submachine Gun, 1x Light MG, 1x 2cm Main Gun and 1x Heavy Armored Car (*Sd.Kfz. 234/3*), 1x Submachine Gun, 1x Light MG, 1x 7.5cm Main Gun	Heavy Armored Car (*Sd.Kfz. 234/1*), 1x Submachine Gun, 1x Light MG, 1x 2cm Main Gun and 1x Heavy Armored Car (*Sd.Kfz. 234/3*), 1x Submachine Gun, 1x Light MG, 1x 7.5cm Main Gun	Heavy Armored Car (*Sd.Kfz. 234/1*), 1x Submachine Gun, 1x Light MG, 1x 2cm Main Gun and 1x Heavy Armored Car (*Sd.Kfz. 234/3*), 1x Submachine Gun, 1x Light MG, 1x 7.5cm Main Gun

Totals: 1x Officer, 11x NCOs, 20x Enlisted Personnel; 20x Pistols, 12x Submachine Guns, 8x Light MG's; 8x Main Guns; 8x Armored Cars

c) 2nd Armored Scout Platoon (Armored Car)

5th Armored Scout Section	6th Armored Scout Section	7th Armored Scout Section

Heavy Armored Car (*Sd.Kfz. 234/1*), 1x Submachine Gun, 1x Light MG, 1x 2cm Main Gun and 1x Heavy Armored Car (*Sd.Kfz. 234/3*), 1x Submachine Gun, 1x Light MG, 1x 7.5cm Main Gun	Heavy Armored Car (*Sd.Kfz. 234/1*), 1x Submachine Gun, 1x Light MG, 1x 2cm Main Gun and 1x Heavy Armored Car (*Sd.Kfz. 234/3*), 1x Submachine Gun, 1x Light MG, 1x 7.5cm Main Gun	Heavy Armored Car (*Sd.Kfz. 234/1*), 1x Submachine Gun, 1x Light MG, 1x 2cm Main Gun and 1x Heavy Armored Car (*Sd.Kfz. 234/3*), 1x Submachine Gun, 1x Light MG, 1x 7.5cm Main Gun

Totals: 9x NCOs, 15x Enlisted Personnel; 15x Pistols, 9x Submachine Guns, 6x Light MG's; 6x Main Guns; 6x Armored Cars

d) 3rd Armored Scout Platoon (Half-track)

8th Armored Scout Section	9th Armored Scout Section	10th Armored Scout Section

Medium Armored Radio Vehicle (*Sd.Kfz. 251/3*), 1x Submachine Gun, 1x Light MG; 1x Medium Armored Personnel Carrier (*M.G.151/20 Drilling*) (*Sd.Kfz. 251/21*), 1x Submachine Gun, 1x Heavy MG; Medium Armored Personnel Carrier (7.5cm Model 40 AT Gun) (*Sd.Kfz. 251/22*), 1x Submachine Gun, 1x Main Gun	Medium Armored Radio Vehicle (*Sd.Kfz. 251/3*), 1x Submachine Gun, 1x Light MG; 1x Medium Armored Personnel Carrier (*M.G.151/20 Drilling*) (*Sd.Kfz. 251/21*), 1x Submachine Gun, 1x Heavy MG; Medium Armored Personnel Carrier (7.5cm Model 40 AT Gun) (*Sd.Kfz. 251/22*), 1x Submachine Gun, 1x Main Gun	Medium Armored Radio Vehicle (*Sd.Kfz. 251/3*), 1x Submachine Gun, 1x Light MG; 1x Medium Armored Personnel Carrier (*M.G.151/20 Drilling*) (*Sd.Kfz. 251/21*), 1x Submachine Gun, 1x Heavy MG; Medium Armored Personnel Carrier (7.5cm Model 40 AT Gun) (*Sd.Kfz. 251/22*), 1x Submachine Gun, 1x Main Gun

Totals: 1x Officer, 11x NCOs, 24x Enlisted Personnel; 9x Rifles, 15x Pistols, 12x Submachine Guns, 3x Light MG's, 6x Main Guns; 9x Armored Cars

Summary

	Officers	NCOs	Enlisted Personnel	Rifles	Pistols (Submachine Guns)	Light MG's	Main Guns	Motorcycles (Sidecar Motorcycles)	Wheeled Vehicles (Trucks)	Armored Cars (Armored Personnel Carriers)
Command Section	1	6	5	5	4 (3)	1	1	2 (1)	2	1
1st Platoon (AC)	1	11	20		20 (12)	8	8			8
2nd Platoon (AC)		9	15		15 (9)	6	6			6
3rd Platoon (Half-track)	1	11	24	9	15 (12)	3	6			(9)
Totals	3	37	64	14	54 (36)	18	21	2 (1)	2	15 (9)

Notes: Light Utility Vehicles (4 Seat) count against Sidecar Motorcycles. Personnel without assigned personal weapons use vehicular small arms as their personal weapon.

LESSONS LEARNED AND FIRSTHAND ACCOUNTS

At the start of the year, there was still considerable give-and-take between the German and Soviet forces, although German offensive actions were usually reactive in nature, launched after the Soviets had seized the initiative somewhere and the offensive needed to be blunted or encircled forces relieved. One of the more famous relief efforts of early 1944 was the attempt to free two trapped army corps in and around Tscherkassy. Although the counteroffensive launched to relieve the forces was ultimately somewhat successful—some 30,000 personnel were able to escape the pocket, at the expense of leaving behind all heavy equipment—the cost was also high on the attacking force. During those operations, the *1. Panzer-Division* used its reconnaissance battalion to serve as an advance guard for its advance:[9]

> While its last mechanized infantry companies were being pulled out of the line southwest of Berditschew, the *1. Panzer-Division* pushed *Panzer-Aufklärungs-Abteilung 1* into the area south of Winograd as its first troop element. After being personally briefed by the Chief-of-Staff of the *1. Panzer-Armee*, *Major* Huppert immediately initiated a reconnaissance-in-force with reinforced armored scout sections in the direction of the pocket and to the southeast.

Once contact was established, the reconnaissance battalion was then used to assist in screening the extended corps flank:[10]

> Up to that point, the commander of *Panzer-Aufklärungs-Abteilung 1* and his brave battalion had screened the long flank of the corps to the south and the southeast practically by itself. The scouts had fulfilled their mission, as always, in exemplary fashion.

Typical actions of the battalion in 1944 are described in these passages, which emphasize the combat role the battalion played, as opposed to scouting and reconnaissance missions. These types of operations had become the norm for reconnaissance battalions in 1944:[11]

> *Panzer-Aufklärungs-Abteilung 1*, which had been sent north, had pushed back enemy elements that had advanced as far as the Sambor–Staryj Sambor road by 1 August 1944, thanks to the aggressive attack conducted by the 3rd Company of *Oberleutnant* Stark. It had also cleared Strzalkowice, which was on that road, of the enemy. Towards midnight, it was attached directly to the *III. Panzer-Korps*. *Major* Huppert received a mission by radio to advance towards Lesko (southeast of Sanok) and establish contact with friendly forces there. Moving quickly, the battalion crossed through Ustryzki, where it refueled. It then moved rapidly along good roads. The *3./Panzer-Aufklärungs-Abteilung 1* assaulted Olsznika after overcoming weak enemy resistance. Likewise, Russian infantry supported by antitank guns in Uherze could be overrun.
>
> It wasn't until three heavy antitank guns in Lesko, the day's objective, were encountered that *Major* Huppert was forced to have his battalion dismount. Supported by the *7./Panzer-Artillerie-Regiment 73*, which had been pushed far forward, and his own 7.5cm *SPW's*, he directed his reconnaissance companies to move against Lesko on foot. That enemy force also withdrew after weak resistance, with the result that the village was soon in friendly hands. Enemy artillery fired from the high ground on the far bank of the San, but it was soon eliminated in an artillery duel. An effort to exploit the initial success by crossing the San was thwarted because the large road bridge over the river had been blown up. Correspondingly, the battalion established outposts to either side of Lesko. The aggressive advance into Lesko earned the battalion a special letter of praise from the Commanding General, *General der Panzertruppen* Breith, as well as the Commander-in-Chief of the *1. Panzer-Armee*, *Generaloberst* Heinrici. The battalion's casualties were unusually light . . .
>
> . . . At the same time, armored scout sections were in constant contact with the enemy and, as a result of their continuous reports, created the prerequisites for the taking of Zuluz (north

of Lesko) by *Hauptmann* Schütt's reinforced *1./Panzer-Aufklärungs-Abteilung 1* in a *coup de main*. On 5 August, the [reconnaissance battalion] advanced further north along the pass road and took Kuzmina, rapidly breaking pockets of resistance. Individual antitank guns at the edge of the village were eliminated through the attack by dismounted elements of the *2./Panzer-Aufklärungs-Abteilung 1*. . . .

. . . Similarly, *Panzer-Aufklärungs-Abteilung 1* was involved in fierce defensive fighting; its [3rd Company] threw back numerous enemy advances and was able to destroy several T-34's in the process . . . The next day, *Panzer-Aufklärungs-Abteilung 1* was relieved by infantry at placed at the disposal of the division; a short time later, it rolled off to the south and then to the southwest. . . .

. . . On 12 August 1944, *Panzer-Aufklärungs-Abteilung 1* moved out to attack north in an effort to form a bridgehead on the north bank of the Vistula at Mdrezechow. The battalion, which was attached to *Kampfgruppe Neumeister*, crossed the river with its [2nd Company] in rafts and was able to establish a bridgehead at Podwale. During the fighting, the commander of the 2nd Company, *Oberleutnant* Reinsberger, was badly wounded. Reinforced by three assault guns and two heavy self-propelled *PaK*, the reconnaissance battalion pressed against the withdrawing enemy in a night attack and established contact with the *24. Panzer-Division* at Trzebiza in a bold advance. At the same time, *Gruppe Schütt*, consisting of his [2nd Company] and seven assault guns, established contact with encircled friendly forces and ensured their safe passage back to German lines. . . .

. . . During that period [of operations in the Great Vistula Bend in late August], the armored scout sections of *Panzer-Aufklärungs-Abteilung 1* were constantly in contact with the enemy while steadily changing areas of operations and engaging in different types of combat situations, in an effort to provide the division with as clear and comprehensive a picture of the enemy and the situation with the neighboring forces as possible or assuming screening and guard missions in the open flanks of attack formations. It was under those circumstances that the newly created Supply Company of *Hauptmann* Huppert's battalion would prove itself through tireless resupply efforts and nimbleness in adapting to changing situations . . .

After a variety of operations, *bewegliche Gruppe Huppert* [Mobile Group "Huppert"] was formed for the attack on Lagow. Reporting directly to the *III. Panzer-Korps*, the group consisted of . . . [*Panzer-Aufklärungs-Abteilung 1*] . . . *Panzer-Aufklärungs-Abteilung 23*, the *I./Panzer-Artillerie-Abteilung 27* and, later, *Panzer-Aufklärungs-Abteilung 17*. Major Huppert, who was awarded the Knight's Cross on 25 August 1944, took Plucki, five kilometers north of Lagow, with the *2./Panzer-Aufklärungs-Abteilung 1* (*Leutnant* Dossner) on 26 August. At the same time, the *3./Panzer-Aufklärungs-Abteilung 1* (*Oberleutnant* Stark) took Zamkowa-Wola. The group then established flank guard for the corps, oriented to the east. The effort to take Lagow in a *coup de main* failed due to the heavy fortified antitank-gun belt that extended all the way around the city. Following the battle group's successful fending off of numerous enemy advances, it was pulled out of the line and then attached to the *17. Panzer-Division* on 27 August. It then took Sedek, five kilometers southwest of the city, whereupon it moved out against Hill 393 in an effort to establish contact with *Gruppe Weiß* (elements of the *97. Jäger-Division*), which was encircled in Sadkow. After initial success in its attack, the effort bogged down at Bardo—halfway to the objective—where a passage point was established and held.

Another effort to relieve the encircled forces failed in the face of heavy enemy tank and antitank-gun belts. In the meantime, however, *Gruppe Weiß* had moved out on its own to break out to the west. At first light on 28 August, it reached the passage point established by *Gruppe Huppert* in Hill 392.9. All efforts of the enemy, who was following in hot pursuit, were able to be turned back and several

T-34's were knocked out by heavy antitank guns (7.5cm towed *PaK*). During the night of 29–30 August, *Gruppe Huppert* was relieved by elements of the *97. Jäger-Division*. From Ponsinowce, the battle group then moved against the patch of woods north of the Opatow–Lagow road. Following the successful attack, the battle group was pulled out of the line and *Panzer-Aufklärungs-Abteilung 1* returned to the *1. Panzer-Division*.

. . . During the night of 10–11 September 1944, the reconnaissance battalion was relieved by elements of *Infanterie-Regiment 1081* (*254. Infanterie-Division*). On 11 and 12 September, back in the fold of the division, the battalion was engaged in fierce fighting for the dominating high ground, Hill 526, outside of Zmigrod, which was occupied extremely heavily by the enemy. A *coup de main* did not succeed, despite the terrific fire support offered by *Panzer-Artillerie-Regiment 73*. After being reinforced by the *1./Panzer-Regiment 1* of *Oberleutnant* Seemann, the [reconnaissance battalion] attacked again, this time in the direction of Lysa Gora at the foot of the dominant terrain. Enemy forces had assembled there in their drive towards the Dukla Pass after penetrating deeply into the front of *Heeresgruppe Nordukraine*. At first light on 13 September, patrols reported that Lysa Gora was occupied by the enemy. In an attack conducted while on the move, the city was taken and the enemy force—about a regiment in number with many trucks and antitank guns—was ejected. Before the visibly surprised enemy could collect itself, *Panzer-Aufklärungs-Abteilung 1*, fielding about 50 men in all, attacked again. After a short firefight, which did not have any artillery or heavy weapons support, *Hauptmann Dr.* Koehler and his scouts soon took Hill 526. Without having any friendly contact to either the right or the left, the men were able to hold out against repeated enemy immediate counterattacks until late in the afternoon, when a battalion from the *101. Jäger-Division* established contact on the right.

The enemy, who realized the importance of the bulwark on Hill 526, undertook repeated counterattacks the following night and on 14 September. These were conducted with vastly superior forces and supported by tanks. Despite that, the enemy was unable to eject the small band of scouts being employed as infantry out of their holes. They continued to unshakably hold their positions even when the enemy succeeded in infiltrating between the boundaries of the [battalion] and the light infantry battalion to the right and into Lysa Gora, where the battalion command post was located. The [battalion's] communications center defended itself with hand grenades and the mounted machine guns on the *SPW's* until a counterattack force consisting of clerks, radio operators and messengers under the command of *Leutnant* Rostan were able to eject the enemy forces and restore the main line of resistance. The division sent a radio message, "Bravo, Koehler!" thus underscoring the importance of the plucky operation of the reconnaissance battalion. The enemy did not give up just yet, however. Additional penetrations could be cleared up by noon, in the process of which *Oberleutnant* Stark's [3rd Company] allowed itself to be overrun repeatedly by enemy tanks. The escort infantry were driven off and a total of four T-34's were destroyed through close combat. On 15 September, it was primarily the [2nd Company] that had to bear the brunt of the defense. Although Lysa Gora had been reduced to a smoking pile of rubble by the heavy enemy fires, the [battalion] was able to maintain its strongpoints and pockets of resistance until it was relieved by *Panzer-Aufklärungs-Abteilung 23* on 20 September.

The Commander-in-Chief of the field-army group, *Generaloberst* Heinrici, acknowledged the brave and decisive operation of *Panzer-Aufklärungs-Abteilung 1* in a telegram [dated 15 September 1944] . . .

During the night of 13–14 September 1944, *Panzer-Aufklärungs-Abteilung 1*, under the leadership of *Hauptmann* Koehler and consisting of 26 men, turned back four consecutive armor-supported attacks of up to battalion strength on Hill 526 east of Lysa Gora in close combat. This was a prerequisite for the initiation of the attack on 14 September 1944 that led to the closure of the gap at Glojsce. Correspondingly, it was an engagement of wide-ranging importance. *Panzer-Aufklärungs-Abteilung 1* should be proud of the fact that it had contributed tremendously to that great success. I commend *Panzer-Aufklärungs-Abteilung 1* and extend it my praise.

/signed/ Heinrici, *Generaloberst*

An indication of the actions and leadership required for a reconnaissance soldier to earn the German Cross in Gold and the Knight's Cross can be gleaned from these award recommendations. This recommendation for the German Cross in Gold for *SS-Obersturmführer* Siegfried Lorenz, written by *SS-Hauptsturmführer* Saalbach, the battalion commander of *SS-Panzer-Aufklärungs-Abteilung 11 "Nordland,"* in November 1944 details five actions in which Lorenz distinguished himself:[12]

Submitted: 16 November 1944
Approved: 30 December 1944
Unit: *1./SS-Panzer-Aufklärungs-Abteilung 11*
Previous Awards: Infantry Assault Badge—February 1941; Iron Cross, 2nd Class—18 August 1941; Iron Cross, First Class—18 October 1941; Eastern medal—1941–1942; Close Combat Clasp in Bronze—1 May 1943; Wound Badge in Black—1 September 1941
Previous assignments: 15 April 1941—Platoon Leader; 22 February 1942—Liaison Officer; 1 October 1942—Adjutant; 24 March 1943—Acting Company Commander; 1 February 1944—Company Commander

Justification and Recommendations of the Intermediate Commanders:
1.) On 26 January 1944, *SS-Obersturmführer* Lorenz had the mission in Gubanitzy, as part of *Kampfgruppe Wengler*, to screen the western portion of Gubanitzy. In spite of extremely heavy enemy armored attacks, Lorenz succeeded in rallying his men to offer every last ounce of resistance again and again through his personal example and in holding the designated line, in accordance with his orders.

During that heavy fighting, he positioned himself personally behind his [lines?—illegible] and, by means of personal example, caused any thought of giving up the threatened position to be snuffed out at its inception. As a result, he contributed significantly in keeping the only supply route available to *Kampfgruppe Wengler* open as long as the tactical situation demanded it.

2.) On 27 January 1944, *SS-Obersturmführer* Lorenz received the mission to occupy the crossroads at Rogowizy, which had been designated as a strongpoint on the right as part of the blocking position outside of Wolossowo. He was to establish contact with armed forces elements there and hold the crossroads at all costs. In the course of the first enemy attack on the crossroads—approximately a battalion-sized element—the armed forces elements pulled back. *SS-Obersturmführer* Lorenz and his battle group stood facing a numerically vastly superior force.

Through pluck and obstinacy, he succeeded in holding the important point for three hours against enemy forces pressing from the north, the east and the south. He did not pull his battle group back 400 meters to the west until the enemy threatened to cut it off.

When a patrol reported that 6 T-34's were blocking the only available route, he broke through the enemy blocking force to his battalion in accordance with his orders. He advanced against the superior enemy force in a bold manner, engaging it with all available weapons. As a result of his brave efforts, he fixed strong Russian forces at an extraordinarily important area and contributed substantially to the delay of the Russian advance, which was threatening to become dangerous at exactly that spot.

3.) On 15 and 16 July 1944, *SS-Obersturmführer* Lorenz had the mission to establish contact between the wings of *Heeresgruppen Nord* and *Mitte*. He led a motorized patrol in a movement lasting both day and night. In addition to important tactical observations, he delivered a report of decisive, operational importance, as was mentioned in the Letter of Recognition written by the Commanding General, *General* Kleffel.

4.) On 17 July 1944, *SS-Obersturmführer* Lorenz received the mission to occupy a line northwest of Lake Scolly at Komai (Lithuania) with a battle group composed of elements of the battalion. He was to hold it against all enemy attacks.

Immediately after the position was occupied, the enemy attempted to break through with strong forces and conduct an intended advance from the flank against Komai. *SS-Obersturmführer* Lorenz, constantly at the hot spots of the defensive fighting, performed the extraordinarily important flank-guard mission for the division, which intended to withdraw through Komai, and eliminated the extremely dangerous threat to the flanks of the division. He did this to the very last moment possible, even after the enemy had blocked his own withdrawal route.

5.) In the course of the enemy's breakthrough at Dorpat, the battalion was employed in a sector spanning 15 kilometers. The left wing of the battalion fought under the command of the Commander of the 5th Company in Mustvee against strong enemy forces. As a result of another breakthrough of the enemy further to the west with tanks and infantry, the battalion received orders to . . . [next line illegible] . . . The connecting route had already been crossed by lead elements of the Russian infantry and a route around them was some 30 kilometers long. Radio contact had been lost. Due to the importance of the [battalion] mission, *SS-Obersturmführer* Lorenz, who himself was the Acting Commander of a company on the right wing, had to attempt to fight his way through to the left wing to lead the battle group fighting there out of being potentially cut off and then guide it to a new area of operations. *SS-Obersturmführer* Lorenz succeeded in doing that through courage and skill. He thus enabled the battalion to conduct an attack against the flank of the enemy armored advance within a very short time.

In the course of executing his mission, *SS-Obersturmführer* Lorenz was wounded in a strafing attack by enemy aircraft.

/signed/ Saalbach

The recommendation for the Knight's Cross for *SS-Hauptsturmführer* Saalbach (later *SS-Sturmbannführer*), the battalion commander, was written by *Oberst* Wengler[13] for actions conducted and leadership displayed while the reconnaissance battalion was attached to Wengler's regiment:[14]

Short Justification and Recommendation of the Intermediate Commander
Copy!
Grenadier-Regiment 366
Regimental Command Post, 5 February 1944

Personnel Section

Acts of Bravery on the Part of
SS-Hauptsturmführer Saalbach
SS-Panzer-Aufklärungs-Abteilung 11

On 26 January 1944, the enemy attacked the village of Gubanitzy with a tank brigade (54 tanks) and accompanying infantry. Saalbach, who was attached with his battalion, so effectively employed his battalion and heavy weapons during all of the critical situations of that day that all of the attacks could be turned back. Always present at the hot spots of the fighting, he continuously gave it his all without regard for himself and mastered every situation. On that day, 34 tanks, including 28 T-34's, were eliminated by the weapons of his battalion.

On 27 January 1944: The enemy attacked the entire day with strong forces. Saalbach was at the hot spots of the fighting again and again and stabilized the situation while callously disregarding his own person. He was an example to his men in all situations.

When the enemy made a dent in the main line of resistance at one location, Saalbach stabilized the situation quickly with rapidly assembled forces.

On 29 January 1944, the enemy attacked the village of Opolje, 2.5 kilometers in front of the main line of resistance, with strong forces and tank support. Saalbach was always at the hot spots of the fighting and turned back all of the enemy attacks with the few men at his disposal until such time as the main line of resistance could be occupied by strong-enough forces.

On orders, he disengaged from the enemy in such a skillful manner that the enemy forces were unable to pursue the withdrawal movements. In the process, two more enemy tanks were destroyed. He was the last one to disengage from the enemy.

FOR THE CORRECTNESS OF THE TRANSCRIPTION:
/signed/ (von Scholz)
SS-Brigadeführer und Generalmajor der Waffen-SS

/signed/
Wengler
Oberst and Regiment Commander

Recommendation of the Division Commander:
The employment and combat operations of *Bataillon Saalbach* in the sector of the friendly division forces to the right was also essential to the successful combat operations enjoyed by the *11. SS-Freiwilligen-Panzer-Grenadier-Division "Nordland."*
/signed/ (von Scholz)
SS-Brigadeführer und Generalmajor der Waffen-SS

The battalion continued to fight hard until the end of the war. Here is a firsthand account from later that summer by *SS-Sturmmann* Heinz Genzow, messenger to the Battalion Commander (Saalbach):[15]

Jekapils/Jakobstadt in Estonia in July 1944

We were with a portion of the headquarters in a barnyard, and the companies were about 2 kilometers in front of us in position. The messenger section, consisting of 3 radio vehicles, 1 *Volkswagen*, 2 sidecar motorcycles and 2 *SPW's*, was at the farmstead. Foxholes and machine-gun positions had been prepared, since the Russians were constantly firing around the area with artillery. Small-arms rounds also whistled past us. Towards noon one day, the artillery fire increased. Our farmstead was hit several times, and the barn burned down. Otherwise, there were no casualties. Then we received a radio message from a company: "The enemy's attacking!" Radio contact was then lost. *Sturmbannführer* Saalbach sent me to the company—that is, I was supposed to go—but that didn't come about. The first *SPW's* from the companies were pulling back to the right of the command post. There was firing everywhere by then. Looking like they had just popped out of the ground, Russian infantry attacked us, the battalion command post. We were able to hold back the initial batch of Russians with our machine guns, but more and more of them kept coming, and we numbered only 15. All of a sudden, we also received fire from the rear. All Hell had broken loose! "Everyone back!" The Battalion Commander ordered. Our *SPW* drivers were on the ball, and everyone attempted to climb aboard. I personally went with the Battalion Commander in the *VW*. The Commander drove the vehicle. I kept my head tucked in and held the submachine gun to the rear and fired off to the side in the middle of the Russians. We moved across fields in the direction of the road. One of the sidecar motorcycles was set alight. The driver was wounded, but he could be brought along. Our *VW* received several hits, but we were able to get through to the road, like the rest. The other companies were also pulling back there.

We had to pull back to the next village, where the Russians were brought to a standstill by means of an immediate counterattack.

Three men were badly wounded and one man was killed during the Russian attack. My comrade and good friend, Motorcycle Messenger Fischer, was among them. He had been hit in the head. The other companies also took casualties. But we had been lucky once again.

Former *SS-Unterscharführer* Franz Bereznyak, who was assigned to the *3./SS-Panzer-Aufklärungs-Abteilung 11*, has provided a firsthand account of fighting in mid-August 1944:[16]

Ignaste, 18 August 1944

After our reconnaissance operations in the area around Dünaburg were over, the 3rd Company, supported by a cannon vehicle from the 5th Company, went into position in Ignaste.

Strong Russian forces, supported by tanks and self-propelled guns, had been directed to take the high ground at Ignaste, in an effort to cut off the forces in Dorpat and vicinity.

The Company Command Post was established in a doctor's house near Ignaste. The company personnel had dug in along high ground. The *SPW's* had also been dug in deeply so that only the machine guns could be seen above the superstructure. We dominated the entire valley and the opposite high ground, where the Russians had assembled for their attack, with our machine guns. From our high ground, we could observe the entire approach march of the Soviets.

The valley was about 100 meters below our positions and about 200 meters wide. The Russians had staged in a small patch of woods on the opposite high ground. Once in the woods, we could only hear the sounds of the enemy tanks. We were wondering what the next few hours would bring.

We didn't have to wait too long. They started coming just after 1300 hours: 15 tanks and self-propelled guns, accompanied by a whole lot of infantry. They didn't have a clue what was awaiting them. We waited tensely for the order to fire. Our Company Commander, *SS-Obersturmführer* Pehrsson, was observing everything through a scissors scope. The Russians came ever closer. They had already crossed the 200-meter-wide valley, and the orders to fire still had not come. When the Russians reached the ascending slope towards us and were about to move up, the thundered order of "Fire!" was given. Everything opened up: all 15 *MG 42*'s, all 15 heavy machine guns mounted on the *SPW's*, a 2cm *Flak*, the 7.6cm cannon of the 5th Company, numerous submachine guns and the mortars to our rear, which were manned by our Swedish comrades.

All Hell had broken loose, and the Russians were sitting in a trap. Only a few were able to save themselves under the cover of the tanks, which were also fleeing back to the protective woods. What had just been a peaceful valley had become a valley of death and destruction. Burning armored vehicles and dead soldiers remained behind.

We thought they wouldn't come again, but we were wrong. Our high ground with its important road was an important objective, and the Russians wanted it, no matter the cost in men or materiel.

Behind the patch of woods, where the Russians had withdrawn, we were able to see a small section of the road that led into the woods. The Russians were now moving down the road in trucks with supplies. I was able to set one truck loaded with ammunition alight. At 1800 hours and after a short artillery preparation on the part of the Russians, the Russians came again. Their artillery fire had been without effect, since we had pulled back behind the high ground. The rounds fired from the Russian tanks went far overhead into the hinterlands.

This time, they attacked with their battle cry, but that assault was also broken up in the valley. We then took the woods under heavy fire for a few hours. Wherever the muzzle flash of a Russian tank was seen, it was soon followed by the sight of a burning Russian tank. Our cannon vehicles put in a terrific performance.

It turned peaceful once again in the pretty valley.

The next three days were also peaceful. The Russians no longer attacked in our sector.

On 23 August, we were relieved by an Army unit and our destination was Dorpat.

Former *SS-Sturmmann* Toni Ging, assigned to the *3./SS-Panzer-Aufklärungs-Abteilung 11*, recounts his experiences in a light half-track in January 1945:[17]

Operations in an *SPW*

After the arrival of the [battalion] outside of Oranienbaum in the middle of December 1943, the 3rd Company was quartered in a small village. We finally received our *SPW's* there. Most of them were open topped, but a few of them had a turret with a 2cm cannon and an *MG 34*. Since I had been trained as a driver, I received a

[*Sd.Kfz. 250/9*]. A *Rottenführer* served as the vehicle commander; the gunner was a Swedish comrade. I cannot remember either name.

The crew was together until around 27 January 1944, and we experienced the armored engagement at Gubanitzy on 25 January. We had orders to render harmless the dismounted crews from knocked-out Russian tanks. Our vehicle was near a 7.5cm cannon vehicle, as well as an antitank gun from the 5th Company. Through my vision slit, I could see the commander of the 5th Company, *SS-Obersturmführer* Langendorf, issue orders to his men.

During the evening of 25 January 1944, we were employed along with additional *SPW's* of the 3rd Company as a rear guard. Our *SPW* was one of the last ones to leave Gubanitzy. While we were pulling back during the night, I saw *SS-Oberscharführer* Nilsson through my vision port several times. He was stamping through the snow, with the sounds of mortar rounds impacting being heard all the time. The next morning, we discovered that [he] had been killed.

On 27 January 1945, we were in position at Wolossowo. Our *SPW* received orders to reconnoiter and determine whether the Russians had already established themselves in the next village. We were accompanied by an *SPW* with mechanized infantry. Our route took us over a narrow trail towards the village. About 100 meters from the village, I moved my *SPW* off to the side on the right so as to be able to give cover to the grenadiers.

The second *SPW* moved on to the edge of the village and the first houses. Up to that point, not a shot had been fired. The *SPW* turned around and returned. It had barely caught up to us, when we were engaged from the direction of the village by heavy small-arms fire.

Just before that happened, I had turned my *SPW* around and also wanted to take off, when the tracks slid in the snow and we found ourselves bottomed out on a pile of rocks that were hidden underneath. The fire was growing more and more intense; we had to get out of there no matter what. First out was the vehicle commander in the turret. The next one was the Swedish gunner. I was the last one out as the driver. Hunched over, we ran to the other *SPW*, which was waiting for us. Before we got there, however, the Swede was hit. Both of us crawled over to him. We dragged him over to the *SPW*, where we put him through the rear door and into the interior of the vehicle. The *Rottenführer* and I positioned ourselves on the hood of the vehicle to be protected from the fire. We moved back as quickly as we could, until we reached the edge of some woods about 300 meters away. We stopped for a moment and saw our abandoned vehicle fly into the air at that instant.

We continued on to the main clearing station, where we turned over the wounded Swede. He died a short while later due to the severe wounding he had taken to his lungs.

That day, the 3rd Company had a combat strength of about 25 men.

Former *SS-Hauptscharführer* Alfred Weiß, the platoon leader of the *PaK-Zug* of the *5./SS-Panzer-Aufklärungs-Abteilung 11*, recounts the fighting around Gubanitzy in late January 1944 that later resulted in the award of the Knight's Cross for the acting company commander:[18]

Impressions of the Armor Engagement on 25–26 January 1944 at Gubanitzy

It was always the same: The monotonous white of the broad Russian countryside, which was only interrupted by the silhouette of a small village, devoid of humans.

We were also clothed in white, and our vehicles and guns had the same color. The snow had frozen hard, and it was cold. Felt boots and padded winter uniforms protected us from the surly and cold weather.

We were sitting on our open armored vehicles and followed nose-to-tail, one behind the other, through the quiet terrain. We knew that the Russians were following us and observing.

That's the way it went, from one blocking position to the next, where we would hold up and show our face to the enemy.

He had figured that out quickly enough and was following us very carefully. You could assume that it would remain quiet at night. Everyone needed and enjoyed his sleep.

It went like that for some time. Everything started to become routine, and everyone knew his role.

The guns of the antitank platoon were distributed among the long march column in such a manner that antiarmor defense was provided up front, to the rear and in the middle. We had moved a considerable distance. As it started to turn dark, the battalion reached the village of Gubanitzy, where we set up for the night.

I arrived there as one of the last ones. I was moving with the gun crew of Broschnowski at the very end. We didn't have a lot of time to seek out quarters, since it would turn dark any minute. So we saw to it that we quickly found a suitable house where we could stretch out our tired limbs and had protection against the cold of the night. My section headquarters had become small. I only had a driver and a captured Russian soldier with me. My good messenger, Hedrich, had to help out elsewhere. Thus we stayed with the gun crew. That was all right with me, since Broschnowski was commanding a gun for the first time. Tired and frazzled, we stretched out.

I became restless as it turned first light. I wanted to go outside and look for the other gun crewmembers. They were still sleeping. I didn't get too far, however. I heard the warning shout of "Tanks!" It was getting louder and louder and was coming down the slope in front of the village. I ran back the few steps I had taken and got the sleepy heads up. In a flash, they were getting their gun into position in an effort to receive the troublemakers. At the same time, I reached for my flare gun to fire off the tank alert. I quickly loaded the gun with a white flare. I pointed it skywards and pulled the trigger. But it didn't do its job. The spring for the bolt only moved forward slowly and sluggishly.

That couldn't be happening: The weapon failed to function in such a decisive moment. I had to set off the alarm somehow and warn the unprepared battalion of what was approaching it. The surprise the Russians intended could not be allowed to happen. But at that moment, I simply couldn't run away from the gun in an effort to warn the others, especially since the gun commander had just been put in charge. What choices did I have?

I cocked the hammer once again. I held the gun firmly, pulled the trigger and slammed the hammer against a fence post at the same time. The blow was enough to set off the round. It flew closely past my nose and in the direction of the middle of the village. I was able to repeat the whole affair one more time, this time with a bundled charge of blue, red and green. That served to warn the battalion. It could start to get ready to throw its reception. The only thing left was the uncertainty of when things would heat up and how they would turn out.

We didn't need to wait very long to find out. Four tanks came racing one behind the other on the road to the left in the village. They were bunched up tightly and coming down the slope towards us. The first one fired its main gun and was able to hit my *SPW*, which had been positioned on the right side of the road the previous evening. It was unmanned and defenseless. That action by the tank gunner turned out to be his last. Just as it was in the process of rolling past us on the road and into the village, the order of "Fire at will!" spelled the end for the tank. The first round that morning was fired from a distance of about 10 meters and tore a hole in the left side of the tank about as big as a man's head. It stopped immediately and took away our field of fire. As a result, the second tank was able to move past to the right and make a getaway. The third and fourth tanks met the same fate as the first one, however.

We thought the engagement had been decided in a few minutes, since there were no more tanks to be seen far and wide. That's where we made a big mistake. We never even considered the thought that what we had seen there was only an advance guard. But we soon knew differently.

All of a sudden, about 15 minutes later, about 50 tanks of the T-34 variety came over the crest of the hill, widely dispersed. The heavy, dark steel giants rolled down the slope in a threatening manner and towards the village, where the battalion had encamped. They probably did not realize that the three other guns of the antitank platoon were waiting for them there. The tanks were escorted by mounted infantry. They were certainly in a position to overrun anything that stood in their way. That's probably how the operation was envisioned. But things turned out differently.

Whoever wanted to survive in this situation had to be steadfast and fight. To prevail or die: There was no other choice. As the steel giants crested the hill and started down the slope, they were taken under fire by all four antitank guns. The range was favorable; each round hit its intended target. The armored force soon went into a state of disarray. When the command tank, which could be determined by the antenna array, was hit, the enemy clearly started to panic. None tried to move forward. They moved back and forth, from left to right, and back again. In the process they rammed and ran into each other. An unimaginable chaos erupted among them and our guns continued to fire their well-aimed rounds. The crews had maintained their nerve when confronted by the steel giants. Everyone else had helped them maintain their composure. Whoever was not engaging enemy infantry came and helped carry ammunition or encourage the crews. Everyone knew what was at stake.

After a while, the tanks had bunched up so close together that they were in each other's way. You could no longer tell which ones were still combat capable. They simply remained where they were and gave up. Their attack had collapsed.

One of them tried to save itself by moving behind a house. But its fate was also sealed there. We helped in that regard by firing a high-explosive round into the house in front of the tank. It tore a huge hole in the clay wall. The second round, an antitank round, hit and penetrated the tank.

We were too far away to see exactly where it had hit, but the loud and joyous outcry of "Target!" from comrades, who were closer by, confirmed our success.

The engagement was decided. It turned quiet again. Everyone needed a break. Quiet observation ensued and continued until the evening.

Then, suddenly, things changed. Concealed by the darkness, three enemy tanks rolled into the village from the other side. The first one was hit by an antitank gun and burned like a torch in the night. The second one succeeded in entering the village, while the third one turned away and disappeared into the night.

Things grew restless in the village. No one had counted on that happening, especially since the tank rammed several battalion vehicles parked along the village street. Was it evil intent or was it due to his driving skills? That was never determined. The tank commander soon lost his nerve, however. Without having caused all that much damage, he turned away and was not seen again.

Approximately 30 enemy tanks had been knocked out. They were scattered out in front of us, silent and taciturn, as if they had all been moved into a junkyard.

Were they really knocked out or only pretending to be?

Either way, the enemy had not succeeded in his attempt. The antitank platoon had received its baptism of fire and garnered so much respect, that enemy tanks only showed themselves from a distance from then on.

The actions described above resulted in a Knight's Cross recommendation by the battalion commander for the acting company commander of the 5th Company, *SS-Untersturmführer* Georg Langendorf, who had been in command less than a week:[19]

Submitted: 8 February 1944

Received at the Office of the *Reichsführer-SS*: 27 February 1944

Approved: 12 March 1944

How long in current position: 22 January 1944

Military Status: Reserves

Date of Entry on Active Duty: 23 November 1939

Date of Rank: 1 September 1943

Awards received in present war: Iron Cross, First Class; Iron Cross, Second Class; Assault Badge; Eastern Medal

Short Rationale and Recommendation of the Intermediate Commanders:
As part of *Kampfgruppe Wengler*, *SS-Panzer-Aufklärungs-Abteilung 11* had the mission of screening the important crossroads at Gubanitzy to the northeast of Wolossowo.

On 26 January 1944, the village was attacked by 56 Russian tanks, most of them T-34's. In addition, there was a battalion of more than 350 men.

SS-Untersturmführer Langendorf, as the Acting Commander of the Heavy Company, screened towards the northeast in the direction of Torosowo with his antitank platoon.

Although no friendly artillery was available and friendly infantry had occupied positions to the rear, Langendorf had his guns manhandled forward in such a manner that he could effectively counter the attack. He did this on his own initiative.

Two assault guns, which only had limited ammunition, had to pull back after a short firefight. That meant that Langendorf's antitank platoon had to bear the brunt of the Russian attack.

Thanks to uncompromising personal involvement in working with his cannon platoon, Langendorf succeeded in knocking out 24 tanks within the space of two hours. Of those, 15 were T-34's. Six additional Russian tanks were also rendered combat ineffective as a result of Langendorf's antitank defense.

Eight Russian tanks were knocked out by the assault guns.

After elimination of the first tank wave, Langendorf employed his cannon platoon and personally led it to the southwestern edge of the village [Gubanitzy], after scattered tanks had advanced. He chased them away and thus held the supply route open during the first part of the engagement.

Once back at the northeastern edge of the village, he collected the slight infantry forces to provide local defense against Russian infantry, and he eliminated additional approaching waves of enemy tanks.

On that day, Langendorf's antitank elements knocked out a total of 31 enemy tanks, among them 22 T-34's, and rendered an additional 6 inoperable.

On 27 January 1944, Langendorf was able to knock out another enemy tank and destroy it.

On 29 January 1944, an additional two enemy tanks were knocked out in Opolje; they were then personally rendered inoperable by Langendorf and blown up.

In the space of those four days, Langendorf and elements of his company eliminated a total of 34 enemy tanks and made 6 tanks combat ineffective.

The total number of "kills" in Gubanitzy on 26 January 1944 made it impossible for the enemy to execute his intention—confirmed by prisoner statements—of advancing on Wolossow through Gubanitzy and taking the former. It also enabled the deliberate withdrawal of the friendly forces on the right.

/signed/ Saalbach
SS-Hauptsturmführer und Battalion Commander

In this account, former *SS-Untersturmführer* Mogens E. Schwartz recalls the time he assumed command of the 4th Company:[20]

SS-Untersturmführer Schwartz Assumes Command of the 4th Company

At the beginning of March 1945, the Company Commander of the 4th Company was killed. On orders of the Battalion Commander, I was directed to assume command of the company. That meant that my time as a liaison officer was over.

I was shown maps for the positions of the 4th Company, and I immediately entered the positions of the individual foxholes, etc. A soldier from the 4th Company, who happened to be at the Battalion Command Post, was directed to lead me there. Both of us took off. But the positions marked on the map had already been evacuated; the right flank was open, presumably marshland. To the left, however, we were supposed to have contact with a unit from the Army, at least according to the Battalion Commander.

We headed off to the left, but there was not a single soul to be seen far and wide. At one place, we had to cross a small, wooden bridge. It was slightly elevated, and we immediately received small-arms fire from the Russians, who had observed us. I had gotten across the bridge without being wounded, but the soldier accompanying me didn't think he had a chance in crossing the footpath and went back to the Battalion Command Post by himself. Since the Russians had seen us, it was also impossible for me to cross the bridge again. Correspondingly, I continued moving. The 4th Company couldn't have just vanished into thin air!

I was only wearing an old, dirty motorcyclist's overcoat. The soldier who had been with me had carried my helmet and submachine gun. The only weapon I had was a 6.35mm pistol under my coat, as well as a hand grenade in my trouser pocket. I looked like a civilian. All of a sudden, three Russian soldiers approached me. They calmly asked me questions, which I did not understand. Unfortunately, the only thing I understood was: *"Nemski Soldaski!"* ("German soldiers!") I patted one of the Russian soldiers on the shoulder in a comradely fashion and pointed off somewhere into the distance. About 100 meters away from them, one man suddenly said something, and the three Russians wanted to grab me. I jumped over a water ditch and found cover behind a single tree. The Russians fired at me, but they only hit the trunk. I saw them conferring amongst themselves.

I took my sole hand grenade and tossed it among the Russians, who were about 10 meters away. I then ran across the open field and reached a wood line. I was on the far side of a small lake, as I later determined, and I hid myself in the lake under a small footbridge. I stayed there until it turned dark. I then moved out in dripping wet clothes and reached friendly defensive positions, where I heard Norwegian. I called out: "Friendly forces. Don't shoot! I am alone."

I heard the word: "Understood!"

The Battalion Command post was far away on the other side of the lake, and I was transported there in an armored vehicle. I laid on the warm hood of the vehicle and was able to dry out my clothes in the process. When I reported to the Battalion Commander, he said to the Battalion Surgeon: "You've lost some *Schnapps*! I told you the Russians wouldn't get Schwartz!"

Genzow continues his personal account with scenes from the fighting in and around Berlin in April 1945:[21]

The Last Days in Berlin

I had almost healed from my first wound. Although I still limped a bit, I wanted to get back to my unit at the front. So I made my way from the field trains to the headquarters of *SS-Panzer-Aufklärungs-Abteilung 11*. At the time, it was in a small village in the vicinity of Schwedt an der Oder.

The Russians had already advanced to the east banks of the Oder, but they still had not attempted an attack across the river.

It was still a bit quiet at the headquarters. That lasted until the day I received orders to go to Schwedt. There was a radio section with *SPW's* there. I was supposed to give it maps and signals instructions.

The exact location of the *SPW's* was unknown, but we eventually found them on a rise outside of Schwedt. From there, we had a good view of the city and the Oder. During the afternoon, we received orders by radio to tear down the site with all of the vehicles and head in the direction of Berlin.

The [battalion] had been pulled out of the line where it had been and sent in the direction of Müncheberg and Seelow outside of Berlin. We still did not know the exact location.

Because of our orders, we moved as stragglers from Schwedt towards the west. The movement went almost without a hitch through municipalities that, in some instances, had already been evacuated by the civilian populace. We passed columns of refugees, who were fleeing from the Russians. The enemy offensive in Germany spread fear and panic everywhere. The German defenses were increasingly collapsing. The Russian breakthrough had one unmistakable objective: Berlin!

We heard the sound of fighting coming from the north, but it was still far away. By then, the Russians had also advanced across the Oder, at least to the north of us, which we did not know at the time.

That surprise did not take long in coming. Just before the entrance to a village, some Russian tanks—T-34's—came out of the woods to the right of the road.

We were able to disappear into the village. In the village proper was a unit of *Volkssturm*. We got out of there in a flash and arrived at Eberswalde in the evening. It was still quiet in that small town. We were forced to take a break, since our fuel was coming to an end. Where would we get some?

We were stranded there for two days. Fuel was impossible to find, even from the local military administration. We did discover, however, that the [battalion] was east of Berlin in the vicinity of Strausberg [approximately 30 kilometers due east of Berlin].

We didn't know quite what to do, and so we agreed to send a couple of men to Berlin on the train. It was 19 April 1945. And so we took off towards Berlin: One *Unterscharführer* and two men, who hailed from Berlin. That meant I was with the group. I secretly entertained the hope of being able to get home one more time.

We got to Berlin's Stettin train station on the night of 20 April 1945. As we later discovered, the ring around Berlin had already been closed by the Russians. Based on that, we were probably among the last ones to head into the trap.

What were we to do at that point in Berlin? The city was in rubble as a result of air attacks; we ourselves experienced one that same night. I don't need to say that it was bad. At least at the front, we knew where the dangers were. But here? Berlin had been transformed into a witch's cauldron . . .

At the *Friedrichsstraße* rail station—a collection point—we discovered that our battalion was in Strausberg. We received marching orders to the battalion. If we hadn't had them, we would have wound up with alert units. No one knew what was going on. The confusion at the collection point was enormous. It did work out that I was able to look up my parents, which the other comrade from Berlin also did. We set up a time to meet the next day, since we wanted to find the battalion. We had to be on our toes to make sure a military patrol didn't nab us. In those cases, no amount of paperwork helped. They took everyone with them.

The next day, we met and attempted to find our unit by heading in the direction of Mahlsberg/Strausberg on a bike. The third man never appeared. The streets were empty, since all of the people were in the basements, seeking shelter from the artillery rounds and the combat aircraft that constantly flew over Berlin.

Lichtenberg was already being fired upon by Russian artillery. We reached the suburb of Friedrichsfelde; it was 22 April 1945. We had already given up looking for our battalion, and we heard machine-gun fire coming from the east. That meant the Russians had already reached the city, but where?

As if pulled by a magnet, we headed in the direction from which the sounds of fighting could be heard.

We reached Alt-Friedrichsfelde, where we ran into elements of [the battalion] at the Marzahn–Mahlsdorf–Frankfurter Allee crossroads. Saalbach's headquarters had set up in a small house. We reported back into the unit and reported on the whereabouts of our section in Eberswalde. It could probably be written off, but it was assumed that the comrades had attempted to make their way to the west. By then, it was evening and it had turned dark . . .

. . . The sound of fighting during the night became louder and louder. The men were generally in the houses; a few were in their armored vehicles, since they had been directed to screen the streets. Towards morning, all Hell broke out. The Russians were coming from the direction of Marzahn with tanks and infantry. In no time at all, everything was in an uproar. The small group that made up the battalion took up the fight. We were able to hold back the Russian infantry. We were also able to knock out a few of the enemy tanks, but we had to bow to the superior numbers and pull back.

The Russians were also coming down the *Frankfurter Allee*; that route back to the middle of the city was cut off. We then headed east, moving along the railway line towards Wühlheide and via Karlshorst and Schönweide towards the city center. We reached the zoo entrance at the *Zoo-Flakbunker* with a few *SPW's* of the headquarters and some of the companies. The trains elements of the battalion were also there. The zoo and the *Flak* tower were already under fire from Russian artillery. As a messenger, I did not get much rest. I received orders to take rations to Britz (Neukölln) with four *SPW's*. There were additional elements of the [battalion] in position there. That was also the last time that I saw comrades from the trains.

Our movement took us through the zoo, *Potsdamer Platz*, Tempelhof and Neukölln. The *Hermann Platz* and *Sonnenallee* were torn up by heavy Russian artillery and the buildings were burning. Despite the danger, civilians were on the streets attempting to grab some foodstuffs wherever they could find them.

We reached the *Kölnische Heide* rail station, where our battalion comrades were in position along the embankment. Together with the other comrades who had just arrived, we took up positions. By then, the Russian infantry had closed dangerously close to the embankment.

In a few places, there was already close-quarters fighting. The situation was more than just a bit murky.

We were but a small and weak battle group that was offering the Soviets determined resistance. It put up a stiff defense. We attempted to fend off the attacks and make the best of that damnable situation, but there was no longer any organized defense. It was more a matter of trying to survive.

I was summoned to the railway station building, where the battalion command post was located. I was with the Battalion Commander and the Battalion Surgeon one more time. Suddenly, however, a salvo of artillery fire from the Russians hit the railway grounds. With it, came my second wounding. At the time the rounds impacted, I was in front of the station, where a few of our vehicles were located. Being out in the open, I got a big blast right in the back. The pain was terrible and there was a lot of blood lost. I passed out. I was taken under cover in the railway station building by a few comrades. There were other casualties as well.

A medic dressed my wounds as best he could. Then the Battalion Surgeon came, followed by the Battalion Commander. He said to me: "Well, kid, take care. It's all over for you. See to it that you get to a hospital and then home."

That was the last time I saw our commander, *SS-Sturmbannführer* Saalbach.

In a school near the [rail station], which had been turned into an emergency hospital, I received medical attention. They took me into the operating room immediately, where the major portion of the shrapnel was removed and I received new dressing.

Through wounded soldiers being brought into the hospital, I discovered that the Russians had advanced to just outside the school. I quickly decided to scram, since I did not want to fall into the hands of the Russians. As I ran through the streets of Neukölln, I saw abandoned military equipment everywhere. The way through the city was marked by the traces of war. Small groups of German soldiers made their way along the streets; all of them wanted to escape that Hell. On several occasions, I had to seek cover when the sounds of incoming artillery could be heard. As the result of my wound, I could barely move. Later on, I was picked up by an ambulance. I wound up in the West End Hospital, which was full of wounded soldiers.

The thought that the war was lost for us and for Germany ran through my head again and again. There was a long, uncertain future ahead of us. I was in the hospital for a week; the war was over. The Russians came and got us, and the road into captivity started. It lasted until January 1950.

SS-Unterscharführer Marienfeld, who was assigned to the 1st Company of *SS-Panzer-Aufklärungs-Abteilung 3 "Totenkopf,"* has provided some insight into armored car operations conducted as part of the initial efforts to relieve Budapest at the beginning of January 1945. The heavy section of the wheeled scout company was given orders late in the afternoon of 2 January 1945 to reconnoiter to the southeast:[22]

It turned night. We moved through Bajot, which was on fire. Our tanks had done a job there. At the fork in the road at the southern edge of the village, things looked nasty: burning Soviet tanks, artillery and vehicles of all types scattered all about. . . . Our armored group was sent in the direction of Bajna. We were directed to reconnoiter along the road that branched off out of the village to the southeast.

Without encountering the Russians, the patrol reached the road from Bajna to Tat, after passing by the large farm at Kls. Szt. Kereszt. Marienfeld continues:

. . . We turned off towards Bajna. Three hundred meters further on was another large farm. The Hungarians who still lived there were relieved when they saw we were German soldiers. "The Russians have fled in the direction of Sari Sap." We radioed the reconnaissance information we had gathered up to that point to the battalion and then moved further south. About one kilometer further, the road moved into a defile after passing a rise in the ground. All of a sudden, Russians in an American Jeep were behind the 8-wheeled car of *Unterscharführer* Schinke. I fired a burst from my submachine gun at the Russians. They jumped out of their vehicle and fled through the vegetation. The Jeep then belonged to us. Once beyond the defile, we halted on the road. The terrain was rising. We figured that Nagysap was behind the hill and it was full of Russians. *Untersturmführer* Goertz, Willi Lidenpütz and I moved forward on foot. We ran into Russians after about 300 meters. Damn it, my submachine gun jammed at first, but then the firefight started. The Russian guards at the outskirts of the village were startled. We went back to our vehicles. All of a sudden, in the darkness, the sound of tracks. T-34's? In the blink of an eye, we moved our vehicles off the road, grabbed our *Panzerfäuste* and took up positions in the defile. But the enemy tanks turned off to the west and took up the route that we had come in on. As we later discovered, even our immediate radio report did not prevent a patrol from the 2nd Company (motorcycle infantry) from moving straight into the arms of those tanks and being wiped out when it unsuspectingly exited some woods. We were also sitting in a trap, since Ivan had cut off the road behind us. Our effort to get back to Bajot in our armored cars by going over the hill at Nagysap failed due to the snowy incline. It was already starting to turn light in the east. It was high time we disappeared. We moved our vehicles into a defile and set up outposts . . .

. . . Russians on horseback patrolled throughout the area. Willi Lidenpütz stopped all outgoing radio traffic. The charger was too loud. We stayed on receive, however. As a result, we heard the tank regiment announce: "We're attacking!" But what was their attack objective? Bajna or Nagysap? Towards morning, a Russian column with antitank guns and mortars headed to the northeast. Presumably, it was the force that had been in Nagysap. We carefully approached the outskirts of the village, where the locals greeted us with joy. Their hospitality with food and drink was in full swing, when there was a tumult on the village street. In a coach with two horses, a commissar was trying to catch up with his forces. He was stopped by the people of the village. He had taken a girl from the village along with him as a hostage. She ran crying to her family. The coach was jammed full of booty, including silver goblets. Our radio message that the Russians had pulled out of Nagysap must not have reached the artillery since friendly artillery rounds were soon slamming into the village. Shrapnel destroyed part of the wheel suspension of *Unterscharführer* Schinke's vehicle. . . . Our driver, Gerd Kracht, knew a few tricks, however. He was able to lash up the wheel that had been affected; the vehicle was able to move. It was time to get out of Nagysap, before we were affected by additional hits from our own artillery.

After returning to the battalion, the heavy armored cars were again dispatched along the same route they had taken the previous day. *SS-Unterscharführer* Marienfeld provides a firsthand account of his scout patrol on 3–4 January. The patrol's objective was to determine whether Epöl was occupied by the enemy:[23]

SS-Untersturmführer Goertz took the route we had taken yesterday. We passed the large farm . . . There was a knocked-out T-34 on the road there. It was always nerve-wracking when you ran into a Russian tank at night. You never knew whether it was intact, knocked out or had been manned again . . .

. . . We moved out on a field path from the Nagysap–Bajna road. We stopped next to the village. *Untersturmführer* Goertz and I continued on foot. There were Russian guards at the outskirts of the village. Well then, the village was occupied. We snuck in from the side and checked out the enemy position as much as we were able. We then departed Epöl through the "emergency exit." When we returned to our vehicles, we radioed our finding to the battalion . . . We then moved back. We reached an improved road at Nagysap.

Our next objective was Sarisap. Moving parallel to us were our self-propelled antitank guns, which were attacking. They knocked out several Russian tanks. It was like we were at a training area. *Untersturmführer* Goertz decided to enter Sarisap by "surprise." We approached the village along a secondary route. About 400–500 meters away from the village, Russian infantry were digging in. They were so preoccupied that they did not even notice us. All of a sudden, there was a bang and a flash inside our vehicle . . . gunpowder . . . a stench. Wood and bits of steel pelted our armored car.

"Back up!"

Did they get our front driver? Hubert Rother fired an entire clip of 2cm rounds into the antitank gun at the edge of the village. Did they hit? Regardless, Ivan stayed quiet in the village. Willi Lidenpütz raced back through the middle of the astonished Russian infantry next to their holes. He was ranting: "Clear my hatch!" Once out of range, we halted. Out of the turret. We saw what had been bestowed upon us. The antitank gun round had hit a tree standing right next to our vehicle. The entire tree, including its crown, had whirled onto our vehicle. It was the tree that had saved us. That was enough for one day.

During the third attempt to relieve Budapest, which started on 18 January 1945, the scouts of the battalion again saw plenty of action. This time,

Marienfeld's driver, *SS-Sturmmann* Kerper, picks up the narrative:[24]

> . . . Our eight-wheeler was ordered to the commander's location to serve as a communications center. We set up behind a haystack. A few meters away was the battalion command post. About 300 meters in front of us, out in the fields, were two "King Tigers" and a *Panzer IV*. Their turrets were at 12 o'clock. They were observing to the front. All of a sudden, we heard the sound of tracks behind us. Moving at high speed, four self-propelled guns raced past us towards the front. We smiled: "Man, they're in a hurry!" Then there was firing from a tank main gun and the sounds of joyous yelling. We ran around the haystack and saw how the self-propelled guns were firing on the "King Tiger" from the rear. They had just knocked out the "King Tiger" on the left. The antitank guns were Russian! They also got the *Panzer IV* on the right. What were we supposed to do with our laughable 2cm guns against 7.62cm cannon? Before we had completed that thought, there was an order: "Mount up!" That was followed by: "Attack!"
>
> "Pepi," the name we had given *SS-Sturmmann* Pribitzer, bolted into the turret. He left the gunner's seat open for Gerd (*SS-Unterscharführer* Marienfeld).
>
> "Move out!"
>
> Out of the corners of my eyes, I observed the battlefield. One of the Russians was steering to the right; another one raced past the *Panzer IV* into a field of corn. The tank commander of the remaining "King Tiger" appeared in the turret. At the same moment, there was a roar. The two other Russians had hit the tank in the rear. A jolt went through the 70-ton giant. The tank commander collapsed in the turret. The main gun sagged; the muzzle pointed towards the ground. The Russians were acting like madmen. Moving at full speed, we emptied an entire magazine of 2cm rounds into the two self-propelled guns. I raced between the two knocked-out tanks with our eight-wheeler, cutting off the path of the two other Russians. Apparently, they were irritated by the loss of their two comrades and were racing around aimlessly. I outmaneuvered them in the cornfield. Our antitank rounds crashed into their left flanks and into their fuel tanks. That was enough . . .

By the middle of March, the Germans began to be pushed back as the Soviets launched their counteroffensive. The following incident occurred on 17 March 1945 and is related again by *SS-Oberscharführer* Marienfeld, who had been ordered at 0400 hours to take his heavy eight-wheeler section to reconnoiter to the northwest and cover the 1- to 1.5-kilometer gap that existed between the battalion and the Hungarian 2nd Armored Division:[25]

> As observed by us, the road in front of the Hungarian positions made a bend to the left and into a valley in the direction of Mor. Two Hungarian *Panzer IV's* were positioned there. We fired against the Russians coming out of the woods. For their part, they answered with antitank rifles. It gradually turned into an uncomfortable situation. Russian artillery was feeling its way forward. There was an Army fortress 88 on the forward slope. Towards noon, we returned to Csokakö and rearmed. . . . [Russian infantry started attacking from out of Csakbereny at the same time.] . . . Our motorcycle infantry chased them away, supported by our other scout cars. Russian artillery started increasing its fire on the village. From the hills to the northwest, Russian mortars began plastering Csokakö. Then Russian infantry started advancing out of the woods there. We had our hands full trying to fend off the Russians attacking from two sides. In the process, we were constantly patrolling between Csokakö and the Hungarian positions, with directed artillery fires following us all the while. The "heavy packages" of the Russians were also impacting among the Hungarian positions. Our allies started to get uneasy. Moreover, we were unable to establish a clear picture of their situation, since the wooded terrain rose to the east and blocked our sight.

Around 1500 hours, we had fired off all of our ammunition again and we moved back to Csokakö to rearm.

After taking ammunition on board, our eight-wheeler pulled forward a bit to allow the second vehicle some room. At that moment—at the same spot we had just been in—it received a direct hit from an artillery round. The vehicle immediately went up in flames. The vehicle commander and the gunner were killed immediately. Both of the drivers were able to dismount. They ran, burning and bleeding, to the medics. At that point, there were just two vehicles, Bullinger and me. We moved out on our "route" again. Our comrades in Csokakö were already receiving main-gun fire from Soviet tanks, which were rolling forward on the western slopes of the Vertes Mountains on the road from Csakbereny. At that point, the Russian antitank riflemen grew ever closer to us. We were still able to hold them at bay. The Russian artillery and mortar fire was literally chasing us back and forth. By then, the pressure on the Hungarian positions must have been strong enough to force the *Honveds* to pull back. Protected by their *Panzer IV's*, they pulled back in a fairly disciplined fashion along the valley road towards Mor. We raced back into Csokakö to render a report.

SS-Hauptsturmführer Berg issued orders: "Stop them!"

I started to object: "They have two *Panzer IV's* with them!"

"Doesn't matter!" He hissed. "Position yourselves between them!"

The devil was already loose in the village. The first T-34's had closed up to the village and were covering the positions of the motorcycle infantry with fire. The heavy weapons that weren't available were replaced by *Panzerfäuste*. Paul Scharfenroth was running towards the forward positions with two of the things clamped under his arms. He didn't react to me when I called out. He probably already felt he wasn't going to leave that village alive. Artillery shrapnel shredded one of the tires of our eight-wheeler. I wanted to change the tire, but we no longer had a spare. Hein Kerper and Willi Lidenpütz called out: "Let's go! Let's get out of here! We don't have any more time!" Pepi Pribitzer, our gunner, quickly loaded the stowage racks. The Russians started coming at us in huge masses, just like in 1941. Their mortars were showering us from the high ground. We had to get out of the village and back on to our "route." It was around 1600 hours . . .

. . . a Russian gun had registered right on the spot of our route back. Its rounds impacted there on a regular basis. We measured the rhythm of the firing and, at a suitable moment, we moved through the dangerous spot. During those moments, we tried to make ourselves as small as possible at our stations. We were lucky and made it through the bottleneck. We observed the Russians storming towards the village, who were literally streaming out of the woods on the high ground. We kept firing into them with our 2cm main gun until Russian artillery chased us away. The huge numerical superiority of the Russians flooded over the village and our comrades there.

It was around 1630 hours, when we arrived at the location of the Hungarian *Panzer IV's*. I intended to talk to the tank commanders to determine how best to hold the position. When I climbed aboard the first tank, I saw that the crew was in the process of rendering it inoperable. All the while, we were receiving heavy fire from the abandoned Hungarian positions. Csokakö was lost. The Russians were advancing from there to the west. We headed into the valley towards Mor. Just outside of the city, we bogged down in mud. After a lot of effort, we were able to free the vehicle and reach our comrades, where our former driver, Kracht, was already waiting with a replacement tire. We quickly changed the tire. We occupied new positions west of Mor.

Employment of the *Sd.Kfz. 250/9* in *KStN 1162c* Armored Scout Companies

Compiled by Martin Block (January 2015)

According to Thomas L. Jentz,[26] three *Sd.Kfz. 250/9* trial vehicles had probably been sent to the Eastern Front by June 1942 for troop trials. During January 1943 the first twenty-seven *Sd.Kfz. 250/9* production vehicles had been completed. By 1 April 1943 a total of thirty-two *Sd.Kfz. 250/9's* were reported available. One month later, the figure had risen to forty-two.

The allocation records for light half-tracks were kept by the Inspectorate of Armored Forces from the second week of May 1943 onward. It is not recorded which units received the first *Sd.Kfz. 250/5's* and *Sd.Kfz. 250/9's* for an armored scout company organized under *KStN 1162c*, but they were probably *SS-Panzer-Grenadier-Division Leibstandarte SS Adolf Hitler*, the *1. Panzer-Division*, and/or the *2. Panzer-Division*. In general, the files do not distinguish between variants of the *Sd.Kfz. 250*, but some allocations were marked with "c-Kp." or "1162c," which indicated the shipments consisted of *Sd.Kfz. 250/5's* and/or *250/9's*.

The listings below are based exclusively on the evaluation of original German records obtained from the Bundesarchiv/Militärarchiv in Freiburg, Germany, and the National Archives and Records Administration in Washington, D.C. The statement "equipment delivered" refers to the full issue for a Type "c" armored scout company in accordance with *KStN 1162c*, that is sixteen *Sd.Kfz. 250/9's* and nine *Sd.Kfz. 250/5's* (in several cases replaced by nine *Sd.Kfz. 250/3's*). Note that in many cases considerable time passed between authorization and actual deliveries.

Armored Divisions, Brigades, and Other Formations (Army and *Luftwaffe*)

Formation / Unit	Authorization / Delivery	Notes
1. Panzer-Division / 2./Panzer-Aufklärungs-Abteilung 1	Mid-February 1943 / late April to early May 1943	The last *Sd.Kfz. 250/9's* used up during February–March 1944. No replacements were received until January 1945, when about four *Sd.Kfz. 250/9* were taken over by the *1./Panzer-Aufklärungs-Abteilung 1* (probably from the *24. Panzer-Division*).
2. Panzer-Division / 2./Panzer-Aufklärungs-Abteilung 2	Mid-March 1943 / late April to early May 1943	Reconstitution was carried out during April 1944 (as the 1st Company). Another reconstitution followed during November 1944. After participation in Ardennes counteroffensive with *Panzer-Brigade 150*, the company was sent to the Milowitz Training Area for yet another reconstitution, but this was apparently not executed.
3. Panzer-Division / Panzer-Aufklärungs-Abteilung 3	(July 1943) / NA	Instead of a Type "c" company, the battalion received a company organized under *KStN 1162b* (parenthetical entry) and issued the *Sd.Kfz. 140/1* (*Aufklärungspanzer 38(t)*).
4. Panzer-Division / Panzer-Aufklärungs-Abteilung 4	(May 1944) / (January 1945)	Instead of a Type "c" company, the battalion received a company organized under *KStN 1162b* (first parenthetical entry) and issued the *Sd.Kfz. 123 Luchs* (*Panzer II, Ausführung L*). In May 1944, a Type "c" company was authorized in case the *Luchs* could not be sustained. Sixteen *Sd.Kfz. 250/9's* were sent to the division on 21 January 1945 (second parenthetical entry) and were distributed among the 2nd, 3rd, and 4th Companies. The division may have also received some additional *Sd.Kfz. 250/9's*, when the battalion was consolidated with *Panzer-Aufklärungs-Abteilung München* (ex-*Panzer-Jagd-Brigade 104*) in March 1945.
5. Panzer-Division / 2./Panzer-Aufklärungs-Abteilung 5	July 1943 (January 1944) / April and May 1943	Parenthetical entry refers to the time period orders actually issued to reorganize the company (as do similar entries throughout the table). Company redesignated as the 1st Company in June 1944.

Formation / Unit	Authorization / Delivery	Notes
6. Panzer-Division / 2./Panzer-Aufklärungs-Abteilung 6	July 1943 (October 1943) / October to December 1943	Parenthetical entry refers to the time period orders actually issued to reorganize the company. The redesignated *1./Panzer-Aufklärungs-Abteilung 6* was reconstituted in the summer of 1944.
7. Panzer-Division / 2./Panzer-Aufklärungs-Abteilung 7	July 1943 (October 1943) / November 1943 to January 1944	The company was redesignated as the *1./Panzer-Aufklärungs-Abteilung 7* in August–September 1944. The last *Sd.Kfz. 250/9's* were used up during January 1945. No replacements were ever recorded as received.
8. Panzer-Division / 2./Panzer-Aufklärungs-Abteilung 8	July 1943 (August 1944) / September 1944	The company was redesignated as the *1./Panzer-Aufklärungs-Abteilung 8* in the summer of 1944.
9. Panzer-Division / Panzer-Aufklärungs-Abteilung 9	NA	The reconnaissance battalion was authorized a *KStN 1162b* company and was issued the *Sd.Kfz. 123* (*Panzer II, Ausführung L Luchs*). Reports about any possible later use of the *Sd.Kfz. 250/9* are unknown to the author.
10. Panzer-Division / Panzer-Aufklärungs-Abteilung 10	NA	The battalion was never authorized a *KStN 1162c* company. It surrendered with the division in North Africa in May 1943.
11. Panzer-Division / 2./Panzer-Aufklärungs-Abteilung 11	July 1943 (October 1943) / October to December 1943	All *Sd.Kfz. 250/9's* were lost in Russia in early 1944. Records do not show any replacements allocated when the division was reconstituted in France starting in May 1944 and thereafter.
12. Panzer-Division / 2./Panzer-Aufklärungs-Abteilung 12	July 1943 (April 1944) / May to July 1944	The company was redesignated as the *1./Panzer-Aufklärungs-Abteilung 8* in the summer of 1944.
13. Panzer-Division / 2./Panzer-Aufklärungs-Abteilung 13	July 1943 (September 1943) / September 1943	The division was later destroyed in Budapest in January–February 1945. Redesignated and reconstituted as *Panzer-Division "Feldherrnhalle 2,"* the division was no longer authorized a *KStN 1162c* company.
14. Panzer-Division / 2./Panzer-Aufklärungs-Abteilung 14	February 1943 (February 1943) / August 1943	Formation of the 2nd Company as a *KStN 1162c* company was authorized and ordered in February 1943, when the division was being reconstituted after its destruction in Stalingrad.
15. Panzer-Division / Panzer-Aufklärungs-Abteilung 15	NA	The battalion was never authorized a *KStN 1162c* company. It surrendered with the division in North Africa in May 1943.
16. Panzer-Division / 2./Panzer-Aufklärungs-Abteilung 16	February 1943 (February 1943) / June 1943	Formation of the 2nd Company as a *KStN 1162c* company was authorized and ordered in February 1943, when the division was being reconstituted after its destruction in Stalingrad. Almost destroyed in early 1945, the division was reconstituted by its consolidation with *Panzer-Division "Jüterbog,"* but did not receive a *KStN 1162c* company again.
17. Panzer-Division / 2./Panzer-Aufklärungs-Abteilung 17	July 1943 (December 1943) / January to March 1944	The company was redesignated as the 1st Company in June 1944. The division suffered serious losses in January 1945, losing most of its armored fighting vehicles. The reconnaissance battalion was reconstituted in mid-March 1945, using the remnants of *Panzer-Aufklärungs-Abteilung "Hirschberg"* (ex-*Panzer-Brigade 103*), which originally also had included a *KStN 1162c* company.
18. Panzer-Division / 2./Panzer-Aufklärungs-Abteilung 18	July 1943 / NA	Reorganization not initiated, since the division itself was redesignated and reorganized as the *18. Artillerie-Division*, which did not have reconnaissance assets.
19. Panzer-Division / 2./Panzer-Aufklärungs-Abteilung 19	July 1943 (July 1944) / August 1944	The company had been redesignated as the 1st Company of the battalion by the time the equipment arrived.
20. Panzer-Division / 2./Panzer-Aufklärungs-Abteilung 20	July 1943 (April 1944) / June 1944	The company had been redesignated as the 1st Company of the battalion by the time the equipment arrived.
21. Panzer-Division (Afrika) / Panzer-Aufklärungs-Abteilung 21	NA	The battalion was never authorized a *KStN 1162c* company. It surrendered with the division in North Africa in May 1943.
21. Panzer-Division (neu) / Panzer-Aufklärungs-Abteilung 21	September 1943 / November 1943	During September 1943 the former *Panzer-Aufklärungs-Lehr-Abteilung* was assigned to the division and redesignated as *Panzer-Aufklärungs-Abteilung 21*. Its 1st Company was already organized as a *KStN 1162c* company and received new equipment during November 1943.
22. Panzer-Division / Kradschützen-Bataillon 24	NA	The battalion was never authorized a *KStN 1162c* company. The division was deactivated in February 1943.

Formation / Unit	Authorization / Delivery	Notes
23. Panzer-Division / 2./Panzer-Aufklärungs-Abteilung 23	July 1943 (October 1943) / December 1943 to January 1944	The company was redesignated as the 1st Company in the late summer of 1944.
24. Panzer-Division / 2./Panzer-Aufklärungs-Abteilung 24	February 1943 (February 1943) / July to August 1943	Formation of the 2nd Company as a *KStN 1162c* company was authorized and ordered in February 1943, when the division was being reconstituted after its destruction in Stalingrad. The company was redesignated as the 1st Company in the late summer of 1944.
25. Panzer-Division / 2./Panzer-Aufklärungs-Abteilung 25	August 1943 / September 1943	When the division was sent to Denmark in May 1944 for reconstitution, the remaining equipment of the company was left behind in Russia. Redesignated as the 1st Company, the unit was reconstituted in October 1944.
26. Panzer-Division / 2./Panzer-Aufklärungs-Abteilung 26	January 1944 / April, June, and August 1944	The *KStN 1162c* company was formed by the redesignation and reorganization of the battalion's former 4th Company. When the unit returned to the division in October 1944, it was as the 1st Company.
27. Panzer-Division / Panzer-Aufklärungs-Kompanie 127	NA	The division was never authorized a *KStN 1162c* company. It was deactivated in February 1943.
116. Panzer-Division / 1./Panzer-Aufklärungs-Abteilung 116	April 1944 / May to June 1944	
Panzer-Lehr-Division / 2./Panzer-Aufklärungs-Lehr-Abteilung	NA / October and December 1943	The *I./Panzergrenadier-Lehr-Regiment* was reassigned to the *Panzer-Lehr-Division* in January 1944 and redesignated as the *Panzer-Aufklärungs-Lehr-Abteilung*. Its 2nd Company was already organized under *KStN 1162c*. The company was redesignated as the 2nd Company in the late summer of 1944.
Fallschirm-Panzer-Division "Hermann Göring" / 2./Fallschirm-Panzer-Aufklärungs-Abteilung "Hermann Göring"	July 1943? / February 1944?	The exact date for the authorization of the 2nd Company could not be established by the author. It probably happened during July 1943. Equipment seems to have been delivered in February 1944, while the company was still forming in Holland. Details about an employment in Italy are currently unknown. After the transfer of the division to the Eastern Front, the company—redesignated as the *1./Fallschirm-Panzer-Aufklärungs-Abteilung "Hermann Göring 1"*—received a complete new set of equipment in late September 1944.
Panzer-Division (-Brigade) Norwegen	NA	The division was never authorized a *KStN 1162c* company.
Panzer-Division "Holstein"	NA	The division was never authorized a *KStN 1162c* company, but the two companies of its *Panzer-Aufklärungs-Abteilung 44* were formed using the equipment of *Reserve-Panzer-Aufklärungs-Abteilung 3* (*233. Reserve-Panzer-Division*). The latter formation had at least two *Sd.Kfz. 250/9's* available at the beginning of 1945, and apparently they were passed on to *Panzer-Division "Holstein."*
Panzer-Division "Jüterbog"	NA	The division was never authorized a *KStN 1162c* company.
Panzer-Division Döberitz ("Schlesien")	NA	The division was never authorized a *KStN 1162c* company.
Panzer-Division "Müncheberg"	NA	The division was never authorized a *KStN 1162c* company.
Panzer-Division Clausewitz	NA	*Panzer-Aufklärungs-Abteilung Elbe* joined the new division in mid-April 1945. Initially it had been named *Panzer-Aufklärungs-Abteilung Döring*, and had been formed from elements of *Panzer-Ausbildungs-und Ersatz-Abteilung 3*, plus a *KStN 1162c* company originally intended for the *4. Kavallerie-Brigade*. *Panzer-Aufklärungs-Abteilung Elbe* consisted of two companies with a total of twenty-four *Sd.Kfz. 250/9's* plus a mix of other *Sd.Kfz. 250* variants and four- and eight-wheeled armored cars.
Panzer-Korps "Feldherrnhalle" / Panzer-Korps-Aufklärungs-Abteilung "Feldherrnhalle"	NA	The battalion was ordered formed in mid-March 1945 using the former armored reconnaissance battalion of *Panzer-Division "Feldherrnhalle,"* which had been at the Milowitz Training Area since October 1944 undergoing reconstitution. In late January 1945, sixteen *Sd.Kfz. 250/9's* had been delivered to the formation.

MECHANIZED INFANTRY DIVISIONS (ARMY AND *LUFTWAFFE*)

Formation / Unit	Authorization / Delivery	Notes
3. Panzergrenadier-Division / 2./Panzer-Aufklärungs-Abteilung 103	February 1943 (February 1943) / July 1943	Formation of the 2nd Company as a *KStN 1162c* company was authorized and ordered in February 1943, when the division was being reconstituted after its destruction in Stalingrad. In the fall of 1944, the company was redesignated as the 1st Company.
		The *10., 15., 16., 18., 20.,* and *25. Panzergrenadier-Divisionen* were never authorized *KStN 1162c* companies for their armored reconnaissance battalions.
29. Panzergrenadier-Division / 2./Panzer-Aufklärungs-Abteilung 129	February 1943 (February 1943) / July 1943	Formation of the 2nd Company as a *KStN 1162c* company was authorized and ordered in February 1943, when the division was being reconstituted after its destruction in Stalingrad. In the fall of 1944, the company was consolidated with the Headquarters Company.
60. Panzergrenadier-Division (Panzergrenadier-Division "Feldherrnhalle") (Panzer-Division "Feldherrnhalle 1") / 2./Panzer-Aufklärungs-Abteilung 160	February 1943 (February 1943) / October 1943	Formation of the 2nd Company as a *KStN 1162c* company was authorized and ordered in February 1943, when the division was being reconstituted after its destruction in Stalingrad (as the *60. Infanterie-Division (mot)*). In the fall of 1944, the company was consolidated with the Headquarters Company. The division (as *Panzer-Division "Feldherrnhalle"*) was effectively destroyed at Budapest in January and February 1945. At the time, the 2nd Company (still a *KStN 1162c* company) was being reconstituted in Germany. Once released to return to the field, the company became a part of *Panzer-Korps "Feldherrnhalle"* (see above), while the newly redesignated and reconstituted division did not receive another *KStN 1162c* company.
90. Panzergrenadier-Division / 2./Panzer-Aufklärungs-Abteilung 190	NA	The battalion was never authorized a *KStN 1162c* company for its armored reconnaissance battalion.
Panzergrenadier-Division "Großdeutschland" / Panzer-Aufklärungs-Abteilung "Großdeutschland"	July 1943 / NA	Although a *KStN 1162c* company was authorized in July 1943, the order was never executed. Instead, the battalion received a *KStN 1162b* company outfitted with the *Sd.Kfz. 140/1 (Aufklärungspanzer 38(t))*.
Panzergrenadier-Division "Brandenburg" / Panzer-Aufklärungs-Abteilung "Brandenburg"	September 1944 / ?	The fielding of the company seems to have remained incomplete. Apparently, only about two-thirds of the equipment were delivered in December 1944 and January 1945.
Panzergrenadier-Division "Kurmark" / Panzer-Aufklärungs-Abteilung 51	? / ?	Surviving strength reports of the division seem to indicate the presence of a few *Sd.Kfz. 250/9's* with the reconnaissance battalion. They may have come from the stocks of *Panzergrenadier-Ersatz-Brigade "Großdeutschland,"* the training and replacement element for the *"Großdeutschland"* formations. Confirmation is still needed.
Fallschirm-Panzergrenadier-Division "Hermann Göring 2" / Fallschirm-Panzer-Aufklärungs-Abteilung "Hermann Göring 2"	NA	The division was never authorized a *KStN 1162c* company for its armored reconnaissance battalion.

ARMORED BRIGADES (ARMY)

Formation / Unit	Authorization / Delivery	Notes
Panzer-Brigaden 101 to *113* were never authorized *KStN 1162c* companies.		
Panzer-Brigade 103 (2nd iteration)	January 1945	In late January 1945, the headquarters detachment of the former *Panzer-Brigade 103* was used as a command and control element for a hastily formed armored battle group that included two armored reconnaissance battalions raised from Replacement Army detachments. One of these was *Panzer-Aufklärungs-Abteilung "Hirschberg,"* which included one, possibly even two *KStN 1162c* companies. The delivery of equipment for one company can be traced in the light half-track allocation files. The brigade was disbanded in mid-March 1945, and *Panzer-Aufklärungs-Abteilung "Hirschberg"* was incorporated into the *17. Panzer-Division.*
Panzer-Brigade 150	NA	During November 1944, the *1./Panzer-Aufklärungs-Abteilung 2* of the *2. Panzer-Division* was attached to the brigade for the upcoming counteroffensive in the Ardennes. This company had been refitting in Germany and just received sixteen *Sd.Kfz. 250/9's*.

Formation / Unit	Authorization / Delivery	Notes
Führer-Grenadier-Brigade (-Division) / Panzer-Späh-Kompanie 101 (Führer-Panzer-Späh-Kompanie 2)	September 1944 / September to October 1944	The brigade/division was authorized to have two platoons of Sd.Kfz. 250/9's.
Führer-Begleit-Brigade (-Division) / Panzer-Späh-Kompanie 102 (Führer-Panzer-Späh-Kompanie 1)	NA	The brigade/division did not have any Sd.Kfz. 250/9 authorizations.
Panzer-Jagd-Brigade 104	NA	Panzer-Aufklärungs-Abteilung München was attached to the brigade. It had received sixteen Sd.Kfz. 250/9's in February 1945. Remnants of the battalion were consolidated with Panzer-Aufklärungs-Abteilung 4 (4. Panzer-Division) in March 1945 (see there).
3. Kavallerie-Brigade (-Division) / Panzer-Aufklärungs-Abteilung 69	March 1945 / April 1945	The battalion was authorized sixteen Sd.Kfz. 250/9's and nine Sd.Kfz. 250/3's in March 1945 while being formed at the Milowitz Training Area. The company left Milowitz on 20 April 1945, but it is unclear whether it actually linked up with its parent division.
4. Kavallerie-Brigade (-Division) / Panzer-Aufklärungs-Abteilung 70	March 1945 / April 1945	The battalion was authorized sixteen Sd.Kfz. 250/9's and nine Sd.Kfz. 250/3's in March 1945 while being formed at the Milowitz Training Area. The vehicles intended for the battalion were instead transferred to elements that eventually made up the reconnaissance assets of Panzer-Division Clausewitz (see there).

ARMORED AND MECHANIZED INFANTRY DIVISIONS OF THE *WAFFEN-SS*

Formation / Unit	Authorization / Delivery	Notes
1. SS-Panzer-Division Leibstandarte SS Adolf Hitler / SS-Panzer-Aufklärungs-Abteilung 1 Leibstandarte SS Adolf Hitler	March 1943? / July 1943 /	A vehicle status report dated 10 March showed the presence of eight Sd.Kfz. 250 mit 2 cm Kwk. The author could not establish when those vehicles had been delivered and which company of the battalion actually used them. A KStN 1162c company was authorized only later (in mid-July 1943), but apparently the formation was not carried out and the equipment was never fully allocated. All of the remaining Sd.Kfz. 250/9's were lost during early 1944. No replacements were allocated thereafter.
2. SS-Panzer-Division "Das Reich" / SS-Panzer-Aufklärungs-Abteilung 2 "Das Reich"	July 1943 / summer 1944	The formation of the 1st Company was apparently not carried out until early summer 1944, but no allocation of any Sd.Kfz. 250/9's was recorded later on.
3. SS-Panzer-Division "Totenkopf" / SS-Panzer-Aufklärungs-Abteilung 3 "Totenkopf"	July 1943 / ?	The reorganization of a company of the battalion into a KStN 1162c company was authorized in mid-July 1943, but it was never apparently executed. It was only much later, during June 1944, that the 1st Company began apparently reporting Sd.Kfz. 250/9's in about platoon strength.
4. SS-Polizei-Panzer-Grenadier-Division / SS-Polizei-Panzer-Aufklärungs-Abteilung	NA	The division was never authorized a KStN 1162c company for its armored reconnaissance battalion.
5. SS-Panzer-Division "Wiking" / 2./SS-Panzer-Aufklärungs-Abteilung "Wiking"	Summer 1943 / September 1944	While the reorganization of a company was authorized in the summer of 1943, the order was not executed and deliveries initiated until the following year. By then the company had been redesignated as the 1st Company.
9. SS-Panzer-Division "Hohenstaufen" /2./SS-Panzer-Aufklärungs-Abteilung 9 "Hohenstaufen"	September 1943 / September to October 1943	The company was redesignated as the 1st Company in the fall of 1944.
10. SS-Panzer-Division "Frundsberg" / 2./SS-Panzer-Aufklärungs-Abteilung 10 "Frundsberg"	September 1943 / September and November 1943	The company was redesignated as the 1st Company in the fall of 1944.
11. SS-Freiwilligen-Panzer-Grenadier-Division "Nordland" / 2./SS-Panzer-Aufklärungs-Abteilung 11 "Nordland"	November 1943 / November 1943	
12. SS-Panzer-Division "Hitlerjugend" / 2./SS-Panzer-Aufklärungs-Abteilung 12 "Hitlerjugend"	October 1943 / December 1943 to February 1944	All remaining Sd.Kfz. 250/9's were incorporated into the new 2nd Company (former 3rd Company) during the fall of 1944.

The 16., 17., and 18. SS-Panzer-Grenadier-Divisionen were never authorized KStN 1162c companies for their armored reconnaissance battalions.

Employment of the *Sd.Kfz. 250/9* in *KStN 1162c* Armored Scout Companies *continued*

In addition to the *Sd.Kfz. 250/9* used by the German military, a full set of equipment for a *KStN 1162c* company was exported to Romania in May 1944 and apparently used by the Romanian 1st Armored Division.

As of 30 December 1944, the Army Quartermaster General reported the following numbers of *Sd.Kfz. 250/9's* on hand:

- Army armored divisions: *5. Panzer-Division*—fifteen; *6. Panzer-Division*—fifteen; *7. Panzer-Division*—three; *8. Panzer-Division*—sixteen; *12. Panzer-Division*—fourteen; *13. Panzer-Division*—one; *14. Panzer-Division*—five; *16. Panzer-Division*—sixteen; *17. Panzer-Division*—sixteen; *19. Panzer-Division*—sixteen; *20. Panzer-Division*—sixteen; *21. Panzer-Division*—seven; *23. Panzer-Division*—thirteen; *24. Panzer-Division*—six; *25. Panzer-Division*—eighteen; *26. Panzer-Division*—seventeen; *116. Panzer-Division*—nine; *233. Reserve-Panzer-Division*—two; *Panzer-Lehr-Division*—thirteen.
- *Luftwaffe* armored formations: *Fallschirm-Panzer-Division "Hermann Göring 1"*—eleven.
- Army mechanized infantry divisions: *3. Panzergrenadier-Division*—eight; *29. Panzergrenadier-Division*—eleven; *Panzergrenadier-Division "Brandenburg"*—ten.
- Army armored brigades: *Führer-Grenadier-Brigade*—seven.
- SS armored divisions: *5. SS-Panzer-Division "Wiking"*—fifteen; *9. SS-Panzer-Division "Hohenstaufen"*—fifteen; *10. SS-Panzer-Division "Frundsberg"*—five; *12. SS-Panzer-Division "Hitlerjugend"*—four.
- SS mechanized infantry divisions: *11. SS-Freiwilligen-Panzer-Grenadier-Division "Nordland"*—eight.

In addition, the Quartermaster General reported an additional seven *Sd.Kfz. 250/9's* on hand at different locations, but these may have been erroneous entries.

This series of images comes from the lens of Ernst Baumann, who was most likely an *SS* war correspondent. He captured the new-equipment training of the *2./SS-Panzer-Aufklärungs-Abteilung 11 "Nordland"* in Croatia in late 1943. In addition to training on its new vehicles, the scouts of the company were employed on a show-of-force mission in an effort to intimidate any insurgents in the region. The field-grade officer seen in many of the images is *SS-Sturmbannführer* Hack, who was overseeing the training of the tankers from both the *"Wiking"* and *"Nordland"* Divisions. Hack later went on to command the reconnaissance battalion of the *"Wiking"* Division in June and August of 1944.[27]

Hack and the vehicle commander take the factory-new *Sd.Kfz. 250/9*, which has an overall coating of dark yellow (*dunkelgelb*), for a test drive cross-county, leaving tracks in the soft earth. In the third and fourth images, the vehicle starts to test its way across a bit more rugged terrain and up a slight incline. The fifth image demonstrates how quickly a tracked vehicle's suspension becomes saturated with mud, even in relatively favorable terrain. Additional images round out the "test ride" sequence. HEINER DUSKE

The business end of the 2cm main gun and coaxial machine gun can be seen clearly, as the turret has been traversed to the fully rearward position. HEINER DUSKE

In this sequence, Hack has been joined by an unidentified officer, who wears typical *SS* camouflage in the form of a smock and field cap. HEINER DUSKE

Hack has returned to the unit's base, where he addresses one of the noncommissioned officers next to the new vehicles, while other scouts continue to work. HEINER DUSKE

This *Sd.Kfz. 250/9* moves out through the local village. In the second image, the very rare *Panzer II, Ausführung J*, which was developed as a fully tracked scout vehicle, can be seen in the background. HEINER DUSKE

Another set of scouts checks out the weaponry on this *Sd.Kfz. 250/9* while taking another ride. HEINER DUSKE

Armored Car Allocations Starting In June 1944

While the *Sd.Kfz. 234* series of armored cars have long fascinated vehicle enthusiasts, relatively few were produced and ultimately introduced into the fighting in the latter stages of the war. The following table is an effort to identify where and when the majority of those vehicles were assigned, as well as other armored cars that were officially out of production but had been recycled through the system as a result of major overhauls or other reasons.[28]

Formation or Entity / Unit	Notes
Divisions	
1. Panzer-Division / Panzer-Aufklärungs-Abteilung 1	December 1944: One *Sd.Kfz. 234/3*
1. SS-Panzer-Division Leibstandarte SS Adolf Hitler / SS-Panzer-Aufklärungs-Abteilung 1 Leibstandarte SS Adolf Hitler	October 1944: Five *Sd.Kfz. 234/1's* and three *Sd.Kfz. 234/3's*[29]
2. SS-Panzer-Division "Das Reich" / SS-Panzer-Aufklärungs-Abteilung 2 "Das Reich"	August 1944: Four *Sd.Kfz. 234/1's* and three *Sd.Kfz. 234/3's* September 1944: Nine *Sd.Kfz. 234/1's* November 1944: Two *Sd.Kfz. 234/1's*
3. SS-Panzer-Division "Totenkopf" / SS-Panzer-Aufklärungs-Abteilung 3 "Totenkopf"	January 1945: Four *Sd.Kfz. 234/1's*
4. Panzer-Division / Panzer-Aufklärungs-Abteilung 4	January 1945: One *Sd.Kfz. 234/1* and six *Sd.Kfz. 234/4's*
4. SS-Polizei-Panzer-Grenadier-Division / SS-Polizei-Panzer-Aufklärungs-Abteilung 4	December 1944: Three *Sd.Kfz. 234/3's*
5. Panzer-Division / Panzer-Aufklärungs-Abteilung 5	September 1944: Four *Sd.Kfz. 232's*, one *Sd.Kfz. 222*, and two *Sd.Kfz. 223's* December 1944: One *Sd.Kfz. 222* and two *Sd.Kfz. 223's*
6. Panzer-Division / Panzer-Aufklärungs-Abteilung 6	June 1944: Three *Sd.Kfz. 234/3's* August 1944: Three *Sd.Kfz. 234/1's* September 1944: Ten *Sd.Kfz. 234/1's*
7. Panzer-Division / Panzer-Aufklärungs-Abteilung 7	December 1944: Three *Sd.Kfz. 232/2's*
8. Panzer-Division / Panzer-Aufklärungs-Abteilung 8	August 1944: Three *Sd.Kfz. 234/3's* September 1944: Thirteen *Sd.Kfz. 234/1's* March 1945: Four armored cars (possibly four *Sd.Kfz. 234/4's*)
9. Panzer-Division / Panzer-Aufklärungs-Abteilung 9	June 1944: Thirteen *Sd.Kfz. 234/1's* July 1944: Three *Sd.Kfz. 234/3's* November 1944: Two *Sd.Kfz. 234/3's* (minus ten *Sd.Kfz. 234/1's* mistakenly sent to the 9. SS-Panzer-Division "Hohenstaufen"; see below)
9. SS-Panzer-Division "Hohenstaufen" / SS-Panzer-Aufklärungs-Abteilung 9 "Hohenstaufen"	November 1944: Four *Sd.Kfz. 234/1's* and three *Sd.Kfz. 234/3's* (plus ten more *Sd.Kfz. 234/1's* intended for the *9. Panzer-Division*)
10. Panzergrenadier-Division / Panzer-Aufklärungs-Abteilung 110	January 1945: Five *Sd.Kfz. 234/4's*
10. SS-Panzer-Division "Frundsberg" / SS-Panzer-Aufklärungs-Abteilung 10 "Frundsberg"	December 1944: Two *Sd.Kfz. 222's*, three *Sd.Kfz. 234/1's*, and three *Sd.Kfz. 234/3's*
11. Panzer-Division / Panzer-Aufklärungs-Abteilung 11	June 1944: Thirteen *Sd.Kfz. 234/1's* July 1944: Three *Sd.Kfz. 234/3's*
12. Panzer-Division / Panzer-Aufklärungs-Abteilung 11	June 1944: Six *Sd.Kfz. 234/2's*
12. SS-Panzer-Division "Hitlerjugend" / SS-Panzer-Aufklärungs-Abteilung 12 "Hitlerjugend"	October 1944: One *Sd.Kfz. 234/1*, three *Sd.Kfz. 234/3's*, three *Sd.Kfz. 223's*, and six *Sd.Kfz. 222's* November 1944: Three *Sd.Kfz. 234/1's*

Formation or Entity / Unit	Notes
Divisions	
13. Panzer-Division (Panzer-Division "Feldherrnhalle 2") / Panzer-Aufklärungs-Abteilung 13 (Panzer-Aufklärungs-Abteilung "Feldherrnhalle 2")	December 1944: Two Sd.Kfz. 234/3's March 1945: Seven armored cars (possibly four Sd.Kfz. 234/1's and three Sd.Kfz. 234/4's)
14. Panzer-Division / Panzer-Aufklärungs-Abteilung 14	September 1944: One Sd.Kfz. 232 and seven Sd.Kfz. 222's
15. Panzergrenadier-Division / Panzer-Aufklärungs-Abteilung 115	March 1945: Eight Sd.Kfz. 222's and four Sd.Kfz. 223's
17. SS-Panzer-Grenadier-Division "Götz von Berlichingen" / SS-Panzer-Aufklärungs-Abteilung 17 "Götz von Berlichingen"	December 1944: Three Sd.Kfz. 234/3's
20. Panzer-Division / Panzer-Aufklärungs-Abteilung 20	September 1944: Three Sd.Kfz. 234/3's[30]
20. Panzergrenadier-Division / Panzer-Aufklärungs-Abteilung 120	October 1944: Four Sd.Kfz. 234/1's, two Sd.Kfz. 234/3's, one Sd.Kfz. 223, and two Sd.Kfz. 222's
21. Panzer-Division / Panzer-Aufklärungs-Abteilung 21	November 1944: One Sd.Kfz. 232 December 1944: One Sd.Kfz. 232 and six Sd.Kfz. 233's
23. Panzer-Division / Panzer-Aufklärungs-Abteilung 23	December 1944: One Sd.Kfz. 234/3
24. Panzer-Division / Panzer-Aufklärungs-Abteilung 24	December 1944: Three Sd.Kfz. 234/3's January 1945: Eight Sd.Kfz. 234/1's and seven Sd.Kfz. 234/3's
25. Panzer-Division / Panzer-Aufklärungs-Abteilung 25	March 1945: Four Sd.Kfz. 234/1's and three Sd.Kfz. 234/4's
25. Panzergrenadier-Division / Panzer-Aufklärungs-Abteilung 125	November 1944: One Sd.Kfz. 223 and two Sd.Kfz. 222's February 1945: Two Sd.Kfz. 234/1's and one Sd.Kfz. 234/3 April 1945: Six armored cars (possibly two heavy and four light)
90. Panzergrenadier-Division / Panzer-Aufklärungs-Abteilung 190	October 1944: Six Sd.Kfz. 222's
116. Panzer-Division / Panzer-Aufklärungs-Abteilung 116	June 1944: Thirteen Sd.Kfz. 234/1's and three Sd.Kfz. 234/3's November 1944: Four Sd.Kfz. 234/1's and one Sd.Kfz. 234/3 April 1945: Six Sd.Kfz. 234/4's (possibly ending up with Panzer-Aufklärungs-Abteilung Döring)
Panzer-Lehr-Division / Panzer-Aufklärungs-Lehr-Abteilung	October 1944: Eight Sd.Kfz. 234/1's[31] November 1944: Two Sd.Kfz. 234/1's
Panzergrenadier-Division "Brandenburg" / Panzer-Aufklärungs-Abteilung "Brandenburg"	October 1944: Three Sd.Kfz. 234/3's December 1944: Four Sd.Kfz. 234/3's January 1945: Two Sd.Kfz. 234/2's and seven Sd.Kfz. 234/4's
Panzer-Division "Feldherrnhalle" (Panzer-Division "Feldherrnhalle 1") / Panzer-Aufklärungs-Abteilung "Feldherrnhalle"	December 1944: One Sd.Kfz. 234/3 January 1945: Two Sd.Kfz. 234/3's March 1945: Five heavy armored cars (possibly three Sd.Kfz. 234/1's and two Sd.Kfz. 234/4's)
Panzergrenadier-Division "Großdeutschland" / Panzer-Aufklärungs-Abteilung "Großdeutschland"	December 1944: Four Sd.Kfz. 232's and two Sd.Kfz. 233's
Panzer-Division "Jüterbog" / Panzer-Aufklärungs-Kompanie "Jüterbog"	February 1945: Three Sd.Kfz. 234/4's
Panzer-Division "Kurmark" / Panzer-Aufklärungs-Abteilung 151	February 1945: Five Sd.Kfz. 234/2's and three Sd.Kfz. 234/4's
Panzer-Division "Müncheberg" / Panzer-Späh-Kompanie "Müncheberg"	March 1945: Four Sd.Kfz. 234/1's and four Sd.Kfz. 234/4's
Panzer-Division "Schlesien" / Panzer-Aufklärungs-Kompanie "Schlesien"	February 1945: Three Sd.Kfz. 234/4's
Führer-Begleit-Division / Panzer-Späh-Kompanie 102	February 1945: Four Sd.Kfz. 234/1's and six Sd.Kfz. 234/4's

Formation or Entity / Unit	Notes
Brigades	
Panzer-Brigade 103 / Panzer-Aufklärungs-Abteilung "Hirschberg" (ex 1./Panzer-Aufklärungs-Abteilung 190)	December 1944: Eight *Sd.Kfz. 234/1*'s and one *Sd.Kfz. 234/3* January 1945: One *Sd.Kfz. 234/1* and two *Sd.Kfz. 234/3*'s
Panzer-Jagd-Brigade 104 / Panzer-Aufklärungs-Abteilung München	January 1945: Two *Sd.Kfz. 234/1*'s, one *Sd.Kfz. 234/3*, and five *Sd.Kfz. 222*'s
Panzer-Brigade 150	November 1944: Three *Sd.Kfz. 234/2*'s and three *Sd.Kfz. 234/3*'s
Führer-Grenadier-Brigade / Panzer-Späh-Kompanie 101	September 1944: Six *Sd.Kfz. 234/1*'s
Luftwaffe	
Fallschirm-Panzergrenadier-Division "Hermann Göring 2" / Fallschirm-Panzer-Aufklärungs-Abteilung "Hermann Göring 2"	October 1944: One *Sd.Kfz. 232*, thirteen *Sd.Kfz. 234/1*'s, and three *Sd.Kfz. 234/3*'s
Fallschirm-Panzer-Division "Hermann Göring 1" / Fallschirm-Panzer-Aufklärungs-Abteilung "Hermann Göring 1"	February 1945: Three *Sd.Kfz. 234/4*'s March 1945: Three armored cars (possibly three *Sd.Kfz. 234/4*'s) April 1945: Three armored cars (possibly all heavy)
Miscellaneous	
Replacement Army / *Feld-Unteroffiziersschule*	October 1944: One *Sd.Kfz. 233*
Replacement Army / Unspecified	June 1944: One *Sd.Kfz. 234/2*[32] October 1944: Five *Sd.Kfz. 232*'s, two *Sd.Kfz. 234/2*'s, three *Sd.Kfz. 234/3*'s, and six *Sd.Kfz. 223*'s December 1944: One *Sd.Kfz. 232*, two *Sd.Kfz. 234/3*'s, and three *Sd.Kfz. 223*'s January 1945: One *Sd.Kfz. 232*, six *Sd.Kfz. 234/1*'s, one *Sd.Kfz. 233*, and one *Sd.Kfz. 234/2*
Commander in Chief, *Heeresgruppe B*	December 1944: One *Sd.Kfz. 223*
Panzer-Korps "Feldherrnhalle"	March 1945: Five heavy armored cars (possibly three *Sd.Kfz. 234/1*'s and two *Sd.Kfz. 234/4*'s)
Kampfgruppe Kluge	February 1945: One *Sd.Kfz. 222*
Begleitkompanie z.b.V. (Begleitkompanie I, Kampfgruppe Moews)	March 1945: Three *Sd.Kfz. 234/1*'s and three *Sd.Kfz. 234/4*'s
Aufklärungs-Lehr-Abteilung / Panzer-Aufklärungs-Abteilung-Lehr-Kompanie (not part of *Panzer-Aufklärungs-Lehr-Abteilung* of the *Panzer-Lehr-Division*)	December 1944: Three *Sd.Kfz. 234/3*'s January 1945: Three *Sd.Kfz. 234/1*'s
Armored Reconnaissance Schoolhouse: 5./Panzer-Aufklärungs-Lehr-Abteilung Krampnitz	June 1944: One *Sd.Kfz. 233*
Polizei-Schule Wien[33]	January 1945: Five *Sd.Kfz. 234/1*'s, four *Sd.Kfz. 223*'s or *221*'s, and one *Sd.Kfz. 222*

Death notices for young enlisted scouts, all between the ages of eighteen and twenty, who were assigned to armored reconnaissance battalions and fell in the final twelve months of the war. *Gefreiter* Hans Steinberger, eighteen, died of wounds suffered in combat on 11 May 1944. Ottmar Pösterl, twenty, was killed in action on 19 May 1944. *Gefreiter* Franz Barhammer, nineteen, was killed in action later that year on 22 August 1944, in the vicinity of Sandomierz.

482 TIP OF THE SPEAR

This sequence of images, dated January 1944, shows an unidentified *SS* reconnaissance unit taking fire, apparently from some distance, and responding to it. While the soldiers take cover in a roadside ditch, an *Sd.Kfz. 222* opens up and a 5cm antitank gun takes up position. NATIONAL ARCHIVES.

Images of the *Sd.Kfz. 141* in the field are virtually nonexistent. They were only issued to two reconnaissance battalions: *Panzer-Aufklärungs-Abteilung 3* and *Panzer-Aufklärungs-Abteilung "Großdeutschland."* The first image has been widely circulated on the Internet and purports to be from the latter battalion. The remaining images are taken from one of the last weekly newsreels released—10 February 1945—and show a counterattack in East Prussia in early 1945. These images are also likely from *Panzer-Aufklärungs-Abteilung "Großdeutschland."*

Another vehicle rarely seen, a later version of the *Sd.Kfz. 250/8*, on a railhead at an undisclosed location in 1944. These vehicles are assigned to *Panzer-Aufklärungs-Abteilung "Großdeutschland,"* and the image came from the estate of the late Helmuth Spaeter, a Knight's Cross recipient of the battalion. The heavy cannon platoon was found in an armored heavy company organized as a Model 44 unit. SCOTT PRITCHETT

Scouts assigned to *Panzer-Aufklärungs-Abteilung "Großdeutschland."* The noncommissioned officer in the first image wears the field-gray version of the special-purpose uniform for armored vehicle crewmen. Based on the wear of the *M43* billed field cap, the studio portrait had to be taken sometime in early 1943 or later. The second image shows two other scouts from *Panzer-Aufklärungs-Abteilung "Großdeutschland."* One wears an early first-pattern *Panzer* tunic, a style that was only manufactured through 1936. The other scout wears a modified four-pocket tunic to which *Panzer*-style collar tabs have been attached, a highly unusual modification. SCOTT PRITCHETT

This press-release image, dated 31 May 1944, shows an *Sd.Kfz. 251/3* of a reconnaissance element returning to its unit after being repaired in a maintenance facility. TODD GYLSEN

This press-release image, dated 7 February 1944 and probably taken in Italy, shows an Italian armored car pressed into German service advancing down the road, followed by some grenadiers. TODD GYLSEN

An unidentified armored reconnaissance unit in Transylvania prepares to conduct operations in this 24 October 1944 press-release image. TODD GYLSEN

The crew of either an *Sd.Kfz. 222* or an *Sd.Kfz. 250/9* trains its weapons skyward in this 1944 press-release photograph. TODD GYLSEN

These screen captures of video widely distributed on the Internet show vehicles of the headquarters company of *Panzer-Aufklärungs-Abteilung 20* surrendering to U.S. forces in the Pilsen area of the current Czech Republic in May 1945. The battalion was commanded by *Hauptmann* Petersmann at the time and equipped with a variety of *Sd.Kfz. 234* series armored cars, including the *Sd.Kfz. 234/2 Puma* and the *Sd.Kfz. 234/3*. In one of the images, an *Sd.Kfz. 234/3* has been modified by the removal of its main gun, which was replaced by a 2cm main gun in a hanging mount (*Schwebelafette*), most likely removed from an *Sd.Kfz. 251/17*. This was apparently a "one-off" unit modification.

Appendix 1

School Exercises for Combat Training in Reconnaissance (1939)

SAMPLE EXERCISE

B. THE MISSIONS
(The sketch maps are not drawn to scale and must be considered illustrative only.)

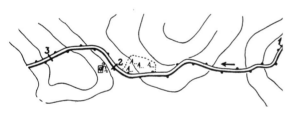

1 = Beginn der Aufgabe.
2 = Ort des Zusammenstoßes mit dem 1. fdl. l.Pz.Sp.Wg.
3 = Ende der Aufgabe. Von hier aus muß im weiteren Straßenverl. der 2. fdl. l.Pz.Sp.Wg. zu sehen sein.
▢ = Platz der Zuschauer.
← = Eigene Vormarschrichtung.

Exercise 3. Legend: 1 = Start of the mission. 2 = Location of the encounter with the first light enemy armored car. 3 = End of the mission. From there, the second enemy light armored car must be able to be seen along the road. 4 = Area for observers. Left arrow = Friendly direction of movement.

3. MEETING ENGAGEMENT WITH LIGHT ENEMY ARMORED CAR (EXERCISE PURPOSE: ATTACK ON THE ENEMY VEHICLE)
3. Meeting engagement with light enemy armored car
   a) **Exercise Purpose:** Attack on the enemy vehicle.
   b) **Type of Vehicle:** One light armored car with armor-defeating weapon.
   c) **Employment of the vehicle as:** Lead vehicle of the light armored car section
   d) **Terrain:** Winding road with limited visibility in hilly terrain
   e) **Opposing force:** 2 light armored cars

   f) **Scenario:** The reconnaissance patrol is moving on the road in enemy territory in an area that is threatened by the enemy. Up to this point, there have been no encounters with the enemy. Enemy contact (reconnaissance patrols) is possible at any time, however. The bound of the reconnaissance patrol goes to the next observation point. (If possible, show in the terrain.) Speed is of the essence.
   g) **Mission:** The light armored car is to move to the designated observation point as the lead vehicle and wait there for the rest of the patrol to close up.
   h) **Start of the Mission:** Displaced as far as possible from the site of the contact so that the vehicle has to pass several curves and blind spots in the road before it encounters the enemy.
   i) **Sequence of Events:** While moving, the advancing vehicle unexpectedly encounters a light enemy armored car approaching it from about 100 meters away. The vehicle attacks the enemy armored car without hesitation, approaches the enemy with increased speed and covers the enemy with fire. The enemy vehicle that has been eliminated is passed, and the vehicle stops at the next good observation point and screens.
   j) **Actions of the Scout:**
   1. After the mission is received, command to the driver: "Prepare for combat." The order is executed.
   2. Orders to the driver as to how he should advance.
   3. Start up the engine upon the command: "*Marsch!*"
   4. When the enemy armored car is identified, orders and call to the driver: "Full speed!"—"Past the enemy!"—"I'm engaging!"
   5. Immediate opening of fire on the enemy armored car. Take up a correct sight picture. Select the proper sight.
   6. When even with the knocked-out enemy armored car, order or command to the driver to move past immediately.
   7. Quick look at the enemy vehicle to determine whether the crew has been put out of action.
   8. Immediate command to the driver where he should move.
   9. Command: "*Marsch!*"

10. Have the vehicle stop at the designated point.
11. Give hand-and-arm signal to the reconnaissance-patrol leader that another enemy armored vehicle has been sighted.

k) **Actions of the Driver:**
1. Execution of all of the commands and orders of the vehicle commander.
2. In case the scout has not seen the approaching vehicle, alert to the vehicle commander.
3. Move tactically properly the entire route. Select the side of the road with the best cover. Move though curves and bends in the road tactically. Maintain a proper speed.

l) **Observe the following during the drill:** The position of the encounter should be selected in such a manner that it is located in a depression that requires the friendly vehicle to continue moving along the road another 100–200 meters after the engagement in order to be able to observe the further course of the road and screen as long as it takes for the remainder of the reconnaissance patrol, which has arrived in the meantime, to search the knocked-out enemy armored vehicle. The second enemy light armored car must be able to be observed at some distance from the bound to the screening position. The second vehicle of the enemy reconnaissance patrol has to halt at the designated point during the mission in such a manner that it cannot intervene in the engagement. The observation and screening halt cannot be allowed to be mistaken for the observation point located much further away (as mentioned under f). Visual contact between the exercise controller and the enemy must be viable so that it can be ensured that the two vehicles do, in fact, encounter one another. To that end, the enemy armored vehicle has to wait with a running engine so as to be able to approach quickly and in a timely manner. Each participant is to be asked at the conclusion of the mission what his estimate of the situation is and what his decision is.

m) **Special Notes for the Enemy:** Do not open fire until the lead vehicle has opened fire. The enemy is supposed to indicate by his actions that he has been surprised. Before the armored car that is undergoing the exercise has reached the area of the enemy vehicle, the enemy vehicle is to halt on the edge of the road (tree or ditch). When the reconnaissance patrol vehicle arrives, the enemy crew is to pretend to be combat ineffective or dead so that the lead vehicle can immediately continue to move on.

n) **Location of the Viewers:** Locate in such a manner that they can observe the encounter without alerting the crew of the approaching lead vehicle.

o) **Special Notes for the Viewers:** Alert the viewers at the start of the commencement of fires and the assumption of a higher rate of speed. Compare this among the individual soldiers. Point out the efforts of the enemy to avoid observation.

p) **Special Points for the After-Action Review:** Emphasize the necessity of still moving **rapidly** even in areas threatened by the enemy, since the average speed sinks considerably as a result of the halting at the individual observation points. Point out that in the case of a meeting engagement, the bolder and more audacious soldier will usually be the victor. Discuss the advantages of a hard-pressed attack even in the case of friendly inferiority in weaponry. Clarify the question of the aiming point when firing. It is preferable to fire short than over. Question the soldiers on their assessment of the situation, especially concerning the time directly following the encounter. Describe the danger of the appearance of additional enemy armored vehicles and the conclusions that are to be drawn as a result. It must be mentioned that the crew of a **reporting** vehicle has to search the knocked-out vehicle and the dead crew for papers, etc. after an encounter with an enemy armored car, inasmuch as this can occur without endangering the friendly vehicle as the result of newly arriving enemy. In the mission illustrated above, however, that is the responsibility of the reconnaissance patrol leader.

q) **Appropriate Paragraphs from Manuals:**
Heeresdienstvorschrift 470/3a = 39, 42, 43, 62, 73, 77, 103 (1st and 2nd sentences), 104, Annexes 1 and 2
Heeresdienstvorschrift 299/5b = 13, 27, 29
Heeresdienstvorschrift 299/5c = 12, 25, 26
Heeresdienstvorschrift 299/5d = 12, 25, 26
Heeresdienstvorschrift 299/5e = 12, 25, 27
Heeresdienstvorschrift 299/5f = 13, 28, 30
Heeresdienstvorschrift 299/8c = 20, 23, 24, 51, 53, 68, 69, Annexes 2 and 3

r) **Modification Options for the Mission:** Numerous modifications are possible by selecting a different type of vehicle, by organizing the reconnaissance patrol differently, by seeking out different types of terrain or just different places in the road and by differing actions on the part of the enemy, e.g., the second enemy armored vehicles follows more closely. For example, the enemy can also move out in the direction of the lead vehicle while firing. He can attempt to escape by setting off a smoke grenade and turning around. Furthermore, he can halt first and then fire. After the enemy stops at the side of the road, the enemy crew also does not have to be combat ineffective. It can continue to fire or it can attempt to flee from its disabled vehicle.

It is recommended that especially instructive modifications be conducted numerous times, even if it has to be done at the same place due to a lack of time and solely as a demonstration for viewers. The basic mission is also to be performed once **at night**. To that end, observe *Heeresdienstvorschrift 470/3a*, paragraphs 81 and 104 (last portion), as well as *Heeresdienstvorschrift 299/8c*, paragraph 56.

An important modification consists of selecting a heavy armored car for the enemy instead of a light armored car. In that case, it must be ensured that the encounter takes place at very close range. The importance of a rapid movement and heavy fire must be emphasized. In that situation, the vehicle needs to turn off the road as soon as possible when it gets past the superior enemy armored vehicle and has broken through. The vehicle may not stop next to the enemy vehicle, because it must be assumed that additional superior enemy armored vehicles will arrive immediately. Whether the enemy heavy armored car will be declared out of action by the light armored vehicle in this modified situation depends on the weaponry on the light armored car and the actions of its crew. The location for this example is to be selected in such a manner that a covered side path leads off from the site of the encounter into which the light armored car can turn. After the vehicle has turned off, the scout must attempt to warn the reconnaissance patrol leader, who was following along the main road, by means of signals or through firing. In most cases, it will be too late to do that or impossible because of the terrain. That point must become a part of the review.

For the enemy, it is imperative to allow the aggressively attacking lead vehicle to pass (purpose of the exercise), even though it is the stronger vehicle. Only in the case of hesitant actions on the part of the light armored car is the enemy allowed to book a partial success (taking the exercise purpose into consideration), which has the scout in the light armored car suffer a grazing wound to the head. In this exercise, the second enemy heavy armored car must be able to be identified at some distance on the main road at the moment that the exercise lead vehicle has moved near the side path.

[Additional sample exercises can be found on the author's website, www.battlebornbooks.com.]

Appendix 2

Reconnaissance Formation Cross-Reference Guide

This listing allows researchers to quickly reference the major command to which division-level reconnaissance assets were assigned. Battalions only in existence before the start of the war are not listed.

Prewar motorized reconnaissance and armored reconnaissance battalions assigned to armored and motorized infantry divisions did not necessarily have the same numerical designator as the division, although most prewar motorcycle infantry battalions assigned to armored divisions had the same numerical designator as the division of assignment. This was also true for some but not all motorcycle infantry battalions assigned to motorized infantry divisions.

In March 1943 motorcycle infantry battalions were officially eliminated from the orders of battle for armored and mechanized infantry divisions and redesignated as armored reconnaissance battalions. In some cases, these changes did not take effect until April or even later. In most cases, the armored reconnaissance battalion bore the numerical designator of the armored division to which it was assigned. In the case of mechanized infantry divisions, the reconnaissance battalions generally had a "1" in front of the numerical designator of the division.

Named formations activated at the end of the war, whose reconnaissance assets bore the same honorific as the division, are not listed, since it is obvious from their designations where they were assigned. (Moreover, they were usually a battalion in name only.) These include: *Panzer-Division Bergen*, *Panzer-Division Clausewitz*, *Panzer-Division Döberitz* (*Holstein / Schlesien*), *Panzer-Division Jüterbog*, *Panzer-Division Kurmark*, *Panzer-Division Müncheberg*, *Panzer-Division Tatra (232. Panzer-Division)*, and the *233. Panzer-Division*. These formations all had nominal *Panzer-Aufklärungs-Abteilungen*.

Reconnaissance assets of the *SS* are not listed, since they generally bore the same honorific as the division under which they served. The same is true for the "*Hermann Göring*" formations of the *Luftwaffe*.

RECONNAISSANCE BATTALIONS

Unit Designation	Major Command	Time Frame
Named		
Panzer-Aufklärungs-Abteilung "Großdeutschland"	Infanterie-Division "Großdeutschland" (mot) / Panzergrenadier-Division "Großdeutschland"	Formed in January 1943 from Kradschützen-Bataillon "Großdeutschland," it served with the division until the end of the war.
Panzer-Aufklärungs-Abteilung "Brandenburg"	Panzergrenadier-Division "Brandenburg"	Formed from other "Brandenburg" elements in September 1944, it served with the division until the end of the war.
Führer-Panzer-Späh-Kompanie	Führer-Begleit-Division	Formed through the redesignation of Panzer-Späh-Kompanie 101, it served with the division until the end of the war.
Panzer-Aufklärungs-Abteilung "Feldherrnhalle" (1st iteration)	Panzergrenadier-Division "Feldherrnhalle"	Formed in June 1943 from remnants of Kradschützen-Bataillon 160 and other elements, it was effectively destroyed in the summer of 1944 during the Soviet Operation Bagration.
Panzer-Aufklärungs-Abteilung "Feldherrnhalle" (2nd iteration)	Panzer-Division "Feldherrnhalle" / Panzer-Division "Feldherrnhalle 1"	Formed in November 1944 from surviving elements of Panzer-Aufklärungs-Abteilung "Feldherrnhalle" of Panzergrenadier-Division "Feldherrnhalle," it became part of the reconstituted and redesignated Panzer-Division "Feldherrnhalle" and, in March 1945, the redesignated Panzer-Division "Feldherrnhalle 1," where it was officially redesignated as Panzer-Aufklärungs-Abteilung "Feldherrnhalle 1."
Panzer-Aufklärungs-Abteilung "Feldherrnhalle 2"	Panzer-Division "Feldherrnhalle 2"	Formed from the redesignation of Panzer-Aufklärungs-Abteilung 13, then the 13. Panzer-Division. The battalion continued to refer to itself as Panzer-Aufklärungs-Abteilung 13, however.
1–5		
Aufklärungs-Abteilung 1 (mot)	(3. Panzer-Division)	A separate reconnaissance battalion at the start of the war, the formation was transferred to the 3. Panzer-Division in early 1941, where it was redesignated as Panzer-Aufklärungs-Abteilung 1.
Panzer-Aufklärungs-Abteilung 1	3. Panzer-Division	Formed from the redesignated Aufklärungs-Abteilung 1 (mot) in early 1941, it consolidated with Kradschützen-Bataillon 3 in April 1942.
Panzer-Aufklärungs-Abteilung 1	1. Panzer-Division	Formed in April 1943 from the redesignated and reorganized Kradschützen-Bataillon 1, it served until the end of the war.
Aufklärungs-Abteilung 2 (mot)	2. Infanterie-Division (mot) / 12. Panzer-Division	Formed prior to the start of the war, the battalion remained with the division when it transitioned into the 12. Panzer-Division in January 1941, where it retained its designation. It was redesignated as Panzer-Aufklärungs- und Voraus-Abteilung 2 in August–November 1941.
Panzer-Aufklärungs-und Voraus-Abteilung 2	12. Panzer-Division	Formed from the consolidation of Aufklärungs-Abteilung 2 (mot) and Kradschützen-Bataillon 22 in August 1941, it was reorganized and redesignated as Kradschützen-Bataillon 22 in November 1941.
Panzer-Aufklärungs-Abteilung 2	2. Panzer-Division	Formed in March 1943 from the redesignated and reorganized Kradschützen-Bataillon 2, it served until the end of the war.
Aufklärungs-Abteilung 3 (mot)	3. Panzer-Division	Activated prior to the war, the battalion was transferred to the 5. leichte Division in January 1941 and assigned to it.
Aufklärungs-Abteilung 3 (mot)	5. leichte Division / 21. Panzer-Division (Afrika)	Previously assigned to the 3. Panzer-Division. Reassigned to the 21. Panzer-Division in August 1941. In February 1943 the battalion was redesignated as Panzer-Aufklärungs-Abteilung 90 and reassigned to the 90. leichte Division.
Panzer-Aufklärungs-Abteilung 3	90. leichte Afrika-Division	Reassigned from the 21. Panzer-Division in February 1943, it was redesignated as Panzer-Aufklärungs-Abteilung 90 and served with the division until the capitulation in May 1943.
Panzer-Aufklärungs-Abteilung 3	3. Panzer-Division	Formed from the redesignation and reorganization of Kradschützen-Bataillon 3 in April 1943, it served with the division until the end of the war.
Aufklärungs-Abteilung 4 (mot)	1. Panzer-Division	Formed prior to the start of the war, it was redesignated as Panzer-Aufklärungs-Abteilung 4 in April 1940
Panzer-Aufklärungs-Abteilung 4	1. Panzer-Division	Formed from April 1940 until June 1942, when it was consolidated with Kradschützen-Bataillon 1.

APPENDIX 2: RECONNAISSANCE FORMATION CROSS-REFERENCE GUIDE

Unit Designation	Major Command	Time Frame
1–5 *continued*		
Panzer-Aufklärungs-Abteilung 4	24. Panzer-Division	Activated in March 1943 when the division was reconstituted, it received a number of personnel from *Kradschützen-Bataillon 4*. It was redesignated as *Panzer-Aufklärungs-Abteilung 24* in April 1943.
Panzer-Aufklärungs-Abteilung 4	4. Panzer-Division	Formed from the redesignation and reorganization of *Kradschützen-Bataillon 34* in April 1943, it served with the division until the end of the war.
Aufklärungs-Abteilung 5 (mot)	2. Panzer-Division	Formed prior to the start of the war, it was redesignated as *Panzer-Aufklärungs-Abteilung 5* in March 1940.
Panzer-Aufklärungs-Abteilung 5	2. Panzer-Division	Deactivated in August 1941 and personnel used to form *Kradschützen-Bataillon 24* of the 22. Panzer-Division.
Panzer-Aufklärungs-Abteilung 5	5. Panzer-Division	Formed from the reorganized and redesignated *Kradschützen-Bataillon 55* in March 1943 and served with the division until the end of the war.
6–10		
Aufklärungs-Abteilung 6 (mot)	1. leichte Division / 6. Panzer-Division	Formed prior to the start of the war, it was reassigned to the 6. Panzer-Division in April 1940, where it was redesignated as *Panzer-Aufklärungs-Abteilung 57*.
Panzer-Aufklärungs-Abteilung 6	6. Panzer-Division	Formed through the redesignation and reorganization of *Kradschützen-Bataillon 6* in April 1943, serving with the division until the end of the war.
Aufklärungs-Regiment 7	2. leichte Division	Deactivated in November 1939.
I./Aufklärungs-Regiment 7		This was the motorcycle infantry battalion. It was transferred to the 7. Panzer-Division and redesignated as *Aufklärungs-Abteilung 37 (mot)*.
II./Aufklärungs-Regiment 7		This was originally the armored scout battalion of the regiment, but when it was transferred to the 7. Panzer-Division and reorganized and redesignated, it became *Kradschützen-Bataillon 7*.
Aufklärungs-Abteilung 7 (mot)	4. Panzer-Division	Formed prior to the start of the war, it was redesignated as *Panzer-Aufklärungs-Abteilung 7* in February 1940.
Panzer-Aufklärungs-Abteilung 7	4. Panzer-Division	Formed from *Aufklärungs-Abteilung 7 (mot)* in February 1940, it was consolidated with *Kradschützen-Bataillon 34* in October 1941 and officially deactivated in December 1941.
Panzer-Aufklärungs-Abteilung 7	7. Panzer-Division	Formed from the reorganization and redesignation of *Kradschützen-Bataillon 7* in April 1943, it served with the division until the end of the war.
Aufklärungs-Regiment 8	3. leichte Division / 8. Panzer-Division	Formed prior to the war and serving initially with the 3. Leichte Division, it was reassigned to the 8. Panzer-Division in November 1939, minus its 1st Battalion (which had been reassigned to the 10. Panzer-Division).
I./Aufklärungs-Regiment 8	(10. Panzer-Division)	This battalion never served with its parent division in combat. It was attached to the 10. Panzer-Division for the campaign in Poland, and assigned to that division after the fighting after being reorganized and redesignated as *Panzer-Aufklärungs-Abteilung 90*.
II./Aufklärungs-Regiment 8		When reassigned to the 8. Panzer-Division, the battalion was reorganized and redesignated as *Aufklärungs-Abteilung 59 (mot)*.
Aufklärungs-Abteilung 8 (mot)	5. Panzer-Division	Formed prior to the start of the war, it was redesignated as *Panzer-Aufklärungs-Abteilung 8* in April 1940.
Panzer-Aufklärungs-Abteilung 8	5. Panzer-Division	Formed in April 1940, it was reorganized, redesignated, and reassigned to the 23. Panzer-Division as *Kradschützen-Bataillon 23* in September 1941.
Panzer-Aufklärungs-Abteilung 8	8. Panzer-Division	Formed from the reorganization and redesignation of *Kradschützen-Bataillon 8* in April 1943, it served with the division until the end of the war.
Aufklärungs-Regiment 9	4. leichte Division / 9. Panzer-Division	After the campaign in Poland, the regiment was reassigned to the 9. Panzer-Division in January 1940, where it participated in the campaign in the West. Its two subordinate battalions formed the division reconnaissance and motorcycle infantry battalions later on.
I./Aufklärungs-Regiment 9	4. leichte Division / 9. Panzer-Division	This was the motorcycle infantry battalion. It was redesignated as *Kradschützen-Bataillon 59* in August 1940 as part of the 9. Panzer-Division.
II./Aufklärungs-Regiment 9	4. leichte Division / 9. Panzer-Division	This was the armored scout battalion of the regiment. It was redesignated as *Aufklärungs-Abteilung 9 (mot)* in August 1940 as part of the 9. Panzer-Division.
Aufklärungs-Abteilung 9 (mot)	9. Panzer-Division	Formed from the reorganized and redesignated *II./Aufklärungs-Regiment 9* in August 1940, it was consolidated with *Kradschützen-Bataillon 59* in March 1942.

Unit Designation	Major Command	Time Frame
6–10 *continued*		
Panzer-Aufklärungs-Abteilung 9	9. Panzer-Division	Formed from the reorganized and redesignated *Kradschützen-Bataillon 59* in April 1943, it served with the division until the end of the war.
Aufklärungs-Abteilung 10 (mot)	10. Infanterie-Division (mot)	Formed from the reorganized and redesignated *Aufklärungs-Abteilung 10* of the *10. Infanterie-Division* in November 1940, it was consolidated with *Kradschützen-Bataillon 40* in July 1940.
Panzer-Aufklärungs-Abteilung 10	10. Panzer-Division	Formed from the reorganized and redesignated *Kradschützen-Bataillon 10* in March 1943, it served with the division until its surrender in Tunisia in May 1943. It was never reactivated.
11–20		
Panzer-Aufklärungs-Abteilung 11	11. Panzer-Division	Formed from the reorganized and redesignated *Kradschützen-Bataillon 61* in April 1943, it served with the division until the end of the war.
Panzer-Aufklärungs-Abteilung 12	12. Panzer-Division	Formed from the reorganized and redesignated *Kradschützen-Bataillon 22* in April 1943, it served with the division until the end of the war.
Aufklärungs-Abteilung 13 (mot)	13. Infanterie-Division (mot)	Formed prior to the start of the war, the battalion moved with its parent division in November 1940 to serve as instructional forces in Romania, where it was referred to as *Lehr-Aufklärungs-Abteilung "R"*. It returned to Germany in May 1941, where it was reorganized and redesignated as *Panzer-Aufklärungs-Abteilung 13*.
Panzer-Aufklärungs-Abteilung 13 (1st iteration)	13. Panzer-Division	Formed from *Aufklärungs-Abteilung 13 (mot)* in May 1941 and consolidated with *Kradschützen-Bataillon 43* in April 1942.
Panzer-Aufklärungs-Abteilung 13 (2nd iteration)	13. Panzer-Division	Formed from the reorganized and redesignated *Kradschützen-Bataillon 43* in April 1943, it served with the division until the end of the war (although officially redesignated *Panzer-Aufklärungs-Abteilung 2 "Feldherrnhalle"* in April 1945, when the division was similarly redesignated).
Aufklärungs-Abteilung 14 (mot)	14. Infanterie-Division (mot)	Formed from personnel levies against a variety of elements in October 1940, it was eventually consolidated with *Kradschützen-Bataillon 54* before the division was demotorized in March 1943.
Panzer-Aufklärungs-Abteilung 14	14. Panzer-Division	Formed from the reorganization and redesignation of *Kradschützen-Bataillon 64* (also short-lived as *Panzer-Aufklärungs-Abteilung 64*) in May 1943.
Panzer-Aufklärungs-Abteilung 16 (1st iteration)	16. Panzer-Division	Formed in August 1940 from various motorized and non-motorized assets, it was consolidated with *Kradschützen-Bataillon 16* in May 1942.
Panzer-Aufklärungs-Abteilung 16 (2nd iteration)	16. Panzer-Division	Formed from the redesignated and reorganized *Kradschützen-Bataillon 16* in April 1943, it served with the division until the end of the war.
Panzer-Aufklärungs-Abteilung 17	17. Panzer-Division	Formed by the redesignation and reorganization of *Kradschützen-Bataillon 17* in May 1943, it served with the division until the end of the war.
Aufklärungs-Abteilung 18 (mot)	18. Infanterie-Division (mot)	Formed from the reconnaissance battalion of the *18. Infanterie-Division* and the *2./Panzer-Aufklärungs-Abteilung 1*, the battalion was consolidated with *Kradschützen-Bataillon 38* in November 1942.
Panzer-Aufklärungs-Abteilung 18	18. Panzer-Division	Formed from *Kradschützen-Bataillon 18* in March 1943, it was reorganized and redesignated as *Schützen-Bataillon 88* of the *18. Artillerie-Division* in October 1943.
Panzer-Aufklärungs-Abteilung 18	18. Panzergrenadier-Division	Formed at the end of March 1945 from the disbanded *Panzer-Aufklärungs-Abteilung 44* of *Panzer-Division Holstein*. This element probably only had a company's worth of assets.
Panzer-Aufklärungs-Abteilung 19 (1st iteration)	19. Panzer-Division	Formed from the reconnaissance elements of the *19. Infanterie-Division* and augmented by the *2./Panzer-Aufklärungs-Abteilung 4*, it was consolidated with *Kradschützen-Bataillon 19* in April 1942.
Panzer-Aufklärungs-Abteilung 19 in (2nd iteration)	19. Panzer-Division	Formed through the reorganization and redesignation of *Kradschützen-Bataillon 19* March 1943, it served with the division until the end of the war.
Aufklärungs-Abteilung 20 (mot)	20. Infanterie-Division (mot)	Activated prior to the start of the war, it was consolidated with *Kradschützen-Bataillon 30* in April 1942
Panzer-Aufklärungs-Abteilung 20	20. Panzer-Division	Formed from the reorganization and redesignation of *Kradschützen-Bataillon 20* in April 1943, it served with the division until the end of the war.
21–30		
Panzer-Aufklärungs-Abteilung 21	21. Panzer-Division (Afrika)	Formed by the redesignation of *Aufklärungs-Abteilung 580 (mot)* in late April 1943, it surrendered with the remaining Axis forces in North Africa on 12 May 1943.

APPENDIX 2: RECONNAISSANCE FORMATION CROSS-REFERENCE GUIDE

Unit Designation	Major Command	Time Frame
21–30 *continued*		
Panzer-Aufklärungs-Abteilung 21	21. Panzer-Division (New)	Formed in July 1943 from personnel levies from *Panzer-Aufklärungs-Kompanie 931* and the *Panzer-Aufklärungs-Lehr-Abteilung*, it served with the division until the end of the war.
Panzer-Aufklärungs-Abteilung 23	23. Panzer-Division	Formed through the redesignation and reorganization of *Kradschützen-Bataillon 23* in April 1943, it served with the division until the end of the war.
Panzer-Aufklärungs-Abteilung 24	24. Panzer-Division	Formed from the redesignated *Panzer-Aufklärungs-Abteilung 4* in April 1943, it served with the division until the end of the war.
Aufklärungs-Abteilung 25 (mot)	25. Infanterie-Division (mot)	Formed in November 1940 primarily from *Aufklärungs-Abteilung 25* of the 25. *Infanterie-Division*, it was consolidated with *Kradschützen-Bataillon 25* in May 1942.
Panzer-Aufklärungs-Abteilung 25 (1st iteration)	25. Panzer-Division	Formed in April 1943 from the redesignated and reorganized *Kradschützen-Bataillon 25*, it was effectively destroyed in February 1944.
Panzer-Aufklärungs-Abteilung 25 (2nd iteration)	25. Panzer-Division	Reconstituted in August 1944 from the former battalion, it served with the division until the end of the war.
Panzer-Aufklärungs-Abteilung 26	26. Panzer-Division	Formed from the redesignation and reorganization of *Kradschützen-Bataillon 26* in April 1943, it served with the division until the end of the war.
Panzer-Aufklärungs-Abteilung 27	17. Panzer-Division	Formed from the reconnaissance battalion of the *17. Infanterie-Division* and the *2./Panzer-Aufklärungs-Abteilung 7*, the battalion was consolidated with *Kradschützen-Bataillon 17* in April 1942.
Aufklärungs-Abteilung 29 (mot)	29. Infanterie-Division (mot)	Formed prior to the start of the war, the battalion was consolidated with *Kradschützen-Bataillon 29* in June 1942.
Panzer-Aufklärungs-Abteilung 29	29. Panzergrenadier-Division	Formed in March 1943 from remnants of *Kradschützen-Bataillon 29* and personnel levies against *Kradschützen-Bataillon 345* of the *345. Infanterie-Division (mot)*, it was redesignated as *Panzer-Aufklärungs-Abteilung 129* in April 1943.
30–100		
Panzer-Aufklärungs-Abteilung 33	15. Panzer-Division	Formed from *Aufklärungs-Abteilung 33* in November 1940, it was redesignated as *Panzer-Aufklärungs-Abteilung 15* at the end of April 1943, only to surrender in Tunisia in May of the same year.
Aufklärungs-Abteilung 36 (mot)	36. Infanterie-Division (mot)	Formed in November 1940 primarily from *Aufklärungs-Abteilung 36* of the 36. *Infanterie-Division*, it was unofficially consolidated with *Kradschützen-Bataillon 36* in October 1941. In November 1941, it was reorganized and redesignated as *Voraus-Abteilung 36*.
Voraus-Abteilung 36	36. Infanterie-Division (mot)	Formed by the consolidation of *Kradschützen-Bataillon 36* and *Aufklärungs-Abteilung 36 (mot)* in November 1941, it was reorganized and redesignated as *Kradschützen-Bataillon 36* in March 1942.
Aufklärungs-Abteilung 37 (mot)	7. Panzer-Division	Formed and redesignated from the *I./Aufklärungs-Regiment 7*, the battalion was redesignated as *Panzer-Aufklärungs-Abteilung 37* in April 1940.
Panzer-Aufklärungs-Abteilung 37	7. Panzer-Division	Formed from *Aufklärungs-Abteilung 37 (mot)* in April 1940, it was consolidated with *Kradschützen-Bataillon 7* in May 1942 (unofficially, the previous fall).
Panzer-Aufklärungs-Abteilung 40	14. Panzer-Division	Formed in August 1940 from personnel levies against a variety of armored reconnaissance assets, it was consolidated with *Kradschützen-Bataillon 40* in April 1942.
Aufklärungs-Abteilung 53 (mot)	3. Infanterie-Division (mot)	Activated in October 1940, it was consolidated with *Kradschützen-Bataillon 53* in March 1942.
Panzer-Aufklärungs-Abteilung 53	3. Panzergrenadier-Division	March–April 1943. Bridge formation between *Kradschützen-Bataillon 53* and *Panzer-Aufklärungs-Abteilung 103*.
Aufklärungs-Abteilung 57 (mot)	6. Panzer-Division	Formed from the redesignated *Aufklärungs-Abteilung 6 (mot)* in April 1940. It was consolidated with *Kradschützen-Bataillon 6* in February 1942.
Panzer-Aufklärungs-Abteilung 59	8. Panzer-Division	Formed and redesignated from the *II./Aufklärungs-Regiment 8*, the battalion was redesignated as *Panzer-Aufklärungs-Abteilung 59* in April 1940. It was consolidated with *Kradschützen-Bataillon 8* in January 1943.

Unit Designation	Major Command	Time Frame
30–100 *continued*		
Panzer-Aufklärungs-Abteilung 88	18. Panzer-Division	Formed in October 1940 through personnel levies against the *Kavallerie-Lehr- und Ersatz-Abteilung*, it was unofficially consolidated with *Kradschützen-Bataillon 18* in November 1941 and officially in January 1942.
Panzer-Aufklärungs-Abteilung 90	10. Panzer-Division	Formed in April 1940 from the *I./Aufklärungs-Regiment 8*, it was consolidated with *Kradschützen-Bataillon 10* in February 1942.
Panzer-Aufklärungs-Abteilung 91	1. Panzer-Division	March 1943. Bridge formation between *Kradschützen-Bataillon 1* and *Panzer-Aufklärungs-Abteilung 1*.
Panzer-Aufklärungs-Abteilung 92	20. Panzer-Division	Formed by personnel levies against replacement detachments and *Panzer-Aufklärungs-Abteilung 37*, it was consolidated with *Kradschützen-Bataillon 20* in January 1942.
101–200		
Panzer-Späh-Kompanie 101*	Führer-Begleit-Division	Formed in late January 1945 from elements of the former brigade, it was redesignated as the *Führer-Panzer-Späh-Kompanie* in March 1945.
Panzer-Späh-Kompanie 102	Führer-Grenadier-Division	Formed from the *17./Führer-Grenadier-Brigade* in January 1945, it was redesignated as the *Führer-Panzer-Späh-Kompanie 2* in March 1945.
Panzer-Aufklärungs-Abteilung 103	3. Panzergrenadier-Division	Formed from the redesignated *Panzer-Aufklärungs-Abteilung 53* in April 1943, it served with the division until the end of the war.
Panzer-Aufklärungs-Abteilung 110	10. Infanterie-Division (mot) / 10. Panzergrenadier-Division	Formed in April 1943 from the redesignation and reorganization of *Kradschützen-Bataillon 40*, it served with the division until the end of the war.
Panzer-Aufklärungs-Abteilung 115	15. Panzergrenadier-Division	Formed in October 1943 from *ad hoc* antecedent formations (*schnelle Abteilung/15. Panzergrenadier Division* and *schnelle Abteilung Sizilien*), it served with the division until the end of the war.
Panzer-Aufklärungs-Abteilung 116 (1st iteration)	16. Infanterie-Division (mot) / 16. Panzergrenadier-Division	Formed through the redesignation and reorganization of *Kradschützen-Bataillon 165* in May 1943, it remained with the division when it transitioned to the *16. Panzergrenadier-Division* in June 1943 and served with it until the division was effectively destroyed and disbanded in May 1944.
Panzer-Aufklärungs-Abteilung 116 (2nd iteration)	16. Panzer-Division	Formed from the remnants of *Panzer-Aufklärungs-Abteilung 116* and personnel levies against *Reserve-Panzer-Aufklärungs-Abteilung 1*, it served with the division until its capitulation in the Ruhr Pocket in April 1945.
Panzer-Aufklärungs-Abteilung 118 (1st iteration)	18. Infanterie-Division (mot) / 18. Panzergrenadier-Division	Formed from the reorganized and redesignated *Kradschützen-Bataillon 38*, it was destroyed with the division in summer 1944.
Panzer-Aufklärungs-Abteilung 118 (2nd iteration)	18. Panzergrenadier-Division	Reconstituted from the original battalion in August 1944, it reached the strength of two companies by February 1945, when the division was disbanded.
Panzer-Aufklärungs-Abteilung 120	20. Infanterie-Division (mot) / 20. Panzergrenadier-Division	Formed from the redesignated and reorganized *Kradschützen-Bataillon 30* in March 1943, it served with the division until the end of the war.
Panzer-Aufklärungs-Abteilung 125 (1st iteration)	25. Infanterie-Division (mot) / 25. Panzergrenadier-Division	Formed through the redesignation and reorganization of *Kradschützen-Bataillon 25* in April 1943, it served until effectively destroyed as part of the Soviet Operation Bagration in the summer of 1944.
Panzer-Aufklärungs-Abteilung 125 (2nd iteration)	25. Panzergrenadier-Division	The battalion was slowly reconstituted, starting in October 1944 with an armored scout platoon. It received a *VW* armored reconnaissance company in November and its remaining line companies in January 1945. It served with the division until the end of the war.
Panzer-Aufklärungs-Kompanie 127	27. Panzer-Division	Formed in November 1942 out of remnants of the *22. Panzer-Division* and personnel levies against *Kradschützen-Ersatz-Bataillon 4*, it was disbanded when the "division" (essentially a *Kampfgruppe*) was disbanded in February 1943.
Panzer-Aufklärungs-Abteilung 129	29. Panzergrenadier-Division	Formed through the redesignation of *Panzer-Aufklärungs-Abteilung 29* in April 1943, it served with the division until the end of the war.
Panzer-Aufklärungs-Lehr-Abteilung 130	Panzer-Lehr-Division	Activated in January 1944 as the *Panzer-Aufklärungs-Lehr-Abteilung*, it was officially redesignated as *Panzer-Aufklärungs-Lehr-Abteilung 130* in April 1944. It surrendered with the division in the Ruhr Pocket in April 1945.

APPENDIX 2: RECONNAISSANCE FORMATION CROSS-REFERENCE GUIDE

Unit Designation	Major Command	Time Frame
101–200 *continued*		
Panzer-Späh-Kompanie 140	22. Panzer-Division	Formed by the division in May 1942 through internal assets, it was apparently intact until November 1942, when its assets were redistributed (probably to the *23. Panzer-Division*).
Panzer-Aufklärungs-Abteilung 151	Panzergrenadier-Division "Kurmark"	Formed at the end of January 1945 from elements of the *"Großdeutschland" Panzergrenadier* replacement brigade, it was most likely a company-size element, effectively wiped out in the Halbe Pocket at the end of the war.
Aufklärungs-Abteilung 160 (mot)	60. Infanterie-Division (mot)	Formed in August 1940 from elements of *Aufklärungs-Abteilung 228*, it was consolidated with *Kradschützen-Bataillon 160* in April 1942.
200–580		
Aufklärungs-Abteilung 220 (mot)	164. leichte Division / 164. leichte Afrika-Division	Formed in April 1942, it was redesignated as *Panzer-Aufklärungs-Abteilung 220* in October of the same year.
Panzer-Aufklärungs-Abteilung 220	164. leichte Afrika-Division	Formed in October 1942 from the redesignation of *Aufklärungs-Abteilung 220 (mot)*, it was redesignated as *Panzer-Aufklärungs-Abteilung 164* in April, serving with the division until its capitulation in May 1943.
Panzer-Aufklärungs-Abteilung 231	11. Panzer-Division	Formed from *Aufklärungs-Abteilung 231* (*231. Infanterie-Division*) in September 1940, it was consolidated with *Kradschützen-Bataillon 61* in December 1941.
Aufklärungs-Abteilung 341 (mot)	16. Infanterie-Division (mot)	Formed in August 1941 from a variety of personnel levies against non-motorized and motorized reconnaissance assets, it was consolidated with *Kradschützen-Bataillon 165* in December 1941.
Gemischte Aufklärungs-Kompanie 580	90. leichte Division / 90. leichte Afrika-Division (May 1942)	Formed in the summer of 1943 from personnel levies against *Wehrkreis III*, it was expanded and redesignated as *Aufklärungs-Abteilung 580 (mot)* in the summer of 1942.
Aufklärungs-Abteilung 580 (mot)	90. leichte Afrika-Division / 21. Panzer-Division (Afrika)	Formed initially as a troop in August 1941, it was expanded to a battalion in summer 1942, known for a short while as *gemischte Aufklärungs-Abteilung 580*. Transferred to the *21. Panzer-Division* in February 1943, it was redesignated as *Panzer-Aufklärungs-Abteilung 21* in April 1943.

*Lexicon der Wehrmacht (accessed 19 July 2014: www.lexikon-der-wehrmacht.de/Gliederungen/Panzergrenadierdivisionen/FuhrerBeglDiv.htm and www.lexikon-der-wehrmacht.de/Gliederungen/Panzergrenadierdivisionen/FuhrerGrenDiv.htm) shows companies 101 and 102 assigned in reverse order.

MOTORCYCLE INFANTRY BATTALIONS

Unit Designation	Major Command	Notes
Named		
Kradschützen-Bataillon "Großdeutschland"	Infanterie-Regiment "Großdeutschland" (mot) / Infanterie-Division "Großdeutschland" (mot)	Formed in March 1942 from the *V./Infanterie-Regiment "Großdeutschland" (mot)*, as well as elements of both the *1.* and *2./Aufklärungs-Abteilung 92* of the *20. Panzer-Division*, it was redesignated and reorganized as *Panzer-Aufklärungs-Abteilung "Großdeutschland"* in January 1943.
1–10		
Kradschützen-Bataillon 1	1. Panzer-Division	With the *1. Panzer-Division* from the start of the war until its redesignation as *Panzer-Aufklärungs-Abteilung 91* in March 1943, then *Panzer-Aufklärungs-Abteilung 1* shortly thereafter.
Kradschützen-Bataillon 2	2. Panzer-Division	With the *2. Panzer-Division* from the start of the war until its redesignation as *Panzer-Aufklärungs-Abteilung 2* in March 1943.
Kradschützen-Bataillon 3	3. Panzer-Division	Formed before the war, the battalion was redesignated and reorganized as Panzer-Aufklärungs-Abteilung 3 in April 1943.
Kradschützen-Bataillon 4	24. Panzer-Division	Formed in December 1941 from *Radfahr-Abteilung 1*, it was effectively destroyed at Stalingrad in January 1943 and never reconstituted.
Kradschützen-Bataillon 6	1. leichte Division / 6. Panzer-Division	Formed prior to the start of the war, it served initially as the *IV./Kavallerie-Schützen-Regiment 4* of the *1. leichte Division* before being redesignated and reorganized as *Kradschützen-Bataillon 6* and reassigned to the *6. Panzer-Division* in October 1939. After consolidating with *Aufklärungs-Abteilung 57 (mot)* in February 1942, it was reorganized and redesignated as *Panzer-Aufklärungs-Abteilung 6* in April 1943.

Unit Designation	Major Command	Notes
1–10 *continued*		
Kradschützen-Bataillon 7	7. Panzer-Division	Formed and redesignated from the *II./Aufklärungs-Regiment 7*, the battalion was reorganized and redesignated as *Panzer-Aufklärungs-Abteilung 7* in March 1943.
Kradschützen-Bataillon 8	8. Panzer-Division	Activated in April 1940 from the reorganization and redesignation of the *II./Kavallerie-Schützen-Regiment 9*, it was reorganized and redesignated as *Panzer-Aufklärungs-Abteilung 8* in April 1943.
Kradschützen-Bataillon 8	10. Panzer-Division	Formed in March 1941, it was redesignated and reorganized as *Panzer-Aufklärungs-Abteilung 10* in March 1943.
11–20		
Kradschützen-Bataillon 15	15. Panzer-Division	Formed in November 1940 from personnel levies against the *13. Infanterie-Division*, it was reassigned to the *21. Panzer-Division* in April 1942, where it was redesignated and reorganized as the *III./Panzergrenadier-Regiment 104*.
Kradschützen-Bataillon 16	16. Panzer-Division	Formed in August 1940 through the redesignation and reorganization of *Maschinengewehr-Bataillon 1*. Effectively destroyed at Stalingrad, the battalion was reconstituted in March 1943 and further redesignated and reorganized as *Panzer-Aufklärungs-Abteilung 16* in March 1943.
Kradschützen-Bataillon 17	17. Panzer-Division	Formed from motorized infantry elements in October 1940, the battalion was redesignated and reorganized as *Panzer-Aufklärungs-Abteilung 17* in May 1943.
Kradschützen-Bataillon 18	18. Panzer-Division	Activated in October 1940 through personnel levies against *Infanterie-Regiment 52 (mot)*, it was reorganized and redesignated as *Panzer-Aufklärungs-Abteilung 18* in March 1943.
Kradschützen-Bataillon 19	19. Panzer-Division	Formed in November 1940 through personnel levies against the *I./Infanterie-Regiment 73 (mot)*, the battalion was consolidated with *Panzer-Aufklärungs-Abteilung 19* in August 1941 (while retaining the latter's designation) and then reverted to its original designation in May 1942. In March 1943 it was redesignated and reorganized as *Panzer-Aufklärungs-Abteilung 19*.
Kradschützen-Bataillon 20	20. Panzer-Division	Formed in November 1940 from personnel levies against the *III./Infanterie-Regiment 115 (mot)*, it was reorganized and redesignated as *Panzer-Aufklärungs-Abteilung 20* in March 1943.
21–30		
Kradschützen-Bataillon 22	2. Infanterie-Division (mot) / 12. Panzer-Division	Activated in August 1940 from personnel levies against infantry and motorized infantry formations, it served for a brief period as *Panzer-Aufklärungs- und Voraus-Abteilung 2* (roughly August–November 1941). It was reorganized and redesignated as *Panzer-Aufklärungs-Abteilung 12* in April 1943.
Kradschützen-Bataillon 23	23. Panzer-Division	Formed in September 1941 from a variety of motorized and armored reconnaissance assets, it was reorganized and redesignated as *Panzer-Aufklärungs-Abteilung 23* in April 1943.
Kradschützen-Bataillon 24	22. Panzer-Division	Formed in September 1941 from a variety of sources, it reorganized as a company in March 1943 before being reorganized, redesignated, and reassigned to the *23. Panzer-Division* as the *2./Kradschützen-Bataillon 23*.
Kradschützen-Bataillon 25	25. Infanterie-Division (mot)	Formed in November 1940 from the *III./Infanterie-Regiment 40*, it was reorganized and redesignated as *Panzer-Aufklärungs-Abteilung 125* in April 1943.
Kradschützen-Bataillon 26	26. Panzer-Division	Formed in September 1942, primarily through the reorganization and redesignation of *Radfahr-Abteilung 23* of the *23. Infanterie-Division*. It was reorganized and redesignated as *Panzer-Aufklärungs-Abteilung 26* in April 1943.
Kradschützen-Bataillon 29	29. Infanterie-Division (mot)	Formed in February 1941 from personnel levies against the division's two motorized infantry regiments, it was effectively destroyed in Stalingrad in January 1943.
31–40		
Kradschützen-Bataillon 30	20. Infanterie-Division (mot)	Formed through the reorganization and redesignation of the *III./Infanterie-Regiment 30 (mot)*, the battalion was redesignated and reorganized as *Panzer-Aufklärungs-Abteilung 120* in March 1943.
Kradschützen-Bataillon 34	4. Panzer-Division	Activated in January 1941, it was redesignated and reorganized as *Panzer-Aufklärungs-Abteilung 4* in April 1943.

APPENDIX 2: RECONNAISSANCE FORMATION CROSS-REFERENCE GUIDE

Unit Designation	Major Command	Notes
31–40 *continued*		
Kradschützen-Bataillon 36	36. Infanterie-Division (mot)	Formed by the reassignment, reorganization, and redesignation of *Maschinengewehr-Bataillon 8* in November 1940, it was consolidated (unofficially) with *Aufklärungs-Abteilung 36 (mot)* in October 1941, and then reorganized and redesignated as *Voraus-Abteilung 36* in November 1941. In March 1942 it reverted to its original designation. In April 1943 it was reorganized and redesignated as *Aufklärungs-Abteilung 36* (division converted to a regular infantry division).
Kradschützen-Bataillon 38	18. Infanterie-Division (mot)	Formed from personnel levies from the *III./Infanterie-Regiment 51*, the battalion was reorganized and redesignated as *Panzer-Aufklärungs-Abteilung 118* in April 1943.
41–60		
Kradschützen-Bataillon 40	10. Infanterie-Division (mot)	Formed in November 1940 from the redesignation and reorganization of *Maschinengewehr-Bataillon 6*, it was further redesignated and reorganized as *Panzer-Aufklärungs-Abteilung 110* in April 1943.
Kradschützen-Bataillon 43	13. Infanterie-Division (mot) / 13. Panzer-Division	Activated in August 1940 through personnel levies from the division's infantry regiments, it was sent with the division to Romania in November 1940 to serve as instructors and trainers, where it was referred to as *Lehr- Kradschützen-Bataillon 43*. Upon return, it served with the division (including its transition into the *13. Panzer-Division*) until its redesignation and reorganization as *Panzer-Aufklärungs-Abteilung 13* in April 1943.
Kradschützen-Bataillon 53	2. Infanterie-Division (mot)	Activated in October 1940, it surrendered at Stalingrad in January 1943.
Kradschützen-Bataillon 54	14. Infanterie-Division (mot)	Formed in October 1940 through personnel levies from the *4. Infanterie-Division*, the battalion was reorganized and redesignated as *Füsilier-Bataillon 14* when the division was demotorized.
Kradschützen-Bataillon 55	5. Panzer-Division	Activated in August 1940, it was redesignated and reorganized as *Panzer-Aufklärungs-Abteilung 5* in March 1943.
Kradschützen-Bataillon 59	9. Panzer-Division	Formed from the reorganized and redesignated *I./Aufklärungs-Regiment 9* in August 1940, it was further redesignated and reorganized as *Panzer-Aufklärungs-Abteilung 9* in April 1943.
61–100		
Kradschützen-Bataillon 61	11. Panzer-Division	Formed in August 1940 from personnel levies against divisional motorized infantry and machine-gun formations, it was further redesignated and reorganized as *Panzer-Aufklärungs-Abteilung 11* in April 1943.
Kradschützen-Bataillon 64	14. Panzer-Division	Formed in August 1940 from personnel levies against motorized infantry formations, it was further redesignated and reorganized as *Panzer-Aufklärungs-Abteilung 64* in May 1943 and, apparently on the same day, as *Panzer-Aufklärungs-Abteilung 14*.
Kradschützen-Bataillon 87	25. Panzer-Division	Formed in October 1942 from the *III./Panzergrenadier-Regiment 146* of the division, it was reorganized and redesignated as *Panzer-Aufklärungs-Abteilung 25* in April 1943.
101–165		
Kradschützen-Bataillon 160	60. Infanterie-Division (mot)	Formed in August 1940 from the reassignment, reorganization, and redesignation of *Maschinengewehr-Bataillon 15*, it was effectively destroyed in Stalingrad in January 1943.
Kradschützen-Bataillon 165	16. Infanterie-Division (mot)	Formed in August 1940 from the redesignation and reorganization of *Maschinengewehr-Bataillon 6*, it was further redesignated and reorganized as *Panzer-Aufklärungs-Abteilung 116* in May 1943.

Appendix 3

The Transition to Increased Firepower: 1932–45

Early prewar armored cars such as the four-wheel *Kfz. 13* were armed with the 7.92mm *MG 13*, an air-cooled, selective-fire light machine gun. This weapon was officially adopted by the German Army as its principal light machine gun from 1932 until 1936, when it was superseded by the excellent *MG 34* with its much higher rate of fire. These early armored cars were intended primarily as training vehicles, not for combat use, although some were used in the Polish, French, and early Russian campaigns, particularly in the reconnaissance battalions of the peacetime infantry divisions.

The *Sd.Kfz. 221* four-wheel armored car, despite being considered a combat-capable vehicle, was initially only armed with a machine gun in a rotating turret. This was originally the *MG 13*, which was replaced by the *MG 34* in 1938. As the machine gun was only effective against infantry, the *Sd.Kfz. 221* was usually escorted by armored cars mounting the 2cm cannon, which was capable of taking on light enemy vehicles of the period.

The shortcomings of the machine-gun-armed *Sd.Kfz. 221* were apparent, and in an attempt to prolong its effective service life, the *Sd.Kfz. 221* was retrofitted with the *2.8cm s.Pz.B. 41*—the 2.8cm *schwere Panzerbüchse* or heavy antitank rifle—mounted in the turret, effective 18 March 1942. The *s.Pz.B. 41* was a tapered-bore weapon, its caliber reduced from 28mm to 20mm with a resultant high velocity of 1,400 meters per second. Armor penetration was a respectable 69mm of plate at 30° from the vertical at 100 meters; at 500 meters, this was reduced to 52mm. This was more than enough to be effective against enemy armored cars and light tanks. A high-explosive round was also provided, with a maximum range of 800 meters. The *s.Pz.B. 41* was also fitted to the half-track *Sd.Kfz. 250/11* issued to some reconnaissance units.

The *Sd.Kfz. 222* was an updated version of the *221* and designed from the outset to mount a 2cm automatic cannon in a rotating armored turret. Although reconnaissance forces used speed and concealment to avoid enemy forces, rather than engage in a firefight, it was evident that heavier armament than a machine gun was required whenever an encounter with enemy units was unavoidable.

The weapon chosen for the *Sd.Kfz. 222* was the *2cm KwK 30*—*Kampfwagen-Kanone 30* or Model 30 main gun—automatic cannon. This gun was developed from the *2cm Flak 30*, a Rheinmetall design developed in conjunction with Solothurn in the late 1920s/early 1930s. This was a robust, reliable weapon with a cyclic rate of fire of 280 rounds per minute and a practical rate of fire of 120 rounds per minute. Both armor-piercing and high-explosive rounds were produced for the *KwK 30*.

Despite the good performance of the *Flak 30*, the *Luftwaffe* required a higher rate of fire; since Rheinmetall had its hands full with other weapon developments, Mauser-Werke was tasked with a redesign of the cannon intended to double the rate of fire. Fortunately, the updated design only required changes to the bolt mechanism, return spring, and accelerator. The result of these relatively minor changes was dramatic, with the rate of fire increasing to 420–480 rounds per minute cyclic and 180–220 rounds per minute sustained. The improved weapon was designated the *2cm Flak 38* and the ground version the *2cm KwK 38*. Externally, the *KwK 30* and *KwK 38* were identical in appearance. They also had the same ballistic performance, as they fired the same ammunition.

The *2cm Kwk 30/38* became the standard onboard weapon for the majority of German armored cars. In addition to the *Sd.Kfz. 222* mentioned above, the 2cm cannon was also fitted to the six-wheeled *Sd.Kfz. 231's* and *232's*, the eight-wheeled *Sd.Kfz. 231's* and *232's*, and the *Sd.Kfz. 234/1*, an improved version of the eight-wheeled *Sd.Kfz. 231* series manufactured from June 1944 to January 1945.

When production of the *Sd.Kfz 222* ceased in June 1943, the replacement vehicle was the half-track *Sd.Kfz 250/9*, which had superior cross-country performance. Early versions of the *Sd.Kfz. 250/9* used the complete turret assembly of the *Sd.Kfz. 222*. The *KwK 38* was also the main armament for the light fully tracked reconnaissance vehicles such as the *Sd.Kfz. 123 (Pz.Kpfw. II Ausf. L "Luchs" (Lynx))* and the *Aufklärer auf Fahrgestell Panzerkampfwagen 38(t) mit 2 cm KwK 38*.

The *KwK 30/38* had a muzzle velocity of 830 meters per second when firing armor-piercing rounds. Its armor penetration with the tungsten-core round *2cm Pzgr.Patr. 40 Leuchtspur*—*Panzergranate-Patrone 40 Leuchtspur* or Model 40 Armor Piercing Round with Tracer—was 40mm of vertical plate at 100 meters.

APPENDIX 3: THE TRANSITION TO INCREASED FIREPOWER: 1932–45

The Germans proved themselves to be masters of improvisation in mounting heavier weapons on relatively light and mobile chassis. The escalation of main gun caliber, velocity, and armor thickness continued, particularly on the Eastern Front. Consequently, there was an accelerated need for reconnaissance vehicles to increase their antipersonnel and—most especially—their antiarmor capabilities.

The 2cm cannon was no longer adequate to deal with the heavier, better-armed enemy vehicles being encountered. Additionally, by 1943 the primary mission of the reconnaissance units had fundamentally changed as they now regularly served as rearguards for the almost continuous German retreats. In this role, stealth and speed were no longer of paramount importance; the ability to engage enemy forces at longer ranges was increasingly necessary. It was common German practice to attach additional assets such as heavier armored vehicles, antitank guns, and artillery to reconnaissance forces for specific missions. However, the need for heavier weapons mounted on the fast-moving reconnaissance vehicles also became an essential requirement.

The *3.7cm PaK 36* was Germany's standard antitank gun at the start of the war, but its lack of penetrating power was evident as early as the 1940 French Campaign. By the start of Barbarossa, the *PaK 36* was totally useless against the Soviet T-34 and KV tanks. However, the *PaK 36* was still a useful weapon, and rather than scrap all the existing stock, the Germans mounted it on the light half-track *Sd.Kfz. 250/10* and the medium *Sd.Kfz. 251/10*. Both vehicles were issued to platoon leaders in order to provide some degree of heavy support within each maneuver platoon.

Firing the standard armor-piercing projectile, the *PaK 36* could penetrate 65mm of vertical plate at 100 meters and 50mm at 30° from the vertical. At 500 meters this decreased to 48mm and 36mm, respectively. Using the tungsten-core *Pzgr.Patr. 40* round at 100 meters, the penetration was 79mm of vertical plate and 68mm at 30°; at 500 meters it was 50mm and 40mm, respectively. The *PaK 36* also fired a useful high-explosive round with an explosive filling of 25 grams of pressed-pellet TNT and a maximum range of 3,000 meters.

The *Schwerer Panzerspähwagen (5cm) Sd.Kfz. 234/2 Puma* was probably the most outstanding armored car of the war: fast, maneuverable, reasonably well protected, and armed with a 5cm high-velocity gun in a fully enclosed turret. The *5cm KwK 39/1 L/60* was the same weapon first mounted in the *Pz.Kpfw. III Ausf. J*.

The standard armor-piercing projectile of the *KwK 39* penetrated 88mm of vertical plate at 250 meters and 67mm at 30° from the vertical; at 500 meters this decreased to 78mm and 61mm, respectively. At 1,000 meters the figures were 61mm vertical and 50mm at 30°. Using the tungsten-core *Pzgr.Patr 40* round at 250 meters, the penetration was an impressive 141mm of vertical plate and 109mm at 30°; at 500 meters it was 120mm and 86mm, respectively. At 1,000 meters the figures were 84mm vertical and 55mm at 30°. This was more than sufficient to deal with most Allied tanks at short and medium ranges, until the appearance of more heavily armored vehicles in late 1944. The *KwK 39* also fired a high-explosive round with an explosive filling of 165 grams of pressed-pellet TNT and a maximum range of 2,650 meters.

With the up-gunning of the *Panzer IV* to the *7.5 cm KwK 40 L43/48*, there was a surplus of the *7.5cm KwK 37 L/24* main guns, and the decision was made to mount them—redesignated the *7.5 cm StuK 37 L/24*, or later the *K 51*—on a variety of chassis in order to increase the antiarmor and area fire capabilities of the units using these vehicles.

The *Sd.Kfz. 233* was a development of the eight-wheeled *Sd.Kfz 231* design. The turret and superstructure roof were removed and the right side of the superstructure cut out to accommodate mounting a *StuK 37*. Thirty-two rounds of fixed ammunition were carried. It was planned for a platoon of six *Sd.Kfz. 233's* to be issued to the armored car companies of the reconnaissance battalions; however, this proved too ambitious, even after the number was reduced to three.

Starting in September 1943, 50 percent of the *Sd.Kfz. 234's* produced were to mount the *7.5 cm Kwk 51 L/24*, with the designation *Sd.Kfz. 234/3*. As of June 1944 the percentage was reduced to 25, reflecting a change in the organization of the reconnaissance troops.

The *7.5cm L/24* was also mounted on the *Sd.Kfz. 250/8* usually issued to the 4th Platoon (Heavy Weapons) of the light armored reconnaissance companies. The larger *Sd.Kfz. 251/9* also carried the *KwK 37/K51(sf)*; the unofficial name for this variant was *Stummel*, or "stump."

Although superseded as a tank main gun, the short *7.5cm* was still a very useful weapon. The standard armor-piercing projectile of the *KwK 37* penetrated 41mm of 30° plate at 100 meters and 39mm at 500 meters, which could hardly be considered formidable. However, a hollow-charge projectile was also developed for the *L/24*, the *Gr.38 H1/C*, that increased armor-penetration capability considerably: At 100 meters, it could defeat 100mm of armor at 30°. With a hollow-charge round, the armor penetration did not reduce with distance, but the maximum range was less than 1,000 meters due to the low velocity of the of the short barrel.

The *KwK 37* also fired a 6-kilogram high-explosive round with an explosive filling of 570 grams of Amatol; the maximum range for this round was 3,500 meters. It is interesting to note that all vehicles armed with the *7.5 cm L/24*—from the *Panzer III Ausf. J/L/M* to the half-tracks and armored cars—were very popular with their crews and provided very effective fire support against infantry, antitank guns, and fortifications.

The largest weapon mounted in a reconnaissance vehicle was the *7.5cm PaK 40*, the standard German antitank gun from 1942 until the end of the war. Powerful and very effective, the *PaK 40* could defeat all Allied armor at medium and long ranges, although the heavier tanks appearing in late 1944—particularly the Soviet "Stalin" series—could only be knocked out at shorter range.

On direct orders from Hitler in December 1944, the *PaK 40* was to be fitted to as many self-propelled chassis as possible. Accordingly, a medium half-track, the *Sd.Kfz. 251/22*, was fitted with the complete *PaK 40* field mount minus the wheels. Since the *PaK 40* was a heavy weapon, the chassis was somewhat overloaded.

As an additional consequence of the December 1944 order, the *PaK 40* also was fitted on a heavy armored car, the newly designated *Sd.Kfz. 234/4*. As with the *Sd.Kfz 251/22*, the whole gun and its field mounting, minus the wheels, was fitted to the open superstructure. These vehicles were issued in limited numbers to armored reconnaissance elements in the closing months of the war and gave much-needed antitank support to the other armored cars.

The standard armor-piercing projectile of the *PaK 40* penetrated 148mm of vertical plate at 100 meters and 120mm at 30° from the vertical; at 500 meters this decreased to 132mm and 104mm, respectively.* Tungsten-core shot was rarely used, as it was discontinued after 1942, but the *Pzgr.Patr. 40* round at 100 meters was capable of penetrating no less than 175mm of vertical plate and 135mm at 30°; at 500 meters it was 154mm and 115mm, respectively.** The *PaK 40* also fired a 9.15-kilogram high-explosive round with an explosive filling of 640 grams of Amatol and maximum range of 7,680 meters.

---

* At 1,000 meters the figures were 116mm vertical and 89mm at 30°; at 1,500 meters they were 102mm vertical and 76mm at 30°.

** At 1,000 meters the figures were 133mm vertical and 96mm at 30°. The maximum engagement range using armor-piercing rounds was 1,800 meters.

With the abandonment of the *Panzer-Brigaden*, the remaining equipment and personnel were incorporated into the regular *Panzer* divisions.* As a consequence, some reconnaissance battalions were issued with the *Sd.Kfz 251/21* armored half-track mounting three coaxially mounted *MG 151* heavy cannon, originally a *Luftwaffe* fighter aircraft weapon. The *MG 151/15* used guns of 15mm caliber and was present in the first fifty vehicles. Subsequently, the *MG 151/20* was introduced, with guns of 20mm caliber. The Germans referred to the tri-mount weapon as the *Drilling* ("triplet"). It was later officially incorporated into some late-war *KStN's*, including those of armored reconnaissance elements in 1945.

Although obviously intended for antiaircraft employment originally, the *Drilling* was generally used for ground engagements, where it was very effective. The three guns were manually cocked and percussion fired. The cannon were mounted on a pedestal mount fixed to the floor of the *Sd.Kfz. 251/21*. Elevation and depression was from -5° to 49° and traverse was 360°. Both elevation/depression and traverse/deflection were manually controlled by the movements of the gunner.

Each belt-fed weapon was capable of firing 700 rounds per minute, with a muzzle velocity of 810 meters per second for high-explosive and 705 meters per second for armor-piercing rounds. The vehicle carried 3,000 rounds of high-explosive and armor-piercing ammunition in an 8 to 1 ratio; ready-use ammunition was 500 rounds for the center gun and 250 rounds for each of the outer guns. The sights consisted of a telescopic sight with 3-power magnification and a field of view of 8°. For antiaircraft fire, there was a simple *Schwebekreisvisier 30* ("cartwheel gun sight"). In addition, a handheld periscope with an 8-power magnification and a field of view of 7.5° was provided for target acquisition.

The *Drilling* was intended to be fired in short bursts of two to three seconds, not continuously; however, the effect of even a relatively short burst from three heavy-caliber, high-velocity automatic weapons must have been devastating. The *Drilling* was very popular with the troops and added considerable firepower to the reconnaissance units fortunate enough to receive them. According to combat reports, it was extremely effective, with targets successfully engaged at 800 meters.[3] Initially deployed to the Eastern Front, the *Drilling* was probably first encountered by the Western Allies in significant numbers during the Battle of the Bulge. In March 1945 two partially destroyed *Drilling* were recovered in the U.S. Third Army area and examined by technical intelligence teams.

COMPARISONS WITH ALLIED ARMORED CARS
The Soviet six-wheeled BA-10 mounted both 37mm and 45mm dual-purpose guns developed from the Rheinmetall *37mm PaK 36*. Considerable numbers were taken into German service.

The British used armored cars extensively and, as a result of their experiences during the disastrous retreat across Belgium and France in 1940, concluded that while machine-gun-armed vehicles were suitable for scouting, they required a heavier armament when acting as rearguards. This was a lesson the Germans were to learn later in the war.

In contrast to their main battle tanks, the British produced very effective, well-armed armored cars. The Mark I Daimler armored car carried a 2-pounder (40mm) cannon in an enclosed, fully rotating turret similar to that designed for the Vickers-Armstrong Mark VII tank. In fact, the Daimler was as well armed as any contemporary British tank.

The AEC Mark I was actually fitted with the same turret as the Valentine tank. Armor protection was good with 30mm maximum, although the vehicle was high at 2.44 meters (8 feet) and heavy at 7 tons.

The 2-pounder was twice the caliber of the standard 2cm German armored car cannon, with both superior range and penetrating power. However, for some inexplicable reason, the British gun was only supplied with armor-piercing ammunition; no high-explosive round was designed for the 2-pounder, thereby severely limiting its effectiveness against infantry and artillery, including antitank guns. This was a deficiency the British learned at the cost of numerous tanks and armored cars and their crews in the Western Desert.

British tanks persisted with the increasingly inadequate 2-pounder and the barely adequate 6-pounder (57 mm) until the advent of the U.S.–supplied M3 Lee/Grant and the M4 Sherman. Armored cars such as the AEC Mark II were up-gunned from the 2-pounder to the 6-pounder, a very powerful weapon for an armored car, and finally supplied with a high-explosive round. Equipped with the new armor-piercing capped ballistic capped (APCBC) ammunition, the 6-pounder penetrated 80mm of vertical armor at 1,000 meters, compared to 62mm for the 75mm main gun of the M4.

Despite this powerful armament, the British reconnaissance units preferred their M3 White half-tracks armed with a 75mm gun, as the M3 had superior cross-country ability compared to the four-wheeled AEC. Eventually, the AEC Mark III was armed with a British 75mm tank gun in an enclosed, fully rotating turret.

The U.S.–supplied four-wheel "Staghound" was armed with a high-velocity 37mm cannon in an open-topped turret. The only six-wheeled armored car fielded by the Western Allies, the M8 "Greyhound," also used that weapon. It was more than adequate to deal with its German counterparts, although such engagements seem to have been comparatively rare occurrences. The British eventually fitted the turret designed for the Crusader tank—up-gunned to 75mm—to the "Staghound," making it, along with the AEC Mark III and the *Sd.Kfz. 234/4*, the most powerfully armed armored car on the World War II battlefield.

---

*This concept was not necessarily bad, but the execution was poor, especially since the separate brigades had no "parent" organization to "own" them. Piecemeal employment and a poor logistics concept were generally their downfall. See the main text for further discussion.

Appendix 4

Errata and Addenda to *Scouts Out*

Page 36: Delete the semicolon in the second paragraph to read: half-track and fully tracked vehicles.

Page 72: Insert the preposition "in" into the first paragraph as indicated: For those used to NATO-style map symbols, the myriad German tactical symbols used in organization charts (and maps) of the World War II era can seem to be a daunting task at first.

Page 78: Insert the phrase "car companies" into the top caption as indicated: *Aufklärungs-Abteilung 373* of the *373. Infanterie-Division (kroat.)* in September 1943. It was later to form two armored car companies out of captured Italian vehicle stocks.

Page 101: Change "251?" to "250" in the following text from the first full paragraph in the right-hand column: had an armored car company, two armored reconnaissance companies (equipped with the *Sd.Kfz. 250*), and a heavy company.[35]

Also, delete the fifth bulleted paragraph from the right-hand column: One armored reconnaissance company (Panzer-Aufklärungs-Kompanie (Krad), (Kettenkrad) or (*VW*)) (4th).

Page 103: Change "251" to "250" in the second bulleted paragraph in the left-hand column: Two armored reconnaissance companies (*Panzer-aufklärungs-Kompanien [gp]*) (3rd and 4th), each equipped with the *Sd.Kfz. 250* and armed with forty-nine light machine guns, three 7.5cm antitank guns, and two medium mortars.

Page 111: In the table at the top of the page concerning field-army assets, there is a *Panzer-Aufklärungs-Abteilung "München."* Thanks to the indefatigable efforts of Martin Block, more information is now available on this formation, which is paraphrased below:[4]

Panzer-Jagd-Brigade 104, formed in the waning months of World War II, included the following (via tactical attachments):
- *Panzer-Aufklärungs-Abteilung München*: new formation.
- *Panzer-Aufklärungs-Abteilung 115*: from the *15. Panzergrenadier-Division*.
- *Sturmgeschütz-Lehr-Brigade 111*: a field army asset.

According to Block, in theory this was a powerful formation that had no fewer than 154 *Jagdpanzer 38(t)'s* and some 60 assault guns of varying types (*Sturmgeschütz III, Sturmgeschütz IV*, and *Sturmhaubitzen*) at its disposal, not to mention armored personnel carriers and armored cars. Block continues: "But actually the brigade was thrown to the front piecemeal practically from the beginning of its existence and thus never served as a complete [formation] even for a single day. The brigade headquarters initially served as [command and control] for various units in the Stargard area and later as sort of a corps headquarters (*Gruppe Munzel*). Subunits were distributed among different field army groups and field army commands and only by exception did any of them work together at all."

Concerning *Panzer-Aufklärungs-Abteilung München*: "This [battalion] was formed by an [an Army High Command] order dated 29 January 1945 using *Panzer-Aufklärungs-Ersatz- und Ausbildungs-Abteilung 4* in Stahnsdorf [and other units from the training base earmarked for the formation of last-ditch formations]. Authorized organization:
- Headquarters with Signals Platoon and Armored Scout Company (in accordance with *KStN 1109 (fG)* dated 1 November 1944).
- 1 Armored Scout Company (Half-track) (in accordance with *KStN 1162c (fG)* dated 1 November 1944).
- 1 Light Armored Reconnassance Company (in accordance with *KStN 1113 (fG)* dated 1 November 1944).
- 1 Heavy Mortar Section (in accordance with *KStN 1126 (fG)* dated 1 November 1944).
- 1 Supply Company (in accordance with *KStN 1180 (fG)* dated 1 November 1944).

The *KStN's* only served as guidelines, with actual equipment dependant on the availability of material."

As could be expected from a formation fielded this late in the war, vehicles came from a variety of sources, including the replacement detachment itself, the Army Signals School, and the Inspectorate of Armored Forces. According to Block, the following were <u>supposed</u> to be provided: two light radio armored cars, five *Sd.Kfz. 222's*, two *Sd.Kfz. 234/1's*, one *Sd.Kfz. 234/2*, one *Sd.Kfz. 234/3*, two light armored cars (radio?), eight *Sd.Kfz. 251/3's*, three Sd.Kfz. 250/3's, and sixteen *Sd.Kfz. 250/9's*. In the middle of February, the battalion was dispatched by rail to the area of operations of *Heeresgruppe Weichsal*, although it appears to have had only one *KStN 1162c* company and one truck-borne light reconnaissance company. By 11 March 1945 the battalion was consolidated with *Panzer-Aufklärungs-Abteilung 4* of the *4. Panzer-Division*.

Page 118: An alert reader from the United Kingdom has provided additional information for the section concerning "Higher Commands," specifically the *Fallschirm-Aufklärungs-Abteilung 12* and *11*:

> Both your narrative and the organizational diagram describes this unit as having five companies, one of *Panzerspähwagen* and three of *SPW's*, plus a supply company.
>
> This has always struck me as an odd organization for an airborne corps, in so much that *Fallschirmjäger* (excepting the *HG* Division of course) were fundamentally infantry, whereas the reconnaissance battalion as described is effectively an armored one and issued armored vehicles. It does not not add up, even though the diagram is German WWII and shows that situation.
>
> As it happens, I have had some recent correspondence with a gentleman who has researched this formation quite deeply, and his research has yielded an entirely different unit structure and one that makes more sense, particularly with regard to the infantry versus armor comments above.
>
> The data are compiled from U.S. Army POW interrogations of personnel who had been assigned to *Fallschirm-Aufklärungs-Abteilung 12* and had been captured in Normandy. They stated that the battalion had the following organization:
>
> Headquarters: 1x 6×6 Italian Armored Car, 3x Italian B4 tanks
> 1st Company (Rifle): 2x *VW Kübelwagen*, 8x trucks, 3x half-tracks (*SPW?*)
> 2nd Company (Rifle): As in the 1st Company
> 3rd Company (Rifle): As in the 1st Company
> 4th Company (Light Antiaircraft): 4x 2cm *Flak* (not verified)
> 5th Company (Heavy Weapons): 1x 12cm mortar, 2x *Pak 40*, 12x trucks
> 6th Company (Maintenance and Supply)
>
> All company commanders are named in these reports, and it is also possible that the half-tracks mentioned might well be something like *Kettenkräder* for gun towing or something similar.
>
> So, as you can see, there is no commonality between the diagram and your narrative that goes with it and these POW statements. As the airborne corps was essentially infantry, the POW descriptions make much more sense. Their poor levels of equipment do very much reflect units put together in 1944.

Page 127: Insert "*20*" into the top caption as indicated: Various armored cars of the *1./Aufklärungs-Abteilung 20 (mot)* move down a fog-shrouded road in this atmospheric scene.

Page 194: Change the last sentence of the bottom caption to read: The men of the *König* ("King") wear a variety of early and late headgear and uniforms, with the vehicle commander wearing the field-gray version of the *Panzer* jacket. Of further interest is the "star" antenna, which indicated a command and control radio set had been installed in this vehicle. (This image comes from a photo album featuring Knight's Cross recipient *Oberfähnrich* Erwin Krüger, featured later in the book.)

Page 206: Change the first sentence of the caption to read: This *Sd.Kfz. 234/1*, attributed to *Panzer-Aufklärungs-Abteilung 4* of the *4. Panzer-Division*, features a distinctive late-war three-tone camouflage pattern.

Page 210: Thanks to the same aforementioned reader from the United Kingdom, the *Puma* in the photograph has been identified. Change the caption to read: This *Puma*, assigned to the *1./Panzer-aufklärungs-Abteilung 2* of the *2. Panzer-Division* in Normandy, has a number of fuel cans mounted on the front in an effort to extend its range.

Page 212: Thanks to the same reader, the *Puma* in the lower photograph has been identified. Change the caption to read: This *Puma* was assigned to the *Stabskompanie of SS-Panzer-Aufklärungs-Abteilung 1* of the *1. SS-Panzer-Division Leibstandarte SS Adolf Hitler*. The image was taken during the fighting in Normandy.

Page 230: Add the following after the vehicle nomenclature:
Sd.Kfz 250/3 (Light Armored Communications Vehicle)
Sd.Kfz. 250/5 (Light Armored Observation Vehicle)
Sd.Kfz. 250/7 (Heavy Mortar or Mortar Ammunition Carrier)

Page 231: Add the following after the vehicle nomenclature:
Sd.Kfz. 250/8 (Light Armored Personnel Carrier with 7.5cm Main Gun)

Page 232: Add the following after the vehicle nomenclature:
Sd.Kfz. 250/9 (Light Scout Armored Personnel Carrier)

Page 234: Add the following after the vehicle nomenclature:
Sd.Kfz 250/10 (Light Armored Personnel carrier with 3.7cm Antitank Gun)
Sd.Kfz. 250/11 (Light Armored Personnel carrier with 2.8cm Antitank Rifle)
Sd.Kfz. 251/1 (Medium Armored Personnel Carrier)
Sd.Kfz. 251/3 (Medium Armored Communications Vehicle)

Page 242: Add the following amplifying comments after the vehicle nomenclature: *Sd.Kfz. 2 (Kettenkrad)*

Page 262: Thanks to the same reader from the United Kingdom, another error was found. Change the last sentence of the bottom caption as follows: Here, the crew of a Krupp Protze prime mover performs maintenance on its vehicle as armored car crews look on.

Page 281: Another alert reader, this one from France, noted that the bottom image was incorrectly captioned. Change the caption to read: The same officer talks to men from his unit. The noncommissioned officer with the binoculars wears a reed-green HBT field uniform with the top tucked into the trousers.

Page 285: The United Kingdom reader has pointed out that the *Puma* seen on this page has the turret number 041, which would place it with *Panzer-Aufklärungs-Abteilung 20* of the *20. Panzer-Division*, a battalion also seen on page 215.

Page 295: The organization for January 1945 for *Panzer-Aufklärungs-Abteilung 1* should be changed as follows: Headquarters (with armored cars), 1st Company (half-track armored scout), 2nd Company (light armored reconnaissance), 3rd Company (light or medium armored reconnaissance) (*Maultier*), and 4th Company (armored heavy).

Page 337: The entries for the *I.* and *II./Aufklärungs-Regiment 9* of the *4. leichte Division* fail to mention that the 1st Battalion (Motorcycle Infantry) was later redesignated and reorganized as *Kradschützen-Bataillon 59* of the *9. Panzer-Division*, while the 2nd (Armored Scout) Battalion was used for the nucleus of *Aufklärungs-Abteilung 9 (mot)* of the same division.

Page 342: Change misspelled text in the bottom caption, third line from the bottom, to: . . . this action earned him the Knight's Cross.

Page 353: The notes section of the entry for *Aufklärungs-Abteilung 8 (mot)* of the *5. Panzer-Division* should read: Originally a separate battalion, it was redesignated and reassigned as the 2nd Battalion of the relatively short-lived *Aufklärungs-Regiment 6* in 1937, which, in turn, became a part of the *1. Leichte Brigade* in

1938. That same year, the battalion was again redesignated as a separate battalion (assuming its original designation). In November 1938 it was assigned to the *5. Panzer-Division*, where it remained until it was redesignated *Panzer-Aufklärungs-Abteilung 8* in April 1940.[5]

Page 354: Change the last portion of the **Organization** section for *Panzer-Aufklärungs-Abteilung 5* in the right-hand column as follows: End of 1944—Headquarters (with armored car sections), 1st Armored Scout Company (half-track), 2nd Light Armored Reconnaissance Company (half-track), and 3rd Armored Reconnaissance Company (half-track)

Page 366: Change the text at the very top of the page in the left-hand column (**Organization** section for *Panzer-Aufklärungs-Abteilung 9*) as follows: April 1944—Headquarters (with armored car sections), 1st Armored Scout Company (*Luchs*), 2nd Light Armored Reconnaissance Company (half-track), 3rd Armored Reconnaissance Company (half-track), 4th Heavy Armored Reconnaissance Company (half-track)

Page 384: Change the misspelled word in the section on *Panzer-Aufklärungs-Abteilung 33*, seventh sentence from the end of the right-hand column: At that point, a vehicle from our patrol broke off and moved towards the *VW* at high speed.

Page 389: Change the text in the **Organization** section for *Panzer-Aufklärungs-Abteilung 17* to read as follows: July 1944—Headquarters (with armored car sections), 1st Armored Scout Company (*Luchs*), 2nd Light Armored Reconnaissance Company (half-track), 3rd Armored Reconnaissance Company (half-track), 4th Heavy Armored Reconnaissance Company (half-track)

Page 412: Change the top caption as follows: Sometimes a bit of military sightseeing was in order, since soldiers of all armies enjoy looking at military equipment. In this instance, the scouts are looking at ex-British Mark IV tanks.

Page 453: Correct the misspelling in the entry for Roth in the **Awards: Knight's Cross** section of *Panzer-Aufklärungs-Abteilung 116*: *Unteroffizier* August Roth, *3./Panzer-Aufklärungs-Abteilung 116* (20 January 1945)

Page 477: The aforementioned reader from the United Kingdom has identified the trucks seen in the bottom image as "ex-British Bedford 15 cwt MWD trucks, all in good order, suggesting a *Wehrmacht* refurbishment after capture in France 1940, so very unlikely to be *SS-Verfügungs-Division* France 1940, more likely later in Russia."

Page 501: Under the **Organization** section in the right-hand column for September 1944, the 2nd Company is mistakenly identified as being a light self-propelled battery. This should read: 2nd Light Reconnaissance Company.

Page 502: Under the **Organization** section for September 1944, the 2nd Company is mistakenly identified as being a light self-propelled battery. This should read: 2nd Light Reconnaissance Company.

Both of these reconnaissance battalions were organized as Model 44 organizations.

Page 511: Insert text as indicated in the sixth line of footnote 12: *Nr. 20* (dated 15 October 1940, paragraph not listed), and *Nr. 17* (dated 1 September 1942, paragraph 309).

Color Section, not paginated: Change caption as indicated on the next-to-last page (concerning Horst Hain): An additional view of the jacket and some details of the insignia. Hain was one of the few personnel in the *Panzertruppe* who was also entitled to wear the *Kreta* cuff title, since he was in *Kradschützen-Bataillon 55*, which participated in the island invasion in 1940. Some of Hain's other high awards and assignments can be gleaned from the job application seen here that he prepared in order to work for the Allies after the war.

New Information: The following concerns a newly identified formation not mentioned in *Scouts Out*: *Gemischte Panzer-Aufklärungs-Abteilung 520*. The information has been provided by Martin Block and is paraphrased here:[6]

On 30 June 1944, the *Organizations-Abteilung* of the Army High Command issued orders to the Replacement Army to form a mixed armored reconnaissance battalion in the area of operations of *Heeresgruppe D* (*Oberbefehlshaber West*) for employment against insurgents. The battalion was to comprise:

- Headquarters for an Armored Reconnaissance Battalion (Armored),
- One Type "C" Light Tank Company,
- One Armored Reconnaissance Company (Motorcycle), and
- One Armored Reconnaissance Company (Armored).

Most of the assets were to be raised from *Wehrkreis IX*, although the light tank company was to be formed from the remnants of *Panzer-Ersatz- und Ausbildungs-Abteilung 100* (an asset from the *Oberbefehlshaber West*). This was based on an order dated 11 July 1944, which indicates that the battalion had yet to be formed. Apparently, another company—a *gekürzte Panzer-Einsatz-Kompanie* ("Truncated Tank Company"), also from *Panzer-Ersatz- und Ausbildungs-Abteilung 100*—was to form a 4th Company of the battalion.

At the beginning of August, unspecified *Sd.Kfz. 251* variants were sent to the battalion, possibly for the 3rd Company, which was to be organized in accordance with *KStN 1114c (gp)*, the medium version of the half-track reconnaissance company. The 1st Company received *Panzer II's* at an unspecified date; the composition of the other tank company is unknown.

Although the battalion or its elements may have seen operations in July and August, it is unknown what they may have been. On 10 September 1944 the *Organizations-Abteilung* ordered the battalion to be deactivated. What was left of the 3rd Company was to be consolidated with (most likely) the *Panzer-Aufklärungs-Lehr-Abteilung* of the *Panzer-Lehr-Division*. Later that month, documents indicate that the light tank company, with eleven *Panzer II's*, had been absorbed by *Panzer-Aufklärungs-Abteilung 2* of the *2. Panzer-Division*.

Notes

CHAPTER 1
1. Robert J. Edwards, Michael H. Pruett, and Michael Olive, *Scouts Out: A History of German Armored Reconnaissance Units in World War II* (Mechanicsburg, PA: Stackpole Books, 2013).
2. *Army Manual 299/10, Training Manual for the Cavalry*. The particular manual referred to here was a draft published in Berlin in 1939. The manual can be read in translation on the author's website, www.battlebornbooks.com.
3. *Kriegstärkenachweisung* = Wartime Strength Authorization, the equivalent of the U.S. Army's Tables of Organization & Equipment. As with all of the organizational charts presented throughout the book, it should be emphasized that these were theoretical constructs. The actual formations frequently looked quite different, based on a number of factors: recent combat activity, adequacy of the supply chain, time available to effect organizational change, etc.
4. The demand for the *Sd.Kfz 260* and *Sd.Kfz 261* could never be met, and wheeled signals vehicles, such as those in the *Kfz 15* series, usually had to take their place.
5. The engagement at the Czajánek Barracks is rather euphemistically called a "battle." The German forces involved were clearly from a reconnaissance element, but they have not been further identified. Indeed, the first battle casualty from the German occupation appears to have been an armored car commander. The fighting force at Czajánek is generally listed as having been the *II./Infanterie-Regiment 84*, which was a part of the *8. Infanterie-Division*. Since both divisions were part of the First Wave, the heavy companies of their reconnaissance battalions may have had an armored car platoon.
6. See AxisHistory.com (http://forum.axishistory.com/viewtopic.php?f=78&t=139116&start=45) concerning the prince.
7. See Tanks Encyclopedia (www.tanks-encyclopedia.com/ww2/czech/Skoda_PA-II_Zelva.php), Škoda PA-II "Želva," for more information concerning Czech armored cars.

CHAPTER 2
1. Veterans of the 3rd Panzer Division, *Armored Bears: The German 3rd Panzer Division in World War II, Vol. 1* (Mechanicsburg, PA: Stackpole Books, 2012), 24–25.
2. Ibid., 29–30.
3. This, of course, was the famous Werner von Fritsch of the Blomberg–Fritsch Affair and prewar intrigue. The author assumes that the readership is well aware of the notoriety of Fritsch, therefore not providing more than a name mention here. Readers interested in Fritsch, the first general officer of the German Army to be killed in the war, can find more information at the Jewish Virtual Library (www.jewishvirtuallibrary.org/jsource/biography/Fritsch.html).
4. Horst Günter Tolmein, *Spähtrupp bleibt am Feind: Die Geschichte der deutschen Panzer-Aufklärungstruppe* (Stuttgart, Germany: Motorbuch Verlag, 1980), 87–89.
5. Ferdinand Bentele, *Im Panzerspähwagen durch Polen, 2nd ed.* (Vienna: Ostmärkischer Landesverlag für Unterricht, Wissenschaft und Kunst, n.d.), 19–20. Although the narratives are generally written in the first person, Bentele frequently does not identify when the narrator is a new one. In each of the extended citations that follow, the first-person narratives are each from different vehicle commanders and scouts.
6. Ibid., 22–23.
7. Ibid., 23–24.
8. Ibid., 27–28.
9. Ibid., 32–33.
10. In typical German prose of the period, the narrator refers to himself in the third person.
11. Bentele, *Im Panzerspähwagen*, 45–48.
12. Hans Cramer, *Die Panzer-Aufklärungs-Lehrabteilung (Kavallerie Lehr- und Versuchsabteilung) von 1937–1940* (Minden, Germany: Albrecht Philler Verlag, n.d.), 14–15. Based on the language of some of the passages quoted from Cramer's short history, they were written during the war (frequent mentions of Jews, Poles referred to as Polacks, and the entire nation referred to sarcastically as a *Kulturvolk*). More information concerning the organization of the battalion and its various permutations during the war can be found in *Scouts Out*.
13. Ibid., 16–19.
14. Ibid., 19.
15. Tolmein, *Spähtrupp*, 89.
16. Ibid., 90–91.

CHAPTER 3
1. Dr. Leo G. Niehorster, *German World War II Organizational Series, Volume 2/II: Mechanized GHQ Units and*

Waffen-SS Divisions (10th May 1940) (Hannover, Germany: Self-published, 1990), 12–13. This organization is a hypothesis by Niehorster.
2. Rolf Stoves, *Die 1. Panzer-Division* (Bad Nauheim, Germany: Verlag Hans-Henning Podzun, 1961), 102 (first passage), 107 (second passage).
3. Ibid., 112.
4. Ibid., 148–49.
5. Ibid., 149.
6. Tolmein, *Spähtrupp*, 92–95, quoted verbatim from an after-action report in the holdings of the German Federal Archives (RH 27-1/17: "Gefechtsbericht über den Angriff auf Hericourt am 1.6.1940").
7. Stoves, *Die 1. Panzer-Division*, 168.
8. 3rd Panzer Division, *Armored Bears 1*, 58–60.
9. Ibid., 62.
10. Ibid., 73.
11. Ibid., 82.
12. Ibid., 101–2.
13. Ibid., 107.
14. Ibid., 109–10 (first passage), 112 (second passage), 113 (third passage).
15. Albert Schick, *Die zehnte P.D.: Die Geschichte der 10. Panzer-Division, 1939–1943* (Cologne, Germany: Self-published by the Veterans' Association of the former 10th Armored Division, 1993), 205–6.
16. Julius Schmidt, ed., *29. Division: 29. Infanterie-Division, 29. Infanterie-Division (mot), 29. Panzergrenadier-Division; das Buch der Falke-Division mit Beiträgen von Joachim Lemelsen, Walter Fries, Wilhelm Schaeffer und vielen anderen Divisionsangehörigen* (Bad Nauheim, Germany: Podzun-Verlag, 1960), 89–92.
17. It was common practice in the German Army to have subordinates repeat orders back to superiors, in an effort to reduce misunderstandings. In this case, the gunner did it on his own, perhaps because he was not certain whether the original order still stood.
18. Cramer, *Die Panzer*, 24. Both of the next two quotations.
19. Ibid., 24–44.
20. Tolmein, *Spähtrupp*, 101–3, quoted verbatim from the after-action report held at the German Federal Archives (RH 27-7/44: "Erfahrungsbericht 7. Panzer-Division").
21. A large number of images from Kreß' photo albums can also be found in *Scouts Out*.

CHAPTER 4

1. See Jürgen Karl, *Aus eigenem Entschluß: Die Ritterkreuzträger der Waffen-SS, 1940–1945, Band I* (Oberhausen, Germany: Adoria-Verlag, 2014) for numerous capsule biographies of some of the more famous participants, including Klingenberg, 246–50; Tychsen, 304–9; and Meyer, 33–40; as well as Meyer's own memories, published in very readable English as *Grenadiers: The Story of Waffen SS General Kurt "Panzer" Meyer* (Mechanicsburg, PA: Stackpole Books, 2005).
2. It appears that the SS motorcycle infantry companies continued to be organized in accordance with *KStN 1111a* of 1 October 1938. As such, they had two more heavy machine guns than their corresponding army counterparts organized under the new *KStN 1112*. All other weapons allocations remained the same. In addition, the three motorized infantry regiments of the division also had limited reconnaissance assets: *SS-Infanterie-Regiment (mot) Deutschland* (with mixed motorcycle infantry/armored car company), *SS-Infanterie-Regiment (mot) Der Führer* (as with *Deutschland*), and *SS-Infanterie-Regiment 11 (mot)* (with motorcycle infantry company). These were probably *ad hoc* organizations.
3. The *1. (Panzer-Späh-)/Panzer-Aufklärungs-Abteilung 5* was lost in its entirety after the campaign when its transport ship was sunk. The company was still being reconstituted when the invasion of the Soviet Union was launched on 22 June 1941.
4. The reconnaissance battalion had two motorcycle infantry companies. It also had an armored car company with a standard headquarters (same as *KStN 1162 / 1 February 1941*) but only two armored car scout platoons (in the form of *KStN 1137 / 1 February 1941*).
5. Anton Detlev von Plato, *Generalleutnant a.D.*, *Die Geschichte der 5. Panzer-Division, 1938 bis 1945* (Regensburg, Germany: Gemeinschaft der Angehörigen der ehemaligen 5. Panzerdivision, 1978), 119–22.
6. Ibid., 127.
7. Ibid., 135–37.
8. Fritz Memminger, *Die Kriegsgeschichte der Windhund-Division, Band 1* (Bochum-Langendreer, Germany: Heinrich Pöppinghaus, 1962), D35–36.
9. Ibid., D38.
10. Ibid., D40–42.
11. Ibid., D59–63.
12. Ibid., D59 footnote: *Oberleutnant* Borchardt, who had already served as an officer in the *Reichswehr*, left active duty in 1934, followed by four years as a military advisor in China, initially with *General* von Seeckt, and then with *General* von Falkenhausen. He reentered active service in the army in 1940. He became the commander of the *1./Aufklärungs-Abteilung 341 (mot)* and was awarded the Knight's Cross in 1941. At the end of July 1941, he was transferred to *Sonderverband 288*, which was later redesignated as *Panzergrenadier-Regiment Afrika*. He was wounded in the fighting outside of Tobruk. At the start of the fighting at El Alamein, he was the commander of *Panzergrenadier-Regiment 125*, but was captured by the British on 28 October 1942. Of further interest is the fact that Borchardt was half Jewish and one of only two Jews to receive the Knight's Cross.

CHAPTER 5

1. The divisional organization chart of March 1941 indicates that the armored car scout company also had an integral reconnaissance platoon with *Volkswagen* utility vehicles. See Veit Scherzer, *Deutsche Truppen im Zweiten Weltkrieg, Band 3, Die Divisionen, Divisionen und Brigaden mit den Nummern 4 bis 8, Gliederung—Kommandeure—Einsatz—Inhaber höchster Auszeichnungen* (Ranis/Jena, Germany: Scherzers Militaer Verlag, 2008), 242.
2. In the interests of relative simplicity, an interim organization, shown in the divisional organization chart for the winter of 1941–42, indicates that the 2nd Company was still organized as a motorcycle infantry company (*KStN 1112* / 1 November 1941) and a heavy company with one engineer platoon and two antitank platoons (one with three towed 37mm antitank guns and one with two towed 50mm antitank guns). See Veit Scherzer, *Deutsche Truppen im Zweiten Weltkrieg, Band 5, Die Divisionen, Divisionen und Brigaden mit den Nummern 15 bis 20, Gliederung—Kommandeure—Einsatz—Inhaber höchster Auszeichnungen* (Ranis/Jena, Germany: Scherzers Militaer Verlag, 2009), 64.
3. Apparently, the light armored reconnaissance company authorized (*KStN 1113 (gp)* / 1 March 1942) was to be filled with captured vehicles. See Scherzer, *Deutsche Truppen, Band 5*, 66.
4. The antitank platoon apparently had a 28mm antitank gun in its establishment as well. See Veit Scherzer, *Deutsche Truppen im Zweiten Weltkrieg, Band 6, Die Divisionen, Divisionen und Brigaden mit den Nummern 21 bis 28, Gliederung—Kommandeure—Einsatz—Inhaber höchster Auszeichnungen* (Ranis/Jena, Germany: Scherzers Militaer Verlag, 2010), 79–80.
5. Ibid.
6. In addition to the usual sources, the authors are indebted to Martin Block, who provided extra background information on this battalion through a posting on the Axis History Forum (http://forum.axishistory.com/viewtopic.php?f=47&t=106132).
7. These were the 2.8cm *schwere Panzerbüchse 41*, featuring a cone-shaped barrel that squeezed the round down from 28mm to 20mm, thus increasing its velocity. A total of 2,797 were produced between 1940 and 1943. For a discussion of the weapon's advantages and disadvantages, see Panzerworld, "*schwere Panzerbüchse 41*" (www.panzerworld.com/s-pz-b-41) and Lexikon der Wehrmacht, "*Panzerbüchsen*" (www.lexikon-der-wehrmacht.de/Waffen/panzerbuchsen-R.htm).
8. More information concerning this unit, along with numerous images, can be found in *Scouts Out*.
9. On the other hand, the memoirs of someone assigned to the battalion has listed the organization of the company somewhat differently:

    Headquarters with radio vehicles and forty 3-ton Opel *Blitz* trucks.

    1st Platoon: Mixed armored car platoon with eight- and four-wheeled armored cars.

    2nd Platoon: Light reconnaissance platoon with *SPW's*

    3rd Platoon: Antitank platoon with towed 5cm antitank guns with 1-ton prime movers (*Sd.Kfz. 10*).

    4th Platoon: Antiaircraft platoon with 2cm *Flak* mounted on 1-ton half-track prime movers (*Sd.Kfz. 10*).

    See Otto Henning, *Als Panzerschütze beim Deutschen Afrika Korps, 1941–1943* (Würzburg, Germany: Verlagshaus Würzburg (Flechsig), 2006), 31. Photos of the rail-loading operation in Germany for deployment to Africa corroborate Henning's assertions. See Henning's photos in his book, starting on page 38, and essentially the same images reproduced in *Scouts Out*.
10. Heinz-Dietrich Aberger, *Die 5. (lei)/21. Panzer-Division in Nordafrika, 1941–1943: Dem Gedenken der gefallenen Kameraden, die in Libyen, Ägypten, Tunesien und auf dem Grunde des Mittelmeeres ruhen und denen, die in Gefangenschaft gestorben sind* (Reutlingen, Germany: Preußischer Militär-Verlag, 1994), 33.
11. Hellmuth Schroetter, *Panzer rollen in Afrika vor, Mit Rommel von Tripolis bis El Alamein* (Wiesbaden and Munich: Limes Verlag, 1985), 24–25.
12. Schroetter is referring to the *Arco dei Fileni*, which had been erected under the orders of Mussolini to commemorate Italian colonization efforts in the region.
13. Schroetter, *Panzer rollen in Afrika*, 18.
14. Ibid., 35–36.
15. Ibid., 84–85.
16. Ibid., 106–7.
17. Ibid., 122, 129.
18. Ibid., 139–40.
19. In German, it rhymes: *In Rußland kämpft das deutsche Heer, in Afrika die Feuerwehr!*
20. Gerhard Fiebig and Johannes Keller, *Pz.A.A. 33 in Nordafrika* (Freiburg im Breisgau: Self-published by the veterans' association, [1988?]), 35–36.
21. Henning, *Als Panzerschütze*, 129–30.

CHAPTER 6

1. Depending on the source, German armor figures number around 4,300 compared to between 15,000 and 25,000 Soviet equivalents. The *Luftwaffe* numbered around 4,400 tactical airframes, while the Red Air Force had some 35,000 to 40,000 aircraft. As always, comparisons are difficult, since not all weaponry on either side was considered suitable for combat employment, but it at least allows an idea of the comparative odds. According to the latest reliable estimates, the *Luftwaffe* fielded around 2,000 operational aircraft compared to some 9,000 Soviet aircraft at the beginning of *Barbarossa*.
2. The armored car company of *Panzer-Aufklärungs-Abteilung 5* had been sunk while being transported from Greece to Italy (May 1941). It was in the process of being reconstituted.

3. Dr. Leo G. Niehorster, *German World War II Organizational Series, Volume 3/I: Mechanized Army Divisions (22nd June 1941)* (Hannover, Germany: Self-published, 1992), 47. According to Niehorster, the battalion signals platoons did not have any armored radio cars, although he does not specify what type of vehicles replaced them (presumably wheeled equivalents). Since all of the Panhard armored cars, except for the radio cars, were armed the same, the distinctions between heavy and light platoons were probably dispensed with as they were no longer relevant. Per Niehorster, all armored cars, except for the *Sd.Kfz. 263* and the *Sd.Kfz. 223*, were replaced by the standard *Panzerspähwagen 178(f)*. The *Sd.Kfz. 263* was replaced with a Panhard outfitted with two machine guns, and the *Sd.Kfz. 223* with a Panhard that had the standard armament but featured a frame antenna. Thus, the armored car company of the battalion had twenty standard Panhards in its line platoons and five radio armored cars in its signals section: in all, twenty-four 25mm automatic cannon and twenty-six machine guns.
4. Dr. Leo G. Niehorster, *German World War II Organizational Series, Volume 3/II: Mechanized GHQ Units and Waffen-SS Divisions (22nd June 1941)* (Hannover, Germany: Self-published, 1992), 68. According to Niehorster, the company headquarters was organized under *KStN 1162*, but there were no line armored car assets. These were filled in by the attachment of two armored car platoons organized under *KStN 1137* (1 February 1941).
5. Stoves, *Die 1. Panzer-Division*, 205.
6. Ibid., 205–6.
7. Ibid., 210–11.
8. Ibid., 222–23.
9. Roughly: Russians above us . . . there's a lot / Diving low and firing their shot / Where is Professor Messerschmitt? / If he doesn't come, we plan to quit. Then, the final verse of doggerel: Hurrah, hurrah, hurrah! / Are those fighters that we saw? / Too bad, no Nazi flyers / Just some more Bolshevik divers!
10. Tolmein, *Spähtrupp*, 129–30.
11. 3rd Panzer Division, *Armored Bears 1*, 154.
12. Ibid., 189.
13. Ibid., 231.
14. Ibid., 269.
15. Hans Schäufler, ed., *Knight's Cross Panzers: The German 35th Panzer Regiment in World War II* (Mechanicsburg, PA: Stackpole Books, 2010), 84–86.
16. Hasso E. V. Von Manteuffel, *General der Panzertruppen a.D., Die 7. Panzer-Division im Zweiten Weltkrieg: Einsatz und Kampf der "Gespenster-Division" 1939–1945* (Friedberg, Germany: Podzun-Pallas-Verlag, 1986, reprint), 162.
17. Ibid., 169.
18. *Die Panzer-Aufklärungs-Abteilung 12*, a collection of writings and documentary materials that were used as handouts at a veterans' meeting in the 1950s and later privately bound. Not paginated.
19. G. W. Jeffke, *Hauptmann a.D., Geschichte, Aufklärungs-Abteilung (tmot) 18—18. Infanterie-Division (tmot)—vom 24.8.1939 bis 1.10.1942* (Münster, Germany: Kameradschaft 8. Reiter, 1992), 71–73.
20. Ibid., 59–60.
21. Ibid., 85–89.
22. Original text has a typo and a missing word, although from context it is clear that this was meant.
23. Ernst August Krag, *An der Spitze im Bild: Späher—Aufklärer—Kradschützen in den Divisionen der Waffen-SS* (Coburg, Germany: Nation Europa Verlag, 2005), 101–4.
24. Original German is *Schlachtfeld*, which carries the duel meaning of "battlefield" and "field of slaughter."
25. Memminger, *Die Kriegsgeschichte, Band I*, D305–9.
26. Ibid., D308.
27. Ibid., D309.
28. Ibid., D319.
29. Ibid., D323.
30. Ibid., D326–27.
31. Ibid., D335.
32. As is typical in accounts such as these, the narrator refers to himself in the third person.
33. Memminger, *Die Kriegsgeschichte, Band I*, D343.
34. Ibid., D349–50.
35. Ibid., D394.
36. Tolmein, *Spähtrupp*, 109–14. This report was taken verbatim from holdings in the German federal Archives in Freiburg/Breisgau found under the call number RH 27-13/45: "Bericht über die Vormarschstraße, 26./27. Juni 1941."
37. Willi Kubik, *Erinnerungen eines Panzerschützen, 1941–1945: Tagebuchaufzeichnungen eines Panzerschützen der Panzer-Aufklärungs-Abteilung 13 im Russlandfeldzug* (Würzburg, Germany: Flechsig, 2004), 20–23.

CHAPTER 7

1. Dr. Leo G. Niehorster, *German World War II Organizational Series, Volume 4/I: Mechanized Army Divisions (28th June 1942)* (Canada: Self-published, 1994), 19. However, see also Veit Scherzer, *Deutsche Truppen im Zweiten Weltkrieg, Band 3, Die Divisionen, Divisionen und Brigaden mit den Nummern 4 bis 8, Gliederung—Kommandeure—Einsatz—Inhaber höchster Auszeichnungen* (Ranis/Jena, Germany: Scherzers Militaer Verlag, 2008), 487; in contrast, Scherzer states that the division had its armored car company. The organizational chart for fall 1942 on page 499 also indicates the presence of an armored car company.
2. Dr. Leo G. Niehorster, *German World War II Organizational Series, Volume 4/II: Mechanized GHQ Units and Waffen-SS Formations (28th June 1942)* (Hannover, Germany: Self-published, 2004), 62. Several other sources consulted do not list the motorcycle infantry company or the attached armored car platoon. See Axis History Forum (http://forum.axishistory.com/

viewtopic.php?t=140401) and the Lexikon of the 2nd World War (www.zweiter-weltkrieg-lexikon.de/index2.php?option=com_content&task=emailform&id=581&itemid=41).

3. Rolf Hinze, *Hitze, Frost und Pulverdampf: Der Schicksalsweg der 20. Panzer-Division* (Bochum, Germany: Heinrich Pöppinghaus Verlag, 1981). The unofficial divisional history is silent on this matter. Correspondence with former unit members has indicated that most of the French armored cars were probably destroyed during the first round of winter fighting. In an organization chart dated 1 September 1942, the armored scout company is listed as "not currently present."
4. This motorized corps was not redesignated as a *Panzer-Korps* until 10 July 1942.
5. This is the theoretical organization. Based on organizational charts shown in Veit Scherzer, *Deutsche Truppen im Zweiten Weltkrieg, Band 6, Die Divisionen, Divisionen und Brigaden mit den Nummern 21 bis 28, Gliederung—Kommandeure—Einsatz—Inhaber höchster Auszeichnungen* (Ranis/Jena, Germany: Scherzers Militaer Verlag, 2010), 159–60, the battalion only had three motorcycle infantry companies in April 1943 and no light armored reconnaissance company. There is one of the latter shown in the organizational chart for October 1942, but it is doubtful this was fielded, since the division had already been decimated in earlier fighting and tasked to provide considerable resources for the activation of the *27. Panzer-Division*.
6. This motorized corps was not redesignated as a *Panzer-Korps* until 9 July 1942.
7. Information provided the authors by Scott Pritchett, extracted from his three-volume history of the division: *Uniforms and Insignia of the Großdeutschland division* (Atglen, PA: Schiffer Publishing, 2010).
8. Niehorster, IV/1, 11, refers to it as a regiment, while Roger James Bender and George A. Petersen, *Hermann Göring from Regiment to Fallschirmpanzerkorps* (Atglen, PA: Schiffer Publishing, 1993), 17, refer to it as a brigade.
9. Bender and Petersen, *Hermann Göring*, 20–24. The armored car platoon was attached to the headquarters company. The armored car company was not earmarked to be activated until April 1943. When deployed to North Africa, only the 1st, 5th, and 6th Companies were sent.
10. As with *Kradschützen-Bataillon 20* of the *20. Panzer-Division*, this battalion had two companies of Panhard armored cars at the start of Barbarossa. Presumably, the battalion was reorganized to the standard armored division model while undergoing reconstitution in France in the summer of 1942.
11. 3rd Panzer Division, *Armored Bears 1*, 305.
12. Ibid., 309–10.
13. Pape was officially presented with the award on 10 February 1942. He later went on to become the 301st recipient of the Oak Leaves to the Knight's Cross of the Iron Cross (15 September 1943). He passed away in his native town of Düsseldorf on 21 January 1986.
14. Veterans of the 3rd Panzer Division, *Armored Bears: The German 3rd Panzer Division in World War II, Vol. 2* (Mechanicsburg, PA: Stackpole Books, 2013), 3.
15. Ibid., 25.
16. Ibid., 51–52.
17. Helmuth Spaeter, *The History of Panzerkorps Großdeutschland, Volume 1* (Winnipeg, Canada: J. J. Fedorowicz Publishing, 1992), 360.
18. *Major* Horst von Usedom was the commander of the motorcycle infantry battalion at the time, while also commanding the division's advance guard.
19. 3rd Panzer Division, *Armored Bears 2*, 78.
20. Kubik, *Erinnerungen eines Panzerschützen*, 199–202.
21. Ibid., 267–68.
22. Dr. F. M. von Senger und Etterlin Jr., *Die 24. Panzer-Division, vormals 1. Kavallerie-Division, 1939–1945* (Friedberg, Germany: Podzun-Pallas-Verlag, 1986), 77–78.
23. Ibid., 92–94.
24. Ibid., 110–11.
25. Ibid., 111–13.
26. Scott Pritchett in correspondence with the authors.

CHAPTER 8

1. Essentially wiped out at Stalingrad, the division was in the process of being reconstituted. This was the proposed organization.
2. This was another so-called "Stalingrad" division, which was still in the process of being reconstituted.
3. Essentially wiped out at Stalingrad, the *29. Panzergrenadier-Division* was also in the process of being reconstituted. This was the proposed organization.
4. This is based on an organization chart dated 1 May 1944. Unfortunately, the authors have been unable to locate an organization chart for 1943. A captured document found in Allied intelligence holdings and dated March 1944 lists a different organization, with the battalion having six companies: one *Volkswagen* company (presumably *KStN 1113 (VW)* of 18 March 1942; one motorcycle infantry company (presumably *KStN 1112* of 1 November 1941); one armored car company (presumably *KStN 1162* of 1 November 1941); one antitank company (unknown composition); one heavy company (not specified whether motorized or armored, but presumably the former); and one antiaircraft company (2cm) (composition unknown). See National Archives, Microfiche T315, Roll 2296.
5. The *Sd.Kfz. 250/3*, the light radio armored personnel carrier, was often issued in lieu of the *Sd.Kfz. 250/5*, as verified by a number of sources from these units.
6. Fiebig and Keller, *Pz.A.A. 33*, 256–61. As with most unit histories, the narrative is intended primarily for former members of the battalion and thus is often an aggregate of individual contributions, which tends to make the narrative frequently disjointed.

7. The battalion continued to operate as part of the *15. Panzergrenadier-Division* in the West, detraining in southwestern Germany in the vicinity of Saarbrücken in early September 1944 and progressively moving farther north, eventually fighting in Holland in October of the same year. In mid-December it was pulled out of the front and transported to the Milowitz Training Area (near Prague), where it underwent a hasty reconstitution, and the armored cars were given the rudiments of an overhaul at the Skoda works. It was then sent to the East, fighting in the Stettin area until March 1945. During that time period, it was separated from the division (which was still in the West). Issued more armored cars, the scout company calibrated its weapons in early April 1945. Lacking fuel, the vehicles were, on one occasion, towed by cows to the edge of a village. The battalion was eventually attached to the *III. SS-Panzer-Korps (germanisches)* and participated in the fighting for Berlin, attached to the *30. Waffen-Grenadier-Division der Waffen-SS Charlemagne*. What remained of the battalion largely succeeded in making it to the Elbe, where it crossed in small groups and surrendered to English and U.S. forces.

CHAPTER 9

1. The divisions listed here were either forming or being reconstituted during the period in question, thus allowing only a "snapshot" view of the organization as it was (or as proposed).
2. Dr. Leo G. Niehorster, *German World War II Organizational Series, Volume 5/I: Mechanized Army Divisions (4th July 1943)* (Crownhill, England: The Military Press, 2004), 30, shows this as the proposed organization for the battalion in July 1943. Although most of the division was receiving French vehicles at the time, it is assumed that the motorcycle reconnaissance companies probably had standard German equipment. By that fall, it had been reorganized as a Model 43 armored reconnaissance battalion. See Scherzer, *Deutsche Truppen, Band 6*, 97.
3. Scherzer, *Deutsche Truppen, Band 6*, 434, 441–42, shows the 4th Company being reorganized from an armored light reconnaissance company into an armored half-track scout company. To that end, the company was detached from the battalion for much of 1944 while it underwent the necessary reorganization and training in Camp Senne and Wildflecken Training Area.
4. Ibid., 293–94, indicates that only the armored car troop remained a reconnaissance element of the division for much of 1944. It reported directly to the division headquarters, while the remainder of the battalion—heavily attrited—was attached to *Panzergrenadier-Regiment 26* of the division.
5. An organization chart dated May 1944 shows a standard Model 43 organization for the reconnaissance battalion. By this time, the division was also redesignated as a *Panzer-Division*.
6. Karl Kollatz, "Fritz Feßmann, ein Schwertertträger der Panzeraufklärer" in *Der Landser Großband, Erlebnisberichte zur Geschichte des Zweiten Weltkriegs* (Rastatt, Germany: Pabel-Moewig Verlag KG, n.d.), 51–55. Karl Kollatz was a pen name of Franz Kurowski. Given Kurowski's penchant for embellishment, it is not entirely certain where Feßmann's account ends and Kurowski's account begins. Nonetheless, it provides a compelling narrative of the fighting around Stalingrad from the perspective of the commander of an armored car company. Fritz Feßmann, born in Urbach on Christmas Day in 1915, received the Knight's Cross to the Iron Cross on 27 October 1941, while serving as a *Leutnant der Reserve* and platoon leader in the *1./Panzer-Aufklärungs-Abteilung 7*. He went on to receive the Oak Leaves to the Knight's Cross on 4 January 1943, while serving as an *Oberleutnant der Reserve* and company commander of the *1./Kradschützen-Bataillon 64* (his award was based on the actions recounted in the narrative), and posthumously received the Swords to the Oak Leaves on 11 October 1944 as the commander of *Panzer-Aufklärungs-Abteilung 5*. He was also posthumously promoted to *Major der Reserve*.
7. Helmuth Spaeter, *The History of Panzerkorps Großdeutschland, Volume 2* (Winnipeg, Canada: J. J. Fedorowicz Publishing, 1995), 61–62. Although the authors do not have access to the original German, some words and phraseology have been changed to more clearly adhere to the intent of the author and common military terminology.
8. 3rd Panzer Division, *Armored Bears 2*, 167–68.
9. Deichen received the award on 10 September 1943. He was also a recipient of the German Cross in Gold, which he received on 8 May 1943, for the time he had served as the company commander of the *2./Kradschützen-Bataillon 3*. Although not noted in the text, Deichen was a *Hauptmann der Reserve* and went on to serve in the *Bundeswehr*, rising to the rank of *Brigade-General*.
10. Wolfgang Vopersal, *Soldaten, Kämpfer, Kameraden: Marsch und Kämpfe der SS-Totenkopfdivision, Band IIIb: Operation "Zitadelle" / Kämpfe am Mius / Abwehrkämpfe westlich und südwestlich Charkow / Rückzugskämpfe auf Krementschug / Berichtigungen zu Band III* (Osnabrück, Germany: Biblio Verlag, 1987), 335.
11. Ibid., 339–40.
12. Ibid., 393–96.
13. Spaeter, *History, Vol. 2*, 136–37.
14. 3rd Panzer Division, *Armored Bears 2*, 177.
15. Vopersal, *Soldaten, Band IIIb*, 478–82.
16. Hax refers to himself as a motorcycle infantryman as a badge of honor. This was quite common among former

motorcycle infantrymen who had made the switch to other vehicles.
17. Vopersal *Soldaten, Band IIIb*, 501–2.
18. Plato, *Die Geschichte*, 288–90.
19. Stoves, *Die 1. Panzer-Division*, 427–28.
20. Schäufler, *Knight's Cross Panzers*, 246–51.
21. Werner Haupt, *Die 8. Panzer-Division im 2. Weltkrieg* (Friedberg, Germany: Podzun-Pallas-Verlag, 1987), 308–9.

CHAPTER 10

1. Kamen Nevenkin, *Fire Brigades: Panzer Divisions 1943–1945* (Winnipeg, Canada: J. J. Fedorowicz Publishing, 2008), 491.
2. J. Dugdale, *Panzer Divisions: Panzer Grenadier Divisions, Panzer Brigades of the Army and the Waffen SS in the West, Autumn 1944–February 1945, Ardennes and Nordwind, Their Detailed and Precise Strengths and Organizations, Volume 1, Part 2, October 1944, Refitting and Re-Equipment* (Milton Keynes, England: The Military Press, 2000), 54. There may be a discrepancy, inasmuch as Dugdale also reports eleven 2cm main guns for the company, two more than the number of *Sd.Kfz. 250/9's* reported as on hand. The next month's strength report indicates two *Sd.Kfz. 222's* on hand, which would account for the missing vehicles, if they were unintentionally not placed on the report and also assigned to the 1st Company.
3. Ibid., 53–54. This is also another potential discrepancy, since the division reported twenty-six armored cars on hand but only nine are reflected in the breakdown of the reconnaissance battalion.
4. Ibid., 51–55.
5. J. Dugdale, *Panzer Divisions, Volume 1, Part 3, November 1944, Refitting and Re-Equipment* (Milton Keynes, England: The Military Press, 2001), 37–39, 44. Dugdale also mentions that there was an *Sd.Kfz. 250* variant assigned to the Supply Company. The actual armored car number may also be off, since the division report indicates fifteen vehicles on hand, of which one was in short-term and three were in long-term maintenance. Those fifteen armored cars are two more than indicated in the specific vehicular breakdown.
6. Mike Wood and J. Dugdale, *Orders of Battle: Waffen-SS Panzer Units in Normandy 1944* (Farnborough, England: Books International, 2000), 134. Wood and Dugdale provide by far the most detailed analysis of the organization status of the formations they study, with the data coming from original documents of the time. Unfortunately, it is difficult to locate this title and the other organizational books published solely by Dugdale. The actual number of *Sd.Kfz. 250/9's* listed may not be correct, since Wood and Dugdale list only eleven 2cm main guns for the company.
7. Niklas Zetterling, *Normandy 1944: German Military Organization, Combat Power and Organizational Effectiveness* (Winnipeg, Canada: J. J. Fedorowicz Publishing, 2000), 350–51. Although enlisted personnel were well over 100 percent, there was a critical shortfall in noncommissioned (44 percent) and commissioned officers (25 percent) within the division. Within the reconnaissance battalion, the percentages were better: officers—23/25 = 92 percent; noncommissioned officers—136/221 = 61 percent; and enlisted—864/690 = 125 percent.
8. Wood and Dugdale, *Orders of Battle*, 124, 126–27, 129–31, 134, 136–38, 142, 145–47, 150. A strength report submitted on 3 August is also discussed, but the overall vehicle status remains about the same.
9. Nevenkin, *Fire Brigades*, 914. Nevenkin reports the appearance of the *Schwimmwagen* in February 1945 in the 3rd Company. In contrast J. Dugdale, *Panzer Divisions, Volume 1, Part 1, September 1944, Refitting and Re-Equipment* (Milton Keynes, England: The Military Press, 2000), 96, 98–99, lists the vehicles on hand in September 1944, and thus being fielded sometime in August.
10. Dugdale, *Panzer Divisions, Vol. 1, Part 2*, 91–93.
11. Dugdale, *Panzer Divisions, Vol. 1, Part 3*, 88, 92. There is a discrepancy in the number of *Schwimmwagen* on hand, with Dugdale initially indicating forty-two and later thirty-three.
12. Ibid., 91–93.
13. Nevenkin, *Fire Brigades*, 764.
14. Dugdale, *Panzer Divisions, Vol. 1, Part 1*, 27–29, 31.
15. Dugdale, *Panzer Divisions, Vol. 1, Part 2*, 5–7.
16. Dugdale, *Panzer Divisions, Vol. 1, Part 3*, 5–7.
17. J. Dugdale, *Panzer Divisions, Volume 1, Part 4a, December 1944, Refitting and Re-Equipment* (Milton Keynes, England: The Military Press, 2002), 5–8, 12. The actual vehicle types are based on the vehicles within the battalion as part of *Kampfgruppe von Fallois* on 16 December 1944.
18. Wood and Dugdale, *Orders of Battle*, 158, 160, 162. The authors provide conflicting information concerning the numbers and types of armored cars within the 1st Company. Based on the reports submitted on 1 June, and not the authors' tabulated data, it appears the company had thirteen *Sd.Kfz. 222's* and five light armored cars, possibly *Sd.Kfz. 223's*.
19. Assuming the company organization was based on *KStN 1113 (VW)*, dated 1 November 1943, it should only have had eighteen light machine guns. The organization chart for 1 June lists twenty on hand, however. In his memoir, Helmut Günther provides a differing organization, which is probably based on the *KStN* for the *Volkswagen*-equipped armored reconnaissance company in November 1944. See Helmut Günther, *The Eyes of the Division: The Reconnaissance Battalion of the 17. SS-Panzer-Grenadier-Division "Götz von*

Berlichingen" (Winnipeg, Canada: J. J. Fedorowicz Publishing, 2012), 249.
20. Wood and Dugdale, *Orders of Battle*, 153, 155–58, 163. On page 163, the authors also show six flamethrowers and a towed 2cm *Flak* for the heavy company.
21. Nevenkin, *Fire Brigades*, 109.
22. Ibid. Nevenkin indicates that this company should have been an armored reconnaissance company organized under *KStN 1114c*, but the vehicles indicate that it was still a light half-tracked reconnaissance company. See the text that follows.
23. Dugdale, *Panzer Divisions, Vol. 1, Part 1*, 34–37.
24. Dugdale, *Panzer Divisions, Vol. 1, Part 2*, 16–20.
25. Nevenkin, *Fire Brigades*, 109, indicates the company was outfitted with bicycles during this period.
26. Dugdale, *Panzer Divisions, Vol. 1, Part 3*, 16–17.
27. Dugdale, *Panzer Divisions, Vol. 1, Part 4a*, 40–41, 46–47.
28. Wood and Dugdale, *Orders of Battle*, 107, 110, 114.
29. Dugdale, *Panzer Divisions, Vol. 1, Part 1*, 87–90.
30. Ibid., 85–87. Dugdale also shows two more *Sd.Kfz. 250* variants assigned to the division than reported for the reconnaissance battalion. Using those figures (sixteen vehicles), six were in short-term maintenance and one in long-term maintenance. Based on the November report, these vehicles may have been issued to the mechanized infantry regiments.
31. Dugdale, *Panzer Divisions, Vol. 1, Part 3*, 81–83. Unlike many of the reconnaissance battalions of the period, the real issue within the *Frundsberg* reconnaissance battalion was manpower shortfalls. The battalion reported only 44 percent personnel end strength, indicating it was heavily involved in direct combat action.
32. Wood and Dugdale, *Orders of Battle*, 77–79, 83.
33. Ibid., 85–88, 92.
34. Dugdale, *Panzer Divisions, Vol. 1, Part 1*, 72–73.
35. Dugdale, *Panzer Divisions, Vol. 1, Part 2*, 72–77.
36. Dugdale, *Panzer Divisions, Vol. 1, Part 3*, 66, 68. Even Dugdale's numbers do not agree here, indicating that one of the reports cited possibly has a wrong date. On page 66, the number of *Sd.Kfz. 250* variants assigned to the company is listed as fourteen; on page 68, it is listed as seven. It should also be noted that the 1st Company did not become a true *Cäsar* company until February 1945 when it received its complement of sixteen *Sd.Kfz. 250/9's*.
37. Ibid. Once again, the numbers for the *Sd.Kfz. 250* do not completely agree, with the total numbers of *Sd.Kfz. 250*s given on page 66 as being fifteen, while the number listed on page 68 is twenty-two.
38. Ibid., 66–69.
39. Dugdale, *Panzer Divisions, Vol. 1, Part 4a*,108–11.
40. Wood and Dugdale, *Orders of Battle*, 104, indicates a total of eighteen 2cm main guns in the company. Assuming that there were actually six *Sd.Kfz. 231's* and *232's*, that would make the remaining armored cars all *Sd.Kfz. 222's*, although the text indicates otherwise.
41. Ibid., 97, 104.
42. Dugdale, *Panzer Divisions, Vol. 1, Part 1*, 77–80.
43. Dugdale, *Panzer Divisions, Vol. 1, Part 2*, 80–81.
44. Dugdale, *Panzer Divisions, Vol. 1, Part 3*, 71–73.
45. Dugdale, *Panzer Divisions, Vol. 1, Part 4a*, 117–19, 125.
46. Wood and Dugdale, *Orders of Battle*, 35, 39, 43, 46. Since numbers relating to light half-tracks were reported in the aggregate on the monthly unit status reports, it is difficult to pinpoint exact numbers of half-tracked vehicles within the companies. The following numbers of *Sd.Kfz. 250's* were on hand on 15 June 1944 (authorized/actual): *Sd.Kfz. 250/1* (22/24), *Sd.Kfz. 250/2* (2/0), *Sd.Kfz. 250/3* (7/2), *Sd.Kfz. 250/5* (16/0), *Sd.Kfz. 250/7* (4/4), and *Sd.Kfz. 250/9* (16/0).
47. Ibid., 48, 50, 54, 61. The following numbers of *Sd.Kfz. 250's* were on hand on 15 June 1944 (authorized/actual): *Sd.Kfz. 250/1* (22/24), *Sd.Kfz. 250/2* (3/0), *Sd.Kfz. 250/3* (4/2), *Sd.Kfz. 250/5* (16/0), *Sd.Kfz. 250/7* (4/4), *Sd.Kfz. 250/8* (2/0), and *Sd.Kfz. 250/9* (16/0).
48. Wood and Dugdale, *Orders of Battle*, 66, 70.
49. Dugdale, *Panzer Divisions, Vol. 1, Part 1*, 66–67.
50. Dugdale, *Panzer Divisions, Vol. 1, Part 2*, 66–67.
51. Dugdale, *Panzer Divisions, Vol. 1, Part 3*, 58–59. Dugdale shows the sole *Sd.Kfz. 222* as having been assigned to the 1st Company. For simplicity, the authors have assigned this vehicle to the Headquarters Company. Of course, the possibility exists that this vehicle was assigned to the personnel unit that was supposed to become the 1st Company. Even though it was to have been a half-tracked scout company, it still needed vehicles on which to train and, by this stage in the war, the *Sd.Kfz. 222* was still available within the training base, even though it had largely been removed from front-line service.
52. Nevenkin, *Fire Brigades*, 598.
53. Dugdale, *Panzer Divisions, Vol. 1, Part 1*, 60–62. There were two *Sd.Kfz. 234/1's* and one *Sd.Kfz. 234/3* on hand. Of the sixteen *Sd.Kfz. 250* variants, six were in short-term maintenance. Included among the *Sd.Kfz. 250* variants were four *Sd.Kfz. 250/9's*. Heinz Guderian, *Das letzte Kriegsjahr im Westen: Die Geschichte der 116. Panzer-Division—Windhund Division—1944–1945* (Sankt Augustin: Self-published, 1994), 569, shows a report dated 15 September with equally drastic numbers. It is interesting to note that two 5cm main guns were also reported, however, indicting the possible presence of two *Sd.Kfz. 234/2's*. On page 570, Guderian shows another strength report, this one dated 0600 hours on 24 September, which shows an increase of four 2cm main guns and no more 5cm main guns.
54. Dugdale, *Panzer Divisions, Vol. 1, Part 2*, 58–59, shows a slight discrepancy, since the division report indicated forty *Sd.Kfz. 250* variants on hand (with four

in short-term and seven in long-term maintenance), whereas Dugdale's tabulated data only shows a total of thirty-four vehicles.
55. Ibid., 57–59.
56. Dugdale, *Panzer Divisions, Vol. 1, Part 3*, 50. This is the only reconnaissance battalion among those listed that reports the presence of the *Drilling*-equipped *Sd.Kfz. 251*. Each mount had three 1.5cm *Flak*.
57. Ibid., 45–47, 50.
58. Nevenkin, *Fire Brigades*, 270–75, 280. Dugdale, in contrast, shows the status report dated 1 September 1944 with figures that indicate a considerably different situation (see entries for September 1944). Part of the reason for the discrepancies may be the fact that the division was generally employed piecemeal during the fighting in Normandy in August and that many of its elements had already been pulled out of the line by the time of the September report, while other elements were still committed.
59. Dugdale, *Panzer Divisions, Vol. 1, Part 1*, 39–44. Dugdale notes that the reconnaissance battalion probably had the most combat power of any battalion in the division at this point.
60. Dugdale, *Panzer Divisions, Vol. 1, Part 2*, 24. The official monthly report, shown in the same book in summarized form on page 25, shows slightly differing figures.
61. The last calculation does not reflect the heavy company, which was in the process of being reconstituted at the time and had been withdrawn from front-line service. Figures for October taken from Dugdale, *Panzer Divisions, Vol. 1, Part 2*, 23–25.
62. Ibid., 21–23.
63. Dugdale, *Panzer Divisions, Vol. 1, Part 4a*, 79–81, 88–89.
64. Hans Stöber, *Die Sturmflut und das Ende: Geschichte der 17. SS-Panzergrenadierdivision "Götz von Berlichingen," Band I: Die Invasion* (Osnabrück, Germany: Munin Verlag GmbH, 1976), 92–96. Günther is a compelling writer, and for those interested in his translated memoirs, see *The Eyes of the Division: The Reconnaissance Battalion of the 17. SS-Panzer-Grenadier-Division "Götz von Berlichingen"* (Winnipeg, Canada: J. J. Fedorowicz Publishing, 2012) and *Hot Motors, Cold Feet: A Memoir of Service with the Motorcycle Battalion of SS-Division "Reich," 1940–1941* (Winnipeg, Canada: J. J. Fedorowicz Publishing, 2004).
65. Götz von Berlichingen was an imperial knight (*Reichsritter*) and mercenary who lived from 1480 to 1561. He was made famous though the eponymous play by Goethe, in which Götz stated to an opponent, " . . . *sag's ihm, er kann mich im Arsche lecken!*" (" . . . tell him he can kiss my ass!"). Needless to say, the common soldiers of the division named after the feisty knight made a lot of mileage out of the saying, which is often called the "Swabian salute."
66. Krag, *An der Spitze im Bild*, 229–30. Although the book also features an adequate translation of the original German, it is included here since many readers may not have access to the German title. This translation is by the authors.
67. Rolf Michaelis, *Die 10. SS-Panzer-Division "Frundsberg"* (Eggolsheim, Germany: Dörfler Verlag GmbH, 2004), 107–8. Unfortunately, the author does not identify the soldier or the source.
68. The awards process, of course, was affected not only by deeds but also by the culture of the unit (e.g., whether awards were recommended/presented profusely or sparingly) and the date (with progressively more awards handed out as Germany's fortunes waned on the battlefield).
69. Veit Scherzer, *Himmlers Militärische Elite: Die höchst dekorierten Angehörigen der Waffen-SS, Band 1: Adam–Kauth* (Bayreuth, Germany: Veit Scherzer Verlag, 2014), 103.
70. Ibid., 147.
71. Ibid., 345.
72. Ibid., 374.
73. Ibid., 423. Born on Christmas day in 1922, Harmstorf was still alive at the time of this writing (January 2015), according to Scherzer.
74. Karl, *Aus eigenem Entschluß*, 473–74. Although the recommendations are not cited directly, the author builds his narrative around them.
75. This footage can be seen on any number of social media sites.

CHAPTER 11

1. See the Axis History website for a complete order of battle for the German Armed Forces for this date (www.axishistory.com/other-aspects/campaigns-a-operations/134-campaigns-a-operations/campaigns-a-operations/1931-15-june-1944-the-battle-between-two-fronts). The estimates for the composition of the armored reconnaissance battalions of the various divisions are gleaned from the Scherzer divisional series, the Nevenkin book, and the various postings and direct correspondence to the authors from Martin Block, unless otherwise referenced.

When no armored cars or light half-tracks are indicated as being in a formation, it does not necessarily mean there were none. In some cases, the author of the report left those figures off or forgot to enter them. These reports were intended to be a "snapshot" of the formation at a point in time and were prone to human error, especially under the stress of combat. Medium half-track strengths are generally not reported, unless exact figures for the reconnaissance element are known, since the number of *Sd.Kfz. 251* variants were reported in the aggregate for all formations across the division.

Formations not listed—even though they may have *Panzer* in the designation—are omitted because they did not have motorized, mechanized, or armored scout or reconnaissance assets, or they had been depleted to such an extent that they were combat ineffective. Likewise, the plethora of *ad hoc* formations created at the very end of the war are not listed because no definitive strength figures are available or they saw combat for only a few days.

2. One of the problems the authors had was in deciding how much information to present on certain formations. Martin Block and Hans Weber, both experts in this particular area, had this additional information concerning *Panzer-Aufklärungs-Abteilung 4* that they had posted on the enthusiast website Feldgrau (www.feldgrau.net/forum/viewtopic.php?f=24&t=15500). Here are some excerpts in slightly abridged—and in some cases rewritten—format:

(Hans Weber, Monday, 27 June 2005 at 1300): [The battalion] never converted to the 1944 organization . . . [It used a Model 43 organization for the rest of the war.] . . . During 1944, it was not pulled out of the front to refresh. This happened only in January 1945. [Weber then goes on to describe the battalion based on the organization chart.] The rightmost symbol is for the *schwerer (s) Panzer-Späh-Zug (7.5cm)*. A unit raised only on special order, which was issued in this case. It was equipped with the older *Sd.Kfz 233*. Six were issued in September 1943, and they were still around more than a year later. One was in repair at the end of 1944, and it seems that the problem proved to be fatal. Thus, only five *Sd.Kfz 233's* were on hand in March 1945, each with a *7.5cm Kwk* [main gun] and one light machine gun. Note that their number is included in the total of twenty-two heavy armored cars.

The *1./Panzer-Aufklärungs-Abteilung 4* was a *Panzerspäh-Kompanie*. As can be expected, not having converted to the type 1944 organization, it did not become part of the Headquarters Company, nor did it have any *Sd.Kfz. 234's* issued prior to 1945. Instead, it had to work with a mixture of light and heavy armored cars the whole year. The standard Model 43 organization consisted of six sections of light four-wheelers, with two *Sd.Kfz 222's* and one *Sd.Kfz. 223* per section and three heavy sections, with one *Sd.Kfz. 231* and one *Sd.Kfz. 232 (Fu)* each, giving the grand total of eighteen light armored cars and six heavy armored cars. At the end of 1944, we still find four *Sd.Kfz. 223's* (light machine gun), five *Sd.Kfz. 222's* (2cm main gun), and three heavy armored cars (2cm main gun). The number of twenty-two heavy armored cars in March is hard to explain. Delivery reports only report the issue of seven heavy armored cars at the end of January (most probably all with 2cm main guns, thus making them the *Sd.Kfz. 234/1* at this date). I haven't found any deliveries of heavy armored cars between March 1944 and this date, when one *Sd.Kfz. 232* was issued (probably to complement the five *Sd.Kfz. 231's/232's* issued in June 1943 and thus bringing the total of heavy armored cars to the six authorized). In my opinion, it is a typo together with the number of light armored cars. It should read thirteen heavy armored cars (six older *Sd.Kfz. 231's/232's* and seven new *Sd.Kfz. 234/1's*) and four light armored cars, giving the correct total of seventeen 2cm main guns.

The *2./Panzer-Aufklärungs-Abteilung 4* is special as it was the only *Luchs* company, together with the *2./Panzer-Aufklärungs-Abteilung 9* in the German armed forces. Of the twenty-four still with the battalion at the end of 1944—albeit with more than 50 percent in maintenance facilities—losses sustained had to be replaced by the more standard *Sd.Kfz. 250/9* by March 1945. This is shown on the organization chart as a separate platoon.

The *3./* and *4./Panzer-Aufklärungs-Abteilung 4* were both mounted on *Sd.Kfz. 250* variants, which were a rare sight by then and again echoes 1943. They were short of roughly a third of their armored transport each. Interestingly, they used the *Sd.Kfz. 250/9* in these reconnaissance companies as well, which was non-standard. It is even more interesting to note that these vehicles seem to have been brand new. Forty-seven *Sd.Kfz. 250* variants were received in January 1945.

The *5./Panzer-Aufklärungs-Abteilung 4* still had an antitank platoon, which had been officially dropped in the 1944 organization. It is hard to tell whether the self-propelled gun is an older *Marder* or an *Sd.Kfz. 251/22*. I suppose the latter, as the presence of another type of armor would probably have been noted next to the twenty-two medium half-tracks shown. The unit then had three *Sd.Kfz. 251/21 Drilling* and six *Sd.Kfz. 251/9's* with the 7.5cm main gun.

Additional material about *Panzer-Aufklärungs-Abteilung 4* was provided by Martin Block on Sunday, 5 March 2005 at 1323:

A detailed armored vehicle status report in the records of the *4. Panzer-Division* shows that the following types of armored cars were on hand on 2 February 1945: four *Sd.Kfz. 222's*, four *Sd.Kfz. 223's*, three *Sd.Kfz. 232's*, six *Sd.Kfz. 233's*, one *Sd.Kfz. 247*, one *Sd.Kfz. 261*, two *Sd.Kfz. 263's*, eighteen *Panzer II, Ausführung L "Luchs"* (including two in long-term maintenance still in Courland), and seven *Sd.Kfz. 234/1's* (en route to the division;

that these were just *Sd.Kfz. 234/1's* is also confirmed by a document of the quartermaster general of *Heeresgruppe Weichsal*. I have read in some publications that the division also received some *Sd.Kfz. 234/4's* with this delivery, but so far records show otherwise).

On the same date the division reported having these *Sd.Kfz. 250* variants available: twenty-two *Sd.Kfz. 250/1's* (plus one in long-term maintenance, still in Courland), seventeen *Sd.Kfz. 250/3's* (plus one in long-term maintenance, still in Courland), thirteen *Sd.Kfz. 250/5's*, and sixteen *Sd.Kfz. 250/9's*.

This includes forty-five vehicles that had just been delivered (twenty-two *Sd.Kfz. 250/1's*, two *Sd.Kfz. 250/3's*, five *Sd.Kfz. 250/5's*, and sixteen *Sd.Kfz. 250/9's*). As Hans already stated, forty-seven light half-tracks were shipped in January. I don't know whether two either just failed to arrive in time before the document was completed or maybe were just lost.

If and how these figures help to explain those given in the 1 March 1945 order of battle, I leave to someone else. At times this can get frustrating!

One additional note: By an order dated 11 March 1945, *Panzer-Aufklärungs-Abteilung "München"* was consolidated with *Panzer-Aufklärungs-Abteilung 4*. I do not know what equipment the former had still left at that time, but originally it was authorised to have the following assets from the following entities:
- *Panzer-Aufklärungs-Ersatz- und Ausbildungs-Abteilung 7*: two 4-wheeled radio armored cars, two light radio armored cars (Horch), and one *Sd.Kfz. 234/2*
- *Heeres-Nachrichten-Schule Halle*: eight *Sd.Kfz. 251/3's* and three *Sd.Kfz. 250/3's*
- *Heeres-Zeugamt Frankfurt/Oder*: two *Sd.Kfz. 234/1's*, one *Sd.Kfz. 234/3*, and five *Sd.Kfz. 222's*
- *Heeres-Zeugamt Frankfurt/Oder*: sixteen *Sd.Kfz. 250/9's*.

I do not know if the replacement detachment and the signals school eventually did provide what they had been ordered to, but the delivery records show that at least the Inspectorate General of the Armored Forces had shipped three heavy armored cars, seven light armored cars (instead of five), and sixteen light half-tracks.

3. Nevenkin, *Fire Brigades*, 135, states that the 2nd Company was probably equipped with *Sd.Kfz. 250* variants. The 3rd Company did not receive these until February 1944.
4. See the Axis History website for a complete order of battle for the German Armed Forces for this date (www.axishistory.com/other-aspects/campaigns-a-operations/134-campaigns-a-operations/campaigns-a-operations/1932-31-december-1944-the-ardennes-aftermath). As with the previous table, the estimates for the composition of the armored reconnaissance battalions of the various divisions are gleaned from the Scherzer divisional series, the Nevenkin book, and Martin Block, unless otherwise referenced.
5. Rudi Zwiener, Einsätze und Erlebnisse der Stabskompanie der Panzer-Aufklärungs-Abteilung 20 der 20. Panzer-Division (Unpublished manuscript dated January 1997). According to the wartime diary of Rudi Zwiener, who was assigned to the Headquarters Company, the company was issued a total of sixteen *Puma* armored cars. The commander's vehicle was numbered 001. There were six vehicles numbered in a 02 series: 021, 022, 023, 024, 025, and 026. Vehicle 025 was lost on 25 July 1944, while vehicles 021 and 022 were written off on 23 August 1944. Vehicle 026 lasted until 1 May 1945. There were six vehicles in a 03 series; they were numbered from 031 to 036. All survived except vehicle 036, which was written off on 23 April 1945. Finally, there were three vehicles in a 04 series: from 041 to 043, of which 043 was lost on 18 August 1944 and 041 on 13 January 1945. The armored cars of the 02 and 03 series were organized in sections of two, with the "odd" vehicle being the section leader (e.g., 021 was commanded by *Leutnant* von Lüttwitz, while 022 was commanded by *Unteroffizier* Zimmer). The 04 series vehicles appeared to possibly have been reserves, since all of the vehicle commanders were *Unteroffiziere*. There were nine *Pumas* destroyed in all, but Zwiener provides no dates for two of them.

There was also a heavy scout section of three *Sd.Kfz. 234/3's*, numbered 051 to 053. Vehicle 051 was recorded as having a barrel burst on 16 February 1945, making it a prime candidate for a field-expedient conversion of the weaponry of the vehicle to a 2cm *Schwebelafette* that is seen in some postwar scrapyard photographs. Some of the personnel of the battalion picked up leather naval uniforms at a supply depot at Löbau Depot on 20 April 1945, thus explaining some of the uniforms seen in the surrender footage at the end of the chapter.
6. See the Axis History website for a complete order of battle for the German Armed Forces for this date (www.axishistory.com/other-aspects/campaigns-a-operations/134-campaigns-a-operations/campaigns-a-operations/1933-12-april-1945-the-final-days-of-the-third-reich). As with the previous table, the estimates for the composition of the armored reconnaissance battalions of the various divisions are gleaned from the Scherzer divisional series, the Nevenkin book, and Martin Block, unless otherwise referenced.
7. Georg Maier, *Drama Between Budapest and Vienna: The Final Battles of the 6. Panzer-Armee in the East, 1945* (Winnipeg, Canada: J. J. Fedorowicz Publishing, 2004), 3–4, argues convincingly that the prefix *SS*

should never be added when discussing this field formation. Since it is used so often, the authors have included it here parenthetically.
8. The same report only listed "half-tracks," not breaking the figures down into light and heavy. The division had a total of seventy half-tracks (of which fifty-seven were operational). It must be assumed that there were still some half-tracks assigned to the battalion.
9. Stoves, *Die 1. Panzer-Division*, 492.
10. Ibid., 513.
11. Ibid., 632–34, 638, 643–44, 648–49.
12. Hans Erlewein, ed., *Kameraden der SS-Panzer-Aufklärungs-Abteilung 11: 11. SS-Freiwilligen-Panzer-Grenadier-Division "Nordland," Schildern Erlebinisse und Eindrücke* (Unknown: Self-published, 1989), 105–8.
13. Maximilian Wengler was likewise a highly decorated officer. He received the Knight's Cross on 6 October 1942 as an *Oberstleutnant der Reserve* and commander of *Infanterie-Regiment 366*. He became the 404th recipient of the Oak Leaves to the Knight's Cross on 22 February 1944 as an *Oberst der Reserve* and in the same capacity. On 21 January 1945, he became the 123rd recipient of the Swords to the Oak Leaves, while serving as a *Generalmajor der Reserve* and commander of the *227. Infanterie-Division*. He was killed in action on 25 April 1945 while serving as the commander of the *83. Infanterie-Division*.
14. Erlewein, *Kameraden*, 17. Rudolf Saalbach, born in Großenhain (Saxony) on 18 March 1911, was killed in action in the fighting around Berlin on 30 April 1945. He was awarded the Knight's Cross on 12 March 1944.
15. Ibid., 44–45.
16. Ibid., 95–97.
17. Ibid., 79–80.
18. Ibid., 176–77.
19. Ibid., 233–35.
20. Ibid., 77.
21. Ibid., 53–57.
22. Wolfgang Vopersal, *Soldaten, Kämpfer, Kameraden, Marsch und Kämpfe der SS-Totenkopfdivision, Band Vb, Abwehrschlachten nordostwärts Warschau / Verlegung nach Ungarn / Entsatzangriffe in Richtung Budapest / Abwehrkämpfe im Raum Stuhlweißenburg / Rückzugskämpfe auf die Reichsschutzstellung / Endkämpfe in Österreich / Auslieferung der Division / Kriegsgefangenschaft / Truppenkameradschaft* (Osnabrück, Germany: Biblio Verlag, 1991), 532, 535–36.
23. Ibid., 541–42.
24. Ibid., 575–76.
25. Ibid., 730–31.
26. Thomas L. Jentz, *Panzer Tracts No. 15-1: Leichter Schützenpanzerwagen, Sd.Kfz. 250, Ausführungen A and B: History of Production, Variants, Organization and Employment from 1941 to 1945* (Boyds, MD: Panzer Tracts Publishing, 2008).
27. For those interested in seeing other previously unpublished images from this series, see *Scouts Out*.
28. The information in this section comes primarily from Hans Weber in his postings on the enthusiast website Feldgrau, in a thread devoted to the *Sd.Kfz. 234* (www.feldgrau.net/forum/viewtopic.php?f=44&t=21678&sid=8cc3a28e6c92930a71f172fd3a91cb24&start=1).
29. The battalion still had eight *Sd.Kfz. 234/2's*. The number of *Sd.Kfz. 234/1's* is slightly different than originally given in the thread, based on personal email correspondence with Hans Weber (1 February 2015).
30. The battalion still had sixteen *Sd.Kfz. 234/2's*.
31. The battalion still had four *Sd.Kfz. 234/2's*.
32. Weber speculates that this might have gone to the *4./Panzer-Aufklärungs-Lehr-Abteilung Krampnitz*.
33. It is not known why these were sent to the Viennese Police Academy, although the school did fight and was destroyed in the battle for Vienna.

APPENDICES

1. The organizations listed in paragraphs 13, 14, and 16 are illustrative only.
2. This may sound odd to American readers, but what is meant is telephonic reporting, since the post offices in all of the European countries held responsibility at that time for telephone communications and had the capacity in each post office to make telephone calls.
3. Thomas Jentz and Hilary Doyle, *Panzer Tracts No. 15-3: Mittlere Schützenpanzerwagen (Sd.Kfz. 251) Ausf. C& D* (Boyds, MD: Panzer Tracts Publishing, 2006), 64.
4. See the Feldgrau website and the following thread for more information: www.feldgrau.net/forum/viewtopic.php?f=24&t=28046&p=196595&hilit=M%C3%BCnchen+Block#p196595.
5. See Lexikon der Wehrmacht website, www.lexikon-der-wehrmacht.de/Gliederungen/PanzerAufklAbt/Gliederung.htm, entry under "Kraftfahrabteilung Potsdam" (accessed 12 July 2014).
6. See the Feldgrau website and the following thread for more information: www.feldgrau.net/forum/viewtopic.php?f=24&t=32574&p=229124&hilit=martin+block#p229124.

Bibliography

PRIMARY SOURCES

Die Panzer-Aufklärungs-Abteilung 12, a collection of writings and documentary materials that were used as handouts at a veterans' meeting in the 1950s.

Panzer-Aufklärungs-Abteilung "Großdeutschland," a collection of writings and documentary materials that were prepared for former members of the battalion. Undated.

Holdings in the U.S. Government National Archives, all in Record Group 242, Publication T78 with individual rolls listed (available through www.sturmpanzer.com as PDF files):

- *Frontnachweiser*, 9th Edition (1943). Roll 402. Sturmpanzer file: T78R402_H1_082a.pdf.
- *Frontnachweiser*, 10th Edition (1944). Roll 400. Sturmpanzer file: T78R400_H1_067.pdf.
- *Gültigkeitslisten der Kriegsstärken- und Ausrüstungsnachweisungen*, files dated 15 July 1944. Roll 391. Sturmpanzer file: T78R391_H1_001.pdf.
- *Gültigkeitslisten der Kriegsstärken- und Ausrüstungsnachweisungen*, files dated 1 April 1943. Roll 397. Sturmpanzer file: T78R397_H1_032.pdf.
- *Kriegsstärkennachweisungen (Heer), Band 3, Aufklärungstruppen, schnelle Truppen, Kavallerie, 1943/1944.* Roll 392. Sturmpanzer file: T78R392_H1_006.pdf.
- *Kriegsstärkennachweisungen (Heer), Band 8, Schnelle Truppen, Panzer-Einheiten, Panzer-Jäger-Einheiten, Panzer-Grenadier-Einheiten, 1943/1944.* Roll 393. Sturmpanzer file: T78R393_H1_012.pdf.
- *Kriegsstärkennachweisungen (Heer), Band 8a, Schnelle Truppen, Panzer-Einheiten, Panzer-Jäger-Einheiten, Panzer-Grenadier-Einheiten, 1943/1944.* Roll 393. Sturmpanzer file: T78R393_H1_012.pdf.
- *Kriegsstärkennachweisungen (Heer)*, A collection of assorted formations and commands. Roll 397. Sturmpanzer file: T78R397_H1_028a.pdf.

SECONDARY SOURCES

Bender, Roger James, and George A. Petersen. *"Hermann Göring": from Regiment to Fallschirmpanzerkorps.* Atglen, PA: Schiffer Publishing, 1993.

Bender, Roger James, and Richard D. Law. *Uniforms, Organization and History of the Afrikakorps.* Mountain View, CA: R. James Bender Publishing, 1973.

Cramer, Hans. *Die Panzer-Aufklärungs-Lehrabteilung (Kavallerie Lehr- und Versuchsabteilung) von 1937–1940.* Minden, Germany: Albrecht Philler Verlag, n.d.

Dugdale, J. *Panzer Divisions, Volume 1, Part 1, September 1944, Refitting and Re-Equipment.* Milton Keynes, England: The Military Press, 2000.

———. *Panzer Divisions: Panzer Grenadier Divisions, Panzer Brigades of the Army and the Waffen SS in the West, Autumn 1944–February 1945, Ardennes and Nordwind, Their Detailed and Precise Strengths and Organizations, Volume 1, Part 2, October 1944, Refitting and Re-Equipment.* Milton Keynes, England: The Military Press, 2000.

———. *Panzer Divisions, Panzer Grenadier Divisions, Panzer Brigades of the Army and the Waffen SS in the West, Autumn 1944–February 1945, Ardennes and Nordwind, Their Detailed and Precise Strengths and Organizations, Volume 1, Part 3, November 1944, Refitting and Re-Equipment.* Milton Keynes, England: The Military Press, 2001.

———. *Panzer Divisions, Panzer Grenadier Divisions, Panzer Brigades of the Army and the Waffen SS in the West, Autumn 1944–February 1945, Ardennes and Nordwind, Their Detailed and Precise Strengths and Organizations, Volume 1, Part 4a, December 1944, Refitting and Re-Equipment.* Milton Keynes, England: The Military Press, 2002.

Edwards, Robert J., Michael H. Pruett, and Michael Olive, *Scouts Out: A History of German Armored Reconnaissance Units in World War II.* Mechanicsburg, PA: Stackpole Books, 2013.

Erlewein, Hans, ed. *Kameraden der SS-Panzer-Aufklärungs-Abteilung 11, 11. SS-Freiwilligen-Panzer-Grenadier-Division "Nordland," Schildern Erlebnisse und Eindrücke.* Unknown: Self-published, 1989.

Fiebig, Gerhard, and Johannes Keller. *Pz.A.A. 33 in Nordafrika*. Freiburg im Breisgau: Self-published by the veterans' association, [1988?].

Guderian, Heinz Günther. *Das letzte Kriegsjahr im Westen: Die Geschichte der 116. Panzer-Division—Windhund-Division—1944–1945*. Sankt Augustin: Self-published, 1994.

Günther, Helmut, *The Eyes of the Division: The Reconnaissance Battalion of the 17. SS-Panzer-Grenadier-Division "Götz von Berlichingen."* Winnipeg, Canada: J. J. Fedorowicz Publishing, 2012.

Haupt, Werner. *Die 8. Panzer-Division im 2. Weltkrieg*. Friedberg, Germany: Podzun-Pallas-Verlag, 1987.

Henning, Otto. *Als Panzerschütze beim Deutschen Afrika Korps, 1941–1943*. Würzburg, Germany: Verlagshaus Würzburg (Flechsig), 2006.

———. *Als Panzer- und Spähtruppführer in der Panzer-Lehr-Division, 1943–1945*. Würzburg, Germany: Verlagshaus Würzburg (Flechsig), 2006.

Hinze, Rolf. *Hitze, Frost und Pulverdampf: Der Schicksalsweg der 20. Panzer-Division*. Bochum, Germany: Heinrich Pöppinghaus Verlag, 1981.

Jeffke, G. W. *Hauptmann a.D. Geschichte, Aufklärungs-Abteilung (tmot) 18—18. Infanterie-Division (tmot)—vom 24.8.1939 bis 1.10.1942*. Münster, Germany: Kameradschaft 8. Reiter, 1992.

Jentz, Thomas L., and Hilary Louis Doyle. *Panzer Tracts No. 11-2: Aufklärungspanzerwagen (Full- and Half-Tracked Armored vehicles), H8H to Vollkettenaufklärer 38*. Boyds, MD: Panzer Tracts, 2003.

———. *Panzer Tracts No. 15-1: Leichter Schützenpanzerwagen, Sd.Kfz. 250, Ausführungen A and B: History of Production, Variants, Organization and Employment from 1941 to 1945*. Boyds, MD: Panzer Tracts Publishing, 2008.

———. *Panzer Tracts No. 13: Panzerspähwagen, Armored Cars, Sd.Kfz. 3 to Sd.Kfz. 263*. Boyds, MD: Panzer Tracts, 2001.

———. *Panzer Tracts No. 20-2-2: Paper Panzers, Aufklärungs-, Beobachtungs- and Flak-Panzer (Reconnaissance, Observation and Antiaircraft)*. Boyds, MD: Panzer Tracts, 2002.

Karl, Jürgen. *Aus Eigenem Entschluss: die Ritterkreuzträger der Waffen-SS, 1940–1945, Band 1*. Oberhausen, Germany: Adoria-Verlag, 2014.

Krag, Ernst August. *An der Spitze im Bild: Späher—Aufklärer—Kradschützen in den Divisionen der Waffen-SS*. Coburg, Germany: Nation Europa Verlag, 2005.

Kubik, Willi. *Erinnerungen eines Panzerschützen, 1941–1945: Tagebuchaufzeichnungen eines Panzerschützen der Panzer-Aufklärungs-Abteilung 13 im Russlandfeldzug*. Würzburg, Germany: Flechsig, 2004.

Von Manteuffel, General der Panzertruppen a.D. Hasso E. V. *Die 7. Panzer-Division im Zweiten Weltkrieg: Einsatz und Kampf der "Gespenster-Division" 1939–1945*. Friedberg, Germany: Podzun-Pallas-Verlag, 1986 (reprint).

Memminger, Fritz. *Die Kriegsgeschichte der Windhund Division, Band I*. Bochum-Langendreer, Germany: Heinrich Pöppinghaus Verlag, 1962.

———. *Die Kriegsgeschichte der Windhund Division, Band III*. Bochum-Langendreer, Germany: Heinrich Pöppinghaus Verlag, n.d.

Michaelis, Rolf. *Die 10. SS-Panzer-Division "Frundsberg."* Eggolsheim, Germany: Dörfler Verlag GmbH, 2004.

Middeldorf, Eike. *Taktik im Rußlandfeldzug: Erfahrungen und Folgerungen*. Frankfurt a.M.: E. S. Mittler & Sohn GmbH, 1956 (2nd expanded edition).

Nafziger, George F. *The German Order of Battle: Panzers and Artillery in World War II*. Mechanicsburg, PA: Stackpole Books, 1999.

———. *The German Order of Battle: Waffen SS and Other Units in World War II*. Conshohocken, PA: Combined Publishing, 2001.

Nevenkin, Kamen. *Fire Brigades: Panzer Divisions 1943–1945*. Winnipeg, Canada: J. J. Fedorowicz Publishing, 2007.

Niehorster, Dr. Leo G. *German World War II Organizational Series, Volume 1/I: Mechanized Army and Waffen-SS Units (1st September 1939)*. Hannover, Germany: Self-published, 1990, 2nd edition.

———. *German World War II Organizational Series, Volume 2/I: Mechanized Army Divisions (10th May 1940)*. Hannover, Germany: Self-published, 1990.

———. *German World War II Organizational Series, Volume 2/II: Mechanized GHQ Units and Waffen-SS Divisions (10th May 1940)*. Hannover, Germany: Self-published, 1990.

———. *German World War II Organizational Series, Volume 3/I: Mechanized Army Divisions (22nd June 1941)*. Hannover, Germany: Self-published, 1992.

———. *German World War II Organizational Series, Volume 3/II: Mechanized GHQ Units and Waffen-SS Divisions (22nd June 1941)*. Hannover, Germany: Self-published, 1992.

———. *German World War II Organizational Series, Volume 4/I: Mechanized Army Divisions (28th June 1942)*. Winnipeg: Self-published (collaborative effort with J. J. Fedorowicz Publishing), 1994.

———. *German World War II Organizational Series, Volume 4/II: Mechanized GHQ Units and Waffen-SS Formations (28th June 1942)*. Hannover, Germany: Self-published, 2004.

———. *German World War II Organizational Series, Volume 5/I: Mechanized Army Divisions (4th July 1943)*. Crownhill, England: The Military Press, 2004.

———. *German World War II Organizational Series, Volume 5/III: Waffen-SS Higher Headquarters and Mechanized Formations (4th July 1943)*. Hannover, Germany: Self-published, 2005.

Schäufler, Hans, ed. *Knight's Cross Panzers: The German 35th Panzer Regiment in World War II*. Mechanicsburg, PA: Stackpole Books, 2010.

Scherzer, Veit. *Deutsche Truppen im Zweiten Weltkrieg, Band 1, Formationsgeschichte des Heeres und des Ersatzheeres 1919–1945, Gliederung—Stärke—Ausstattung—Bewaffnung, Teilband A and Teilband B*. Ranis/Jena, Germany: Scherzers Militaer Verlag, 2007.

———. *Deutsche Truppen im Zweiten Weltkrieg, Band 2, Die Divisionen, Divisionen und Brigaden mit den Nummern 1 bis 3, Gliederung—Kommandeure—Einsatz—Inhaber höchster Auszeichnungen*. Ranis/Jena, Germany: Scherzers Militaer Verlag, 2007.

———. *Deutsche Truppen im Zweiten Weltkrieg, Band 3, Die Divisionen, Divisionen und Brigaden mit den Nummern 4 bis 8, Gliederung—Kommandeure—Einsatz—Inhaber höchster Auszeichnungen*. Ranis/Jena, Germany: Scherzers Militaer Verlag, 2008.

———. *Deutsche Truppen im Zweiten Weltkrieg, Band 4, Die Divisionen, Divisionen und Brigaden mit den Nummern 9 bis 14, Gliederung—Kommandeure—Einsatz—Inhaber höchster Auszeichnungen*. Ranis/Jena, Germany: Scherzers Militaer Verlag, 2008.

———. *Deutsche Truppen im Zweiten Weltkrieg, Band 5, Die Divisionen, Divisionen und Brigaden mit den Nummern 15 bis 20, Gliederung—Kommandeure—Einsatz—Inhaber höchster Auszeichnungen*. Ranis/Jena, Germany: Scherzers Militaer Verlag, 2009.

———. *Deutsche Truppen im Zweiten Weltkrieg, Band 6, Die Divisionen, Divisionen und Brigaden mit den Nummern 21 bis 28, Gliederung—Kommandeure—Einsatz—Inhaber höchster Auszeichnungen*. Ranis/Jena, Germany: Scherzers Militaer Verlag, 2010.

———. *Deutsche Truppen im Zweiten Weltkrieg, Band 7, Die Divisionen, Divisionen und Brigaden mit den Nummern 29 bis 50, Gliederung—Kommandeure—Einsatz—Inhaber höchster Auszeichnungen*. Ranis/Jena, Germany: Scherzers Militaer Verlag, 2011.

———. *Himmlers Militärische Elite: Die höchst dekorierten Angehörigen der Waffen-SS, Band 1: Adam–Kauth*. Bayreuth, Germany: Veit Scherzer Verlag, 2014.

———. *Die Ritterkreuzträger, Die Inhaber des Ritterkreuzes des Eisernen Kreuzes, 1939–1945*. Ranis/Jena, Germany: Scherzers Militaer Verlag, 2005.

Schmitz, Peter, et al. *Die deutschen Divisionen, 1939–1945, Heer / Landgestützte Kriegsmarine / Luftwaffe / Waffen-SS, Band 1, Die Divisionen 1–5*. Osnabrück, Germany: Biblio Verlag, 1993.

———. *Die deutschen Divisionen, 1939–1945, Heer / Landgestützte Kriegsmarine / Luftwaffe / Waffen-SS, Band 2, Die Divisionen 6–10*. Osnabrück, Germany: Biblio Verlag, 1994.

———. *Die deutschen Divisionen, 1939–1945, Heer / Landgestützte Kriegsmarine / Luftwaffe / Waffen-SS, Band 3, Die Divisionen 11–16*. Osnabrück, Germany: Biblio Verlag, 1996.

———. *Die deutschen Divisionen, 1939–1945, Heer / Landgestützte Kriegsmarine / Luftwaffe / Waffen-SS, Band 4, Die Divisionen 17–25*. Osnabrück, Germany: Biblio Verlag, 2000.

Spaeter, Helmuth. *The History of Panzerkorps Großdeutschland, Volume 1*. Winnipeg, Canada: J. J. Fedorowicz Publishing, 1992.

———. *The History of Panzerkorps Großdeutschland, Volume 2*. Winnipeg, Canada: J. J. Fedorowicz Publishing, 1995.

Stöber, Hans. *Die Sturmflut und das Ende, Geschichte der 17. SS-Panzergrenadierdivision "Götz von Berlichingen", Band I: Die Invasion*. Osnabrück, Germany: Munin Verlag, 1976.

Stoves, Rolf. *Die 1. Panzer-Division*. Bad Nauheim, Germany: Verlag Hans-Henning Podzun, 1961.

Strauß, Franz Josef. *Geschichte der 2. (Wiener) Panzer-Division*. Friedberg, Germany: Podzun-Pallas-Verlag, 1987 (updated reprint).

Tolmein, Horst Günter. *Spähtrupp bleibt am Feind: Die Geschichte der deutschen Panzer-Aufklärungstruppe*. Stuttgart, Germany: Motorbuch Verlag, 1980.

Veterans of the 3rd Panzer Division. *Armored Bears: The German 3rd Panzer Division in World War II, Volume 1*. Mechanicsburg, PA: Stackpole Books, 2012.

———. *Armored Bears: The German 3rd Panzer Division in World War II, Volume 2*. Mechanicsburg, PA: Stackpole Books, 2013.

Vopersal, Wolfgang. *Soldaten, Kämpfer, Kameraden, Marsch und Kämpfe der SS-Totenkopfdivision, Band IIIb: Operation "Zitadelle" / Kämpfe am Mius / Abwehrkämpfe westlich und südwestlich Charkow / Rückzugskämpfe auf Krementschug / Berichtigungen zu Band III*. Osnabrück, Germany: Biblio Verlag, 1987.

———. *Soldaten, Kämpfer, Kameraden, Marsch und Kämpfe der SS-Totenkopfdivision, Band Vb, Abwehrschlachten nordostwärts Warschau / Verlegung nach Ungarn / Entsatzangriffe in Richtung Budapest / Abwehrkämpfe im Raum Stuhlweißenburg / Rückzugskämpfe auf die Reichsschutzstellung / Endkämpfe in Österreich / Auslieferung der Division / Kriegsgefangenschaft / Truppenkameradschaft*. Osnabrück, Germany: Biblio Verlag, 1991.

Wood, Mike, and J. Dugdale. *Orders of Battle: Waffen-SS Panzer Units in Normandy 1944*. Farnborough, England: Books International, 2000.

Zetterling, Niklas. *Normandy 1944: German Military Organization, Combat Power and Organizational Effectiveness*. Winnipeg, Canada: J. J. Fedorowicz Publishing, 2000.

Zwiener, Rudi. *Einsätze und Erlebnisse der Stabskompanie der Panzer-Aufklärungs-Abteilung 20 der 20. Panzer-Division*. Unpublished manuscript dated January 1997.

INTERNET SOURCES

niehorster.orbat.com. Dr. Leo Niehorster's excellent site devoted to researching the orders of battle of all of the combatants of World War II.

www.afrika-korps.de. Highlights all aspects of the *Deutsches Afrika-Korps* and is highly recommended.

www.feldgrau.org. A general forum on all things related to the German military in World War II. Its threads often provide additional information not contained elsewhere.

www.panzer-archiv.de. Primarily a German-language site, but a treasure trove of information on all things related to German armor in World War II.

www.sturmpanzer.com. Although the focus is on the *Sturmpanzer IV*, there are invaluable links and downloads available at the site concerning the microfiche records of the German Army held at the U.S. National Archives (see above under primary sources).

www.wwiidaybyday.com. Christoph Awender's site uses primary documents to discuss a number of topics concerning the Germany Army, among which are his excellent graphics for the *KStN's*.